CRIME AND JUSTICE IN SOCIETY

CRIME AND JUSTICE IN SOCIETY

Richard Quinney

New York University

Little, Brown and Company · Boston

Preface

Men have their ideals. The myth is that they are realized in practice. *Justice* is such an ideal. The American colonists, imbued with the liberal thought of the European enlightenment, made justice the basis of their democratic government. The Massachusetts Bill of Rights of 1780 captured the essence of the ideal: "It is essential to the preservation of the rights of every individual, his life, liberty, property, and character, that there be an impartial interpretation of the laws, and administration of justice." A similar notion of justice was written into the Declaration of Independence and the American Bill of Rights.

The ideal of justice is fundamental to criminal law. Whenever the legal category *crime* is used, it is assumed that justice weighs all men impartially on her scales in deciding the criminality of each. Criminal law in practice, it follows, is the achievement of criminal justice. Yet, through our experiences and observations we know that criminal law does not operate impartially. The complicated machinery of the legal system contains devices whereby cases are necessarily individualized according to numerous extralegal factors. Partly by design, legal actions are hidden behind a system that dispenses the law according to its own administrative rules. Only in the public drama that surrounds the criminal law are we presented with an image of the credibility of justice.

Guided by the ideal of justice, we are currently being led to inquire into the nature of criminal law. A consideration of justice is in large measure responsible for the intellectual rapprochement that is occurring between the social sciences and law. Persons in various disciplines are now asking: How is criminal law formulated and administered? As a consequence, a considerable body of research is accumulating in an area that may be called the *sociology of criminal law*.

In this book I have brought together a good portion of the research on the sociology of criminal law. I have organized the material according to stages of the legal process. The book is thus divided into sections on formulation of criminal law, enforcement of criminal law, judicial administration of criminal law, and administration of penal and correctional policy. All the selections pertain to criminal justice in that law is being practiced. But more important, the findings and discussions are directed toward justice as an ideal.

Before presenting the research, I have attempted to formulate a *sociological theory of criminal law*. In a reformulation of sociological jurisprudence, I have proposed a sociological theory of interests. The theory consists of a number of propositions about criminal law in politically organized society, the interest structure of society, the unequal distribution of power and the conflict which characterize the interest structure, and the formulation and administration of criminal law within the interest structure of politically organized society. The

v

theory is intended to provide a perspective for the integration and synthesis of the research presented here on the sociology of criminal law.

Crime and Justice in Society is intended to serve several needs. First, the book provides a needed supplement for college and university courses in criminology, social problems, and sociology of law. Criminal law cannot be ignored in these courses: criminal law gives behavior its quality of criminality. Second, the book furnishes the law student with a sociological approach to criminal law. Third, the practicing lawyer should benefit from the sociological approach and the research findings. Fourth, the book will be of interest to the general reader. Criminal law is not only that which is found in statutes, court decisions, and administrative rulings; it is also a process. An understanding of criminal law in action is a primary objective of the book. But ultimately we are led to questions that are provoked by a sense of justice.

I am obviously indebted to all those who have paved the way for a sociology of criminal law. I want to thank the persons who have given me permission to include their works in this book.

Richard Quinney

Contents

Section 4. Administration of Penal and Correctional Policy

Introduction:
Toward a Sociology
of Criminal Law

What is crime? As the history of criminology indicates, this is a crucial question. Indeed, definitions have guided criminologists in selecting subject matter and developing theoretical perspectives. Today, as always, one's feelings about the word "crime" provide one with the vision for studying crime. Currently we are involved in reformulating criminology; our endeavors are increasing in scope. Let us, then, sketch the trends in theoretical criminology, review recent research that broadens criminology, and present a sociological theory that integrates and synthesizes the sociology of criminal law.

TRENDS IN
THEORETICAL CRIMINOLOGY

A history of the study of crime would show a progression from an absolute conception to a relativistic one. In early studies and writings we find that the observer's standard determined what constituted crime. That conception was consistent with the criminologist's interest in "the criminal." In the last few years, however, realizing that crime is defined differently by each legal system, students of crime increasingly have relied upon society's legal definitions as the standards for the study of crime. Thus, criminologists have expanded their investigation to include not only criminally defined persons and behaviors, but also the ways in which persons and behaviors are defined as criminal. Awareness of criminal law and inquiries into its formulation, enforcement, and administration are perhaps the most significant developments in the modern sociological study of crime.

Criminal law was studied only sporadically by criminologists before this recent trend. For a time in the eighteenth century, before crime came to be studied "scientifically," the relationship of man to the state's legal structure received considerable attention.[1] Reacting against contemporary legal practice, writers in the so-called "classical school" protested the inconsistencies and injustices in the criminal law, proposing reforms that were in keeping with a humanitarian, rationalistic conception of man. It was important for theoretical criminology that these writers defined crime strictly according to legal terms. Central to the classical school was the doctrine of *nullum crimen sine lege* — no crime without a legally defined harm.

---

[1] See C. Ray Jeffery, "The Historical Development of Criminology," in Hermann Mannheim (ed.), *Pioneers in Criminology* (London: Stevens & Sons, 1960), pp. 364–394.

1

As scientific methods began to be applied to human behavior, the legal definition of crime receded into obscurity in the latter part of the nineteenth century, remaining there well into this century. The "positive school" of criminology that developed at the end of the nineteenth century, especially among several Italian students of crime, turned criminologists from their interest in the law and violation of specific legal codes to the study of "criminals." The positivists, attempting to overcome the criminal law's relativism, resorted to a nonlegal concept of crime. Crime, thus, began to be regarded as an act against the law of nature.

The nonlegal conception of crime has dominated American criminology. Revisions of the nonlegal conception have, nevertheless, been suggested on occasion. The need for returning to a legal conception of crime was illustrated dramatically in the early 1930's with a report by Michael and Adler on the state of knowledge in criminology.[2] Critical of the past research directed toward the etiology of criminal behavior, Michael and Adler suggested that it was the criminal law that defined the scope and boundaries of criminology. They wrote: "If crime is merely an instance of conduct which is proscribed by the criminal code it follows that the criminal law is the formal cause of crime. That does not mean that the law produces the behavior which it prohibits, although, as we shall see, the enforcement or administration of the criminal law may be one of the factors which influence human behavior, it means only that the criminal law gives behavior its quality of criminality."[3] Michael and Adler forcefully observed that "the most precise and least ambiguous definition of crime is that which defines it as behavior which is prohibited by the criminal code" and, further, that "this is the only possible definition of crime."[4]

A strong adherent of a legal definition of crime was the legally trained sociologist, Paul W. Tappan. Though he advocated explaining an offender's behavior, Tappan warned, "Our definitions of crime cannot be rooted in epithets, in minority value judgments or prejudice, or in loose abstractions."[5] Tappan recognized that a person is a criminal only because his behavior has been defined as criminal by the state. In answering his own question, "Who is the Criminal?" Tappan went so far as to propose that "only those are criminals who have been adjudicated as such by the courts."[6]

Several criminologists subsequently have called for a sociological study

2 Jerome Michael and Mortimer J. Adler, *Crime, Law and Social Science* (New York: Harcourt, Brace, 1933).
3 Michael and Adler, *Crime, Law and Social Science,* p. 5.
4 Michael and Adler, *Crime, Law and Social Science,* p. 2.
5 Paul W. Tappan, *Crime, Justice and Correction* (New York: McGraw-Hill, 1960), p. 10.
6 Paul W. Tappan, "Who Is the Criminal?" *American Sociological Review,* 12 (February, 1947), p. 100.

of criminal law. C. Ray Jeffery, after reviewing diverse definitions of crime, suggested that crime should be studied within the framework of the criminal law.[7] From the criminal law we would be able to ascertain under what conditions behavior becomes defined as criminal and how legal codes interact with other normative systems. Jeffery's concluding statement succinctly expressed his concern for a sociology of criminal law:

> The sociology of criminal law would provide us with a framework for the study of crime, and at the same time it would enable us to differentiate between the criminal and the non-criminal. The legal criterion is the only standard that differentiates the two groups. Further studies of the personality makeup of the offender, of the type engaged in for the past fifty years, are never going to furnish a differential. An explanation of criminal behavior is going to depend upon an explanation of behavior. Such an explanation necessarily involves many non-sociological factors. It is to be questioned at this time whether the sociologist has to be so concerned with human motivation. It seems to the writer that the sociologist would do better to be more concerned with group reactions to certain types of behavior. The study of social structure is sociological; the study of human motivation is only quasi-sociological. A study of social systems in relation to the topic "law and society" would eventually lead to a theory of crime.[8]

Vold illustrated how important criminal law is to the study of crime in observing that there exists a dual problem of explanation in criminology: "Crime always involves both human behavior (acts) and the judgment or definitions (laws, customs, mores) of fellow human beings as to whether specific behavior is appropriate and permissible, or is improper and forbidden. Crime and criminality lie in the area of behavior that is considered improper and forbidden. There is, therefore, always a dual problem of explanation — that of accounting for the behavior, *as behavior,* and equally important, accounting *for the definitions* by which specific behavior comes to be considered as crime or non-crime."[9]

In considering this dual problem further, Turk observed that the problem that is distinctly criminological is the study of *criminality.*[10] He argued that

---

[7] C. Ray Jeffery, "The Structure of American Criminological Thinking," *Journal of Criminal Law, Criminology and Police Science,* 46 (January-February, 1956), pp. 658–672.

[8] Jeffery, "The Structure of American Criminological Thinking," p. 672.

[9] George C. Vold, *Theoretical Criminology* (New York: Oxford University Press, 1958), pp. v–vi. For recent discussions of the dual problems of behavior and definition, see David J. Bordua, "Recent Trends: Deviant Behavior and Social Control," *Annals of the American Academy of Political and Social Science,* 369 (January, 1967), pp. 149–163; Jack P. Gibbs, "Conceptions of Deviant Behavior: the Old and the New," *Pacific Sociological Review,* 9 (Spring, 1966), pp. 9–14; Ronald L. Akers, "Problems in the Sociology of Deviance: Social Definitions and Behavior," *Social Forces,* 46 (June, 1968), pp. 455–465.

[10] Austin T. Turk, "Prospects for Theories of Criminal Behavior," *Jour-*

the criminal law determines the criminal status of persons and behavior, and only an explanation of such criminality is an explanation of crime. Thus, because the legal definition of behavior determines what is regarded as criminal, it is necessary for the criminologist to study how criminal law is formulated and administered.[11]

In addition to the writers in theoretical criminology, many sociologists and social scientists have become interested in the law as a subject for study. Most important, the social sciences and law are converging in an intellectual movement which defines and combines the mutual interests of social scientists and legal scholars.[12] To ensure the exchange of ideas between the various disciplines attending to legal matters, the Law and Society Association was formed in 1964. In the first issue of the Association's journal, the editor described the new convergence of law and the social sciences:

> During the past decade, each of the social sciences has found it necessary to face legal policy issues of highest relevance to the disciplines themselves and to the society as a whole. In political science, the decision process in the courts and administrative agencies has been explored to an extent which parallels earlier and continuing work on the legislatures. Political scientists have also turned their attention to the implementation of legal decisions, especially where the institutions of government have been seen as an important determinant of the impact of law. Sociologists, too, are showing increasing interest in the legal process. Their studies have been concerned with the manner in which the population is affected by law in such areas as civil rights, poverty, and crime. Both professions have joined with the anthropologists in studying the relationship between society and culture on the one hand and the nature and operation of legal institutions on the other. In addition, other professional groups — notably economists, social workers, clinical and social psychologists, and psychiatrists — are increasingly called upon for information thought to be of value in the formulation of legal policy. Above all, the legal profession has moved from a position of reluctant consumer of such information to an active participant in the research process.[13]

The research resulting from this convergence and the recent research in criminology form the basis for a sociology of criminal law. New theoretical frameworks for studying crime are certain to be the consequence.

---

nal of Criminal Law, Criminology and Police Science, 55 (December, 1964), pp. 454–461.

[11] Richard Quinney, "Crime in Political Perspective," *American Behavioral Scientist,* 8 (December, 1964), pp. 19–22; Richard Quinney, "Is Criminal Behavior Deviant Behavior?" *British Journal of Criminology,* 5 (April, 1965), pp. 132–142.

[12] See Gilbert Geis, "Sociology, Criminology, and Criminal Law," *Social Problems,* 7 (Summer, 1959), pp. 40–47.

[13] Richard D. Schwartz, "From the Editor," *Law and Society Review,* 1 (November, 1966), p. 6.

RESEARCH IN
THE SOCIOLOGY OF CRIMINAL LAW

Roughly a decade of labor by social scientists has resulted in extensive empirical research on criminal law, a good portion of which is included in this book. This research can be reviewed and presented according to the *stages* of the legal process. For analytical and practical purposes these stages may be divided into the formulation of criminal law, enforcement of criminal law, judicial administration of criminal law, and administration of penal and correctional policy.

FORMULATION OF CRIMINAL LAW

Criminal law, as an aspect of public policy, is established to govern the lives and affairs of the inhabitants of a politically organized society. The concept of criminal law emerged only when the custom of private vengeance was replaced by the principle that the community as a whole is injured when one of its members is harmed. Thus, the right to act against a wrongdoing was taken out of the hands of the immediate victim and his family and was, instead, granted to the state as the representative of the people.

The turning point in the emergence of criminal law in the Western world occurred in Athens at the beginning of the sixth century B.C. when in order to forestall a possible revolution, the ruling aristocrats granted citizens the right to initiate prosecutions with the support of the state.[14] This step protected citizens from one another and from government itself, in this case the lower class of Athens from aggression by the rich and powerful.

In other societies criminal law could develop only with the achievement of a political unity that allowed a law to be established and administered in the name of a centralized government. In England, therefore, the country's political development also marked the development of criminal law. According to Jeffery, important change began in the latter part of the eleventh century and continued throughout the twelfth.[15] With the Norman invasion of 1066 and the strong rule of the Norman kings, the old tribal-feudal system of law was replaced by a criminal law that lay in the hands of a central authority, the Crown. In order to place law under the jurisdiction of the King's government, several types of courts were created, writs were devised to carry cases out of baronial courts and into the King's courts, and eventually a "common law"

---

[14] See George M. Calhoun, *The Growth of Criminal Law in Ancient Greece* (Berkeley: University of California Press, 1927).

[15] C. Ray Jeffery, "The Development of Crime in Early English Society," *Journal of Criminal Law, Criminology and Police Science,* 47 (March-April, 1957), pp. 647–666.

was established for the justice of all men. This new system determined offenses which clearly violated the peace of the King and country.

It was during the fifteenth century in England that the modern law of theft was formulated into criminal law by a case known as the "Carrier's Case." As documented and interpreted by Jerome Hall,[16] the Carrier's Case of 1473 demonstrates how changing social conditions and emerging social interests bring about the formulation of a criminal law. The judges in the case departed from precedent by introducing the notion that a person trusted with another's property could commit a trespass upon that property. According to Hall, the legal reformulation of trespass was shaped by fifteenth-century England in the following ways:

We are now in a position to visualize the case and the problem presented to the judges as a result of the legal, political and economic conditions described above. On the one hand, the criminal law at the time is clear. On the other hand, the whole complex aggregate of political and economic conditions described above thrusts itself upon the court. The more powerful forces of the time were interrelated very intimately and at many points: the New Monarchy and the *nouveau riche* — the mercantile class; the business interests of both and the consequent need for a secure carrying trade; the wool and textile industry, the most valuable, by far, in all the realm; wool and cloth, the most important exports; these exports and the foreign trade; this trade and Southampton, chief trading city with the Latin countries for centuries; the numerous and very influential Italian merchants who bought English wool and cloth inland and shipped them from Southampton. The great forces of an emerging modern world, represented in the above phenomena, necessitated the elimination of a formula which had outgrown its usefulness. A new set of major institutions required a new rule. The law, lagging behind the needs of the times, was brought into more harmonious relationship with the other institutions by the decision rendered in the Carrier's Case.[17]

Another basic legal concept that developed in early English law is that of vagrancy. In analyzing the law of vagrancy, Chambliss has shown how the vagrancy statutes changed in England according to emerging social interests.[18] The first full-fledged vagrancy law, enacted in 1349, regulated the giving of alms to able-bodied, unemployed persons. After the Black Death and the flight of workers from landowners, the law was reformulated in order to force laborers to accept employment at a low wage. By the sixteenth century, with increased emphasis on commerce and industry, the vagrancy statutes were revived and strengthened. In other words, formulations and changes in the vagrancy statutes were brought about by powerful interest groups.

[16] Jerome Hall, *Theft, Law and Society,* 2nd ed. (Indianapolis: Bobbs-Merrill, 1952).
[17] Hall, *Theft, Law and Society,* p. 33.
[18] William J. Chambliss, "A Sociological Analysis of the Law of Vagrancy," *Social Problems,* 12 (Summer, 1964), pp. 67–77.

The vagrancy laws emerged in order to provide the powerful landowners with a ready supply of cheap labor. When this was no longer seen as necessary and particularly when the landowners were no longer dependent upon cheap labor nor were they a powerful interest group in society the laws became dormant. Finally a new interest group emerged and was seen as being of great importance to the society and the laws were then altered so as to afford some protection to this group.[19]

Eventually the vagrancy laws came to serve, as they do today, the purpose of controlling persons and activities regarded as undesirable to the community.

The laws of the American colonies developed, for the most part, within the tradition of the English common law.[20] Yet local conditions shaped some of the colonial laws. The Massachusetts Bay Colony was faced with the critical problem of finding the proper place for law in a religious community. While the colony had been chartered as a commercial enterprise in 1630, the principal objectives of the settlers clearly were religious and social. Relating law to such objectives was resolved by constructing a legal system based on Biblical authority. The Scriptures served as the most appropriate source for establishing a government in accordance with God's word. As Haskins has shown, most provisions in the Puritan's legal code were annotated by chapter and verse from the Old Testament, and many incorporated biblical phraseology.[21] In such a fashion, the state's authority was condoned and supported by religion. Ultimately, this meant that the welfare of the whole, rather than that of the individual, was the state's chief concern.

One of the most dramatic modern attempts to control morality through law is found in the enactment of the Volstead Act and its ratification in the Eighteenth Amendment in 1920. In a social history of prohibition, Sinclair observed that the movement to place a ban on drinking and the liquor trade was an assertion of the rural Protestant mind against the emerging urban culture. The successful activities of the dry interest groups instituted the era of prohibition:

Through the many roots of prohibition — rural mythology, the psychology of excess, the exploited fears of the mass of the people, the findings of science and medicine, the temper of reform, the efficiency of the dry pressure groups, their mastery of propaganda, the stupidity and self-interest of the brewers and distillers, the necessary trimming of politicians, and the weakness of the elected representatives of the people — through all these channels the sap of the dry tree rose until

---

[19] Chambliss, "A Sociological Analysis of the Law of Vagrancy," p. 77.

[20] See Roscoe Pound, "The Development of American Law and Its Deviation from English Law," *Law Quarterly Review,* 67 (January, 1951), pp. 49–66.

[21] George Lee Haskins, *Law and Authority in Early Massachusetts* (New York: Macmillan, 1960), pp. 141–162. Also see Kai T. Erikson, *Wayward Puritans: A Study in the Sociology of Deviance* (New York: John Wiley & Sons, 1966); Edwin Powers, *Crime and Punishment in Early Massachusetts* (Boston: Beacon Press, 1966).

the legal prohibition of the liquor trade burst out new and green in the first month of 1920. The roots had been separate; yet they were all part of a common American seed. They combined and contributed to the strength of the whole. The Anti-Saloon League, bent on its particular reform, was the heir and beneficiary of many interactions in American life. As the drys stood on the threshold of victory at the opening of the twenties, they could see manifest destiny in the success of their cause. They seemed to be the darling army of the Lord. Behind them appeared to lie one mighty pattern and purpose. Before them hung the sweet fruits of victory.[22]

But prohibition failed as law just as it failed as a noble cause. An outdated morality could not be enforced through criminal law.

Some criminal laws, not unlike other passions and conveniences, experience periods of popularity. The formulation of sexual psychopath laws is an instance of such fashion in law. Beginning in the late 1930's and extending into the 1950's, over half the states in the United States enacted sexual psychopath laws. In analyzing the diffusion of these laws, Sutherland noted that certain phases preceded the enactment of the laws,[23] such as arousal of fear by a few serious sex crimes, agitation stemming from fear within the community, and the appointment of a committee to study the problem and to make recommendations. Sutherland further observed that the principal interest group backing the sexual psychopath laws, as determined by the composition of the investigation and proposal committees, has been that of psychiatry. The provisions of the sexual psychopath laws thus promote the occupational interests of psychiatrists.

Behind the formulation of all laws is an enterprising group that stands to benefit in some way from a particular law. As both Becker and Lindesmith have documented, criminal laws that regulate the sale and possession of drugs reflect actions of the Federal Bureau of Narcotics.[24] Its role in the enactment of the Harrison Act of 1914 and the Marihuana Tax Act of 1937 has created public suspicion and fear of drug use. Today the use of any type of drug by a segment of the population — be the drug addictive or not, a narcotic drug, marihuana, or a psychedelic drug — arouses the public to such an extent that it often calls for repressive legislation. The Federal Bureau of Narcotics has defined its interests as total restriction of drugs and complete enforcement of the law. These interests have become the standards by which the public now judges the use of drugs.

Research on criminal law has demonstrated that criminal laws are formu-

---

[22] Andrew Sinclair, *Era of Excess: A Social History of the Prohibition Movement* (New York: Harper & Row, 1964), p. 170.

[23] Edwin H. Sutherland, "The Diffusion of Sexual Psychopath Laws," *American Journal of Sociology*, 56 (September, 1950), pp. 142–148.

[24] Howard S. Becker, *Outsiders: Studies in the Sociology of Deviance* (New York: The Free Press of Glencoe, 1963), pp. 135–146; Alfred R. Lindesmith, *The Addict and the Law* (Bloomington: Indiana University Press, 1965), pp. 3–34.

lated within a social context that involves the promotion of the interests of certain groups in society. This is the social nature of criminal law.

LAW ENFORCEMENT

Criminal law does not provide specific instructions for the enforcement of the law. In spite of popular conception, law enforcement, as LaFave has indicated, is largely a matter of discretion.[25] The arrest of a person is an operational step that involves a decision to interfere with the freedom of someone suspected of criminal conduct. Police discretion in law enforcement rarely becomes known to the public. Recently, however, social scientists have turned their attention to the study and explanation of law enforcement. We are now beginning to understand the nature of law enforcement.

Each police department operates within a community. Generally, however, the police in all communities must function in a sphere of their own, isolated within the community. The requirements of law enforcement, as Clark describes the situation, contribute to this isolation.[26] Among the forces that come into play are the intrusion of police activity into the private interests of citizens, resentment against the police, the reminder that the police expose deviance in the community, and the secretive operations of the police.

Yet, in spite of the inevitable isolation of the police in communal life, to view police activity solely in terms of community hostility and strict enforcement of the law misses an important aspect of the role of the police, since one of its principal functions is to promote peace in the community.[27] Each day the policeman may be as much a "peace officer" as a "law officer." The supportive role of the police has been documented in a study of the telephone calls received at the desk of a metropolitan police department.[28] An analysis of the calls showed that nearly half were requests for support of some kind, such as requests for assistance in personal problems, requests for health services, and assistance in handling problems of children and incapacitated persons. The police, thus, are engaged in many activities that are not directly related to law enforcement, but which uphold the community's welfare.

Studies of police activity in different communities sustain the fact that the police have functions other than law enforcement. Esselstyn, in a study of the

[25] Wayne R. LaFave, *Arrest: The Decision to Take a Suspect into Custody* (Boston: Little, Brown, 1965), pp. 63–82.

[26] John P. Clark, "Isolation of the Police: A Comparison of the British and American Situations," *Journal of Criminal Law, Criminology and Police Science,* 56 (September, 1965), pp. 307–319.

[27] Michael Banton, *The Policeman in the Community* (London: Tavistock, 1964), p. 127.

[28] Elaine Cumming, Ian Cumming, and Laura Edell, "Policeman as Philosopher, Guide and Friend," *Social Problems,* 12 (Winter, 1965), pp. 276–286.

county sheriff in a county in southern Illinois, found that the primary function of the sheriff was to conserve the peace.[29] The rule of thumb was public safety, and arresting a person was not always the best way to provide for that safety. Similarly, in a study of police activity in skid-row areas of large cities, Bittner observed that the primary objective of police work in these areas is "keeping the peace."[30] As with law enforcement, however, peace-keeping is often accomplished by using discretion, and there are no clear legal mandates for the fulfillment of this function.

In addition to community expectations and requirements, the behavior of the police is greatly influenced by the organization of police departments. Organizational considerations are always present when a decision is made to enforce the criminal law. One of the most important organizational aspects of law enforcement is police bureaucratization.[31] While social relations within police departments are arranged according to a hierarchy of command, the communications center of the modern metropolitan police department is the principal source of organizational control. Furthermore, through internal organization and control, the police are integrated into an occupational community that furnishes a commitment which takes precedence over extra-occupational demands. Because of bureaucratic and occupational organization, the police develop within departments their own rules and procedures of law enforcement.

Because of the role the police play in the community and the particular organization that is molded for that role, a special ideology develops among the police. The occupational ideology of the police, in relation to their social role and occupational organization, has been described by Westley as follows:

> The policeman finds his most pressing problems in his relationships to the public. His is a service occupation but of an incongruous kind, since he must discipline those whom he serves. He is regarded as corrupt and inefficient by, and meets with hostility and criticism from, the public. He regards the public as his enemy, feels his occupation to be in conflict with the community, and regards himself to be a pariah. The experience and the feeling give rise to a collective emphasis on secrecy, an attempt to coerce respect from the public, and a belief that almost any means

[29] T. C. Esselstyn, "The Social Role of the County Sheriff," *Journal of Criminal Law, Criminology and Police Science,* 44 (July-August, 1953), pp. 177–184.

[30] Egon Bittner, "The Police on Skid-Row: A Study of Peace Keeping," *American Sociological Review,* 32 (October, 1967), pp. 699–715.

[31] David J. Bordua and Albert J. Reiss, Jr., "Command, Control and Charisma: Reflections on Police Bureaucracy," *American Journal of Sociology,* 72 (July, 1966), pp. 68–76. Also see Arthur L. Stinchcombe, "Institutions of Privacy in the Determination of Police Administrative Practice," *American Journal of Sociology,* 69 (September, 1963), pp. 150–160; James Q. Wilson, "The Police and the Delinquent in Two Cities," in Stanton Wheeler (ed.), *Controlling Delinquents* (New York: John Wiley & Sons, 1968), pp. 9–30; Robert Edward Mitchell, "Organization as a Key to Police Effectiveness," *Crime and Delinquency,* 12 (October, 1966), pp. 344–353.

are legitimate in completing an important arrest. These are for the policeman basic occupational values. They arise from his experience, take precedence over his legal responsibilities, are central to an understanding of his conduct, and form the occupational contexts within which violence gains its meaning.[32]

The "rookie" policeman is faced with the dilemma of choosing between the professional ideals acquired during his academy training and the pragmatic approach of the precinct. In the first weeks of duty, as Niederhoffer has found, the new policeman must learn to make arrest decisions by resolving the conflict between the ideals learned in training and the requirements of his job.[33] It becomes obvious to him that every law on the book cannot be enforced and that laws are to be enforced with discretion according to the norms of his department, the ideology of his occupation, and the expectations of the community.

When an arrest is made, complex personal interactions and perceptions come into play. The definition of "criminal" is not based so much on behavior in obvious violation of a specific criminal law as it is on circumstances present in the encounter between policeman and suspect. The policeman, using a probabilistic model of law enforcement, looks for characteristics in the suspect that may indicate "criminal behavior." Thus, the outward appearance and demeanor of the suspect are most important. A study by Piliavin and Briar of how juvenile cases are handled showed that the decision of whether or not to bring a boy to the station and other decisions made at the station "were based largely on cues from which the officer inferred the youth's character."[34] The cues included the youth's demeanor, group affiliations, age, race, grooming, and dress. Uncooperative youths, members of known delinquent gangs, older boys, Negroes, and youths with well-oiled hair, black jackets, and soiled denims or jeans received the more serious dispositions. Obviously, more than the initial act of the suspect is considered whenever an arrest is made.

To observe and explain police discretion is also to realize that enforcement of criminal law takes place within tenuous social control and legal regulation. Police practices tend to be affected minimally by legal considerations. The police, because of such factors as community expectations, bureaucratic organization, and occupational ideology, operate according to extralegal directives. At best, procedural law regulating police activities is affected by the

---

[32] William A. Westley, "Violence and the Police," *American Journal of Sociology,* 59 (July, 1953), p. 35.

[33] Arthur Niederhoffer, *Behind the Shield: The Police in Urban Society* (Garden City, New York: Doubleday, 1967), pp. 52–56.

[34] Irving Piliavin and Scott Briar, "Police Encounters with Juveniles," *American Journal of Sociology,* 70 (September, 1964), p. 210. For other findings, see Robert M. Terry, "The Screening of Juvenile Offenders," *Journal of Criminal Law, Criminology and Police Science,* 58 (June, 1967), pp. 173–181.

social role of the police. With this in mind, Skolnick has argued that ultimately the regulation of law enforcement must come from sources other than
the law. The police themselves bear part of the responsibility of safeguarding
the rights of the citizen while at the same time maintaining order in the
community.

The needed philosophy of professionalism must rest on a set of values conveying the idea that the police are as much an institution dedicated to the achievement
of legality in society as they are an official social organization designed to control
misconduct through the invocation of punitive sanctions. The problem of police in
a democratic society is not merely a matter of obtaining newer police cars, a higher
order technical equipment or of recruiting men who have to their credit more years
of education. What must occur is a significant alteration in the ideology of police,
so that police "professionalization" rests on the values of a democratic legal order,
rather than on technological proficiency.[35]

JUDICIAL ADMINISTRATION

The administration of justice, contrary to common belief, is not "above
politics" but is by its very nature political. Administration of criminal law is
political in that public policy is being interpreted and affirmed. Justice, then,
is political because the administration of criminal law involves the making
of decisions in the name of the state. Judicial decision-making without discretionary actions is inconceivable.

In the judiciary, decisions must be made at various stages in the judicial
process. Once a case has been admitted to the judicial system, after an arrest,
a series of decisions are made regarding the fate of the accused. The stages
consist of the first judicial appearance (including the preliminary hearing),
the formal charge (including indictment and filing of information), the arraignment (including pretrial motions and applications), the trial or nontrial
adjudication, the sentence, and final release from the legal system. At each
stage the decision reached by certain officials limits the alternatives for decisions in the subsequent stages.

Judicial decision-making is being investigated and explained by social scientists. Such research is removing the "purple curtain" of justice from the
activities of the judicial system. The criminal court, as Blumberg has shown,
has a social organization and an operation of its own outside of public scrutiny and beyond legal considerations: "The court, unlike most other formal
organizations, functions as a genuinely 'closed community' in that it successfully conceals the true nature of its routine operations from the view of outsiders — and sometimes even from some of the participants themselves. It
socializes its members and participants toward compliance with specific ob-

---

[35] Jerome H. Skolnick, *Justice Without Trial: Law Enforcement in Democratic Society* (New York: John Wiley & Sons, 1966), pp. 238–239.

jectives which are not part of the official goals of justice and due process."[36]

Extra-legal considerations are evident at the very first judicial stage. The principal function of the initial judicial appearance is to provide for the defendant's release pending further proceedings. The first appearance does not determine whether there is sufficient evidence for prosecution, but establishes a means of assuring that the defendant will be available for further judicial consideration. Bail — the traditional method of insuring the reappearance of the defendant — is determined by a number of interacting parties, namely the judge, the prosecuting attorney, and the defense attorney. As Suffet observed in a study of courtroom bailsetting, each party makes bail suggestions for different purposes.[37] The final decision on the terms of bail serves to diffuse the responsibility for the defendant's release. Beyond the interactions and the decisions, the practice of bail itself discriminates against those who cannot afford to pay the bail fee, fosters a shady bail-bond business, and promotes the use of questionable judicial procedures.[38]

Important as the criminal trial is as an ideal in the administration of justice, the fact remains that the most commonly used method in settling cases is adjudication without benefit of trial. Roughly 90 per cent of criminal convictions are made on the basis of guilty pleas which are adjudicated without a trial.[39] Because of a tremendous case load, the judicial system has come to depend upon the use of the practice known as "plea bargaining." The negotiation of the guilty plea results in a compromise conviction that is reached by the state and the accused for the benefit of both.

In a study of plea negotiations and convictions, Newman found that the accused, directly or through an attorney, offered to plead guilty to the offense for which he was arrested, providing the charge was reduced in kind or degree, and exchanged for a certain length of sentence.[40] The subsequent conviction agreements followed several patterns according to the bargains involved. Sudnow, in another study of plea negotiation, observed that the interactions and perceptions of the prosecutor and the defense are critical in

---

[36] Abraham S. Blumberg, *Criminal Justice* (Chicago: Quadrangle Books, 1967), p. 70. For other observations on the social organization of the administration of criminal justice, see Jerome H. Skolnick, "Social Control in the Adversary System," *Journal of Conflict Resolution*, 11 (March, 1967), pp. 52–70. On the juvenile court, see Aaron V. Cicourel, *The Social Organization of Juvenile Justice* (New York: John Wiley & Sons, 1968).

[37] Frederic Suffet, "Bail Setting: A Study of Courtroom Interaction," *Crime and Delinquency,* 12 (October, 1966), pp. 318–331.

[38] See Caleb Foote, "The Bail System and Equal Justice," *Federal Probation,* 23 (September, 1959), pp. 43–48; Ronald Goldfarb, *Ransom: A Critique of the American Bail System* (New York: Harper & Row, 1965).

[39] Donald J. Newman, *Conviction: The Determination of Guilt or Innocence Without Trial* (Boston: Little, Brown, 1966), pp. 3–4.

[40] Donald J. Newman, "Pleading Guilty for Considerations: A Study of Bargain Justice," *Journal of Criminal Law, Criminology and Police Science,* 46 (March-April, 1956), pp. 780–790.

arriving at a charge.[41] In the course of their repeated interactions and negotiations, prosecution and defense develop unstated guides, outside of the penal
code, for the reduction of original charges to lesser charges.

When negotiation between legal representatives has failed to result in the
defendant's plea of guilt, or when the defendant pleads not guilty without
any attempt at bargaining, a criminal trial provides the setting for adjudication. The criminal trial is a process of constructing a reality of the case at
hand. Social and subjective factors enter into the arguments of the attorneys,
the testimony of witnesses, the deliberations of jurors, and the actions of the
judge. The criminal trial is not strictly an exercise in fact finding and logical
deduction, but is a product of human perception and action.

Both the prosecution and defense utilize witnesses that will affect their
case favorably. Testimony that is often included in the criminal trial is that
of the so-called "expert." Criminal procedure today relies especially upon the
testimony of the psychiatrist. During the trial the psychiatrist may be asked
to make a judgment as to the responsibility or the mental condition of the
defendant and he may thus have a crucial role because he can supposedly
provide information about the defendant. Because of the importance attached
to his judgment and the element of uncertainty in his practice, the role of the
psychiatrist in the criminal trial and pretrial proceedings has been seriously
questioned in recent years.[42] Whatever the future use of "expert" testimony
in the judicial process, presently the fate of the defendant is vitally affected
by the evaluations of psychiatrists.

In regard to the jury, the assumption is that defendants are tried by a representative body of the citizenry. However, research has shown that social
and economic biases operate in the methods by which jurors are selected and
in the ways in which they deliberate. Lower occupational groups tend to be
excluded from juries systematically, and foremen are often selected on the
basis of their social position in the community.[43] Furthermore, the social
status and sex of an individual juror are related to his participation and influence in jury deliberations. Studies of mock juries have shown that men and

[41] David Sudnow, "Normal Crimes: Sociological Features of the Penal
Code in a Public Defender Office," *Social Problems,* 12 (Winter, 1965), pp.
255–276.

[42] Seymour L. Halleck, "A Critique of Current Psychiatric Roles in the
Legal Process," *Wisconsin Law Review* (Spring, 1966), pp. 379–401. Also
see Thomas S. Szasz, *Psychiatric Justice* (New York: Macmillan, 1965).

[43] W. S. Robinson, "Bias, Probability, and Trial by Jury," *American
Sociological Review,* 15 (February, 1950), pp. 73–78; Fred L. Strodtbeck,
Rita M. James, and Charles Hawkins, "Social Status and Jury Delibera-
tions," *American Sociological Review,* 22 (December, 1957), pp. 713–719;
William Bevan, Robert S. Albert, Pierre R. Loiseaux, Peter N. Mayfield, and
George Wright, "Jury Behavior as a Function of the Prestige of the Fore-
man and the Nature of His Leadership," *Journal of Public Law,* 7 (Fall,
1958), pp. 419–449.

persons of higher social status have higher participation and influence in jury deliberations.[44]

Jurors also differ in the kinds of things they focus upon during the deliberation. In general, as indicated in another jury study, jurors spend about half their time exchanging experiences and opinions related to the trial.[45] About a quarter of the time is devoted to procedural matters, with about 15 per cent spent on reviewing the facts of the case and about 8 per cent spent on court instructions. The more educated jurors give relatively more emphasis to procedure and instructions; the less educated emphasize testimony, personal and daily experiences, and opinions based on the trial. The same researcher found that in reaching a verdict in insanity trials, lower class jurors are more likely to favor the defendant. Women jurors, on the other hand, are more sympathetic toward the defendant than men, but are likely to qualify their verdict according to the offense.[46]

At the end of jury deliberation, the verdict reached by the jurors may not be the same as the trial judge would have rendered. The extent to which the verdicts of jurors and judges differ has been researched by Kalven and Zeisel.[47] The research consisted of an investigation and analysis of 3,576 actual jury verdicts and the matching hypothetical verdicts of the judges involved in the particular cases. The major finding of the research was that the judge and jury *agreed* in 75.4 per cent of the trials. Whenever the judge and jury disagreed, the disagreement was predominantly in one direction: the jury was more likely than the judge to acquit. Practically, the defense strategy, in selecting a type of trial, directly affects the conviction.

An indication of the factors that enter into orienting a judge toward the defense was obtained by Nagel in a study of state and federal supreme court judges.[48] Each judge was given a decision score representing the number of times he favored the defense. Judges who were more defendant-minded were likely to be Democrats rather than Republicans, nonmembers rather than members of the American Bar Association, lawyers who had not been prosecutors rather than former prosecutors, Catholics rather than Protestants, and relatively liberal as measured by off-the-bench attitudes. Thus, because of

[44] Fred L. Strodtbeck and Richard D. Mann, "Sex Role Differentiation in Jury Deliberations," *Sociometry,* 19 (March, 1956), pp. 3–11; Strodtbeck, James, and Hawkins, "Social Status in Jury Deliberations," pp. 713–719.

[45] Rita M. James, "Status and Competence of Jurors," *American Journal of Sociology,* 64 (May, 1959), pp. 563–570.

[46] Rita James Simon, *The Jury and the Defense of Insanity* (Boston: Little, Brown, 1967), pp. 98–119.

[47] Harry Kalven, Jr., and Hans Zeisel, *The American Jury* (Boston: Little, Brown, 1966).

[48] Stuart S. Nagel, "Judicial Backgrounds and Criminal Cases," *Journal of Criminal Law, Criminology and Police Science,* 53 (September, 1962), pp. 333–339.

certain background and attitudinal characteristics, judges appear to be disposed to make particular kinds of judicial decisions.

Following conviction of the defendant, a decision is made regarding the sentence that will be attached to the conviction. Sentencing involves the manipulations and use of discretion by a number of persons. Even when sentencing is the province of the judge, other persons participate in making the decision. In many jurisdictions a presentence investigation is made by personnel of the probation department attached to the court. The report, which covers the defendant's personal and social background, his criminal record, and his mental and physical condition, includes the probation department's recommendations for sentencing. With the report and recommendations in hand, the judge then imposes a sentence. Carter and Wilkins, in a study of the relation between presentence reports and dispositions, have shown that in most cases judges sentence according to the recommendations provided by the probation department.[49] While the final sentencing decision may belong to the judge, the decisions of others are important in the actual disposition of the sentence.

Sentencing statistics and studies indicate that criminal court judges differ in their use of discretion in sentencing. Gaudet, in a study of sentences assigned in nearly 7,500 criminal cases handled by six judges over ten years in a county in New Jersey, reported that the judges differed considerably in the frequency, length, and type of sentence they assigned to convicted offenders.[50] Other studies have shown that sentences differ according to characteristics of the defendants. Bullock, in studying the length of prison sentences (assigned in this case by juries), found that the sentences varied in length according to the race of the defendant.[51] Even when nonracial characteristics were controlled in the analysis, Negroes tended to receive longer prison sentences than whites.

Sentencing decisions, whether reached by judges, juries, or on the basis of probation department recommendations, are probably made, as Green has argued in a study of the sentencing practices of criminal court judges, within the framework provided by the law.[52] Nevertheless, even within the bound-

---

[49] Robert M. Carter and Leslie T. Wilkins, "Some Factors in Sentencing Policy," *Journal of Criminal Law, Criminology and Police Science,* 58 (December, 1967), pp. 503–514.

[50] Frederick J. Gaudet, "The Difference Between Judges in Granting Sentences of Probation," *Temple Law Quarterly,* 19 (April, 1946), pp. 471–484; Frederick J. Gaudet, "Individual Differences in Sentencing Tendencies of Judges," *Archives of Psychology,* 32 (1938); Frederick J. Gaudet, G. S. Harris, and C. W. St. John, "Individual Differences in Penitentiary Sentences Given by Different Judges," *Journal of Applied Psychology,* 8 (October, 1934), pp. 675–680.

[51] Henry Allen Bullock, "Significance of the Racial Factor in the Length of Prison Sentence," *Journal of Criminal Law, Criminology and Police Science,* 52 (November-December, 1961), pp. 411–417.

[52] Edward Green, "Sentencing Practices of Criminal Court Judges in

aries of the law, there is opportunity for making decisions on the basis of extra-legal considerations. The criminal sanctions that are ultimately imposed on convicted defendants are influenced by such extra-legal matters as the nature of the judges that assign the sentences, the norms that regulate sentencing, the social organization of the judiciary, and the responses and cues provided by the defendant himself. In other words, even while sentencing operates within a legal framework, extra-legal or social factors play their parts in the decision-making process.

ADMINISTRATION OF PENAL AND CORRECTIONAL POLICY

The criminal sentence is administered within a very general legal framework. Whether the sentence is penal or correctional in nature, legal policy serves only as a guideline for its administration.

The legal framework varies in accordance with the emphasis placed on the punishment or treatment aims of the policy. In a study of the punishment-treatment orientation in the administration of penal and correctional policy of several jurisdictions, Hayner found that the practices differed considerably from one jurisdiction to another.[53] Differentials in the penal and correctional practices of jurisdictions are apparently related to the value structures of the respective jurisdictions.

In the United States, in particular, treatment orientation has been perhaps the most significant development in criminal justice in the last fifty years. The use of probation and parole, the creation of the juvenile court, the development of treatment programs, and the establishment of treatment within the prison all mark what Allen has called "the rehabilitative ideal."[54] Yet, as Allen has observed, the results of the rehabilitative ideal have not been in all cases as humanitarian as intended. In fact, the schemes that have emerged from the rehabilitative ideal have often led to more severe penal measures. Many of the original aims of the rehabilitative ideal have been debased and practices have been instituted which conflict with the value of individual liberty. Nevertheless, in the administration of penal and correctional policy, the consequences of the two separate orientations of punishment and treatment have not been as disparate as expected.

Whatever the general aims of penal and correctional policy, the criminal sentence may be administered, served, and completed in a number of ways. If the sentence is a fine, payment of the fine removes the criminal status from

Philadelphia," *American Journal of Correction,* 22 (July-August, 1960), pp. 32–35.

[53] Norman S. Hayner, "Correctional Systems and National Values," *British Journal of Criminology,* 3 (October, 1962), pp. 163–175.

[54] Francis A. Allen, "Criminal Justice, Legal Values and the Rehabilitative Ideal," *Journal of Criminal Law, Criminology and Police Science,* 50 (September-October, 1959), pp. 226–232.

the convicted offender. If the judge imposes a period of probation, the satisfactory completion of the sentence is dependent upon the offender's "good behavior" and conformity to the stipulated conditions of probation. The removal of the criminal status is then determined by the recommendations of the probation officer assigned to the offender. As Reed and King have shown in an experiment of decision-making among probation officers, officers differ in their decisions and rationalizations.[55] Differences were related to the characteristics and orientations of the officers, the extenuating circumstances of the cases, the relative roles of officer and offender, and the involvement of other legal agents in the cases.

Special problems characterize the administration of a sentence of imprisonment. The prison is an organization unto itself. It is, as some have said, a "closed system," a "total institution," or a "system of total power."[56] Furthermore, prisons contain several different, and often contradictory, hierarchical organizations. Regarding these separate organizations, Cressey has written:

> In all prisons there is a line organization of custodial ranks, ranging from warden to guard, and salary differentials and descriptive titles indicate that a chain of command is expected within this hierarchy. However, while all employees are responsible to the warden, there is no clear expectation that the institution shall consist *solely* of a hierarchy of custodial ranks in reference to which all positions are integrated. Systems of nonline positions, such as those of professional personnel and industrial foremen and superintendents, are essentially separate and have their own salary differentials and titles. They are neither part of the custodial chain of command nor staff organizations. Noncustodial personnel are not advisers to the custodians in the sense that the experts of various sorts who make up the staff organization of factories are advisers, providing specialized knowledge to assist the line organization with its task of production. The structure of prisons provides for three principal hierarchies — devoted respectively to *keeping, using,* and *serving* inmates — but not for the integration of their divergent purposes. The separate organizations concerned with keeping and with serving inmates, for example, are not merely overlapping, but have entirely different and partly contradictory purposes.[57]

Each type of organization, in turn, shows a special relationship between its staff and the inmates and a specific pattern of authority, communication, and

[55] John P. Reed and Charles E. King, "Factors in Decision-Making of North Carolina Probation Officers," *Journal of Research in Crime and Delinquency,* 3 (July, 1966), pp. 120–128.

[56] See, in particular, Erving Goffman, *Asylums* (New York: Doubleday, 1961); Gresham M. Sykes, *The Society of Captives* (Princeton: Princeton University Press, 1958).

[57] Donald R. Cressey, "Limitations on Organization of Treatment in the Modern Prison," in Richard A. Cloward, *et al., Theoretical Studies in Social Organization of the Prison* (New York: Social Science Research Council, 1960), pp. 79–80.

decision-making. But the persons most affected by the divergent organizations of the prison are the inmates. Differences in handling the affairs and fate of inmates result primarily from the organizational problems inherent in the prison.

Eventually most inmates are released from prison. Some are released only when their prison sentence expires. The majority, however, leave prison by means of parole. The decision to parole an inmate is usually made by a parole board, staffed either by personnel from the prison or by members of a statewide board of parole. The offender's future is settled by the discretion of others. And the ways in which such decisions are made, as the President's Commission on Law Enforcement and Administration of Justice has argued, are not especially laudable:

Except for sentencing, no decision in the criminal process has more impact on the convicted offender than the parole decision, which determines how much of his maximum sentence a prisoner must serve. This again is an invisible administrative decision that is seldom open to attack or subject to review. It is made by parole board members who are often political appointees. Many are skilled and conscientious, but they are generally able to spend no more than a few minutes on a case. Parole decisions that are made in haste and on the basis of insufficient information, in the absence of parole machinery that can provide good supervision, are necessarily imperfect decisions, and since there is virtually no appeal from them, they can be made arbitrarily or discriminatorily.[58]

As in the case of probation, the parolee must maintain a relation with a legal agent, the parole officer. Decisions by the parole officer determine whether or not the parolee will complete the conditions of his parole. The parole officer has a unique role, as Johnson has observed.[59] He must fulfill the authoritarian function of representing the state, but must simultaneously be oriented to the rehabilitation of the offender. As a middleman, or as a person who plays the role of "stranger," the parole officer must elicit the participation of the parolee and of the community in integrating the parolee into community life. The role that the parole officer plays is both a handicap and a resource in accomplishing his diverse tasks.

The dual considerations of protecting the public and helping the parolee have given rise to different types of performance by parole officers. Glaser has observed that parole officers are variously oriented toward the demands of control and assistance.[60] Some parole officers emphasize both control and

[58] President's Commission on Law Enforcement and Administration of Justice, *The Challenge of Crime in a Free Society* (Washington, D. C.: U. S. Government Printing Office, 1967), p. 12.

[59] Elmer H. Johnson, "The Parole Supervisor in the Role of Stranger," *Journal of Criminal Law, Criminology and Police Science,* 50 (May-June, 1959), pp. 38–43.

[60] Daniel Glaser, *The Effectiveness of a Prison and Parole System,* Indianapolis, Ind.: Bobbs-Merrill, 1964, pp. 429–442.

assistance ("paternal" officers), whereas others pay little attention to either ("passive" officers). In addition, some officers emphasize assistance but not control ("welfare" officers), and finally others emphasize control but not assistance ("punitive" officers). Each officer style has associated with it a different kind of personal background and a different way of perceiving and evaluating parolees. The offender's fate is thus determined by the type of parole officer who happens to be assigned to him.

For inmates who are not released at the expiration of their sentence or by parole, there are other alternatives. The original sentence may be modified by the executive by a pardon, commutation, or amnesty. As a last resort, an inmate may be executed in prison. As with all decisions, extra-legal factors would be expected to affect this, the ultimate of decisions. In studying the execution of condemned inmates, Wolfgang, Kelly, and Nolde found characteristics that distinguish those inmates who are executed from those who have their execution orders commuted.[61] The offender's race was the most important factor in determining whether a person awaiting execution on death row was executed or had his sentence commuted. We cannot regard as overstatement the researcher's conclusion that "Negroes have not received equal consideration for commutation of the death penalty."[62] Findings and conclusions such as these illustrate not only that research in the sociology of criminal law can uncover and explain the workings of the criminal law, but also that such research frequently paves the way for legal reform.

A SOCIOLOGICAL THEORY
OF CRIMINAL LAW

In spite of considerable research in recent years, a theory of criminal law has not developed. We do not yet have the theoretical means to generalize beyond the research studies or to formulate research hypotheses. In what follows, I will propose a sociological theory of criminal law to assist in these tasks. This theory is based upon a particular theoretical orientation within sociology and incorporates the research in the sociology of criminal law.

FROM SOCIOLOGICAL JURISPRUDENCE
TO SOCIOLOGY OF CRIMINAL LAW

The paradox today is that in the convergence of law and social science the theoretical orientation to legal matters is no more apparent than it was half a

---

[61] Marvin E. Wolfgang, Arlene Kelley, and Hans C. Nolde, "Comparison of the Executed and the Commuted Among Admissions to Death Row," *Journal of Criminal Law, Criminology and Police Science,* 53 (September, 1962), pp. 301–311.

[62] Wolfgang, Kelly, and Nolde, "Comparison of the Executed and the Commuted Among Admissions to Death Row," p. 311.

century ago. From a historical point of view, the rapprochement of law and social science that we are currently witnessing is not novel. There was a similar occurrence in the United States shortly after the turn of the century. At that time social scientists, the early American sociologists in particular, were incorporating law into their scheme of things. E. A. Ross referred to law as "the most specialized and highly furnished engine of control employed by society."[63] Lester F. Ward, an advocate of government control and social planning, foresaw a day when legislation would undertake to solve "questions of social improvement, the amelioration of the condition of all the people, the removal of whatever privations may still remain, and the adoption of means to the positive increase of the social welfare, in short the organization of human happiness."[64] The possibility of social reform, through legal means available to the state, was also emphasized by Albion W. Small.[65]

The ideas of the early sociologists directly influenced the development of the school of legal philosophy that became a major force in American legal thought — sociological jurisprudence. Roscoe Pound, the principal figure in sociological jurisprudence, drew from the early sociologists in asserting that law should be studied as a social institution.[66] Pound saw law as a specialized form of social control which brings pressure to bear upon each man "in order to constrain him to do his part in upholding civilized society and to deter him from anti-social conduct, that is, conduct at variance with the postulates of social order."[67]

Central to Pound's sociological jurisprudence was his theory of interests, according to which the law functions to accomplish socially worthwhile purposes. Besides the programmatic and teleological aspects of his work, Pound provided in his theory of interests one of the few starting points for the study of law as a social phenomenon.

A vast amount of writing and research has accumulated in recent years documenting the role of interest groups in the political process. There have been discussions on the techniques and tactics of interest groups, relations between groups, internal organization and politics of interest groups, and

[63] E. A. Ross, *Social Control* (New York: Macmillan, 1922), p. 106 (originally published in 1901).

[64] Lester F. Ward, *Applied Sociology* (Boston: Ginn, 1906), p. 339.

[65] Albion W. Small, *General Sociology* (Chicago: University of Chicago Press, 1925).

[66] The relation between early American sociologists and the development of Pound's sociological jurisprudence is discussed in Gilbert Geis, "Sociology and Jurisprudence: Admixture of Lore and Law," *Kentucky Law Journal,* 52 (Winter, 1964), pp. 267–293. Also see Edwin M. Schur, *Law and Society* (New York: Random House, 1968), pp. 17–50.

[67] Roscoe Pound, *Social Control Through Law* (New Haven: Yale University Press, 1942), p. 18. Earlier statements by Pound are found in Roscoe Pound, *An Introduction to the Philosophy of Law* (New Haven: Yale University Press, 1922) ; Roscoe Pound, *Outline of Lectures on Jurisprudence* (Cambridge: Harvard University Press, 1928).

overlapping group membership.[68] In addition, studies have been conducted on the operation of specific interest groups.[69] In spite of all these efforts, research on the role of interests in formulating and administering law has been almost nonexistent.[70] Moreover, few have attempted to revise Pound's theory of interests to reflect recent sociological developments. As Geis has commented, "Sociologists to date have paid virtually no attention to Pound's doctrine, either in terms of rejecting it, refining it for their purposes, or supplementing it with sociological material of more recent vintage."[71]

In the current movement toward research into law by social scientists and the use of social science research by lawyers, the role of interests might well be considered in an attempt to construct a theory of criminal law that would integrate the existing research findings and provide direction for future research. For sociological purposes, however, Pound's approach necessarily requires reformulation and extension into a sociological theory of criminal law.

Law is not merely a complex of rules and procedures; Pound taught us

[68] Donald C. Blaisdell, *American Democracy Under Pressure* (New York: Ronald Press, 1957); V. O. Key, Jr., *Politics, Parties, and Pressure Groups* (New York: Thomas Y. Crowell, 1959); Earl Latham, *Group Basis of Politics* (Ithaca, N.Y.: Cornell University Press, 1952); David B. Truman, *The Governmental Process* (New York: Alfred A. Knopf, 1951); Henry W. Ehrmann (ed.), *Interest Groups on Four Continents* (Pittsburgh: University of Pittsburgh Press, 1958); Henry A. Turner, "How Pressure Groups Operate," *Annals of the American Academy of Political and Social Science,* 319 (September, 1958), pp. 63–72; Richard W. Gable, "Interest Groups as Policy Shapers," *Annals of the American Academy of Political and Social Science,* 319 (September, 1958), pp. 84–93; Murray S. Stedman, "Pressure Groups and the American Tradition," *Annals of the American Academy of Political and Social Science,* 319 (September, 1958), pp. 123–129.

[69] Robert Engler, *The Politics of Oil* (New York: Macmillan, 1961); Oliver Garceau, *The Political Life of the American Medical Association* (Cambridge: Harvard University Press, 1941); Charles M. Hardin, *The Politics of Agriculture: Soil Conservation and the Struggle for Power in Rural America* (New York: The Free Press of Glencoe, 1962); Grant McConnell, *Private Power and American Democracy* (New York: Alfred A. Knopf, 1966); Harry A. Millis and Royal E. Montgomery, *Organized Labor* (New York: McGraw-Hill, 1945); Warner Schilling, Paul Y. Hammond, and Glenn H. Snyder, *Strategy, Politics and Defense* (New York: Columbia University Press, 1962); William R. Willoughby, *The St. Lawrence Waterway: A Study in Politics and Diplomacy* (Madison: University of Wisconsin Press, 1961).

[70] Other social orientations to the law may be found among sociological jurists, among the so-called legal realists, and among current legal historians. See, in particular, Oliver Wendell Holmes, "The Path of the Law," *Harvard Law Review,* 10 (March, 1897), pp. 457–478; Thurman W. Arnold, *Symbols of Government* (New Haven: Yale University Press, 1935); Jerome Frank, *Courts on Trial* (Princeton: Princeton University Press, 1949); K. N. Llewellyn and E. Adamson Hoebel, *The Cheyenne Way: Conflict and Case Law in Primitive Jurisprudence* (Norman: University of Oklahoma Press, 1941); J. Willard Hurst, *Law and Economic Growth: The Legal History of the Lumber Industry in Wisconsin, 1836–1915* (Cambridge, Mass.: The Belknap Press, 1964).

[71] Geis, "Sociology and Sociological Jurisprudence: Admixture of Lore and Law," p. 292.

that in his call for the study of "law in action" as distinguished from the study of law in the books. For some purposes it may be useful to view law as autonomous to society, developing according to its own internal logic and proceeding along its own lines. But law also operates simultaneously as a reflection of society and as an influence in society. Thus, in a social sense, law is both social product and social force. In Pound's juristic approach, however, law as both a product and a force was viewed in a very special way. In jurisprudence, law as a social product is conceived as law which reflects the consciousness of the total society. This *consensus* model of law, regarding criminal law, is described thus: "The state of criminal law continues to be — as it should — a decisive reflection of the social consciousness of a society. What kind of conduct an organized community considers, at a given time, sufficiently condemnable to impose official sanctions, impairing the life, liberty, or property of the offender, is a barometer of the moral and social thinking of a community."[72] Similarly, Pound, in formulating his theory of interests, looked upon law as reflecting the needs of the well-ordered society. In fact, the law was a form of "social engineering" in a civilized society:

For the purpose of understanding the law of today I am content to think of law as a social institution to satisfy social wants — the claims and demands involved in the existence of civilized society — by giving effect to as much as we may with the least sacrifice, so far as such wants may be satisfied or such claims given effect by an ordering of human conduct through politically organized society. For present purposes I am content to see in legal history the record of a continually wider recognizing and satisfying of human wants or claims or desires through social control; a more embracing and more effective securing of social interests; a continually more complete and effective elimination of waste and precluding of friction in human enjoyment of the goods of existence — in short, a continually more efficacious social engineering.[73]

Thus, the interests Pound had in mind were those which would maintain and, ultimately, improve the social order. His was a *teleological* as well as consensus theory of interests: There are interests which man and society must fulfill for the good of the whole society. These interests are to be achieved through law. In Pound's theory, only the right law could emerge in a civilized society.

Jurisprudence has generally utilized a *pluralistic* model with respect to law as a social force in society. Accordingly, law regulates social behavior and establishes social organization. Law orders human relations by restraining individual actions and by settling disputes in social relations. In recent juris-

[72] Wolfgang Friedmann, *Law in a Changing Society* (Harmondsworth, England: Penguin Books, 1964), p. 143. A similar statement is found in Michael and Adler, *Crime, Law and Social Science*, pp. 2–3.
[73] Pound, *An Introduction to the Philosophy of Law*, pp. 98–99.

tic language, law functions "first, to establish the general framework, the rules of the game so to speak, within and by which individual and group life shall be carried on, and secondly, to adjust the conflicting claims which different individuals and groups of individuals seek to satisfy in society."[74] For Pound, the law adjusts and reconciles conflicting interests:

> Looked at functionally, the law is an attempt to satisfy, to reconcile, to harmonize, to adjust these overlapping and often conflicting claims and demands, either through securing them directly and immediately, or through securing certain individual interests, or through delimitations or compromises of individual interests, so as to give effect to the greatest total of interests or to the interests that weigh most in our civilization, with the least sacrifice of the scheme of interests as a whole.[75]

In Pound's theory of interests, therefore, it is assumed that the legal order is created in society to regulate and adjust the conflicting desires and claims of men. The law provides the general framework within which individual and group life is carried on, according to the postulates of social order. Moreover, as a legal historian has written, "The law defines the extent to which it will give effect to the interests which it recognizes, in the light of other interests and of the possibilities of effectively securing them through law; it also devises means for securing those that are recognized and prescribes the limits within which those means may be employed."[76] In the interest theory of sociological jurisprudence, then, law is regarded as an instrument which controls interests according to the requirements of social order.

Pound's theory of interests included a threefold classification of interests: (1) individual interests, (2) public interests, and (3) social interests. "Individual interests are claims or demands or desires involved immediately in the individual life and asserted in the title of that life. Public interests are claims or demands or desires involved in life in a politically organized society and asserted in the title of that organization. They are commonly treated as the claims of a politically organized society thought of as a legal entity. Social interests are claims or demands or desires involved in social life in a civilized society and asserted in the title of that life. It is not uncommon to treat them as the claims of the whole social group as such."[77] While Pound delineated three kinds of interests secured by the legal order, he warned that the types

---

[74] Carl A. Auerbach, "Law and Social Change in the United States," *U.C.L.A. Law Review,* 6 (July, 1959), pp. 516–532. Similarly, see Julius Stone, *The Province and Function of Law* (Cambridge: Harvard University Press, 1950), Part III; Julius Stone, *Social Dimensions of Law and Justice* (Stanford: Stanford University Press, 1966), chaps. 4–8.

[75] Roscoe Pound, "A Survey of Social Interests," *Harvard Law Review,* 57 (October, 1943), p. 39.

[76] George Lee Haskins, *Law and Authority in Early Massachusetts,* p. 226.

[77] Pound, "A Survey of Social Interests," pp. 1–2.

are overlapping and interdependent and that most claims, demands, or desires can be placed in all the categories, depending upon one's purpose. However, he argued that it is often expedient to put claims, demands, and desires in their most general form; that is, into the category of social interests.

Surveying the claims, demands, and desires found in legal proceedings and in legislative proposals, Pound suggested that the most important social interest appears to be the interest in security against actions that threaten the social group.[78] Other social interests consist of the interest in the security of social institutions, including domestic, religious, economic, and political; the interest in morals; the interest in conservation of social resources; the interest in general progress, including the development of human powers and control over nature for the satisfaction of human wants; and the interest in individual life, especially the freedom of self-assertion. According to Pound, the nature of any legal system depends upon the way in which these interests are incorporated into law.

Although the *sociological theory of interests* that I am developing is in the general tradition of the interest theory of sociological jurisprudence, it departs from that tradition in a number of ways. First, the interest theory I am proposing is based on a particular conception of society. Society is characterized by diversity, conflict, coercion, and change, rather than by consensus and stability. Second, law is a *result* of the operation of interests, rather than an instrument which functions outside of particular interests. Though law may operate to control interests, it is in the first place *created* by interests. Third, law incorporates the interests of specific persons and groups in society. Seldom is law the product of the whole society. Rather than representing the interests of all members of society, law consists of the interests of only specific segments of the population. Law is made by men, particular men representing special interests, who have the power to translate their interests into public policy. In opposition to the pluralistic conception of politics, law does not represent the compromise of the diverse interests in society, but supports some interests at the expense of others. Fourth, the sociological theory of interests is devoid of teleological connotations. The social order may require certain functions for its maintenance and survival, but such functions will not be considered as inherent in the interests involved in formulating particular substantive laws. Fifth, the theory proposed here includes a conceptual scheme for analyzing interests in the law. Sixth, the theory is systematically constructed according to an arrangement of propositions. Finally, construc-

[78] Pound, "A Survey of Social Interests," 1–39. Other aspects of the theory of interests are discussed by Pound in the following publications: *The Spirit of the Common Law* (Boston: Marshall Jones, 1921), pp. 91–93, 197–203; *An Introduction to the Philosophy of Law*, pp. 90–96; *Interpretations of Legal History* (New York: Macmillan, 1923), pp. 158–164; *Social Control through Law*, pp. 63–80.

tion of the sociological theory of interests is based on findings from current social science research.

A Sociological Theory of Interests

These characteristics of a sociological approach to law serve as the basis for constructing a sociological theory of interests. The theory consists of four propositions. Each proposition is presented with supporting rationale.

1. *Law is the creation and interpretation of specialized rules in a politically organized society.*

Authority relationships are present in all social collectivities: some persons are always at the command of others. In establishing order in a society, several systems of control develop to regulate the conduct of various groups of persons. Human behavior, thus, is subject to restraint by varied agencies, institutions, and social groupings — families, churches, social clubs, political organizations, labor unions, corporations, educational systems, and so forth.

The control systems vary considerably in the forms of conduct they regulate, and most of them provide means for assuring compliance to their rules. Informal means, spontaneously employed by some persons, such as ridicule, gossip, and censure, may ensure conformity to some rules. Control sytems may, in addition, rely upon formal and regularized means of sanction.

The *legal system* is the most explicit form of social control. The law consists of (1) specific rules of conduct, (2) planned use of sanctions to support the rules, and (3) designated officials to interpret and enforce the rules.[79] Furthermore, law becomes more important as a system of control as societies increase in complexity. Pound wrote that "in the modern world law has become the paramount agent of social control. Our main reliance is upon force of a politically organized state."[80]

Law is not only a system of formal social control but also a body of specialized rules created and interpreted in a *politically organized society*. Politically organized society, or the state, is a territorial organization with the authorized power to govern the lives and activities of all the inhabitants. Though other types of organized bodies may possess formal rules, only the specialized rule systems of politically organized societies are regarded here as systems of law.[81]

Law, as a special kind of institution that exists in particular societies, is more than an abstract body of rules. Rather than being autonomous to so-

---

[79] F. James Davis, "Law as a Type of Social Control," in F. James Davis, Henry H. Foster, Jr., C. Ray Jeffery, and E. Eugene Davis, *Society and the Law* (New York: The Free Press of Glencoe, 1962), p. 43.

[80] Pound, *Social Control through Law,* p. 20.

[81] The rule systems of other than politically organized society may be adequately referred to, for comparative purposes, in any number of quasi-legal ways, such as nonstate law, primitive law, or lawways. Perhaps, even better, such systems of rules could be described simply as tradition, norma-

ciety and developing according to its own internal logic, law is an integral part of society, operating as a force in society and as a social product. The law is not only that which is written as statutes and recorded as court opinions and administrative rulings, but is also a method or *process* of doing something.[82] As a process, law is a dynamic force that is continually being *created* and *interpreted*. Thus, law in action involves the making of specialized (legal) decisions by various *authorized agents*. In politically organized society, human actions are regulated by those invested with the authority to make certain decisions in the name of the society.

Furthermore, law in operation is an aspect of politics. That is, law is one of the methods in which *public policy* is formulated and administered for governing the lives and activities of the inhabitants of the state. As an act of politics, law does not represent the norms and values of all persons in the society. Legal decisions, rather, incorporate the interests of only some persons. Whenever a law is created or interpreted, the values of some are necessarily assured and the values of others are either ignored or negated. The *politicality of law* is basic to the sociological theory of interests.

2. *Politically organized society is based on an interest structure.*

Modern societies are characterized by an organization of differences. The social differentiation of society, in turn, provides the basis for the political life of the state. To be specific, the governing process in a politically organized society operates according to the interests that characterize the socially differentiated positions. Because various kinds of interests are distributed among the positions, and because the positions are differently equipped with the ability to command, public policy represents certain interests in the society. Politically organized society, therefore, may be viewed as a differentiated *interest structure*.

Each *segment* of society has its own values, norms, and ideological orientations. When these concerns are considered as important for the existence and welfare of the respective positions, they may be defined as *interests*.[83] Further, interests can be categorized according to the ways in which activities are generally pursued in society; that is, according to the *institutional orders* of society. The following may then serve as a definition of interests: *the in-*

tive system, or custom. The concept of law is expanded to include the control systems of other than politically organized society among such writers as Bronislaw Malinowski, *Crime and Custom in Savage Society* (London: Routledge and Kegan Paul, 1926); E. Adamson Hoebel, *The Law of Primitive Man* (Cambridge: Harvard University Press, 1954); William M. Evan, "Public and Private Legal Systems," in William M. Evan (editor), *Law and Sociology* (New York: The Free Press of Glencoe, 1962), pp. 165–184; Philip Selznick, "Legal Institutions and Social Controls," *Vanderbilt Law Review,* 17 (December, 1963), pp. 79–90.

[82] For this conception of law, as applied to criminal law, see Henry M. Hart, Jr., "The Aims of the Criminal Law," *Law and Contemporary Problems,* 23 (Summer, 1958), pp. 401–441.

[83] The view here that interests are not distributed randomly in society

stitutional concerns of the segments of society. Thus, interests are grounded in the segments of society and represent the institutional concerns of the segments.

The institutional orders within which interests operate may be classified into fairly broad categories.[84] For our purposes, these orders will be delimited: (1) *the political order,* which regulates the distribution of power and authority in society; (2) *the economic order,* which regulates the production and distribution of goods and services; (3) *the religious order,* which regulates the relationship of man to a conception of the supernatural; (4) *the kinship order,* which regulates sexual relations, family patterns, and the procreation and rearing of children; (5) *the educational order,* which regulates the formal training of the members of society; and (6) *the public order,* which regulates the protection and maintenance of the community and its citizens. Each segment of society has its own orientation to these institutional orders. Some segments, because of their authority position in the interest structure, are able to have their interests represented in public society.

The segments of society differ in the extent to which their interests are organized. The segments themselves are broad statistical aggregates containing persons of similar age, sex, class, status, occupation, race, ethnicity, religion, or the like. All these segments have *formal interests;* that is, interests which are advantageous to the segment but which are not consciously held by the incumbents and are not organized for action. *Active interests,* on the other hand, are interests that are manifest to persons in the segments and are sufficiently organized to serve as the basis for representation in policy decisions.[85]

Within the segments, groups of persons may organize to promote their common interests. These groups may be simply called *interest groups.* Thus, it is within the broad segments of society that groups become aware of their common concerns and organize to promote their interests. Public policy, in turn, is the result of the success of these groups. These are the dynamics of the interest structure in a politically organized society.

3. *The interest structure of politically organized society is characterized by unequal distribution of power and by conflict.*

Basic to the interest structure is a conception of unequal distribution of

---

but are related to one's position in society follows Marx's theory of economic production and class conflict. See Ralf Dahrendorf, *Class and Class Conflict in Industrial Society* (Stanford: Stanford University Press, 1959), especially pp. 3–35.

[84] The conception of institutional orders closely follows that of Hans Gerth and C. Wright Mills, *Character and Social Structure* (New York: Harcourt, Brace, 1953), especially pp. 25–26.

[85] The distinction between formal interests and active interests is similar to the distinction Dahrendorf makes between latent and manifest interests. See Dahrendorf, *Class and Class Conflict in Industrial Society,* pp. 173–179.

power and *conflict* between the segments of politically organized society. The interest structure is differentiated not only by diverse interests, but also according to the ability of the segments to translate their interests into public policy. Furthermore, the segments are in continual conflict over their interests. Thus, interests are structured according to differences in power and are in conflict.

Power and conflict are inextricably linked in this conception of interest structure. Power, as the ability to shape public policy, produces conflict between the competing segments, and conflict, in turn, produces differences in the distribution of power. Coherence in the interest structure is thus assured by the exercise of force and constraint by the conflicting segments of the interest structure.[86] In the conflict-power model of interest structure, therefore, politically organized society is held together by conflicting elements and functions according to the coercion of some segments by others.

The conflict-power conception of interest structure implies that public policy results from differential distribution of power and conflict between the segments of society. Diverse segments with specialized interests become so highly organized that they are able to influence the policies that affect all persons in the state. Groups that have the power to gain access to the decision-making process are able to translate their interests into public policy. Thus, the interests represented in the formulation and administration of public policy are those treasured by the dominant segments of the society. Hence, public policy is created because segments with power differentials are in conflict with one another. Public policy itself is a manifestation of an interest structure in politically organized society.

4. *Law is formulated and administered within the interest structure of a politically organized society.*

Law is a form of public policy that regulates the behavior and activities of all members of a society. Law is *formulated* and *administered* by the segments of society that are able to incorporate their interests into the creation and interpretation of public policy. Rather than representing the institutional concerns of all segments of society, law secures the interests of particular segments. Law supports one point of view at the expense of others.

Thus, the content of the law, including the substantive regulations and the procedural rules, represents the interests of segments of society that have the power to shape public policy. Formulation of law allows some segments of society to protect and perpetuate their own interests. By formulating law, some segments are able to control others to their own advantage.

---

[86] The sociological theory of interests is based upon the coercion model of society as opposed to the integrative model. See Ralf Dahrendorf, "Out of Utopia: Toward a Reorientation in Sociological Analysis," *American Journal of Sociology,* 67 (September, 1958), pp. 115–127.

The interests that the power segments of society attempt to maintain enter into all stages of legal administration. Since legal formulations do not provide specific instructions for interpreting law, administration of law is largely a matter of discretion on the part of *legal agents* (police, prosecutors, judges, juries, prison authorities, parole officers, and others). The decisions reached tend to support the interests of some segments of society while impeding the interests of others. Though implementation of law necessarily is influenced by such matters as localized conditions and the occupational organization of legal agents, the interest structure of politically organized society is responsible for the general design of the administration of justice.

Finally, since law is formulated and administered within the interest structure of politically organized society, it follows that law changes with modifications in that structure. New and shifting demands require new laws. When the interests that underlie a law no longer are relevant to groups in power, the law will be reinterpreted or changed to incorporate the dominant interests. The social history of criminal law can be described according to alterations in the interest structure of society.

CONCLUSION

The scope of criminology has been broadened in recent years to include the process by which persons and behaviors become defined as criminal. That is, the criminal law — including its formulation and administration — no longer is taken for granted, but serves as a major orientation for the study of crime. Research in the last decade has substantiated the importance of criminal law in criminology. Much of the research is presented in this book.

In order to provide a theoretical perspective for presenting and interpreting the research in the sociology of criminal law, a theory of law has been constructed. This theory, a sociological theory of interests, has been inspired by Roscoe Pound's juristic approach. It departs from Pound's approach by postulating, among other things, that law is created by interests, by assuming a conflict-power model of society, and by proposing a conceptual scheme for analyzing the relationship between law and interests.   —

Most important, the sociological theory of interests has been systematically constructed according to propositions which state that law consists of specialized rules that are created and interpreted in politically organized society, that such a society is based on an interest structure, that an interest structure is characterized by unequal distribution of power and by conflict, and that law is formulated and administered within the interest structure of politically organized society. This theory is consistent with and is supported by findings from current empirical investigations of crime, law, and administration of justice.

1

FORMULATION OF
CRIMINAL LAW

A Rule to Walk By

GEORGE LEE HASKINS

"In all their administrations," wrote John Winthrop in defense of the constitutionality of the early Massachusetts government, "the Officers of this Bodye Politick have a Rule to walk by . . . which Rule is the *Worde of God.* . . ."[1] The basic content of that rule, in Puritan eyes, was to be found in the Bible, wherein God had provided an immutable constitution not only, as John Cotton said, "for the right ordering of a private mans soule to everlasting blessednes with himselfe, but also for the right ordering of a mans family, yea, of the commonwealth too, so farre as both of them are subordinate to spiritual ends. . . ."[2]

That the word of God provided the mainspring for the colony mission is hardly open to doubt. The reform and purification of church discipline and doctrine through a return to the principles of the primitive apostolic church was not only the deliberate and unswerving aim of the early Puritans in England but the primary purpose of the founding of the Bay Colony. To God's word as declared in Scripture the colonists consistently turned for guidance and justification, both in matters of church polity and in the framing and administration of their laws. The decisions of the courts were expected to conform to that Word, and an order of the General Court in 1636 had expressly so provided in situations for which no positive law had been established.[3] Moreover, the Epistle to the Code of 1648 proclaimed that it had been "no small priviledge, and advantage to us in New-England . . . to frame our civil Politie, and lawes according to the rules of [God's] most holy word,"[4] and the capital laws therein contained were specifically annotated to chapter and verse of the Old Testament. Several of those provisions, as well as other enactments, incorporated literal biblical phraseology into the body of statutory law.[5]

The colonists' reliance upon biblical precedent and authority, apparent in the pronouncements of their leaders and in the fabric of the legal system, has led some scholars to conclude that the law of early Massachusetts was

Reprinted with permission of the author and The Macmillan Company from *Law and Authority in Early Massachusetts* by George Lee Haskins. Copyright by George Lee Haskins 1960.

[1] *Winthrop Papers* IV, 472.
[2] Quoted in P. Miller and T. H. Johnson, *The Puritans* (New York, 1938) 209.
[3] *Mass. Records* I, 174–175.
[4] *Laws and Liberties,* Epistle.
[5] See *infra,* pp. 146 *et seq.*

essentially biblical,[6] and even to characterize the colony as the "Bible Commonwealth."[7] Although such generalizations are not without foundation, their value is lessened by failure to examine them from the standpoint of the law as a whole and with reference both to the special conditions of settlement and to the social, political, and legal inheritance which the Puritans shared in common with other seventeenth century Englishmen.

At the outset, it should be observed that influential as the Bible was in the lives of the colonists, it also held a position of extraordinary importance for their English contemporaries. Recourse to, and reliance upon, the teachings of Scripture was by no means confined to the Puritans and was common throughout England in the sixteenth and seventeenth centuries. By the time of the settlement of Massachusetts, the Bible in English translation had been widely available for nearly a century.[8] Henry VIII had at one point sought to stem developing interest therein through a prohibition against its being read by servants and women; yet the impetus of the English Reformation so stimulated popular demand for free access to the Scriptures that by the 1530's Bible reading was actively encouraged by the Tudor government. In 1538 it was ordered that every parish in the country should purchase a copy of the Bible in English, to be set up in each church, "where the parishioners might most commodiously resort to the same and read it."[9] As the century wore on, the Bible, in cheap and readily available editions, had become the common property of all classes of English society. Children in school were taught to read from books studded with scriptural selections,[10] and by the beginning of the seventeenth century virtually every literate English household had its own copy.[11] The rich imagery of its texts quickened the imagination and left an indelible imprint upon English speech and letters, while its precepts and parables, no longer buried in the obscurities of the Latin tongue or meted out at the discretion of a priestly caste, became a powerful force not only in molding religious ideas but in shaping the everyday conduct of English people in all walks of life.

By the end of the sixteenth century, critical study of biblical texts and of

[6] E.g., P. S. Reinsch, "The English Common Law in the Early American Colonies," *Select Essays in Anglo-American Legal History* (Boston, 1907) I, 367 at 372–376.

[7] E.g., T. J. Wertenbaker, *The Puritan Oligarchy* (New York, 1947) Chap. 2.

[8] William Tyndale's English translation of the New Testament, printed on the Continent, was circulated in England as early as the late 1520's; Miles Coverdale's translation of the entire Bible was published under a royal license in 1537. See *The Cambridge History of English Literature* (eds. A. W. Ward and A. R. Waller: New York, 1909), 46–49.

[9] W. S. Churchill, *A History of the English-Speaking Peoples* (London, 1956) II, 61.

[10] H. M. and M. Dexter, *The England and Holland of the Pilgrims* (Boston, 1905) 26.

[11] F. A. Inderwick, *The Interregnum* (London, 1891) 126.

Christian philosophy was an important feature of the curricula of the English universities, particularly at Cambridge, and theology and church polity had become leading intellectual interests of the day.[12] Ecclesiastics of all persuasions turned to the Bible in defense or in support of their views. Bishop Jewel, an apologist for the Elizabethan establishment, was convinced no less than his Puritan opponents that he had searched out of the Bible "one sure form of religion," returning thereby "unto the primitive church of the ancient fathers and apostles."[13] In the eagerness and intensity with which the Puritans studied the Bible, and in the conclusions they drew therefrom, the Puritans did, however, differ from their contemporaries. The renaissance of Hebrew studies which had accompanied the Reformation particularly affected them, since the ancient texts helped to provide a key to the word of God. Such men as John Cotton, Nathaniel Ward, and John Eliot read Hebrew as well as Latin, and its study was made a part of the required curriculum at Harvard College; but it should be observed that this interest is as much attributable to then current English standards of education as to the specific influence of Puritanism.[14]

Hardly less striking was the influence of the Bible upon English law and legal thinking. Belief in the Scriptures as a source of law was widespread among educated Englishmen, partly because of the persisting influence of mediaeval scholasticism and partly because of the tendency of Protestant theologians to equate natural law with Mosaic law.[15] English exiles who had lived at Geneva during the reign of Mary had seen at firsthand a legal system that owed much to biblical precepts,[16] and the influence of Calvinism in Scotland had resulted in the enactment of the eighteenth chapter of Leviticus as the positive law of the northern kingdom.[17] As part of the effort to prove the English Church's claim to apostolic succession, the sixteenth century had seen the publication and widespread praise of the early code of Alfred the Great, which incorporated the Decalogue and much of four chapters of Exodus as part of the laws of England.[18] Thomas Cromwell, Henry VIII's Chief Minister, had even ordered the reading of the Ten Commandments at the end of every Sabbath service.[19]

[12] S. E. Morison, *The Puritan Pronaos* (New York, 1936) 17–21.
[13] P. Miller, *Orthodoxy in Massachusetts, 1630–1650* (Cambridge, Mass., 1933) 25.
[14] Morison, *op. cit. supra* n. 12, at 41–42; L. I. Newman, *Jewish Influence on Christian Reform Movements* (New York, 1925) 635–636.
[15] J. T. McNeill, "Natural Law in the Teaching of the Reformers," *Journal of Religion* XXVI, 168–182 (1946).
[16] D. Neal, *History of the Puritans* (London, 1837), I, 76–83.
[17] *The Acts of the Parliaments of Scotland* (London, 1814) III, 26 (December 20, 1567).
[18] J. Goebel, Jr., "King's Law and Local Custom in Seventeenth Century New England," *Columbia Law Review* XXXI, 416, 424, n. (1931).
[19] *Ibid.*

Among lawyers belief in the Bible as a source of law was given special cogency by the wide popularity of St. Germain's *Doctor and Student* and other texts which sought to demonstrate that the law of England was grounded upon the law of God.[20] As early as 1551, the king's attorney argued before the Exchequer Chamber that "the Christian Kings of this realm in former times have made their laws as neer to the laws of God as they could," and then proceeded to cite Deuteronomy as authority for the rule for which he was contending.[21] The argument merely reflected the tendency of the age, for reliance upon and reference to the Bible was habitual among English judges and legal writers during this period. Lord Chancellor Ellesmere, in the reign of James I, began an opinion with the words: "The law of God speaks for the plaintiff, Deut. XXVIII.30."[22] In a manslaughter case in 1611, a justice of the King's Bench cited, in Latin, Christ's warning that he who lives by the sword shall perish by the sword.[23] Coke's report of Ratcliff's Case, decided in Queen's Bench in 1592, noted that the court's conclusion that inheritances may lineally descend, but not ascend, was reinforced by the argument "that in this Point as almost in all others the Common Law was grounded upon the Law of God . . . as it appeareth in the 27 Chap. of *Numbers*," the relevant text of which was summarized and quoted in the report.[24]

Justices of the peace, according to Lambarde, customarily addressed their charges to the jury under heads corresponding to the Ten Commandments[25] — a practice which was also followed in Massachusetts.[26] The exhortation to the jury outlined in Kitchin's standard manual for the conduct of courts leet begins: "Feare God and keepe his Commandements," and goes on to cite or quote the Old and the New Testament ten times in the course of a small printed page.[27] The peroration of the charge to the jury printed in Fitzherbert's manual for justices of the peace is explicit as to the application of God's laws to the affairs of man:

Saint *Iames* saith, *He that knoweth how to doe well, and doth it not, to him it is sinne.* And the *Gospell* saith, *He that knoweth his Masters will, and doth not per-*

---

[20] See W. S. Holdsworth, *A History of English Law* (London, 1942) IV, 275–276, 279–281, and *id.* V (1942) 266–269, for an account of the influence of the *Doctor and Student* upon the development of equity jurisdiction in England during the sixteenth century.

[21] *Reniger v. Fogossa*, 1 Plowden's Reports 1, 8 (King's Bench 1551).

[22] Earl of Oxford's Case, quoted in Z. Chafee, Jr., Introduction, "Records of the Suffolk County Court, 1671–1680," *Col. Soc. Mass. Coll.* XXIX, xxxii (1933).

[23] *Bradley v. Banks*, 1 Bulstrode's Reports 141, 142 (King's Bench 1611).

[24] Ratcliff's Case, 3 Coke's Reports 37a, 40a (Queen's Bench 1592).

[25] W. Lambarde, *Eirenarcha, or Of the Office of the Iustices of Peace* (London, 1607) 401.

[26] T. Lechford, "Plain Dealing: or, Newes from New-England," *Mass. Hist. Soc. Coll.* (3rd. ser.) III, 55, 84 (1833).

[27] J. Kitchin, *Jurisdictions: or, The Lawful Authority of Courts Leet, Courts Baron, Court of Marshallseyes, Court of Pypowder, and Ancient mesne* (London, 1653) 13.

fome the same, shall be beaten with many stripes. Which places of Scripture, although they chiefly pertain to the Transgressors of the Law Divine: yet sith Subiects are bounden in conscience to keepe the Lawes of their Princes and Countries, which are not against the Lawes of God, it is not impertinent to applie the said places of Scripture to the breakers of the same Lawes.[28]

Unquestionably, therefore, Englishmen of the sixteenth and seventeenth centuries were thoroughly conversant with the Bible and accustomed to looking upon it as authority. It is equally without question that the influence of the Bible upon conceptions of what the law ought to be was more pronounced and more inclined toward literalism among the English Puritans than among their non-Puritan countrymen. The former saw themselves as children of Israel, openly imitated Hebraic practices, and likened their persecutions to the misery of the Jews at the hands of Antiochus.[29] By the same token, they were convinced that much of the law that God had given to ancient Israel continued to bind the people whom He had chosen as His own in the England of Elizabeth and James. "So soon as God had set up Politicall Government among his people Israel," recites the Epistle to the Code of 1648, "hee gave them a body of lawes for judgement both in civil and criminal causes. These were breif and fundamental principles, yet withall so full and comprehensive as out of them clear deductions were to be drawne to all particular cases in future times."[30] Pursuant to this kind of thinking, Thomas Cartwright, in the time of Elizabeth, had urged the necessity of the death penalty for blasphemers and unruly children;[31] and Puritan reformers of the Interregnum were to employ the same reasoning in pressing for the literal enactment of the Mosaic code.[32]

None of the Massachusetts laws more clearly reflects biblical influence than do the provisions of the capital laws contained in the Code of 1648. Idolatry, witchcraft, blasphemy, bestiality; sodomy, adultery, rape, man stealing, treason, false witness with intent to take life, cursing or smiting of a parent, stubbornness or rebelliousness on the part of a son against his parents, and homicide committed with malice prepense, by guile or poisoning, or "suddenly in . . . anger or cruelty of passion" — all were punishable with death.[33] Each of these provisions, with the exception of that relating to rape, was annotated to some chapter and verse of the Pentateuch, and several exactly reproduced its language. No more striking proof of literal reliance upon the Bible in this

---

[28] A. Fitzherbert, *Loffice Et auctoritie de Iustices de Peace* (London, 1617) iv.

[29] Newman, *op. cit. supra* n. 14, at 631–635.

[30] *Laws and Liberties,* Epistle.

[31] J. Strype, *Life and Acts of John Whitgift* (Oxford, 1822) III, 235, 237.

[32] See, e.g., the "Post-Script" printed at the end of *Examen Legum Angliae: or, the Laws of England Examined, By Scripture, Antiquity, and Reason* (London, 1656) No. 5 (blasphemy), No. 16 (disobedient children).

[33] *Laws and Liberties* 5–6. See also *id.* at 4–5 (theft).

area of the law can be found than in the law relating to rebellious sons,[34] which is here quoted in full, to the right of the text of Deuteronomy 21:18–21:

<table>
<tr>
<td>

If a man have a stubborn and rebellious son, which will not obey the voice of his father, or the voice of his mother, and that, when they have chastened him, will not hearken unto them: Then shall his father and his mother lay hold on him, and bring him out unto the elders of his city, and unto the gate of his place; And they shall say unto the elders of his city, This our son is stubborn and rebellious, he will not obey our voice; he is a glutton, and a drunkard. And all the men of his city shall stone him with stones, that he die . . .

</td>
<td>

If a man have a stubborn or REBELLIOUS SON, of sufficient years & understanding (*viz*) sixteen years of age, which will not obey the voice of his Father, or the voice of his Mother, and that when they have chastened him will not harken unto them; then shal his Father & Mother being his natural parents, lay hold on him, & bring him to the Magistrates assembled in Court & testifie unto them, that their Son is stubborn & rebellious & will not obey their voice and chastisement, but lives in sundry notorious crimes, such a son shal be put to death.

</td>
</tr>
</table>

Other capital laws contain clauses, phrases, or words taken directly from the Old Testament. Thus, the witchcraft provision defined a witch as one that "hath or consulteth with a familiar spirit"[35] in terms of Leviticus 20:27 and Deuteronomy 18:11, which speak respectively of one "that hath a familiar spirit" and of "a consulter with familiar spirits." Again, it is prescribed in Leviticus 20:15 and 16 that "if a man lie with a beast, he shall surely be put to death: and ye shall slay the beast," and a similar punishment was provided "if a woman approach unto any beast, and lie down thereto"; by comparison, the bestiality law of Massachusetts states that "If any man or woman shall LYE WITH ANY BEAST, or bruit creature, by carnall copulation; they shall surely be put to death: and the beast shall be slain, & buried, and not eaten."[36] In the same chapter of Leviticus, 20:13, it is stated that "If a man also lie with mankind, as he lieth with a woman, both of them have committed an abomination"; the colony law against sodomy prescribes that "If any man LYETH WITH MAN-KINDE as he lieth with a woman, both of them have committed abomination. . . ."[37] In Exodus 21:16 it is declared that "he that stealeth a man, and selleth him, or if he be found in his hand, he shall surely be put to death"; in Massachusetts law, "If any man STEALETH A MAN, or Man-kinde, he shall surely be put to death."[38] Finally, the colonial provision that "If any child, or children . . . shall CURSE, or SMITE their natural FATHER, or MOTHER; he or they shall be put to death:"[39] is paralleled by

---

[34] *Id.* at 6.
[35] *Id.* at 5.
[36] *Ibid.*
[37] *Ibid.*
[38] *Id.* at 6
[   ] *Ibid.*

Exodus 21:15 and 17, to the effect that "he that smiteth his father, or his mother . . . And he that curseth his father, or his mother, shall surely be put to death."

At the same time, even those capital laws which are unequivocally based upon the Bible contain evidence of substantial non-Scriptural influences. The sodomy law, for example, is qualified by an exception in favor of one who was "forced (or be under fourteen years of age in which case he shall be severely punished)."[40] This exception demonstrates that in the course of revising an earlier law, first enacted in the Body of Liberties, the colonists not only took account of the element of intent but introduced the recognized English legal presumption that a boy under fourteen years of age was deemed to be legally incapable of committing sodomy.[41] Significantly, legal presumptions based upon age are also apparent in the colony law against cursing or smiting of parents and in that dealing with stubborn and rebellious sons. Those laws, which were originally enacted by the General Court in November, 1646, were made applicable, respectively, to "any child, or children, above sixteen years old, and of sufficient understanding,"[42] and to a son "of sufficient years & understanding (*viz*) sixteen years of age."[43] In the former law a second qualification of Scripture was introduced for cases in which "it can be sufficiently testified that the Parents have been very unchristianly negligent in the education of such children; or so provoked them by extream, and cruel correction; that they have been forced therunto to preserve themselves from death or maiming."[44] This qualification appears to represent, as the absolute biblical injunction does not, an effort to accommodate the community's interest in ensuring the observance of God's command that parents be honored with the Puritan view that parents should provide their children with a proper moral and religious education, and should use moderation in correcting them.

Like the sodomy statute, the blasphemy statute was amended in important respects between its original enactment in 1641[45] and its incorporation into the Code in 1648.[46] The 1648 version is quoted in full, with the additions

---

40 *Id.* at 5–6.

41 E. Coke, *Institutes* (Part III) Chap. X: "If the party buggered be within the age of discretion, it is no felony in him but in the agent only." To the same effect, Sir Matthew Hale: "If buggery be committed upon a man of the age of discretion, both are felons within this law. But if with a man under the age of discretion, *viz*. fourteen years old, then the buggerer only is the felon" (*Historia Placitorum Coronae* [London, 1736] I, 670).

42 *Laws and Liberties* 6; *Mass. Records* II, 179.

43 *Ibid.*

44 *Ibid.*

45 *Body of Liberties* 94.

46 *Laws and Liberties* 5. The amended statute quoted in the text was originally enacted in substantially the same form as it appears in the *Laws and Liberties* on November 4, 1646 (*Mass. Records* II, 176–177).

italicized in order to demonstrate the extent to which the draftsmen consciously applied considered policy to its revision:

If any person *within this Jurisdiction whether Christian or Pagan shall wittingly and willingly presume to* BLASPHEME the *holy* Name of God, Father, Son or Holy-Ghost, with direct, expresse, presumptuous, or high-handed blasphemy, *either by wilfull or obstinate denying the true God, or his Creation, or Government of the world:* or shall curse God in like manner, *or reproach the holy Religion of God as if it were but a politick device to keep ignorant men in awe; or shal utter any other kinde of Blasphemy of the like nature & degree they* shall be put to death.

The first of the three amendments specifically extends the reach of the capital law to the Indians, pursuant to biblical authority afterward cited that "as well the stranger, as he that is born in the land, when he blasphemeth the name of the Lord, shall be put to death."[47] The second, as well as the first amendment, introduces the fundamental Puritan idea of the offender's moral responsibility for a criminal act, based upon his knowing and deliberate choice. Equally important is the third addition, which requires that the offenders be "wilfull or obstinate," and emphasizes the Puritan belief, apparent in other aspects of the colony's criminal law, that persistent criminal conduct, in the face of clear warning and exhortation, was more deserving of punishment than the single commission of a wrongful act.[48] The remainder of the additions specify the kinds of utterances which are to be punished as blasphemous and are not greatly at variance with the common-law definition of blasphemy that appears in Blackstone at the end of the eighteenth century.[49]

Curiously, the language of the colony's homicide provisions, which were enacted originally in 1641 and reenacted without change in the 1648 codification, contains few biblical terms. "Wilfull murder," "manslaughter," and "premeditated malice" were common-law terms, as were "mere casualty against will" and "mans necessary and just defence."[50] The substance of at least one of these provisions, however, was not English but biblical. Homicide committed "suddenly in . . . ANGER, or CRUELTY of passion," was a mandatory capital crime pursuant to Numbers 35:20,[51] whereas under English law homicide under such circumstances was manslaughter and a clergyable offense.[52] Whether the murder statute, which appears on its face to make self-defense and lack of intention complete defenses, was based upon biblical

---

[47] Leviticus 24:16. The preamble to the amended statute of November 4, 1646, justifies the extension of the law to the Indians by reference to natural law (*Mass. Records* II, 176).

[48] See Chap. XI, pp. 206 *et seq., infra.*

[49] W. Blackstone, *Commentaries on the Laws of England* (Oxford, 1769) IV, 59.

[50] Hale, *op. cit. supra* n. 41, at I, 424–434.

[51] *Laws and Liberties* 5.

[52] Coke, *op. cit. supra* n. 41, at 55–56; M. Dalton, *The Countrey Justice* (London, 1622) 222.

authority is not entirely clear, but under English law homicide *se defendendo* and *per infortunium* were nevertheless crimes, although not felonies.[53]

The colonial prescription of the death penalty for adultery reflected not only biblical influence but the Puritan view that the family was the cornerstone of church and commonwealth. Hence, any threat to the sanctity and integrity of the family unit deserved the most serious punishment of which God's law approved.[54] Three generations of Puritan pamphleteers in England had advocted that adultery be punished by death instead of by the small fines and penances which the Archdeacon's Court normally imposed,[55] and even Winthrop, for all his leniency in many directions, regarded as absurd the notion that "we may passe by Murders, Adulteryes, Idolatryes, etc: without Capitall punishments. . . ."[56] Hence, the colonial law provided that "If any person committ ADULTERIE with a married, or espoused wife; the Adulterer & Adulteresse shal surely be put to death."[57] Here, again, the Bible provided the substantive formulation of, and the penalty for, the crime. In accordance with Mosaic law, Massachusetts defined adultery in terms of the matrimonial status of the woman, ignoring that of the man; whereas under English ecclesiastical law adultery was committed whenever either participant in the illicit act was married.[58] A second departure from the English definition of adultery was the extension of the crime to include intercourse with a woman espoused but not yet married.[59] This extension was clearly based upon the prescription of Deuteronomy 22:23 and 24, cited as authority both in the Cotton draft of laws and in the Body of Liberties,[60] to the effect, "If a damsel that is a virgin be betrothed unto an husband, and a man find her in the city, and lie with her; Then ye shall bring them both out unto the gate of that city, and ye shall stone them with stones that they die. . . ."

The Massachusetts rape statute is the only one of the capital laws for which scriptural authority is not cited, and the reason for the omission appears to be that by the laws of Moses the offense was punishable not by death but by payment of damages and by an injunction to marry the victim.[61]

---

[53] Dalton, *op. cit. supra* n. 52, at 225.

[54] E. S. Morgan, *The Puritan Family* (Boston, 1944) 78–80.

[55] The Court of High Commission apparently imposed heavy fines, sometimes exceeding £500, upon offenders of superior rank (J. Stephen, *A History of the Criminal Law of England* [London, 1883] II, 422–423).

[56] *Winthrop Papers* IV, 477.

[57] *Laws and Liberties* 6.

[58] A seventeenth century abridgement of the English ecclesiastical law states that adultery could be committed "in a threefold manner, either *ex parte viri, vel feminae, vel utriusq,* always supposing that one or both are Matrimonaliz'd." J. Godolphin, *Repertorium Canonicum, or an Abridgment of the Ecclesiastical Laws of this Realm,* etc. (London, 1680) 475.

[59] Cf. *ibid.* with *Laws and Liberties* 6.

[60] *The Hutchinson Papers* (Albany, 1865) I, 199; *Body of Liberties* 94(9). The text of the Cotton draft is also printed in *Mass. Hist. Soc. Coll.* (1st ser.) V, 173 *et seq.* (1798).

[61] Deuteronomy 22:28 and 29. See n. 33, *supra.*

At common law, rape was defined as consensual or forcible copulation with a female under ten and nonconsensual intercourse with a female over ten; the offense was a felony and punishable by death.[62] By the 1640's, the increase of sexual crime had become a source of grave concern to the Massachusetts authorities, and Winthrop had argued that "by the equity of the law against sodomy" intercourse with a child should be punished with death, "for it is against nature as well as sodomy. . . ."[63] When the shocking case of John Humfry's daughters came to light and it was discovered that between the ages of seven and nine the elder had had sexual relations with three servants of her father, "so as she was grown capable of man's fellowship, and took pleasure in it," the colony was in an uproar.[64] By English law, the man would have been hanged, and many in the General Court strongly urged the death penalty. Ultimately, after consultation with all the elders of Massachusetts, Plymouth, Connecticut, and New Haven, the court concluded that because the crime was not expressly capital by the word of God or by any express law of the colony the principal offender should be fined and have his nostrils slit and seared and should be required to wear a noose of rope around his neck.[65] The other two men were also fined and ordered to be severely whipped.[66] However, on the same day that sentence was passed, the General Court enacted its first addition to the capital laws of the Body of Liberties in the form of statutes prescribing mandatory death penalties for sexual intercourse, consensual or otherwise, with a child under ten and for forcible intercourse with a woman "married or contracted," and a discretionary death penalty for rape of any single woman above the age of ten.[67]

These enactments afford striking illustrations of the interplay of cultural forces in the shaping of the colony law. The inference is clear that the General Court, shocked and inflamed by the Humfry case, formulated a definition of rape that bore a close similarity to the common-law crime but justified it on the basis of scriptural authority for the punishment of sodomy.[68] From this standpoint, the subsequent history of the rape statutes is instructive. In the revision of the capital laws that preceded the codification of 1648, the two provisions imposing the mandatory death penalty were dropped from the capital laws, leaving only the law which related to forcible intercourse with a maid or single woman above the age of ten years and which decreed "death, or . . . some other grievous punishment according to circumstances

---

[62] Coke, *op. cit. supra* n. 41, at Chap. XI.
[63] Winthrop, *Journal* II, 38.
[64] J. Winthrop, *History of New England* (ed. J. Savage: Boston, 1826) II, 46.
[65] *Mass. Records* II, 12–13.
[66] *Ibid.*
[67] *Mass. Records* II, 21.
[68] Winthrop, *Journal* II, 38.

as the Judges, or General court shal determin."[69] It seems probable that the scruples about a "warrant" from the word of God that had saved the lives of the defendants in the Humfry case had sufficiently revived so that the General Court was unwilling to retain a mandatory death penalty which had no specific biblical authority.

The provisions of the Massachusetts capital laws have been discussed in some detail because they illustrate not only the colonists' extensive reliance upon Scripture but also their unwillingness to follow its precepts when contrary to their own ethical and moral conceptions. Despite their dependence upon the word of God and the close connection that they saw between sin and crime, they were demonstrably reluctant to prescribe death for every offense that the Bible ordered so punished. Had they regarded the Bible's pronouncements as dogmatic injunctions, literally to be followed under all circumstances, the criminal laws should have embraced at least as many capital offenses as John Cotton included in his draft code.[70] In fact, the laws of Massachusetts prescribed relatively mild punishments for a number of such offenses, and the colonists' position seems to have been that no divine warrant was needed for the infliction of penalties that were *less* severe than those prescribed in the Bible. They were even more reluctant to extend the death penalty to offenses which were not expressly capital by the word of God, as the Humfry case illustrates. The General Court's decision in that case was entirely consistent with Puritan thinking on capital punishment. The author of the *Examen Legum Angliae,* who proposed reforms in the laws of England on the basis of biblical authority, stated it as "a Rule without Exception, given by the Learned, That no humane law can justly take away the life of a man for any offence, without a general or particular warrant from God's word; because mans life is onely at God's disposing."[71]

In the criminal law, therefore, the authority of the Bible appears to have been sought less as a dogmatic rule to be blindly followed than as a justification, or "warrant" as the colonists termed it, for the infliction of death upon a fellow man. Within the limits and for the reasons suggested, they apparently felt free to determine what offenses should be so punished. Hence, the scriptural annotations to the capital laws provided the justification, although not necessarily the reason, for their choice. In this connection it is worth observing that before 1650 there were but few convictions under any of the capital

[69] *Laws and Liberties* 6.
[70] Compare *The Hutchinson Papers, supra* n. 60, at I, 196–199, with *Laws and Liberties* 5–6. See T. Hutchinson, *The History of the Colony and Province of Massachusetts Bay* (ed. L. S. Mayo: Cambridge, Mass., 1936) I, 373, note, in which the author states that he saw a copy of the Cotton draft, corrected in John Winthrop's hand, whereon he had erased the death penalty for numerous offenses.
[71] *Examen Legum Angliae, supra* n. 32, at 54.

laws and, under some of them, none.[72] This suggests that to a substantial extent, at least, those laws were believed, like the Decalogue, to fulfill a hortatory or *in terrorem* function, which is further emphasized by the order of the General Court that children be taught to read so that they would know the capital laws.[73]

Among the reasons for the paucity of convictions under the capital laws was the insistence of the courts upon clear and palpable proof of the commission of crime. That insistence resulted partly from general Puritan reluctance to take human life and partly from the precept of Deuteronomy 17:6 that "At the mouth of two witnesses, or three witnesses, shall he that is worthy of death be put to death; but at the mouth of one witness he shall not be put to death." The colony law specifically prescribed that "no man shall be put to death without the testimonie of two or three *witnesses*, or that which is equivalent therunto."[74] Although in the seventeenth century the two-witness rule was customarily followed in the English ecclesiastical courts and in the Star Chamber,[75] the common-law courts were moving away from the requirement of a fixed number of witnesses except in cases of treason and perjury.[76] That tendency, together with the colonists' discussion and use of the rule, emphasizes its biblical basis.[77] Not only were they sufficiently concerned about its scope to refer the problem to the elders of the churches,[78] but they were prepared to, and apparently did, extend it, in accordance with the provision in John Cotton's draft code, to civil as well as criminal cases.[79] Nevertheless, the adoption of the two-witness rule probably owed something to the colonists' English experience, and it is not without significance that Sir John Fortescue's fifteenth century treatise in praise of the laws of England re-

---

[72] Cf. *Mass. Records* II, 243; *Assistants Records* II, 108, for two situations in which the death penalty was not exacted.

[73] Heads of households were required "to teach by themselves or others, their children & apprentices so much learning as may inable them perfectly to read the english tongue, & knowledge of the Capital lawes. . . ." (*Laws and Liberties* 11.)

[74] *Id.* at 54.

[75] J. H. Wigmore, *A Treatise on the Anglo-American System of Evidence in Trials at Common Law* (Boston, 1940) VII, 274.

[76] Holdsworth, *op. cit. supra* n. 20, at IX (1944) 203–211.

[77] See Winthrop, *Journal* II, 257–258, for an account of the trial of a man and woman for adultery in 1645 which resulted in their acquittal of the capital crime because of scruples of the magistrates and jury about the two-witness requirement. Winthrop, *op. cit. supra* n. 64, at II, 47, for Winthrop's summary of the answers of the New England clergy to the question put to them by Governor Bellingham in 1641, "whether two vocal witnesses be always necessary for conviction and sentencing an offender?" However, William Schooler, was convicted of murder and hanged in 1637 upon circumstantial evidence. Winthrop, *Journal* I, 236–238; *Assistants Records* II, 69.

[78] See n. 77 *supra*.

[79] *Hutchinson Papers, supra* n. 60, at I, 201–202; *Essex Records* I; *passim*.

ferred to the law of God as forbidding proof by fewer than two witnesses.[80]

The capital laws are by no means the only part of the colonial criminal law that reflect biblical influence. The limitation on whipping sentences to forty stripes,[81] in contrast with the English formula "until his body be bloody,"[82] was apparently based upon Deuteronomy 25:2 and 3. Similarly, the fornication statute, which empowered the magistrates to enjoin the parties to marriage,[83] was clearly agreeable to the Word as set forth in Exodus 22:16, as contrasted with the then current practice of English justices of the peace, who were primarily concerned with the economic problem of fixing responsibility for support of a bastard child upon its reputed father.[84] The Massachusetts law, however, had a further purpose in prescribing the marriage of the guilty parties, and that was the moral issue connected with the colonists' belief in the sanctity of the family unit and their conception of its role in community life. Here, again, in the adoption of the biblical rule, can be seen their insistence upon conforming their laws to the patterns of right living that had been developed in the colony.

Another striking departure from English law which apparently owed much to biblical authority was the colonists' adoption of multiple restitution and involuntary servitude for theft. At common law, the theft of a shilling, like other felonies, was punishable by hanging, and theft of a lesser amount by whipping.[85] Under a number of English statutes, restitution — single, double, or treble — was a common penalty imposed by justices of the peace for a variety of specified property crimes.[86] The Bible, however, prescribed multiple restitution as the penalty of the thief in most cases, or "if he have nothing, then he shall be sold for his theft."[87]

From the beginning, the colonial magistrates regularly followed the biblical patterns, imposing double restitution when the offender was capable thereof,[88] and requiring thieves unable to make restitution otherwise to satisfy the

---

[80] J. Fortescue, *De Laudibus Legum Anglie* (ed. S. B. Chrimes: Cambridge, 1942) 73.

[81] *Laws and Liberties* 50.

[82] See, e.g., *Calendar to the Sessions Records, County of Middlesex* (ed. W. Le Hardy: London, 1935) (new ser.) I, 188; *Quarter Sessions Records for the County of Somerset* (ed. E. H. Bates: London, 1907) I, 211.

[83] *Laws and Liberties* 23.

[84] See the statute of 18 Elizabeth I, c. 3. Study of the Somersetshire quarter sessions records for the early seventeenth century shows that the reputed father was ordinarily ordered to pay six or eight pence each week, and that the mother was ordered to contribute money to the support of the child if she could not keep the child herself. So long as the child's upbringing was not chargeable to the parish, she was not committed to the workhouse. See *Quarter Sessions Records for the County of Somerset* (ed. E. H. Bates: London, 1907) I, *passim*.

[85] Coke, *op. cit. supra* n. 41, at 109.

[86] E.g., stats. 37 Henry VIII, c. 6; 7 James I, c. 7.

[87] Exodus 22:3.

[88] See Index to *Assistants Records* II and to *Essex Records* I.

court's sentence by a term of service.[89] The exaction of these penalties was without specific statutory authority until 1646.[90] Prior thereto, the colonial treatment of theft furnishes an example of the shaping of law by magisterial discretion in the way favored by Winthrop. When restitution was feasible, it was usually the only punishment imposed,[91] but the courts did not hesitate to combine it with one or more of a variety of other penalties, ranging through whipping,[92] the stocks,[93] a fine to the court,[94] and degradation from the rank of gentleman.[95] Servants, and others incapable of making restitution in money or in kind, were generally whipped,[96] but theft by a servant from his own master appears to have been punished almost invariably by restitution, which was sometimes exacted in the form of an extension of the servant's term of service.[97] Significantly, when the colonists enacted the theft act of 1646,[98] they not only displaced the magistrates' discretionary power to vary penalties to which they had so long been opposed but adopted the English statutory penalty of treble restitution with which they had been familiar in rural England.[99] Thus, while the early use of restitution as a penalty for theft can be attributed with reasonable assurance to biblical influence, its later statutory prescription is reflective of English ways. The colonial practice in this area again vividly illustrates the interplay of the two cultural forces.

The foregoing account of the role of the Bible in shaping the criminal law of the colony demonstrates that its influence was important but not always controlling. When we turn from the criminal to the civil law of the colony, however, the apparent influence of the Bible is much less clear. Aside from the double portion allowed to the eldest son in cases of intestacy,[100] and the prohibitions against bond slavery and usury,[101] few provisions in the civil law can be attributed to scriptural influences. In one respect, however — namely, in the law of master and servant — those influences are unmistakable.

As already stated, a master was not only privileged, but under a duty, to correct his servant, and the servant might resort to the courts for protection against unjust or excessive correction. One of the provisions of the Body of

---

[89] E.g., *Assistants Records* II, 94, 99, 118.
[90] *Mass. Records* II, 180; *Laws and Liberties* 5.
[91] *Assistants Records* II, *passim; Essex Records* I, *passim.*
[92] E.g., *Assistants Records* II, 9, 14, 53, 59, 62, 72, 98; *Essex Records* I, 25.
[93] E.g., *Assistants Records* II, 53; *Essex Records* I, 110.
[94] E.g., *Assistants Records* II, 16, 81; *Essex Records,* I, 59.
[95] Josias Plastowe, who stole "4 basketts of corne from the Indians," was ordered in 1631 to "returne them 8 basketts againe be ffined V £ & hereafter to be called by the name of Josias & not Mr. as formerly hee vsed to be" (*Assistants Records* II, 19).
[96] *Assistants Records* II, *passim; Essex Records* I, *passim.*
[97] E.g., *Assistants Records* II, 70, 86, 131, 137; *Essex Records* I, 57, 84.
[98] *Mass. Records* II, 180; *Laws and Liberties* 5.
[99] See n. 86, *supra.*
[100] *Laws and Liberties* 53–54.
[101] *Id.* at 4, 52.

Liberties, retained without substantial change in the Code of 1648,[102] provided:

If any servants shall flee from the Tiranny and crueltie of their masters to the howse of any freeman of the same Towne, they shall be there protected and susteyned till due order be taken for their relife. Provided due notice thereof be speedily given to their masters from whom they fled. And the next Assistant or Constable where the partie flying is harboured.

The provision had a sound biblical precedent in Deuteronomy 25:15 and 16:

Thou shalt not deliver unto his master the servant which is escaped from his master unto thee; He shall dwell with thee, even among you, in that place which he shall choose in one of thy gates, where it liketh him best: thou shalt not oppress him.

Characteristically, however, the Massachusetts law expanded the biblical rule by limiting the permissible grounds for self-help to "Tiranny and crueltie," and by ensuring the observance of due process of law through the requirement that proper notice be given to the servant's master and to an officer of the court. The effect of the colonial act was thus to give the oppressed servant an effective means of invoking the jurisdiction of the court to correct abuses, while also protecting the master's contractual rights.

A further provision of the colony laws which had explicit scriptural authority, decreed:

If any man smite out the eye or tooth of his man-servant, or maid servant, or otherwise mayme or much disfigure him, unlesse it be by meere casualtie, he shall let them goe free from his service. And shall have such further recompense as the Court shall allow him.[103]

A corresponding passage in Exodus 21:26–27 states that

. . . if a man smite the eye of his servant, or the eye of his maid, that it perish; he shall let him go free for his eye's sake. And if he smite out his manservant's tooth, or his maidservant's tooth; he shall let him go free for his tooth's sake.

Again the colonists expanded the scriptural formula. Restating verbatim the eye-and-tooth provisions, the Massachusetts law nevertheless used them as the basis for framing a general rule that servants should be freed in any case of maiming or "much" disfigurement, and added the important qualification that the master's act must be deliberate.

Still another of the "Liberties of Servants" enacted in 1641 and incorporated into the Code[104] declared:

Servants that have served deligentlie and faithfully to the benefitt of their maisters seaven years, shall not be sent away emptie. And if any have been unfaithfull,

---

[102] *Body of Liberties* 85; *Laws and Liberties* 39.
[103] *Body of Liberties* 87; *Laws and Liberties* 39.
[104] *Body of Liberties* 88; *Laws and Liberties* 39.

negligent or unprofitable in their service, notwithstanding the good usage of their maisters, they shall not be dismissed till they have made satisfaction according to the Judgement of Authoritie.

Deuteronomy 15:12–14, had said that servants were to be freed upon completion of seven years' service:

. . . in the seventh year thou shalt let him go free from thee. And when thou sendest him out free from thee, thou shalt not let him go away empty: Thou shalt furnish him liberally out of thy flock, and out of thy floor, and out of thy winepress: of that wherewith the Lord thy God hath blessed thee thou shalt give unto him.

Once more, and characteristically, the Massachusetts law incorporated inferences drawn from the bare text of Scripture. Only the good and faithful servant was entitled to a provision upon departing his master's service; more importantly, the negligent, unfaithful, or unprofitable servant was deemed obligated to make satisfaction for his shortcomings.

For all the biblical flavor of the colonial master-servant legislation, the Massachusetts courts' procedures for resolving disputes in this area did not greatly differ from contemporary English practices under the Statute of Labourers. In such cases, a single justice of the peace was empowered to "take such order and direction between the said master and his apprentice, as the equity of the cause shall require."[105] Appeal was allowed by either party to the next sessions of the peace, where four justices were empowered to put an end to the indentures between master and apprentice, or "if the default shall be found to be in the apprentice, then the said justices . . . shall cause such due correction and punishment to be ministered unto him, as by their wisdom and discretions shall be thought meet."[106] The Massachusetts rule, which permitted the mistreated servant to flee to the protection of a neighbor, who was thereupon obliged to notify the judicial authorities and the servant's master, had no statutory counterpart in England, but the disposition of such cases by the courts followed much the same pattern on both sides of the ocean. At Salem in 1645, Daniel Rumble, who confessed to striking Henry Hall in the head with a hand hammer, was fined and admonished for "Crueltie in Correcting" his servant.[107] By comparison, in Worcestershire in 1637 a man was presented at the sessions of the peace "for immoderately beating and misusing Owen Brown his apprentice."[108] In 1640 the Court of Assistants, finding that Samuel Hefford had "bene much misused by his master Jonathan Wade," freed him from Wade's service and put him out to

---

[105] Stat. 5 Elizabeth I, c. 4.
[106] *Ibid.*
[107] *Essex Records* I, 83.
[108] *Calendar of the Quarter Sessions Papers* (Worcestershire) (ed. J. W. W. Bund: Worcester, 1900) I, 645.

another master for the remainder of his time.[109] Similarly, an order of a Somerset quarter sessions in 1630 declared:

Whereas it hath appeared unto this Court that William Culverhouse of Greinton, Blacksmith, hath misused and beaten ffrancis Sheppard *als.* Townsend his apprentice to the great hurt of the said apprentice we doe therefore for preventinge of further mischeife which may happen absolutely free, acquit and discharge the said ffrancis Sheppard the apprentice from his apprenticehood. . . .[110]

Thus, both the English and the Massachusetts systems enforced obedience, respect, and industry on the part of the servant, as well as rough standards of fair and humane treatment on the part of the master. The criteria applied in the colony undoubtedly owed as much to English precedent as to the Bible's texts. At the same time, the substantive similarity that each system bore to biblical precept suggests that Elizabethan legislators, like those of Massachusetts, were also influenced, though to a lesser degree, by the biblical inheritance in which they both shared.

At this point, it must be emphasized that the influence of the Bible apparent upon the face of the 1648 Code was only one, and by no means the most important, of its many manifestations in the colony's law. The spirit of the Bible, in the form of ethical rules and attitudes, no less than its detailed injunctions, was reflected in every phase of colony life; "the matter of the scripture," said Winthrop, "be always a Rule to vs, yet not the phrase."[111] That spirit, expounded in public preaching, and applied through brotherly admonition and communal vigilance, underlay the entire formal structure of the law and ensured its substantial acceptance. English Puritanism, from its earliest days, had been marked by a striking insistence upon its ethical elements. Elizabethan Puritans, accepting Calvin's teaching that every man was predestined to sainthood or damnation and hence utterly powerless to save himself by righteous conduct, nevertheless ordered their lives in accordance with strict moral principles.[112] The same concern over right conduct was likewise characteristic of the Puritans of Massachusetts, whose covenant theology, positing that man's free compliance with the moral law was required by the terms of his covenant with God as the consideration for the gift of grace, ensured that the role of moral obedience in Puritan society had sound theological footing.[113] God had provided, in the moral laws of the Scriptures and

---

[109] *Assistants Records* II, 101.
[110] *Quarter Sessions Records for the County of Somerset* (ed. E. H. B. Harbin: London, 1908) II, 109.
[111] *Winthrop Papers* IV, 348.
[112] *Two Elizabethan Puritan Diaries (Richard Rogers and Samuel Ward)* (ed. M. M. Knappen: Chicago, 1933) 1–16. The editor of these two early Puritan diaries concludes that "the most striking feature of the Puritan way of life as revealed in these diaries is the overwhelming predominance of the ethical element" (*id.* at 2).
[113] P. Miller, *The New England Mind: the Seventeenth Century* (New York, 1939) 384–385.

in the judicial laws appendant thereto, a rule whereby mankind, with the aid of right reason, could fulfill his covenant by walking in God's way. Puritan theology thus invoked the Bible directly as a guide to human behavior, but reliance upon it was as much a symptom of the longstanding Puritan absorption with moral conduct as it was a cause thereof. The pervasiveness of its influence within the community served to furnish both workable rules for the informal adjustment of neighborhood disputes, and simple standards of righteousness as guides for communal vigilance against sinful conduct.

Biblical influence also made itself felt in the law of the colony through the concept of a fundamental, divinely inspired natural law, which the colony leaders shared with educated Europeans generally. Familiar conceptions of natural and positive law were intimately related in their thinking to specifically Puritan ideas with respect to the threefold division of Mosaic law into its "moral," "judicial," and "ceremonial" aspects.[114] They believed that God's law was either natural or positive. The former embraced those precepts for the guidance of human behavior which could be immediately apprehended, or logically arrived at, by human reason; it was regarded as something instilled in the soul of man by God himself, and hence immutable. Commonly, natural law was equated with the law of reason.[115] "There is nothing in them," wrote William Ames of the Ten Commandments, "but what may be well enjoined from clear reason. . . ."[116]

God's positive law, on the other hand, was that law which was added to the natural law by some special revelation of God. It could be received, but not be arrived at, by reason. Moreover, unlike the natural law, it was not immutable, but "mutable and various according to God's good pleasure."[117] Specifically, God's positive law might, and did, vary between the Old Testament and the New; much of the positive law given to the Jews by God — the so-called "judicial" and "ceremonial" laws — was abrogated by the New Testament dispensation. All of the "ceremonial" laws — the dietary injunctions, the intricate Levitical rules as to worship and the like — were so abrogated because they were viewed as pertaining only to the Israel of the Old Testament. Many of the judicial laws of Moses, on the other hand, so commended themselves to reason that they clearly partook of the eternally binding nature of God's natural, moral law itself, and these laws were not abrogated, but remained in force because, "when the special intrinsical and proper reason of the law is moral, then it always follows that the law itself

---

[114] W. Ames, *Conscience With the Power and Cases Thereof* (London, 1639) Book 5, Chap. 1, reprinted in *Puritanism and Liberty* (ed. A. S. P. Woodhouse: Chicago, 1951) 187 at 190–191.

[115] J. Dickinson, *Administrative Justice and the Supremacy of Law in the United States* (Cambridge, Mass., 1927) 86–88 and authorities there cited.

[116] Ames, *op. cit. supra* n. 114, at 190.

[117] *Ibid.* at 187.

must needs be moral."[118] This aspect of the law of God — divine injunctions to the children of Israel, proved by their evident reasonableness to be meant to bind no less than the moral law of the Decalogue — was the principal source and justification of the biblical literalism that is evident in the colonial law of Massachusetts. As the Epistle to the Code recites, "These were breif and fundamental principles, yet withall so full and comprehensive as out of them clear deductions were to be drawne to all particular cases in future times."[119]

Finally, aside from the law of God in its natural and positive aspects, there were human laws, enacted by men for their various societies. In the Augustinian view accepted by Christians generally, man's perception of the moral law instilled in him by God was clouded by original sin. Human laws were particular applications of the natural, moral law (insofar as fallen man's reason was capable of perceiving it) to the varying needs of human states. The corruption of man's nature assured that no human law could ever perfectly reflect the moral law; but, to the extent that such human laws did reflect the moral law, they were as binding as natural law itself.

Puritan reconciliation of traditional natural-law ideas with the notion of the threefold nature of the Mosaic law was susceptible to varying emphases. John Cotton, for instance, consistently took the position that most, if not all, of the "judicial" laws of Moses reflected the moral law, and hence were as eternally binding as the Decalogue itself.[120] His emphasis upon obedient acceptance of explicit divine precepts is reflected in the literalism of his proposed code of laws. John Winthrop, on the other hand, emphasized those aspects of the orthodox theory which asserted the dependence of all civil laws upon natural law, and implied that a test of the law of nature was its agreement with the needs of the society to which it is applied.[121] Cotton, with small faith in the ability of man's corrupted reason to frame a just law, stated, "The more any Law smells of man the more unprofitable."[122] Winthrop did not quarrel with the idea that lawmaking was a divine function or that man's role was solely one of interpretation and application; but to that end, God had given "power and gifts to men to interprett his Lawes: and this belonges principally to the highest Authoritye: in a Common Wealth, and subordinately to other magistrates and Judges accordinge to their severall places."[123]

These ideas of Winthrop's were very similar to those expressed by common-law judges and lawyers who, since the Middle Ages, had affirmed that law

---

[118] *Ibid.* at 191.

[119] *Laws and Liberties,* Epistle.

[120] W. C. Ford, "Cotton's 'Moses his Judicials,' " *Mass. Hist. Soc. Proc.* (2nd ser.) XVI, 274, 280–284 (1903).

[121] *Winthrop Papers* IV, 486–487.

[122] Ford, *loc. cit. supra* n. 120, at 284.

[123] *Winthrop Papers* IV, 480.

was eternal and immutable, and hence could only be found by man but not made.[124] Despite their apparent consignment of a purely ministerial function to the human legislator, the practical effect of these beliefs was enormously to enhance the prestige of human laws. As expressed in the concluding words of the Epistle to the 1648 Code:

> . . . when the Authoritie is of God and that in way of an Ordinance *Rom. 13.1* and when the administration of it is according to deductions, and rules gathered from the word of God, and the clear light of nature in civil nations, surely there is no humane law that tendeth to common good (according to those principles) but the same is mediately a law of God, and that in way of an Ordinance which all are to submit unto and that for conscience sake. *Rom. 13.5.*[125]

One consequence of this type of thinking was to free the framers of the Massachusetts legal system from the necessity of literal adherence to scriptural precepts, by virtue of an idea which was itself biblically inspired and theologically orthodox; it echoes the thinking of John Calvin, who believed that all nations had liberty to enact the particular laws that they deemed expedient, and that such enactments, to the extent that they followed "the perpetual rule of love," were valid, "however they may differ from the Jewish law or from each other."[126]

Winthrop, arguing in a recognizably Thomistic vein, but citing Scripture for support, maintained that "law" and "penalty" were totally different concepts; the former was eternal and binding, the latter temporary, and belonging to the magistrates' discretion.[127] John Cotton, on the other hand, believed that the judicial laws of the Pentateuch, in which God had further elaborated upon the moral laws of the Ten Commandments and had prescribed penalties for their breach, were of a force in civil society equal to that of the laws of the Decalogue.[128] Neither man, if pressed, would have denied the validity of the other's view, so that the difference between them emerges as one of emphasis upon two widely held Puritan beliefs. Winthrop's conception of the office of a magistrate in a godly society, of which his ideas about "law" and "penalty" were but one manifestation, was at least as important in the shaping of the colony law as Cotton's relative literalism. Winthrop's view, however, implied a place for human reason in the shaping of law that was notably larger than that ordinarily assigned to it by men such as Cotton, who reflected a more orthodox Puritan view.

---

[124] Dickinson, *op. cit. supra* n. 115, at 85–86; G. L. Haskins, *The Statute of York and the Interest of the Commons* (Cambridge, Mass., 1935) 29 *et seq.* The idea is an ancient one and appears in Herodotus, *Histories,* III, 31.
[125] *Laws and Liberties,* Epistle.
[126] Quoted in *John Calvin on God and Political Duty* (ed. J. T. McNeill: New York, 1950) 62–63.
[127] *Winthrop Papers* IV, 478.
[128] See note 120 *supra.*

At the same time, and somewhat paradoxically, the use of reason was a crucial part of even the strictest Puritan literalism. If the word of God furnished a perfect guide for man's righteous conduct in civil society, and for the laws required for its enforcement, the fact remained that the Word was knowable only by the instrument of human reason. Not every pronouncement of the Bible was binding upon all men in all places, and not every manifestation of God's word was apparent in the Bible's literal text. Moreover, the Puritans were not bound to apply the same standards in accepting or rejecting the Bible's nontheological dictates as they applied to its teachings on church polity, or upon divine grace and redemption. In theology, the Bible as expounded by learned divines was the supreme and unquestioned authority. Careful application to revelation was indispensable because the principles of divinity were not deemed to be in man from nature: "None can learn it by the book of nature, for there are some lessons in Religion which are not to be found in the book of Creation."[129] It was, however, characteristic of the Puritan mind that in the pursuit of politics, natural science, and every other human art dealing with God's creatures, as opposed to God's revelations, man must look to natural objects, using the Bible not as the fountainhead and authority which it was for theology, but as the confirmation or justification of rational conclusions drawn from natural premises. Even the "science" of ethics was not regarded by the Puritans as contained within the covers of the Bible, although its influence in this sphere was predominant for obvious reasons. Outside the field of divinity, revelation, in Professor Miller's words, only served "incidentally to substantiate and reinforce the patterns of ideas upon which the natural universe had been constructed."[130]

In law, too, aside from the Decalogue, the Bible was not so much binding precedent as enormously persuasive authority, and, like any persuasive force, the extent to which it swayed the lawmaker in a given instance was inversely proportional to the force of the exigencies of circumstance and the reasonableness of the arguments to whose thrust it was opposed. Because the colonists' use of specific biblical precepts in framing laws was selective, those parts of the Scripture that they rejected or ignored are no less significant for an understanding of the role of "revelation" in the law than the parts that they embodied in it. Even when they professed and appeared to be following God's word most literally, they were influenced by their English inheritance, intellectual as well as legal, and by pragmatic or expedient considerations growing out of the conditions of settlement. The same kind of eclecticism that was motivated, guided, and made coherent by the distinctive ethic that marked Puritan scholarship generally is clearly apparent in the shaping of

---

[129] Quoted in Miller, *op. cit. supra* note 113, at 189.
[130] *Ibid.*, at 188–189.

Massachusetts law.[131] For all their reverence for the Scriptures, the colonists almost never enacted literal Bible texts as law before those texts had passed a rigorous logical justification.

The Bible in Massachusetts was an indispensable touchstone, but not the cornerstone, of Puritan legal thinking. Central as was its position in Puritan life and thought, it was only one influence among many in a rich cultural heritage which was quickened by the challenge of new problems in a new land.

[131] See the penetrating analysis of Professor Miller, *ibid.* at 89 *et seq.*

A Sociological Analysis of the Law of Vagrancy

WILLIAM J. CHAMBLISS

With the outstanding exception of Jerome Hall's analysis of theft[1] there has been a severe shortage of sociologically relevant analyses of the relationship between particular laws and the social setting in which these laws emerge, are interpreted, and take form. The paucity of such studies is somewhat surprising in view of widespread agreement that such studies are not only desirable but absolutely essential to the development of a mature sociology of law.[2] A fruitful method of establishing the direction and pattern of this mutual influence is to systematically analyze particular legal categories, to observe the changes which take place in the categories and to explain how these changes are themselves related to and stimulate changes in the society. This paper is an attempt to provide such an analysis of the law of vagrancy in Anglo-American Law.

LEGAL INNOVATION: THE EMERGENCE OF THE LAW OF VAGRANCY IN ENGLAND

There is general agreement among legal scholars that the first full fledged vagrancy statute was passed in England in 1349. As is generally the case with legislative innovations, however, this statute was preceded by earlier laws which established a climate favorable to such change. The most significant forerunner to the 1349 vagrancy statute was in 1274 when it was provided:

Because that abbies and houses of religion have been overcharged and sore grieved, by the resort of great men and other, so that their goods have not been

Reprinted from *Social Problems,* Vol. 12, No. 1, pp. 67–77, by permission of the author and The Society for the Study of Social Problems.

For a more complete listing of most of the statutes dealt with in this report the reader is referred to Burn, *The History of the Poor Laws.* Citations of English statutes should be read as follows: 3 Ed. 1. c. 1. refers to the third act of Edward the first, chapter one, etc.

[1] Hall, J., *Theft, Law and Society* (Bobbs-Merrill, 1939). See also, Alfred R. Lindesmith, "Federal Law and Drug Addiction," *Social Problems,* Vol. 7, No. 1, 1959, p. 48.

[2] See, for example, Rose, A., "Some Suggestions for Research in the Sociology of Law," *Social Problems,* Vol. 9, No. 3, 1962, pp. 281–283, and Geis, G., "Sociology, Criminology, and Criminal Law," *Social Problems,* Vol. 7, No. 1, 1959, pp. 40–47.

sufficient for themselves, whereby they have been greatly hindered and impoverished, that they cannot maintain themselves, nor such charity as they have been accustomed to do; it is provided, that none shall come to eat or lodge in any house of religion, or any other's foundation than of his own, at the costs of the house, unless he be required by the governor of the house before his coming hither.[3]

Unlike the vagrancy statutes this statute does not intend to curtail the movement of persons from one place to another, but is solely designed to provide the religious houses with some financial relief from the burden of providing food and shelter to travelers.

The philosophy that the religious houses were to give alms to the poor and to the sick and feeble was, however, to undergo drastic change in the next fifty years. The result of this changed attitude was the establishment of the first vagrancy statute in 1349 which made it a crime to give alms to any who were unemployed while being of sound mind and body. To wit:

Because that many valiant beggars, as long as they may live of begging, do refuse to labor, giving themselves to idleness and vice, and sometimes to theft and other abominations; it is ordained, that none, upon pain of imprisonment shall, under the colour of pity or alms, give anything to such which may labour, or presume to favour them towards their desires; so that thereby they may be compelled to labour for their necessary living.[4]

It was further provided by this statute that:

. . . every man and woman, of what condition he be, free or bond, able in body, and within the age of threescore years, not living in merchandize nor exercising any craft, nor having of his own whereon to live, nor proper land whereon to occupy himself, and not serving any other, if he in convenient service (his estate considered) be required to serve, shall be bounded to serve him which shall him require. . . . And if any refuse, he shall on conviction by two true men, . . . be commited to gaol till he find surety to serve.

And if any workman or servant, of what estate or condition he be, retained in any man's service, do depart from the said service without reasonable cause or license, before the term agreed on, he shall have pain of imprisonment.[5]

There was also in this statute the stipulation that the workers should receive a standard wage. In 1351 this statute was strengthened by the stipulation:

And none shall go out of the town where he dwelled in winter, to serve the summer, if he may serve in the same town.[6]

By 34 Ed. 3 (1360) the punishment for these acts became imprisonment for fifteen days and if they "do not justify themselves by the end of that time, to be sent to gaol till they do."

---

[3] 3 Ed. 1. c. 1.
[4] 35 Ed. 1. c. 1.
[5] 23 Ed. 3.
[6] 25 Ed. 3 (1351).

A change in official policy so drastic as this did not, of course, occur simply as a matter of whim. The vagrancy statutes emerged as a result of changes in other parts of the social structure. The prime-mover for this legislative innovation was the Black Death which struck England about 1348. Among the many disastrous consequences this had upon the social structure was the fact that it decimated the labor force. It is estimated that by the time the pestilence had run its course at least fifty per cent of the population of England had died from the plague. This decimation of the labor force would necessitate rather drastic innovations in any society but its impact was heightened in England where, at this time, the economy was highly dependent upon a ready supply of cheap labor.

Even before the pestilence, however, the availability of an adequate supply of cheap labor was becoming a problem for the landowners. The crusades and various wars had made money necessary to the lords and, as a result, the lord frequently agreed to sell the serfs their freedom in order to obtain the needed funds. The serfs, for their part, were desirous of obtaining their freedom (by "fair means" or "foul") because the larger towns which were becoming more industrialized during this period could offer the serf greater personal freedom as well as a higher standard of living. This process is nicely summarized by Bradshaw:

> By the middle of the 14th century the outward uniformity of the manorial system had become in practice considerably varied . . . for the peasant had begun to drift to the towns and it was unlikely that the old village life in its unpleasant aspects should not be resented. Moreover the constant wars against France and Scotland were fought mainly with mercenaries after Henry III's time and most villages contributed to the new armies. The bolder serfs either joined the armies or fled to the towns, and even in the villages the free men who held by villein tenure were as eager to commute their services as the serfs were to escape. Only the amount of "free" labor available enabled the lord to work his demesne in many places.[7]

And he says regarding the effect of the Black Death:

> . . . in 1348 the Black Death reached England and the vast mortality that ensued destroyed that reserve of labour which alone had made the manorial system even nominally possible.[8]

The immediate result of these events was of course no surprise: Wages for the "free" man rose considerably and this increased, on the one hand, the landowner's problems and, on the other hand, the plight of the unfree tenant. For although wages increased for the personally free laborers, it of course did not necessarily add to the standard of living of the serf, if anything it made

---

[7] Bradshaw, F., *A Social History of England,* p. 54
[8] *Ibid.*

his position worse because the landowner would be hard pressed to pay for the personally free labor which he needed and would thus find it more and more difficult to maintain the standard of living for the serf which he had heretofore supplied. Thus the serf had no alternative but flight if he chose to better his position. Furthermore, flight generally meant both freedom and better conditions since the possibility of work in the new weaving industry was great and the chance of being caught small.[9]

It was under these conditions that we find the first vagrancy statutes emerging. There is little question but that these statutes were designed for one express purpose: to force laborers (whether personally free or unfree) to accept employment at a low wage in order to insure the landowner an adequate supply of labor at a price he could afford to pay. Caleb Foote concurs with this interpretation when he notes:

> The anti-migratory policy behind vagrancy legislation began as an essential complement of the wage stabilization legislation which accompanied the breakup of feudalism and the depopulation caused by the Black Death. By the Statutes of Labourers in 1349–1351, every able-bodied person without other means of support was required to work for wages fixed at the level preceding the Black Death; it was unlawful to accept more, or to refuse an offer to work, or to flee from one county to another to avoid offers of work or to seek higher wages, or go give alms to able-bodied beggars who refused to work.[10]

In short, as Foote says in another place, this was an "attempt to make the vagrancy statutes a substitute for serfdom."[11] This same conclusion is equally apparent from the wording of the statute where it is stated:

> Because great part of the people, and especially of workmen and servants, late died in pestilence; many seeing the necessity of masters, and great scarcity of servants, will not serve without excessive wages, and some rather willing to beg in idleness than by labour to get their living: it is ordained, that every man and woman, of what condition he be, free or bond, able in body and within the age of threescore years, not living in merchandize, (etc.) be required to serve. . . .

The innovation in the law, then, was a direct result of the aforementioned changes which had occurred in the social setting. In this case these changes were located for the most part in the economic institution of the society. The vagrancy laws were designed to alleviate a condition defined by the lawmakers as undesirable. The solution was to attempt to force a reversal, as it were, of a social process which was well underway; that is, to curtail mobility of laborers in such a way that labor would not become a commodity for which the landowners would have to compete.

---

[9] *Ibid.*, p. 57.
[10] Foote, C., "Vagrancy Type Law and Its Administration," *Univ. of Pennsylvania Law Review* (104), 1956, p. 615.
[11] *Ibid.*

Statutory Dormancy:
A Legal Vestige

In time, of course, the curtailment of the geographical mobility of laborers was no longer requisite. One might well expect that when the function served by the statute was no longer an important one for society, the statutes would be eliminated from the law. In fact, this has not occurred. The vagrancy statutes have remained in effect since 1349. Furthermore, as we shall see in some detail later, they were taken over by the colonies and have remained in effect in the United States as well.

The substance of the vagrancy statutes changed very little for some time after the first ones in 1349–1351 although there was a tendency to make punishments more harsh than originally. For example, in 1360 it was provided that violators of the statute should be imprisoned for fifteen days[12] and in 1388 the punishment was to put the offender in the stocks and to keep him there until "he find surety to return to his service."[13] That there was still, at this time, the intention of providing the landowner with labor is apparent from the fact that this statute provides:

. . . and he or she which use to labour at the plough and cart, or other labour and service of husbandry, till they be of the age of 12 years, from thenceforth shall abide at the same labour without being put to any mistery or handicraft: and any covenant of apprenticeship to the contrary shall be void.[14]

The next alteration in the statutes occurs in 1495 and is restricted to an increase in punishment. Here it is provided that vagrants shall be "set in stocks, there to remain by the space of three days and three nights, and there to have none other sustenance but bread and water; and after the said three days and nights, to be had out and set at large, and then to be commanded to avoid the town."[15]

The tendency to increase the severity of punishment during this period seems to be the result of a general tendency to make finer distinctions in the criminal law. During this period the vagrancy statutes appear to have been fairly inconsequential in either their effect as a control mechanism or as a generally enforced statute.[16] The processes of social change in the culture generally and the trend away from serfdom and into a "free" economy obvi-

---

[12] 34 Ed. 3 (1360).
[13] 12 R. 2 (1388).
[14] *Ibid.*
[15] 11 H. & C. 2 (1495).
[16] As evidenced for this note the expectation that " . . . the common gaols of every shire are likely to be greatly pestered with more numbers of prisoners than heretofore . . . " when the statutes were changed by the statute of 14 Ed. c. 5 (1571).

ated the utility of these statutes. The result was not unexpected. The judiciary did not apply the law and the legislators did not take it upon themselves to change the law. In short, we have here a period of dormancy in which the statute is neither applied nor altered significantly.

A SHIFT
IN FOCAL CONCERN

Following the squelching of the Peasant's Revolt in 1381, the services of the serfs to the lord " . . . tended to become less and less exacted, although in certain forms they lingered on till the seventeenth century. . . . By the sixteenth century few knew that there were any bondmen in England . . . and in 1575 Queen Elizabeth listened to the prayers of almost the last serfs in England . . . and granted them manumission."[17]

In view of this change we would expect corresponding changes in the vagrancy laws. Beginning with the lessening of punishment in the statute of 1503 we find these changes. However, instead of remaining dormant (or becoming more so) or being negated altogether, the vagrancy statutes experienced a shift in focal concern. With this shift the statutes served a new and equally important function for the social order of England. The first statute which indicates this change was in 1530. In this statute (22 H. 8. c. 12 1530) it was stated:

If any person, being whole and mighty in body, and able to labour, be taken in begging, or be vagrant and can give no reckoning how he lawfully gets his living; . . . and all other idle persons going about, some of them using divers and subtle crafty and unlawful games and plays, and some of them feigning themselves to have knowledge of . . . crafty sciences . . . shall be punished as provided.

What is most significant about this statute is the shift from an earlier concern with laborers to a concern with *criminal* activities. To be sure, the stipulation of persons "being whole and mighty in body, and able to labour, be taken in begging, or be vagrant" sounds very much like the concerns of the earlier statutes. Some important differences are apparent however when the rest of the statute includes those who " . . . can give no reckoning how he lawfully gets his living"; "some of them using divers subtil and unlawful games and plays." This is the first statute which specifically focuses upon these kinds of criteria for adjudging someone a vagrant.

It is significant that in this statute the severity of punishment is increased so as to be greater not only than provided by the 1503 statute but the punishment is more severe than that which had been provided by *any* of the pre-

---

[17] Bradshaw, *op. cit.*, p. 61.

1503 statutes as well. For someone who is merely idle and gives no reckoning of how he makes his living the offender shall be:

> . . . had to the next market town, or other place where they [the constables] shall think most convenient, and there to be tied to the end of a cart naked, and to be beaten with whips throughout the same market town or other place, till his body be bloody by reason of such whipping.[18]

But, for those who use "divers and subtil crafty and unlawful games and plays," etc., the punishment is ". . . whipping at two days together in manner aforesaid."[19] For the second offense, such persons are:

> . . . scourged two days, and the third day to be put upon the pillory from nine of the clock till eleven before noon of the same day and to have one of his ears cut off.[20]

And if he offend the third time ". . . to have like punishment with whipping, standing on the pillory and to have his other ear cut off."

This statute (1) makes a distinction between types of offenders and applies the more severe punishment to those who are clearly engaged in "criminal" activities, (2) mentions a specific concern with categories of "unlawful" behavior, and (3) applies a type of punishment (cutting off the ear) which is generally reserved for offenders who are defined as likely to be a fairly serious criminal.

Only five years later we find for the first time that the punishment of death is applied to the crime of vagrancy. We also note a change in terminology in the statute:

> and if any ruffians . . . after having been once apprehended . . . shall wander, loiter, or idle use themselves and play the vagabonds . . . shall be eftsoons not only whipped again, but shall have the gristle of his right ear clean cut off. And if he shall again offend, he shall be committed to gaol till the next sessions; and being there convicted upon indictment, he shall have judgment to suffer pains and execution of death, as a felon, as an enemy of the commonwealth.[21]

It is significant that the statute now makes persons who repeat the crime of vagrancy a felon. During this period then, the focal concern of the vagrancy statutes becomes a concern for the control of felons and is no longer primarily concerned with the movement of laborers.

These statutory changes were a direct response to changes taking place in England's social structure during this period. We have already pointed out that feudalism was decaying rapidly. Concomitant with the breakup of feudalism was an increased emphasis upon commerce and industry. The com-

---

[18] 22 H. 8. c. 12 (1530).
[19] *Ibid.*
[20] *Ibid.*
[21] 27 H. 8. c. 25 (1535).

mercial emphasis in England at the turn of the sixteenth century is of particular importance in the development of vagrancy laws. With commercialism came considerable traffic bearing valuable items. Where there were 169 important merchants in the middle of the fourteenth century there were 3,000 merchants engaged in foreign trade alone at the beginning of the sixteenth century.[22] England became highly dependent upon commerce for its economic support. Italians conducted a great deal of the commerce of England during this early period and were held in low repute by the populace. As a result, they were subject to attacks by citizens and, more important, were frequently robbed of their goods while transporting them. "The general insecurity of the times made any transportation hazardous. The special risks to which the alien merchant was subjected gave rise to the royal practice of issuing formally executed covenants of safe conduct through the realm."[23]

Such a situation not only called for the enforcement of existing laws but also called for the creation of new laws which would facilitate the control of persons preying upon merchants transporting goods. The vagrancy statutes were revived in order to fulfill just such a purpose. Persons who had committed no serious felony but who were suspected of being capable of doing so could be apprehended and incapacitated through the application of vagrancy laws once these laws were refocused so as to include " . . . any ruffians . . . [who] shall wander, loiter, or idle use themselves and play the vagabonds . . . . "[24]

The new focal concern is continued in 1 Ed. 6. c. 3 (1547) and in fact is made more general so as to include:

Whoever man or woman, being not lame, impotent, or so aged or diseased that he or she cannot work, not having whereon to live, shall be lurking in any house, or loitering or idle wandering by the highway side, or in streets, cities, towns, or villages, not applying themselves to some honest labour, and so continuing for three days; or running away from their work; every such person shall be taken for a vagabond. And . . . upon conviction of two witnesses . . . the same loiterer (shall) be marked with a hot iron in the breast with the letter V, and adjudged him to the person bringing him, to be his slave for two years. . . .

Should the vagabond run away, upon conviction, he was to be branded by a hot iron with the letter S on the forehead and to be thenceforth declared a slave forever. And in 1571 there is modification of the punishment to be inflicted, whereby the offender is to be "branded on the chest with the letter V" (for vagabond). And, if he is convicted the second time, the brand is to be made on the forehead. It is worth noting here that this method of punishment, which first appeared in 1530 and is repeated here with somewhat more

[22] Hall, *op. cit.*, p. 21.
[23] *Ibid.*, p. 23.
[24] 27 H. 8. c. 25 (1535).

force, is also an indication of a change in the type of person to whom the law is intended to apply. For it is likely that nothing so permanent as branding would be applied to someone who was wandering but looking for work, or at worst merely idle and not particularly dangerous *per se*. On the other hand, it could well be applied to someone who was likely to be engaged in other criminal activities in connection with being "vagrant."

By 1571 in the statute of 14 Ed. c. 5 the shift in focal concern is fully developed:

All rogues, vagabonds, and sturdy beggars shall . . . be committed to the common gaol . . . he shall be grievously whipped, and burnt thro' the gristle of the right ear with a hot iron of the compass of an inch about. . . . And for the second offense, he shall be adjudged a felon, unless some person will take him for two years in to his service. And for the third offense, he shall be adjudged guilty of felony without benefit of clergy.

And there is included a long list of persons who fall within the statute: "proctors, procurators, idle persons going about using subtil, crafty and unlawful games or plays; and some of them feigning themselves to have knowledge of . . . absurd sciences . . . and all fencers, bearwards, common players in interludes, and minstrels . . . all juglers, pedlars, tinkers, petty chapmen . . . and all counterfeiters of licenses, passports and users of the same." The major significance of this statute is that it includes all the previously defined offenders and adds some more. Significantly, those added are more clearly criminal types, counterfeiters, for example. It is also significant that there is the following qualification of this statute: "Provided also, that this act shall not extend to cookers, or harvest folks, that travel for harvest work, corn or hay."

That the changes in this statute were seen as significant is indicated by the following statement which appears in the statute:

And whereas by reason of this act, the common gaols of every shire are like to be greatly pestered with more number of prisoners than heretofore hath been, for that the said vagabonds and other lewd persons before recited shall upon their apprehension be committed to the said gaols; it is enacted. . . .[25]

And a provision is made for giving more money for maintaining the gaols. This seems to add credence to the notion that this statute was seen as being significantly more general than those previously.

It is also of importance to note that this is the first time the term *rogue* has been used to refer to persons included in the vagrancy statutes. It seems, *a priori*, that a "rogue" is a different social type than is a "vagrant" or a "vagabond"; the latter terms implying something more equivalent to the

[25] 14 Ed. c. 5. (1571).

idea of a "tramp" whereas the former (rogue) seems to imply a more disorderly and potentially dangerous person.

The emphasis upon the criminalistic aspect of vagrants continues in Chapter 17 of the same statute:

Whereas divers *licentious* persons wander up and down in all parts of the realm, to countenance their *wicked behavior;* and do continually assemble themselves armed in the highways, and elsewhere in troops, *to the great terror* of her majesty's true subjects, *the impeachment of her laws,* and the disturbance of the peace and tranquility of the realm; and whereas many outrages are daily committed by these dissolute persons, and more are likely to ensue if speedy remedy be not provided. (Italics added.)

With minor variations (*e.g.,* offering a reward for the capture of a vagrant) the statutes remain essentially of this nature until 1743. In 1743 there was once more an expansion of the types of persons included such that "all persons going about as patent gatherers, or gatherers of alms, under pretense of loss by fire or other casualty; or going about as collectors for prisons, gaols, or hospitals; all persons playing of betting at any unlawful games; and all persons who run away and leave their wives or children . . . all persons wandering abroad, and lodging in alehouses, barns, outhouses, or in the open air, not giving good account of themselves," were types of offenders added to those already included.

By 1743 the vagrancy statutes had apparently been sufficiently reconstructed by the shifts of concern so as to be once more a useful instrument in the creation of social solidarity. This function has apparently continued down to the present day in England and the changes from 1743 to the present have been all in the direction of clarifying or expanding the categories covered but little has been introduced to change either the meaning or the impact of this branch of the law.

We can summarize this shift in focal concern by quoting from Halsbury. He has noted that in the vagrancy statutes:

. . . elaborate provision is made for the relief and incidental control of destitute wayfarers. These latter, however, form but a small portion of the offenders aimed at by what are known as the Vagrancy Laws, . . . many offenders who are in no ordinary sense of the word vagrants, have been brought under the laws relating to vagrancy, and the great number of the offenses coming within the operation of these laws have little or no relation to the subject of poor relief, but are more properly directed towards the prevention of crime, the preservation of good order, and the promotion of social economy.[26]

Before leaving this section it is perhaps pertinent to make a qualifying remark. We have emphasized throughout this section how the vagrancy stat-

---

[26] Earl of Halsbury, *The Laws of England* (Butterworth & Co., Bell Yard, Temple Bar, 1912), pp. 606–607.

utes underwent a shift in focal concern as the social setting changed. The shift in focal concern is not meant to imply that the later focus of the statutes represents a completely new law. It will be recalled that even in the first vagrancy statute there was reference to those who "do refuse labor, giving themselves to idleness and vice and sometimes to theft and other abominations." Thus the possibility of criminal activities resulting from persons who refuse to labor was recognized even in the earliest statute. The fact remains, however, that the major emphasis in this statute and in the statutes which followed the first one was always upon the "refusal to labor" or "begging." The "criminalistic" aspect of such persons was relatively unimportant. Later, as we have shown, the criminalistic potential becomes of paramount importance. The thread runs back to the earliest statute but the reason for the statutes' existence as well as the focal concern of the statutes is quite different in 1743 than it was in 1349.

VAGRANCY LAWS
IN THE UNITED STATES

In general, the vagrancy laws of England, as they stood in the middle eighteenth century, were simply adopted by the states. There were some exceptions to this general trend. For example, Maryland restricted the application of vagrancy laws to "free" Negroes. In addition, for *all* states the vagrancy laws were even more explicitly concerned with the control of criminals and undesirables than had been the case in England. New York, for example, explicitly defines prostitutes as being a category of vagrants during this period. These exceptions do not, however, change the general picture significantly and it is quite appropriate to consider the U. S. vagrancy laws as following from England's of the middle eighteenth century with relatively minor changes. The control of criminals and undesirables was the *raison d'être* of the vagrancy laws in the U. S. This is as true today as it was in 1750. As Caleb Foote's analysis of the application of vagrancy statutes in the Philadelphia court shows, these laws are presently applied indiscriminately to persons considered a "nuisance." Foote suggests that " . . . the chief significance of this branch of the criminal law lies in its quantitative impact and administrative usefulness."[27] Thus it appears that in America the trend begun in England in the sixteenth, seventeenth and eighteenth centuries has been carried to its logical extreme and the laws are now used principally as a mechanism for "clearing the streets" of the derelicts who inhabit the "skid roads" and "Bowerys" of our large urban areas.

Since the 1800's there has been an abundant source of prospects to which

[27] Foote, *op. cit.*, p. 613. Also see in this connection, Irwin Deutscher, "The Petty Offender," *Federal Probation*, XIX, June, 1955.

the vagrancy laws have been applied. These have been primarily those persons deemed by the police and the courts to be either actively involved in criminal activities or at least peripherally involved. In this context, then, the statutes have changed very little. The functions served by the statutes in England of the late eighteenth century are still being served today in both England and the United States. The locale has changed somewhat and it appears that the present day application of vagrancy statutes is focused upon the arrest and confinement of the "down and outers" who inhabit certain sections of our larger cities but the impact has remained constant. The lack of change in the vagrancy statutes, then, can be seen as a reflection of the society's perception of a continuing need to control some of its "suspicious" or "undesirable" members.[28]

A word of caution is in order lest we leave the impression that this administrative purpose is the sole function of vagrancy laws in the U.S. today. Although it is our contention that this is generally true it is worth remembering that during certain periods of our recent history, and to some extent today, these laws have also been used to control the movement of workers. This was particularly the case during the depression years and California is of course infamous for its use of vagrancy laws to restrict the admission of migrants from other states.[29] The vagrancy statutes, because of their history, still contain germs within them which make such effects possible. Their main purpose, however, is clearly no longer the control of laborers but rather the control of the undesirable, the criminal and the "nuisance."

DISCUSSION

The foregoing analysis of the vagrancy laws has demonstrated that these laws were a legislative innovation which reflected the socially perceived necessity of providing an abundance of cheap labor to landowners during a period when serfdom was breaking down and when the pool of available labor was depleted. With the eventual breakup of feudalism the need for such laws eventually disappeared and the increased dependence of the economy upon industry and commerce rendered the former use of the vagrancy statutes unnecessary. As a result, for a substantial period the vagrancy statutes were dormant, undergoing only minor changes and, presumably, being applied infrequently. Finally, the vagrancy laws were subjected to considerable alteration through a shift in the focal concern of the statutes. Whereas in their inception the laws focused upon the "idle" and "those refusing to

---

[28] It is on this point that the vagrancy statutes have been subject to criticism. See for example, Lacey, Forrest W., "Vagrancy and Other Crimes of Personal Condition," *Harvard Law Review* (66), p. 1203.

[29] *Edwards v. California*, 314 S. 160 (1941).

labor" after the turn of the sixteenth century and emphasis came to be upon "rogues," "vagabonds," and others who were suspected of being engaged in criminal activities. During this period the focus was particularly upon "roadmen" who preyed upon citizens who transported goods from one place to another. The increased importance of commerce to England during this period made it necessary that some protection be given persons engaged in this enterprise and the vagrancy statutes provided one source for such protection by re-focusing the acts to be included under these statutes.

Comparing the results of this analysis with the findings of Hall's study of theft we see a good deal of correspondence. Of major importance is the fact that both analyses demonstrate the truth of Hall's assertion that "The functioning of courts is significantly related to concomitant cultural needs, and this applies to the law of procedure as well as to substantive law."[30]

Our analysis of the vagrancy laws also indicates that when changed social conditions create a perceived need for legal changes that these alterations will be effected through the revision and refocusing of existing statutes. This process was demonstrated in Hall's analysis of theft as well as in our analysis of vagrancy. In the case of vagrancy, the laws were dormant when the focal concern of the laws was shifted so as to provide control over potential criminals. In the case of theft the laws were re-interpreted (interestingly, by the courts and not by the legislature) so as to include persons who were transporting goods for a merchant but who absconded with the contents of the packages transported.

It also seems probable that when the social conditions change and previously useful laws are no longer useful there will be long periods when these laws will remain dormant. It is less likely that they will be officially negated. During this period of dormancy it is the judiciary which has principal responsibility for *not* applying the statutes. It is possible that one finds statutes being negated only when the judiciary stubbornly applies laws which do not have substantial public support. An example of such laws in contemporary times would be the "Blue Laws." Most states still have laws prohibiting the sale of retail goods on Sunday yet these laws are rarely applied. The laws are very likely to remain but to be dormant unless a recalcitrant judge or a vocal minority of the population insist that the laws be applied. When this happens we can anticipate that the statutes will be negated.[31] Should there arise a perceived need to curtail retail selling under some special circum-

---

[30] Hall, *op. cit.,* p. XII.

[31] Negation, in this instance, is most likely to come about by the repeal of the statute. More generally, however, negation may occur in several ways including the declaration of a statute as unconstitutional. This later mechanism has been used even for laws which have been "on the books" for long periods of time. Repeal is probably the most common, although not the only, procedure by which a law is negated.

stances, then it is likely that these laws will undergo a shift in focal concern much like the shift which characterized the vagrancy laws. Lacking such application the laws will simply remain dormant except for rare instances where they will be negated.

This analysis of the vagrancy statutes (and Hall's analysis of theft as well) has demonstrated the importance of "vested interest" groups in the emergence and/or alteration of laws. The vagrancy laws emerged in order to provide the powerful landowners with a ready supply of cheap labor. When this was no longer seen as necessary and particularly when the landowners were no longer dependent upon cheap labor nor were they a powerful interest group in the society the laws became dormant. Finally a new interest group emerged and was seen as being of great importance to the society and the laws were then altered so as to afford some protection to this group. These findings are thus in agreement with Weber's contention that "status groups" determine the content of the law.[32] The findings are inconsistent, on the other hand, with the perception of the law as simply a reflection of "public opinion" as is sometimes found in the literature.[33] We should be cautious in concluding, however, that either of these positions are necessarily correct. The careful analysis of other laws, and especially of laws which do not focus so specifically upon the "criminal," are necessary before this question can be finally answered.

In conclusion, it is hoped that future analyses of changes within the legal structure will be able to benefit from this study by virtue of (1) the data provided and (2) the utilitization of a set of concepts (innovation, dormancy, concern and negation) which have proved useful in the analysis of the vagrancy law. Such analyses should provide us with more substantial grounds for rejecting or accepting as generally valid the description of some of the processes which appear to characterize changes in the legal system.

---

[32] M. Rheinstein, *Max Weber on Law in Economy and Society* (Harvard University Press, 1954).

[33] Friedman, N., *Law in a Changing Society* (Berkeley and Los Angeles: University of California Press, 1959).

The Law of Prohibition

ANDREW SINCLAIR

Liquor was a power in Congress before prohibition was. The fondness of Washington legislators for the bottle was supplemented by the lobby of the liquor trade. The Internal Revenue Act of 1862 put a license fee of twenty dollars on retail liquor dealers and a tax of one dollar a barrel on beer and twenty cents a gallon on spirits. The drys always accused this act, signed by Abraham Lincoln himself, of making an evil traffic legitimate and of corrupting politics for half a century. However true this accusation, it is undeniable that the United States Brewers' Association was formed in the same year. The object of the association was to prosecute its interests "vigorously and energetically" before the legislative and executive branches of the nation and to defeat the maneuvers of the temperance party.[1] After less than a year of pressure, the Association managed to secure a cut in the beer tax to sixty cents a barrel. By 1866, a permanent committee had been set up at Washington, on such cordial terms with the Commissioner of Internal Revenue that it helped to revise the Federal Excise Tax Law of that year.

Other organizations were also set up to exert pressure at Washington on behalf of the liquor trade. There was the National Wholesale Liquor Dealers' Association, the National Retail Liquor Dealers' Association, the National Association of Wine and Spirit Representatives, the United States Manufacturers' and Merchants' Association, and various other pressure groups, often misnamed civic or liberty leagues. These associations, although they were mainly concerned with influencing Congress, also aimed to secure the elections of sympathetic Congressmen. A resolution of the National Brewers' and Distillers' Association stated in 1882 that it was pledged to work harmoniously and assiduously at the ballot box against any party which favored a prohibition amendment to the Constitution.[2] In New York the following year, the local brewers employed a technique which would have defeated the drys in perpetuity, if it had been properly exploited; they asked all political candidates where they stood on temperance matters and fought the silent along with the drys at the polls.[3]

Reprinted from *Prohibition: The Era of Excess* by Andrew Sinclair, by permission of Atlantic-Little, Brown and Co. and Faber and Faber Limited. Copyright © 1962 by Andrew Sinclair.

[1] *Proceedings of the Ninth Brewers' Congress, 1869*, p. 13.
[2] H. Asbury, *The Great Illusion* (New York, 1951), pp. 105–106.
[3] S. Unger, *A History of the National Women's Christian Temperance Union* (Ph.D., Ohio State Univ., 1933), p. 63.

The scandals caused by the connection of the liquor trade and the politicians were nasty and frequent. As Mr. Dooley knew, the friendship of the great was worse than their enmity.[4] The exposure of the Whisky Ring under President Grant, of the Whisky Trust in 1887, and of the conspiracies of the brewers in Texas elections showed the political skulduggery of the liquor trade. The aim of the trade to control Congress, even if it lost the support of the majority of Americans, was manifest. A final damning indictment of the brewers was reported to the Senate in 1919. The report disclosed that the brewers had bought large sections of the press, had influenced campaigns, had exacted pledges from candidates prior to election, had boycotted the goods of their enemies, had formed their own secret political organization, had subsidized the banned German-American Alliance, "many of the membership of which were disloyal and unpatriotic," had formed a secret agreement with the distillers to split political expenses, and had done their utmost to subvert the processes of democracy.[5] This disclosure coincided with the passage of the Volstead Act through the Senate, and was the final nail in the coffin of the liquor trade.

With such powerful opponents behind the scenes in Washington, the drys had to organize a strong lobby of their own. Although the first Congressional Temperance Society was begun by the Reverend Justin Edwards in 1833, and eight abortive attempts to pass a national prohibition amendment were made by Senators Blair and Plumb between 1876 and 1885, no strong political pressure was exerted by the drys in the national capital until 1899. In that year, the first legislative superintendent of the Anti-Saloon League, Edwin C. Dinwiddie, arrived in Washington. After a period of trial and error, the political power and *expertise* of the League grew, and Congress leaped to do its bidding.[6] For twenty years after 1913, the League lobby under Dinwiddie and his successor, Wayne B. Wheeler, was the most powerful and successful reform lobby in Washington.

The first major triumph of the Anti-Saloon League was the passage of the Webb-Kenyon Law in 1913. The law used the federal power in interstate commerce to prevent liquor dealers from sending liquor in packages into dry states. Before the passage of the law, a mail-order liquor business had flourished in dry states, using such advertising slogans as "Uncle Sam Is Our Partner."[7] Although the bill was bitterly denounced in Congress as the work

---

[4] F. Dunne, *Dissertations by Mr. Dooley* (New York, 1906), p. 277.

[5] *Cong. Record,* 66 Cong., 1 Sess., p. 4909. There are good descriptions of the political corruption engineered by the liquor trade in P. Odegard, *Pressure Politics* (New York, 1928), pp. 244–266; F. Dobyns, *The Amazing Story of Repeal* (New York, 1940), pp. 213–245; and D. Leigh Colvin, *Prohibition in the United States* (New York, 1926). The last two books must be partially discounted, since they show bias towards the dry cause.

[6] There is a full and detailed account of the pressure of the Anti-Saloon League on Congress in P. Odegard, *op. cit.,* pp. 127–180.

[7] *Cong. Record,* 62 Cong., 3 Sess., p. 761.

of "a few rabid, misguided, professional prohibitionists," it was passed over Taft's veto by a vote of 63 to 21 in the Senate and 246 to 95 in the House of Representatives.[8] All but two Senators of the dry majority came from the South and West, where the dry cause was strong. Although the wets hoped that the Supreme Court would declare the measure unconstitutional, they were forced to concede that the drys had won a great victory. It was "the impressive fact that in the face of the united effort of all branches of the alcoholic liquor trade, the National Congress voted for the bill."[9] Four years later, the Supreme Court upheld the law.[10]

The first classic debate on the subject of national prohibition came with the vote on the Hobson resolution in the House on December 22, 1914. The resolution called for a national prohibition amendment to the Constitution. Kelly, of Pennsylvania, opened the dry case. He said that the drys were the real friends of liberty — not the false personal liberty which meant license to do wrong. They would grant every liberty save that of injuring the rights of others. Congress should pass the Hobson resolution because of the very forces against it:

. . . the allied powers that prey, the vultures of vice, the corrupt combinations of politics, the grafters and gangsters, the parasites that clothe themselves in the proceeds of woman's shame, the inhuman ones that bathe themselves in the tears of little children, the wastrels who wreck and ruin material things while they contaminate childhood, debauch youth, and crush manhood; the plunder-laden ones who fatten themselves upon the misery and want and woe that their own greed has created, the Hessians in the black-bannered troop whose line of march is over wrecked homes and broken hearts and ruined lives.

Hobson himself followed up by condemning the alcohol poison which attacked "the tender tissues associated with reproduction both in male and female." Hulings, of Pennsylvania, and Tribble, of Georgia, said that the resolution was not an attack on states' rights but a confirmation of them; for the constitutional amendment would be referred to the legislatures of the various states. Garrett, of Texas, regretted the inevitable progress of boys from high-class beer gardens to the doggery. Lindquist, of Michigan, called for the support of patriots; zeppelins, submarines, bombs, and siege guns were not the only things that could destroy a nation; the treasonable conspiracy of the liquor trade had already captured the great cities of America, and was devastating the land and robbing it of its manhood. And Hobson concluded with his famous speech on "Alcohol, the Great Destroyer."

Cantrill, of Kentucky, began the defense of the wets. He denied the capacity of national prohibition to prohibit. The Hobson resolution should

[8] *Ibid.*, p. 2836.
[9] G. Muller, *National Liquor Dealers' Journal*, April 2, 1913.
[10] *Clark Distilling Co. v. Western Maryland R. Co.*, 242 U.S. 311 (1917).

really be called "a resolution legalizing the unlimited manufacture of intoxicating liquor without taxation." Underwood, of Alabama, spoke up for the fundamental beliefs of the Republic, for individual liberty, states' rights, and the rights of property. He denied that the drys represented the forces of temperance, because all men believed in temperance; they were a mere faction "that would tear down the very fabric of the Government itself and destroy the foundation stones on which it rests." Kahn, of California, also pointed out that temperance applied to all things in life, not only to liquor. Prohibition generally resulted in making men liars, sneaks, and hypocrites. If men wanted liquor, they could invariably get it. "We are trying to regulate all human conduct by laws, laws, laws. Efforts of that character are as old as the world. And they have invariably resulted in failure."

Vollmer, of Iowa, scoffed at the great American superstition, "belief in the miraculous potency of the magical formulae: Be it resolved, and Be it enacted." He stood beside George Washington, the brewer; Thomas Jefferson, the distiller; Abraham Lincoln, the saloonkeeper; and Jesus Christ of Nazareth, who had turned water into wine. For him, the policeman's club was not a moral agent; morality which was not self-imposed was not morality. Vicious propensities that could not find an outlet in liquor would find another; they would not be prohibited. Johnson, of Kentucky, said that he was not concerned with the merits of prohibition, but with its economic effects. The measure would destroy property worth billions of dollars, while the wets would have to pay increased taxes to make up the lost revenue. Moreover, the sacred American principle of home rule would be attacked. Finally, Morrison, of Indiana, objected that the House was being stampeded by the Anti-Saloon League and was being forced to reform under fire. Prohibition, even if put into the Constitution, could never be enforced, when Sears, Roebuck catalogues were advertising home distilling kits for less than five dollars an outfit.[11]

At the close of the debate, the vote was taken. The Hobson resolution was passed by 197 votes to 190. Since a two-thirds majority was necessary for the passage of a constitutional amendment, the resolution failed. The drys, however, had given a further demonstration of their growing power. And, significantly, the word "saloon" was never mentioned in the debate except in a derogatory sense. Indeed, Colonel Gilmore admitted in *Bonfort's Wine and Spirit Circular* that the saloon was now doomed.[12]

The widespread prohibition legislation of the powers engaged in the Great War and the certainty that America would enter that war gave the drys a strong lever. When Europe was starving, how could America in God's name turn its grain into sinful drink? In 1917, under the pressure of patriotism,

[11] *Cong. Record,* 63 Cong., 3 Sess., pp. 498–616.
[12] Quoted in P. Odegard, *op. cit.,* p. 158.

Congress passed the Eighteenth Amendment to the Constitution. It also passed other laws giving prohibition to Alaska and Puerto Rico, setting up dry zones around Army camps and Naval bases, and banning soldiers and sailors from all liquor.[13] In addition, three further laws were passed, which showed the political trafficking of both wets and drys at their worst.

The first of these three laws was the Reed Bone-dry Amendment to a bill to exclude liquor advertisements from the mails. Senator Reed, of Missouri, was a dripping wet; but he decided to confound the cautious Anti-Saloon League lobby by making it an offense to use imported liquor in dry territory, as well as to transport or sell it. The use of imported liquor had not been forbidden by the Webb-Kenyon Law. The League was caught napping. Its chief lobbyist, Dinwiddie, advised against voting for Reed's amendment; but Congress, voting freely for the first time for some years, passed the amendment, as much to show their independence of the League as to demonstrate their belief in the tricks of Senator Reed. The League then claimed credit for the measure. Indeed, the position of Reed and the wets was worsened by such a stringent law, especially as its provisions caused no revulsion of moderate support away from the dry cause.

The second law was the District of Columbia Prohibition Law, which banned the legal liquor trade in the capital. The drys refused to hold a referendum on this matter for fear of the popular vote going against them. Moreover, despite the Reed Bone-dry Amendment, the law only prohibited the traffic in liquor, not its use by members of Congress and others.[14]

The third law passed in 1917 was a prohibition clause in the Food Control Bill. The drys were holding up this vital war measure in Congress by threatening to tack onto it various clauses forbidding food to be made into alcohol for drinking purposes. In fact, the drys were so insistent that prohibition was necessary to win the war that Woodrow Wilson was forced to write a letter to Bishop James Cannon, Jr., who was head of the legislative committee of the Anti-Saloon League. He appealed to the Bishop's patriotism: "I regard the immediate passage of the [Food] bill as of vital consequence to the safety and defense of the nation. Time is of the essence." Cannon replied the next day that the League would compromise. If the manufacture of distilled spirits should be forbidden, the President could stop the supply of food to the brewers and winemakers at his own discretion. Wilson replied that he appreciated the Anti-Saloon League's attitude, which was "a very admirable proof of their patriotic motives."[15]

---

[13] The drys passed the third law, which dried up the Army and Navy, by tacking a clause onto the Selective Service Draft Act.

[14] See W. Graham, "After National Prohibition — What?" *North American Review,* April, 1917.

[15] *Woodrow Wilson: Life and Letters* (R. Baker, ed., 8 vols., New York, 1927–1939), VII, pp. 137–138.

Wilson, however, failed to use his discretionary powers, and received a rebuke from the Anti-Saloon League. Its legislative committee wrote to him on April 1, 1918, pointing out that:

... the people have been requested to have heatless days, meatless days, wheatless days and to eliminate waste in every possible way, and yet the breweries and saloons of the country continue to waste food-stuffs, fuel and man-power and to impair the efficiency of labor in the mines, factories and even in munition plants near which saloons are located.[16]

After hearing nothing from Wilson and getting nowhere with him in a conference at the White House, the League used the same device and tacked total wartime prohibition onto the Agricultural Appropriation Bill. All use of foods in the making of spirits, beer, and wine was banned. One report said that Wilson felt so strongly about the matter that he would have vetoed the prohibition measure, if he could have got the rest of the bill through in any other way.[17] But he could not. Wartime prohibition was passed by Congress. The manufacture of liquor in the United States was legally prohibited after June 30, 1919, unless demobilization were to be completed before that date.

A majority in Congress seemed to be inspired by the same false logic that made Senator Myers, of Montana, declare, "There is nothing to understand except one thing, and that is that bread will help us win this war more than whisky. That is the only thing that it is necessary to understand."[18] In face of such implacable reasoning, Wilson had to act. Dry pressure was too great. On Colonel House's advice, he did not veto the Agricultural Appropriation Bill. On September 16, he issued a proclamation that forbade the use of food in making beer. But he did not exercise the authority given him by the Agricultural Appropriation Bill to declare "dry zones" at once in strategical mining and industrial areas. He still supported the flow of such strong drink as could be got for the factory workers. Like any good democrat, he was conscious of the need not to offend too much or too many. This meant the simultaneous gift of sops to the wets and sponges to the drys.

THE EIGHTEENTH AMENDMENT

The Wilson administration was often blamed for the passage through Congress of the Eighteenth Amendment and the Volstead Act. Actually, Wilson had nothing to do with these measures. They were put through, despite the

---

[16] Quoted in J. Steuart, *Wayne Wheeler, Dry Boss* (New York, 1928), pp. 106–107.

[17] J. Tumulty, *Woodrow Wilson as I Know Him* (New York, 1921), p. 413.

[18] *Cong. Record,* 65 Cong., 1 Sess., p. 2171. Prohibition was also extended to Hawaii during the war.

urgency of the war, by the power of the dry lobby in Congress. At the same time that the Anti-Saloon League was helping to defeat the Kaiser by sobering up America, it was also preparing to win the peace by making a land fit for heroes to live in. Its remedy for demobilization and the future was national prohibition.

Professor Irving Fisher, of Yale, a notable dry apologist and statistician, revealed that the Anti-Saloon League knew some of the wet Senators were psychologically prepared to accept national prohibition after the preliminary failure of the war prohibition measure in the Food Control Bill. It is even possible that the League made a deal with them.[19] However that was, Fisher wrote that the League "very astutely took advantage of the situation to propose the act submitting the Eighteenth Amendment. . . . It was easy even for wet Senators to let this act pass, on the theory that it did not really enact Prohibition, but merely submitted it to the States." Then, once the Eighteenth Amendment was safely through Congress, wartime prohibition was reintroduced and passed, "as a means of filling in the gap between the adoption of Constitutional Prohibition and its taking effect. This was pretty hard on the brewers."[20] In other words, by playing on the urge of Congress to escape responsibility for national prohibition, and by yielding ground on wartime prohibition only to revive it again once peacetime prohibition had passed Congress, the dry lobby showed itself guilty of political genius and bad faith.

During the debate on the Eighteenth Amendment in the Senate and the House, various deals were made between the wets and the drys. As Wheeler put it, "we traded jackknives with them."[21] The willing and mindless Senator Harding, of Ohio, was the go-between. In return for a year's grace for the liquor trade to wind up its affairs after possible ratification of the amendment by the states, the wets agreed to put a time limit of six, and then seven, years on ratification. With this limit, the wets in Congress were lulled into a sense of false security. Thirty-six states had to ratify the amendment for it to become part of the Constitution. The wets counted on holding at least thirteen state legislatures. Only twenty-seven states had passed state prohibition laws. The drys would have to gain nine more for their side, as well as convincing the legislatures of the twenty-seven that national prohibition was necessary. The Eighteenth Amendment appeared as a heaven-sent opportunity for wet Senators to wash their hands of the whole affair and to be left in peace at the polls by the Anti-Saloon League.

[19] P. Odegard, *op. cit.*, p. 171.
[20] I. Fisher, *Prohibition at Its Worst* (rev. ed., New York, 1927), pp. 12–13. Fisher was in a position to know about the backstage negotiations at this time, since he was serving at Washington on the Council of National Defense.
[21] New York *Times*, March 31, 1926.

In the debate on the amendment in the Senate, Harding summed up in his heartfelt and confused way the sentiments of many middle-of-the-road Senators. He said that he was not a prohibitionist and had never pretended to be, although he did claim to be a temperance man. He did not see prohibition as a great moral question, but he did see its ethical and economic side. The need for concord in wartime and the fact prohibition would never be effective made him think that the timing of the proposed Eighteenth Amendment was "unwise, imprudent, and inconsiderate"; but he would vote for it, since he was fed up with seeing every politician measured by the wet and dry yardstick. It was high time for the question to be settled. In this way, the people, through their state legislatures, would settle the issue. Although he preferred that compensation be paid to the breweries, he would not insist on this clause.[22] And yet Harding, after declaring himself for the drys, was one of only four Senators who voted for Hardwick's attempt to wreck the passage of the amendment by making it illegal to purchase and use liquor, as well as to manufacture, sell, or transport it.

The Anti-Saloon League lobby, which did much to write the Eighteenth Amendment, was careful to pussyfoot on the question of the use of liquor, as they had done with the Webb-Kenyon Law and with the District of Columbia Prohibition Act. They wanted to punish makers and sellers of liquor, not respectable drinkers. Moreover, they could not afford to alienate the majority of the Senators, who were drinkers. They had to represent the measure as an economic and patriotic necessity. It was no reflection on the personal habits of the legislators of the nation. It was the liquor trade that did evil, not those decent people who supported the trade. In this way, the League could and did gain moderate support in both Senate and House, especially as the blackmail of the open ballot threatened retribution at the polls for the foes of the Eighteenth Amendment.

The extreme drys in the Senate ignored the careful approach of the League and the objections of moderates such as Norris to "this ill-advised attempt."[23] Sheppard, of Texas, set the tone of the Senate debate on the amendment with a full-blooded denunciation of alcohol as the cause of venereal disease, blighted babies, fallen women, and waste to the toiling millions. Kenyon, of Iowa, shook blood out of the flag with his unanswered queries, "If liquor is a bad thing for the boys in the trenches, why is it a good thing for those at home? When they are willing to die for us, should we not be willing to go dry for them?" Jones, of Washington, denied the brewers' charges that prohibition would produce anger, resentment, and disaffection among millions

---

[22] Cong. Record, 65 Cong., 1 Sess., p. 5648.

[23] Like Harding and Borah, who protested over the constitutionality of the time-limit clause to the Eighteenth Amendment, Norris voted for the amendment after speaking against it.

as "a base libel on American workers," who were "as loyal and patriotic a class as we have." Intelligent labor knew that prohibition was being passed for its benefit. Moreover, those opposed to prohibition would live to bless prohibition. Ashurst, of Arizona, saw the amendment as a great referendum to the states. Sherman, of Illinois, remembered his many liberal friends of thirty years past who had been killed off by the saloons and had died "with strange complaints, seeing strange things in the air and hearing strange voices." Kirby, of Arkansas, did not doubt that through the ages one increasing purpose ran. And Myers, of Montana, rounded off the dry case with his declaration that the world was steadily becoming better. He suggested that the momentous day when the Senate passed the amendment should be observed as another Fourth of July, a second Declaration of Independence.

The drys could afford rhetoric, for they were certain that their cause was won. But the wets were forced to appeal to reason, for they knew that they had lost. Underwood, of Alabama, warned the Senate that the tyranny of corruption could be replaced by the subtler, less tangible, more enduring tyranny of reform. Moreover, the propaganda of the drys that Congress should pass its responsibility on to the states was subversive of the spirit of republican government. Lodge, of Massachusetts, gave a prophetic denunciation of the impossibility of enforcing national prohibition. Without a prepared public sentiment, all prohibition could hope to effect was the destruction of every control on the liquor traffic. People would resent the dry law as a gross and tyrannical interference with personal liberty. Respect for justice would vanish. "Where large masses of the people would consider it even meritorious — at least quite venial — to evade and break the law, the law would inevitably be broken constantly and in a large and effective way." Lodge doubted that there could be an army large enough to enforce absolute prohibition. The measure was "the worst thing that could be done to advance temperance and total abstinence among the people." But the wet protests were unavailing. The amendment passed the Senate by a vote of 65 to 20.[24]

One new idea came out of the House debate on the Eighteenth Amendment, and a legion of old ideas. While the Senate's version of the amendment had provided for the prohibition of the manufacture, sale, or transportation of intoxicating liquors, Congressman Webb introduced the phrase, "the Congress and the several States shall have concurrent power to enforce this article by appropriate legislation." By his term "concurrent power," Webb meant to protect states' rights, for "nobody desires that the Federal Congress shall take away from the various States the right to enforce the prohibition laws of those States." He also intended that the states should take much of the burden off the federal government in law enforcement. "We do not want

---

[24] *Cong. Record,* 65 Cong., 1 Sess., pp. 5548–5560, 5585–5627, 5636–5667.

10,000 Federal officers, with all the expense of salaries, going over the country enforcing these laws when the States have their own officers to do so and are willing to do so." In answer to questions, Webb denied that there would be a conflict of jurisdiction between state and federal courts. A man ought not to be tried twice for the same offense. "One punishment ought to be sufficient." He said that he was not afraid to trust the states to enforce the amendment. "I never saw one that went counter to the United States Consitution, or whose law officers failed to enforce the law." Yet, whatever Webb's reasons, the inclusion of the term "concurrent power" in the amendment led to a myriad of later legal complications.

Webb also referred to the letter which Samuel Gompers, head of the American Federation of Labor, had written to the newspapers that morning, December 17, 1917. Gompers had complained that prohibition would throw two million people out of work; it was also a class law against the beer of the workingman. Webb replied that the jobs of only about sixty thousand people directly connected with the liquor trade would be affected. He quoted William Jennings Bryan, that it was a slander to intimate that the great laboring classes of America measured their patriotism by the quart or by the schooner.

After many other loyal dry appeals, Robbins, of Pennsylvania, reminded the House that there were three constitutional amendments pending, those of prohibition and woman suffrage and writing the name of God into the Constitution. All three should be referred to the states, for *vox populi vox Dei.* Little, of Kansas, raised laughter when he referred to a gentleman from "some semi-civilized foreign colony in New York City" who damned prohibition as a mere reform from "the outlying settlements." According to Little, the outlying settlements provided all the reforms that New York City would ever get. Norton, of North Dakota, would have gone so far as to send all the wet spokesmen to the front, for their arguments showed them to be "marvelously great camouflage artists."

In face of these patriotic and rural appeals, the wets in the House countered with some reason and some wit. Gard, of Ohio, said that the Eighteenth Amendment would substitute "controversy for sure settlement." The President had it in his power to forbid the use of food in making liquor by proclamation. Congress should not waste time debating the amendment, but should help the President in winning the war. Magee, of New York, made the good point that the question was "not temperance versus intemperance, but whether we are willing to use the condition of war as the chief instrument in attempting to bring about Nation-wide prohibition at this particular time." In fact, no grain would be conserved by the passage of the amendment, since it probably would not go into effect until the war was over. As for himself, he had no brief for wets or drys, but a brief for "his country first, last, and all the time."

Walsh, of Massachusetts, observed that temperance in thought and speech was sometimes as wise as temperance in the use of food and drink. Small, of North Carolina, said that the dry effort to get the House to pass responsibility for the measure on to the states was pernicious, for "we are not mere automatons to register the will of the Anti-Saloon League or any other organization of reformers." Slayden, of Texas, warned that a constitutional amendment would perpetuate the tyranny of a temporary majority in the country. McArthur, of Oregon, said that the League would be better off spending its money on educating people against liquor, while Gordon, of Ohio, resented the attack of rural morality on the large cities. The vote on the amendment would, anyway, not be an honest one, as Gallagher, of New York, pointed out. A secret ballot would show the drys that their majorities came from fear.[25]

When the vote was taken, the Eighteenth Amendment passed the House by 282 votes to 128. It was then referred to the states for ratification. Lengthy extracts from the speeches in Congress on the issue have been included to demonstrate the charged atmosphere in which the measure was passed, and the arguments which were repeated *ad nauseam* by both wets and drys in the years preceding and following the amendment. The extracts also show that boredom played some part in the passage of the amendment.[26] The members of Congress were sick of being badgered by the Anti-Saloon League and their dry constituents. They ignored Heflin, of Alabama, who said that no member of the House could dispose of the question simply by saying he was tired of being bothered with it.[27] It was unfortunate for Congress that the Eighteenth Amendment was only the beginning of dry fuss about the liquor issue.

A comparative analysis of the vote on the Hobson resolution and the Eighteenth Amendment in the House shows how and where the drys gained support between 1914 and 1917, and how the speeches of Congressmen were motivated less by party consideration than by geography. The drys gained 85 votes in this period. Their largest gain was a block of 39 Republican votes from Midwestern states, where the Anti-Saloon League had its most powerful political organization and where the Democratic party was associated with the liquor interests. During these three years, with the help of the League, the Republican party in the Midwest doubled its strength, while the Demo-

[25] *Cong. Record,* 65 Cong., 2 Sess., pp. 422–470.

[26] C. Merz, *The Dry Decade* (New York, 1931), p. 76. Merz's book is the only good general account of prohibition. It is based largely on newspaper files. Unfortunately, it was published before the release of the *Wickersham Report,* although Walter Lippmann considered it better than the report, praising it for its "mastery of material, intellectual candor and restrained brilliance of statement."

[27] *Cong. Record,* 65 Cong., 2 Sess., p. 458.

crats, despite Woodrow Wilson's victory of 1916 against Hughes, lost 37
seats in the House of Representatives.

Yet the League was a nonpartisan organization. It supported drys in both
parties. The votes on the Hobson resolution and the Eighteenth Amendment
were not party matters. In the first case, 120 Democrats and 73 Republicans
voted for the measure, 141 Democrats and 47 Republicans against. In the
second case, 140 Democrats and 138 Republicans voted for the measure, 64
Democrats and 62 Republicans against. The vote proved correct both the
Anti-Saloon League's assertion that the only way to obtain national prohibition was to support drys in both of the major parties, and also the Prohibition party's objection that both of the major parties were too divided on the
issue to enforce national prohibition wholeheartedly. Prohibition was a party
matter only on a sectional basis. Northern Democrats, whose support was
based on the wet cities, were opposed by the Anti-Saloon League and the
Republican party, while Southern Democrats in the dry and one-party South
were helped by the League. The nonpartisan approach of that powerful dry
organization helped to build the irreparable split in the Democratic party on
the prohibition issue. Meanwhile, the Republican party, freed of the gar-
rulous conscience of the South, was able to straddle the issue more circum-
spectly during conventions and elections.

The vote on the Hobson resolution shows clearly on what a rock the dry
congressional group was founded. Of the 197 members of the House who
voted for the Hobson resolution, 129 were from cities of less than 10,000
people, while 64 of them were from country villages of less than 2500 people.
Only 13 were from cities containing a population of more than 100,000. Of
the 190 opponents to the resolution, 109 were from cities of more than 25,000
people, and only 25 from villages with less than 2500 inhabitants. In fact,
national prohibition was a measure passed by village America against urban
America. This conclusion is confirmed by the fact that San Francisco, St.
Louis, St. Paul, Chicago, Cincinnati, Cleveland, Detroit, and Boston all rejected prohibitory laws during the period when the Eighteenth Amendment
was being considered by Congress and the states.[28]

An analysis of the Senate vote on the amendment also proves the rural
support of the measure. Of course, both in the United States Senate and in
the various state senates the country was overrepresented at the expense of
the cities, as Senator Calder pointed out.[29] This was the reason why the drys
wanted prohibition to be passed by the legislatures as an amendment to the

---

[28] C. Merz, *op. cit.*, p. 71.

[29] For instance, over the question of ratification of prohibition in the New
York state assembly, one voter in rural Putnam County had as much representation as four voters in Rochester, five in Syracuse, and seven in parts
of Manhattan.

Constitution, rather than by state referendum. For the populous cities often upset dry majorities in country areas during state referendums. Ohio itself, the headquarters and home state of the Anti-Saloon League leaders, did not pass state-wide prohibition until 1918, owing to the opposition of Cincinnati and other wet cities. But if the League could only cow the lower houses of the various states into passing a constitutional amendment, they could rely on the country majorities in the senates to support them.

While the vote in the House of Representatives on the Eighteenth Amendment gave the measure a bare two-thirds majority, in the Senate the measure passed by a majority of more than three to one. Of the twenty Senators who opposed the measure, nine came from the populous Atlantic states, seven from the South, ever eager to protect the doctrine of states' rights, and the remaining four from states whose beer or wine interests would suffer from the amendment. A similar disproportion is shown when the votes of the senates and lower houses of the ratifying states are compared. While the combined senates of the forty-six ratifying states voted 1310 to 237 to carry the amendment, the combined lower houses voted 3782 to 1035.[30] Where the country was more heavily represented than the cities, the drys could count on more support for dry measures.

The drys reversed their tactics to secure the ratification of the Eighteenth Amendment by the states. While they had told Congress that the amendment was a democratic measure because the question of national prohibition had to be referred to the states, they told the state legislatures that their duty was to ratify the Eighteenth Amendment, since it had been approved by a two-thirds majority of both houses of Congress. Moreover, it was easier for the drys to get the states to ratify, for they needed only a straight majority in each house of three-quarters of the states. The necessary thirty-six states ratified within fourteen months, forty-five within sixteen months. New Jersey ratified in 1922, but Connecticut and Rhode Island never ratified.

The terms of the Eighteenth Amendment show the great care of the dry lobby not to push legislators too far too fast. The amendment read:

Section 1. After one year from the ratification of this article the manufacture, sale, or transportation of intoxicating liquors within, the importation thereof into, or the exportation thereof from the United States and all territory subject to the jurisdiction thereof for beverage purposes is hereby prohibited.

Section 2. The Congress and the several States shall have concurrent power to enforce this article by appropriate legislation.

Section 3. This article shall be inoperative unless it shall have been ratified as an amendment to the Constitution by the legislatures of the several States, as provided in the Constitution, within seven years from the date of the submission hereof to the States by the Congress.

[30] C. Merz, *op. cit.,* Appendix D, pp. 315–316.

If the prohibitionists had insisted on total prohibition of liquor in America, they would not have allowed the Eighteenth Amendment to be presented in this form. But the Anti-Saloon League was more concerned with enshrining the practice of prohibition in the Constitution than with enacting a stringent and unequivocal measure. The first step was to pass the amendment in any form; the second was to pass a severe law to enforce it. The League was always occupied with the possible in politics, although it favored the eternal in propaganda.

There were many flaws in the wording of the Eighteenth Amendment. As in the Webb-Kenyon Law, the amendment did not forbid the purchase or use of liquor — only four Senators could be found to support Hardwick's motion to this effect. Therefore, any man who could afford to fill his cellars before the amendment became legal could serve liquor to his guests perfectly legitimately until his stocks were exhausted. Also, the fact that the amendment gave the liquor trade a year to wind up its business destroyed the dry argument that the liquor trade was criminal. No criminal organization would be guaranteed by Congress a year to put its affairs in order. Moreover, instruments for manufacturing liquor in the home were not banned, and the bootlegger was given ample time to prepare for his future profession. Again, the amendment served to increase class hatred, for it was only the poor who could not afford to stock up liquor. In Samuel Gompers's words, "The workers who have no cellars and have not the opportunity of gratifying a normal even though temporary rational desire learn to hate their more fortunate fellow citizens more bitterly and uncompromisingly."[31]

The failure of the Eighteenth Amendment to include a purchase clause was a further weakness. Since there was no penalty attached to buying liquor, people were prepared to buy. The threat of putting bootleggers in jail hardly deterred their respectable patrons, who ran no risk at all. Thus the amendment allowed a safe demand for liquor to exist, and only persecuted the suppliers of that demand. The consciences of many good citizens was salved by the consideration that they were not legally breaking the letter of the Constitution themselves, nor even aiding and abetting others to break it. When only the trade in liquor was criminal and liquor itself not so, legal reasons for abstaining did not exist.

There were additional flaws in the amendment. The words "concurrent power" were ambiguous and set the stage for a long legal battle between the states and the federal government. Furthermore, the omission of the word "alcoholic" from the amendment in favor of the word "intoxicating," despite the protests of the Prohibition party, allowed many cases in the law courts to be dismissed. Proof that liquor was "intoxicating" was harder to demonstrate

---

[31] Quoted in F. Dobyns, *op. cit.*, p. 253. Dobyns gives a full-scale assault on the Eighteenth Amendment from the point of view of a fanatical dry.

than proof that liquor was "alcoholic" and had been sold. Although the Volstead Act later defined "intoxicating" as one-half of 1 per cent of alcohol by volume, an amendment to the Volstead Act, such as the Cullen Bill of 1933, could allow the sale of beer before the Eighteenth Amendment had been repealed.

In the debate on the Eighteenth Amendment in the House, Congressman Graham, of Pennsylvania, had said that the wet argument of the unconstitutionality of the amendment was a bugaboo. The Supreme Court later upheld his wisdom in the National Prohibition Cases.[32] But Graham was even wiser in his succeeding remarks, when he detailed his reasons for voting against the measure. For him, the Eighteenth Amendment destroyed the purpose of the Constitution. That fundamental law was only a declaration of principles, never of policy.[33]

THE VOLSTEAD ACT

In 1930, a journalist unkindly suggested that the whole history of the United States could be told in eleven words: Columbus, Washington, Lincoln, Volstead, Two flights up and ask for Gus.[34] In a sense, his cheap wit was truer than he knew. For if the speak-easy and the bootlegger were aided by the loopholes of the Volstead Act, those loopholes were only in the act because of the whole tradition of American history.

Although the prohibitionists had written prohibition into the fundamental law of America, that fundamental law prevented them from enforcing it. The Constitution guaranteed Americans certain rights. The Volstead Act and other means of enforcing the Eighteenth Amendment seemed to deny Americans their heritage. The Fourth Amendment gave people the right to be secure in their persons, houses, papers, and effects against unreasonable searches and seizures. The Fifth Amendment prevented people from being forced to be witnesses against themselves or from being tried twice for the same offense. The Sixth Amendment guaranteed "a speedy and public trial by an impartial jury." Yet these individual rights were attacked by the Volstead Act and its successors. Moreover, those states that by tradition or conviction opposed the increasing power of the federal government, were never persuaded that the Eighteenth Amendment did not violate the Tenth, which reserved all powers not delegated to the United States by the Constitution to the states or to the people.

Yet Congress, once the Eighteenth Amendment had been ratified by the states, had to provide for its token enforcement. The amendment could not be

[32] See 253 U.S. 350 (1920).
[33] *Cong. Record,* 65 Cong., 2 Sess., pp. 463–464.
[34] H. Phillips, in the New York *Evening Sun,* March 12, 1930.

properly enforced without a bill, which would invade American liberties intolerably. The American people and Congress were not prepared for this. Thus the drys had to put through a measure which would deter without terrifying too much, and compromise without excusing everything. The principal author of this unhappy mish-mash of the possible and the desirable was the Anti-Saloon League Washington attorney, Wayne B. Wheeler. Despite the jealous opposition of Bishop Cannon, he drafted such a complex measure that he gave himself great power for the nine years before his death.[35] He was the only man who could understand and interpret the code of enforcement. Like Moses, he interpreted the commandments of his law to the faithful. The sponsor of his law was Representative Andrew Volstead, of Minnesota. Volstead lost his seat in Congress four years later for his pains.[36]

The original Volstead Bill was considerably more severe than the amended act of sixty-seven sections, later supplemented by another six sections, which evolved out of the debates on the measure in Congress. First, the House Judiciary Committee weakened the clauses of the bill that dealt with search and seizure, with the soliciting of orders for liquor, and with the report of arrests for drunkenness by local officers. House amendments, although partially restoring the search and seizure clauses, provided for severe penalties against the wrongful issue of search warrants, and allowed the possession of liquor in private homes and the sale of sacramental wine. The amended bill was passed in the House by a vote of 287 to 100, a loss to the wets of 28 votes since the division in the Eighteenth Amendment owing to dry and Republican victories in the elections of 1918.

The bill was then referred to a Senate Judiciary Subcommittee and the Senate Judiciary Committee. Further amendments were passed. Dwellings where people could possess liquor without fear of reprisals were defined as including residences, apartments, hotels, or similar places of abode. Individuals were still allowed to store and consume liquor and, in addition, to manufacture light wine and cider at home. Although the provision defining "intoxicating" at such a trivial volume of alcohol was upheld, the Senate insisted that the government must bear "the burden of proof" in the prosecution of liquor violations. The Senate then passed the bill without roll call and returned it to the House, which refused to accept the Senate's amendments. A conference was set up between the houses to reach an agreement. At the con-

---

[35] In his autobiography, *Bishop Cannon's Own Story* (R. Watson, ed., Duke Univ., 1955), p. 289, Cannon says that Wheeler was the principal author of the Volstead Act. This is also confirmed in J. Steuart, *op. cit.*, pp. 149–152.

[36] Although the Anti-Saloon League exerted itself in 1920 to save Volstead's seat, it was unable to win the election for him in 1922. The wets and moderates hated him too much. He was unseated after twenty successive years in Congress, and became legal adviser to the chief of the North Western Dry Enforcement District.

ference, the Senate won virtually every one of its liberal provisions, even in minor matters, such as striking out the clause penalizing drunkards on public vehicles, allowing alcoholics to be given liquor while under hospital treatment, and legalizing the manufacture of beer before it was made into near-beer.

The Volstead Act, as passed by Congress, was a curious document. Although the Armistice had been signed for eight months, the Act provided for the enforcement of wartime prohibition. The drys maintained that the period of demobilization was so difficult that it should be considered as part of the war; the wets said that the clause was a dishonest attempt by the drys to go back on their promise to give the liquor trade a year to wind up its business. For, by the device of prolonging wartime prohibition, the Volstead Act closed up the gap between its passage in 1919 and the start of national prohibition under the Eighteenth Amendment on January 16, 1920. However this was, Woodrow Wilson used the anomaly of the clauses relating to wartime prohibition to veto the Volstead Act on October 27, 1919. In his message to Congress, he added the cryptic warning that in all matters having to do with the personal habits and customs of large numbers of people, the established processes of legal change had to be followed.[37] But he did not express specifically in his veto message either approval or disapproval of the Eighteenth Amendment or of the main body of the Volstead Act. The House and the Senate immediately reacted by passing the act over Wilson's veto.

In brief, the amended Volstead Act provided for the manufacture of industrial alcohol by permits, and its denaturing to render it unfit for human consumption. The use of beverage alcohol was restricted to the patients of doctors, communicants at religious services, and makers of vinegar and cider. The Commissioner of Internal Revenue was charged with administering the enforcement of the act. The Commissioner and his assistants were given powers to investigate offenders and report them to United States attorneys, who would prosecute them before the federal courts. Penalties for bootleggers were set at a maximum fine of $1000 and six months in jail for first offenders, and $10,000 and five years in jail for second offenders. Places selling liquor illegally could be padlocked by court injunction for one year. Personal property used for the transportation of liquor, such as automobiles, boats, and airplanes, could be seized and sold by public auction to help defray the costs of enforcement. The purchase of liquor, however, did not make the purchaser liable for prosecution under the law of conspiracy.[38]

The Volstead Act was full of flaws. It was the result of compromises in the

---

[37] The full text of the message is contained in *The Standard Encyclopedia of the Alcohol Problem* (Westerville, Ohio, 1930), VI, p. 2782.

[38] For the full text of the Volstead Act, see *U.S. Statutes*, Vol. 41, Pt. 1, pp. 305–322.

House and the Senate between the determined dry lobbyists and a majority of the members of Congress who did not desire that the Eighteenth Amendment should be rigidly enforced. Even the drys in Congress did not want to jeopardize the amendment by making the Volstead Act too severe and by causing a public revulsion against national prohibition. Only three members of the House voted for an amendment to the Volstead Act on July 21 to make the home possession of liquor unlawful; both drys and wets opposed such a stringent provision. The aim of the Act was to secure as much enforcement as the country would endure, not total enforcement.

The faults in the framing of the Volstead Act were quickly revealed, once national prohibition was put into effect. Yet these shortcomings were no reflection on the sincerity of the drys. They wanted prohibition to be enforced as efficiently as possible; but they knew that Congress and the wet cities would not allow them to get all they wanted. Even so, by the compromise of the Volstead Act, they did the dry cause great damage. They did not secure the blessings of good law enforcement for their supporters, and they gave great cause for resentment to their opponents. The provision that allowed the making of home cider and light wines seemed a monstrous discrimination in favor of the farm against the town. As Congressman Barkley pointed out, if fermented apple juice and grape juice were legal, "how about corn juice?" Congressman McKiniry further saw in the legislation the "malicious joy" of the rural districts of America in "inflicting this sumptuary prohibition legislation upon the great cities. It preserves their cider and destroys the city workers' beer."[39]

But perhaps Congressman Crago, of Pennsylvania, best put the objections of those old-fashioned Americans whom the Volstead Act was designed to protect. He feared that the law would breed "a discontent and disrespect for law in this country beyond anything we have ever witnessed before." The Act refused trial by jury in some cases; it confiscated personal property; it extended the power of the judiciary beyond anything since the shameful days of Judge Jeffreys in England; it invaded the sanctity of the home; and it made "crimes of the ordinary harmless housekeeping acts of nearly every family in our country."[40]

In this way, the Eighteenth Amendment and the Volstead Act became the law of the land. Through the many roots of prohibition — rural mythology, the psychology of excess, the exploited fears of the mass of the people, the findings of science and medicine, the temper of reform, the efficiency of the dry pressure groups, their mastery of propaganda, the stupidity and self-interest of the brewers and distillers, the necessary trimming of politicians, and the weakness of the elected representatives of the people — through all

[39] *Cong. Record,* 66 Cong., 1 Sess., pp. 2869, 2894.
[40] *Ibid.,* p. 2956.

these channels the sap of the dry tree rose until the legal prohibition of the liquor trade burst out new and green in the first month of 1920. The roots had been separate; yet they were all part of a common American seed. They combined and contributed to the strength of the whole. The Anti-Saloon League, bent on its particular reform, was the heir and beneficiary of many interactions in American life. As the drys stood on the threshold of victory at the opening of the twenties, they could see manifest destiny in the success of their cause. They seemed to be the darling army of the Lord. Behind them appeared to lie one mighty pattern and purpose. Before them hung the sweet fruits of victory.

The Diffusion of
Sexual Psychopath Laws

EDWIN H. SUTHERLAND

This paper is an analysis of the diffusion of sexual psychopath laws from the point of view of collective behavior. Since 1937 twelve states and the District of Columbia have enacted sexual psychopath laws. With minor variations they provide that a person who is diagnosed as a sexual psychopath may be confined for an indefinite period in a state hospital for the insane. This confinement is not ordered by a criminal court as a punishment for crime but by a probate court for the protection of society against persons who are believed to have irresistible sexual impulses.[1]

Implicit in these laws is a series of propositions which have been made explicit in an extensive popular literature, namely, that the present danger to women and children from serious sex crimes is very great, for the number of sex crimes is large and is increasing more rapidly than any other crime; that most sex crimes are committed by "sexual degenerates," "sex fiends," or "sexual psychopaths" and that these persons persist in their sexual crimes throughout life; that they always give warning that they are dangerous by first committing minor offenses; that any psychiatrist can diagnose them with a high degree of precision at an early age, before they have committed serious sex crimes; and that sexual psychopaths who are diagnosed and identified should be confined as irresponsible persons until they are pronounced by psychiatrists to be completely and permanently cured of their malady.[2]

Most of these propositions can be demonstrated to be false and the others questionable. More particularly, the concept of the "sexual psychopath" is so vague that it cannot be used for judicial and administrative purposes with-

Reprinted from *American Journal of Sociology*, 56 (September 1950), pp. 142–148, by permission of The University of Chicago Press. Copyright 1950 by The University of Chicago.

[1] In some states conviction of a sex crime is a prerequisite to the operation of this law. Even in this case the significant characteristic of the law is that it takes the criminal out of the realm of ordinary punishment and treats him as a patient with a mental malady.

[2] J. Edgar Hoover, "How Safe Is Your Daughter?" *American Magazine*, CXLIV (July, 1947), 32–33; David G. Wittels, "What Can We Do about Sex Crimes?" *Saturday Evening Post*, CCXXI (December 11, 1948), 30 ff.; C. J. Dutton, "Can We End Sex Crimes?" *Christian Century*, XLIV (December 22, 1937), 1594–95; F. C. Waldrup, "Murder as a Sex Practice," *American Mercury* (February, 1948), 144–58; Charles Harris, "A New Report on Sex Crimes," *Coronet* (October, 1947), 3–9; Howard Whitman, "Terror in Our Cities: No. I, Detroit," *Collier's*, November 19, 1949, pp. 13–15, 64–66.

out the danger that the law may injure the society more than do the sex crimes which it is designed to correct. Moreover, the states which have enacted such laws make little or no use of them. And there is no difference in the trend in rates of serious sex crimes, so far as it can be determined, between the states which enact such laws and adjoining states which do not.[3]

These dangerous and futile laws are being diffused with considerable rapidity in the United States. Michigan first enacted such a law in 1937.[4] Illinois followed in 1938, and California and Minnesota in 1939. Thus four states have had these laws for ten years. In 1943 Vermont passed a sexual psychopath law; in 1945 Ohio; in 1947 Massachusetts, Washington, and Wisconsin; in 1948 the District of Columbia; and in 1949 Indiana, New Hampshire, and New Jersey. They continue to spread, with no indication of abatement. What is the explanation of this diffusion of laws which have little or no merit?

First, these laws are customarily enacted after a state of fear has been aroused in a community by a few serious sex crimes committed in quick succession. This is illustrated in Indiana, where a law was passed following three or four sexual attacks in Indianapolis, with murder in two. Heads of families bought guns and watchdogs, and the supply of locks and chains in the hardware stores of the city was completely exhausted.[5]

The sex murders of children are most effective in producing hysteria. Speaking of New York City in 1937, after four girls had been murdered in connection with sexual attacks, Austin H. MacCormick says:

> For a while it was utterly unsafe to speak to a child on the street unless one was well-dressed and well-known in the neighborhood. To try to help a lost child, with tears streaming down its face, to find its way home would in some neighborhoods cause a mob to form and violence to be threatened.[6]

The hysteria produced by child murders is due in part to the fact that the ordinary citizen cannot understand a sex attack on a child. The ordinary citizen can understand fornication or even forcible rape of a woman, but he concludes that a sexual attack on an infant or a girl of six years must be the act of a fiend or maniac. Fear is the greater because the behavior is so incomprehensible.

A protracted man-hunt following a sex attack arouses additional fear. The newspapers report daily on the progress of the chase, and every real or imag-

---

[3] These appraisals of the sexual psychopath laws have been elaborated in my paper in the *Journal of Criminal Law and Criminology,* XL (January-February, 1950), 534–54.

[4] This law as declared unconstitutional, but a revised law was enacted in 1939.

[5] *Time,* November 24, 1947, pp. 29–30.

[6] "New York's Present Problem," *Mental Hygiene,* XX (January, 1938), 4–5.

ined sex attack, from near and far, is given prominence. In the case of Fred Stroble in Los Angeles in November, 1949, three days elapsed between the discovery of the mutilated body of his victim and his capture. A description of the crime and of the suspected criminal was sent to all adjoining cities and counties, and blockades were set up along the Mexican border. Watches were set at hotels, motels, bus stations, railway stations, and saloons. Hundreds of reports came to the police from Los Angeles and from other cities. Timid old men were pulled off streetcars and taken to police stations for identification, and every grandfather was subject to suspicion. The body of a drowned man, recovered from the ocean, was at first reported to be Stroble. The history of Stroble's molestations of other girls was reported. A detailed description of seven other cases of sex murders of girls in Los Angeles since 1924 was published. At the end of the week, twenty-five other cases of molestations of girls in Los Angeles had been reported to the Los Angeles police.[7] After three days it appeared that Stroble had gone to Ocean Park, on the edge of Los Angeles, and had stayed in hotels there. He then returned to Los Angeles with the intention of surrendering to the police. He went into a bar after alighting from a bus and was recognized and pointed out to a policeman. The picture of the policeman who made the arrest was published in scores of newspapers over the United States as the "capturer of the sex fiend." After his capture, other details of the case and of related cases kept the community in a state of tension. As soon as the district attorney secured from Stroble an account of the manner of the murder, he went to the assembled reporters and repeated the story, "with beads of sweat standing on his face and neck." The psychiatrist's diagnosis of Stroble was published: he loved this little girl because he was a timid and weak old man, insufficiently aggressive to approach grown women; the murder of the girl was merely an incident due to fear of being caught and punished.

Fear is seldom or never related to statistical trends in sex crimes. New York City's terror in 1937 was at its height in August, although that was not the month when sex crimes reached their peak. The number of sex crimes known to the police of New York City was 175 in April, 211 in May, 159 in August, and 177 in September.[8] Ordinarily, from two to four spectacular sex crimes in a few weeks are sufficient to evoke the phrase "sex crime wave."

Fear is produced more readily in the modern community than it was earlier in our history because of the increased publicity regarding sex crimes. Any spectacular sex crime is picked up by the press associations and is distributed to practically all the newspapers in the nation; in addition, it is often de-

---

[7] "Molestation" is a weasel word and can refer to anything from rape to whistling at a girl.

[8] Citizens' Committee for the Control of Crime in New York, "Sex Crimes in New York City," quoted in *Journal of Criminal Law and Criminology,* XXIX (May, 1938), 143–44.

scribed in news broadcasts. Then weekly and monthly journals publish general articles on sex crimes. All this produces a widespread uneasiness which, given a few local incidents, readily bursts into hysteria.

Although this condition of fear has been found in all the states prior to the enactment of their sexual psychopath laws, it is not a sufficient explanation of the laws. For generations communities have been frightened by sex crimes and have not enacted sexual psychopath laws. In the present generation the states which have not enacted sexual psychopath laws have had similar fears.

A second element in the process of developing sexual psychopath laws is the agitated activity of the community in connection with the fear. The attention of the community is focused on sex crimes, and people in the most varied situations envisage dangers and see the need of and possibility for their control. When a news broadcaster, in connection with the Stroble case, expressed the belief over the radio that something should be done, he received more than two hundred telegrams agreeing with him. The mother of the murdered girl demanded punishment for the daughter of Stroble, who had harbored him without notifying the parents of girls in the neighborhood that he was a dangerous criminal. A woman spoke in condemnation of strip-tease and other lewd shows as stimulating sex fiends and demanded that they be closed. Letters to the editors demanded that sex criminals be castrated; others recommended whipping. The City Council of Los Angeles adopted a resolution demanding that the legislature of the state be called in special session to enact laws which would punish sex crimes more severely and would make sex criminals ineligible for parole. The attorney-general of the state sent a bulletin to all sheriffs and police chiefs urging them to enforce strictly the laws which required registration of all sex criminals. The judiciary committee of the state legislature appointed a subcommittee to study the problem of sex crimes and to make recommendations to a special session of the legislature. The superintendent of city schools urged, among other things, that sex offenders who loitered around the schools should be prosecuted. The grand jury met and started a general investigation of sex crimes. The Juvenile Protective Committee urged an appropriation of $50,000 for medical and clinical treatment of sex offenders, and the County Probation Department energetically requested the authorizing of a psychiatric clinic for the study and supervision of sex offenders. It was reported that some psychiatrists in the city opposed these suggestions for psychiatric clinics as "socialized medicine" and "statism."

In the meantime, organization developed in other directions. The sheriff's office set up a special detail on sex offenses, with a staff to co-ordinate all police activities on sex offenses in the county. The Parent-Teacher Association sponsored mass meetings, with blanks on which interested persons could enroll as members of an organization which would continue its efforts until effective action for control of sex crimes was taken. At the first mass meeting, attended by about eight hundred people, speakers were scheduled to explain the existing laws and procedures and to suggest programs for improvement. The news of the Stroble crime and of subsequent events was carried over the nation by the press associations and produced national reactions. J. Edgar Hoover was quoted as calling for an all-out war against sex criminals. The Associated Press's science editor wrote a syndicated column on the views of leaders in the nation regarding methods of controlling sex crimes.

The third phase in the development of these sexual psychopath laws has been the appointment of a committee. The committee gathers the many conflicting recommendations of persons and groups of persons, attempts to determine "facts," studies procedures in other states, and makes recommendations, which generally include bills for the legislature. Although the general fear usually subsides within a few days, a committee has the formal duty of following through until positive action is taken. Terror which does not result in a committee is much less likely to result in a law. The appointment of a committee is a conventional method of dealing with any problem. Even during the recent agitations in California and Michigan, which have had sexual psychopath laws for ten years, committees have been appointed to study sex crimes and to make recommendations.

These committees deal with emergencies, and their investigations are relatively superficial. Even so, the community sometimes becomes impatient. Before a committee appointed by the Massachusetts legislature had had time for even a superficial investigation, the impatient legislature enacted a sexual psychopath law. The committee report several months later recommended that the statute which had just been enacted should be repealed on the ground that sex crimes should not be considered apart from the general correctional system of the state.[9] Similarly, the legislature of New Jersey enacted a sexual psychopath law in 1949 and also appointed a committee to investigate sex crimes and to suggest a policy. In New York City, on the other hand, the mayor took certain emergency actions in 1937 and did not appoint a committee until several months after the crisis. This committee made a very thorough study of all sex crimes in New York City in the decade 1930–39 and did not report for two or three years. The result was that New York State did not enact a sexual psychopath law; and, in fact, the committee was divided in its recommendation that such a law should be enacted.

In some states, at the committee stage of the development of a sexual psychopath law, psychiatrists have played an important part. The psychiatrists, more than any others, have been the interest group back of the laws. A com-

[9] Massachusetts, "Report of the Commission for Investigation of the Prevalence of Sex Crimes," *House Reports,* Nos. 1169 and 2169, 1948.

mittee of psychiatrists and neurologists in Chicago wrote the bill which became the sexual psychopath law of Illinois; the bill was sponsored by the Chicago Bar Association and by the state's attorney of Cook County and was enacted with little opposition in the next session of the state legislature.[10] In Minnesota all of the members of the governor's committee except one were psychiatrists. In Wisconsin the Milwaukee Neuropsychiatric Society shared in pressing the Milwaukee Crime Commission for the enactment of a law. In Indiana the attorney-general's committee received from the American Psychiatric Association copies of all of the sexual psychopath laws which had been enacted in other states.

Such actions by psychiatrists are consistent in some respects with their general views. Most psychiatrists assert that serious sex crimes are the result of mental pathology, although few of them would make such unqualified statements as that attributed to Dr. A. A. Brill at the time of the panic in New York City in 1937: "Sex crimes are committed only by people of defective mentality. All mental defectives have either actual or potential sex abnormalities."[11] Also, psychiatrists almost without exception favor the view that criminals should be treated as patients. Moreover, since the sexual psychopath laws usually specify that the diagnosis for the court shall be made by psychiatrists, they have an economic interest in the extension of this procedure.

While psychiatrists have often played an important part in the promotion of sexual psychopath laws, many prominent psychiatrists have been forthright in their opposition to them. They know that the sexual psychopath cannot be defined or identified. Probably most of the psychiatrists in the nation have been indifferent to legislation; they have exerted themselves neither to promote nor to oppose enactment.

The function of the committee is to organize information. The committee, dealing with emergency conditions, customarily takes the information which is available. Much of this has been distributed through popular literature, which contains the series of propositions outlined above. The latter are customarily accepted without firsthand investigation by the committee and are presented to the legislature and the public as "science." Although these propositions are all false or questionable, they have nevertheless been very effective in the diffusion of the laws. Bills are presented to the legislature with the

---

[10] W. S. Stewart, "Concerning Proposed Legislation for the Commitment of Sex Offenders," *John Marshall Law Quarterly*, III (March, 1938), 407–21; W. H. Haines, H. R. Hoffman, and H. A. Esser, "Commitments under the Criminal Sexual Psychopath Law in the Criminal Court of Cook County, Illinois," *American Journal of Psychiatry*, CV (November, 1948), 422.

[11] Quoted in *Time*, August 23, 1937, pp. 42–44. If the Kinsey Report is trustworthy, all males, whether defective or not, "have either actual or potential sex abnormalities."

explanation that these are the most enlightened and effective methods of dealing with the problem of sex crimes and that the states which have sexual psychopath laws have found them effective. Very little discussion occurs in the legislature. When the bill for the District of Columbia was presented in Congress, the only question asked was whether this bill, if enacted, would weaken or strengthen the sex laws; the questioner was satisfied with a categorical reply that the bill would strengthen them.[12]

The law is similarly presented to the public as the most enlightened and effective method of dealing with sex offenders. After the sexual psychopath bill had been drafted in Indiana, the *Indianapolis Star* had the following editorial:

Indiana today is one step nearer an enlightened approach to the growing menace of sex crimes. A proposed new law to institutionalize sexual psychopathics until pronounced permanently recovered has been drafted by a special state citizens' committee which helped the attorney general's office to study the problem. . . . Such a law should become a realistic, practical answer to the sex crime problem. This type of legislation has succeeded elsewhere and is long overdue in Indiana.[13]

The diffusion of sexual psychopath laws, consequently, has occurred under the following conditions: a state of fear developed, to some extent, by a general, nation-wide popular literature and made explicit by a few spectacular sex crimes; a series of scattered and conflicting reactions by many individuals and groups within the community; the appointment of a committee, which in some cases has been guided by psychiatrists, which organizes existing information regarding sex crimes and the precedents for their control and which presents a sexual psychopath law to the legislature and to the public as the most scientific and enlightened method of protecting society against dangerous sex criminals. The organization of information in the name of science and without critical appraisal seems to be more invariably related to the emergence of a sexual psychopath law than is any other part of this genetic process.

The most significant reason for the specific content of the proposals of these committees — treatment of the sex criminal as a patient — is that it is consistent with a general social movement.[14] For a century or more two rival policies have been used in criminal justice. One is the punitive policy; the other is the treatment policy. The treatment policy is evidenced by probation, parole, the indeterminate sentence, the juvenile court, the court clinic, and the facilities in correctional institutions for education, recreation, and

[12] *Congressional Record,* XCIV (April 26, 1948), 4886.
[13] December 8, 1948.
[14] See Herbert Blumer, "Social Movements," chap. xxiii in *New Outline of the Principles of Sociology,* edited by A. M. Lee (New York: Barnes & Noble, 1946).

religion. The treatment policy has been gaining, and the punitive policy has been losing, ground.

The trend toward treatment and away from punishment is based on cultural changes in the society. The trend away from punishment in criminal justice is consistent with the trend away from punishment in the home, the school, and the church. The trend toward treatment is consistent with a general trend toward scientific procedures in other fields, as illustrated by medicine, with its techniques of diagnosis and with treatment and prevention based on scientific knowledge of the causes of disease. The trend away from punishment toward treatment is not, however, based on a demonstration that treatment is more effective than punishment in protecting society against crime, for no such demonstration is available. Also, the fact that the trend in punishment is consistent with trends in other aspects of culture is not an adequate explanation of the trend in punishment. A general theory of social change must include more than a showing that one part of a culture changes consistently with other parts of a culture.

Not only has there been a trend toward individualization in treatment of offenders, but there has been a trend also toward psychiatric policies. Treatment tends to be organized on the assumption that the criminal is a socially sick person; deviant traits of personality, regarded as relatively permanent and generic, are regarded as the causes of crime. Since the time of Lombroso, at least, the logic of the typological schools of criminology has remained constant, while the specific trait used as the explanation of criminal behavior has changed from time to time. The first school held that criminals constitute a physical type, either epileptoid or degenerate in character; the second, that they are feeble-minded; the third, and current, school holds that criminals are emotionally unstable. All hold that crime can be caused only by a mental pathology of some type. The professionally trained persons other than lawyers who are employed in the field of criminal justice, whether as social workers, psychologists, psychiatrists, or sociologists, tend toward the belief that emotional traits are the explanation of crime. This conclusion likewise has not been demonstrated, and the body of evidence in conflict with the conclusion is increasing.

A specific aspect of this trend toward treatment of offenders as patients is the provision for psychotic and feeble-minded criminals. When such persons do the things prohibited by criminal law, they may be held to be irresponsible from the legal point of view and may still be ordered to confinement in institutions for the protection of society. All the states have some provision for psychotic criminals, and several have provisions for feeble-minded criminals. In some European nations the provisions for psychotic and feeble-minded criminals have been expanded and generalized under the name of "social security" laws: some have included sexual criminals under their social security measures, and the latter are the direct precedents for the sexual psychopath laws of the United States.

One of the questions in criminal law has been the criterion of responsibility. The courts have generally held that "knowledge of right and wrong" is the most satisfactory criterion. The psychiatrists have generally opposed this; they have argued that 90 per cent of the inmates of state hospitals for the insane can distinguish right from wrong but are, nevertheless, legally irresponsible. The important consideration, they argue, is that the psychotic person has impulses which he cannot control and that "irresistible impulse" should be substituted for "knowledge of right and wrong" as the criterion. The psychiatrists, however, have not been able to make their criterion clear cut for practical purposes.

The trend away from punishment and toward treatment of criminals as patients is to some extent a "paper" trend. Laws are enacted which provide for treatment rather than punishment; but the treatment goes on within a framework of punishment, and in many respects the punitive policies continue, despite changes in legislation. Probation, for instance, is upheld from the constitutional point of view as a suspension of punishment rather than as a method co-ordinate with punishment and is regarded by some persons as effective primarily because of the threat implied in it that punishment will follow violation of probation.

The sexual psychopath laws are consistent with this general social movement toward treatment of criminals as patients. Some laws define sexual psychopaths as "patients"; they provide for institutional care similar to that already provided for psychotic and feeble-minded criminals; they substitute the criterion of "irresistible impulse" for the criterion of "knowledge of right and wrong"; and they reflect the belief that sex criminals are psychopathic. The consistency with a general social movement provides a part of the explanation of the diffusion of sexual psychopath laws.

In the United States the connection between the enactment of sexual psychopath laws and the development of treatment policies is, at best, vague and loose. This is obvious from a consideration of the distribution of the laws. Three New England states, one Middle Atlantic state, and two Pacific Coast states have passed such laws; but the remainder — half of all the states with sexual psychopath laws — are in the North Central region. These laws, in fact, have been enacted in a solid block of North Central states: Ohio, Indiana, Illinois, Michigan, Wisconsin, and Minnesota. On the other hand, no state in the southern, South Central, or Mountain regions has a sexual psychopath law. These regions also are less committed to treatment policies than are the regions which have sexual psychopath laws. While this association may be found when large regions are compared, it is not found when specific states are compared; New York State, for instance, has had an extensive development of treatment policies but no sexual psychopath law. Similarly, the states which have sexual psychopath laws are not differentiated clearly from states which do not have such laws by any statistical variable which has been discovered: they are not differentiated by the rate of rape, by the racial composition of the population, by the proportion of immigrants in the population, by the sex ratio in the population, or by the extent of industrialization or urbanization.

The Marihuana
Tax Act

It is generally assumed that the practice of smoking marihuana was imported into the United States from Mexico, by way of the southwestern states of Arizona, New Mexico, and Texas, all of which had sizable Spanish-speaking populations. People first began to notice marihuana use in the nineteen-twenties but, since it was a new phenomenon and one apparently confined to Mexican immigrants, did not express much concern about it. (The medical compound prepared from the marihuana plant had been known for some time, but was not often prescribed by U.S. physicians.) As late as 1930, only sixteen states had passed laws prohibiting the use of marihuana.

In 1937, however, the United States Congress passed the Marihuana Tax Act, designed to stamp out use of the drug. According to the theory outlined above, we should find in the history of this Act the story of an entrepreneur whose initiative and enterprise overcame public apathy and indifference and culminated in the passage of Federal legislation. Before turning to the history of the Act itself, we should perhaps look at the way similar substances had been treated in American law, in order to understand the context in which the attempt to suppress marihuana use proceeded.

The use of alcohol and opium in the United States had a long history, punctuated by attempts at suppression.[1] Three values provided legitimacy for attempts to prevent the use of intoxicants and narcotics. One legitimizing value, a component of what has been called the Protestant Ethic, holds that the individual should exercise complete responsibility for what he does and what happens to him; he should never do anything that might cause loss of self-control. Alcohol and the opiate drugs, in varying degrees and ways, cause people to lose control of themselves; their use, therefore, is evil. A person intoxicated with alcohol often loses control over his physical activity; the centers of judgment in the brain are also affected. Users of opiates are more likely to be anesthetized and thus less likely to commit rash acts. But

Reprinted with permission of the author and The Macmillan Company from *Outsiders* by Howard S. Becker. Copyright by The Free Press of Glencoe, a Division of The Macmillan Company, 1963.

[1] See John Krout, *The Origins of Prohibition* (New York: Columbia University Press, 1928); Charles Terry and Mildred Pellens, *The Opium Problem* (New York: The Committee on Drug Addiction with the Bureau of Social Hygiene, Inc., 1928); and *Drug Addiction: Crime or Disease?* Interim and Final Reports of the Joint Committee of the American Bar Association and the American Medical Association on Narcotic Drugs (Bloomington, Indiana: Indiana University Press, 1961).

they become dependent on the drug to prevent withdrawal symptoms and in this sense have lost control of their actions; insofar as it is difficult to obtain the drug, they must subordinate other interests to its pursuit.

Another American value legitimized attempts to suppress the use of alcohol and opiates: disapproval of action taken solely to achieve states of ecstasy. Perhaps because of our strong cultural emphases on pragmatism and utilitarianism, Americans usually feel uneasy and ambivalent about ecstatic experiences of any kind. But we do not condemn ecstatic experience when it is the by-product or reward of actions we consider proper in their own right, such as hard work or religious fervor. It is only when people pursue ecstasy for its own sake that we condemn their action as a search for "illicit pleasure," an expression that has real meaning to us.

The third value which provided a basis for attempts at suppression was humanitarianism. Reformers believed that people enslaved by the use of alcohol and opium would benefit from laws making it impossible for them to give in to their weaknesses. The families of drunkards and drug addicts would likewise benefit.

These values provided the basis for specific rules. The Eighteenth Amendment and the Volstead Act forbade the importation of alcoholic beverages into the United States and their manufacture within the country. The Harrison Act in effect prohibited the use of opiate drugs for all but medical purposes.

In formulating these laws, care was taken not to interfere with what were regarded as the legitimate interests of other groups in the society. The Harrison Act, for instance, was so drawn as to allow medical personnel to continue using morphine and other opium derivatives for the relief of pain and such other medical purposes as seemed to them appropriate. Furthermore, the law was carefully drawn in order to avoid running afoul of the constitutional provision reserving police powers to the several states. In line with this restriction, the Act was presented as a revenue measure, taxing unlicensed purveyors of opiate drugs at an exorbitant rate while permitting licensed purveyors (primarily physicians, dentists, veterinarians, and pharmacists) to pay a nominal tax. Though it was justified constitutionally as a revenue measure, the Harrison Act was in fact a police measure and was so interpreted by those to whom its enforcement was entrusted. One consequence of the passage of the Act was the establishment, in the Treasury Department, of the Federal Bureau of Narcotics in 1930.

The same values that led to the banning of the use of alcohol and opiates could, of course, be applied to the case of marihuana and it seems logical that this should have been done. Yet what little I have been told, by people familiar with the period, about the use of marihuana in the late 'twenties and early 'thirties leads me to believe that there was relatively lax enforcement of the existing local laws. This, after all, was the era of Prohibition and the police had more pressing matters to attend to. Neither the public nor law enforcement officers, apparently, considered the use of marihuana a serious problem. When they noticed it at all, they probably dismissed it as not warranting major attempts at enforcement. One index of how feebly the laws were enforced is that the price of marihuana is said to have been very much lower prior to the passage of Federal legislation. This indicates that there was little danger in selling it and that enforcement was not seriously undertaken.

Even the Treasury Department, in its report on the year 1931, minimized the importance of the problem:

A great deal of public interest has been aroused by newspaper articles appearing from time to time on the evils of the abuse of marihuana, or Indian hemp, and more attention has been focused on specific cases reported of the abuse of the drug than would otherwise have been the case. This publicity tends to magnify the extent of the evil and lends color to an inference that there is an alarming spread of the improper use of the drug, whereas the actual increase in such use may not have been inordinately large.[2]

The Treasury Department's Bureau of Narcotics furnished most of the enterprise that produced the Marihuana Tax Act. While it is, of course, difficult to know what the motives of Bureau officials were, we need assume no more than that they perceived an area of wrongdoing that properly belonged in their jurisdiction and moved to put it there. The personal interest they satisfied in pressing for marihuana legislation was one common to many officials: the interest in successfully accomplishing the task one has been assigned and in acquiring the best tools with which to accomplish it. The Bureau's efforts took two forms: cooperating in the development of state legislation affecting the use of marihuana, and providing facts and figures for journalistic accounts of the problem. These are two important modes of action available to all entrepreneurs seeking the adoption of rules: they can enlist the support of other interested organizations and develop, through the use of the press and other communications media, a favorable public attitude toward the proposed rule. If the efforts are successful, the public becomes aware of a definite problem and the appropriate organizations act in concert to produce the desired rule.

The Federal Bureau of Narcotics cooperated actively with the National Conference of Commissioners on Uniform State Laws in developing uniform laws on narcotics, stressing among other matters the need to control mari-

---

[2] U.S. Treasury Department, *Traffic in Opium and Other Dangerous Drugs for the Year ended December 31, 1931* (Washington: Government Printing Office, 1932), p. 51.

huana use.[3] In 1932, the Conference approved a draft law. The Bureau commented:

The present constitutional limitations would seem to require control measures directed against the intrastate traffic in Indian hemp to be adopted by the several State governments rather than by the Federal Government, and the policy has been to urge the State authorities generally to provide the necessary legislation, with supporting enforcement activity, to prohibit the traffic except for bona fide medical purposes. The proposed uniform State narcotic law . . . with optional text applying to the restriction of traffic in Indian hemp, has been recommended as an adequate law to accomplish the desired purposes.[4]

In its report for the year 1936, the Bureau urged its partners in this cooperative effort to exert themselves more strongly and hinted that Federal intervention might perhaps be necessary:

In the absence of additional Federal legislation the Bureau of Narcotics can therefore carry on no war of its own against this traffic . . . the drug has come into wide and increasing abuse in many states, and the Bureau of Narcotics has therefore been endeavoring to impress upon the various States the urgent need for vigorous enforcement of local cannabis [marihuana] laws.[5]

The second prong of the Bureau's attack on the marihuana problem consisted of an effort to arouse the public to the danger confronting it by means of "an educational campaign describing the drug, its identification, and evil effects."[6] Apparently hoping that public interest might spur the States and cities to greater efforts, the Bureau said:

In the absence of Federal legislation on the subject, the States and cities should rightfully assume the responsibility of providing vigorous measures for the extinction of this lethal weed, and it is therefore hoped that all public-spirited citizens will earnestly enlist in the movement urged by the Treasury Department to adjure intensified enforcement of marihuana laws.[7]

The Bureau did not confine itself to exhortation in departmental reports. Its methods in pursuing desired legislation are described in a passage dealing with the campaign for a uniform state narcotic law:

[3] *Ibid.,* pp. 16–17.
[4] Bureau of Narcotics, U.S. Treasury Department, *Traffic in Opium and Other Dangerous Drugs for the Year ended December 31, 1932* (Washington: Government Printing Office, 1933), p. 13.
[5] Bureau of Narcotics, U.S. Treasury Department, *Traffic in Opium and Other Dangerous Drugs for the Year ended December 31, 1936* (Washington: Government Printing Office, 1937), p. 59.
[6] *Ibid.*
[7] Bureau of Narcotics, U.S. Treasury Department, *Traffic in Opium and Other Dangerous Drugs for the Year ended December 31, 1935* (Washington: Government Printing Office, 1936), p. 30.

Articles on Marihuana Indexed in The Reader's Guide to Periodical
Literature

Time period	Number of articles
January, 1925-December, 1928	0
January, 1929-June, 1932	0
July, 1932-June, 1935	0
July, 1935-June, 1937	4
July, 1937-June, 1939	17
July, 1939-June, 1941	4
July, 1941-June, 1943	1
July, 1943-April, 1945	4
May, 1945-April, 1947	6
May, 1947-April, 1949	0
May, 1949-March, 1951	1

Articles were prepared in the Federal Bureau of Narcotics, at the request of a number of organizations dealing with this general subject [uniform state laws] for publication by such organizations in magazines and newspapers. An intelligent and sympathetic public interest, helpful to the administration of the narcotic laws, has been aroused and maintained.[8]

As the campaign for Federal legislation against marihuana drew to a successful close, the Bureau's efforts to communicate its sense of the urgency of the problem to the public bore plentiful fruit. The number of articles about marihuana which appeared in popular magazines indicated by the number indexed in the *Reader's Guide,* reached a record high. Seventeen articles appeared in a two-year period, many more than in any similar period before or after.

Of the seventeen, ten either explicitly acknowledged the help of the Bureau in furnishing facts and figures or gave implicit evidence of having received help by using facts and figures that had appeared earlier, either in Bureau publications or in testimony before the Congress on the Marihuana Tax Act. (We will consider the Congressional hearings on the bill in a moment.)

One clear indication of Bureau influence in the preparation of journalistic articles can be found in the recurrence of certain atrocity stories first reported by the Bureau. For instance, in an article published in the *American Magazine,* the Commissioner of Narcotics himself related the following incident:

· An entire family was murdered by a youthful [marihuana] addict in Florida. When officers arrived at the home they found the youth staggering about in a

[8] Bureau of Narcotics, U.S. Treasury Department, *Traffic in Opium and Other Dangerous Drugs for the Year ended December 31, 1933* (Washington: Government Printing Office, 1934), p. 61.

human slaughterhouse. With an ax he had killed his father, mother, two brothers, and a sister. He seemed to be in a daze. . . . He had no recollection of having committed the multiple crime. The officers knew him ordinarily as a sane, rather quiet young man; now he was pitifully crazed. They sought the reason. The boy said he had been in the habit of smoking something which youthful friends called "muggles," a childish name for marihuana.[9]

Five of the seventeen articles printed during the period repeated this story, and thus showed the influence of the Bureau.

The articles designed to arouse the public to the dangers of marihuana identified use of the drug as a violation of the value of self-control and the prohibition on search for "illicit pleasure," thus legitimizing the drive against marihuana in the eyes of the public. These, of course, were the same values that had been appealed to in the course of the quest for legislation prohibiting use of alcohol and opiates for illicit purposes.

The Federal Bureau of Narcotics, then, provided most of the enterprise which produced public awareness of the problem and coordinated action by other enforcement organizations. Armed with the results of their enterprise, representatives of the Treasury Department went to Congress with a draft of the Marihuana Tax Act and requested its passage. The hearings of the House Committee on Ways and Means, which considered the bill for five days during April and May of 1937, furnish a clear case of the operation of enterprise and of the way it must accommodate other interests.

The Assistant General Counsel of the Treasury Department introduced the bill to the Congressmen with these words: "The leading newspapers of the United States have recognized the seriousness of this problem and many of them have advocated Federal legislation to control the traffic in marihuana."[10] After explaining the constitutional basis of the bill — like the Harrison Act, it was framed as a revenue measure — he reassured them about its possible effects on legitimate businesses:

The form of the bill is such, however, as not to interfere materially with any industrial, medical, or scientific uses which the plant may have. Since hemp fiber and articles manufactured therefrom [twine and light cordage] are obtained from the harmless mature stalk of the plant, all such products have been completely eliminated from the purview of the bill by defining the term "marihuana" in the bill so as to exclude from its provisions the mature stalk and its compounds or manufacturers. There are also some dealings in marihuana seeds for planting purposes and for use in the manufacture of oil which is ultimately employed by the

[9] H. J. Anslinger, with Courtney Ryley Cooper, "Marihuana: Assassin of Youth," *American Magazine,* CXXIV (July, 1937), 19, 150.
[10] *Taxation of Marihuana* (Hearings before the Committee on Ways and Means of the House of Representatives, 75th Congress, 1st Session, on H.R. 6385, April 27–30 and May 4, 1937), p. 7.

paint and varnish industry. As the seeds, unlike the mature stalk, contain the drug, the same complete exemption could not be applied in this instance.[11]

He further assured them that the medical profession rarely used the drug, so that its prohibition would work no hardship on them or on the pharmaceutical industry.

The committee members were ready to do what was necessary and, in fact, queried the Commissioner of Narcotics as to why this legislation had been proposed only now. He explained:

Ten years ago we only heard about it throughout the Southwest. It is only in the last few years that it has become a national menace. . . . We have been urging uniform State legislation on the several States, and it was only last month that the last State legislature adopted such legislation.[12]

The commissioner reported that many crimes were committed under the influence of marihuana, and gave examples, including the story of the Florida mass-murderer. He pointed out that the present low prices of the drug made it doubly dangerous, because it was available to anyone who had a dime to spare.

Manufacturers of hempseed oil voiced certain objections to the language of the bill, which was quickly changed to meet their specifications. But a more serious objection came from the birdseed industry, which at that time used some four million pounds of hempseed a year. Its representative apologized to the Congressmen for appearing at the last minute, stating that he and his colleagues had not realized until just then that the marihuana plant referred to in the bill was the same plant from which they got an important ingredient of their product. Government witnesses had insisted that the seeds of the plant required prohibition, as well as the flowering tops smokers usually used, because they contained a small amount of the active principle of the drug and might possibly be used for smoking. The birdseed manufacturers contended that inclusion of seed under the provisions of the bill would damage their business.

To justify his request for exemption, the manufacturers' representative pointed to the beneficial effect of hempseed on pigeons:

[It] is a necessary ingredient in pigeon feed because it contains an oil substance that is a valuable ingredient of pigeon feed, and we have not been able to find any seed that will take its place. If you substitute anything for the hemp, it has a tendency to change the character of the squabs produced.[13]

Congressman Robert L. Doughton of North Carolina inquired: "Does that

---

[11] *Ibid.*, p. 8.
[12] *Ibid.*, p. 20.
[13] *Ibid.*, pp. 73–74.

seed have the same effect on pigeons as the drug has on human beings?" The manufacturers' representative said: "I have never noticed it. It has a tendency to bring back the feathers and improve the birds."[14]

Faced with serious opposition, the Government modified its stern insistence on the seed provision, noting that sterilization of the seeds might render them harmless: "It seems to us that the burden of proof is on the Government there, when we might injure a legitimate industry."[15]

Once these difficulties had been ironed out, the bill had easy sailing. Marihuana smokers, powerless, unorganized, and lacking publicly legitimate grounds for attack, sent no representatives to the hearings and their point of view found no place in the record. Unopposed, the bill passed both the House and Senate the following July. The enterprise of the Bureau had produced a new rule, whose subsequent enforcement would help create a new class of outsiders — marihuana users.

I have given an extended illustration from the field of Federal legislation. But the basic parameters of this case should be equally applicable not only to legislation in general, but to the development of rules of a more informal kind. Wherever rules are created and applied, we should be alive to the possible presence of an enterprising individual or group. Their activities can properly be called *moral enterprise,* for what they are enterprising about is the creation of a new fragment of the moral constitution of society, its code of right and wrong.

Wherever rules are created and applied we should expect to find people attempting to enlist the support of coordinate groups and using the available media of communication to develop a favorable climate of opinion. Where they do not develop such support, we may expect to find their enterprise unsuccessful.[16]

And, wherever rules are created and applied, we expect that the processes of enforcement will be shaped by the complexity of the organization, resting on a basis of shared understandings in simpler groups and resulting from political maneuvering and bargaining in complex structures.

[14] *Ibid.*

[15] *Ibid.*, p. 85.

[16] Gouldner has described a relevant case in industry, where a new manager's attempt to enforce rules that had not been enforced for a long time (and thus, in effect, create new rules) had as its immediate consequence a disruptive wildcat strike; he had not built support through the manipulation of other groups in the factory and the development of a favorable climate of opinion. See Alvin W. Gouldner, *Wildcat Strike* (Yellow Springs, Ohio: Antioch Press, 1954).

2

LAW ENFORCEMENT

Police Discretion

WAYNE R. LA FAVE

Because the exercise of discretion involves decision-making not strictly governed by legal rules, but rather with a significant element of personal judgment,[1] it is sometimes said to be totally improper in criminal law enforcement, where the consequences of official action directly affect a citizen's freedom and property.[2]

No one would assert that law enforcement agencies have a right to exercise discretion beyond the outer boundaries of the law defining criminal conduct, such as by arresting for conduct which the legislature has not declared to be a crime. The issue is rather whether discretion within these boundaries, exemplified by the common police decision not to arrest in some situations where criminal conduct has occurred, is proper. Some assert that the two situations are essentially the same and that both involve an abuse of power: "[T]he rule of law [means] . . . that the citizen should be free from arbitrary power. A discretion to withhold a punishment may result in just as much arbitrary power as discretion to use extra-legal punishment."[3]

Whatever their status in principle, it is clear that the two situations are dealt with differently in current practice. It is not common to arrest a person

Reprinted from *Arrest: The Decision to Take a Suspect into Custody,* by Wayne R. LaFave, pp. 63–84 (Boston: 1964), by permission of the author and Little, Brown and Company. Some footnotes have been abridged.

[1] Roscoe Pound defines discretion as "an authority conferred by law to act in certain conditions or situations in accordance with an official's or an official agency's own considered judgment and conscience. It is an idea of morals, belonging to the twilight zone between law and morals." Pound, "Discretion, Dispensation and Mitigation: The Problem of the Individual Special Case," 35 *N.Y.U.L. Rev.* 925, 926 (1960). Judge Breitel defines it as "the power to consider all circumstances and then determine whether any legal action is to be taken. And if so taken, of what kind and degree, and to what conclusion." Breitel, "Controls in Criminal Law Enforcement," 27 *U. Chi. L. Rev.* 427 (1960). A typical dictionary definition of discretion is the "ability to make decisions which represent a responsible choice and for which an understanding of what is lawful, right, or wise may be presupposed." Webster, *Third New International Dictionary* 647 (1961). . . .

[2] "Nobody disputes the fact that, in order to make efficient use of the means at its disposal, the government must exercise a great deal of discretion. But, to repeat, under the rule of law the private citizen and his property are not an object of administration by the government, not a means to be used for its purposes. It is only when the administration interferes with the private sphere of the citizen that the problem of discretion becomes relevant to us; and the principle of the rule of law, in effect, means that the administrative authorities should have no discretionary powers in this respect." Hayek, *The Constitution of Liberty* 213 (1960). See also Hayek, *The Road to Serfdom* 72 (1944).

[3] Hargrove, "Police Discretion," 25 *Sol.* 337 (1958), stating the views of Dicey.

unless he is at least suspected of having engaged in criminal conduct. It is common for some persons not to be arrested even though it can easily be proved that they have engaged in criminal conduct.[4]

CURRENT ATTITUDES TOWARD POLICE DISCRETION

There has been a traditional failure to recognize the existence and importance of police discretion. This results, at least to some degree, from attitudes about (1) the mandate of the substantive criminal law; (2) the proper allocation of power between the legislative, judicial, and administrative agencies in American government; (3) the requirements of the rule of law or principle of legality; (4) the extent to which there is an actual necessity for discretion in the existing system; and (5) the extent to which any needed discretion can be exercised by the prosecutor.

1. *The mandate of the substantive law.* The substantive criminal law, insofar as it is addressed to the public, consists of a series of "thou shalt not's." Less clear is the extent to which it must be read as a mandate to law enforcement agencies to proceed against all conduct which is defined as criminal. While some view the substantive law as such a mandate,[5] other observers of the process have characterized it in different terms. Thurman Arnold has said that the criminal law should be looked upon by the law enforcers "not as something to be enforced because it governs society, but as an arsenal of weapons with which to incarcerate certain dangerous individuals who are bothering society."[6] Others have stated the duty of the law enforcement agency to be enforcement only when "in the public interest . . . , [considering] the effect . . . upon public morale and order and all other considerations affecting public policy";[7] enforcement "in such manner that the greatest degree of social protection will be secured";[8] enforcement only when it will

---

[4] A considerable part of the formal law is devoted to protecting innocent persons from arrest, charging, or conviction. . . . Another substantial segment of the law concerns improper police methods.

[5] Goldstein, "Police Discretion Not to Invoke the Criminal Process: Low-Visibility Decisions in the Administration of Justice," 69 *Yale L.J.* 543, 557 (1960). The Goldstein article is a thoughtful and detailed presentation of the view that discretion in the police agency not to invoke the process is highly undesirable.

[6] Arnold, *The Symbols of Government* 153 (1935). He says: "[T]he problem of the police and prosecutor is the suppression of the occasional dangerous individual. For this purpose the ideal that all laws should be enforced without a discretionary selection is impossible to carry out. It is like directing a general to attack the enemy on all fronts at once." *Ibid.*

[7] Devlin, *The Criminal Prosecution in England* 23–24 (1958).

[8] Smith, *Police Systems in the United States* 21 (1940). Smith goes on to say that by following this objective: "The degree of enforcement and the method of application will vary with each neighborhood and community. There are no set rules, nor even general guides to policy, in this regard."

secure "the real purpose of a police service, the prevention of crime";[9] or enforcement which will "winnow and sift from the offenders those who are the most guilty."[10] These attitudes reflect a view of the substantive criminal law as something less than a mandate for enforcement in all cases.[11]

2. *The proper allocation of power between legislature, court, and administrative agency.* It has been common in the criminal law field, particularly in recent decades, to assume that the legislature should play an almost exclusive role in deciding what conduct is criminal. The proper system is often said to be one in which the legislature makes the policy decisions reflected in the enactment of criminal statutes, the court is limited to the resolution of ambiguities in these statutes, and the administrative agency merely executes the policy which has been legislatively prescribed. This position is consistent with the often stated rule that the legislature cannot constitutionally delegate the power to define criminal conduct.[12]

In other fields of law, particularly the field of governmental regulation of economic behavior, it is commonly recognized that administrative agencies do have major responsibility for important policy decisions.[13] In part this results from the fact that legislators sometimes avoid policy determinations, particularly those likely to have political repercussions greater than their importance

---

Each policeman must, in a sense, determine the standard which is to be set in the area for which he is responsible." *Ibid.*

[9] Dunning, "Discretion in Prosecution," 1 *Police J.* 39, 47 (1928).

[10] Crownhart, "Address to the Meeting of the District Attorneys' Convention," 16 Ops. Wis. Atty. Gen. xlix (1927). Justice Crownhart was of the view that there should be strict enforcement as to offenses mala in se, but that considerable discretion might be exercised with regard to those mala prohibita.

[11] But whether a court will consider the law on the books or the law as actually enforced as the true criminal law will depend upon the context within which this question arises. If a defendant attempts a defense based upon lack of enforcement of a particular provision of the criminal law, then the answer is: "The failure of the executive branch to enforce a law does not result in its modification or repeal. . . . The repeal of laws is as much a legislative function as their enactment." *District of Columbia v. John R. Thompson Co.,* 346 U.S. 100, 113–114, 73 Sup. Ct. 1007, 1014, 97 L. Ed. 1480, 1492 (1953). . . .

[12] 1 Davis, *Administrative Law* § 2.13 (1958); Dession, *Criminal Law, Administration and Public Order* 24 (1948); Schwenk, "The Administrative Crime, Its Creation and Punishment by Administrative Agencies," 42 *Mich. L. Rev.* 51 (1943). Compare: "The law placed before an administrative official represents merely a statement of policy. Even if couched in mandatory language, it is still subject to administrative interpretation." Roucek, *Social Control* 87–88 (1947).

[13] "The executive and judicial branches of the government are and must be coordinate branches not only for carrying out policies determined by the legislative branch but also for determining basic policy." 1 Davis, *supra,* § 2.05 (1958). The current legislative practice of sharing policy-making responsibilities with the executive and administrative agencies is a product of historic development. See Hurst, *The Growth of American Law: The Law Makers,* chaps. 2 and 3 (1950).

warrants.[14] In part it also results from the obvious fact that there are limitations upon a legislature's ability to decide in advance all of the important policy issues which may arise. Roscoe Pound has observed:

No lawmaker has been able to foresee more than the broad outlines of the clash of interests or more than the main lines of the courses of conduct to which the law even of his own time must be applied. Moreover, a legal system which seeks to cover everything by a special provision becomes cumbrous and unworkable.[15]

These factors are also applicable to the field of criminal law administration, and, therefore, the explanation for the different attitude toward criminal justice agencies and other governmental agencies must be found elsewhere.

Perhaps there is an assumption that the other agencies are more competent to make important policy decisions than is the average police department. Perhaps the assumption is that discretion in the hands of a regulatory agency is proper when the sanction is noncriminal but improper when the sanction is criminal prosecution. The difficulty with this latter explanation is that economic regulatory agencies have been expressly delegated discretion to define as criminal any conduct falling within limits set in advance by the legislature,[16] provided that no conduct is subjected to a criminal penalty unless it has been defined as criminal by a precise, pre-existing, and published administrative regulation.[17] Similarly, where the legislature has itself defined the conduct which is criminal, there have been delegations to these agencies of power to declare exemptions to general statutory prohibitions or power to suspend the operation of a statute or regulation for a time, if a sufficiently definite legislative standard is provided.[18]

There has been no express legislative delegation of discretion to the police, although it is arguable that such a delegation would be constitutional because police are in a position comparable to other administrative agencies. Such a delegation might even be implied, particularly where the substantive criminal law is ambiguous. However, police have not claimed to have this kind of discretion; rather, they exercise a wide range of discretion without attempting to give explicit justification for the practice. As a consequence, police cur-

---

[14] Gross, *The Legislative Struggle* 106 (1953). For other references to studies of the limitations of the legislative process as a policy-making device, see Remington and Rosenblum, "The Criminal Law and the Legislative Process," 1960 *U. Ill. L.F.* 481, 481–482 n.2. . . .

[15] Pound, *Criminal Justice in America* 40–41 (1930).

[16] The Supreme Court, in *United States v. Grimaud,* 220 U.S. 506, 522, 31 Sup. Ct. 480, 485, 55 L. Ed. 563, 570 (1911), upheld an express delegation of power to define criminal conduct because "A violation of . . . [the administrative provision] is made a crime, not by the Secretary, but by Congress. The statute, not the Secretary, fixes the penalty." . . .

[17] See Gellhorn and Byse, *Cases on Administrative Law* 142 (4th ed. 1960).

[18] See cases cited *id.* at 119–124, and Note, 87 *U. Pa. L. Rev.* 201 (1938). . . .

rently function differently from other administrative agencies. While even broadly defined criminal statutes are more precise in setting outer limits of discretion than are many statutes delegating authority to regulatory agencies, enforcement policies of these agencies are often explicit, whereas enforcement by the police is seldom preceded by an announcement indicating specifically what conduct the police intend to subject to enforcement. Also the common police practice of suspending the effective operation of certain penal statutes or of creating exemptions to them occurs without any standards having been prescribed in advance by the legislature.

3. *The rule of law or principle of legality.* Undoubtedly the exercise of discretion in the administration of the criminal law raises more difficult issues than the exercise of discretion in other areas because of the American commitment to the "rule of law"[19] or "principle of legality."[20]

These concepts are said to be inconsistent with the exercise of discretion in deciding not to arrest the person who has committed a crime.[21] Jerome Hall has stated this position:

. . . there is an inevitable incompatibility between the principle of legality and complete exculpation even in marginal cases where very good motivation combines with a minimum of the proscribed harm. . . . If we agree that it is preferable to have a legal system with the attendant guarantees against official abuse, then we are bound to accept the limitations of any such system and recognize that mitigation, not exculpation, is the relevant recourse in meritorious cases.[22]

On the other hand, adherence to the principle of legality may require only that criminal sanctions not be imposed without fair notice that the conduct is susceptible to the sanction. Thus the boundaries of the criminal law must be drawn in advance of their application and with sufficient precision to allow compliance.[23] The exercise of discretion not to enforce the law would not depart from the principle of legality because there need be no advance notice of the boundaries of exculpation.[24]

[19] The term "rule of law" is rather nebulous, and may be used to mean (1) law and order, (2) fixed rules, (3) elimination of discretion, (4) due process or fairness, (5) natural law, (6) preference for judges, or (7) judicial review. See 1 Davis, *Administrative Law* § 1.08 (1958).

[20] "The essence of this principle of legality is limitation on penalization by the State's officials, effected by the prescription and application of specific rules. That is the actual meaning of the principle of legality so far as the criminal law is concerned." Hall, *General Principles of Criminal Law* 28 (2d ed. 1960).

[21] See quotation from Hayek, *supra* note 2; and from Hargrove, *supra* note 3.

[22] Hall, *General Principles of Criminal Law* 55 (2d ed. 1960).

[23] "In order that there be no doubt regarding the meaning of the principle, it has two important corollaries: penal statutes must be strictly construed, and they must not be given retroactive effect." *Ibid.* at 28.

[24] Thus, in a criminal case, the defendant's complaint that other persons

There are obviously middle positions between the refusal to recognize any right to exercise of discretion and the recognition as proper of any discretion within the outer limits of conduct defined as criminal by the legislature. "Fair notice" may require advance notice not only of what conduct might be treated as criminal but also of what conduct is treated as criminal according to existing enforcement policy. It is certainly arguable that exculpation must be based upon differential factors which might properly have been considered by the legislature in drawing the line between criminal and noncriminal conduct.[25] Thus race or religion would clearly be an improper basis upon which to rest the decision not to enforce.

Whatever the proper position is, the concern and uncertainty about the "rule of law" or "principle of legality" has tended to prevent explicit recognition of police discretion and has, to that extent, contributed to the lack of an adequate understanding of the function of police discretion in current criminal justice administration.

4. *The need for discretion.* It is obvious that in practice some discretion must be employed somewhere in the existing criminal justice system. The exercise of discretion in interpreting the legislative mandate[26] is necessary because no legislature has succeeded in formulating a substantive criminal code which clearly encompasses all conduct intended to be made criminal and which clearly excludes all other conduct. Poor draftsmanship and a failure to revise the criminal law to eliminate obsolete provisions[27] have contributed to existing ambiguities.[28] However, even where care has been taken, it has not been possible to draft substantive provisions which are entirely free from ambiguity. This is a result not only of limitations upon the effectiveness of language but also of the inability of a legislature to envisage all of the day-to-day law enforcement problems[29] which may arise.

have not been proceeded against will usually be dismissed, e.g., *People v. Flanders,* 140 Cal. App. 2d 765, 296 P.2d 13 (Dist. Ct. App. 1956).

[25] Such was the view taken in one case in which the defendant in a criminal prosecution raised equal protection arguments because other violators were not proceeded against. *Taylor v. City of Pine Bluff,* 226 Ark. 309, 289 S.W.2d 679 (1956).

[26] Sometimes it is assumed that such exercise of discretion can be adequately controlled. "In acting under the rule of law the administrative agencies will often have to exercise discretion as the judge exercises discretion in interpreting the law. This, however, is a discretionary power which can and must be controlled by the possibility of a review of the substance of the decision by an independent court." Hayek, *The Constitution of Liberty* 213 (1960). However, currently decisions not to invoke the process based upon interpretation of statutes are not likely to be reviewed by a court.

[27] Wechsler, "The Challenge of a Model Penal Code," 65 *Harv. L. Rev.* 1097, 1101 (1952); Remington and Rosenblum, "The Criminal Law and the Legislative Process," 1960 *U. Ill. L.F.* 481, 483–487.

[28] Wechsler, *supra,* at 1113.

[29] See quotation from Pound, *supra* note 15.

Even more important is the fact that not enough financial resources are allocated to make possible enforcement of all the laws against all offenders.[30] The legislative body responsible for granting appropriations makes a general decision as to how much it is willing to pay for law enforcement, but usually provides no guidance as to how this sum is to be expended.[31] Allocation of resources to enforcement agencies is ordinarily decided by a municipal legislative body, while the criminal law is defined by the state legislature, which often leaves the administrator subject to conflicting legislative mandates. The same conflict occurs when the state legislature appropriates money to a state police unit, since the crime-defining and budget decisions are essentially unrelated even within the same unit of government. Because of the obvious dilemma created by limited resources and lack of established priorities for enforcement, the necessity of discretionary enforcement on this basis has received some recognition.[32] Yet there are no suggested principles to guide the exercise of such discretion.[33]

Finally, the exercise of discretion seems necessary in the current criminal justice system for reasons unrelated to either the interpretation of criminal statutes or the allocation of available enforcement resources. This is because of the special circumstances of the individual case, particularly the characteristics of the individual offender which "differentiate him from other offenders in personality, character, sociocultural background, the motivations of his crime, and his particular potentialities for reform or recidivism."[34] The in-

---

[30] Although this lack of resources is generally recognized, there is no agreement on what would be a proper level of enforcement. See Goldstein, "Police Discretion Not to Invoke the Criminal Process: Low-Visibility Decisions in the Administration of Justice," 69 *Yale L.J.* 543, 561 nn.31, 32 (1960).

[31] It has been suggested that the maximum sentence authorized for the various offenses might be some guide to enforcement priorities. *Id.* at 568. It might also be said that, to the extent that local legislative bodies actually prescribe in detail the structure of the law enforcement agencies (e.g., setting by ordinance the size of the police department vice bureau or narcotics squad), some guidance is being given. . . .

[32] See Pound, *Criminal Justice in America* 19–20, 62–63 (1930); Wilson, *supra*, at 20; Breitel, "Controls in Criminal Law Enforcement," 27 *U. Chi. L. Rev.* 427, 431 (1960); Hall, "Police and Law in a Democratic Society," 28 *Ind. L.J.* 135, 149–150 (1953). Even those generally opposed to recognition of discretion in the hands of law enforcers are apt to make an exception here, e.g., Hayek, *The Constitution of Liberty* 213 (1960); Goldstein, "Police Discretion Not to Invoke the Criminal Process: Low-Visibility Decisions in the Administration of Justice," 69 *Yale L.J.* 543, 560–561 (1960).

[33] Police materials are usually devoted to *how* to make an arrest and *when* to arrest in terms of probability of guilt, with the allocation of resources problem completely ignored. An exception is California State Department of Education, California Police Officers' Training Bulletin No. 71, *Police Supervisory Control* 26–27 (1957): "Finally, note must be made of one insurmountable obstacle to supervisory control which confronts every chief of police: the fact that it is absolutely impossible to enforce all laws. . . .

[34] Glueck, "Predictive Devices and the Individualization of Justice," 23 *Law & Contemp. Prob.* 461 (1958).

finite variety of individual circumstances complicates administration by mere application of rules.[35] Justice Charles D. Breitel, who has had extensive administrative, legislative, and judicial experience, stresses this point:

> If every policeman, every prosecutor, every court, and every post-sentence agency performed his or its responsibility in strict accordance with rules of law, precisely and narrowly laid down, the criminal law would be ordered but intolerable.[36]

Individualized treatment of an offender, based upon the circumstances of the particular case, is well recognized at the sentencing stage, where discretion is provided.[37] These same circumstances may be apparent at the arrest stage and may seem to the police to dictate that the criminal process not be invoked against a particular offender. While sentence discretion is widely recognized, arrest discretion is not. This may reflect an assumption that, while individual circumstances may justify mitigation, the individualization of criminal justice should never go so far as to result in the complete exoneration of a particular offender.[38] The contrary view is that the individual circumstances sometimes make conviction and even arrest excessive,[39] so that proper administration requires the exercise of discretion at the early as well as at subsequent stages in the process.

5. *The extent to which necessary discretion can be exercised by the prosecutor.* It has been traditional to give explicit recognition to the propriety of discretion on the part of the prosecutor and either to deny or, more commonly, to ignore the issue of police discretion. To some extent this attitude

---

[35] "Although an important group of neo-analytical jurists still think of law as a body of rules attaching prescribed detailed sanctions to prescribed details of socially undesired conduct, it has become generally well perceived that the judicial process cannot be held solely to rules. . . . All legal experience shows that the power of adjusting the operations of legal precepts to the exigencies of special circumstances is unavoidable if there is to be a complete system of justice according to law." Pound, "Discretion, Dispensation and Mitigation: The Problem of the Individual Special Case," 35 *N.Y.U.L. Rev.* 925–926, 936–937 (1960).

[36] Breitel, "Controls in Criminal Law Enforcement," 27 *U. Chi. L. Rev.* 427 (1960).

[37] See Glueck, "Predictive Devices and the Individualization of Justice," 23 *Law & Contemp. Prob.* 461 (1958); Goldstein, "Police Discretion Not to Invoke the Criminal Process: Low-Visibility Decisions in the Administration of Justice," 69 *Yale L.J.* 543, 549 n.12 (1960). Treatment of this will also be found in the volume on Sentencing.

[38] See quotation from Hall, *supra* notes 20 and 22.

[39] Sometimes dispensation has been postponed until after conviction because of a view that the pardon is the only appropriate device to take care of such situations. . . . See Pound, "Discretion, Dispensation and Mitigation: The Problem of the Individual Special Case," 35 *N.Y.U.L. Rev.* 925, 936 (1960).

is based upon an assumption that the prosecutor is qualified to exercise discretion[40] while the average police agency is not.[41] This may result from the fact that the prosecutor has ordinarily been better educated than most police officers and, unlike most police, is directly responsible to the electorate.

The effect upon traditional attitudes of assumptions about the comparative competence of the prosecutor and the police is difficult to assess. Different educational requirements may be the result rather than the cause of the different attitudes about their respective responsibilities. There is, however, reason to believe that the assumption that the average municipal police agency lacks any special competence to make policy decisions is an important current factor. For example, the United States Supreme Court held it proper for the Federal Trade Commission to follow a policy of proceeding criminally against only major violators because there were insufficient resources to proceed against all violators.[42] This kind of judgment was said to be within the expertness of the enforcement agency, which is familiar with the economic problems being dealt with. Under similar circumstances, a Philadelphia court held an identical policy of the Philadelphia Police Commissioner to be improper.[43] The Philadelphia court gave no indication that it believed that the police commissioner was particularly qualified to decide how best to allocate the limited enforcement resources made available to him.

Although it is theoretically possible to have a system in which all discretion is exercised by the prosecutor, this would be difficult, perhaps impossible, to implement in practice. There are a number of alternatives:

(a) The police could make no arrests until the matter had been reviewed by the prosecutor. Referrals often are made in doubtful cases,[44] but the feasibility of doing so is limited by the need to make an immediate arrest in some cases[45] and the fact that prior consultation in all cases would place a

---

[40] See the series of articles by Baker and DeLong, 23–26 *J. Crim. L., C. & P.S.* (1933-1936). . . .

[41] Parratt, "How Effective Is a Police Department?," 199 *Annals* 153 (Sept. 1938).

[42] The Federal Trade Commission obtained a cease and desist order against one firm engaging in illegal pricing. The firm contended that the order should be suspended because certain of its competitors were engaged in the same practices but had not been proceeded against, with the result that this one firm suffered serious financial loss. The court held it would not disturb the FTC decision to put the order into operation immediately. . . . *Moog Industries, Inc. v. FTC,* 355 U.S. 411, 413, 78 Sup. Ct. 377, 379, 2 L. Ed. 2d 370, 373 (1958).

[43] *Bargain City U.S.A., Inc. v. Dilworth,* 29 U.S.L. Week 2002 (Pa. C.P., June 10, 1960). Compare the statement in *Gowan v. Smith,* 157 Mich. 443, 473, 122 N.W. 286, 297 (1909). . . .

[44] For example, questions involving difficult interpretation are often referred to the prosecutor in obscene literature and negligent homicide cases.

[45] For the reasons why immediate arrest may be essential, see LaFave, *Arrest,* chap. 9 (1965).

considerably greater strain on police resources than does the current practice.[46]

(b) The police could arrest all violators, leaving to the prosecutor the responsibility for exercising discretion when he decides whether to charge the suspect.[47] Carried to its extreme, this would require the police to construe all criminal statutes liberally, leaving it to the prosecutor to decide whether ambiguity ought to be resolved in favor of prosecution or release.[48] As a consequence, more persons would be arrested and later determined not to have violated the statute than is the case under current practice. The police would thus be liable for damages, at least in theory, because current tort law seems clearly to hold the officer liable for any mistake in the determination of the meaning of a criminal statute.[49] The imposition on the persons arrested would be great,[50] particularly in cases where arrest in itself is damaging to reputation.[51] To the extent that such a practice would require more arrests to be made, it would necessitate the allocation of greater resources to law enforcement, an expense which municipalities would probably not be willing to incur for the purpose of eliminating police discretion.[52]

[46] Particularly in the numerous cases in which the officer and offender are face to face, it is far less time consuming to make an immediate arrest than to consult with a prosecutor or magistrate.

[47] Because police training materials rarely deal with the invocation-discretion problem, few opinions have been expressed on this point. An exception is found in the Oakland, California, Police Academy materials, advising that "we should . . . remember that it's our job to turn in the evidence and it's the Prosecuting Attorney's job to determine when a complaint will be issued." See Goldstein, "Police Discretion Not to Invoke the Criminal Process: Low-Visibility Decisions in the Administration of Justice," 69 *Yale L.J.* 543, 560 n.28 (1960).

[48] Jerome Hall has cautioned the police that, where the law is uncertain, "the law that must be enforced is the narrow, strict interpretation of the relevant statutes and decisions. . . . This does not oppose the standard that the police must enforce definite law impartially and regardless of their private opinion of its merits." Hall, "Police and Law in a Democratic Society," 28 *Ind. L.J.* 133, 171 (1953). A less than broad interpretation is also implied by Goldstein, who notes that full enforcement by the police is not a realistic expectation due to ambiguities in the substantive law. Goldstein, *supra,* at 543, 560.

[49] See LaFave, *Arrest* 86 (1965).

[50] This is sometimes conceded by opponents of discretion by the police. Thus Goldstein, who is of the view that the "ultimate answer is that the police should not be delegated discretion not to invoke the criminal law," admits that full enforcement now would be improper because too many persons have come to rely upon nonenforcement. Goldstein, "Police Discretion Not to Invoke the Criminal Process: Low-Visibility Decisions in the Administration of Justice," 69 *Yale L.J.* 543, 586, 588 (1960).

[51] See LaFave, *Arrest* 137 (1965).

[52] It is not clear whether the police are, or should be, aware of the limited resource problems of the subsequent agencies in the criminal justice process and whether they exercise invocation discretion on this basis. Certainly the burden upon these agencies is lessened by the various kinds of decisions not to invoke which are made. However, no evidence has been found which indicates that the police follow a particular pattern of nonenforcement specifically to avoid a strain upon the resources of another

(c) Police could confine their decisions to policies made known in advance by the prosecutor and courts. The formulation of self-executing policies presents the same kind of difficulty as is presented by the effort to draft self-executing statutes. The range of individual variations is so great that it is difficult to deal with all of them in a brief verbal formulation. If the policy statements are elaborate, police training would need to be greatly improved to communicate effectively these statements to the individual officer. Most important, perhaps, is the fact that the prosecutor's policies may not adequately take account of limited police resources, particularly since the prosecutor, a county officer, is not directly concerned with the fiscal policies of the cities in the county, upon which most police departments in the area must rely for their support.

POLICE DISCRETION AND THE LAW

Police decisions not to enforce the law rarely become known to the public. Consequently, these decisions are seldom challenged either in the legislature[53] or in the trial or appellate courts.[54] Where there is challenge in court, the person making the challenge is confronted with a very difficult burden of proof[55] and often by the lack of an available remedy.[56]

1. *Legislation on police discretion.* Almost every state has some legislation relevant to police discretion. However, there is a distinct lack of originality

agency. General observations about the police knowledge of and sympathies concerning these related agencies suggests that such action, if it demonstrates any concern at all, occurs only with regard to the burden upon the prosecutor's office.

[53] Legislative action presupposes a number of persons sufficiently interested in obtaining legislative declaration of a given principle that they will work together toward that end. Interest groups objecting to police discretion have not taken form, and while the police might be expected to work toward an express legislative grant of discretion, they have been satisfied to exercise it without explicit authorization and in such a manner that it is not brought to general attention.

[54] Of the cases observed, most involved nonenforcement which was clearly a result of corruption or neglect of duty, rather than an attempt to exercise discretion of the kind to be described herein. These opinions rarely refer to the problem of noninvocation in the absence of such circumstances.

[55] The problem of proof may be a considerable one. In *People v. Winters,* 171 Cal. App. 2d Supp. 876, 342 P.2d 538 (Sup. Ct. 1959), a trial judge's dismissal of a case on grounds of discriminatory enforcement of gambling laws against Negroes was reversed on the basis that such intentional and purposeful discrimination had to be proved, judicial notice not being sufficient. In *Bargain City U.S.A., Inc. v. Dilworth,* 29 *U.S.L. Week* 2002 (Pa. C.P., June 10, 1960), prosecution under the Sunday blue laws was enjoined because of a deliberate policy of selective enforcement, but the case is unusual in that the police commissioner, because of limitations in resources, had previously articulated a policy of enforcement directed only at large retail establishments. . . .

[56] See LaFave, *Arrest* 157 (1965).

in the statutes defining the powers and duties of the police agencies. It is obvious that the question of police discretion has not received careful legislative attention. Most of the statutes have existed for many years, usually without the benefit of judicial interpretation. Therefore, while a good case can be made for the proposition that the state legislatures have generally denied the police authority to exercise discretion,[57] a review of all the applicable laws leaves the matter in some doubt.

The most convincing evidence that the police have been denied discretion is found in statutes which set forth the duties of various police agencies. Some impose a duty upon sheriffs[58] or city police[59] to arrest "all" violators of the criminal law. Others employ more limited terms, declaring it the officer's responsibility to arrest "all felons"[60] or "all persons committing an offense in his presence."[61] A lesser number state a duty to enforce "all" the criminal laws.[62] Seldom are the statutes phrased in permissive terms.[63]

Statutes frequently impose a duty of full enforcement in particularly sensitive areas of the criminal law such as gambling,[64] prostitution,[65] narcotics,[66] or liquor[67] violations. While these provisions do seem to demonstrate a special

---

[57] See Goldstein, "Police Discretion Not to Invoke the Criminal Process: Low-Visibility Decisions in the Administration of Justice," 69 *Yale L.J.* 543, 557 (1960).

[58] Ariz. Rev. Stat. Ann. §11-441 (1956); Ark. Stat. Ann. §12-1110 (1947); Cal. Govt. Code §26601 (1943); Hawaii Rev. Laws §31-5 (1955); Idaho Code §31-2202 (1961); N.D. Cent. Code §11-15-03 (1960); Utah Code Ann. §17-22-2 (1962); Wash. Rev. Code §36.28.010 (1961).

[59] Colo. Rev. Stat. §139-3-15 (1953); Hawaii Rev. Laws §150-10(b) (1955); Iowa Code Ann. §748.4 (1950); Mo. Ann. Stat. §74.203 (1952); Neb. Rev. Stat. §16-323 (1954); Utah Code Ann. §10-6-66 (1962); Wyo. Stat. §7-155 (1957).

[60] Minn. Stat. Ann. §387.03 (Supp. 1960); Mo. Ann. Stat. §57.100 (1959); N.M. Stat. Ann. §15-40-2 (1953).

[61] Ill. Rev. Stat., chap. 38, §655 (1961); Ind. Stat. Ann. §48-6107 (1950), §49-2802 (1951); Neb. Rev. Stat. §27-1706 (1956); Ohio Rev. Code Ann. §2935.03 (1954).

[62] Alaska Comp. Laws Ann. §40-12-8 (Supp. 1958); Ark. Stat. Ann. §19-1705 (Supp. 1961); Colo. Rev. Stat. §139-75-5 (1953); Del. Code Ann., tit. 11, §8303 (1953); Hawaii Rev. Laws §150-9 (1955); Idaho Code §19-4804 (1948); Ky. Rev. Stat. Ann. §70.570 (1960); Mich. Stat. Ann. §5-1752 (1952); Mo. Ann. Stat. §85.060 (1952); Ohio Rev. Code Ann. §737.11 (1954); Va. Code §15-557 (Supp. 1960); W. Va. Code §509 (1961). . . .

[63] The closest approach to express recognition of discretion in the police duty statutes is found in N.M. Stat. §39-1-1 (1953), which makes it a police duty "to investigate all violations of the criminal laws . . . which are called to the attention of any such officer or of which he is aware, and it is also declared the duty of every such officer to diligently file a complaint or information, if the circumstances are such as to indicate to a reasonably prudent person that such action should be taken. . . ." . . .

[64] E.g., Cal. Penal Code §335 (1960); Miss. Code Ann. §2478 (1942).

[65] E.g., N.D. Cent. Code §44-04-06 (1960).

[66] E.g., Ore. Rev. Stat. §475.120 (1959).

[67] E.g., Okla. Stat. Ann., tit. 37, §88 (1953); R.I. Gen. Laws §3-12-1 (1956).

legislative desire for full enforcement in these areas, it is questionable whether one can properly infer from them a recognition that discretion does exist in regard to crimes not specifically mentioned. In practice, police do tend to conform to specific commands for full enforcement while at the same time exercising considerable discretion in other enforcement areas.[68]

Over two-thirds of the states have passed general arrest statutes prescribing the circumstances under which police can make an arrest without warrant. A great majority are in permissive terms, usually indicating that the police "may" arrest upon a given quantum of evidence.[69] By comparison, only a few states have declared that police "shall" arrest when such evidence exists.[70] Occasionally courts have suggested that even the permissive language must be read as imposing a duty to arrest when the officer obtains the necessary evidence.[71] A similar assertion has been made with regard to common law arrest powers.[72]

Statutes commonly make it a criminal offense for an officer to refuse or neglect to make an arrest pursuant to a warrant directed to him.[73] This is understandable. Once the prosecutor or magistrate has decided that an arrest should be made, the police officer has only the ministerial duty of executing the warrant.[74] It may be of some significance that there are few comparable

[68] Thus, while the police in Michigan exercise considerable discretion, the Director of the Enforcement Division of the Michigan State Liquor Commission noted that local officers were resisting pressures for nonenforcement of the liquor laws because a duty of full enforcement is stated in the Liquor Control Act, Mich. Stat. Ann. §18.971 (1937).

[69] Ala. Code, tit. 15, §154 (1958); Alaska Comp. Laws Ann. §66-5-30 (1958); Ariz. Rev. Stat. Ann. §13-1403 (1956); Ark. Stat. Ann. §19-1706 (1947); Cal. Penal Code §836 (1960); Colo. Rev. Stat. §39-2-20 (Perm. Supp. 1960); D.C. Code §4-141 (1961); Fla. Stat. Ann. §530.15 (1960); Hawaii Rev. Laws §255-5 (1955); Idaho Code §19-603 (1961); Ill. Rev. Stat., chap. 38, §657 (1961); Ind. Stat. §9-1024 (1956); Iowa Code Ann. §755.4 (1950); La. Rev. Stat. §15:60 (1950); Mass. Ann. Laws, chap. 276, §28 (1956); Mich. Stat. Ann. §28.874 (1938); Minn. Stat. Ann. §629.34 (1947); Miss. Code Ann. §2470 (1956); Mont. Rev. Codes §94-6003 (1947); Nev. Rev. Stat. §171.235 (1957); N.Y. Code Crim. Proc. §177 (Supp. 1961); N.D. Cent. Code §29-06-15 (1960); Ohio Rev. Code Ann. §2935.04 (1954); Okla. Stat. Ann., tit. 22, §196 (1937); Ore. Rev. Stat. §133.310 (1959); R.I. Gen. Laws §12-7-4 (1956); S.C. Code §17-253 (1952); S.D. Code §45.1133 (Supp. 1960); Tenn. Code Ann. §40-803 (1955); Tex. Code Crim. Proc., art. 215 (1954); Utah Code Ann. §77-13-3 (1953); Va. Code §52-20 (1958); W. Va. Code §489 (1961); Wis. Stat. Ann. §954.03 (1961). . . .

[70] Conn. Gen. Stat. Ann. §6-49 (1961); Me. Rev. Stat., chap. 147, §4 (1954); Neb. Rev. Stat. §29-401 (1956); N.C. Gen. Stat. §15-41 (Supp. 1959); Wyo. Stat. §7-155 (1957). Of these, only the Connecticut and North Carolina statutes refer to persons other than those "found" violating the law.

[71] *Lees v. Colgan,* 120 Cal. 262, 52 Pac. 502 (1898); *Monson v. Boyd,* 81 Idaho 575, 348 P.2d 93 (1959); *Schultz v. United States Fidelity & Guaranty Co.,* 134 App. Div. 260, 118 N.Y.S. 977 (1909), aff'd, 201 N.Y. 230, 94 N.E. 601 (1909).

[72] E.g., *Hoch v. State,* 199 Wis. 63, 225 N.W. 191 (1929).

[73] E.g., N.M. Stat. §40-31-09 (1953); N.D. Cent. Code §12-17-02 (1960).

[74] Consequently, it is generally agreed that the police officer can incur no liability if the warrant is fair on its face and he acts in accordance with it.

statutes dealing with the failure of an officer to arrest without warrant.[75] A few western states make it a crime if an officer "willfully refuses to . . . arrest any person charged with a criminal offense,"[76] but it is not clear whether "charged" means charged by the prosecutor, charged by a private complainant, or merely that sufficient evidence exists to make a legal arrest without warrant.[77] In a few states it is an offense only if the officer should "neglect making any arrest for an offense . . . committed in his presence."[78] Similarly, only a few states expressly declare failure to make an arrest to be grounds for removal from office.[79]

The Wisconsin statutes suggest that there is a duty to arrest,[80] while equivalent provisions in Kansas[81] and Michigan[82] are in permissive terms. However, it seems likely that the choice of language was fortuitous.

    2. The courts and police discretion. Generally, appellate courts have not recognized the propriety of police discretion. In part this is due to the fact

[75] Of course, it can hardly be contended that this conclusively establishes the existence of police discretion. It would be questionable policy, in an area such as this where the officer himself must weigh the evidence to determine if he can arrest, to leave the officer open to tort liability, if he erred in making an arrest, and to criminal liability, if he erred in the other direction. Yet criminal liability could be limited to those instances where the police officer, knowing he could lawfully arrest, failed to do so. See statutes cited in note 76.

[76] Cal. Penal Code §142 (1960); Colo. Rev. Stat. §40-7-34 (1953); Idaho Code §18-701 (1947); Nev. Rev. Stat. §281.280 (1959).

[77] In the only case found in which an appellate court interpreted this term in such a statute, it was observed that "it may be said that the words 'charged with criminal offense' limit the application of this statute to cases in which a formal charge has been made. . . ." *Monson v. Boyd,* 81 Idaho 575, 348 P.2d 93 (1959).

[78] D.C. Code §4-143 (1961); Tex. Penal Code, art. 382 (1952).

[79] Okla. Stat. Ann., tit. 11, §577 (1959), removal for refusal to "make an arrest in the proper case"; W. Va. Code §509 (1961), for violation of the "duty to . . . arrest . . . any offender"; Wyo. Stat. §7-13 (1957), for failure to arrest for a violation in the officer's presence.

[80] The statute on constables states as a duty: "To cause to be prosecuted all violations of law of which he has knowledge or information," Wis. Stat. §60.54(6) (1955), incorporated by reference in the city police and village marshal statutes, Wis. Stat. §§61.28, 62.09(13) (1955). City police and village marshals are further directed in these statutes to "arrest . . . every person found . . . violating any law of the state or ordinance" of the city or village. Conservation wardens shall ". . . cause proceedings to be instituted if the proofs at hand warrant it." Wis. Stat. §29.05(2) (1955). The statute on sheriffs and their aides is less clear, although it indicates that they ". . . shall keep and preserve the peace in their respective counties. . . ." Wis. Stat. §59.24 (1955). . . .

[81] Kan. Gen. Stat. §§13-623, 14-819 (1949), on police of first and second class cities. But see Kan. Gen. Stat. §19-813 (1949), on the county sheriff, drafted in language similar to the Wisconsin sheriff provision. . . .

[82] The general peace officer statute, Mich. Stat. Ann. §28.874 (1938), is permissive, as are many dealing with the duties of particular officers, e.g., Mich. Stat. Ann. §4.436 (1952), on state police, and Mich. Stat. Ann. §13.1226 (1951), on conservation officers.

that strong language denying the propriety of such discretion has been used in opinions in cases involving a clear abuse of authority. For example, in a Kansas case the court stated emphatically: "There is a discretion to be exercised, but that discretion is reposed in [the legislature and city council]. They have left no room for the exercise of discretion on the part of officials charged especially with the duty of seeing that the laws are enforced."[83] This use of unqualified language makes it difficult to reach a different result in situations where the exercise of discretion is more defensible.

Even within a single case a court may treat as identical a clearly improper decision not to arrest and a decision not to arrest for which a sensible reason can be given. For example, the Wisconsin court recently reviewed the conviction of a sheriff on counts which included allowing prostitution to continue in return for certain favors and failing to make an arrest in an assault case where the victim, who was the adult son of the offender, told the sheriff that he did not want to sign a complaint against his father.[84] A decision not to arrest in a case like the latter is certainly not unusual in current practice.[85] Yet the court held that the failure to arrest the father for assault justified conviction under a statute punishing a public official who "intentionally fails or refuses to perform a known mandatory, nondiscretionary, ministerial duty of his office."[86] The court, therefore, apparently assumed that the sheriff's decision in this situation was as improper as it was in the prostitution case.

Some other courts have nevertheless expressly recognized that some discretion, such as that involved in interpreting the meaning of a statute defining the crime, must be exercised by the police.[87] However, this right has been carefully limited, and where the legislative mandate is clear and unambiguous, it has been held that the police are not justified in concluding that the legislature did not contemplate enforcement against conduct clearly within the scope of the statute.[88] But there are cases suggesting that such an assumption

[83] *State ex rel. Parker v. McKnaught,* 152 Kan. 689, 107 P.2d 693 (1940).
[84] *State v. Lombardi,* 8 Wis. 2d 421, 99 N.W.2d 829 (1959).
[85] See LaFave, *Arrest* 121 (1965).
[86] Wis. Stat. §946.12(1) (1955).
[87] Thus, an officer has "the duty . . . of interpreting the statutes he is called upon to enforce. He must act according to his best lights." *State ex rel. Pacific American Fisheries v. Darwin,* 81 Wash. 1, 13, 142 Pac. 441, 444 (1914). See also *Jumonville v. Herbert,* 170 So. 497 (La. App. 1936).
[88] Thus a city ordinance providing that no person shall sell liquor without first obtaining a license may not be interpreted to exclude wholesale liquor dealers on the basis that it was the legislative intent that it apply only to saloon keepers. Such an ordinance imposes on the police "an official duty . . . purely ministerial. No judicial discretion is anywhere involved." *State ex rel. School District of Omaha v. Cummings,* 17 Neb. 311, 313, 22 N.W. 545, 546 (1885). But see *Rohrer v. Hastings Brewing Co.,* 83 Neb. 111, 119, 119 N.W. 27, 30 (1908), where the court, engaging in statutory interpretation under similar circumstances, relied on nonenforcement. . . .

by the police is justified if the legislation has remained unenforced for a substantial period of time.[89]

There has rarely been judicial recognition of the right of police not to enforce certain laws where available resources make full enforcement possible. An exception is the Michigan case of *Gowan v. Smith*,[90] where the court declared that the police commissioner

... is bound to use the discretion with which he is clothed. He is charged not alone with the execution of the liquor laws of the State within the city of Detroit, but he is likewise charged with the suppression of all crime and the conservation of the peace. To enable him to perform the duties imposed upon him by law, he is supplied with certain limited means. It is entirely obvious that he must exercise a sound discretion as to how those means shall be applied for the good of the community.[91]

Other courts have reached the opposite conclusion.[92]

Where discretion is recognized as proper, courts have not indicated what standards ought to control the exercise of such discretion. One court did suggest that police might appropriately divert resources away from those cases in which the possibility of conviction seems slight.[93] However, other courts have insisted that the police have a duty to arrest even when reasonably certain the prosecutor or judge will dismiss.[94] Some have held it improper to divert resources away from the enforcement of laws which do not enjoy public support.[95]

Certainly enforcement criteria must accord with constitutional guarantees such as the right to equal protection. However, the state cases on equal pro-

[89] Thus, in refusing to mandamus the police, one court observed that "the ordinance [in question] seems, whether for adequate or inadequate reasons, to have been a dead letter for a number of years." *Carmody v. City of Elmira,* 160 Misc. 916, 290 N.Y.S. 1021, 1023 (Sup. Ct. 1936).

[90] 157 Mich. 443, 122 N.W. 286 (1909).

[91] 157 Mich. at 470, 122 N.W. at 297. While opinions expressly recognizing police discretion in this fashion are most unusual, it might be said that a number of courts have accomplished approximately the same result by denying to the relator the extraordinary writ requested, on the grounds that such a remedy was not available to him. . . .

[92] After the Philadelphia Police Commissioner, because of lack of funds and personnel, adopted a policy of limiting enforcement of the blue laws to large retail establishments, the Philadelphia Court of Common Pleas enjoined prosecution of a complaining defendant. *Bargain City U.S.A., Inc. v. Dilworth,* 29 U.S.L. Week 2002 (Pa. C.P., June 10, 1960).

[93] "If it be true that petit jurors will not convict in such cases, it might well be doubted whether it would be best to summarily arrest the parties. . . ." *Graham v. Gaither,* 140 Md. 330, 345, 117 Atl. 858, 863 (1922).

[94] Thus, "derelictions of other officials cannot excuse . . . failure to do what the law plainly required. . . ." *State ex rel. Thompson v. Reichman,* 8 Tenn. 653, 680, 188 S.W. 225, 232 (1916) (claimed courts would not convict). See also *Goodell v. Woodbury,* 71 N.H. 378, 52 Atl. 855 (1902) (suggested prosecutor would not charge).

[95] *Clark v. Police Board of Columbus,* 10 Ohio Dec. 256, 19 *Wkly. L. Bull.* 341 (C.P. 1888).

tection in law enforcement are not consistent. Aside from those cases holding that the equal protection clause has no application to discriminatory penal enforcement, the only agreement is that the prohibition is of purposeful and intentional discrimination. It is probably accurate to conclude that the constitutional requirement is only that the enforcement agency refrain from using classifications impermissible to the legislature, such as race or religion, although some courts have stated other tests. Wherever the line is ultimately drawn, the equal protection cases neither specifically affirm nor deny the propriety of police discretion. Rather they serve only to identify certain enforcement criteria as unconstitutional.

The exercise of discretion by the police, which seems inevitable in current criminal justice administration, continues unrecognized. In practice, policies to guide the individual officer in deciding whether to make an arrest are not formally developed within the police agency, and no sustained effort is made to subject existing practices to re-evaluation. This being so, the first step toward better understanding of the problem is identification and analysis of the criteria presently employed in practice.

Isolation of the Police:
A Comparison of the British
and American Situations

JOHN P. CLARK

Policing in most societies exists in a state of "dynamic tension" between forces that tend to isolate it and those that tend to integrate its functioning with other social structures. In its broadest sense, the concept of isolation-integration is used here to denote the degree to which policing contributes to the overall unity and welfare of a society as measured by its own diverse sets of standards. More specifically, the police may be said to be isolated when the relationships between themselves and others involved in social control activities are less frequent or of a different nature than those thought to be desirable, or when conceptions of proper police action vary significantly between the police and some other segment of the population, or when actual police action varies from that desired by specified others. Police isolation often means the lack of social interaction on the behavioral level, but it also refers to the lack of consensus regarding proper police functioning.

It is the purpose of this paper to identify some forces that contribute to the isolation and integration of policing and to suggest their consequences to police organizations and general society. Further, the results of a study which attempted to measure the nature of police isolation in three medium-sized cities in Illinois are presented and compared with similar recently published data about the British police.[1]

FORCES THAT CONTRIBUTE
TO THE ISOLATION OF POLICING

Certainly, those who have experienced restrictive action by the police (and even those who perceive themselves as potential police clients) resent this intrusion upon the pursuit of their private interests.[2] This resentment may foster efforts to neutralize further police activity and frequently sensitizes

Reprinted by special permission of the author and *The Journal of Criminal Law, Criminology and Police Science,* Copyright © 1965 by the Northwestern University School of Law, Vol. 56 (September 1965), pp. 307–319.

[1] The data in British police-public relations are taken largely from the Royal Commission on the Police, Morton-Williams, *Relations between the Police and the Public* (Appendix IV) (1962). Readers may also be interested in the final recommendations made in the *Final Report* by the Royal Commission.

[2] For an extremely insightful analysis concerning resentment to police activity see Stinchcombe, *The Control of Citizen Resentment in Police Work* (undated, unpublished monograph).

both parties involved to differences in their conceptions of desirable police work — both reactions being likely contributors to police isolation. The potency of this isolating force is probably proportional to the importance placed upon the behavior actually or potentially being curtailed, the projected social consequences of this kind of police-public contact, the availability of "isolating resources," and the predispositions of those involved regarding the proper role of formal social control agencies.

A second force that contributes to police isolation is the social reaction to recurrences of the historic problems of policing. The history of local police forces both here and in Great Britain is liberally endowed with incompetence, brutality, corruption, and the influence of private interests, although there is considerably less of this in Great Britain since about the middle of the nineteenth century.[3] The extensive documentation of policing in totalitarian countries frequently reinforces our worst fears of relatively uncontrolled police power. Our recent preoccupation with the emotion-laden issues of racial segregation, civil liberties, increased official crime rates, and corruption of those in authority (especially the police) has re-sensitized us to questions of the quality of police forces and their social responsiveness.[4] The accumulative effects of fear, mistrust, and disdain overshadow relationships between the police and others and result in restricted interaction between the two factions and incomplete cooperation and distorted perceptions of police motives and operations on the part of the public.

Thirdly, police officers and their operations tend to be set apart because they are visible reminders of the seamy and recalcitrant portions of human behavior. In societies where a generalized stigmatization of the individual and perhaps his associates is the prevalent reaction to social deviance and where there is a pervasive orientation that "getting caught" is the crucial determinant of this degradation, the consequences of police detection and apprehension loom large, indeed. Lawyers, judges, probation officers, and social workers are associated with deviants, in a sense, *after* social sanction which occurs in a very real sense during the investigative and accusative operations of policing. The maneuvers and hagglings of prosecutors, defense attorneys, judges and correctional personnel in the vast majority of cases are not primarily concerned with *whether* social sanction should be applied but *what form* formal sanctions will take. Obviously, not only does the latter depend upon the former, but "post-police" handling is likely to be less important to the actual or potential offender. Therefore, prudence demands that actual or

---

[3] For brief histories of the development of modern police forces in the U.S. and Britain see Germann, *Introduction to Law Enforcement* 37–67 (1962); Chapman, *The Police Heritage in England and America* (1962).

[4] Examples are "Our Streets of Violence," *The New Republic* (September 5, 1964); "How Cops Behave in Harlem," *The New Republic* (August 22, 1964); "Who Cares," *Look* (September 8, 1964).

potential police clients construct maximum insulation between themselves and the police who are the pivotal figures in the application of social sanctions. The reservoir of possible police clients has grown immensely with the proliferation of legal regulations.[5] Positive reaction notwithstanding, thoughts of policing to this segment of the population may conjure up images of surveillance, inconvenience, embarrassment, frustration and indignation. Though the presence of police may serve as a positive socializing symbol for social control,[6] it may also be a constant reminder that the police must be isolated in order to reduce the risk of social sanction.

The rapid growth of professional expertise in a complex industrialized society has had its effect upon policing. Modern crime detection techniques, police administrative procedures, techniques of handling mass demonstrations and riots, and communication networks have contributed to the increased differentiation of the role of policing. Good policemen must be trained and re-trained. To the extent that such socialization creates an occupational structure with its own standards of behavior and a body of specialized knowledge, this occupation may be thought of as a profession. Professionalization to the point of being granted license to determine the content of policing provides both the condition and the impetus whereby the profession may become isolated from other occupations and the general public. Whereas the professionalization of other occupations might be looked upon as very desirable by the general population, its emergence here serves to aggravate an already sensitive relationship between the police and the public. Becoming more expert and unreproachable in the restriction of behavior may be interpreted quite negatively, especially by those who were not in sympathy initially with police procedures and philosophies. This same isolating force may operate to mutually isolate the police and other organizations in the social control system (e.g., social welfare agencies and schools) whose philosophy of operation is not sympathetic to the professionalization of certain police activities.

One of the most important contributions to police isolation stems from the general policy (official or unofficial) of policing organizations themselves. That is, in the interest of "good police work," officers are often advised to isolate themselves from certain segments of the public in order to avoid entangling or contaminating relationships. In fact, becoming closely identified with any segment of the public is frequently condemned because of the increased vulnerability to charges of favoritism and the fear of incurring obligations that subsequently could become detrimental to police operations.

---

[5] See Gourley, "Police Public Relations," 291 *Annals* 135 (1954); Parker, "The Police Challenge in Our Great Cities," 291 *Annals* 5 (1954).

[6] See Wenninger & Clark, "A Theoretical Orientation for Police Studies," in Klein & Myerhoff, *Juvenile Gangs in Context: Theory, Research, and Action* 178–191 (undated), monograph in the Youth Studies Center of the University of Southern California.

For at least these reasons, policing in our society tends to be isolated in both the behavioral and normative sense. However, in most societies, and especially those more or less committed to democracy, numerous counterpressures contribute to the integration of policing.

FORCES THAT TEND
TO INTEGRATE POLICING

First of all, a large proportion of the population accepts the legitimacy of policing as an integral part of the social structure. Though this may be an elementary observation, it is probably this basic orientation that provides the fundamental integration of police forces and their operations into most communities. To most, not having a body of functionaries who will intercede in certain social control situations that are thought to be damaging to the individual or the community, however rare the occasion, is unthinkable. Outcries against the police demand their reform, not abolition. The public and those in other parts of the social control system recognize that the police cannot be totally isolated and perform their fundamental functions. This minimum of acceptance, although variously defined, assures the police of continued existence and integration.

A second force which mediates against police isolation is the fear of what police agencies might become if they were not integrated in the sense of being responsive to the dominant will of those policed. As was mentioned above, however, this same fear may prompt police isolation, because of the possibility of negative consequences from interaction with the police who are not totally responsive to public desires. This fear of uncontrolled police activity appears to create an "approach-avoidance" situation which might better be termed a state of *social ambivalence*. The manifestations of this ambivalent orientation toward the police are numerous. For example, episodes of flirtation with the police (e.g., having them speak at service club meetings and school assemblies) alternate with widespread general condemnation of police officers and their activities and demands for investigations. At times, police are forced to be subservient to "civilian" police commissions or advisory boards to insure police integration, while at other times they are surrounded by an apathetic local government and public who may even strongly encourage them "to do whatever you think best."[7] In yet another area, many communities demand

---

[7] See Royal Commission on the Police, *Final Report* 22–24; 51–55 (1962); Johnson, *Crime, Correction and Society* 440–461 (1964); Gourley, *op. cit. supra* note 5 at 135; Smith, *Police Systems in the United States* 15–23 (1960). Germann, *op. cit. supra* note 3 at 67–103. For a sample of police reaction to restriction of their power see Wilson, "Police Authority in a Free Society," 54 *J. Crim. L., C. & P.S.* 175 (1963) and Day, "Criminal Law Enforcement and a Free Society," 54 *J. Crim. L., C. & P.S.* 360 (1963).

that police officers be recruited only from within the local jurisdictions to assure police sensitivity to their unique circumstances, yet expect the officers to be free of any entangling social relationships that might bias their work — all this with little or no formal training in policing!

A more specific source of pressure toward the integration of policing is the process of accommodation which occurs between the police and the policed. The subversion of police activity by the policed through purposefully placing the police in a position of indebtedness or obligation to them tends to bind the two parties involved more closely together. Those at high police risk, such as tavern operators, professional criminals, cab drivers, prostitutes, and drug addicts, are famous for such operations.[8] The police are equally renowned for their efforts to create "contacts" among these same populations. One consequence of such activity is the creation of integrative tissue between the police and their potential and actual clientele. It should be noted here that greater police integration with certain populations may result in the isolation of the police from other segments of society, as was suggested above. Therefore, this specific process may explain both the integration and isolation of the police, depending upon the portion of the citizenry or the quality of policing being considered.

Somewhat similarly, those portions of the public who are likely to request more than ordinary police services may be more solicitous than others of police personnel and may initiate relationships that in some fashion bind the police closely to them. For example, managers of financial establishments, theatre owners, operators of "teen-age hangouts," certain property owners, and tavern operators, have particular need for rapid and reliable access to police services. Through their efforts to obtain these, they entwine the police into the social fabric.

Also, the occupation of policing holds considerable glamour for significant numbers of people. Characteristics of policing such as danger, public prominence, power, "being in on the know," and handling the "bad guys," appear to attract portions of the public. This probably accounts for some efforts by the public to interact with the police, and the latter's willingness to respond. A latent function of such activity is the greater integration of the police with the public.

One of the most obvious and powerful social forces of police integration is the effort of police officers themselves to keep the role they occupy in fundamental agreement with their cultural heritage and that of the community within which they work. Although the power of this pressure varies with the selection, training, and retention policies of the police, there is strain toward

---

[8] The classic documentation being Whyte, *Street Corner Society* 111–146. See also Wilson, "The Police and Their Problems: A Theory," 12 *Pub. Pol.* 203–204. Deutsch, *The Trouble With Cops* 75–84, 96–106 (1955).

consistency between the work and private attitudes and values of police officers. Of course, to the extent that police recruiting, training, and retention create a body of individuals who hold a unique set of values and attitudes, consistency between private and occupational orientations may help explain the lack of police integration into the larger society.

Police officers have occupational reasons for avoiding their own isolation. Most aspects of policing require the uncoerced cooperation of the public.[9] Since the criminal code is at best only a crude guide to police action, the major responsibility for determining when and how to activate police power lies squarely upon the shoulders of the police.[10] Therefore, when police initiate action, they do so with the knowledge that their action is condoned by the significant public and the legal system which may ultimately become involved, and frequently by the offenders themselves.[11] Such efforts to act safely within the boundaries of expectations of others cannot help but exert pressure toward a closer integration of policing into the larger society. On an operational level the police depend upon their working relationships with the public as sources of information, as indicators of public sentiment, and in the more informal aspects of social control, as their colleagues.

Policing leads a turbulent existence as a result of the strains imposed upon it by the various forces which tend both to isolate and integrate it within society.[12] Changes in the relative strength of one or more of these forces may bring about a significant change in the character of police isolation. The consequences of such isolation have been the subject of a few scientific investigations. Although these efforts have been focused primarily upon the dysfunctions of police isolation and even include suggestions as to how "the problem might be solved," several positive consequences of this isolation are identifiable.

POSITIVE CONSEQUENCES
OF THE ISOLATION OF POLICING

Among these would be the probability that up to a certain ill-defined point the smaller the involvement of police personnel with those who are to be

[9] Parker, *op. cit. supra* note 5; Gourley, *op. cit. supra* note 5; Wilson, *op. cit. supra* note 7.

[10] See Royal Commission, *op. cit. supra* note 7 at 31; 34–50; LaFave, "The Police and Non-Enforcement of the Law—Parts I and II" (1962) *Wis. L. Rev.* 104, 179. See also LaFave, *Arrest: The Decision to Take a Suspect Into Custody* (1965).

[11] Banton, *The Policeman in the Community* 144–146 (1964); Goldman, "The Differential Selection of Juvenile Offenders for Court Appearance," *National Council on Crime and Delinquency* 101–108 (1963).

[12] Wilson, *op. cit. supra* note 8 at 191–193; Ehrlich, *The Analysis of Role Conflicts in a Complex Organization: The Police,* 1959 (unpublished doctoral thesis in Michigan State University Library); Deutsch, *op. cit. supra* note 8 at 21–37.

policed (especially the more habitual and traditional offenders), the freer the former feel to detect, harass, and apprehend the latter. Obviously, there is a real danger of overstating and distorting this point, but there is evidence to indicate that the police have some practical difficulty in restricting the behavior of those with whom they are clearly identified or by whom they have been, in a sense, co-opted.[13] This is not meant to imply that good police work consists of dispassionate detection and apprehension, but merely that certain degrees of detachment from clients may be conducive to more objective evaluation and more aggressive action in police situations. When one considers the great variation in the demands placed upon municipal police forces and the equally diverse motivations for these expectations, there is a real reason to doubt whether "good police work" can be accomplished for the whole society. For example, as a practical matter, it is difficult to see how police forces in areas experiencing severe racial turmoil can retain sufficient isolation from the white population and enough integration with the Negro population to effect "good police work" with either. Here the unenviable role of the police as "the agency between" becomes sharply defined.[14]

Secondly, to the extent that police forces are used as positive agents of social change, they are likely to represent but a portion of society (likely the dominant political forces), and therefore, will be asked to force compliance with new regulations upon large segments of the population.[15] The relatively threat-free sanctuary of being somewhat isolated from the public, and perhaps not as vulnerable or responsive to its criticism, contributes to more aggressive action to effect social change.

In his discussion of role-set, Merton alludes to another possible function of some degree of police isolation. He suggests that the "mechanism of insulating role-activities from observability by members of the role-set" may contribute to social stability by allowing those in the same role-set who are differently located in the social structure to play their individual roles without overt conflict.[16] In this sense, police isolation may be said to permit the "peaceful co-existence" of police operations and anti-police sentiments and actions.

One of the most frequently offered panaceas to "police problems" is that of professionalization.[17] To the extent that this concept implies the accumula-

[13] Whyte, *op. cit. supra* note 8; Wilson, *op. cit. supra* note 8; Deutsch, *op. cit. supra* note 8 at 75–106.

[14] Police agencies may be viewed as standing between efforts to maximize individual desires and the need of social protection, between law breakers and their actual and potential victims.

[15] For a brief discussion of the role of the police as change agent see Wenninger and Clark, *op. cit. supra* note 6.

[16] Merton, *Social Theory and Social Structure* 374–376 (1957).

[17] Germann, *op. cit. supra* note 3 at 213–221; Deutsch, *op. cit. supra* note 8 at 226–233; Wilson, *op. cit. supra* note 8 at 200–211; Smith, *op. cit. supra* note 7 at 14–15.

tion of practices recognized as desirable by significant numbers of policemen and serving as a major guide to police behavior, then freedom from entangling social relationships with those who do not have similar orientations is functional to its growth. At least in the short run, the detachment from certain segments of the larger society may go hand-in-hand with or be a necessary pre-condition of increased police professionalization, given the myriad of standards for police work held within society.

NEGATIVE CONSEQUENCES OF ISOLATION OF POLICING

The listing of benefits derived from police isolation for either the police themselves or other segments of the community should not overshadow the social costs of such isolation. One prominent police chief has chastised his fellow officers for their retreat into "minoritism" and their "near-fatal inability to recognize police dependence on public opinion" and cooperation.[18] Police officer morale is thought to be severely damaged by feelings of isolation, yet high morale of police forces is considered to be a major factor in aggressive police work.[19] Gourley maintains that the lack of a "spirit of free cooperation" between the public and the police decreases police morale and cripples their service. He points out further that without the assistance of the public, police convictions become difficult if not impossible, a state which tends to regenerate poor morale on the part of the police department as well as negative attitudes on the part of the public toward the police.[20] One might generalize such observations and predict the probable negative consequences of the isolation of the municipal police from other community social control agencies such as the courts, social welfare, and the schools as well.

Westley attributes much of the rationale for police violence and secrecy to their perceived isolation. The development of a rigidly defined "in-group," not well monitored by other social structures, allows the development and persistence of certain abuses of police power that their more complete integration might prevent, according to this author:

"[The policeman] . . . regards the public as his enemy, feels his occupation to be in conflict with the community and regards himself to be a pariah. The experience and the feeling give rise to a collective emphasis on secrecy, an attempt to coerce respect from the public and a belief that almost any means are legitimate in completing an important arrest."[21]

Although such an interpretation is clearly within the tradition of suspicion of police power and stems from the study of one metropolitan police department,

[18] Parker, *op. cit. supra* note 5 at 5.
[19] Wilson, *op. cit. supra* note 8 at 191–192.
[20] Gourley, *op. cit. supra* note 5 at 135.
[21] Westley, "Violence and the Police," *Am. J. Soc.* 35 (1953).

it is undeniable that the police have unique opportunities to abuse the power of the state. To the extent that forces exist that result in police malpractice if not controlled through their close integration with the larger society, isolation of the police may be looked upon as dysfunctional to society.

In a study of the discretionary power of the police in their contact with juveniles, Goldman found that the more integrated the police were into the community, the greater the number of "arrests" of juveniles but the less frequently their cases resulted in official action.[22] This conclusion suggests that the juvenile delinquency rate (as measured from court statistics) may be more a measure of police isolation than the misbehavior of youngsters. Apparently the integrative structure between the police and other facets of the local community provides avenues of informal adjustment among the offender, the offended, and the police. When such routes are not available, there is little time (and perhaps desire) to establish them and formal channels are more likely to be utilized. Once official channels have been activated, official disposition is often imminent.[23] Therefore, if reduction of the official juvenile delinquency rate is a social goal, police isolation is dysfunctional.

A STUDY OF POLICE ISOLATION

Having identified some of the forces which tend to isolate or integrate the police within society and some of the resultant consequences, questions arise as to the measurement of the degree and exact nature of such isolation. The phenomenon might be measured, using a variety of indicators depending upon the aspect of policing chosen for examination. In the research reported here data were collected on the following indicators of isolation:

1. The social isolation of police officers and their families.
2. The quality and quantity of police interaction with other agencies of social control.
3. The consensus among the public, police, and other social control agency personnel on certain moral attitudes.
4. The consensus among the public, police, and other social control agency personnel on the conception of proper police action in "police situations."

Data regarding these indicators were gathered during 1963–64 as part of a larger study of the role of the police in social control.[24] Data were collected

---

[22] Goldman, *op. cit. supra* note 11.

[23] For an illustration of this process see Scheff, "The Societal Reaction to Deviance: Ascriptive Elements in the Psychiatric Screening of Mental Patients in a Midwestern State," 2 *Soc. Prob.* 401–413 (1964).

[24] Essentially the larger study is focused upon the image the public and police have of policing, the attitudes social control agency personnel (including the police) have toward related agency personnel and the behavioral consequences of these attitudes.

Table 1: Distribution of Respondents by Source in Three Illinois Communities

Municipal police	313
Public	598
Social control agency personnel (including)	430
Prosecutors	8
School officials	64
Court personnel	26
Clergymen	192
Public social workers	66
Private help agency personnel	74

in three Illinois cities of 80,000 to 130,000 population from three sources: (1) the total universe of municipal police, (2) a random sample of the public age 15 and over (approximately 200 from each city), and (3) the total universe of those in other social control agencies who were likely to have direct interaction with the police through the normal pursuit of their occupation. Police officers and those in the other social control agencies (operationally defined as prosecutors, school officials, court personnel, clergymen, public social workers, and private help agency personnel) responded to anonymous questionnaires.[25] The members of the public were individually interviewed. Part of the questionnaire to which the police and public responded was a replication of a recent survey of public-police relations conducted for the Royal Commission on the Police in Great Britain,[26] which involved interviews of a sample of 2605 members of the public (age 18 and upwards) and a sample of 611 police officers. The recent publication by Banton of a comparative study of a few police departments in Scotland and the United States[27] provides further information for cross-cultural comparison.

FINDINGS AND DISCUSSION

1. *Social Isolation of the Police.* Perhaps the most obvious indication of the lack of integration of the police into the larger society is the isolation of the officers and their families. Although police officers may restrict their social relations with the non-police public for a variety of reasons, social inter-

[25] Police officers completed questionnaires in small groups. Other agency personnel completed their questionnaires privately. Clergymen (a 2 in 3 sample) responded to a mailed questionnaire with a return rate of 46 per cent.

[26] Royal Commission on the Police, *Minutes of Evidence* (1962). All respondents in the British study were individually interviewed. The public sample was drawn randomly from 60 police administrative districts in England, Scotland, and Wales. Approximately 10 police officers were drawn at random from each of these 60 districts.

[27] Banton, *op. cit. supra* note 11.

action is further restricted by the public. In this study, the officers were asked if being policemen made any difference in their friendships with non-police persons. Forty per cent replied that it did and 35 per cent added that it affected their immediate family's relationships with the general public as well. In his extremely provocative study, Banton concludes that "the American policeman in his public and private roles is less set apart from society than his British counterpart."[28] Therefore, one would expect to find a larger proportion of the British officers who felt socially isolated than was found in our study. This hypothesis is supported by the British survey results which reveal 67 per cent of the police officers indicated their occupational role contributed to their social estrangement.[29] Although these findings are not directly indicative of the *distance* between the police and the public, they provide a measure of the pervasiveness of such feelings on the part of the officers which may vary directly with the distance.

American police explain their segregation on the grounds of their peculiar working hours, other unique demands of police work, and the public dislike for those who represent arbitrary authority. British police seldom mention these factors specifically but over half (58 per cent) of them felt the public to be suspicious, reserved and guarded in their presence.[30] Only 7 per cent of the American police noted this factor, indicating a possible difference between the two societies either in the public's reaction to police (more relaxed in America) or in the sensitivity of the police to incomplete public acceptance (more sensitive in Great Britain), or both. These findings seem to support Banton's contention that the British police officer is seen as a representative of the police establishment and not as an individual whereas his American counterpart is more likely to receive particularistic treatment from the public.[31]

Responses to questions concerning social isolation suggest that police officers and their immediate families are segregated from those in their own neighborhoods and social strata. For example, many of the Illinois police officers perceive their occupation to be a cause of ridicule of their children and the reason for members of the community to expect flawless behavior from the officer and his family. Probably few other occupational groups experience this isolation in social relationships from those "on their own level."

2. *Police Isolation from Other Social Control Agencies.* If we conceive

[28] Banton, *op. cit. supra* note 11 at 219.
[29] Royal Commission on Police, *Minutes of Evidence* (1962).
[30] *Ibid.*
[31] Banton, *op. cit. supra* note 11 at Chapters 7 and 8.

social control to be a *system* of relationships which pervade a community,[32] and if we agree that part of the policing function is to effect social control, then we might logically expect police personnel to interact with other organizations who also play social control roles. Both formal regulations and informal understandings require interaction between the municipal police and other control agencies under certain circumstances although the great majority of such contacts are left to the discretion of the agencies involved. The failure of the police to initiate interaction with another control agency when situations dictate they should, or for the other agency not to establish contact with the police in similar situations, would indicate something of the quality and quantity of police isolation in a given community.

Members of both the police department and the other social control agencies were asked to indicate the frequency with which they failed to interact with the other on official matters because the personnel of the other agency's not being "what they should be." Failure to interact was operationally defined to mean (1) avoiding or ignoring a situation which might result in the need for interaction, or (2) turning to somebody else for assistance, or (3) handling the matter themselves without the assistance of others.

The data in Table 2 demonstrate that a significant portion of the police *and* other agency personnel manage to curtail indicated interaction in official matters, and therefore, mutually isolate each other within the social control system. This phenomenon is particularly noticeable between the police and public social workers,[33] which may reflect the presence of conflicting operating ideologies, lack of professional respect, and ignorance of the other's operations.

One may only speculate on the relative isolation of the police from other control agencies in Great Britain. The greater overall integration of the British society and the commonly accepted notion of greater respect for police and their operations in Britain suggest that isolation of the police might not be as great there.

3. *Isolation of the Police on Moral Attitudes.* Banton suggests that the isolation of the British police has resulted in their espousing a value system

---

[32] We stress again that the social control activities of police, although few in number when compared to total social control efforts, are important to the total efforts and must be integrated into them for greater efficiency. See Clinard, *Sociology of Deviant Behavior* 148–152 (1963).

[33] The author was impressed, as others have been with the institutionalized hostility between those in police work and those in social work. The nature of "inter-institutional conflict" will be examined in a later article. See Miller, "Inter-Institutional Conflict as a Major Impediment to Delinquency Prevention," *Human Organization* 20–23 (1958). A paper, "The Control of Delinquent Behavior by Police and Probation Officers," by Peter G. Garabedian and read at the 1964 annual meetings of the Society for the Study of Social Problems, reports an extremely interesting study of the differential commitment these two categories of officials have to punitive reactions toward legal offenders which may have direct relevance here.

Table 2: Percentage of Avoidance of Interaction Between Police and Other Social Control Agencies[a]

	Avoided or ignored the situation		Turned to somebody else		Took care of things personally	
	Agency avoidance of police	Police avoidance of agency	Agency avoidance of police	Police avoidance of agency	Agency avoidance of police	Police avoidance of agency
Prosecutors	63	27	50	30	87	31
School officials	25	23	24	34	31	32
Court personnel	21	26	26	39	22	30
Clergymen	33	20	39	26	45	26
Public social workers	42	37	47	50	50	47
Private help agencies	33	27	40	39	30	40

[a]*Percentages are those who failed to interact "sometimes," "often," or "almost always."*

somewhat different (more traditional) than that held by the general public.[34] To the extent that the American police are also isolated, one might expect to discover similar differences between the police and public in this country, although of smaller magnitude if it is assumed that American police are more socially integrated than their British counterparts. Unfortunately there are no comparable British data to compare with those gathered in our research on this aspect of police isolation. However, data are available in this study to measure divergence in moral value orientations between the police and those in other social control agencies and the general public in the three Illinois communities.

All respondents were presented with six hypothetical situations which might involve police action. These situations were constructed so as to be brief, free of direct involvement of juveniles, and ranging from instances where it was thought most would agree that no police action was required to those where most would agree that police action was appropriate. These six situations were:

1. A police officer finds a grocery store illegally open for business on Sunday.
2. A Negro meets a police officer on a street and tells him that he has just been refused service in a nearby restaurant. He says that he is willing to do whatever is necessary to take action against the owner of the restaurant.
3. A police officer learns of card games being played for large amounts of

[34] Banton, *op. cit. supra* note 11 at Chapters 7 and 8.

money in a private home. The card games are being run by professional gamblers although the games are not crooked. No juveniles are
involved.

4. A police officer discovers a couple of bums who had been drinking in
the alley and are pretty drunk. The officer knows both because he has
found them many times before in the same condition.

5. A police officer finds out about a woman who is charging men to sleep
with her. No juveniles are involved.

6. A police officer learns that a person is in town selling obscene magazines. These magazines are written and have pictures for the purpose
of being sexually exciting. As far as the officer can tell, no juveniles are
involved.

All respondents were asked to reply to several questions about each of the
six hypothetical situations. One such question was, "Do you believe this kind
of thing is morally wrong?" As demonstrated in Table 3, there is great similarity between the distribution of the public and police responses, indicating
the absence of a unique moral orientation of policemen and suggesting no
significant isolation in this regard. However, there are some interesting differences between the distributions of responses among the municipal police
and certain other social control agencies. The police were more likely than
any other category of respondents measured to indicate that the case of racial
prejudice was not morally wrong. However, a higher proportion of police
officers interpreted gambling and being a drunken bum to be moral transgressions than did the public social workers and private help agency personnel.
To some extent then, the police appear to be isolated, although cultural integration of all agencies is the predominant indication from this comparison.

Table 3: Percentage of Respondents Who Believed the Content of
Hypothetical Police Situations to be Morally Wrong

Situations	Police	Public	Prose-cutors	School officials	Court officials	Clergy-men	Public social workers	Private help per-sonnel
1. Sunday blue laws	13	28	0	19	11	58	20	25
2. Racial prejudice	62	71	25	81	96	87	82	92
3. Gambling	68	72	25	69	85	91	55	60
4. Drunken bums	85	86	38	78	93	93	69	68
5. Prostitution	90	94	63	100	96	99	89	92
6. Obscene literature	94	96	63	97	100	97	88	89

4. *Police Isolation on Conception of Police Work.* One of the most direct indicators of the isolation of policing is the dissensus existing between the police and others on the conceptions of proper police activity. It is not realistic to expect the public to exhibit expertness on the allocation of police resources. Yet, however misinformed it may be, public opinion provides the foundation for actions concerning the police. Isolation of the police is keenly felt when considerable discrepancy exists between police and public expectations of policing, although the magnitude of this discrepancy is at best an imperfect indicator of the magnitude of the reaction by the police and the public to this difference.

The Illinois public was asked if there are any areas in which the police should spend more of their time or less of it. A significant portion indicated they did not know (20 and 35 per cent, respectively), which may in itself suggest a lack of sufficient police integration to prompt minimal knowledge or concern on the part of the public. Nearly one-half of the public sample stated that there were areas where the police should spend more time, while only 15 per cent responded that the police should spend less of their time on certain matters. Obviously more persons see circumstances in which additional police activity is thought appropriate than where it should be diminished or eliminated — a provocative finding! This phenomenon is not as evident in the British data where about 38 and 28 per cent of the public note areas where police should spend, respectively, more and less time.[35] These data suggest that there is considerable discrepancy between the conception of proper police operations and the perception of actual police operations in the mind of the public.

As would be expected, policemen gave more specific responses to the above two questions as revealed in Table 4. Eighty-two per cent of the Illinois officers believed that there were areas where more of their time should be spent, although somewhat similar to the Illinois public, a much smaller proportion identified areas in which police effort should be curtailed. These data suggest that in any police officer's opinion there are discrepancies between the conception of the ideal police role and the real one. The situation in Great Britain appears to be similar.

In the sense that the police and public *agree* in principle that the roles of the police on the desired and real levels are far from being identical, one could say that the police and public conceptions are integrated. However, to the extent that the character of this discrepancy is different for the police and public, then isolation exists. After noting the difference in proportion of police and public respondents who indicated that the allocation of police

[35] Royal Commission, *op. cit. supra* note 29 at 19.

Table 4: Comparison of Public and Police Responses in Great Britain
and United States on Questions Regarding the Role of Policing[a]

Question and response	Public		Police	
	U.S. %	G.B. %	U.S. %	G.B. %
1. Are there any things you think the police should spend *more* time on than they do now? (YES responses)	47	38	82	73
2. Are there any things you think the police should spend *less* time on than they do now? (YES responses)	15	28	52	75
3. Do you think there is anything the public should do to help the police more to prevent crime or enforce the law? (YES responses)	76	73	88	97
4. Do you think that in general the public helps as much as they should when they see a policeman in trouble, for example in dealing with violent drunks or gangs? (NO responses)	60	75	87	87
5. Have you ever been asked by the police to testify as a witness in a case? (OF THOSE WHO RESPONDED YES) Did you agree to be a witness? (NO responses)	24	10		

[a]*Data on public and police respondents gleaned from Royal Commission on the Police, Appendix IV to the* Minutes of Evidence, *"Relations between the Police and the Public," by R. Morton-Williams (London: H.M.S.O., 1962).*

effort should be modified, it is interesting to discover that there is basic agreement between the public and police *within each country* on the areas wherein police efforts should be altered. The Illinois police officers agreed with members of the public that the police should spend more time on "crime prevention and detection" and "improving relations with the public," and less time on "being on duty at public affairs," and "office work."[36] The British public and police agreed that the officers should devote additional time to "foot patrols" and less to "enforcement of licensing regulations," "office work," and "traffic control and supervision."[37] Again, these crude data reveal basic integration of public and police disposition on desired police operations. It

[36] The Illinois public also indicated the police should spend *more* time on "traffic control and supervision" and the police suggested *less* time should be spent on "checking buildings to see if they are locked." To this extent the public and police conceptions of the ideal police role are different.

[37] Royal Commission, *op. cit. supra* note 29 at 35–36.

would appear that portions of the police role, as they are now being performed, are somewhat isolated from the preferred role content as viewed by
large segments of both the public and police.

The role of policing society has traditionally included public assistance to
law enforcement agencies under certain circumstances. As mentioned previously, there is recurrent concern about a seeming decrease in the willingness
of the public to perform this role. Banton concludes that police officers in the
United States are more likely than their British counterparts to have "to go
it alone."[38] In both the British and American surveys respondents were asked
if the public should assist the police more in prevention of crime and enforcing the law. Table 4 demonstrates that the large majority of both the police
and public answered affirmatively. Although a slightly smaller majority answered negatively, the public and the police in both this country and Great
Britain went so far as to declare that the public does not help as much as they
should to assist policemen in difficulties, e.g., in dealing with violent drunks
or gangs. An extremely high proportion of the British respondents (especially
the police) felt the public was not responsive enough to police needs. Although it might be concluded that there is limited cooperation between the
public and police, these findings might also reflect deep concern on the part
of both parties of some slight change in what traditionally has been a very
close relationship. The responses to a further question tend to support the
latter conclusion. In response to an inquiry of those who had been asked at
some time by the police to serve as a witness, a relatively small number of
the British respondents had refused to do so compared to about one-fourth
of those asked in Illinois. Although other forces than commitment to police
assistance probably affect these decisions, it would appear that the British
police receive more assistance from the public than is the case in Illinois,
although Britishers tend to be more concerned about the lack of public-
police cooperation.

In summary, there is a consistent response pattern of both the public and
police in both countries regarding the desirable character of the policing role.
To this extent the police do not appear to be isolated. However, since such
high proportions of public and, particularly, the police, would suggest changes
in actual policing activities, there is an overpowering suggestion that the
police are isolated by the manner in which they perform their operations.

Further data pertaining to this tentative conclusion were gathered through
the use of the six hypothetical situations mentioned previously. With each
situation all respondents were asked several questions concerning the nature
of police action dictated and usually received in their local community.

---

[38] Banton, *op. cit. supra* note 11 at 100–101; 110–114.

Table 5: Percentage of Respondents Who Indicated the Police Should Take Action in the Hypothetical Situations

Situations	Police	Public	Prose-cutors	School officials	Court officials	Clergy-men	Public social workers	Private help personnel
1. Blue laws	2	6	0	9	4	7	0	7
2. Racial prejudice	58	55	75	48	48	54	54	63
3. Gambling	91	71	0	83	85	87	78	76
4. Drunken bums	99	94	100	97	96	96	94	100
5. Prostitution	95	89	100	98	93	98	83	93
6. Obscene literature	95	92	100	94	100	93	88	92

Great divergence between the orientations of the police and others toward the role of the police in these circumstances would indicate police isolation from the larger society.

As the data in Table 5 demonstrate, the proportions of the public, police, and those in other social control agencies who would have the police take action in each situation is rather uniform. Almost all would have the police take no action in the Sunday blue-law case. Conversely, almost all would have the police take some sort of action in the situations concerning drunken bums, prostitution, and obscene literature. Nearly all categories of respondents were equally divided on the issue of police intervention in the instance of racial prejudice, and a significantly greater proportion of the police (91 per cent) than the public (71 per cent) believe the police should take action in the gambling situation. Once again, the data reveal the public, and other control agencies in essential agreement about the desired role of the police in these hypothetical situations. Obviously, this measure is not sensitive to the intensity of police-public or police-other control agency conflict that might occur between those of conflicting persuasions.

Knowing that the ecological distributions of the police, public, and control agencies are similar on whether action should be taken does not assure us that there is commensurate integration of orientation on the nature of the action to be taken. Cries for action do not necessarily provide useful guides to the exact police performance expected. Police officers were asked what they believed the people in the commmunity wanted them to do, and the public was asked what they really would like the police to do in each of the situations. Although the possible responses were somewhat tailored to each situation, in each case a response was available which focused upon (1) doing nothing, (2) mediating, (3) harassing, (4) warning, (5) arresting, or doing "something else."[39] Evidence of significant discrepancies between the distribution of responses across these possible answers is submitted as evidence of a type of police isolation. Table 6 summarizes the results.

Again, the percentage distributions are somewhat similar in many cases, which signifies certain similarity between public desires of policing and the police perception of these desires. However, there is the noticeable tendency for the police to misperceive public desires between the warning and arresting of offenders. In almost all cases a significantly larger proportion of the public wished to have the police warn the offenders than was judged to be the case by the police, and in four of the six hypothetical situations a significantly smaller portion of the public would like to see arrests made than was perceived by the police. As mentioned previously, these data are not extremely helpful in predicting the outcome of encounters between those of different persuasions, but there is clear evidence that a greater proportion of the public than of the police is likely to wish police effort which stops short of formal arrest, however untenable this position may appear to police officials. Police officers are more likely to be aware of a series of events which precede their making an arrest, while the knowledge of the private citizen is more likely limited to the immediate incident. Based only upon the single incident the judgment that a warning is sufficient may seem to be the most appropriate action. Whatever the reason for the difference in orientation, the police can be said to be isolated in their perception of public desires regarding the arrest of certain offenders.

The final evidence regarding conceptions of the policing role as an indicator of police isolation from other aspects of society is the discrepancy between the police action desired by the public and that which the police actually perform. With each of the six situations, all police officers were asked to disclose the action usually taken by their department in such circumstances. These responses were compared to the public's declared desires for police action (see Table 6). In most situations the actual police performance is noticeably different from the desires of the public for it. In all cases except the racial segregation issue, reported police action becomes much more unified into a single response. Apparently police action is much more likely to be an actual arrest than public desires would dictate, and even more likely than the police perception of community desires would suggest. The blue-law situation is an exception, but even here, there is much greater consensus

---

[39] For example, in Situation No. 1, the possible responses were:
  1. Do nothing at all.
  2. Keep them off the streets.
  3. Keep the pressure on people like this until they move on.
  4. Warn them that if they keep doing this they will be arrested.
  5. Arrest them and book them for legal action.
  6. Something else (what?) ——————.

Table 6: Comparisons Among Police Perceptions of Public's Expectations, Actual Public Expectations, and Actual Police Role Performance in Six Hypothetical Situations

Situations	Do nothing	Mediate	Harass	Warn	Arrest	Something else
1. Blue laws						
Police perceive public	75	17	1	0	0	7
Public desires	67	23	3	2	1	4
Police performance	93	3	0	0	1	3
2. Racial prejudice						
Police perceive public	24	46	1	7	4	18
Public desires	17	52	9	10	4	8
Police performance	24	41	1	10	8	16
3. Gambling						
Police perceive public	10	5	14	4	61	6
Public desires	9	13	12	23	41	2
Police performance	10	2	7	3	74	4
4. Drunken bums						
Police perceive public	1	42	6	3	43	5
Public desires	2	15	7	31	33	12
Police performance	1	12	4	5	77	1
5. Prostitution						
Police perceive public	2	10	6	2	76	4
Public desires	4	5	7	24	57	3
Police performance	3	1	3	1	89	3
6. Obscene literature						
Police perceive public	2	8	4	5	79	2
Public desires	2	8	11	18	59	2
Police performance	5	2	3	5	83	2

among the police on their taking no action in such cases than is warranted by expressed public desires or of the police perceptions of them.

When it comes to actual behavior, then, the police tend to act in a unitary manner and somewhat differently from what a large segment of the public desires in these situations. The findings are clear enough to suggest the strong influence of separate organizational (and perhaps professional) standards to guide police operations. As was hinted in the comparison just prior to this, the closer one's measures approach actual police operations, the greater the isolation of the police from the larger society.

CONCLUSION

Probably as a result of some of the forces identified at the beginning of this article, policing in the United States (Illinois) and Great Britain occupies a position of some isolation within their respective societies. The character of this isolation is somewhat peculiar to the specific society but considerable similarity between the two situations exists.

A large proportion of the policemen sampled in both countries feel socially isolated although the British officers are more likely to notice the lack of social integration.

Illinois policemen frequently avoid interaction with other social control agencies and these organizations reciprocate in kind. The quality of certain moral value orientations appears to be similarly distributed among police officers and the general public, although the police officers as an organization occasionally differ on certain moral issues from other social control agencies.

Both the British and Illinois police and public agree in principle on the content of the ideal police role, but at least in Illinois, police role performance differs significantly from this common ideal. The data suggest that the police knowingly perform their function somewhat differently than their own individual convictions or their perception of public desires would dictate.

Policeman as Philosopher, Guide and Friend

ELAINE CUMMING, IAN CUMMING, AND LAURA EDELL

This is the fourth report from a group of studies designed to throw some light upon the division of labor among the social agents whose central role is concerned with maintaining social integration by controlling various forms of deviant behavior.[1]

In earlier reports, we have adopted the convention of looking at social agents and agencies in terms of their relatively supportive or relatively controlling character. We have assumed that it is difficult for an agent to exercise both support and control at the same time and that any agent tends, therefore, to specialize in one or the other aspect of the integrative process.[2] Even when he is specialized, such an agent may be considered controlling when he is compared with some agents, and supportive when compared with others. Thus, the probation officer is more on the client's side, that is, supportive to him, than the policeman, but less so than the psychiatrist. Furthermore, the agent may be seen as supportive by the layman but experienced as controlling by the client, and vice versa. For example, the prisoner remanded by the court for psychiatric treatment may well experience his hospitalization as incarceration. Conversely, a chronic alcoholic may be grateful, in mid-winter, for a night in prison.

There is another aspect to this duality in the handling of deviance. While it is probably impossible to perform acts of support and control simulta-

Reprinted from *Social Problems,* Vol. 12, No. 3, pp. 276–286, by permission of the authors and The Society for the Study of Social Problems. A more recent version of this article has appeared in *Systems of Social Regulation* by Elaine Cumming, published by Atherton Press, Inc., N.Y.

[1] Earlier reports include: Elaine Cumming, "Phase Movement in the Support and Control of the Psychiatric Patient," *Journal of Health and Human Behavior,* 3 (Winter, 1962), pp. 235–241; Isabel McCaffrey, Elaine Cumming and Claire Rudolph, "Mental Disorders in Socially Defined Populations," *American Journal of Public Health,* 53 (July, 1963), pp. 1025–1030; Elaine Cumming and Charles Harrington, "Clergyman as Counselor," *American Journal of Sociology,* LXIX (November, 1963), pp. 234–243.

[2] This assumption is derived in part from studies of the division of labor in small groups (see, for example, Bales' "The Equilibrium Problem in Small Groups," in T. Parsons and R. F. Bales, *Working Papers in the Theory of Action,* [Glencoe: The Free Press, 1953]), and upon theories of role conflict (see, for example, W. J. Goode, "A Theory of Role Strain," *American Sociological Review,* 25 [August, 1960], pp. 483–495). At another level of analysis, of course, we all control and support one another — by showing disapproval when our expectations are not met and by friendliness, responsiveness, understanding and sympathy when they are.

neously, support without control is overprotection and invites passivity and dependency, while control without support is tyranny and invites rebellion. While the agent may specialize in one aspect of social control of deviance, the other must, nevertheless, be part of his repertoire.[3] Thus while physicians and clergymen are generally supportive of people in pain or trouble, such people are expected, in return, to perform appropriately the role of patient or parishioner. The support is overt, the control is latent. In general, the agent's training and professional ethics focus on the skills needed for the overt part of his role; the latent aspects are derived from and governed by general norms and values. Role conflict can be avoided in part by keeping the "contradictory" side of a role latent.

The policeman's role in an integrative system is, by definition and by law, explicitly concerned with control — keeping the law from being broken and apprehending those who break it — and only latently with support. For example, if you break the law, you can expect to be arrested, but if you go along quietly, you can, unless there is a special circumstance, expect to be treated reasonably.[4] In the course of controlling one member of society, moreover, the policeman often provides indirect support to another. For example, when he apprehends, and thus controls a wife-beating husband, he supports the wife, just as, in a reverse situation, the doctor controls the behavior of those attending a patient when he prescribes rest and sympathy. Finally, besides latent support, the policeman often gives direct help to people in certain kinds of trouble. When he does this, the balance between support and control has shifted, and he is acting overtly as a supportive agent and only latently in his controlling role. He has, at the same time, changed from a professional to an amateur. This paper reports a study of the requests for help received by a city police department and the policeman's response to them, with special attention to what is assumed here to be the latent side of his role.

METHOD OF STUDY

Because there seems to be no systematic account of the day-to-day activities of policemen, two specific questions were posed: (1) What kinds of calls for help do policemen get, and (2) How do they answer them? Two kinds of

---

[3] Certain highly skilled agents, such as psychoanalysts, may be able to phase their activities so that they are supportive in certain phases of the treatment and controlling in others. It is doubtful if this is feasible in the ordinary run of events because of the ambiguity it would generate in social interaction; see, for example, Gregory Bateson, D. D. Jackson, J. Haley and J. Weakland, "Toward a Theory of Schizophrenia," *Behavioral Science*, 1 (October, 1956), pp. 251–264.

[4] For an excellent discussion of the many problems inherent in the controlling function of the police, see Claude R. Sowle (ed.), *Police Power and Individual Freedom* (Chicago: Aldine, 1962).

data were collected. First, a total of 801 incoming telephone calls at the police complaint desk in a metropolitan police department were observed over a total of 82 hours. These hours were not evenly distributed around the 24 hours, for reasons connected with the field worker, not with the Police Department. As each complaint was received and disposed of, a description was dictated into a tape recorder. Fourteen selected prowl car calls were then observed. At the end of this phase of the study, the worker submitted field notes concerned with the general culture of the police station. Secondly, interviews were conducted with detectives concerning their special assignments. A formulation of the nature of the policeman's supporting role was then constructed from these data.

RESULTS

The Complaint Desk

Figure 1 shows the hourly distribution of police calls. The daily peak activity is between the evening hours of seven and eight o'clock excepting for Thursday, Friday and Saturday when it is between nine and ten. (Because

Figure 1: Average Police Calls per Hour, First Part of the Week (6 A.M. Sunday to 5 A.M. Thursday) and Second Part of the Week (6 A.M. Thursday to 5 A.M. Sunday)

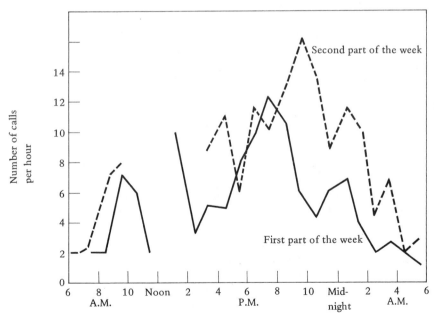

Table 1: Classification of Calls to the Complaint Desk of a Metropolitan Police Department During 82 Selected Hours in June and July, 1961

Type of call	Number of calls	Percentage of total
Total	801	100.0
Calls included in analysis	652	81.4
1. Calls about "things"	255	31.8
2. Calls for support	397	49.6
Persistent personal problems	230	28.7
a. Health services	81	10.1
b. Children's problems	83	10.4
c. Incapacitated people	33	4.1
d. Nuisances	33	4.1
Periodic personal problems	167	20.9
a. Disputes	63	7.9
b. Violence	43	5.4
c. Protection	29	3.6
d. Missing persons	11	1.4
e. Youths' behavior	21	2.6
Calls excluded from analysis	149	18.6
Information only	33	4.1
Not police business	28	3.5
Feedback calls	88	11.0

of the gaps in the data, there is a possibility that there is a peak at about noon in the first part of the week, but on both theoretical and common-sense grounds, it seems unlikely.) The last part of the week also shows a greater volume of calls than the first. In general, the high rate of calls in the evening and on weekends suggests that problems arise when the social pulse is beating fast — when people are coming and going, regrouping, and, of course, engaging in informal rather than formal activities.

In order to interpret these rhythms further, the 801 calls were classified according to their content, as Table I shows. One hundred and forty-nine, or 18.6 per cent of the calls, were excluded from analysis; 88 of these were call-backs on earlier complaints, 33 were requests for information only, and 28 were outside this police department's jurisdiction.[5] The remaining 652 calls were for service within the purview of these police. They are treated as independent, but the unit of analyses is the call, and not the caller, and results must be interpreted with this in mind.

The 652 calls included in the study were divided into two major groups: the first included calls for service in connection with things or possessions,

[5] The latter two groups (61 calls) were excluded because there was no chance of a car being sent, and therefore they could not be compared with the remainder.

while the second included calls for support or assistance with regard to problems of health, safety or interpersonal relationships.[6]

The first (nearly one-third of the total of 801 calls) include traffic violations, reports of losses or thefts, calls about unlocked doors, fallen power wires and so on. These are part of the regular controlling function of the police and are not the main focus of this paper. The second major group (about one-half of all calls) is concerned with personal problems and therefore may reasonably be expected to include the need or desire for some form of support. These calls were subdivided into two types: (1) persistent problems occurring throughout the week; and (2) periodic problems occurring mainly on the weekend.

As Table I shows, the first type comprises 230 calls, of which about one-third are requests for health services, that is, ambulance escorts, investigation of accidents, suicide attempts, and so on; another third are children's problems, usually complaints about trespassing, or destructive behavior; and the remainder are divided equally between incapacitated people, usually described over the phone as drunk or "psycho," and nuisances, usually noisy behavior.

Periodic problems comprise 167 calls of which more than a third are about disputes and quarrels of all kinds, both in families and among unrelated people. Almost half are concerned with violence or protection from potential violence[7] and the remainder are about missing persons or gangs of youths and hot-rodders.

Table II shows the distribution of the calls, by type, through the days of the week and the period of the day. It now appears that the heaping up of calls in the last part of the week is made up of two effects: first, routine police business and persistent interpersonal calls occur most frequently on Thursday, while periodic interpersonal problems heap up on Friday night. The meaning of this finding is not clear, but it may be that the tensions associated with the instrumental activity of the working week are increasing by Thursday and are then let go on Friday — payday — and on the weekend, when formal constraints are fewer. Because fewer of the other agents are available at these times, the policeman takes over many emergency health and welfare services, a kind of division of labor through time.

Almost three quarters of all 652 calls were answered by dispatch of a patrolman in a squad car to the scene, while about 8 per cent received vari-

---

[6] It was surprisingly easy to classify the calls on these two major dimensions and coders had no trouble getting over 90 per cent agreement. Differences were reconciled in conferences.

[7] Most "protection" calls are for a "clothing escort," that is, for a policeman to accompany a person who has left his home, or been thrown out of it, into the house to get his clothing.

Table II: Number of Calls to the Complaint Desk of a Metropolitan Police Department, by Type of Problem,[a] Day of Week, Time of Day, and Hours of Observation During 82 Selected Hours in June and July, 1961

Time of day, hours of observation, and type of call	Total	Sun.	Mon.	Tue.	Wed.	Thur.	Fri.	Sat.
All calls	652	50	69	55	76	95	54	253
(hours observed)	(82)	(8)	(14)	(9)	(9)	(9)	(6)	(27)
12:01 A.M.-5:00 A.M.	91	16	18					57
(hours observed)	(14)	(2)	(5)	(0)	(0)	(0)	(0)	(7)
Routine	28	4	8					16
Persistent	21	4	4					13
Periodic	42	8	6					28
5:01 A.M.-noon	52		9	19		17		7
(hours observed)	(13)	(0)	(4)	(3)	(0)	(3)	(0)	(3)
Routine	36		6	11		15		4
Persistent	10		2	4		2		2
Periodic	6		1	4		0		1
12:01 P.M.-6:00 P.M.	187	18		36	38	38	31	26
(hours observed)	(26)	(4)	(0)	(6)	(5)	(3)	(4)	(4)
Routine	88	9		12	18	18	16	15
Persistent	68	6		17	11	16	12	6
Periodic	31	3		7	9	4	3	5
6:01 P.M.-midnight	322	16	42		38	40	23	163
(hours observed)	(29)	(2)	(5)	(0)	(4)	(3)	(2)	(13)
Routine	103	4	13		17	15	2	52
Persistent	131	5	22		18	17	7	62
Periodic	88	7	7		3	8	14	49

[a]Departures from uniformity:

1. Periodic interpersonal calls occur more often than chance would indicate on Friday evening ($x^2 = 24.1$, d.f. = 5, P < .01) and the early hours of Saturday ($x^2 = 8.4$, d.f. = 2, P = .02).

2. Both routine police calls and persistent interpersonal calls occur more frequently than chance would indicate on Thursday, the former in the morning ($x^2 = 12.3$, d.f. = 3, P < .01) and the latter in the afternoon ($x^2 = 13.1$, d.f. = 5, P = .05).

ous kinds of advice or information, and about 4½ per cent were referred to another source of help. Of the 29 referrals, one was to a medical service, one to a social service, 19 to other legal services and the remaining eight to commercial concerns, such as the Telephone Company. Almost 15 per cent of the calls were terminated — that is, service was withheld for reasons not determined, occasionally because no car was available.

In Table III, we see that the probability of a car being sent out is inversely related to the rate at which calls are coming in. During the six time

Table III: Percentage of Calls to Which Cars Sent, by Hours of the Day, Days of the Week and Type of Call, and Number of Calls Received per Hour; 82 Selected Hours at the Complaint Desk of a Metropolitan Police Department, June and July, 1961

Time of day, type of call, and calls/hr.	Total		Sun.-Wed.[a]		Thursday		Fri.-Sat.[a]	
	Calls	Percentage to which car sent	Calls	Percentage to which car sent	Calls	Percentage to which car sent	Calls	Percentage to which car sent
Total calls (total/hr.)	652 (8.0)	72.1	250 (6.3)	72.8	95 (10.6)	71.6	307 (9.3)	70.0
12:01 A.M.-5:00 A.M. (calls/hour)	91 (6.5)	80.2	34 (4.9)	85.3			57 (8.1)	77.2
Routine	28	85.7	12	91.7			16	81.3
Persistent	21	71.4	8	87.5			13	61.5
Periodic	42	81.0	14	78.6			28	82.1
5:01 A.M.-Noon (calls/hour)	52 (4.0)	86.5	28 (4.0)	89.3	17 (5.7)	88.2	7 (2.3)	71.4
Routine	36	88.9	17	94.1	15	86.7	4	75.0
Persistent	10	90.0	6	83.3	2	100.0	2	100.0
Periodic	6	66.7	5	80.0	0	—	1	—
12:01 P.M.-6:00 P.M. (calls/hour)	187 (7.2)	73.8	92 (6.1)	70.7	38 (12.7)	71.0	57 (7.1)	80.7
Routine	88	69.3	39	66.7	18	66.7	31	74.2
Persistent	68	80.9	34	76.5	16	75.0	18	94.4
Periodic	31	71.0	19	68.4	4	75.0	8	75.0
6:01 P.M.-midnight (calls/hour)	322 (11.1)	66.5	96 (8.7)	65.6	40 (13.3)	65.0	186 (12.4)	67.2
Routine	103	60.2	34	58.8	15	40.0	54	66.7
Persistent	131	72.5	45	73.3	17	76.4	69	71.0
Periodic	88	64.8	17	58.8	8	87.5	63	57.1

Table IV: Disposition of 397 Calls to the Complaint Desk of a Metropolitan Police Department Regarding Interpersonal Problems, by Sub-Category of Complaint; 82 Selected Hours in June and July, 1961

Type of call	*Total calls*	*Percentage car sent*
Total calls	397	76.8
Persistent problems	230	79.1
a. Health services	81	86.4
b. Children's problems	83	85.5
c. Incapacitated people	33	75.8
d. Nuisances	33	48.5
Periodic problems	167	73.7
a. Disputes	63	50.8
b. Violence	43	95.3
c. Protection	29	79.3
d. Missing persons	11	81.8
e. Youths' behavior	21	85.7

periods in which a total of 235 calls were received at a rate of fewer than eight calls per hour, 78 per cent of them were responded to with cars. During the five time periods in which 417 calls were received at a rate of more than eight calls per hour, cars were sent only 68 per cent of the time. This difference is highly significant ($X^2 = 7.54$, d.f. $= 1$), and suggests that cars are sent on a simple supply-and-demand basis. Furthermore, there is no difference among the three major categories with regard to the likelihood of a car being sent. Nevertheless, certain sub-categories of complaint are more likely to get service than others. As Table IV shows, calls regarding violence (control), children and youths (support and control), and illness (support) are the most likely to be responded to with a car, although the likelihood of the law being broken — which defines the police mandate — is greater for some of these complaints than for others.

When the complainant reports a nuisance or a dispute, he has only one chance in two of getting more than advice — albeit professional advice. Thus, a man calls to say that he has had a fight with his girl and she hasn't come to see him, although he knows she is off duty from the hospital; the policeman says he can't make her come to his house — perhaps she doesn't want to — and goes on to advise the man that that's the way life is sometimes.

It is possible that some of the calls about violence are later stages of these unanswered dispute calls. For example, to one complaint, "My boy friend is mad at me and is going to beat me up," the answer was, "Call us again when he does."[8]

It is quite apparent that the policeman must often exercise a kind of clinical judgement about these complaints, and that this judgement reflects his own values. The field notes suggest, for example, that policemen are sincerely, if sentimentally, concerned about children, and that negligent parents are likely to find the police at their most truculent. The following example is taken from the notes:

A call came from a very kindly sounding Italian man at about 11 o'clock in the evening. He was reporting that he had found a little boy from next door wandering in the street . . . and he thought the police ought to know about the situation. A car was dispatched and reported that there was nobody home, and in fact, there were three smaller children in the house. . . . The captain dispatched a camera crew, child placement was notified and the children were immediately placed in a temporary placement home. A stake-out was set for the parents. Meanwhile the pictures had been developed and they showed four under-nourished, under-clothed little children lying in their own feces on a mattress on the floor. The refrigerator contained two cans of condensed milk and some rotten vegetables; the place was filthy and unheated. As the time went by, anger began to rise and when at about four o'clock in the morning the parents were brought in to the station everybody was in an ugly mood. . . . Had they been the least bit smart, glib, or said almost anything other than "yes" or "no" while they were issued tickets, they would have gotten poked.

All-out support for the children is accompanied by the barest minimum of support to the parents in the form of approval for appropriately docile behavior.

THE SQUAD CAR

Certain calls are considered serious enough to warrant a captain following the squad car to the scene.[9] The following thumb-nail summaries represent 14 calls made by the captains in a 23-hour period. Half of them were not considered serious, but the field worker asked the captain to go to the scene.

(1) A man, reported by his ex-wife as dangerous and perhaps mentally ill, is found asleep; his ex-wife and her mother are in an agitated state. They report that when the ex-wife came to the home the husband shook his fist under her nose and said, "I have divorced you, I want you out of this goddam house by morning." The police officer woke up the man who once again threatened his ex-wife, and the officer then

---

[8] Police Chief Murphy describes this entry as "poor police practice."

[9] The field worker could not go with the regular prowl car owing to a rule forbidding the officers to carry passengers. It is also possible that the captain did not want the field worker to see episodes that he did not himself monitor.

told her that since it was his house and she was legally divorced from him, she and her mother should "please leave, and not cause any more trouble."

(2) A car accident severely injures a woman and the police supervise her removal to hospital.

(3) A bartender asks for, and receives, help in closing up so that there will be no problems — a routine "preventive" police service usually given by the car on the beat.

(4) A man has beaten up his female neighbor earlier in the day and she has called the police and preferred charges. At the time of this call, the man's wife had threatened this woman with a knife. All are drunk and are taken to the station for further investigation.

(5) A call from a woman about neighborhood children bullying a small boy who wears glasses. The field notes read, "There was a lot of argument and a lot of screaming back and forth, nothing was particularly accomplished, the three policemen (captain and two officers from a squad car) stood around for awhile, questioned people, did a little shouting, got shouted at, then the whole thing sort of dissolved and was resolved in a manner that I don't understand."

(6) A woman complains that her husband doesn't bring home enough of his money to feed the kids. She is advised to go to Children's Court.

(7) Field notes read: "Husband destroying property at his house. He's drunk and he and his wife got in an argument over the children . . . the wife smashed the gift he had given her for Mothers' Day. This set the incident off. He fought the officers, they handcuffed him, and is taken to the station — a psycho."

(8) A slightly drunk man is an unwelcome visitor in his ex-wife's home. Police send him home in a cab.

(9) An ex-patient from a mental hospital is missing from her relative's home. They will broadcast a missing persons call.

(10) A drunk man claims he has been slugged, but cannot amplify so no action is taken. "This is a low IQ street," says the policeman.

(11) A woman in her pajamas and covered with mud says her husband threw her out. He is at home drunk with the children. As he has a police record, two cars are dispatched, one with a tear-gas gun. The house is found in a shambles. The wife is taken to hospital, children to a shelter, and the husband is booked for investigation and possible psychiatric treatment.

(12) Fight in a third floor apartment between a man and his wife. Policeman settles it in some undiscernible fashion.

(13) A man has "gone out of his mind over a girl" and has gone berserk with a gun. The man is shipped to hospital and witnesses are taken in because the gun makes the affair a felony.

(14) The call is "see if an ambulance is needed." A young Negro in a filthy, crowded house appears to be in agony. Police examine him for knife wounds and being satisfied that he has not been stabbed, and that no further investigation is needed, send him to hospital in an ambulance.

There seem to be three types of cases here. In the first, the police act as guides or conveyors to the courts and hospitals, giving indirect support meanwhile. In the second, they appear to resolve problems by giving concrete in-formation and guidance about what is and is not possible under the law. Here both indirect and overt support are given. In the third type, they appear to settle problems through some consensual method based on mutual under-standing between the police and the people involved. Here support is fairly overt but control is, of course, latent because of the policeman's representa-tion of law and order. Occasionally, the police give outright friendly support, as in the following incident from the field notes:

Sitting in the police station is an old man, a citizen wanderer who is on his way to Oregon, and has become dissatisfied with the Rescue Mission and walked out. He's going to spend the night out of the rain until the morning when he's going over to the Salvation Army.

It is, of course, not possible to say what proportion of the policeman's re-sponses to citizens fall into these three types, nor indeed, to know what other types there may be, because of the method of selecting the squad car calls.

DETECTIVES

Four detectives of the twenty in the department, selected only because they were on duty at the time of the field worker's visit, were asked to describe their ten most recent cases. It was felt that they might be assigned the more "professional" and hence controlling tasks. Two of them were specialists in theft and forgery and so their cases were, indeed, of this character. However, fifteen out of twenty cases described by the two general detectives fell into our two personal-problem categories, and were similar to the complaint calls except that they were being further investigated because of more serious breaches of the law.

Another detective, in charge of services to alcoholics, reported that in 1956 the police department sent him to Yale for training in the handling of alco-holics. He says, "As a police officer I saw people being arrested for drunk and re-arrested for drunk and I thought it was a pretty medieval way of going about trying to help a person with a basic problem and illness that the pub-lic was just kicking in the corner and that's how I wound up here." This officer handles about 900 alcoholics a year. Of these, he takes about 150 charged persons on suspended sentence from the court and tries to arrange for some agency to carry them — an outright supportive service.

Missing persons: The sergeant in charge of this service estimates that he locates about 600 missing people from this area in a year, about half of them children. He further estimates that from 3 to 5 per cent are mentally dis-turbed adults. This particular officer says that he sometimes counsels with children that he has traced after they have been returned home. At the same time, he complains to the interviewer that children don't respect police of-ficers the way they did when he was young.

Detectives in charge of homicide and those on duty with the vice squad were not interviewed, so it is impossible to say what proportion of all detective work is supportive. These data suggest that it is similar to the patrolman's.

POLICE CULTURE

The field worker reports several impressions that are relevant to our interests. Although they cannot be demonstrated from these data, some of them are similar to findings from other studies. First, poor, uneducated people appear to use the police in the way that middle-class people use family doctors and clergymen — that is, as the first port of call in time of trouble. Second, the policeman must often enforce unpopular laws among these poor people at the same time he sees these laws being flouted by those in positions of power.[10] Third, many policemen are themselves recruited from, and sympathetic to, the class of people from whom most of the "interpersonal" calls for assistance come.[11]

Fourth, the police have little knowledge of, and liaison with, social or even medical agencies, and seem to feel that these agencies' activities are irrelevant to the problems they, themselves, face.

Fifth, the police appear to have a concern not only for children but also for those they define as disturbed and ill. They are tolerant, for example, about many crank calls, and will, if a car is available, help a paranoid old lady search her house for the malignant intruder she feels sure is hiding there. Nevertheless, it is possible to see, both in episodes of prejudice against minorities, and in less dramatic ways, how their own values transcend the individual's rights. A field note says, for example, "A woman wants protection from her doctor who is trying to commit her to a mental institution; the officer replies, 'That's not police business, lady. The police cannot go against any doctor.'"[12]

Finally, many policemen are bitter about their low pay, the label "punitive" applied to them in a world that values "warmth," the conflicting de-

---

[10] This seems to be most true of the vice squad and it was not covered here. Nevertheless, a lot of police station conversation was on this topic.

[11] This becomes less true, of course, as the police department becomes more professionalized, and is probably less true of this department now than it was in 1961 when these data were collected.

[12] This attitude is, of course, construed by some as a denial of the basic rights of the mentally ill person. See, in this regard, Thomas Szasz, *The Myth of Mental Illness* (New York: Harper, 1961). A trickle of manifestly disturbed people may be turned down for other reasons at the complaint desk. One agitated man complained that his back yard was full of snails; the officer replied, "What do you want me to do, come and shoot them?" Even so, the field worker reports that if the complaint officer had had a car available, he would probably have sent it out.

mands of their jobs, and the ingratitude of the public. This bitterness is reflected, in this police force, in a catch phrase, "I hate citizens."[13]

SUMMARY AND DISCUSSION

We return now to our starting questions: What calls are made on the police and how do they respond? More than one-half of the calls coming routinely to the police complaint desk, and perhaps to detectives, appear to involve calls for help and some form of support for personal or interpersonal problems. To about three-quarters of these appeals, a car is sent. When the policeman reaches the scene, the data suggest that he either guides the complainant to someone who can solve his problem or tries to solve it himself. To do this, he must often provide support, either by friendly sympathy, by feeding authoritative information into the troubled situation, or by helping consensual resolution to take place. We started with the assumption that these activities belonged to the latent aspect of his role, and he is certainly an amateur — these policemen have no training for this kind of service. Why, then, are they called upon to exercise their amateur talents half of the time?

The reasons are probably complex. First, the policeman has to do much of what he does because he is on duty at times of the day when no other agent is available. Second, he deals with the problems of a group of people — the poor and the ignorant — that studies of our own and others have shown no other agent to be anxious to serve[14] and, third, he has knowledge of, and access to, very few other agents. In other words, he is part of an integrative system in which the labor is divided not so much on the basis of function as on the basis of the time of day and the nature of the target population. All citizens can count on emergency help from the police when there is sudden illness at night, but only a certain kind of citizen takes his marital troubles to them.

The policeman's supportive acts are not only the latent and hence amateur part of his role, they are also latent in not being recognized and legitimated by the other agents in the integrative system. These others, our own studies show, prefer to recognize the policeman's professional controlling function, which they both need and often call upon.[15] Thus, it is as an agent of control

---

[13] It may be that the higher respect for policemen in England is related to the higher value on order and the lower value on warmth.

[14] See, for a discussion of this problem in this community, Claire Rudolph and John Cumming, "Where are Psychiatric Services Most Needed?" *Social Work,* 7 (July, 1962), pp. 15–20.

[15] There is reason to believe that most social workers, clergymen, and doctors have no conception of the amount of support policemen give during a day's work. There is also reason to believe that they do not want the burden of the "unmotivated" poor and ignorant whom they believe to be increasing in number.

that the policeman participates in a divided labor with social workers, doctors, clergymen, lawyers and teachers in maintaining social integration. The problems he faces appear to be a *failure of integration within the integrative system,* so that he cannot mobilize the other agents when he needs them.

Some modern advocates of "professionalization" of police work recognize that the policeman on the beat spends about half his time as an amateur social worker and they hope, instead of improving the referral process, to equip him with the skills of a professional. The policeman will then have a role containing both overtly supportive and overtly controlling elements. If our assumption that these are incompatible activities is correct, this development would lead to a division of labor within police work that would tend once more to segregate these elements. This, in turn, would result in a basic shift in the relationship of the police to the rest of the integrative system. All of this might remove the policeman's present reasons for hating citizens, but it would not guarantee that they would not be replaced with others.

The Social Role
of a County Sheriff

T. C. ESSELSTYN

Rural crime is a neglected field in criminology. Standard texts devote scant space to it. Few research projects have focused upon it. Rural sociologists are concerned with other matters. Pertinent tables in the *Uniform Crime Reports* are sometimes based on data from communities as large as 25,000 inhabitants.[1]

For these and for many other reasons, it would seem that some idea of space and function should be substituted for the term rural in criminology. The substitute offered in this present article is the *open country*. It would be defined as the region beyond the metropolis as measured by daily commuting and marketing. Agriculture and other extractive industries are prominent features of its economy and these enterprises play an important part in the attitudes and social organization of all the people who live there. It includes the towns, villages, and small cities — the trade and service centers of varying size that stud it. This is the composite region on which the relevant tables in the *Uniform Crime Reports* are actually based. It has not been studied systematically by criminologists. This area is what we probably have in mind when we say "rural."

An open country crime would be any crime on which an open country law enforcement officer takes action. One way to study such crime would be to see how that officer acts. Several types of officers could be selected but the one recommended is the county sheriff because for many parts of the United States he is still important in open country crime control. A convenient method for this purpose would be to follow Znaniecki's concept of a social role, breaking it down into its four components: the social circle, the social person, the social status or office, and the social function.[2]

What follows is a summary of a larger study in which this method was used.[3] The region selected was "Star County," Illinois, a fictitious name for an actual county which lies in the open country as defined earlier. The

Reprinted by special permission of the author and *The Journal of Criminal Law, Criminology and Police Science,* Copyright © 1953 by the Northwestern University School of Law, Vol. 44 (July-August 1953), pp. 177–184.

[1] See *Reporting Handbook* (May, 1947), p. 28. See also Table 34, "Rural Crime Rates," *Annual Bulletin* for 1951, where 10,000 is taken as the working population base.

[2] Znaniecki, Florian W., *The Social Role of the Man of Knowledge* (New York: Columbia University Press, 1940).

[3] Esselstyn, T. C., *Crime and Its Control in the Hinterland* (unpublished dissertation submitted in partial fulfillment of the requirements for the degree of Doctor of Philosophy, New York University, February, 1952).

sheriff whose role was analysed served there between 1946 and 1950. No pretense is made that what obtains in Star County obtains in all open country areas, for a sufficient body of inductive studies executed along similar lines is not at hand. What is offered here is a method by which such studies might proceed and an indication of some of the results that can be expected if it were applied.

STAR COUNTY, ILLINOIS

The principal city of Star County is Hopkins, the county seat with some 37,000 inhabitants. Hopkins is an independent police district. Apart from operating the county jail there, the sheriff carries on none of his peace-keeping functions within its limits. The remaining 50,000 persons in the population are dispersed among twenty-two minor civil divisions and eighteen towns including the rural areas. A little over twelve percent of the employed population is engaged in agriculture. This is the largest single field of employment.

The historical development of Star County can not be traced here. It may be characterized briefly as a wealthy corn belt county with a cash-grain economy in which corn and livestock are the principal features. Money, volume output, quick turnover, and high profits from farm produce mark the worthy man. The pattern setter in the social order of Star County is the successful farmer. There is a continual drift from his ranks to the villages and small cities where he takes up residence in his declining years. He brings with him the values and attitudes of responsibility, individualism, initiative, and the outward evidences of success and favor by which these are shown. His influence thus permeates all levels of Star County life and he is perhaps the chief referent in the "social circle" whom the sheriff serves.

The class structure discernible here appears to follow in general the four-way split discovered in other regions in Illinois.[4] This comes to bear on the sheriff because law breaking often involves class-linked behavior patterns. As to the adult, the social and recreational outlets available to Classes I and II are seldom policed. The counterparts for Classes III and IV are usually taverns and these the sheriff watches closely, not only on his own initiative but also on demand of the proprietors. Trouble is expected and trouble happens. The result is that adult crime in Star County, like crime elsewhere, is preponderantly associated with the less privileged.

As to the juvenile, the reaction pattern of the parent shows a generally stable connection with class position. Parents from Classes I and II characteristically rally to the side of the juvenile or express a readiness to take

---

[4] Warner, W. Lloyd, *et al., Democracy in Jonesville* (New York: Harper and Brothers, 1949).

remedial action. Parents from Classes III and IV are usually overwhelmed or are resigned in the face of the child's delinquency to the point of relative inaction. The result is an overloading of court cases and juveniles in the county jail from the latter two classes. Popularly, this result is attributed to favoritism. Functionally, the consequence flows from patterns acquired by the parent largely through class membership.

Social groups are perhaps of greater importance to law enforcement in Star County than social class. The number and kinds of groups are legion. Some, like the churches, certain occupational groups, service clubs, school boards, fraternal orders, and the like, are important agents for transmitting the value scheme. Open country life is channeled, controlled, and structured by their activities. Where the sheriff fails to take cognizance of their activities, he risks his strength.

Other groups are important because they exert a measure of strategic dominance over open country law enforcement. There are several groups of this kind but the only one that will be mentioned here is the political party. This is a kind of closed corporation, wherein assignments and duties are distributed with an eye to group victory on election day. Obligations incurred during the campaign are discharged by appointments as deputies or jailers, court house jobs, and other types of patronage. Yet curiously, the spoils system is self-limiting. There is a recognized point beyond which these preferential agreements violate the central values of personal worth and individualism, and thus constitute a threat to party survival. Short of that, the effect of the political party can be seen in the constituency of the sheriff's force.

THE SHERIFF AS A SOCIAL TYPE

Before the spring primaries in 1950, an effort was made to learn something of the voting habits of Star County. Informants were asked what kind of a man they felt would best fill the office of sheriff. The replies stressed a reputation for "fairness and good judgment." He should know the county intimately and should be fairly mature. He show know "how to get along with people." A candidate would present evidence of this by prosperity and success in business or farming.

The incumbent sheriff replied independently and in quite the same way. Looking back upon his own victory in 1946, he felt that the candidate should symbolize success in life first of all, for this aroused the voter's confidence and was an index of reliability. He should be mature and, of course, free of scandal. Beyond these —

Experience in law enforcement would come last. The people assume your ability to be a good sheriff if they check you off on the other three things. If you can show you have got along with people all your life, that you are moral and are old enough to be a little wise about things, they will be able to judge whether you will be a sheriff who is stern and mean and hard on people, or whether you will be kind and decent and treat people right, yet all the time honest and doing the job the best way you can. You can say what you would do if you were sheriff, but usually in Star County the candidates never have had experience in law enforcement and the public doesn't expect it.[5]

The social type that the voters have in mind as an ideal construct is thus almost identical to the construct which the sheriff had derived. He himself conformed to the desired social type. When he went before the people in 1946, he had thirty years' experience in the wholesale and retail meat trades, had prospered also as a handler of bulk petroleum products, and had held minor public offices by which he had established himself with the political party. He was well-known in the county, was equipped with many of the criteria on which Star County judges the worthy man, and could point to his business success as proof that he knew "how to get along with people." The "social person" in large measure reflected the values of the "social circle" by these means.

THE OFFICE OF SHERIFF

Sheriffs throughout the nation have been criticized so often in the popular press and in learned journals that a restatement would serve no purpose. Yet it should be clear by now that in many parts of the country, the office is almost impregnable.

In Illinois, the powers and duties of the sheriff are set forth in Chapter 125 of the revised statutes but these are extended and modified by other provisions liberally sprinkled elsewhere in the law. The resulting confusion places the sheriff in a position where he can interpret his job however he will. This means that he must exercise discretion, and in the process both the favored and the disaffected tend to regard him as both arbitrary and corrupt at one and the same time. The dilemma is especially marked over such issues as gambling and prostitution. Complaints are made to the sheriff ". . . but no one will swear out a warrant. We can't just go in there on suspicion. This is a free country. You can't search without a warrant and if no one will sign a complaint we can't do anything." Whatever the merits of this position, the point is that it prevails among sheriffs in Illinois and will persist until relevant statutes are codified. In the meanwhile, the sheriff is immune from at-

---

[5] Elsewhere in Illinois the political tradition is for the sheriff and his chief deputy or the sheriff and the county treasurer to alternate in office. In those counties prior experience in law enforcement is part of voter appeal. These regularities have not been established in Star County and, hence, prior experience is not demanded. It might even be a detriment.

tack on this score because this interpretation has the backing of both custom and court decisions.

From another point of view, the office is impregnable in Illinois because of the vital part it plays in the system of county government. The reference here is not to the way in which it controls crime, but to the jobs and moneys involved in its share of the local bureaucracy. In Star County, twenty-two persons were awarded jobs on the deputy force, in the jail, and in the court house in partial recognition of support to the sheriff during the 1946 campaign. As to finance, the annual reports of the county auditor, on at least one interpretation, suggest that the sheriff directed the income and outgo of about $100,000 a year during his term. Some of this went to salaries and allowed fees. About 60 per cent of the income was applied to expenses incurred in court house and jail maintenance. The implication is not that these payments were improper or excessive. The only inference is that many middlemen participate in the sheriff's affairs. They have an understandable stake in the perpetuation of the office as a fixture and can be relied upon to support it regardless of how well or how poorly it controls crime.

A third support to the office can be found in open country attitudes. Here the sheriff is seen as symbolizing local control over local problems — another bulwark against the encroachments of centralized state power. A fourth support grows out of the associations, both local and statewide, which the sheriff sets up while in office. In the discharge of duty, he maintains local contacts which can be depended upon to further whatever other political hopes he may have. Formal contacts beyond the county line with other sheriffs and informal contacts through the Illinois Sheriff's Association help entrench the office. By these means it becomes the repository for specialized police crafts with exclusive dominance over open country crime control. Coupled with the legal chaos which surrounds it and the control it holds over jobs and finances, these factors make the sheriff's office one of the most powerful links in the system of county government. Against these defenses, the assaults of critics avail but little.

CONSERVING THE PEACE

The social function of conserving the peace is influenced by the three broad components just reviewed. It is influenced also by the actual experience of peace-keeping. Within the sheriff's ranks a body of knowledge significant for open country law enforcement is gradually built up by trial and error. Prominent in this lore are the following six elements: terrain features and climatic changes; shifting public demand; the amenability of deputies to superior orders; their individual initiative; their knowledge of typical habit patterns; and a general guide for conduct in all trouble-cases.

The first five are self-explanatory. The last is more complex. In order to guard against the needless dissipation of energies, every sheriff must devise some effective principle to show him when to act. The Star County sheriff developed the following solution:

Public safety is our rule. If you were driving sixty miles an hour through a zoned area late at night with no traffic in the road, it would be against the law, but it's not morally wrong and you wouldn't be hurting the public safety. So we don't arrest you. But if you did that in day time when a lot of cars are on the highway, you would be a menace to yourself and everyone else. We would have to pull you in not only for the public's safety but for yours too. That's how we decide all these things.

This is another word for discretion. As stated earlier, its exercise becomes extremely involved when the conflict of interest is more subtle.

The dynamics of crime control in Star County are traceable to these six factors. Their product is what the *Uniform Crime Reports* call "offenses known." What of offenses not known? Informants who had reported offenses were interviewed and in almost every case they disclosed other offenses which they had not reported. As a general practice, the rule of silence is invoked in four circumstances: where the theft or offense "didn't amount to much," or where it was felt that a report "won't do any good"; where the threat of a report is countered by an apology, an offer of marriage, or restitution; where there is fear of reprisal, real or imagined; and where a report might threaten community harmony. This last involves extreme cases such as un- explained deaths, suspected incest, fires or explosions of unknown origin, and the like. It is impossible to get specific facts in these instances. However, ac- counts of these events are transmitted to the young and to the objective in- vestigator in a context designed to show the limits beyond which it is re- garded as unwise to resort to formal legal sanctions — unwise because it is felt that ultimate justice has or will be done, or because of the fear that group life will be shattered if neighbor must testify against neighbor.

In these "offenses not known" there is the suggestion that the open coun- try has a fairly high tolerance for lawlessness. A further issue remains. Of- fenses associated with the conduct of agriculture are often reported in the local press and in various local farm journals. These take many forms and many are embraced by the criminal code.[6] None was ever reported to the sheriff and he made no arrests for these offenses between 1946 and 1950. When committed, such offenses are handled by administrative agencies. The effect is to so condition local attitudes as to regard offenses running with agri-

[6] See Hannah, H. W., *Law For the Illinois Farmer,* Circular No. 632 (Col- lege of Agriculture, University of Illinois, Urbana, 1948).

culture as something other than crimes. There is an important extension here of Sutherland's earlier views on white collar crime.[7]

CONCLUSIONS:
TENTATIVE CHARACTERISTICS
OF OPEN COUNTRY CRIME

An analysis of 5,700 offenders arrested by the sheriff in Star County between 1945 and 1949 shows many things, a few of which are these:

1. The annual arrest rate for persons from Hopkins (population 37,000) who committed offenses beyond the city limits was 1373.62 per 100,000. The comparable rate for all other Star County residents was 448.43.

It is doubtful whether these figures by themselves confirm older views on the excessive criminality of the urban dweller. The rate may be normal for an open country town like Hopkins. Then too, factors such as class status and the pattern of leisure time behavior need to be considered before the excess can be established generally.

2. Rates for reported offenses occurring *in* the open country vary according to the characteristics of each community. Communities in Star County outside of Hopkins varied in their average annual reported rates from 691.0 to 8,000.0.

3. The relatively high proportion of offenses against the person, long cited for rural areas, seems to hold for Star County viewed as an open country region. Thirteen per cent of all arrests were for offenses against the person, the rest were for offenses against property. This would probably change if the reporting habits of the open country were considered. The inclusion of offenses against property not now reported would reduce the ratio.

4. Persons engaged in agriculture are represented among known offenders in about one half their chance share. However, a whole host of offenses associated with agriculture are eliminated from the sheriff's function by custom. If these were included, the crime rate of the agricultural class would go up.

5. Offenders arrested by the Star County sheriff appear to be from three to five years younger on the average than for the country as a whole. This seems to be due chiefly to the jail confinement of juveniles, whose inclusion in this study depressed the mean. Any sheriff in Illinois can probably refuse to receive juveniles in his jail on the grounds that the intent of the "Dependent, Neglected, and Delinquent Children's Act" makes it unlawful. However, such refusals are unknown.

[7] Sutherland, E. H., *White Collar Crime* (New York: Dryden Press, 1950).

6. The preponderant tendency is for all offenders to leave the jail at the end of the second day. Seventy-five per cent leave within ten days. About 3 per cent of all offenders are sentenced to jail as punishment. An additional 5 per cent are sentenced to the state penal farms for periods of less than one year. Thus 8 per cent of all offenders receive a jail or like sentence.

In the main, offenders are disposed of in routine fashion. There is little concern over the causes of their crimes or the conditions surrounding their occurrence. As is true everywhere else, the administration of criminal justice in Star County is trapped by ritual. This is a commentary, not upon the sheriff nor upon the county judge nor the local state's attorney. It is a commentary upon the system of which they are parts.

These findings from Star County suggest that open country crime does not conform in all particulars to general ideas of crime beyond the metropolis thus far advanced. However, generalizations can hardly be made until further studies have been conducted along similar lines. Important by-products of such studies will probably be a fresh understanding of the law and of law enforcement. These may be even more important than the actual delineation of open country crime.[8]

[8] Llewellyn, Karl N., "Law and the Social Sciences," *American Sociological Review,* Vol. 14, No. 4, August 1949, pp. 451–462.

The Police on Skid-Row:
A Study
of Peace Keeping

EGON BITTNER

The prototype of modern police organization, the Metropolitan Police of London, was created to replace an antiquated and corrupt system of law enforcement. The early planners were motivated by the mixture of hard-headed business rationality and humane sentiment that characterized liberal British thought of the first half of the nineteenth century.[1] Partly to meet the objections of a parliamentary committee, which was opposed to the establishment of the police in England, and partly because it was in line with their own thinking, the planners sought to produce an instrument that could not readily be used in the play of internal power politics but which would, instead, advance and protect conditions favorable to industry and commerce and to urban civil life in general. These intentions were not very specific and had to be reconciled with the existing structures of governing, administering justice, and keeping the peace. Consequently, the locus and mandate of the police in the modern polity were ill-defined at the outset. On the one hand, the new institution was to be a part of the executive branch of government, organized, funded, and staffed in accordance with standards that were typical for the entire system of the executive. On the other hand, the duties that were given to the police organization brought it under direct control of the judiciary in its day-to-day operation.

The dual patronage of the police by the executive and the judiciary is characteristic for all democratically governed countries. Moreover, it is generally the case, or at least it is deemed desirable, that judges *rather than* executive officials have control over police use and procedure.[2] This prefer-

Reprinted from *American Sociological Review*, 32 (October 1967), pp. 699–715, by permission of the author and the American Sociological Association.

[1] The bill for a Metropolitan Police was actually enacted under the sponsorship of Robert Peel, the Home Secretary in the Tory Government of the Duke of Wellington. There is, however, no doubt that it was one of the several reform tendencies that Peel assimilated into Tory politics in his long career. Cf. J. L. Lyman, "The Metropolitan Police Act of 1829," *Journal of Criminal Law, Criminology and Police Science*, 55 (1964), 141–154.

[2] Jerome Hall, "Police and Law in a Democratic Society," *Indiana Law Journal*, 28 (1953), 133–177. Though other authors are less emphatic on this point, judicial control is generally taken for granted. The point has been made, however, that in modern times judicial control over the police has been asserted mainly because of the default of any other general controlling authority, cf. E. L. Barrett, Jr., "Police Practice and the Law," *California Law Review*, 50 (1962), 11–55.

ence is based on two considerations. First, in the tenets of the democratic creed, the possibility of direct control of the police by a government in power is repugnant.[3] Even when the specter of the police state in its more ominous forms is not a concern, close ties between those who govern and those who police are viewed as a sign of political corruption.[4] Hence, mayors, governors, and cabinet officers — although the nominal superiors of the police — tend to maintain, or to pretend, a hands-off policy. Second, it is commonly understood that the main function of the police is the control of crime. Since the concept of crime belongs wholly to the law, and its treatment is exhaustively based on considerations of legality, police procedure automatically stands under the same system of review that controls the administration of justice in general.

By nature, judicial control encompasses only those aspects of police activity that are directly related to full-dress legal prosecution of offenders. The judiciary has neither the authority nor the means to direct, supervise, and review those activities of the police that do not result in prosecution. Yet such other activities are unavoidable, frequent, and largely within the realm of public expectations. It might be assumed that in this domain of practice the police are under executive control. This is not the case, however, except in a marginal sense.[5] Not only are police departments generally free to determine what need be done and how, but aside from informal pressures they are given scant direction in these matters. Thus, there appear to exist two relatively independent domains of police activity. In one, their methods are constrained by the prospect of the future disposition of a case in the courts; in the other, they operate under some other consideration and largely with no structured and continuous outside constraint. Following the terminology suggested by Michael Banton, they may be said to function in the first instance as "law officers" and in the second instance as "peace officers."[6] It must be emphasized that the designation "peace officer" is a residual term, with only some vaguely presumptive content. The role, as Banton speaks of

---

[3] A. C. German, F. D. Day and R. R. J. Gallati, *Introduction to Law Enforcement* (Springfield, Ill.: C. C Thomas, 1966); "One concept, in particular, should be kept in mind. A dictatorship can never exist unless the police system of the country is under the absolute control of the dictator. There is no other way to uphold a dictatorship except by terror, and the instrument of this total terror is the secret police, whatever its name. In every country where freedom has been lost, law enforcement has been a dominant instrument in destroying it" (p. 80).

[4] The point is frequently made; cf. Raymond B. Fosdick, *American Police Systems* (New York: Century Company, 1920); Bruce Smith, *Police Systems in the United States*, 2nd rev. ed. (New York: Harper, 1960).

[5] The executive margin of control is set mainly in terms of budgetary determinations and the mapping of some formal aspects of the organization of departments.

[6] Michael Banton, *The Policeman in the Community* (New York: Basic Books, 1964), pp. 6–7 and 127 ff.

it, is supposed to encompass all occupational routines not directly related to making arrests, without, however, specifying what determines the limits of competence and availability of the police in such actions.

Efforts to characterize a large domain of activities of an important public agency have so far yielded only negative definitions. We know that they do not involve arrests; we also know that they do not stand under judicial control, and that they are not, in any important sense, determined by specific executive or legislative mandates. In police textbooks and manuals, these activities receive only casual attention, and the role of the "peace officer" is typically stated in terms suggesting that his work is governed mainly by the individual officer's personal wisdom, integrity, and altruism.[7] Police departments generally keep no records of procedures that do not involve making arrests. Policemen, when asked, insist that they merely use common sense when acting as "peace officers," though they tend to emphasize the elements of experience and practice in discharging the role adequately. All this ambiguity is the more remarkable for the fact that peace keeping tasks, i.e., procedures not involving the formal legal remedy of arrest, were explicitly built into the program of the modern police from the outset.[8] The early executives of the London police saw with great clarity that their organization had a dual function. While it was to be an arm of the administration of justice, in respect of which it developed certain techniques for bringing offenders to trial, it was also expected to function apart from, and at times in lieu of, the employment of full-dress legal procedure. Despite its early origin, despite a great deal of public knowledge about it, despite the fact that it is routinely done by policemen, no one can say with any clarity what it means to do a good job of keeping the peace. To be sure, there is vague consensus that when policemen direct, aid, inform, pacify, warn, discipline, roust, and do whatever else they do without making arrests, they do this with some reference to the circumstances of the occasion and, thus, somehow contribute to the maintenance of the peace and order. Peace keeping appears to be a solution to an unknown problem arrived at by unknown means.

The following is an attempt to clarify conceptually the mandate and the practice of keeping the peace. The effort will be directed not to the formulation of a comprehensive solution of the problem but to a detailed consideration of some aspects of it. Only in order to place the particular into the overall domain to which it belongs will the structural determinants of keep-

---

[7] R. Bruce Holmgren, *Primary Police Functions* (New York: William C. Copp, 1962).

[8] Cf. Lyman, *op. cit.,* p. 153; F. C. Mather, *Public Order in the Age of the Chartists* (Manchester: Manchester University Press, 1959), chapter IV. See also Robert H. Bremer, "Police, Penal and Parole Policies in Cleveland and Toledo," *American Journal of Economics and Sociology,* 14 (1955), 387–398, for similar recognition in the United States at about the turn of this century.

ing the peace in general be discussed. By structural determinants are meant the typical situations that policemen perceive as *demand conditions* for action without arrest. This will be followed by a description of peace keeping in skid-row districts, with the object of identifying those aspects of it that constitute a *practical skill*.

Since the major object of this paper is to elucidate peace keeping practice as a skilled performance, it is necessary to make clear how the use of the term is intended.

Practical skill will be used to refer to those methods of doing certain things, and to the information that underlies the use of the methods, that *practitioners themselves* view as proper and efficient. Skill is, therefore, a stable orientation to work tasks that is relatively independent of the personal feelings and judgments of those who employ it. Whether the exercise of this skilled performance is desirable or not, and whether it is based on correct information or not, are specifically outside the scope of interest of this presentation. The following is deliberately confined to a description of what police patrolmen consider to be the reality of their work circumstances, what they do, and what they feel they must do to do a good job. That the practice is thought to be determined by normative standards of skill minimizes but does not eliminate the factors of personal interest or inclination. Moreover, the distribution of skill varies among practitioners in the very standards they set for themselves. For example, we will show that patrolmen view a measure of rough informality as good practice vis-à-vis skid-row inhabitants. By this standard, patrolmen who are "not rough enough," or who are "too rough," or whose roughness is determined by personal feelings rather than by situational exigencies, are judged to be poor craftsmen.

The description and analysis are based on twelve months of field work with the police departments of two large cities west of the Mississippi. Eleven weeks of this time were spent in skid-row and skid-row-like districts. The observations were augmented by approximately one hundred interviews with police officers of all ranks. The formulations that will be proposed were discussed in these interviews. They were recognized by the respondents as elements of standard practice. The respondents' recognition was often accompanied by remarks indicating that they had never thought about things in this way and that they were not aware how standardized police work was.

STRUCTURAL DEMAND CONDITIONS
OF PEACE KEEPING

There exist at least five types of relatively distinct circumstances that produce police activities that do not involve invoking the law and that are only in a trivial sense determined by those considerations of legality that determine law enforcement. This does not mean that these activities are illegal but merely that there is no legal directive that informs the acting policeman whether what he does must be done or how it is to be done. In these circumstances, policemen act as all-purpose and terminal remedial agents, and the confronted problem is solved in the field. If these practices stand under any kind of review at all, and typically they do not, it is only through internal police department control.

1. Although the executive branch of government generally refrains from exercising a controlling influence over the direction of police interest, it manages to extract certain performances from it. Two important examples of this are the supervision of certain licensed services and premises and the regulation of traffic.[9] With respect to the first, the police tend to concentrate on what might be called the moral aspects of establishments rather than on questions relating to the technical adequacy of the service. This orientation is based on the assumption that certain types of businesses lend themselves to exploitation for undesirable and illegal purposes. Since this tendency cannot be fully controlled, it is only natural that the police will be inclined to favor licensees who are at least cooperative. This, however, transforms the task from the mere scrutiny of credentials and the passing of judgments, to the creation and maintenance of a network of connections that conveys influence, pressure, and information. The duty to inspect is the background of this network, but the resulting contacts acquire additional value for solving crimes and maintaining public order. Bartenders, shopkeepers, and hotel clerks become, for patrolmen, a resource that must be continuously serviced by visits and exchanges of favors. While it is apparent that this condition lends itself to corrupt exploitation by individual officers, even the most flawlessly honest policeman must participate in this network of exchanges if he is to function adequately. Thus, engaging in such exchanges becomes an occupational task that demands attention and time.

Regulation of traffic is considerably less complex. More than anything else, traffic control symbolizes the autonomous authority of policemen. Their commands generally are met with unquestioned compliance. Even when they issue citations, which seemingly refer the case to the courts, it is common practice for the accused to view the allegation as a finding against him and to pay the fine. Police officials emphasize that it is more important to be circumspect than legalistic in traffic control. Officers are often reminded that a large segment of the public has no other contacts with the police, and that the field lends itself to public relations work by the line personnel.[10]

2. Policemen often do not arrest persons who have committed minor offences in circumstances in which the arrest is technically possible. This prac-

[9] Smith, *op. cit.*, pp. 15 ff.
[10] Orlando W. Wilson, "Police Authority in a Free Society," *Journal of Criminal Law, Criminology and Police Science*, 54 (1964), 175–177.

tice has recently received considerable attention in legal and sociological literature. The studies were motivated by the realization that "police decisions not to invoke the criminal process determine the outer limits of law enforcement."[11] From these researches, it was learned that the police tend to impose more stringent criteria of law enforcement on certain segments of the community than on others.[12] It was also learned that, from the perspective of the administration of justice, the decisions not to make arrests often are based on compelling reasons.[13] It is less well appreciated that policemen often not only refrain from invoking the law formally but also employ alternative sanctions. For example, it is standard practice that violators are warned not to repeat the offense. This often leads to patrolmen's "keeping an eye" on certain persons. Less frequent, though not unusual, is the practice of direct disciplining of offenders, especially when they are juveniles, which occasionally involves inducing them to repair the damage occasioned by their misconduct.[14]

The power to arrest and the freedom not to arrest can be used in cases that do not involve patent offenses. An officer can say to a person whose behavior he wishes to control, "I'll let you go this time!" without indicating to him that he could not have been arrested in any case. Nor is this always deliberate misrepresentation, for in many cases the law is sufficiently ambiguous to allow alternative interpretations. In short, not to make an arrest is rarely, if ever, merely a decision not to act; it is most often a decision to act alternatively. In the case of minor offenses, to make an arrest often is merely one of several possible proper actions.

3. There exists a public demand for police intervention in matters that contain no criminal and often no legal aspects.[15] For example, it is commonly assumed that officers will be available to arbitrate quarrels, to pacify the unruly, and to help in keeping order. They are supposed also to aid people in trouble, and there is scarcely a human predicament imaginable for which police aid has not been solicited and obtained at one time or another. Most authors writing about the police consider such activities only marginally related to the police mandate. This view fails to reckon with the fact that the availability of these performances is taken for granted and the police assign a substantial amount of their resources to such work. Although this work can-

[11] Joseph Goldstein, "Police Discretion Not to Invoke the Criminal Process," *Yale Law Journal,* 69 (1960), 543.

[12] Jerome Skolnick, *Justice Without Trial* (New York: Wiley, 1966).

[13] Wayne LaFave, "The Police and Nonenforcement of the Law," *Wisconsin Law Review* (1962), 104–137 and 179–239.

[14] Nathan Goldman, *The Differential Selection of Juvenile Offenders for Court Appearance* (National Research and Information Center, National Council on Crime and Delinquency, 1963), pp. 114 ff.

[15] Elaine Cumming, Ian Cumming and Laura Edell, "Policeman as Philosopher, Guide and Friend," *Social Problems,* 12 (1965), 276–286.

not be subsumed under the concept of legal action, it does involve the exercise of a form of authority that most people associate with the police. In fact, no matter how trivial the occasion, the device of "calling the cops" transforms any problem. It implies that a situation is, or is getting, out of hand. Police responses to public demands are always oriented to this implication, and the risk of proliferation of troubles makes every call a potentially serious matter.[16]

4. Certain mass phenomena of either a regular or a spontaneous nature require direct monitoring. Most important is the controlling of crowds in incipient stages of disorder. The specter of mob violence frequently calls for measures that involve coercion, including the use of physical force. Legal theory allows, of course, that public officials are empowered to use coercion in situations of imminent danger.[17] Unfortunately, the doctrine is not sufficiently specific to be of much help as a rule of practice. It is based on the assumption of the adventitiousness of danger, and thus does not lend itself readily to elaborations that could direct the routines of early detection and prevention of untoward developments. It is interesting that the objective of preventing riots by informal means posed one of the central organizational problems for the police in England during the era of the Chartists.[18]

5. The police have certain special duties with respect to persons who are viewed as less than fully accountable for their actions. Examples of those eligible for special consideration are those who are under age[19] and those who are mentally ill.[20] Although it is virtually never acknowledged explicitly, those receiving special treatment -include people who do not lead "normal" lives and who occupy a pariah status in society. This group includes residents of ethnic ghettos, certain types of bohemians and vagabonds, and persons of known criminal background. The special treatment of children and of sick persons is permissively sanctioned by the law, but the special treatment of others is, in principle, opposed by the leading theme of legality and the tenets of the democratic faith.[21] The important point is not that such persons are

---

16 There is little doubt that many requests for service are turned down by the police, especially when they are made over the telephone or by mail, cf. LaFave, *op. cit.*, p. 212, n. 124. The uniformed patrolman, however, finds it virtually impossible to leave the scene without becoming involved in some way or another.

17 Hans Kelsen, *General Theory of Law and State* (New York: Russell & Russell, 1961), pp. 278–279; H. L. A. Hart, *The Concept of Law* (Oxford: Clarendon Press, 1961), pp. 20–21.

18 Mather, *op. cit.;* see also, Jenifer Hart, "Reform of the Borough Police, 1835–1856," *English History Review*, 70 (1955), 411–427.

19 Francis A. Allen, *The Borderland of Criminal Justice* (Chicago: University of Chicago Press, 1964).

20 Egon Bittner, "Police Discretion in Emergency Apprehension of Mentally Ill Persons," *Social Problems*, 14 (1967), 278–292.

21 It bears mentioning, however, that differential treatment is not unique with the police, but is also in many ways representative for the administra-

arrested more often than others, which is quite true, but that they are perceived by the police as producing a special problem that necessitates continuous attention and the use of special procedures.

The five types of demand conditions do not exclude the possibility of invoking the criminal process. Indeed, arrests do occur quite frequently in all these circumstances. But the concerns generated in these areas cause activities that usually do not terminate in an arrest. When arrests are made, there exist, at least in the ideal, certain criteria by reference to which the arrest can be judged as having been made more or less properly, and there are some persons who, in the natural course of events, actually judge the performance.[22] But for actions not resulting in arrest there are no such criteria and no such judges. How, then, can one speak of such actions as necessary and proper? Since there does not exist any official answer to this query, and since policemen act in the role of "peace officers" pretty much without external direction or constraint, the question comes down to asking how the policeman himself knows whether he has any business with a person he does not arrest, and if so, what that business might be. Furthermore, if there exists a domain of concerns and activities that is largely independent of the law enforcement mandate, it is reasonable to assume that it will exercise some degree of influence on how and to what ends the law is invoked in cases of arrests.

Skid-row presents one excellent opportunity to study these problems. The area contains a heavy concentration of persons who do not live "normal" lives in terms of prevailing standards of middle-class morality. Since the police respond to this situation by intensive patrolling, the structure of peace keeping should be readily observable. Needless to say, the findings and conclusions will not be necessarily generalizable to other types of demand conditions.

THE PROBLEM OF
KEEPING THE PEACE
IN SKID-ROW

Skid-row has always occupied a special place among the various forms of urban life. While other areas are perceived as being different in many ways, skid-row is seen as completely different. Though it is located in the heart of civilization, it is viewed as containing aspects of the primordial jungle, calling

tion of justice in general; cf. J. E. Carlin, Jan Howard and S. L. Messinger, "Civil Justice and the Poor," *Law and Society*, 1 (1966), 9–89; Jacobus tenBroek (ed.), *The Law of the Poor* (San Francisco: Chandler Publishing Co., 1966).

[22] This is, however, true only in the ideal. It is well known that a substantial number of persons who are arrested are subsequently released without ever being charged and tried, cf. Barret, *op. cit.*

for missionary activities and offering opportunities for exotic adventure. While each inhabitant individually can be seen as tragically linked to the vicissitudes of "normal" life, allowing others to say "here but for the Grace of God go I," those who live there are believed to have repudiated the entire role-casting scheme of the majority and to live apart from normalcy. Accordingly, the traditional attitude of civic-mindedness toward skid-row has been dominated by the desire to contain it and to salvage souls from its clutches.[23] The specific task of containment has been left to the police. That this task pressed upon the police some rather special duties has never come under explicit consideration, either from the government that expects control or from the police departments that implement it. Instead, the prevailing method of carrying out the task is to assign patrolmen to the area on a fairly permanent basis and to allow them to work out their own ways of running things. External influence is confined largely to the supply of support and facilities, on the one hand, and to occasional expressions of criticism about the overall conditions, on the other. Within the limits of available resources and general expectations, patrolmen are supposed to know what to do and are free to do it.[24]

Patrolmen who are more or less permanently assigned to skid-row districts tend to develop a conception of the nature of their "domain" that is surprisingly uniform. Individual officers differ in many aspects of practice, emphasize different concerns, and maintain different contacts, but they are in fundamental agreement about the structure of skid-row life. This relatively uniform conception includes an implicit formulation of the problem of keeping the peace in skid-row.

In the view of experienced patrolmen, life on skid-row is fundamentally different from life in other parts of society. To be sure, they say, around its geographic limits the area tends to blend into the surrounding environment, and its population always encompasses some persons who are only transitionally associated with it. Basically, however, skid-row is perceived as the natural habitat of people who lack the capacities and commitments to live

[23] The literature on skid-row is voluminous. The classic in the field is Nels Anderson, *The Hobo* (Chicago: University of Chicago Press, 1923). Samuel E. Wallace, *Skid-Row as a Way of Life* (Totowa, N.J.: The Bedminster Press, 1965), is a more recent descriptive account and contains a useful bibliography. Donald A. Bogue, *Skid-Row in American Cities* (Chicago: Community and Family Center, University of Chicago, 1963), contains an exhaustive quantitative survey of Chicago skid-row.

[24] One of the two cities described in this paper also employed the procedure of the "round-up" of drunks. In this, the police van toured the skid-row area twice daily, during the mid-afternoon and early evening hours, and the officers who manned it picked up drunks they sighted. A similar procedure is used in New York's Bowery and the officers who do it are called "condition men." Cf. *Bowery Project,* Bureau of Applied Social Research, Columbia University, Summary Report of a Study Undertaken under Contract Approved by the Board of Estimates (1963, mimeo.), p. 11.

"normal" lives on a sustained basis. The presence of these people defines the nature of social reality in the area. In general, and especially in casual encounters, the presumption of incompetence and of the disinclination to be "normal" is the leading theme for the interpretation of all actions and relations. Not only do people approach one another in this manner, but presumably they also expect to be approached in this way, and they conduct themselves accordingly.

In practice, the restriction of interactional possibilities that is based on the patrolman's stereotyped conception of skid-row residents is always subject to revision and modification toward particular individuals. Thus, it is entirely possible, and not unusual, for patrolmen to view certain skid-row inhabitants in terms that involve non-skid-row aspects of normality. Instances of such approaches and relationships invariably involve personal acquaintance and the knowledge of a good deal of individually qualifying information. Such instances are seen, despite their relative frequency, as exceptions to the rule. The awareness of the possibility of breakdown, frustration, and betrayal is ever-present, basic wariness is never wholly dissipated, and undaunted trust can never be fully reconciled with presence on skid-row.

What patrolmen view as normal on skid-row — and what they also think is taken for granted as "life as usual" by the inhabitants — is not easily summarized. It seems to focus on the idea that the dominant consideration governing all enterprise and association is directed to the occasion of the moment. Nothing is thought of as having a background that might have led up to the present in terms of some compelling moral or practical necessity. There are some exceptions to this rule, of course: the police themselves, and those who run certain establishments, are perceived as engaged in important and necessary activities. But in order to carry them out they, too, must be geared to the overall atmosphere of fortuitousness. In this atmosphere, the range of control that persons have over one another is exceedingly narrow. Good faith, even where it is valued, is seen merely as a personal matter. Its violations are the victim's own hard luck, rather than demonstrable violations of property. There is only a private sense of irony at having been victimized. The overall air is not so much one of active distrust as it is one of irrelevance of trust; as patrolmen often emphasize, the situation does not necessarily cause all relations to be predatory, but the possibility of exploitation is not checked by the expectation that it will not happen.

Just as the past is seen by the policeman as having only the most attenuated relevance to the present, so the future implications of present situations are said to be generally devoid of prospective coherence. No venture, especially no joint venture, can be said to have a strongly predictable future in line with its initial objectives. It is a matter of adventitious circumstance whether or not matters go as anticipated. That which is not within the grasp of momentary control is outside of practical social reality.

Though patrolmen see the temporal framework of the occasion of the moment mainly as a lack of trustworthiness, they also recognize that it involves more than merely the personal motives of individuals. In addition to the fact that everybody *feels* that things matter only at the moment, irresponsibility takes an *objectified* form on skid-row. The places the residents occupy, the social relations they entertain, and the activities that engage them are not meaningfully connected over time. Thus, for example, address, occupation, marital status, etc., matter much less on skid-row than in any other part of society. The fact that present whereabouts, activities, and affiliations imply neither continuity nor direction means that life on skid-row lacks a socially structured background of accountability. Of course, everybody's life contains some sequential incongruities, but in the life of a skid-row inhabitant every moment is an accident. That a man has no "address" in the future that could be in some way inferred from where he is and what he does makes him a person of *radically reduced visibility*. If he disappears from sight and one wishes to locate him, it is virtually impossible to systematize the search. All one can know with relative certainty is that he will be somewhere on some skid-row and the only thing one can do is to trace the factual contiguities of his whereabouts.

It is commonly known that the police are expert in finding people and that they have developed an exquisite technology involving special facilities and procedures of sleuthing. It is less well appreciated that all this technology builds upon those socially structured features of everyday life that render persons findable in the first place.

Under ordinary conditions, the query as to where a person is can be addressed, from the outset, to a restricted realm of possibilities that can be further narrowed by looking into certain places and asking certain persons. The map of whereabouts that normally competent persons use whenever they wish to locate someone is constituted by the basic facts of membership in society. Insofar as memberhip consists of status incumbencies, each of which has an adumbrated future that substantially reduces unpredictability, it is itself a guarantee of the order within which it is quite difficult to get lost. Membership is thus visible not only now but also as its own projection into the future. It is in terms of this prospective availability that the skid-row inhabitant is a person of reduced visibility. His membership is viewed as extraordinary because its extension into the future is *not* reduced to a restricted realm of possibilities. Neither his subjective dispositions, nor his circumstances, indicate that he is oriented to any particular long-range interests. But, as he may claim every contingent opportunity, his claims are always seen as based on slight merit or right, at least to the extent that interfering with them does not constitute a substantial denial of his freedom.

This, then, constitutes the problem of keeping the peace on skid-row. Considerations of momentary expediency are seen as having unqualified priority as maxims of conduct; consequently, the controlling influences of the pursuit of sustained interests are presumed to be absent.

THE PRACTICES OF
KEEPING THE PEACE
IN SKID-ROW

From the perspective of society as a whole, skid-row inhabitants appear troublesome in a variety of ways. The uncommitted life attributed to them is perceived as inherently offensive; its very existence arouses indignation and contempt. More important, however, is the feeling that persons who have repudiated the entire role-status casting system of society, persons whose lives forever collapse into a succession of random moments, are seen as constituting a practical risk. As they have nothing to foresake, nothing is thought safe from them.[25]

The skid-row patrolman's concept of his mandate includes an awareness of this presumed risk. He is constantly attuned to the possibility of violence, and he is convinced that things to which the inhabitants have free access are as good as lost. But his concern is directed toward the continuous condition of peril *in the area* rather than *for society in general*. While he is obviously conscious of the presence of many persons who have committed crimes outside of skid-row and will arrest them when they come to his attention, this is a peripheral part of his routine activities. In general, the skid-row patrolman and his superiors take for granted that his main business is to keep the peace and enforce the laws *on skid-row*, and that he is involved only incidentally in protecting society at large. Thus, his task is formulated basically as the protection of putative predators from one another. The maintenance of peace and safety is difficult because everyday life on skid-row is viewed as an open field for reciprocal exploitation. As the lives of the inhabitants lack the prospective coherence associated with status incumbency, the realization of self-interest does not produce order. Hence, mechanisms that control risk must work primarily from without.

---

[25] An illuminating parallel to the perception of skid-row can be found in the more traditional concept of vagabondage. Cf. Alexandre Vexliard, *Introduction à la Sociologie du Vagabondage* (Paris: Librairie Marcel Rivière, 1956), and "La Disparition du Vagabondage comme Fléau Social Universel," *Revue de L'Institut de Sociologie* (1963), 53–79. The classic account of English conditions up to the 19th century is C. J. Ribton-Turner, *A History of Vagrants and Vagrancy and Beggars and Begging* (London: Chapman and Hall, 1887).

External containment, to be effective, must be oriented to the realities of existence. Thus, the skid-row patrolman employs an approach that he views as appropriate to the *ad hoc* nature of skid-row life. The following are the three most prominent elements of this approach. First, the seasoned patrolman seeks to acquire a richly particularized knowledge of people and places in the area. Second, he gives the consideration of strict culpability a subordinate status among grounds for remedial sanction. Third, his use and choice of coercive interventions is determined mainly by exigencies of situations and with little regard for possible long range effects on individual persons.

The Particularization of Knowledge

The patrolman's orientation to people on skid-row is structured basically by the presupposition that if he does not know a man personally there is very little that he can assume about him. This rule determines his interaction with people who live on skid-row. Since the area also contains other types of persons, however, its applicability is not universal. To some such persons it does not apply at all, and it has a somewhat mitigated significance with certain others. For example, some persons encountered on skid-row can be recognized immediately as outsiders. Among them are workers who are employed in commercial and industrial enterprises that abut the area, persons who come for the purpose of adventurous "slumming," and some patrons of second-hand stores and pawn shops. Even with very little experience, it is relatively easy to identify these people by appearance, demeanor, and the time and place of their presence. The patrolman maintains an impersonal attitude toward them, and they are, under ordinary circumstances, not the objects of his attention.[26]

Clearly set off from these outsiders are the residents and the entire corps of personnel that services skid-row. It would be fair to say that one of the main routine activities of patrolmen is the establishment and maintenance of familiar relationships with individual members of these groups. Officers emphasize their interest in this, and they maintain that their grasp of and control over skid-row is precisely commensurate with the extent to which they "know the people." By this they do not mean having a quasi-theoretical understanding of human nature but rather the common practice of individualized and reciprocal recognition. As this group encompasses both those who render services on skid-row and those who are serviced, individualized interest is not always based on the desire to overcome uncertainty. Instead, relations with

[26] Several patrolmen complained about the influx of "tourists" into skid-row. Since such "tourists" are perceived as seeking illicit adventure, they receive little sympathy from patrolmen when they complain about being victimized.

service personnel become absorbed into the network of particularized attention. Ties between patrolmen, on the one hand, and businessmen, managers, and workers, on the other hand, are often defined in terms of shared or similar interests. It bears mentioning that many persons live *and* work on skid-row. Thus, the distinction between those who service and those who are serviced is not a clearcut dichotomy but a spectrum of affiliations.

As a general rule, the skid-row patrolman possesses an immensely detailed factual knowledge of his beat. He knows, and knows a great deal about, a large number of residents. He is likely to know every person who manages or works in the local bars, hotels, shops, stores, and missions. Moreover, he probably knows every public and private place inside and out. Finally, he ordinarily remembers countless events of the past which he can recount by citing names, dates and places with remarkable precision. Though there are always some threads missing in the fabric of information, it is continuously woven and mended even as it is being used. New facts, however, are added to the texture, not in terms of structured categories but in terms of adjoining known realities. In other words, the content and organization of the patrolman's knowledge is primarily ideographic and only vestigially, if at all, nomothetic.

Individual patrolmen vary in the extent to which they make themselves available or actively pursue personal acquaintances. But even the most aloof are continuously greeted and engaged in conversations that indicate a background of individualistic associations. While this scarcely has the appearance of work, because of its casual character, patrolmen do not view it as an optional activity. In the course of making their rounds, patrolmen seem to have access to every place, and their entry causes no surprise or consternation. Instead, the entry tends to lead to informal exchanges of small talk. At times the rounds include entering hotels and gaining access to rooms or dormitories, often for no other purpose than asking the occupants how things are going. In all this, patrolmen address innumerable persons by name and are in turn addressed by name. The conversational style that characterizes these exchanges is casual to an extent that by non-skid-row standards might suggest intimacy. Not only does the officer himself avoid all terms of deference and respect but he does not seem to expect or demand them. For example, a patrolman said to a man radiating an alcoholic glow on the street, "You've got enough of a heat on now; I'll give you ten minutes to get your ass off the street!" Without stopping, the man answered, "Oh, why don't you go and piss in your own pot!" The officer's only response was, "All right, in ten minutes you're either in bed or on your way to the can."

This kind of expressive freedom is an intricately limited privilege. Persons of acquaintance are entitled to it and appear to exercise it mainly in routinized encounters. But strangers, too, can use it with impunity. The safe way of gaining the privilege is to respond to the patrolman in ways that do not challenge his right to ask questions and issue commands. Once the concession is made that the officer is entitled to inquire into a man's background, business, and intentions, and that he is entitled to obedience, there opens a field of colloquial license. A patrolman seems to grant expressive freedom in recognition of a person's acceptance of his access to areas of life ordinarily defined as private and subject to coercive control only under special circumstances. While patrolmen accept and seemingly even cultivate the rough *quid pro quo* of informality, and while they do not expect sincerity, candor, or obedience in their dealings with the inhabitants, they do not allow the rejection of their approach.

The explicit refusal to answer questions of a personal nature and the demand to know why the questions are asked significantly enhances a person's chances of being arrested on some minor charge. While most patrolmen tend to be personally indignant about this kind of response and use the arrest to compose their own hurt feelings, this is merely a case of affect being in line with the method. There are other officers who proceed in the same manner without taking offense, or even with feelings of regret. Such patrolmen often maintain that their colleagues' affective involvement is a corruption of an essentially valid technique. The technique is oriented to the goal of maintaining operational control. The patrolman's conception of this goal places him hierarchically above whomever he approaches, and makes him the sole judge of the propriety of the occasion. As he alone is oriented to this goal, and as he seeks to attain it by means of individualized access to persons, those who frustrate him are seen as motivated at best by the desire to "give him a hard time" and at worst by some darkly devious purpose.

Officers are quite aware that the directness of their approach and the demands they make are difficult to reconcile with the doctrines of civil liberties, but they maintain that they are in accord with the general freedom of access that persons living on skid-row normally grant one another. That is, they believe that the imposition of personalized and far-reaching control is in tune with standard expectancies. In terms of these expectancies, people are not so much denied the right to privacy as they are seen as not having any privacy. Thus, officers seek to install themselves in the center of people's lives and let the consciousness of their presence play the part of conscience.

When talking about the practical necessity of an aggressively personal approach, officers do not refer merely to the need for maintaining control over lives that are open in the direction of the untoward. They also see it as the basis for the supply of certain valued services to inhabitants of skid-row. The coerced or conceded access to persons often imposes on the patrolman tasks that are, in the main, in line with these persons' expressed or implied interest. In asserting this connection, patrolmen note that they frequently help people to obtain meals, lodging, employment, that they direct them to welfare and health services, and that they aid them in various other ways. Though patrolmen tend to describe such services mainly as the product of their own altruism, they also say that their colleagues who avoid them are simply doing a poor job of patrolling. The acceptance of the need to help people is based on the realization that the hungry, the sick, and the troubled are a potential source of problems. Moreover, that patrolmen will help people is part of the background expectancies of life on skid-row. Hotel clerks normally call policemen when someone gets so sick as to need attention; merchants expect to be taxed, in a manner of speaking, to meet the pressing needs of certain persons; and the inhabitants do not hesitate to accept, solicit, and demand every kind of aid. The domain of the patrolman's service activity is virtually limitless, and it is no exaggeration to say that the solution of every conceivable problem has at one time or another been attempted by a police officer. In one observed instance, a patrolman unceremoniously entered the room of a man he had never seen before. The man, who gave no indication that he regarded the officer's entry and questions as anything but part of life as usual, related a story of having had his dentures stolen by his wife. In the course of the subsequent rounds, the patrolman sought to locate the woman and the dentures. This did not become the evening's project but was attended to while doing other things. In the densely matted activities of the patrolman, the questioning became one more strand, not so much to be pursued to its solution as a theme that organized the memory of one more man known individually. In all this, the officer followed the precept formulated by a somewhat more articulate patrolman: "If I want to be in control of my work and keep the street relatively peaceful, I have to know the people. To know them I must gain their trust, which means that I have to be involved in their lives. But I can't be soft like a social worker because unlike him I cannot call the cops when things go wrong. I am the cops!"[27]

THE RESTRICTED RELEVANCE OF CULPABILITY

It is well known that policemen exercise discretionary freedom in invoking the law. It is also conceded that, in some measure, the practice is unavoidable. This being so, the outstanding problem is whether or not the decisions are in line with the intent of the law. On skid-row, patrolmen often make decisions based on reasons that the law probably does not recognize as valid. The problem can best be introduced by citing an example.

---

[27] The same officer commented further, "If a man looks for something, I might help him. But I don't stay with him till he finds what he is looking for. If I did, I would never get to do anything else. In the last analysis, I really never solve any problems. The best I can hope for is to keep things from getting worse."

A man in a relatively mild state of intoxication (by skid-row standards) approached a patrolman to tell him that he had a room in a hotel, to which the officer responded by urging him to go to bed instead of getting drunk. As the man walked off, the officer related the following thoughts: Here is a completely lost soul. Though he probably is no more than thirty-five years old, he looks to be in his fifties. He never works and he hardly ever has a place to stay. He has been on the street for several years and is known as "Dakota." During the past few days, "Dakota" has been seen in the company of "Big Jim." The latter is an invalid living on some sort of pension with which he pays for a room in the hotel to which "Dakota" referred and for four weekly meal tickets in one of the restaurants on the street. Whatever is left he spends on wine and beer. Occasionally, "Big Jim" goes on drinking sprees in the company of someone like "Dakota." Leaving aside the consideration that there is probably a homosexual background to the association, and that it is not right that "Big Jim" should have to support the drinking habit of someone else, there is the more important risk that if "Dakota" moves in with "Big Jim" he will very likely walk off with whatever the latter keeps in his room. "Big Jim" would never dream of reporting the theft; he would just beat the hell out of "Dakota" after he sobered up. When asked what could be done to prevent the theft and the subsequent recriminations, the patrolman proposed that in this particular case he would throw "Big Jim" into jail if he found him tonight and then tell the hotel clerk to throw "Dakota" out of the room. When asked why he did not arrest "Dakota," who was, after all, drunk enough to warrant an arrest, the officer explained that this would not solve anything. While "Dakota" was in jail "Big Jim" would continue drinking and would either strike up another liaison or embrace his old buddy after he had been released. The only thing to do was to get "Big Jim" to sober up, and the only sure way of doing this was to arrest him.

As it turned out, "Big Jim" was not located that evening. But had he been located and arrested on a drunk charge, the fact that he was intoxicated would not have been the real reason for proceeding against him, but merely the pretext. The point of the example is not that it illustrates the tendency of skid-row patrolmen to arrest persons who would not be arrested under conditions of full respect for their legal rights. To be sure, this too happens. In the majority of minor arrest cases, however, the criteria the law specifies are met. But it is the rare exception that the law is invoked merely because the specifications of the law are met. That is, compliance with the law is merely the outward appearance of an intervention that is actually based on altogether different considerations. Thus, it could be said that patrolmen do not really enforce the law, even when they do invoke it, but merely use it as a resource to solve certain pressing practical problems in keeping the peace. This observation goes beyond the conclusion that many of the lesser norms of the criminal law are treated as defeasible in police work. It is patently not the case that skid-row patrolmen apply the legal norms while recognizing many exceptions to their applicability. Instead, the observation leads to the conclusion that in keeping the peace on skid-row, patrolmen encounter certain matters they attend to by means of coercive action, e.g., arrests. In doing this, they invoke legal norms that are available, and with some regard for substantive appropriateness. Hence, the problem patrolmen confront is not which drunks, beggars, or disturbers of the peace should be arrested and which can be let go as exceptions to the rule. Rather, the problem is whether, when someone "needs" to be arrested, he should be charged with drunkeness, begging, or disturbing the peace. Speculating further, one is almost compelled to infer that virtually any set of norms could be used in this manner, provided that they sanction relatively common forms of behavior.

The reduced relevance of culpability in peace keeping practice on skid-row is not readily visible. As mentioned, most arrested persons were actually found in the act, or in the state, alleged in the arrest record. It becomes partly visible when one views the treatment of persons who are not arrested even though all the legal grounds for an arrest are present. Whenever such persons are encountered and can be induced to leave, or taken to some shelter, or remanded to someone's care, then patrolmen feel, or at least maintain, that an arrest would serve no useful purpose. That is, whenever there exist means for controlling the troublesome aspects of some person's presence in some way alternative to an arrest, such means are preferentially employed, provided, of course, that the case at hand involves only a minor offense.[28]

The attenuation of the relevance of culpability is most visible when the presence of legal grounds for an arrest could be questioned, i.e., in cases that sometimes are euphemistically called "preventive arrests." In one observed instance, a man who attempted to trade a pocket knife came to the attention of a patrolman. The initial encounter was attended by a good deal of levity and the man willingly responded to the officer's inquiries about his identity and business. The man laughingly acknowledged that he needed some money to get drunk. In the course of the exchange it came to light that he had just arrived in town, traveling in his automobile. When confronted with the demand to lead the officer to the car, the man's expression became serious and he pointedly stated that he would not comply because this was none of the

---

[28] When evidence is present to indicate that a serious crime has been committed, considerations of culpability acquire a position of priority. Two such arrests were observed, both involving checkpassers. The first offender was caught *in flagrante delicto*. In the second instance, the suspect attracted the attention of the patrolman because of his sickly appearance. In the ensuing conversation the man made some remarks that led the officer to place a call with the Warrant Division of his department. According to the information that was obtained by checking records, the man was a wanted checkpasser and was immediately arrested.

officer's business. After a bit more prodding, which the patrolman initially kept in the light mood, the man was arrested on a charge involving begging. In subsequent conversation the patrolman acknowledged that the charge was only speciously appropriate and mainly a pretext. Having committed himself to demanding information he could not accept defeat. When this incident was discussed with another patrolman, the second officer found fault not with the fact that the arrest was made on a pretext but with the first officer's own contribution to the creation of conditions that made it unavoidable. "You see," he continued, "there is always the risk that the man is testing you and you must let him know what is what. The best among us can usually keep the upper hand in such situations without making arrests. But when it comes down to the wire, then you can't let them get away with it."

Finally, it must be mentioned that the reduction of the significance of culpability is built into the normal order of skid-row life, as patrolmen see it. Officers almost unfailingly say, pointing to some particular person, "I know that he knows that I know that some of the things he 'owns' are stolen, and that nothing can be done about it." In saying this, they often claim to have knowledge of such a degree of certainty as would normally be sufficient for virtually any kind of action except legal proceedings. Against this background, patrolmen adopt the view that the law is not merely imperfect and difficult to implement, but that on skid-row, at least, the association between delict and sanction is distinctly occasional. Thus, to implement the law naively, i.e., to arrest someone *merely* because he committed some minor offense, is perceived as containing elements of injustice.

Moreover, patrolmen often deal with situations in which questions of culpability are profoundly ambiguous. For example, an officer was called to help in settling a violent dispute in a hotel room. The object of the quarrel was a supposedly stolen pair of trousers. As the story unfolded in the conflicting versions of the participants, it was not possible to decide who was the complainant and who was alleged to be the thief, nor did it come to light who occupied the room in which the fracas took place, or whether the trousers were taken from the room or to the room. Though the officer did ask some questions, it seemed, and was confirmed in later conversation, that he was there not to solve the puzzle of the missing trousers but to keep the situation from getting out of hand. In the end, the exhausted participants dispersed, and this was the conclusion of the case. The patrolman maintained that no one could unravel mysteries of this sort because "these people take things from each other so often that no one could tell what 'belongs' to whom." In fact, he suggested, the terms owning, stealing, and swindling, in their strict sense, do not really belong on skid-row, and all efforts to distribute guilt and innocence according to some rational formula of justice are doomed to failure.

It could be said that the term "curb-stone justice" that is sometimes applied to the procedures of patrolmen in skid-rows contains a double irony. Not only is the procedure not legally authorized, which is the intended irony in the expression, but it does not even pretend to distribute deserts. The best among the patrolmen, according to their own standards, use the law to keep skid-row inhabitants from sinking deeper into the misery they already experience. The worst, in terms of these same standards, exploit the practice for personal aggrandizement or gain. Leaving motives aside, however, it is easy to see that if culpability is not the salient consideration leading to an arrest in cases where it is patently obvious, then the practical patrolman may not view it as being wholly out of line to make arrests lacking in formal legal justification. Conversely, he will come to view minor offense arrests made solely because legal standards are met as poor craftsmanship.

The Background of Ad Hoc Decision Making

When skid-row patrolmen are pressed to explain their reasons for minor offense arrests, they most often mention that it is done for the protection of the arrested person. This, they maintain, is the case in virtually all drunk arrests, in the majority of arrests involving begging and other nuisance offenses, and in many cases involving acts of violence. When they are asked to explain further such arrests as the one cited earlier involving the man attempting to sell the pocket knife, who was certainly not arrested for his own protection, they cite the consideration that belligerent persons constitute a much greater menace on skid-row than any place else in the city. The reasons for this are twofold. First, many of the inhabitants are old, feeble, and not too smart, all of which makes them relatively defenseless. Second, many of the inhabitants are involved in illegal activities and are known as persons of bad character, which does not make them credible victims or witnesses. Potential predators realize that the resources society has mobilized to minimize the risk of criminal victimization do not protect the predator himself. Thus, reciprocal exploitation constitutes a preferred risk. The high vulnerability of everybody on skid-row is public knowledge and causes every seemingly aggressive act to be seen as a potentially grave risk.

When, in response to all this, patrolmen are confronted with the observation that many minor offense arrests they make do not seem to involve a careful evaluation of facts before acting, they give the following explanations: First, the two reasons of protection and prevention represent a global background, and in individual cases it may sometimes not be possible to produce adequate justification on these grounds. Nor is it thought to be a problem of great moment to estimate precisely whether someone is more likely to come to grief or to cause grief when the objective is to prevent the proliferation of troubles. Second, the patrolmen maintain that some of the seemingly spur-of-the-moment decisions are actually made against a background of knowledge of facts that are not readily apparent in the situations. Since experience not only contains this information but also causes it to come to mind, patrolmen claim to have developed a special sensitivity for qualities of appearances that allow an intuitive grasp of probable tendencies. In this context, little things are said to have high informational value and lead to conclusions without the intervention of explicitly reasoned chains of inferences. Third, patrolmen readily admit that they do not adhere to high standards of adequacy of justification. They do not seek to defend the adequacy of their method against some abstract criteria of merit. Instead, when questioned, they assess their methods against the background of a whole system of ad hoc decision making, a system that encompasses the courts, correction facilities, the welfare establishment, and medical services. In fact, policemen generally maintain that their own procedures not only measure up to the workings of this system but exceed them in the attitude of carefulness.

In addition to these recognized reasons, there are two additional background factors that play a significant part in decisions to employ coercion. One has to do with the relevance of situational factors, and the other with the evaluation of coercion as relatively insignificant in the lives of the inhabitants.

There is no doubt that the nature of the circumstances often has decisive influence on what will be done. For example, the same patrolman who arrested the man trying to sell his pocket knife was observed dealing with a young couple. Though the officer was clearly angered by what he perceived as insolence and threatened the man with arrest, he merely ordered him and his companion to leave the street. He saw them walking away in a deliberately slow manner and when he noticed them a while later, still standing only a short distance away from the place of encounter, he did not respond to their presence. The difference between the two cases was that in the first there was a crowd of amused bystanders, while the latter case was not witnessed by anyone. In another instance, the patrolman was directed to a hotel and found a father and son fighting about money. The father occupied a room in the hotel and the son occasionally shared his quarters. There were two other men present, and they made it clear that their sympathies were with the older man. The son was whisked off to jail without much study of the relative merits of the conflicting claims. In yet another case, a middle-aged woman was forcefully evacuated from a bar even after the bartender explained that her loud behavior was merely a response to goading by some foul-mouth youth.

In all such circumstances, coercive control is exercised as a means of coming to grips with situational exigencies. Force is used against particular persons but is incidental to the task. An ideal of "economy of intervention" dictates in these and similar cases that the person whose presence is most likely to perpetuate the troublesome development be removed. Moreover, the decision as to who is to be removed is arrived at very quickly. Officers feel considerable pressure to act unhesitatingly, and many give accounts of situations that got out of hand because of desires to handle cases with careful consideration. However, even when there is no apparent risk of rapid proliferation of trouble, the tactic of removing one or two persons is used to control an undesirable situation. Thus, when a patrolman ran into a group of four men sharing a bottle of wine in an alley, he emptied the remaining contents of the bottle into the gutter, arrested one man — who was no more and no less drunk than the others — and let the others disperse in various directions.

The exigential nature of control is also evident in the handling of isolated drunks. Men are arrested because of where they happen to be encountered. In this, it matters not only whether a man is found in a conspicuous place or not, but also how far away he is from his domicile. The further away he is, the less likely it is that he will make it to his room, and the more likely the arrest. Sometimes drunk arrests are made mainly because the police van is available. In one case a patrolman summoned the van to pick up an arrested man. As the van was pulling away from the curb the officer stopped the driver because he sighted another drunk stumbling across the street. The second man protested saying that he "wasn't even half drunk yet." The patrolman's response was "OK, I'll owe you half a drunk." In sum, the basic routine of keeping the peace on skid-row involves a process of matching the resources of control with situational exigencies. The overall objective is to reduce the total amount of risk in the area. In this, practicality plays a considerably more important role than legal norms. Precisely because patrolmen see legal reasons for coercive action much more widely distributed on skid-row than could ever be matched by interventions, they intervene not in the interest of law enforcement but in the interest of producing relative tranquility and order on the street.

Taking the perspective of the victim of coercive measures, one could ask why he, in particular, has to bear the cost of keeping the aggregate of troubles down while others, who are equally or perhaps even more implicated, go scot-free. Patrolmen maintain that the ad hoc selection of persons for attention must be viewed in the light of the following consideration: Arresting a person on skid-row on some minor charge may save him and others a lot of trouble, but it does not work any real hardships on the arrested person. It is difficult to overestimate the skid-row patrolman's feeling of certainty that his coercive and disciplinary actions toward the inhabitants have but the most passing significance in their lives. Sending a man to jail on some charge that will hold him for a couple of days is seen as a matter of such slight importance to the affected person that it could hardly give rise to scruples.

Thus, every indication that a coercive measure should be taken is accompanied by the realization "I might as well, for all it matters to him." Certain realities of life on skid-row furnish the context of this belief in the attenuated relevance of coercion in the lives of the inhabitants. Foremost among them is that the use of police authority is seen as totally unremarkable by everybody on skid-row. Persons who live or work there are continuously exposed to it and take its existence for granted. Shopkeepers, hotel clerks, and bartenders call patrolmen to rid themselves of unwanted and troublesome patrons. Residents expect patrolmen to arbitrate their quarrels authoritatively. Men who receive orders, whether they obey them or not, treat them as part of life as usual. Moreover, patrolmen find that disciplinary and coercive actions apparently do not affect their friendly relations with the persons against whom these actions are taken. Those who greet and chat with them are the very same men who have been disciplined, arrested, and ordered around in the past, and who expect to be thus treated again in the future. From all this, officers gather that though the people on skid-row seek to evade police authority, they do not really object to it. Indeed, it happens quite frequently that officers encounter men who welcome being arrested and even actively ask for it. Finally, officers point out that sending someone to jail from skid-row does not upset his relatives or his family life, does not cause him to miss work or lose a job, does not lead to his being reproached by friends and associates, does not lead to failure to meet commitments or protect investments, and does not conflict with any but the most passing intentions of the arrested person. Seasoned patrolmen are not oblivious to the irony of the fact that measures intended as mechanisms for distributing deserts can be used freely because these measures are relatively impotent in their effects.

SUMMARY AND CONCLUSIONS

It was the purpose of this paper to render an account of a domain of police practice that does not seem subject to any system of external control. Following the terminology suggested by Michael Banton, this practice was called keeping the peace. The procedures employed in keeping the peace are not determined by legal mandates but are, instead, responses to certain demand conditions. From among several demand conditions, we concentrated on the one produced by the concentration of certain types of persons in districts known as skid-row. Patrolmen maintain that the lives of the inhabitants of the area are lacking in prospective coherence. The consequent reduction in the temporal horizon of predictability constitutes the main problem of keeping the peace on skid-row.

Peace keeping procedure on skid-row consists of three elements. Patrolmen seek to acquire a rich body of concrete knowledge about people by cultivating personal acquaintance with as many residents as possible. They tend to proceed against persons mainly on the basis of perceived risk, rather than on the basis of culpability. And they are more interested in reducing the aggregate total of troubles in the area than in evaluating individual cases according to merit.

There may seem to be a discrepancy between the skid-row patrolman's objective of preventing disorder and his efforts to maintain personal acquaintance with as many persons as possible. But these efforts are principally a tactical device. By knowing someone individually the patrolman reduces ambiguity, extends trust and favors, but does not grant immunity. The informality of interaction on skid-row always contains some indications of the hierarchical superiority of the patrolman and the reality of his potential power lurks in the background of every encounter.

Though our interest was focused initially on those police procedures that did not involve invoking the law, we found that the two cannot be separated. The reason for the connection is not given in the circumstance that the roles of the "law officer" and of the "peace officer" are enacted by the same person and thus are contiguous. According to our observations, patrolmen do not act alternatively as one or the other, with certain actions being determined by the intended objective of keeping the peace and others being determined by the duty to enforce the law. Instead, we have found that *peace keeping occasionally acquires the external aspects of law enforcement.* This makes it specious to inquire whether or not police discretion in invoking the law conforms with the intention of some specific legal formula. The real reason behind an arrest is virtually always the actual state of particular social situations, or of the skid-row area in general.

We have concentrated on those procedures and considerations that skid-row patrolmen regard as necessary, proper, and efficient relative to the circumstances in which they are employed. In this way, we attempted to disclose the conception of the mandate to which the police feel summoned. It was entirely outside the scope of the presentation to review the merits of this conception and of the methods used to meet it. Only insofar as patrolmen themselves recognized instances and patterns of malpractice did we take note of them. Most of the criticism voiced by officers had to do with the use of undue harshness and with the indiscriminate use of arrest powers when these were based on personal feelings rather than the requirements of the situation. According to prevailing opinion, patrolmen guilty of such abuses make life unnecessarily difficult for themselves and for their co-workers. Despite disapproval of harshness, officers tend to be defensive about it. For example, one sergeant who was outspokenly critical of brutality, said that though in general brutal men create more problems than they solve, "they do a good job in some situations for which the better men have no stomach." Moreover, supervisory personnel exhibit a strong reluctance to direct their subordinates in the particulars of their work performance. According to our observations, control is exercised mainly through consultation with superiors, and directives take the form of requests rather than orders. In the background of all this is the belief that patrol work on skid-row requires a great deal of discretionary freedom. In the words of the same sergeant quoted above, "a good man has things worked out in his own ways on his beat and he doesn't need anybody to tell him what to do."

The virtual absence of disciplinary control and the demand for discretionary freedom are related to the idea that patrol work involves "playing by ear." For if it is true that peace keeping cannot be systematically generalized, then, of course, it cannot be organizationally constrained. What the seasoned patrolman means, however, in saying that he "plays by ear" is that he is making his decisions while being attuned to the realities of complex situations about which he has immensely detailed knowledge. This studied aspect of peace keeping generally is not made explicit, nor is the tyro or the outsider made aware of it. Quite to the contrary, the ability to discharge the duties associated with keeping the peace is viewed as a reflection of an innate talent of "getting along with people." Thus, the same demands are made of barely initiated officers as are made of experienced practitioners. Correspondingly, beginners tend to think that they can do as well as their more knowledgeable peers. As this leads to inevitable frustrations, they find themselves in a situation that is conducive to the development of a particular sense of "touchiness." Personal dispositions of individual officers are, of course, of great relevance. But the license of discretionary freedom and the expectation of success under conditions of autonomy, without any indication that the work of the successful craftsman is based on an acquired preparedness for the task, is ready-made for failure and malpractice. Moreover, it leads to slipshod practices of patrol that also infect the standards of the careful craftsman.

The uniformed patrol, and especially the foot patrol, has a low preferential value in the division of labor of police work. This is, in part, at least, due to the belief that "anyone can do it." In fact, this belief is thoroughly mistaken. At present, however, the recognition that the practice requires preparation, and the process of obtaining the preparation itself, is left entirely to the practitioner.

Command, Control,
and Charisma:
Reflections on Police Bureaucracy

DAVID J. BORDUA AND ALBERT J. REISS, JR.

Bureaucratization can be regarded as an organizational technique whereby civic pressures are neutralized from the standpoint of the governing regime. In the development of the modern police, bureaucratization has been a major device to commit members to the occupational organization, to the occupational community, and to its norms of subordination and service to a degree where these commitments take precedence over extra-occupational ones to family and community.

The political neutrality and legal reliability of the police in modern societies are less a matter of the social sources of their recruitment than of the nature of internal organization, training, and control. While this, of course, is true for all government organizations under a civil service or tenure system, it is true for the police not primarily because they are civil servants in the restricted sense but because of their allegiance to an occupationally organized community that sets itself apart. The situation is particularly crucial for the police since they often are called upon to enforce laws that are unpopular with the public or for which they have no personal sympathy, while at the same time they are armed and organized. Perhaps this fundamental significance of police bureaucratization can be seen by the fact that given a well-organized, well-disciplined, and internally well-regulated police, civil authorities can count on the police if they are assured of the political loyalty or neutrality of the commander. Indeed, the modern police emerged under conditions whereby they were an organized source of stability between the elites and the masses, serving to draw hostility from the elites to themselves and thereby permitting more orderly relations among the elites and the masses.[1]

COMMAND SYSTEMS

To our knowledge, there is no detailed empirical description of command processes in a police department. It is necessary, therefore, to rely largely on

Reprinted from *American Journal of Sociology*, 72 (July 1966), pp. 68–76, by permission of the authors and The University of Chicago Press. Copyright 1966 by The University of Chicago.

[1] Alan Silver, "On the Demand for Order in Civil Society: A Review of Some Themes in the History of Urban Crime, Police and Riot in England" (to be published in David J. Bordua [ed.], *The Police* [New York: John Wiley & Sons, 1966]), p. 11.

published discourses that give information on the rhetoric of command and control and that are of variable and unknown validity as descriptions of behavior.[2]

Police literature emphasizes the quasi-military nature of police-command relations, and casual observation in metropolitan police departments indicates that police officials are highly sensitive to "orders from above" and to probabilities of official disapproval of behavior. In principle and in rhetoric, a police organization is one characterized by strict subordination, by a rigid chain of command, by accountability of command, and more doubtfully, by a lack of formal provision for consultation between ranks.

Before accepting this description of its structure uncritically, it is necessary to say that such statements are meaningful only by comparison. We have relatively little data comparing the operating as opposed to the rhetorical nature of command in different types of organizations. In many ways, policing is a highly decentralized operation involving the deployment of large numbers of men alone or in small units where control by actual command, that is, by issuing orders, is difficult. This problem is generally recognized by top police administrators, leading to their stressing the importance of accountability of command to achieve control. O. W. Wilson puts it this way:

Authority is delegated by some form of command; responsibility is effectively placed by some form of control. . . . The effective placing of responsibility or the act of holding accountable involves an evaluation of the manner in which the authority was exercised, hence the rule of control: *He who gives an order must ascertain that it has been properly executed.*

It is relatively easy to delegate authority by giving a command, but to ascertain the manner in which the order was carried out so that the subordinate may be held responsible is often difficult.[3]

Other evidence from the police literature suggests that the description is overdrawn, that both internal and external transactions structure the effective range of command and control. Moreover, as J. Q. Wilson points out, it seems clear that the variations between "system-oriented" as opposed to "professionalized" departments include fundamental differences in styles of control.[4]

Historical changes in the nature of police work and organization have increased the importance of more subtle and perhaps more important developments in methods of control. In the dialectic of dispersion versus cen-

[2] See, for example, Bruce Smith, *Police Systems in the United States,* 2nd rev. ed. (New York: Harper & Brothers, 1960), esp. chaps. vii–ix.

[3] O. W. Wilson, *Police Administration* (New York: McGraw-Hill Book Co., 1950), p. 59.

[4] James Q. Wilson, "The Police and Their Problems: A Theory," in Carl J. Friedrich and Seymour E. Harris (eds.), *Public Policy, XII* (Cambridge, Mass.: Harvard University Press, 1963), pp. 189–216.

tralization of command, every development in the technology for police control of the population is accompanied by changes in the capacity of the organization to control its members. Originally the bell, creaker, or rattle watches were limited in summoning help to the effective range of their "noise"; the addition of "calling the hours" served to monitor the behavior of the patrol (quite generally open to question).[5] Here we see evidence of a classic and continuing dilemma in organizations — that to control subordinates they must be required to make themselves visible. For the police, this means that when they become visible they likewise become more calculable to potential violators. Control of the dispersed police was really difficult before the call box that simultaneously enabled patrolmen to summon help and enabled commanders to issue calls and require periodic reporting.[6] The cruising car with two-way radio enabled still greater dispersion and flexibility in the allocation of patrols, while at the same time bringing the patrolman or team more nearly within the range of constant control. It is now a fundamental duty of the radio patrol officer to remain "in contact," that is, controllable.

More important, perhaps, is the fact that a centralized radio communication system, where telephoned complaints are received and commands given, makes it possible for top management to have independent knowledge of complaints and of who is assigned to them before either subordinate commanders or the patrol team does. A minimum of centralized control is available, then, not simply by the direct issuance of commands from superior to subordinate but by means of a paper-matching process whereby the complaint board's written record can be matched with the written record the patrolman is required to generate. This pattern of control by centralized communication and internal organizational audit is highly dependent upon the distribution of telephones in the population. The citizen's telephone enables the police commander to enlist the complainant — on a routine basis — as part of the apparatus for control of the policeman. A citizen's opportunity to mobilize the police is intricately balanced with that of the commander.

Added to these matters of task organization, in large police departments, the chief's power to command and control is limited by a complex system of "due process" that protects subordinates. This, of course, is true of all

---

[5] Selden D. Bacon, "The Early Development of American Municipal Police: A Study of the Evolution of Formal Controls in a Changing Society" (unpublished Ph.D. dissertation, Yale University, 1939).

[6] The innovation of the police patrol and signal service in Chicago in 1880 brought forth considerable resistance and indignation from the police patrol precisely because it made possible closer supervision of the patrol (see John Joseph Flynn, *History of the Chicago Police: From the Settlement of the Community to the Present Time* [Chicago: Police Book Fund, 1887], chap. xx).

civil service organizations. The strong interest in keeping the police "out of politics" coupled with the interest of the rank and file in job security, however, creates a situation where, formally, the department head must contend with legally empowered authorities in the selection, promotion, and discharge of personnel. Even in matters of internal assignment and definition of task, decisions may impinge on the civil service classifications system. Police employee organizations, likewise, are quite effective in seeing to it that the system of "due process" continues to protect them. The individual officer, furthermore, when accused of wrongdoing or a crime, demands all the legal safeguards he may deny to those whom he accuses of committing a crime.

Not all police operations are constituted in the fashion of this highly oversimplified picture of so-called routine patrol. Detectives, for example, are less subject to such control. But these considerations of due-process barriers to centralized command and historical changes in control procedures that rely less on actual command as a form of control are intended to raise questions about the sociological meaning of the stress generally placed on command and to lay the ground for a somewhat more systematic analysis of it.

FORMS OF LEGITIMATION

Thus far, "command" has been used in two senses. In one, "command" refers to a technique of control in organizations that consists of "giving commands." The directive communication between superior and subordinate may be called "a command," or, if more impersonally clothed, "an order." In another sense, however, "command" means neither a specific technique of control nor an instance of its use, but something more general — a principle that legitimates orders, instructions, or rules. Orders, then, are obeyed *because* they are "commanded."

Sociologists are familiar with discussions of this type ever since Weber.[7] In Weberian terms, the police department "as an order" is legitimated by the principle of command. Each form of legitimation, however, as Weber so clearly saw, has a correlative requirement of "attitude" on the part of those subject to its sway. In the case of "an order" legitimated by a rhetoric of command, the correlative expectation is "obedience" — again not as a situational expectation in the case of a given specific command but as a principle relating member to organization. To be "obedient" in this sense carries the same general sense of principle as in the "poverty, chastity, and obedience" of the monk's vow. In a system so legitimated, we can expect that commitment to obedience will be displayed as a sign of membership.

[7] Talcott Parsons (ed.), *Max Weber: The Theory of Social and Economic Organization* (New York: Oxford University Press, 1947), pp. 324 ff.

It is not surprising, then, that social scientists who are based in organizations where independence is legitimated, rehabilitation workers based in those where professional discretion and supportiveness are legitimated, and police who are based in organizations where obedience is legitimated so often fail to communicate with one another when they are engaged in exchanges of ideologies.

We may point out as well that in orders legitimated by command and exacting obedience, the classic status reward is "honor." The morale and public-relations problems of the American police can be more clearly understood as an attempt to substitute public prestige sought in an occupational performance market for the Weberian status regard sought and validated in the "honor market." The American police are denied both, for the public seems unwilling to accord the police status either in the European sense of status honor as representatives of the State or in the more typically American sense of prestige based on a claim to occupational competence.

Command as a basis for legitimacy can be located under any of the three basic types of legitimation discussed by Weber — the rational-legal, the traditional, and the charismatic. Inherently, however, command as a principle focuses on the commander, and the exact nature of the concrete "order" legitimated by the principle of command will depend on the role of the specific commander. Because of this commander focus, the command principle is likely to lead to a mystique of the personal commander and an organizational stress on legitimating specific orders or even general rules as emanating from him.

COMMAND AND TASK ORGANIZATION

To regard a metropolitan police system solely in terms of the classic features of the hierarchically oriented command bureaucracy would be mistaken, however. Although the more traditional police departments in American cities are organized on quasi-military command principles, modernized ones display features of other control systems, particularly those of centralized and professional control structures.

The core of the modern metropolitan police system is the communications center, linking as it does by radio dispatch the telephoned demands of a dispersed population with a dispersed police in mobile units. The technology of the radio, the telephone, the recorder, and the computer permits a high degree of central control of operating units in the field. The more modern police departments, for example, have tape records of all citizen phone complaints, the response of dispatch to them, and the action of mobile units. This technology also makes possible reporting directly to a centralized records unit. Indeed, the more rationalized police-command systems make extensive use of the computer as a centralized intelligence system to which mobile units can make virtually direct inquiry, as a "decision-maker" about which units are to be dispersed for what service, and as a source of intelligence on the output of personnel and units in the department. Such a centralized and direct system of command and control makes it possible to bypass many positions in the hierarchical command structure, particularly those in the station command. More and more, those in the line of authority assume work supervision of informal adjudicatory rather than strictly command roles.

There undeniably is considerable variability among internal units of a police department in the degree to which they are centrally commanded such that routine patrol is more subject to central command than are tactical or investigation units. Yet, all in all, there is a growing tendency for all internal units to operate under programed operations of a central command rather than under local commanders. Orders not only originate with the central command but pass directly from it.

The centralization of command and control is one of the major ways that American police chiefs have for coping with the tendency toward corruption inherent in traditional hierarchically organized departments. Chiefs no longer need rely to the same extent upon the station commander to implement the goals of the department through the exercise of command. Indeed, a major way that corrupt departments are reformed these days is to reduce the command operations of local commanders, replacing them with centralized command and control. Yet it is precisely in those operations where corruption is most likely to occur, namely, the control of vice, that a centralized command is least effective. The main reason for this is that a centralized command lends itself best to a reactive strategy, whereas a professionalized or hierarchically organized command lends itself to a proactive strategy. Vice requires an essentially proactive strategy of policing in the modern metropolis, whereas the citizens' command for service demands an essentially reactive strategy and tactics.

A central command not only bypasses traditional hierarchical command relations but, like the hierarchical command, creates problems for the developing professionalized control in police systems. A professionalized model of control respects a more or less decentralized decision-making system where the central bureaucracy, at best, sets general policy and principles that guide the professional. Indeed, many police tasks and decisions would appear to lend themselves to a professional as well as technical role relationship with the client.

Yet, the institutionalized and legally defined role of the police formally denies professional discretion to them in decisions of prosecution and adjudication, granting them to professional lawyers. The "professionalizing" police, therefore, are formally left only with certain decisions regarding public order, safety, service, and arrest. These formal prohibitions coupled with the new technology and centralized command (developed under the banner of professionalization of the police) both serve to decrease rather than enhance discretionary decision-making by subordinates. Police organizations become "professionalized," not their members.

COMMAND AND OCCUPATIONAL CULTURE

The internal organizational life of American police departments displays features which distinguish the police from other organizations and which have important implications for the nature of organizational command. These features are the familial and/or ethnic inheritance of occupation, the almost exclusive practice of promotion from within, the large number of formal voluntary organizations that cut across organizational membership, and, finally, the existence of legal protections for tenure which inhere in civil service regulations.

Specific police jobs differ; yet it is quite important to recognize that, fundamentally, police status overrides these differentiations. Not only does the basic status override lateral differentiations, but it also tends to override differences in rank. Police occupational culture, unlike the situation in industry, unites rather than divides ranks.

This is perhaps the most fundamental significance of the practice of promoting from within. The fact that all police-command personnel came up through the ranks means not only that there is relatively little class distinction among police but that the sharp differences between managers and workers in industry is less apparent for the police.[8]

In addition to the vertical spread of police occupational culture due to promotion from within, local recruitment tends to entrench any specific department's version of the more general occupational culture. This combination of occupational culture and organizational culture produces what J. Q. Wilson referred to as "system-oriented" departments.[9]

Interlinked with the features of local recruitment and internal promotion is the factor of familial and ethnic inheritance of the police occupation. Many occupations are strongly based in ethnicity, and many organizations have widespread kinship bonds; indeed, some companies advertise the fact. The consequences, however, the more exaggerated in the police, partly because

---

[8] The more professionalized a police department, however, the more it displays manager-worker differences common in industry. The police in the line symbolize this by referring to those on the staff as "empty holster ————." The occupational culture holds, nevertheless, for police personnel in staff and line versus the non-sworn personnel, the latter commonly being referred to as "civilians."

[9] James Q. Wilson, *op. cit.*

police culture emphasizes distance between the occupation and the general community but, more importantly we suspect, because of the relative lack of vertical differentiation. Thus, police corruption can become spread up precisely because of this lack of differentiation.

Finally, the development of civil service can mean that a rather rigid formal, legal shell is erected around occupational and organizational cultures in a way that makes the exercise of command from the top even more difficult than it would otherwise be. The reform chief must choose his command from among those who began tenure under his predecessors. And except for retirement, "resignation," or formal dismissal proceedings, he is left with the cadre of the "old department."

It should be noted, however, that occupational and organizational cultures and the reinforcing solidarities provided by formal organizations like the Fraternal Order of Police and by the legal protections of civil service have another side. They make possible the existence of police systems which function at least moderately well over long periods in a society notoriously inhospitable to police; indeed, they are partially a defensive response to that inhospitability. While they may inhibit modernization and reform, they do insure that the job will get done somehow. More importantly, they provide the irreplaceable minimum structural conditions for at least the basic elements of status honor. They provide the essential precondition for a sense of honor — a relatively closed, secure community (not just organization) of functionaries who can elaborate and apply honor-conferring criteria.

These internal solidarities create special barriers to the effective exercise of command over and above the features of task organization previously discussed. They become particularly significant in attempts at modernization or reform. The police commander ignores this internal culture at his peril. It can confront him with an opposition united from top to bottom.

The modernizing chief is constrained, therefore, to make at least symbolic obeisance to police solidarity by demonstrating that he is a "cop's cop" as well as a devotee of systems analysis and psychological screening of applicants. One of the ways he does so is by emphasis in his dress and bearing — the policeman's chief social tool — the ability to command personal respect.[10] At least during a period of change, personal charisma and "presence" are of particular significance. He must also make his orders stick, of course.

The reform chief's charisma is of special significance because of the objective uncertainty of obedience but also because reform depends on the cooperation of a cadre of immediate subordinates whose careers may depend upon the chief's success. His certainty becomes their hope.

---

[10] The ability to command respect personally is more necessary in America than in Britain where police command more respect officially (see Michael Banton, *The Policeman in the Community* [New York: Basic Books, 1965]).

COMMAND AND CIVIL ACCOUNTABILITY

The structure of command is affected not only by elements of task organization and technology and by the features of occupational and organizational culture discussed above but also by the relationship between the chief and his civil superiors. In the case of the American municipality, police chiefs, at least traditionally, both at law and in practice, are politically accountable officials who ordinarily stand or fall with the fortunes of their civilian superiors (who are lodged in external systems). Given the often controversial nature of police work, and the often "irrational" and unpredictable nature of political fortunes in municipal government, the American police chief who is responsible to a politically elected official comes close to the position of a "patrimonial bureaucrat" in Weber's terms. His tenure as chief, though not necessarily his tenure in the department, depends on continuing acceptability to the elected official(s).

We have alluded to some of the dimensions along which police departments and their command processes seem to vary—using terms like "modernized," "rationalized," "reformed." It would be possible to indicate other dimensions which intersect these by referring to department age, growth rate, and other variables as well as environmental context variables such as variations in civic culture — comparing, for example, Los Angeles and San Francisco. It is not our intention, however, to attempt a systematic comparative scheme. In the case of the problem of civic accountability, however, it is possible to use some of the material presented thus far to begin development of such a scheme.

The relations of police commanders to civil superiors are actually more varied and complex than those depicted above. We shall discuss briefly only the two most important dimensions of variation: the security of tenure of the chief commander and the degree to which he is held strictly accountable by a mayor. Given strict accountability plus insecurity of tenure, we can expect a kind of obsession with command and a seemingly "irrational" emphasis on the twinned symbols of the visibility of the commander and the obedience of the force. Some of the rhetoric of command in the police literature likely arises from an attempt to "protect" the chief by the compulsive effort to "overcontrol" subordinates, almost any of whom can get him fired. This amounts to saying that as civil superiors increase the formal accountability of the police chief *without changing* the tenure features of the role, the increasing bureaucratization of the American municipal police stressed by J. Q. Wilson leads to the development of an organization animated by a principle of the commanding person.[11] This "personalized subordination" to

[11] James Q. Wilson, *op. cit.*

Table 1: Types of Police Departments

	Tenure of chief	
Relation to mayor	*Secure*	*Insecure*
Strictly accountable	Command bureaucracy	Personalized command bureaucracy
Feudal allegiance	Command feudality	Personalized "political" feudality

the "Hero Chief" can become an operating, if not a formal, principle of organization.[12]

Increased professionalization can be another accommodative strategy in such a situation, but this time aimed not at control of the force but at control of the mayor by changing the grounds of accountability. One of the first jobs of the "professionalizing" police chief often is to convince his civil superior that "you can't win 'em all" and that it is irrational and "unprofessional" to dismiss a police chief or commissioner because of failure to solve some particular crime. Perhaps, in the long run, it is hard to have a professionalized police without a professionalized mayor. Perhaps also, this would lead us to expect different kinds of command styles where a professional city manager intervenes between the chief and the mayor.

If the civil superior, for whatever reason, does not demand accountability from the chief, the quasi-formalized obsession with "command" as a principle of control may be replaced by a complex system of feudal loyalties. In this situation, ties of personal political fealty between chief and mayor — or between chief and the local "powers" — may become prominent and "keep your nose clean" the principle of subordination. When this trend goes beyond a certain point, the department is commonly described as politically corrupt. Finally, to the degree that the chief is secure in his tenure, we would expect the obsession with command and the emphasis on personalized subordination to decrease.

On the basis of this analysis of command and the position of the chief we may distinguish the four types of departments (Table 1).

We have consciously chosen words such as "feudality" with outrageously large quotas of surplus meaning since the concern here is to direct attention to features of police organization that receive relatively little attention and

---

[12] One study reports that, as compared with welfare workers and school teachers, policemen were more likely to personalize authority (Robert L. Peabody, "Perceptions of Organizational Authority: A Comparative Analysis," *Administrative Science Quarterly*, VI [March, 1962], 477–80; see also Elaine Cumming, Ian M. Cumming, and Laura Edell, "Policeman as Philosopher, Guide and Friend," *Social Problems*, XII [Winter, 1965], 276–97).

to questions of fundamental differences in the consequences of organizational membership between police and other organizations.[13]

A word about two of these types seems in order. The command-feudality type seems a contradiction in terms (and indeed derives from the cross-classification itself). Some small municipal and sheriff's departments, where the tenure of the chief in the local "feudal political structure" is secure, may fall here. Because everyone is secure in a relatively non-bureaucratic system, the operating principle of subordination can be command. Such an arrangement possibly characterizes the exceptionally long-tenure chiefs discovered in Lunden's study in Iowa.[14]

The "personalized command bureaucracy" seems likely to occur where an insecure reform head is in office. To reform successfully he must bureaucratize and rationalize administrative operations. To do this against the inevitable internal resistance he must emphasize the principle of command. To make clear that status quo–oriented commanders have been superseded he must emphasize *his* command and his *capacity* to command. In *short*, he must exercise what Selznick defines as one of the crucial functions of leadership in administration. He must define the emerging character of the institution.[15]

CONCLUSION

We have discussed features of American police systems that may account for variations in and possible changes in command structures and also features that account for both a rhetorical and behavioral emphasis not on one or the other formal command system but on something which seemingly appears as alien and contradictory — the personal charisma of the chief and the emphasis on personalized command as a symbolic, if not actual, principle of order.

Command, obedience, and honor ring strangely in analysis of organizational life in America except, perhaps, for the military. Yet it seems to us that meaningful analysis of the police must touch upon them as well as upon duty, courage, and restraint. The self-image of the police is different because of them. We have already alluded to the fact that the status reward for obedience is honor and that the maintenance of honor requires a status community — not simply a formal organization.[16]

[13] This typology owes much to the analysis of labor unions in Harold L. Wilensky, *Intellectuals in Labor Unions* (Glencoe, Ill.: Free Press, 1956).

[14] Walter A. Lunden, "The Mobility of Chiefs of Police," *Journal of Criminal Law, Criminology and Police Science,* XLIX (1958), 178–83.

[15] Philip Selznick, *Leadership in Administration* (New York: Row, Peterson & Co., 1957).

[16] Military honor is similarly communal and not just organizational (Morris Janowitz, *The Professional Soldier* [Glencoe, Ill.: Free Press, 1960], esp. chaps. iv and v).

The significance of honor is that it lies at the heart of the necessary police virtues — courage, devotion to duty, restraint, and honesty. In the absence of ritually symbolic auspices such as the European State or the English Crown, the personal charisma of chiefs is a necessary transitional step to an occupationally based community of honor. In the long run, such status honor, not only occupational prestige, is one fundamental answer to police corruption.[17] In the short run, it means that successful police commanders must attempt not to have the police reflect the society but transcend it.

[17] M. McMullen, "A Theory of Corruption," *Sociological Review,* IX (1961), 181–201.

Violence and
the Police

WILLIAM A. WESTLEY

Brutality and the third degree have been identified with the municipal police of the United States since their inauguration in 1844. These aspects of police activity have been subject to exaggeration, repeated exposure, and virulent criticism. Since they are a breach of the law by the law-enforcement agents, they constitute a serious social, but intriguing sociological, problem. Yet there is little information about or understanding of the process through which such activity arises or of the purposes which it serves.[1]

This paper is concerned with the genesis and function of the illegal use of violence by the police and presents an explanation based on an interpretative understanding of the experience of the police as an occupational group.[2] It shows that (*a*) the police accept and morally justify their illegal use of violence; (*b*) such acceptance and justification arise through their occupational experience; and (*c*) its use is functionally related to the collective occupational, as well as to the legal, ends of the police.

The analysis which follows offers both an occupational perspective on the use of violence by the police and an explanation of policing as an occupation, from the perspective of the illegal use of violence. Thus the meaning of this use of violence is derived by relating it to the general behavior of policemen as policemen, and occupations in general are illuminated through the delineation of the manner in which a particular occupation handles one aspect of its work.

The technical demands of a man's work tend to specify the kinds of social relationships in which he will be involved and to select the groups with whom these relationships are to be maintained. The social definition of the occupation invests its members with a common prestige position. Thus, a man's occupation is a major determining factor of his conduct and social identity. This being so, it involves more than man's work, and one must go beyond the technical in the explanation of work behavior. One must discover the oc-

Reprinted from *American Journal of Sociology,* 49 (July 1953), pp. 34–41, by permission of the author and The University of Chicago Press. Copyright 1953 by The University of Chicago.

[1] This paper presents part of a larger study of the police by the writer. For the complete study see William A. Westley, "The Police: A Sociological Study of Law, Custom, and Morality" (unpublished Ph.D. dissertation, University of Chicago, Department of Sociology, 1951).

[2] Interpretative understanding is here used as defined by Max Weber (see *The Theory of Social and Economic Organization,* trans. Talcott Parsons [New York: Oxford University Press, 1947], pp. 88).

cupationally derived definitions of self and conduct which arise in the involvements of technical demands, social relationships between colleagues and with the public, status, and self-conception. To understand these definitions, one must track them back to the occupational problems in which they have their genesis.[3]

The policeman finds his most pressing problems in his relationships to the public. His is a service occupation but of an incongruous kind, since he must discipline those whom he serves. He is regarded as corrupt and inefficient by, and meets with hostility and criticism from, the public. He regards the public as his enemy, feels his occupation to be in conflict with the community, and regards himself to be a pariah. The experience and the feeling give rise to a collective emphasis on secrecy, an attempt to coerce respect from the public, and a belief that almost any means are legitimate in completing an important arrest. These are for the policeman basic occupational values. They arise from his experience, take precedence over his legal responsibilities, are central to an understanding of his conduct, and form the occupational contexts within which violence gains its meaning. This then is the background for our analysis.[4]

The materials which follow are drawn from a case study of a municipal police department in an industrial city of approximately one hundred and fifty thousand inhabitants. This study included participation in all types of police activities, ranging from walking the beat and cruising with policemen in a squad car to the observation of raids, interrogations, and the police school. It included intensive interviews with over half the men in the department who were representative as to rank, time in service, race, religion, and specific type of police job.

DUTY AND VIOLENCE

In the United States the use of violence by the police is both an occupational prerogative and a necessity. Police powers include the use of violence, for to them, within civil society, has been delegated the monopoly of the legitimate means of violence possessed by the state. Police are obliged by their duties to use violence as the only measure adequate to control and apprehension in the presence of counterviolence.

Violence in the form of the club and the gun is for the police a means of persuasion. Violence from the criminal, the drunk, the quarreling family, and

---

[3] The ideas are not original. I am indebted for many of them to Everett C. Hughes, although he is in no way responsible for their present formulation (see E. C. Hughes, "Work and the Self" in Rohrer and Sherif, *Social Psychology at the Crossroads* [New York: Harper & Bros., 1951]).

[4] The background material will be developed in subsequent papers which will analyze the occupational experience of the police and give a full description of police norms.

the rioter arises in the course of police duty. The fighting drunk who is damaging property or assailing his fellows and who looks upon the policeman as a malicious intruder justifies for the policeman his use of force in restoring order. The armed criminal who has demonstrated a casual regard for the lives of others and a general hatred of the policeman forces the use of violence by the police in the pursuit of duty. Every policeman has some such experiences, and they proliferate in police lore. They constitute a commonsense and legal justification for the use of violence by the police and for training policemen in the skills of violence. Thus, from experience in the pursuit of their legally prescribed duties, the police develop a justification for the use of violence. They come to see it as good, as useful, and as their own. Furthermore, although legally their use of violence is limited to the requirements of the arrest and the protection of themselves and the community, the contingencies of their occupation lead them to enlarge the area in which violence may be used. Two kinds of experience — that with respect to the conviction of the felon and that with respect to the control of sexual conduct — will illustrate how and why the illegal use of violence arises.

1. THE CONVICTION OF THE FELON

The apprehension and conviction of the felon is, for the policeman, the essence of police work. It is the source of prestige both within and outside police circles, it has career implications, and it is a major source of justification for the existence of the police before a critical and often hostile public. Out of these conditions a legitimation for the illegal use of violence is wrought.

The career and prestige implication of the "good pinch"[5] elevate it to a major end in the conduct of the policeman. It is an end which is justified both legally and through public opinion as one which should be of great concern to the police. Therefore it takes precedence over other duties and tends to justify strong means. Both trickery and violence are such means. The "third degree" has been criticized for many years, and extensive administrative controls have been devised in an effort to eliminate it. Police persistence in the face of that attitude suggests that the illegal use of violence is regarded as functional to their work. It also indicates a tendency to regard the third degree as a legitimate means for obtaining the conviction of the felon. However, to understand the strength of this legitimation, one must include other factors: the competition between patrolman and detectives and the publicity value of convictions for the police department.

The patrolman has less access to cases that might result in the "good

---

[5] Policemen, in the case studied, use this term to mean an arrest which (*a*) is politically clear and (*b*) likely to bring them esteem. Generally it refers to felonies, but in the case of a "real" vice drive it may include the arrest and *conviction* of an important bookie.

pinch" than the detective. Such cases are assigned to the detective, and for their solution he will reap the credit. Even where the patrolman first detects the crime, or actually apprehends the possible offender, the case is likely to be turned over to the detective. Therefore patrolmen are eager to obtain evidence and make the arrest before the arrival of the detectives. Intimidation and actual violence frequently come into play under these conditions. This is illustrated in the following case recounted by a young patrolman when he was questioned as to the situations in which he felt that the use of force was necessary:

One time Joe and I found three guys in a car, and we found that they had a gun down between the seats. We wanted to find out who owned that gun before the dicks arrived so that we could make a good pinch. They told us.

Patrolmen feel that little credit is forthcoming from a clean beat (a crimeless beat), while a number of good arrests really stands out on the record. To a great extent this is actually the case, since a good arrest results in good newspaper publicity, and the policeman who has made many "good pinches" has prestige among his colleagues.

A further justification for the illegal use of violence arises from the fact that almost every police department is under continuous criticism from the community, which tends to assign its own moral responsibilities to the police. The police are therefore faced with the task of justifying themselves to the public, both as individuals and as a group. They feel that the solution of major criminal cases serves this function. This is illustrated in the following statement:

There is a case I remember of four Negroes who held up a filling station. We got a description of them and picked them up. Then we took them down to the station and really worked them over. I guess that everybody that came into the station that night had a hand in it, and they were in pretty bad shape. Do you think that sounds cruel? Well, you know what we got out of it? We broke a big case in ————. There was a mob of twenty guys, burglars and stick-up men, and eighteen of them are in the pen now. Sometimes you have to get rough with them, see. The way I figure it is, if you can get a clue that a man is a pro and if he won't cooperate, tell you what you want to know, it is justified to rough him up a little, up to a point. You know how it is. You feel that the end justifies the means.

It is easier for the police to justify themselves to the community through the dramatic solution of big crimes than through orderly and responsible completion of their routine duties. Although they may be criticized for failures in routine areas, the criticism for the failure to solve big crimes is more intense and sets off a criticism of their work in noncriminal areas. The pressure to solve important cases therefore becomes strong. The following statement, made in reference to the use of violence in interrogations, demonstrates the point:

If it's a big case and there is a lot of pressure on you and they tell you you can't go home until the case is finished, then naturally you are going to lose patience.

The policeman's response to this pressure is to extend the use of violence to its illegal utilization in interrogations. The apprehension of the felon or the "good pinch" thus constitutes a basis for justifying the illegal use of violence.

2. Control of Sexual Conduct

The police are responsible for the enforcement of laws regulating sexual conduct. This includes the suppression of sexual deviation and the protection of the public from advances and attacks of persons of deviant sexual tendencies. Here the police face a difficult task. The victims of such deviants are notoriously unwilling to co-operate, since popular curiosity and gossip about sexual crimes and the sanctions against the open discussion of sexual activities make it embarrassing for the victim to admit or describe a deviant sexual advance or attack and cause him to feel that he gains a kind of guilt by association from such admissions. Thus the police find that frequently the victims will refuse to identify or testify against the deviant.

These difficulties are intensified by the fact that, once the community becomes aware of sexual depredations, the reports of such activity multiply well beyond reasonable expectations. Since the bulk of these reports will be false, they add to the confusion of the police and consequently to the elusiveness of the offender.

The difficulties of the police are further aggravated by extreme public demand for the apprehension of the offender. The hysteria and alarm generated by reports of a peeping Tom, a rapist, or an exhibitionist result in great public pressure on the police; and, should the activities continue, the public becomes violently critical of police efficiency. The police, who feel insecure in their relationship to the public, are extremely sensitive to this criticism and feel that they must act in response to the demands made by the political and moral leaders of the community.

Thus the police find themselves caught in a dilemma. Apprehension is extremely difficult because of the confusion created by public hysteria and the scarcity of witnesses, but the police are compelled to action by extremely public demands. They dissolve this dilemma through the illegal utilization of violence.

A statement of this "misuse" of police powers is represented in the remarks of a patrolman:

Now in my own case when I catch a guy like that I just pick him up and take him into the woods and beat him until he can't crawl. I have had seventeen cases like that in the last couple of years. I tell that guy that if I catch him doing that again I will take him out to those woods and I will shoot him. I tell him that I carry a second gun on me just in case I find guys like him and that I will plant it in his hand and say that he tried to kill and that no jury will convict me.

This statement is extreme and is not representative of policemen in general. In many instances the policeman is likely to act in a different fashion. This is illustrated in the following statement of a rookie who described what happened when he and his partner investigated a parked car which had aroused their suspicions:

He [the partner] went up there and pretty soon he called me, and there were a couple of fellows in the car with their pants open. I couldn't understand it. I kept looking around for where the woman would be. They were both pretty plastered. One was a young kid about eighteen years old, and the other was an older man. We decided, with the kid so drunk, that bringing him in would only really ruin his reputation, and we told him to go home. Otherwise we would have pinched them. During the time we were talking to them they offered us twenty-eight dollars, and I was going to pinch them when they showed the money, but my partner said, "Never mind, let them go."

Nevertheless, most policemen would apply no sanctions against a colleague who took the more extreme view of the right to use violence and would openly support some milder form of illegal coercion. This is illustrated in the statement of another rookie:

They feel that its okay to rough a man up in the case of sex crimes. One of the older men advised me that if the courts didn't punish a man we should. He told me about a sex crime, the story about it, and then said that the law says the policeman has the right to use the amount of force necessary to make an arrest and that in that kind of a crime you can use just a little more force. They feel definitely, for example, in extreme cases like rape, that if a man was guilty he ought to be punished even if you could not get any evidence on him. My feeling is that all the men on the force feel that way, at least from what they have told me.

Furthermore, the police believe, and with some justification it seems, that the community supports their definition of the situation and that they are operating in terms of an implicit directive.

The point of this discussion is that the control of sexual conduct is so difficult and the demand for it so incessant that the police come to sanction the illegal use of violence in obtaining that control. This does not imply that all policemen treat all sex deviants brutally, for, as the above quotations indicate, such is not the case. Rather, it indicates that this use of violence is permitted and condoned by the police and that they come to think of it as a resource more extensive than is included in the legal definition.

LEGITIMATION OF VIOLENCE

The preceding discussion has indicated two ways in which the experience of the police encourages them to use violence as a general resource in the achievement of their occupational ends and thus to sanction its illegal use. The experience, thus, makes violence acceptable to the policeman as a generalized means. We now wish to indicate the particular basis on which this general resource is legitimated. In particular we wish to point out the extent to which the policeman tends to transfer violence from a legal resource to a personal resource, one which he uses to further his own ends.

Seventy-three policemen, drawn from all ranks and constituting approximately 50 per cent of the patrolmen, were asked, "When do you think a policeman is justified in roughing a man up?" The intent of the question was to get them to legitimate the use of violence. Their replies are summarized in Table 1.

An inspection of the types and distribution of the responses indicates (1) that violence is legitimated by illegal ends (A, C, E, F, G) in 69 per cent of the cases; (2) that violence is legitimated in terms of purely personal or group ends (A) in 37 per cent of the cases (this is important, since it is the largest single reason for the use of violence given); and (3) that legal ends are the bases for legitimation in 31 per cent of the cases (B and D). However, this probably represents a distortion of the true feelings of some of these men, since both the police chief and the community had been severely critical of the use of violence by the men, and the respondents had a ten-

Table 1:[a] Bases for the Use of Force Named by 73 Policemen

Type of response		Frequency	Percentage
(A)	Disrespect for police	27	37
(B)	When impossible to avoid	17	23
(C)	To obtain information	14	19
(D)	To make an arrest	6	8
(E)	For the hardened criminal	5	7
(F)	When you know man is guilty	2	3
(G)	For sex criminals	2	3
	Total	73	100

[a]*Many respondents described more than one type of situation which they felt called for the use of violence. The "reason" which was either* (a) *given most heatedly and at greatest length and/or* (b) *given first was used to characterize the respondent's answer to the question. However, this table is exhaustive of the types of replies which were given.*

dency to be very cautious with the interviewer, whom some of them never fully trusted. Furthermore, since all the men were conscious of the chief's policy and of public criticism, it seems likely that those who did justify the use of violence for illegal and personal ends no longer recognized the illegality involved. They probably believed that such ends fully represented a moral legitimation for their use of violence.

The most significant finding is that at least 37 per cent of the men believed that it was legitimate to use violence to coerce respect. This suggests that policemen use the resource of violence to persuade their audience (the public) to respect their occupational status. In terms of the policeman's definition of the situation, the individual who lacks respect for the police, the "wise guy" who talks back, or any individual who acts or talks in a disrespectful way, deserves brutality. This idea is epitomized in admonitions given to the rookies such as, "You gotta make them respect you" and "You gotta act tough." Examples of some of the responses to the preceding question that fall into the "disrespect for the police" category follow:

Well, there are cases. For example, when you stop a fellow for a routine questioning, say a wise guy, and he starts talking back to you and telling you you are no good and that sort of thing. You know you can take a man in on a disorderly conduct charge, but you can practically never make it stick. So what you do in a case like that is to egg the guy on until he makes a remark where you can justifiably slap him and, then, if he fights back, you can call it resisting arrest.

Well, it varies in different cases. Most of the police use punishment if the fellow gives them any trouble. Usually you can judge a man who will give you trouble though. *If there is any slight resistance,* you can go all out on him. You shouldn't do it in the street though. Wait until you are in the squad car, because, even if you are in the right and a guy takes a poke at you, just when you are hitting back somebody's just likely to come around the corner, and what he will say is that you are beating the guy with your club.

Well, a prisoner deserves to be hit when he goes to the point where he tries to put you below him.

You gotta get rough when a man's language becomes very bad, when he is trying to make a fool of you in front of everybody else. I think most policemen try to treat people in a nice way, but usually you have to talk pretty rough. That's the only way to set a man down, to make him show a little respect.

If a fellow called a policeman a filthy name, a slap in the mouth would be a good thing, especially if it was out in the public where calling a policeman a bad name would look bad for the police.

There was the incident of a fellow I picked up. I was on the beat, and I was taking him down to the station. There were people following us. He kept saying that I wasn't in the army. Well, he kept going on like that, and I finally had to bust him one. I had to do it. The people would have thought I was afraid otherwise.

These results suggest (1) that the police believe that these private or group ends constitute a moral legitimation for violence which is equal *or superior* to the legitimation derived from the law and (2) that the monopoly of violence delegated to the police, by the state, to enforce the ends of the state has been appropriated by the police as a personal resource to be used for personal and group ends.

THE USE OF VIOLENCE

The sanctions for the use of violence arising from occupational experience and the fact that policemen morally justify even its illegal use may suggest that violence is employed with great frequency and little provocation. Such an impression would be erroneous, for the actual use of violence is limited by other considerations, such as individual inclinations, the threat of detection, and a sensitivity to public reactions.

Individual policemen vary of course in psychological disposition and past experience. All have been drawn from the larger community which tends to condemn the use of violence and therefore have internalized with varying degrees of intensity this other definition of violence. Their experience as policemen creates a new dimension to their self-conceptions and gives them a new perspective on the use of violence. But individual men vary in the degree to which they assimilate this new conception of self. Therefore, the amount of violence which is used and the frequency with which it is employed will vary among policemen according to their individual propensities. However, policemen cannot and do not employ sanctions against their colleagues for using violence,[6] and individual men who personally condemn the use of violence and avoid it whenever possible[7] refuse openly to condemn acts of violence by other men on the force. Thus, the collective sanction for the use of violence permits those men who are inclined to its use to employ it without fear.

All policemen, however, are conscious of the dangers of the illegal use of violence. If detected, they may be subject to a lawsuit and possibly dismissal from the force. Therefore, they limit its use to what they think they can get away with. Thus, they recognize that, if a man is guilty of a serious crime, it is easy to "cover up" for their brutality by accusing him of resisting arrest, and the extent to which they believe a man guilty tends to act as a precondition to the use of violence.[8]

---

[6] The emphasis on secrecy among the police prevents them from using legal sanctions against their colleagues.

[7] Many men who held jobs in the police station rather than on beats indicated to the interviewer that their reason for choosing a desk job was to avoid the use of violence.

[8] In addition, the policeman is aware that the courts are highly critical of confessions obtained by violence and that, if violence is detected, it will "spoil his case."

The policeman, in common with members of other occupations, is sensitive to the evaluation of his occupation by the public. A man's work is an important aspect of his status, and to the extent that he is identified with his work (by himself and/or the community) he finds that his self-esteem requires the justification and social elevation of his work. Since policemen are low in the occupational prestige scale, subject to continuous criticism, and in constant contact with this criticizing and evaluating public, they are profoundly involved in justifying their work and its tactics to the public and to themselves. The way in which the police emphasize the solution of big crimes and their violent solution to the problem of the control of sexual conduct illustrate this concern. However, different portions of the public have differing definitions of conduct and are of differential importance to the policeman, and the way in which the police define different portions of the public has an effect on whether or not they will use violence.

The police believe that certain groups of persons will respond only to fear and rough treatment. In the city studied they defined both Negroes and slum dwellers in this category. The following statements, each by a different man, typify the manner in which they discriminate the public:

In the good districts you appeal to people's judgment and explain the law to them. In the South Side the only way is to appear like you are the boss.

You can't ask them a question and get an answer that is not a lie. In the South Side the only way to walk into a tavern is to walk in swaggering as if you own the place and if somebody is standing in your way give him an elbow and push him aside.

The colored people understand one thing. The policeman is the law, and he is going to treat you rough and that's the way you have to treat them. Personally, I don't think the colored are trying to help themselves one bit. If you don't treat them rough, they will sit right on top of your head.

Discriminations with respect to the public are largely based on the political power of the group, the degree to which the police believe that the group is potentially criminal, and the type of treatment which the police believe will elicit respect from it.

Variations in the administration and community setting of the police will introduce variations in their use of violence. Thus, a thoroughly corrupt police department will use violence in supporting the ends of this corruption, while a carefully administered nonpolitical department can go a long way toward reducing the illegal use of violence. However, wherever the basic conditions here described are present, it will be very difficult to eradicate the illegal use of violence.

Given these conditions, violence will be used when necessary to the pursuit of duty or when basic occupational values are threatened. Thus a threat to the respect with which the policeman believes his occupation should be regarded or the opportunity to make a "good pinch" will tend to evoke its use.

CONCLUSIONS

This paper sets forth an explanation of the illegal use of violence by the police based on an interpretative understanding of their occupational experience. Therefore, it contains a description and analysis of *their* interpretation of *their* experience.

The policeman uses violence illegally because such usage is seen as just, acceptable, and, at times, expected by his colleague group and because it constitutes an effective means for solving problems in obtaining status and self-esteem which policemen as policemen have in common. Since the ends for which violence is illegally used are conceived to be both just and important, they function to justify, to the policeman, the illegal use of violence as a general means. Since "brutality" is strongly criticized by the larger community, the policeman must devise a defense of his brutality to himself and the community, and the defense in turn gives a deeper and more lasting justification to the "misuse of violence." This process then results in a transfer in property from the state to the colleague group. The means of violence which were originally a property of the state, in loan to its law-enforcement agent, the police, are in a psychological sense confiscated by the police, to be conceived of as a personal property to be used at their discretion. This, then, is the explanation of the illegal use of violence by the police which results from viewing it in terms of the police as an occupational group.

The explanation of the illegal use of violence by the police offers an illuminating perspective on the social nature of their occupation. The analysis of their use of brutality in dealing with sexual deviants and felons shows that it is a result of their desire to defend and improve their social status in the absence of effective legal means. This desire in turn is directly related to and makes sense in terms of the low status of the police in the community, which results in a driving need on the part of policemen to assert and improve their status. Their general legitimation of the use of violence *primarily* in terms of coercing respect and making a "good pinch" clearly points out the existence of occupational goals, which are independent of and take precedence over their legal mandate. The existence of such goals and patterns of conduct indicates that the policeman has made of his occupation a preoccupation and invested in it a large aspect of his self.

On the Job

ARTHUR NIEDERHOFFER

THE ROOKIE AT THE PRECINCT

The recruit reports to his precinct with some anxiety, but in general ready to practice what has been preached to him at the Academy [New York City Police Academy]. According to the general code of deportment, which covers the behavior of the newcomer, he is expected to be a good listener, quiet, unassuming, and deferential without being obsequious toward his superior officers. Despite a good deal of hazing as part of the breaking-in period the recruit usually adapts to these standards without difficulty.

For a month or so, he receives lenience and sympathy for routine mistakes. After that he is on trial and carefully watched to see how he measures up to the challenge of police patrol. His reputation is made in the next few weeks and will shadow him for the rest of his police career: no matter where or when he is transferred, a phone call will precede his arrival, reporting the evaluation that was made of his handling of his first few important cases.

On these cases the new patrolman must resolve the dilemma of choosing between the professional ideal of police work he has learned at the Academy and the pragmatic precinct approach. In the Academy, where professionalism is accented, the orientation is toward that of the social sciences and opposed to the "lock-them-up" philosophy. But in the precinct a patrolman is measured by his arrest record. Thus the new man is needled when he shows signs of diffidence in arresting or asserting his authority. Over and over again well-meaning old-timers reiterate, "You gotta be tough, kid, or you'll never last." Fifteen years ago Westley observed this phenomenon in the police force he studied and explained the basic rationalization behind the slogan:

Expecting the excuse, the argument, the evasion, the officer tries to get tough first, to treat them tough, to make them respect the law, a particular judgment of the law. . . . This is the origin of the get tough, make them respect you thesis which predominates throughout police work.[1]

It is disconcerting to find that a similar solution to the practitioner-client problem is widely accepted in other service professions, that have none of the authoritarian flavor of the police force. In probation and parole work Lloyd Ohlin found that

From *Behind the Shield* by Arthur Niederhoffer. Copyright © 1967 by Arthur Niederhoffer. Reprinted by permission of the author and Doubleday & Company, Inc.

[1] William A. Westley, "The Police: A Sociological Study of Law, Custom, and Morality," unpublished Ph. D. dissertation, University of Chicago, 1951, p. 112.

The (social) worker experiences widespread pressure by the police and other official functionaries to define his role as that of the enforcement officer who should
use control measures to restrict the client's freedom and coercion to punish him
for wrongdoing. When he attempts to resist these pressures, he finds probation
and parole interpreted as leniency and himself identified as a "sob sister."[2]

According to Howard S. Becker's analysis of the teacher-pupil relationship,
some teachers adopt the same attitude toward their charges:

You can't ever let them get the upper hand on you or you're through. So I start
out tough. . . . You've got to start out tough then you can ease up as you go along.
If you start out easy-going, when you try to get tough, they'll just look at you and
laugh.[3]

That a "get tough" ideology dominates many workers in the major institutions devoted to the education, control, and welfare of the public is of prime
importance to sociologists. Why should the field practitioner, in actual contact
with the clientele he is supposed to serve, develop a philosophy so contrary
to the creed of altruism and service that his profession exalts? Apparently,
practical experience leads to the acceptance of a Hobbesian model of the social
system.

In the case of the young policeman the choice between professionalism and
pragmatism is apt to depend largely on the circumstances of the case. It is,
for example, no great feat for a policeman working in an upper-class neighborhood to protect the rights of his white clientele. It is much more difficult
in a lower-class community. In a slum area the professional ethic loses most
of the time: the civil rights of lower-class individuals do not count as much
as the necessity to accomplish a staggering amount of police work as ex-
peditiously as possible. Shifting from idealism to pragmatism, the newcomer
to a lower-class precinct house enters a new reference group whose members
are a little contemptuous of all the Academy represents.

LEARNING THE ROPES: LANGUAGE

The identification with this new group is revealed in many facets of behavior and personality. Speech patterns increasingly reflect the loss of influence of Academy training, which demanded a decent level of grammar and
vocabulary. Police terminology, which substitutes broad stereotypes for precise distinctions, becomes a linguistic crutch. The colloquialism "desperate"
means anything bad, unpleasant, or derogatory. "Radical" is used to label

[2] Lloyd E. Ohlin, H. Piven, and Don Pappenfort, "Major Dilemmas of
the Social Worker in Probation and Parole," *National Probation and Parole
Association Journal,* 2 (July, 1956), p. 221.
[3] Howard S. Becker, "Social Class Variations in the Teacher-Pupil Relationship," *Journal of Educational Sociology,* 25 (1951–1952), p. 459.

anyone who is not reactionary, or at least conservative, even those policemen who are articulate in protesting about long-accepted conditions in the department. A "detail" is a special job or assignment — usually a desirable one. "Rabbi" means a person with influence in the department. Although Jewish policemen suspect the dark origins of this neologism, they cannot help being amused when they overhear conversations like the following:

"Say, did you hear that O'Grady finally got that detail to the Detective Division?"

"No. But I knew that he had a contract in. Who was his rabbi?"

"His rabbi? Why his uncle, the priest, of course." The word "contract" is very important in the police world. It can mean any obligation, debt, errand, request, agreement, or arrangement.[4]

A whole class of colorful idioms is derived from parts of the body. "Hairy" stands for smart, shrewd, and conniving. "On the arm," and "egghead" are fairly well known in common parlance. A courageous policeman who stands up for his rights is complimented with the description, "he has a lot of balls."[5]

In the precinct even the well-educated officers adopt this slovenly jargon, sometimes consciously, to merge their identities with those of the "common men" on the force. They purposely say mischiev-*i*-ous and mispronounce other common words in order to belong and conform.[6] The police role and its special argot cannot, however, be donned for eight hours a day without making serious inroads: when the time comes for the intellectual to slough off his occupational speech patterns, he is often unsuccessful, to his great embarrassment.

Although official police policy strongly condemns any reciprocity between policemen and criminal elements, it nonetheless exists and is mirrored in a shared vocabulary. This social interaction is unwittingly recognized as unavoidable by the authoritative *FBI Law Enforcement Bulletin*. The editors, listing a glossary of several hundred words and phrases commonly used by the underworld, are forced to justify the fact that at least one-half of the list is included in the police lexicon:

Just as the newspaperman, the short-order cook, or the baseball player has a

---

[4] There are varying degrees of obligation in each contract. When it is performed, a reciprocal obligation arises to fulfill a contract in return. Sometimes, in the performance of a contract, several intermediaries are approached in order to attain the final result. Each of these middlemen becomes enmeshed in this contractual web. Thus, it forms an unofficial system of rights and obligations that often controls interpersonal relations more stringently than do bureaucratic protocol and hierarchy.

[5] For a parallel study of the use of "body" terms in the jargon of an all-male society, see Henry Elkin, "Aggressive and Erotic Tendencies in Army Life," *American Journal of Sociology*, 51 (1945–1946), pp. 411–412.

[6] In "The Intellectuals and the Language of Minorities," *American Journal of Sociology*, 64 (1958–1959), pp. 25–35, Melvin Seeman has shown that where intellectuals are minorities, they often employ defensive tactics of this type.

specialized manner of expressing himself, so has the juvenile gang member, the
criminal and, by necessity, the police officer. . . .

The words on pages 24, 25 are included in the jargon of the violator as well as
that of the law enforcement officer, since it is difficult to separate one from the
other. The policeman, finding it necessary to be cognizant of the criminal's lingo,
frequently absorbs it as part of his own speech and uses the terms and phrases in his
general police activities, as well as contributing to it many colorful forms of expression of his own.[7]

RITUAL

Along with a new vocabulary, the new patrolman also picks up a series of
rituals, several of them vital to the world of the policeman. One — the "coffee
and" ritual which began each tour of duty — operated with unforgettable
potency during the time I was on the beat. Each day en route to his post the
patrolman stopped almost compulsively at his favorite luncheonette or cafe-
teria for coffee and cake. Even when a tough "shoofly"[8] was reported in the
vicinity, a "real" cop felt obliged to risk the chance of receiving a complaint
to stop for his coffee. Since the ritual was followed even on sweltering summer days, it could not be related to his desire to warm up. It had nothing to
do with hunger because in most cases the men came to work just after a
heavy meal. It was not a "break" to relieve fatigue; the tour was just starting. In some manner the coffee seemed to allay the vestige of anxiety every
thinking policeman carries with him on his tour of patrol. Life and death are
so closely bound up with police work that the ceremonious interruption, like
a religious duty, may have constituted a libation to the gods.

FOOT PATROL

The basic job of the police force is patrol, where most recruits start. The
patrolman pounding his beat is the proletarian of the department, and, like
proletarians in most countries, accorded a very low status. His position has
been realistically described in the *Police Management Review,* issued by the
Planning Bureau of the New York City Police Department:

Yet, more than anyone else in the Department, the foot patrolman is prone to
boredom and inertia. Young and initially enthusiastic men are often bored at a
time when a proportion of the Force is overworked.[9]

---

[7] "Juvenile Gangs and Underworld Have Own Lingo," *FBI Law Enforcement Bulletin,* 30 (January, 1961), pp. 22–23.
[8] A "shoofly" is a supervisor of patrol who purposely dresses in civilian
clothes rather than in proper uniform in order to avoid being spotted by the
men on patrol.
[9] Lieutenant Matthew J. Neary, "Motivating the Foot Patrolman," *Police
Management Review* (November, 1963), p. 5.

The working hours of the foot patrolman, the recurrent bad publicity, the indifferent attitudes of the public, the fact that promotion and earnings are almost completely divorced from the performance of his duties, all constitute an imposing array of anti-motivating factors.[10]

The patrolman can find little satisfaction in his work when something goes wrong on his post; although the investigation starts at the very top, inevitably the "buck" is passed down until the final responsibility and blame come to rest upon him. When, however, praise is lavished, some superior officer or member of the force in a special assignment appears from nowhere to accept the accolade. Moreover, the patrolman, although he does a little of everything, is being increasingly restricted to trivialities because police work is constantly developing specialties that only trained experts can handle. Just when the work becomes most interesting, a specialist is assigned to replace the lowly "man on the post."

In the exciting cases, such as homicides or serious felonies, the patrolman on post must notify the station house as soon as he discovers the incident. Within minutes, a superior officer from the Detective Division assumes command. From then on the patrolman is a supernumerary. Detectives swarm over the scene searching for clues, interviewing witnesses and suspects, handling specific parts of the investigation. The Photo Unit arrives to take pictures. The Mobile Laboratory rolls up and scientific instruments are trundled into the crime area. The patrolman, shunted to one side, is sometimes allowed to guard the scene, by which time he may be wondering just how necessary he really is. It may, however, be worth noting that even the detective who supplants the patrolman will have only a moment of glory if he solves the case. The computer has invaded the world of the police. Soon the only record of his achievement will be a few holes punched on an I.B.M. card stockpiled in some basement storeroom. Alienation may not be as universal a condition in contemporary society as some social critics allege, but a computerized milieu fosters foreboding uneasiness.

The foot patrolman with heavy responsibility but no prestige either on or off the job becomes first bitter, then apathetic. Many times I have asked a young patrolman how many years he has had on the job. A common response is, "I have seventeen years, four months, two weeks, and three days to go until retirement." Small wonder that the score of foot patrolmen on the cynicism questionnaire was significantly higher than the mean score of the total sample.

KEEPING THE LAW

Another potent source of cynicism is the new policeman's realization that it is literally impossible to enforce every law "on the book" — the jails would

[10] *Ibid.,* p. 7.

be too small to hold the prisoners — and that one of the important arts he must master is the sense of when to take action and, perhaps more important, when not to. An officer who brings too many trivial cases into the station house is considered incompetent, but an officer who brings in too few is considered a shirker.

The conventional wisdom of the job sets the standard. The old sages of the station house dispense didactic tales to which new members of the force listen avidly, thereby learning that typical incidents to be settled on the street, or occasionally even dodged, are the annoying drunk, the case of disorderly conduct involving adolescents who congregate on street corners, and quarrels between: husband and wife, taxi driver and his fare, neighbor and neighbor, store owner and customer, and landlord and tenants.

When an officer clearly observes a serious violation of law, his discretion is limited; he must arrest. But the average crime is not committed in full view of the policeman. He must conduct a preliminary investigation which places him in the middle of a labyrinth, following conflicting reports of witnesses into blind alleys. Each suspect denies any connection with the crime. Perpetrators claim to be victims. From time to time progress is barred by a wall of silence. Shall he make an arrest or not? Which of the suspects should he arrest? Just when he needs them most, the usual guideposts are silent. His wisest procedure is to trust no one. Cynicism improves his technique as an investigator.[11]

It is the individual policeman's responsibility to decide if and how the law should be applied, and he searches for the proper combination of cues on which to base his decision. These are derived from the typical sociological variables: class, education, clarity of role prescriptions, reference groups, self-conception, and visibility. Because the application of the law depends to a large degree on the definition of the situation and the decision reached by the patrolman, he, in effect, makes the law; it is his decision that establishes the boundary between legal and illegal.

Always searching for this tenuous and blurred dividing line in the behavior of others, the policeman frequently loses the ability to distinguish between law and license in himself. As the result of United States Supreme Court decisions, kaleidoscopic changes in the practical application of the law have confused the average patrolman until he is often uncertain of the proper course of action. His ignorance dims the luster of the law because the policeman learns to manipulate law in the name of expediency, and this loss of respect, in turn, breeds more cynicism.

In the administration of justice, the poor, the minorities, and the deviants

---

[11] Despite his typical mistrust, the average policeman fancies himself a keen psychologist, who can by intuition, and/or experience, sense when a person being interrogated is lying or telling the truth.

need all the protection possible. They suffer most when the police fail to take proper action. In busy precincts covering sections inhabited by Negroes or Puerto Ricans, this sphere of inaction is large. Incidents that would cause commotion and consternation in quiet precincts seem so common in ghetto neighborhoods that they are often not reported. The police rationalize this avoidance of duty with theories that the victim would refuse to prosecute because violence has become the accepted way of life for his community, and that any other course would result in a great loss of time in court, which would reduce the efficiency of other police functions. These decisions are rarely subjected to review, a particularly disturbing situation to men who are interested in creating a better system of justice.[12]

Police decisions not to invoke the criminal process largely determine the outer limits of law enforcement. By such decisions, the police define the ambit of discretion throughout the process of other decision-makers — prosecutor, grand and petit jury, judge, probation officer, correction authority, and parole and pardon boards. These police decisions, unlike their decisions to invoke the law, are of extremely low visibility and consequently are seldom the subject of review. Yet an opportunity for review and appraisal of non-enforcement decisions is essential to the functioning of the rule of law in our system of criminal justice.[13]

When the professionals attack this non-enforcement of the law, the articulate defender of the status quo has a powerful riposte: he can plead that the social sciences so profusely quoted by the professionals also teach the lesson of cultural relativity. This doctrine encourages an observer from one culture to respect the integrity of another, although its standards of behavior may be different from his own. The implication is that the policeman has some justification for accepting a minority group's way of life on its own terms, and thus for acting the way he does. There is no easy answer to this paradox.

A harsher indictment of the police officer's neglect or refusal to enforce the law has been pronounced by Martin Luther King who holds that nonfeasance amounts to malfeasance:

The most grievous charge against municipal police is not brutality, although it exists. Permissive crime in ghettos is the nightmare of the slum family. Permissive crime is the name for the organized crime that flourishes in the ghetto — designed, directed, and cultivated by white national crime syndicates operating numbers, narcotics, and prostitution rackets freely in the protected sanctuaries of the ghet-

---

[12] Joseph Goldstein, "Police Discretion Not to Invoke the Criminal Process: Low Visibility Decisions in the Administration of Justice," *The Yale Law Journal*, 69 (1960), pp. 574–575. See also Herman Goldstein, "Police Discretion: The Ideal Versus the Real," *Public Administration Review*, 23 (September, 1963), pp. 140–148; and Wayne R. LaFave, *Arrest: The Decision to Take a Suspect into Custody* (Boston: Little, Brown and Co., 1965).

[13] Joseph Goldstein, *op. cit.*, p. 543.

tos. Because no one, including the police, cares particularly about ghetto crime, it pervades every area of life.[14]

THE SUMMONS

Even the routine, apparently trivial duties that the young policeman must learn to handle may easily escalate into a near riot unless he controls them properly. Take, for example, the serving of a summons on a peddler. The public observing this event is apt to react with hostility toward the policeman. The officer himself may feel a little guilty.

This appears to be a universal dilemma for policemen. Anatole France has written a short story, "Crainquebille,"[15] which depicts the repercussions in the life of a French vegetable seller when Constable 64 arrests him for peddling. When the policeman orders Crainquebille to move on, the vendor mutters something under his breath which sounds to the policeman like *"Mort aux Vaches,"* in those days, a vile insult that meant literally "Death to the Cows," but was interpreted as "Down with the Cops."[16]

During World War II, a New York City policeman had an equally harrowing experience with a peddler, selling pretzels, who set up her daily shop in front of a well-known department store. One of the patrolman's important duties was to keep the post clear of peddlers, by no means an easy assignment on a busy shopping day. Although Molly, as we shall call her, was small and elderly, she had the strength and speed of an athlete. She dexterously threaded her way through the crowds, unseen by the police until she set down her basket at a suitable spot. No matter how many times she was chased away, she always reappeared.

One day the patrolman became so exasperated that he decided to serve her with a summons. At the sight of his summons book, Molly began to scream, "Murderer! He's killing me! Why doesn't he catch criminals instead of ruining a poor woman who is trying to make an honest living? Nazi!" With this she threw herself down on the ground, and rolled around in a fit of fury or despair, never stopping the stream of epithets. The policeman (who was Jewish himself) was thoroughly embarrassed by the obvious rancor of the crowd of hundreds gathered to watch the show. Arrest seemed the only answer, and in desperation he asked a bystander to call the precinct for a patrol wagon.

After a struggle, he placed Molly and her heavy pretzel basket into the

---

[14] Martin Luther King, "Beyond the Los Angeles Riots: Next Stop: The North," *Saturday Review,* 48 (November 13, 1965), p. 34.

[15] Anatole France, "Crainquebille," in *Golden Tales of Anatole France* (New York: Dodd Mead and Co., 1926), pp. 215–257.

[16] It is interesting to note that in France the police were called "cows" in the vernacular, but to Americans the police are "bulls."

wagon, climbed in himself, and signaled the driver to proceed. Suddenly he noticed a transformation in the prisoner. The histrionics had stopped. As they slowly pulled away from the scene, Molly peered intently through the rear grating, a quiet smile of triumph on her face. The officer glanced out. From the subway kiosk Molly's husband, Abie, was emerging, loaded down with an overflowing basket of pretzels, certain of a couple of uninterrupted hours of brisk sales. It was impossible to escape the suspicion of prearrangement.

Police management hotly denies the existence of a summons quota. Men at the patrol level are not so sure about this. In November 1960 there was a well-publicized altercation between then New York Police Commissioner Kennedy and Patrolman John J. Cassese, the president of the Patrolmen's Benevolent Association. Patrolman Cassese bought advertising space in the New York City press in which he alleged that there was definitely a quota system, and that he could prove it.[17] Thereupon the delegates to the P.B.A. were given questionnaires demanding whether or not they knew of any summons quota system. According to the *Herald Tribune,* delegates who answered negatively admitted later that they had lied[18] to keep from having to reveal the names of the superior officers responsible for ordering the quota system. The so-called "rat rule" requires a member of the force having knowledge of a violation of departmental regulations to report it to a superior officer, but these policemen preferred to perjure themselves rather than be known as informers.[19]

GRAFT

Every policeman patrolling the streets sooner or later faces the temptation of a "payoff." As in most other large organizations, there are the few who have their price, but their betrayal of the public trust has unjustifiably tarnished the whole department. The image of the crooked cop projected in literature has fortified this misconception. In *The Iceman Cometh,* Eugene O'Neill described ex-Lieutenant Pat McGloin as "the biggest drunken grafter that ever disgraced the police force." McGloin's former position lures him, and his one hope is to be reinstated because "there's fine pickings these

---

[17] It is of interest that Commissioner Kennedy on December 9, 1959, sent a teletype message to all commands explaining why there could not be a quota: "Inasmuch as there is no quota on persons killed and injured, there cannot be and there is no quota on enforcement." See New York *Herald Tribune,* November 29, 1960, p. 15.

[18] New York *Herald Tribune,* November 29, 1960, pp. 1, 15.

[19] A statement concerning the existence of a summons quota was included in the cynicism questionnaire. Well over half the patrolmen, and more than forty per cent of the superior officers apparently do believe that a summons quota exists.

days."[20] Actual policemen seem to accept graft for other reasons than avarice. Often the first transgression is inadvertent. Or, they may be gradually indoctrinated by older policemen. Step by step they progress from a small peccadillo to outright shakedown and felony.

A Denver policeman involved in the police burglary scandal of 1961 recalls his downfall.

> So the rookie . . . is turned over to a more experienced man for breaking in. . . .
>
> He knows he is being watched. . . . He is eager to be accepted.
>
> He does what he can to show he has guts. He backs up his partner in any way he can. . . .
>
> It may happen like this: the older man stops at a bar, comes out with some packages of cigarettes. He does this several times. He explains that this is part of the job. . . .
>
> So he, the rookie, goes into a Skid Row bar and stands uncomfortably at the end, waiting for the bartender to acknowledge his presence and disdainfully toss him two packages of butts.
>
> The feeling of pride slips away, and a hint of shame takes hold.
>
> One thing leads to another for the rookies. After six months they have become conditioned to accept free meals, a few packs of cigarettes, turkeys at Thanksgiving and liquor at Christmas from the respectable people in their districts. . . .[21]

Lincoln Steffens, one of the great muckrakers, studied police corruption in New York and other cities at the end of the nineteenth century.[22] His report of the Schmittberger saga is documented by the records of the Lexow Commission. The blemished hero of the story is a baker named Schmittberger who became a member of the New York City Police Department and was assigned to the Tenderloin district. He was so honest, and so dumb, that when someone came up to him one day and put ten dollars in his hand while he was on patrol, he immediately turned it over to his captain. The captain was so impressed by this honesty, that he rewarded Schmittberger in the most fitting way possible — by making him his graft collection man. Schmittberger showed great talent for his new job. Finally he turned State's evidence during the Lexow investigation and thus retained his job. Theodore Roosevelt, the new Police Commissioner, was eager to eliminate vice in the city and corruption in the department. Steffens advised him to rely upon Schmittberger

---

[20] Eugene O'Neill, *The Iceman Cometh* (New York: Random House, 1946), pp. 55, 57.

[21] Mort Stern, "What Makes a Policeman Go Wrong?" *Journal of Criminal Law, Criminology and Police Science,* 53 (March, 1962), pp. 98–99.

[22] Lincoln Steffens, *The Shame of the Cities* (New York: McClure Phillips & Co., 1904); Lincoln Steffens, *The Autobiography of Lincoln Steffens* (New York: Harcourt, Brace & Co., 1931). For one of the latest of the many books on the subject of police corruption, see Ralph L. Smith, *The Tarnished Badge* (New York: Thomas Y. Crowell Co., 1965).

as the spearhead of the campaign. Schmittberger, the most assiduous collector of graft under the former regime, responded by devoting his tremendous energy and experience to the problem of arresting or outlawing gamblers and prostitutes.

Schmittberger's initial encounter with graft was not unique. The pattern has repeated itself through the years. A similar case from the 1940's, involved a young policeman who held a college degree. The commanding officer of the precinct, favorably impressed by the patrolman's obvious attempt to do a good job, called him into his office to discuss the problem of organized gambling in the precinct and shortly after assigned him to a special park post to arrest, if possible, the suspected bookmakers who were supposed to operate in the area.

The park was as famous as Hyde Park in London. Radicals and political dissenters of every persuasion made it their headquarters. On the crosswalks, rival speakers harangued listeners and thundered against each other, the system, and the "lackeys of the ruling class." Our college-trained patrolman grew so familiar with the appellation that he did not even flinch at it, but thought it odd that they were berating him for protecting their right to fulminate against the power elite. He was in his element. College had prepared him for such an assignment.

Among the various groups — some arguing vociferously, others deeply immersed in the latest *Daily Worker* — the officer walked his post with a smug sense of accomplishment. What other officer could mediate so well among Stalinists, Trotskyites, Lovestone-ites, Nazis, and Fascists? Whether it was dialectic materialism, united front, permanent revolution, or any of the other current political clichés, our hero could handle himself well.

He became a species of referee to whom disputants would appeal for redress. A supporter of the Fascists would accost him and whisper to him that a dangerous "Red" with a knife had threatened to stab him. A Trotskyite might slip him a note containing allegations against a Nazi. He did a wonderful job of controlling the political tempers and wars in the park. But he never noticed any sign of bookmaking or gambling.

This went on for several months. One winter night about 6:00 P.M. almost everyone had deserted the park because it was raining heavily. One persistent group, however, was still busily engaged in a discussion of some abstruse point in the *Worker*. The patrolman approached them and, wanting to get them out of the park so he could "grab a fast cup of coffee," called out roughly, "Why don't you go home? Here you are trying to settle the world's problems and you don't even know enough to get out of the rain." The apparent leader of the group said, "Officer, I'll speak to you later." The officer, anticipating the usual accusations against rival groups in the park, responded,

"Don't bother speaking to me at all. Just pack up and get out of here." Then he turned and walked away.

He heard someone follow him from the group and felt a wad of paper thrust stealthily into his hand. Certain that it was another "piece of vital information" he looked at it contemptuously. He was shocked to see that this time there were two bills in his palm.

When he saw his side partner, Big Fred, he eagerly told the story. Big Fred looked at him queerly and said, "That was Izzy, the bookie. Do you mean to tell me you've been working in the park this whole time and don't know Izzy?" At that moment the rookie saw how far he had to travel before he became a real "cop." The bookie and his horseplayers had been busy all those weeks discussing, not the Third International at Moscow but the Third Invitational at Hialeah. Behind every *Daily Worker* had been a copy of the *Daily Racing Form*.

The strange thing is that a policeman can take the payoff and still consider himself an honest or innocent man. The Denver policeman reacted to graft by saying:

that this is okay, that all the men accept these things, that this is a far cry from stealing and they can still be good policemen.[23]

Lincoln Steffens gives a more involved explanation to the same effect.

The collections, he, Schmittberger, was to make for his captain were the regular monthly payments by gamblers, prostitutes, saloons — all law-breakers — for the privilege of breaking the law, rightly called police protection. . . .

The big business was the regular graft that Schmittberger handled for years, all in the day's work, without losing either his honesty or, it seemed to me, all his innocence. I often afterward reviewed this part of his experience; it bore upon my old interest in moral and ethical psychology. My note was that the process of corruption had begun so quietly with the first tip and proceeded so gradually in an environment where it was all a matter of course, that this man never realized what he was doing till the Lexow Committee's exposure.[24]

Knowing that the Penal Law and the police regulations clearly prohibit such malfeasance, how is it possible for an experienced policeman to accept money, and at the same time maintain that he is innocent of any wrongdoing? Such psychological prestidigitation can be accomplished only by artful casuistry based on cynicism. The policeman rationalizes with twisted logic: "I am not hurting anyone. Everyone is doing the same thing. Most people are much worse. The public thinks a policeman is dishonest whether he is or not. Therefore, I am not doing anything wrong by taking graft."

---

[23] Mort Stern, *op. cit.*, p. 99.
[24] Lincoln Steffens, *The Autobiography of Lincoln Steffens, op. cit.*, pp. 272–273.

THE ARREST

The function of the police department that justifies the claim of professional status is crime prevention. This special function is measured, validly or not, by the "good pinch." Not only the public, but also the police themselves accept this standard; as a result, they glorify the felony arrest.

The apprehension of the felon then represents for these men a source of prestige in the police department . . . and in the community.[25]

Yet according to the research division of the International Association of Chiefs of Police, "the percentage of the police effort devoted to the traditional criminal law matters probably does not exceed ten per cent."[26] Police forces have been overwhelmed with onerous administrative and regulative duties which keep them from devoting their major attention to preventing crime. Moreover, the advocates of professionalism, by stressing the qualities of police integrity rather than mere performance, have given a curious twist to the act of arrest. It is well known that gambling syndicates are the commonest source of police corruption. Thus the professionals on the force hail the arrest of a known gambler or bookie as a great feat and often allow it to assume more significance than an arrest for a serious felony. The patrolman, not sharing the professionals' artificial viewpoint on this subject, never considers the bookie as a criminal in the same class with a rapist or a mugger, and explains the peculiar reversal of values in which a "bookie's" arrest is a cause for more celebration than a felony arrest is by abscribing either stupidity or hypocrisy to the "big brass."

One overpowering reason for cynicism among patrolmen is that it stimulates an outstanding arrest record. The very cynical officer rejects the possibility of decent impulses in others. By undertaking many investigations and never letting up in his relentless justification of this morbid distrust, he is following the advice laid down by the experts. For example, in the obituary of James Leggett, former Chief of Detectives of the New York City Police Department, the *New York Times* reported that Leggett frequently urged his subordinates to probe, probe, probe, until they came up with the answers.

[25] Westley, "The Police: A Sociological Study of Law, Custom, and Morality," *op. cit.*, p. 225.

[26] Richard A. Myren and Lynn D. Swanson, *Police Contacts with Juveniles: Perspectives, Guidelines, 2nd Review Draft*, June 1961 (Washington, D.C.: Children's Bureau, United States Department of Health, Education and Welfare, 1961), pp. 1–4. In an empirical study of the Syracuse Police Department, 801 incoming telephone calls were analyzed over a period of eighty-two hours in the summer of 1961. Only 20 per cent of the calls were related to crime or violence. See Elaine Cumming, Ian M. Cumming, and Laura Edell, "Policeman as Philosopher, Guide and Friend," *Social Problems*, 12 (Winter, 1965), p. 279.

You have to be nosey, use your eyes and your ears, and continually ask questions. . . .

Keep saying to yourself, over and over, "What's the answer?" Take nothing for granted. . . .[27]

A high arrest record reinforces the cynicism that inspired it in the first place, while often establishing a policeman's reputation for initiative and efficiency. His superiors recommend him for assignment to the detective division. This route to promotion appeals to many young policemen who have little hope of passing a written competitive test for promotion, and impels many of them to adopt cynicism as a rational and functional way to advancement.

THE FIVE YEAR MAN

By the time a patrolman has had five years on the force, he has usually started casting about for a "good detail" in order to escape from foot patrol duty. Upon hearing rumors of impending transfers, patrolmen seek to arrange "contracts with rabbis." The lower ranks tend to believe that special assignments depend on "whom you know," and not on merit.[28]

In most cases, detective work is the detail preferred above all others. However, most policemen will accept any detail "as long as I get 'out of the bag' (uniform)." Defining this as simply the desire for upward mobility would be short-sighted. The implications go much deeper to reveal the policemen's urge to escape from foot patrol duty in uniform, not only because of its low status, but also because a large proportion of the men become "fed up" with this basic job of all police systems. Their service motivation has become extinguished: they want to remove the uniform that publicly identifies them as policemen.

This desire impels many officers to prepare for the second ladder of upward mobility, the civil service promotion test. Day after day the patrolman studying for the sergeant's examination plods his way to the "cram" school, sometimes to two or three schools on consecutive days. There are men who have been attending such classes for twenty years, and are still optimistic.

All too quickly, the policeman moves along his career line. Until his twelfth year there is the possibility of leaving police work for a more attractive and remunerative position. After this, he realizes that in only eight more years he will be entitled to a pension, and his desire to leave quickly diminishes. . . .

---

[27] *New York Times,* January 17, 1962, p. 33.

[28] In the study of cynicism 40 per cent of the patrolmen shared this view, in the face of strong protestations to the contrary by top officials of the department.

THE DETECTIVE

Crime novels often portray police department detectives as stupid, sadistic, lecherous, and altogether second-rate when compared with the "private eye" — that omniscient and ithyphallic standard-bearer of all that is noble. Erle Stanley Gardner, who mass-produces "whodunits" and qualifies as an expert on this phase of American culture, has some interesting and relevant opinions:

And as far as detective fiction is concerned, the "dumb" cop is a fixture because the public demands him! In fact, it is as necessary to have a "dumb" cop in a detective story as it is to have a clever detective.

For some years now, I have been interested in better law enforcement and my conscience got to bothering me about the manner in which Perry Mason pulled an intellectual razzle-dazzle on the dumb cops I had created in my books. Therefore, I decided to write a book in which I would show the police in their true colors and in which Mason would race neck and neck to a solution with the character who had previously taken the part of the dumb cop. The result was that the publisher was literally deluged with letters of protest from book dealers and public alike.[29]

Contrary to the fantasies of the paperback thrillers, the public actually accords great respect and prestige to the detective, far more than it grants to the uniformed beat patrolman. A detective's clothes, mannerisms, easy familiarity with superior officers, and snobbish aloofness from uniformed patrolmen are all part of his impressive front, helping him to dramatize his status and work performance. Within the police hierarchy the detective also enjoys an exalted status. Almost every cop dreams of the day when he will "make the bureau" and become a "big dick." Commissioners grant assignment to the detective bureau as a reward for exceptional performance. All members of the force know the benefits of detective work. Most imagine many more than exist, but there are three immediately apparent advantages: higher salary, more interesting work, and "getting out of the bag."

Nearly every patrolman who comes into the department dreams of one day "making the bureau." He glories in thoughts of working in street clothes, sometimes in the most deceptive disguises, tracking down a dangerous gunman, searching for a clue at the scene of a homicide, lifting a fingerprint from a bloodied axe handle. . . .[30]

Candidates for detective units are usually given some preparatory training at the Police Academy. Their anticipatory socialization immediately displays itself. Their clothes take on an "Ivy" look: jackets, hats, carefully knotted

[29] Erle Stanley Gardner, "The Need for New Concepts in the Administration of Criminal Justice," *Journal of Criminal Law, Criminology and Police Science,* 50 (May–June, 1959), p. 22.
[30] *Spring 3100,* 30 (July–August, 1959), p. 15.

ties, and trench coats replace the sweaters, lumberjackets, and hunters' caps worn by the less fortunate patrolmen.

Detectives are the upper class of police society and haughtily guard their special status and privileges. Their quarters are separate from those of the uniformed force. Within this private domain democratic camaraderie eliminates the social distance that ordinarily divides the various ranks of a bureaucratic hierarchy. A lower-ranking detective may call a detective captain by his first name without causing any surprise; he may walk arm-in-arm with a detective inspector (a very high superior officer), while discussing an important case.

Some cynics explain this nonchalant disregard of organizational protocol as the result of nepotism in department appointments. They claim that since almost every detective must have an important "rabbi," to get in the division no clever operator would risk antagonizing some unknown and powerful sponsor by being rude to his protégé, and thus adopts a friendly and democratic policy toward subordinates.

Because of the higher status of detectives within the department, a new policeman tends to assume that they are superior to uniformed men in intelligence or motivation. A strong minority on the force asserts on the contrary that a detective's value and future success depend on the private sources of information at his disposal, and his willingness to do the necessary leg work. They support this opinion by citing the many brilliant detectives in police history who could never have passed an I.Q. test, could hardly write an intelligible report, and whose techniques of investigation constantly violated every recommended principle of scientific detection.

Unexpected corroboration for this minority belief comes from a fabled detective whose heyday was forty years ago. As head of New York City's famed Italian Squad, which successfully battled the Mafia, Lieutenant Fiaschetti spoke with authority about the requirements for success as a detective, and evaluated the storybook detective intellectual rather pungently:

> It makes me tired to read how those bulls in books solve mysteries with their deductions. In the honest-to-God story of how the detective gets his man, stool pigeon's the word.[31]

It is also true that ambitious detectives strive to build up a private circle of informers which automatically connects them to the criminal underworld.

This interaction between detective and criminal is by no means confined to the American police force. In London, Scotland Yard sometimes depends on streetwalkers for tips. The effectiveness of this liaison was demonstrated

---

[31] Michael Fiaschetti, *You Gotta Be Rough* (New York: Doubleday Doran & Co., 1930), p. 27.

after prostitutes were forbidden to solicit on the streets. As one Scotland Yard detective complained,

> One quite eccentric result of the street clearing was shown almost immediately by a series of successful jewel robberies at night in London which caught the police unprepared. "It's the fault of that Act," said one of the detectives to the press. "The girls used to notice when anything funny was up — they hadn't much else to do walking about — and they'd tip us off." Nowadays, the police depend on the ordinary marks, and have to do without streetgirl volunteers. It wasn't a very wide or reliable source of information; but it was something.[32]

The freedom of the detective division to form and utilize contacts with the criminal world underlines the peculiarly open structure of this segment of the police force. With its easygoing approach to interpersonal relations, its lack of concern for the formal regulations that hamstring the rest of the department, and its informal discipline, the division forms what might be called a mock bureaucracy.[33] It is of special significance that this high-status unit, to which every member of the lower echelon aspires, performs best when disregarding formal regulations and official procedures. Adopting detectives as models, other members of the force do not remain as fervently dedicated to these official rules and procedures as they might if they lacked this example.

THE SUPERIOR OFFICER

Superior officers of the old regime were autocrats. Patrolmen responded fearfully to their wrath and would not have risked approaching them casually. Supervisors were quick to register complaints, generally about subordinates who failed to acknowledge a superior's innate charisma.

In contemporary police culture, democratization and demilitarization have replaced the formerly rigid code, for several reasons. In the first place, there is no police counterpart of West Point at which the superior officer may be trained (although the National Academy of the Federal Bureau of Investigation gradually has attained an equivalence). In America police superiors rise from the ranks and have no aura of glamour, upper-class background, or unique endowments with which to impress the rank and file. A superior's

---

[32] Raymond Postgate, "London: Goodbye to Hullo, Darling," *Holiday Magazine,* 28 (November, 1960), p. 50.

[33] In *Patterns of Industrial Bureaucracy* (Glencoe: The Free Press, 1954), Alvin Gouldner describes three theoretical types of bureaucracy: the punishment-centered, the representative, and the mock. All three types can be found among police departments. The traditional police force with its authoritarian structure corresponds to the punishment-centered bureaucracy. The professional force stresses a persuasive, more democratic kind of discipline, and can be equated to the representative type. The detective division, of course, fits nicely into the description of the mock bureaucracy.

reputation precedes him; he cannot expect to be treated with rigid deference.

The influx of college men into police work during and after the Great Depression upset the established pattern of upward mobility within the ranks. Educated policemen were able to shorten by half the time required for promotion to sergeant. After World War II, many men transferred from the armed forces to the police. Fed up with ostentatious rituals, combat veterans coined barbed epithets for those who insisted on exaggerated compliance with protocol, and consequently helped to democratize patterns of interaction in the police system. Professionalization also accelerated this process. Policemen, regarding themselves as experts and leaders, become involved in role conflicts. Trying to impress the public with his leadership, the policeman only perfunctorily salutes or otherwise recognizes differences in rank, and thus compromises his professional self-conception and the demands of protocol.

The current loosening of rigid discipline is so evident that police administrators are beginning to classify the sergeant as a foreman in industry who has allied himself with labor rather than with management. Some police experts, unwilling or unable to accept the sergeant's reduced prestige, consider it a damaging blow to the force and to the community. In the following comments, Paul Weston, a high-ranking police officer before he became a college professor of Police Administration, expresses the sentiments of the old regime.

A slow eating or wearing away of the responsibility and authority of a patrol sergeant has been taking place. If it is not halted, this deterioration will undermine the entire hierarchy of any police unit, contribute to the waste of human resources, and interfere with attempts to gain objectives which will provide a community with a climate of law and order.[34]

While top level management and even friendly sergeants may be somewhat responsible for this transformation, Weston feels that the true miscreants are industrial sociologists and psychologists, who

preach the creed that a happy worker is an efficient and productive worker. "Fear," they said, "should never rule." Requests and suggestions, instead of orders, would keep the workers happy.

These experts in human relations in industry say that supervision should not be brutal and reign through fear, and that supervisors must like people, help them, and constantly strive to get along with them. While it is true that brutality has no place in supervision, it is possible that fear can have its constructive aspects.

Every police department has one or more "tough" sergeants. Men who appear to dislike people, offer little apparent help, and seem to have little or no interest in getting along with them. This type of supervisor commands respect despite the environment of fear he creates, and though he sets high standards of performance,

[34] Paul Weston, "The Role of the Patrol Sergeant," *Law and Order,* 7 (September, 1959), p. 31.

he is usually as demanding of himself as he is of his subordinates. Men may not like him, but they like working for him, and he develops subordinates as he spurs them to peak performance.[35]

THE ADMINISTRATORS

The higher echelons of large police forces assume a chauvinistic posture in order to defend their organization. They decry the lack of respect for law and order, and the difficulties created by the courts that seem to the police to be over-protective of criminals. At the same time police administrators are quick to take offense when criticized.

To maintain at all costs the virtue of their force, the administrators must sometimes do an abrupt about-face. For example, their most popular proof of police efficiency is an impressive statistical report. But if other statistics indicate a reduction in efficiency, they must somehow cushion the impact of figures. A good illustration of such a reversal occurred when the FBI published data for the first nine months of 1965 showing a 6.5 per cent rise for New York City crime over the comparable period of 1964. The *New York Times* reported that "a spokesman for the Police Department here declined to concede that this proved an 'unusually high' incidence of crime here,"[36] and quoted a deputy commissioner:

[The statistics] were only three-quarters of the picture and reflect a crime bulge from the summer months.

[The statistics] might show a drop at the end of the year and that could create a whole new average. Until you get the whole picture of the full year, you have only statistics.[37]

When statistics imply discredit, administrators either attack their source or devalue the statistics *per se*. In this case, since it is next to impossible for any police department to discredit the FBI, the statistics become the target. Police officials are not so lenient with critics of law enforcement.

When the Federal Narcotics Bureau was condemned for its treatment of suspects, the Bureau's answer was (according to Benjamin DeMott) a propaganda line hinting that "Any man who interests himself in the problem of 'unknown criminals' must have unsavory reasons for doing so."[38]

When civil rights groups criticized the FBI for its ambivalence in circumventing Mississippi segregationists, J. Edgar Hoover countered that Martin Luther King, Jr., was "the most notorious liar in the country."[39]

[35] *Ibid.*
[36] *New York Times,* December 1, 1965, p. 95.
[37] *Ibid.*
[38] "The Great Narcotics Muddle," *Harper's,* 214 (March, 1962), p. 50.
[39] *New York Times,* November 20, 1964, p. 1.

Former New York City Police Commissioner Michael Murphy followed the same pattern in defending the action of his department in the civil rights disorders during the summer of 1964. Describing the frustration of the police who were "puzzled, bitter, and deeply resentful," he moved to the attack, asserting

that the public image of law enforcement — particularly as it involved the police — was unfairly "distorted and smeared today as never before in our history."

He said part of the picture was caused by "certain groups determined to weaken the democratic process."[40]

Probably the zenith of this administrative tropism was exemplified by Commissioner Vincent Broderick, the successor to Commissioner Murphy. Suffused by this extraordinary spirit of bureaucratic loyalty, he fought Mayor Lindsay himself, at the eventual cost of his job. The expected twist became apparent when the Commissioner elected publicly to interpret the mayor's call for a Civilian Review Board as an unwarranted political interference with the internal workings of the department, rather than to accept it as an idealistic innovation to honor a campaign pledge to promote better relations between the police and the city's minority groups.[41]

Police officials in this country envy the sacrosanct status enjoyed by Scotland Yard and the bobbies. But even these latter institutions seem to be losing their power to induce faith and silence criticism. In recent years Scotland Yard has had to cope with an England that can no longer be characterized as a nation of quiet, law-abiding citizens. The crime rate is rapidly increasing; the clearance rate is decreasing; sensational train robberies surpass TV thrillers; armed criminals kill policemen; race riots and teen-age gang rumbles signal social distress. Fleets of motorcycles roar through once peaceful communities. Traffic volume overwhelms the narrow streets of historic towns, and the police have antagonized the motoring public by traffic summons campaigns. Scandals have rocked the government.

These indications of disquiet are underlined by British press reports of bribery, brutality, forced confessions, racial discrimination, and illegally planted evidence. It is becoming difficult to attract capable recruits. When British police administrators submit annual reports, they are forced to defend certain obvious inadequacies. The British Police Superintendents' Association recently complained in a memorandum to the Home Secretary that

Britain's Bobbies are being pilloried, bullied, restricted and increasingly unjustifiably criticized by members of the public in all walks of life . . . traditional

[40] *New York Times,* August 23, 1964, p. 48.
[41] It is notable that former Police Commissioners Francis Adams and Michael Murphy support Commissioner Broderick in his stand. *New York Times,* February 10, 1966, p. 1.

British respect for the law [is] dwindling and . . . the police [can] not cope with a growing criminal element under present conditions.[42]

It is somewhat ironic, but nonetheless a testimonial to the efficiency and prestige of our own great police forces, that Roy Jenkins, the British Home Secretary, charged with responsibility for his country's police establishment, came to New York and Chicago on a police fact-finding mission.[43] It will certainly prove interesting to New York City police officials that there were more than nine thousand complaints lodged against Britain's police in 1965, and that as a result the influential *Economist* has proposed the formation of a civilian-dominated review board "on New York City's model."[44]

THE OLD-TIMER

Walking the streets, climbing stairs, lifting stretchers, and searching basements for armed criminals, the beat patrolman leads an active life that keeps him physically fit. It is a wrench the first time a rookie or youngster on his post calls him "Pop." Yet with fifteen years of service behind him, he is fast entering the circle of old-timers. In many of the personal interviews with policemen of this group, the men demonstrated a peculiar soul-searching type of introspection. Looking back over the years, they experienced a revulsion in reviewing all the distasteful acts of omission and commission in which they had participated.

They gradually assume the older statesman role and transmit the wisdom of the job to the new men. Seniority entitles them to the easier assignments, which allow them time to regale the younger men with endless reminiscences of the good old days when a cop could really be a cop. When arguments occur, the split reveals a conflict of generations, each group paying allegiance to a different value system.

They recall with nostalgia, their early years on the job and often wonder at their former brashness. More and more their conversation becomes larded with the typical refrain of the aging, "When I was a rookie, things were different." Until this stage, the majority of the men talk confidently of retiring as soon as possible. However, at the approach of the twenty year retirement limit old-timers often begin to waver. What can the ordinary veteran policeman offer a prospective employer? His main talent, if he has one, is that of a low-level practitioner of applied psychology or sociology.

The typical position available to a former policeman is that of bank guard, night watchman, mail room clerk, or messenger. This demoralizing situation impels the policeman to stay with the force,[45] where he can be somewhat

42 *New York Times,* October 26, 1965, p. 13.
43 *New York Times,* October 1, 1966, p. 16.
44 *The Economist,* August 20, 1966, p. 711.
45 Appointments to the force are reported in the department's Annual

satisfied in knowing that he earns a salary many professional men would envy.

Even when they retire, most policemen preserve some connection with the force. Many former officers keep their revolvers, for which they must now obtain a permit. The retired patrolman's organization issues shields somewhat like those worn by active members of the force. Frequently, the retired men find new employment in security jobs requiring general police skills.

Significantly, disillusioned and threatened by his exposure to the job-hunter's world, the old-timer renews his commitment to the police occupation he probably deprecated as a recruit. The graph of cynicism patterns over twenty years' service reflects this change among veterans approaching the twenty year milestone. Their degree of cynicism is consistently lower than that of men with less time on the job.

Reports. Retirements can be found in the magazine *Spring 3100*. With the aid of these sources I traced a cohort of 1,674 policemen from appointment to the time of eligibility for retirement, covering a twenty-four-year period from 1941 until 1965. Counting all retirements except those for medical reasons, I found that more than 50 per cent of the cohort was still on the job at the beginning of 1965 when the cohort's average service was twenty-two and one-half years.

Police Encounters
with Juveniles

IRVING PILIAVIN AND SCOTT BRIAR

As the first of a series of decisions made in the channeling of youthful offenders through the agencies concerned with juvenile justice and corrections, the disposition decisions made by police officers have potentially profound consequences for apprehended juveniles. Thus arrest, the most severe of the dispositions available to police, may not only lead to confinement of the suspected offender but also bring him loss of social status, restriction of educational and employment opportunities, and future harassment by law-enforcement personnel.[1] According to some criminologists, the stigmatization resulting from police apprehension, arrest, and detention actually reinforces deviant behavior.[2] Other authorities have suggested, in fact, that this stigmatization serves as the catalytic agent initiating delinquent careers.[3] Despite their presumed significance, however, little empirical analysis has been reported regarding the factors influencing, or consequences resulting from, police actions with juvenile offenders. Furthermore, while some studies of police encounters with adult offenders have been reported, the extent to which the findings of these investigations pertain to law-enforcement practices with youthful offenders is not known.[4]

The above considerations have led the writers to undertake a longitudinal study of the conditions influencing, and consequences flowing from, police actions with juveniles. In the present paper findings will be presented indicat-

Reprinted from *American Journal of Sociology,* 70 (September 1964), pp. 206–214, by permission of the authors and The University of Chicago Press. Copyright 1964 by The University of Chicago.

[1] Richard D. Schwartz and Jerome H. Skolnick, "Two Studies of Legal Stigma," *Social Problems,* X (April, 1962), 133–42; Sol Rubin, *Crime and Juvenile Delinquency* (New York: Oceana Publications, 1958); B. F. McSally, "Finding Jobs for Released Offenders," *Federal Probation,* XXIV (June, 1960), 12–17; Harold D. Lasswell and Richard C. Donnelly, "The Continuing Debate over Responsibility: An Introduction to Isolating the Condemnation Sanction," *Yale Law Journal,* LXVIII (April, 1959), 869–99.

[2] Richard A. Cloward and Lloyd E. Ohlin, *Delinquency and Opportunity* (Glencoe, Ill.: Free Press, 1960), pp. 124–30.

[3] Frank Tannenbaum, *Crime and the Community* (New York: Columbia University Press, 1936), pp. 17–20; Howard S. Becker, *Outsiders: Studies in the Sociology of Deviance* (New York: Free Press of Glencoe, 1963), chaps. i and ii.

[4] For a detailed accounting of police discretionary practices, see Joseph Goldstein, "Police Discretion Not To Invoke the Criminal Process: Low Visibility Decisions in the Administration of Justice," *Yale Law Journal,* LXIX (1960), 543–94; Wayne R. LaFave, "The Police and Non-enforcement of the Law—Part I," *Wisconsin Law Review* (January, 1962), pp. 104–37; S. H. Kadish, "Legal Norms and Discretion in the Police and Sentencing Processes," *Harvard Law Review,* LXXV (March, 1962), 904–31.

ing the influence of certain factors on police actions. Research data consist primarily of notes and records based on nine months' observation of all juvenile officers in one police department.[5] The officers were observed in the course of their regular tours of duty.[6] While these data do not lend themselves to quantitative assessments of reliability and validity, the candor shown by the officers in their interviews with the investigators and their use of officially frowned-upon practices while under observation provide some assurance that the materials presented below accurately reflect the typical operations and attitudes of the law-enforcement personnel studied.

The setting for the research, a metropolitan police department serving an industrial city with approximately 450,000 inhabitants, was noted within the community it served and among law-enforcement officials elsewhere for the honesty and superior quality of its personnel. Incidents involving criminal activity or brutality by members of the department had been extremely rare during the ten years preceding this study; personnel standards were comparatively high; and an extensive training program was provided to both new and experienced personnel. Juvenile Bureau members, the primary subjects of this investigation, differed somewhat from other members of the department in that they were responsible for delinquency prevention as well as law enforcement, that is, juvenile officers were expected to be knowledgeable about conditions leading to crime and delinquency and to be able to work with community agencies serving known or potential juvenile offenders. Accordingly, in the assignment of personnel to the Juvenile Bureau, consideration was given not only to an officer's devotion to and reliability in law enforcement but also to his commitment to delinquency prevention. Assignment to the Bureau was of advantage to policemen seeking promotions. Consequently, many officers requested transfer to this unit, and its personnel comprised a highly select group of officers.

In the field, juvenile officers operated essentially as patrol officers. They cruised assigned beats and, although concerned primarily with juvenile offenders, frequently had occasion to apprehend and arrest adults. Confrontations between the officers and juveniles occurred in one of the following three ways, in order of increasing frequency: (1) encounters resulting from officers' spotting officially "wanted" youths; (2) encounters taking place at or near the scene of offenses reported to police headquarters; and (3) encounters oc-

---

[5] Approximately thirty officers were assigned to the Juvenile Bureau in the department studied. While we had an opportunity to observe all officers in the Bureau during the study, our observations were concentrated on those who had been working in the Bureau for one or two years at least. Although two of the officers in the Juvenile Bureau were Negro, we observed these officers on only a few occasions.

[6] Although observations were not confined to specific days or work shifts, more observations were made during evenings and weekends because police activity was greatest during these periods.

curring as the result of officers' directly observing youths either committing offenses or in "suspicious circumstances." However, the probability that a confrontation would take place between officer and juvenile, or that a particular disposition of an identified offender would be made, was only in part determined by the knowledge that an offense had occurred or that a particular juvenile had committed an offense. The bases for and utilization of nonoffenses related criteria by police in accosting and disposing of juveniles are the focuses of the following discussion.

SANCTIONS FOR DISCRETION

In each encounter with juveniles, with the minor exception of officially "wanted" youths,[7] a central task confronting the officer was to decide what official action to take against the boys involved. In making these disposition decisions, officers could select any one of five discrete alternatives:

1. outright release
2. release and submission of a "field interrogation report" briefly describing the circumstances initiating the police-juvenile confrontation
3. "official reprimand" and release to parents or guardian
4. citation to juvenile court
5. arrest and confinement in juvenile hall.

Dispositions 3, 4, and 5 differed from the others in two basic respects. First, with rare exceptions, when an officer chose to reprimand, cite, or arrest a boy, he took the youth to the police station. Second, the reprimanded, cited, or arrested boy acquired an official police "record," that is, his name was officially recorded in Bureau files as a juvenile violator.

Analysis of the distribution of police disposition decisions about juveniles revealed that in virtually every category of offense the full range of official disposition alternatives available to officers was employed. This wide range of discretion resulted primarily from two conditions. First, it reflected the reluctance of officers to expose certain youths to the stigmatization presumed to be associated with official police action. Few juvenile officers believed that correctional agencies serving the community could effectively help delinquents. For some officers this attitude reflected a lack of confidence in rehabilitation techniques; for others, a belief that high case loads and lack of professional training among correctional workers vitiated their efforts at treatment. All officers were agreed, however, that juvenile justice and correctional processes were essentially concerned with apprehension and punishment rather

---

[7] "Wanted" juveniles usually were placed under arrest or in protective custody, a practice which in effect relieved officers of the responsibility for deciding what to do with these youths.

than treatment. Furthermore, all officers believed that some aspects of these processes (e.g., judicial definition of youths as delinquents and removal of delinquents from the community), as well as some of the possible consequences of these processes (e.g., intimate institutional contact with "hard-core" delinquents, as well as parental, school, and conventional peer disapproval or rejection), could reinforce what previously might have been only a tentative proclivity toward delinquent values and behavior. Consequently, when officers found reason to doubt that a youth being confronted was highly committed toward deviance, they were inclined to treat him with leniency.

Second, and more important, the practice of discretion was sanctioned by police-department policy. Training manuals and departmental bulletins stressed that the disposition of each juvenile offender was not to be based solely on the type of infraction he committed. Thus, while it was departmental policy to "arrest and confine all juveniles who have committed a felony or misdemeanor involving theft, sex offense, battery, possession of dangerous weapons, prowling, peeping, intoxication, incorrigibility, and disturbance of the peace," it was acknowledged that "such considerations as age, attitude and prior criminal record might indicate that a different disposition would be more appropriate."[8] The official justification for discretion in processing juvenile offenders, based on the preventive aims of the Juvenile Bureau, was that each juvenile violator should be dealt with solely on the basis of what was best for him. Unofficially, administrative legitimation of discretion was further justified on the grounds that strict enforcement practices would overcrowd court calendars and detention facilities, as well as dramatically increase juvenile crime rates — consequences to be avoided because they would expose the police department to community criticism.

In practice, the official policy justifying use of discretion served as a demand that discretion be exercised. As such, it posed three problems for juvenile officers. First, it represented a departure from the traditional police practice with which the juvenile officers themselves were identified, in the sense that they were expected to justify their juvenile disposition decisions not simply by evidence proving a youth had committed a crime — grounds on which police were officially expected to base their dispositions of non-juvenile offenders[9] — but in the *character* of the youth. Second, in disposing of juvenile offenders, officers were expected, in effect, to make judicial rather than ministerial decisions.[10] Third, the shift from the offense to the offender

---

[8] Quoted from a training manual issued by the police department studied in this research.

[9] In actual practice, of course, disposition decisions regarding adult offenders also were influenced by many factors extraneous to the offense per se.

[10] For example, in dealing with adult violators, officers had no disposition alternative comparable to the reprimand-and-release category, a disposition which contained elements of punishment but did not involve mediation by the court.

as the basis for determining the appropriate disposition substantially increased the uncertainty and ambiguity for officers in the situation of apprehension because no explicit rules existed for determining which disposition different types of youths should receive. Despite these problems, officers were constrained to base disposition decisions on the character of the apprehended youth, not only because they wanted to be fair, but because persistent failure to do so could result in judicial criticism, departmental censure, and, they believed, loss of authority with juveniles.[11]

DISPOSITION CRITERIA

Assessing the character of apprehended offenders posed relatively few difficulties for officers in the case of youths who had committed serious crimes such as robbery, homicide, aggravated assault, grand theft, auto theft, rape, and arson. Officials generally regarded these juveniles as confirmed delinquents simply by virtue of their involvement in offenses of this magnitude.[12] However, the infraction committed did not always suffice to determine the appropriate disposition for some serious offenders;[13] and, in the case of minor offenders, who comprised over 90 per cent of the youths against whom police took action, the violation per se generally played an insignificant role in the choice of disposition. While a number of minor offenders were seen as serious delinquents deserving arrest, many others were perceived either as "good" boys whose offenses were atypical of their customary behavior, as pawns of undesirable associates or, in any case, as boys for whom arrest was regarded as an unwarranted and possibly harmful punishment. Thus, for nearly all minor violators and for some serious delinquents, the assessment of character — the distinction between serious delinquents, "good" boys, misguided youths, and so on — and the dispositions which followed from these assessments were based on youths' personal characteristics and not their offenses.

Despite this dependence of disposition decisions on the personal characteristics of these youths, however, police officers actually had access only to very limited information about boys at the time they had to decide what to do with them. In the field, officers typically had no data concerning the past offense records, school performance, family situation, or personal adjustment

[11] The concern of officers over possible loss of authority stemmed from their belief that court failure to support arrests by appropriate action would cause policemen to "lose face" in the eyes of juveniles.

[12] It is also likely that the possibility of negative publicity resulting from the failure to arrest such violators — particularly if they became involved in further serious crime — brought about strong administrative pressure for their arrest.

[13] For example, in the year preceding this research, over 30 per cent of the juveniles involved in burglaries and 12 per cent of the juveniles committing auto theft received dispositions other than arrest.

of apprehended youths.[14] Furthermore, files at police headquarters provided data only about each boy's prior offense record. Thus both the decision made in the field — whether or not to bring the boy in — and the decision made at the station — which disposition to invoke — were based largely on cues which emerged from the interaction between the officer and the youth, cues from which the officer inferred the youth's character. These cues included the youth's group affiliations, age, race, grooming, dress, and demeanor. Older juveniles, members of known delinquent gangs, Negroes, youths with well-oiled hair, black jackets, and soiled denims or jeans (the presumed uniform of "tough" boys), and boys who in their interactions with officers did not manifest what were considered to be appropriate signs of respect tended to receive the more severe dispositions.

Other than prior record, the most important of the above clues was a youth's *demeanor*. In the opinion of juvenile patrolmen themselves the demeanor of apprehended juveniles was a major determinant of their decisions for 50–60 per cent of the juvenile cases they processed.[15] A less subjective indication of the association between a youth's demeanor and police disposition is provided by Table 1, which presents the police dispositions for sixty-six youths whose encounters with police were observed in the course of this study.[16] For purposes of this analysis, each youth's demeanor in the encounter was classified as either co-operative or unco-operative.[17] The results clearly reveal a marked association between youth demeanor and the severity of police dispositions.

The cues used by police to assess demeanor were fairly simple. Juveniles who were contrite about their infractions, respectful to officers, and fearful

[14] On occasion, officers apprehended youths whom they personally knew to be prior offenders. This did not occur frequently, however, for several reasons. First, approximately 75 per cent of apprehended youths had no prior official records; second, officers periodically exchanged patrol areas, thus limiting their exposure to, and knowledge about, these areas; and third, patrolmen seldom spent more than three or four years in the juvenile division.

[15] While reliable subgroup estimates were impossible to obtain through observation because of the relatively small number of incidents observed, the importance of demeanor in disposition decisions appeared to be much less significant with known prior offenders.

[16] Systematic data were collected on police encounters with seventy-six juveniles. In ten of these encounters the police concluded that their suspicions were groundless, and consequently the juveniles involved were exonerated; these ten cases were eliminated from this analysis of demeanor. (The total number of encounters observed was considerably more than seventy-six, but systematic data-collection procedures were not instituted until several months after observations began.)

[17] The data used for the classification of demeanor were the written records of observations made by the authors. The classifications were made by an independent judge not associated with this study. In classifying a youth's demeanor as co-operative or unco-operative, particular attention was paid to: (1) the youth's responses to police officers' questions and requests; (2) the respect and deference — or lack of these qualities — shown by the youth toward police officers; and (3) police officers' assessments of the youth's demeanor.

Table 1: Severity of Police Disposition, by Youth's Demeanor

Severity of police disposition	Youth's demeanor		Total
	Co-op-erative	Unco-op-erative	
Arrest (most severe)	2	14	16
Citation or official reprimand	4	5	9
Informal reprimand	15	1	16
Admonish and release (least severe)	24	1	25
Total	45	21	66

of the sanctions that might be employed against them tended to be viewed by patrolmen as basically law-abiding or at least "salvageable." For these youths it was usually assumed that informal or formal reprimand would suffice to guarantee their future conformity. In contrast, youthful offenders who were fractious, obdurate, or who appeared nonchalant in their encounters with patrolmen were likely to be viewed as "would-be tough guys" or "punks" who fully deserved the most severe sanction: arrest. The following excerpts from observation notes illustrate the importance attached to demeanor by police in making disposition decisions.

1. The interrogation of "A" (an -18-year-old upper-lower-class white male accused of statutory rape) was assigned to a police sergeant with long experience on the force. As I sat in his office while we waited for the youth to arrive for questioning, the sergeant expressed his uncertainty as to what he should do with this young man. On the one hand, he could not ignore the fact that an offense had been committed; he had been informed, in fact, that the youth was prepared to confess to the offense. Nor could he overlook the continued pressure from the girl's father (an important political figure) for the police to take severe action against the youth. On the other hand, the sergeant had formed a low opinion of the girl's moral character, and he considered it unfair to charge "A" with statutory rape when the girl was a willing partner to the offense and might even have been the instigator of it. However, his sense of injustice concerning "A" was tempered by his image of the youth as a "punk," based, he explained, on information he had received that the youth belonged to a certain gang, the members of which were well known to, and disliked by, the police. Nevertheless, as we prepared to leave his office to interview "A," the sergeant was still in doubt as to what he should do with him.

As we walked down the corridor to the interrogation room, the sergeant was stopped by a reporter from the local newspaper. In an excited tone of voice, the reporter explained that his editor was pressing him to get further information about this case. The newspaper had printed some of the facts about the girl's disappearance, and as a consequence the girl's father was threatening suit against the paper for defamation of the girl's character. It would strengthen the newspaper's position, the reporter explained, if the police had information indicating that the girl's associates, particularly the youth the sergeant was about to interrogate, were persons of disreputable character. This stimulus seemed to resolve the sergeant's uncertainty. He told the reporter, "unofficially," that the youth was known to be an undesirable person, citing as evidence his membership in the delinquent gang. Furthermore, the sergeant added that he had evidence that this youth had been intimate with the girl over a period of many months. When the reporter asked if the police were planning to do anything to the youth, the sergeant answered that he intended to charge the youth with statutory rape.

In the interrogation, however, three points quickly emerged which profoundly affected the sergeant's judgment of the youth. First, the youth was polite and co-operative; he consistently addressed the officer as "sir," answered all questions quietly, and signed a statement implicating himself in numerous counts of statutory rape. Second, the youth's intentions toward the girl appeared to have been honorable; for example, he said that he wanted to marry her eventually. Third, the youth was not in fact a member of the gang in question. The sergeant's attitude became increasingly sympathetic, and after we left the interrogation room he announced his intention to "get 'A' off the hook," meaning that he wanted to have the charges against "A" reduced or, if possible, dropped.

2. Officers "X" and "Y" brought into the police station a seventeen-year-old white boy who, along with two older companions, had been found in a home having sex relations with a fifteen-year-old girl. The boy responded to police officers' queries slowly and with obvious disregard. It was apparent that his lack of deference toward the officers and his failure to evidence concern about his situation were irritating his questioners. Finally, one of the officers turned to me and, obviously angry, commented that in his view the boy was simply a "stud" interested only in sex, eating, and sleeping. The policeman conjectured that the boy "probably already had knocked up half a dozen girls." The boy ignored these remarks, except for an occasional impassive stare at the patrolmen. Turning to the boy, the officer remarked, "What the hell am I going to do with you?" And again the boy simply returned the officer's gaze. The latter then said, "Well, I guess we'll just have to put you away for a while." An arrest report was then made out and the boy was taken to Juvenile Hall.

Although anger and disgust frequently characterized officers' attitudes toward recalcitrant and impassive juvenile offenders, their manner while processing these youths was typically routine, restrained, and without rancor. While the officers' restraint may have been due in part to their desire to avoid accusation and censure, it also seemed to reflect their inurement to a frequent experience. By and large, only their occasional "needling" or insulting of a boy gave any hint of the underlying resentment and dislike they felt toward many of these youths.[18]

---

[18] Officers' animosity toward recalcitrant or aloof offenders appeared to stem from two sources: moral indignation that these juveniles were self-righteous and indifferent about their transgressions, and resentment that

PREJUDICE IN APPREHENSION AND DISPOSITION DECISIONS

Compared to other youths, Negroes and boys whose appearance matched the delinquent stereotype were more frequently stopped and interrogated by patrolmen — often even in the absence of evidence that an offense had been committed[19] — and usually were given more severe dispositions for the same violations. Our data suggest, however, that these selective apprehension and disposition practices resulted not only from the intrusion of long-held prejudices of individual police officers but also from certain job-related experiences of law-enforcement personnel. First, the tendency for police to give more severe dispositions to Negroes and to youths whose appearance corresponded to that which police associated with delinquents partly reflected the fact, observed in this study, that these youths also were much more likely than were other types of boys to exhibit the sort of recalcitrant demeanor which police construed as a sign of the confirmed delinquent. Further, officers assumed, partly on the basis of departmental statistics, that Negroes and juveniles who "look tough" (e.g., who wear chinos, leather jackets, boots, etc.) commit crimes more frequently than do other types of youths.[20] In this sense, the police justified their selective treatment of these youths along epidemiological lines: that is, they were concentrating their attention on those youths whom they believed were most likely to commit delinquent acts. In the words of one highly placed official in the department:

If you know that the bulk of your delinquent problem comes from kids who, say, are from 12 to 14 years of age, when you're out on patrol you are much more likely to be sensitive to the activities of juveniles in this age bracket than older

these youths failed to accord police the respect they believed they deserved. Since the patrolmen perceived themselves as honestly and impartially performing a vital community function warranting respect and deference from the community at large, they attributed the lack of respect shown them by these juveniles to the latters' immorality.

[19] The clearest evidence for this assertion is provided by the overrepresentation of Negroes among "innocent" juveniles accosted by the police. As noted, of the seventy-six juveniles on whom systematic data were collected, ten were exonerated and released without suspicion. Seven, or two-thirds of these ten "innocent" juveniles were Negro, in contrast to the allegedly "guilty" youths, less than one-third of whom were Negro. The following incident illustrates the operation of this bias: One officer, observing a youth walking along the street, commented that the youth "looks suspicious" and promptly stopped and questioned him. Asked later to explain what aroused his suspicion, the officer explained, "He was a Negro wearing dark glasses at midnight."

[20] While police statistics did not permit an analysis of crime rates by appearance, they strongly supported officers' contentions concerning the delinquency rate among Negroes. Of all male juveniles processed by the police department in 1961, for example, 40.2 per cent were Negro and 33.9 per cent were white. These two groups comprised at that time, respectively, about 22.7 per cent and 73.6 per cent of the population in the community studied.

or younger groups. This logic in our case is the same except that our delinquency problem is largely found in the Negro community and it is these youths toward whom we are sensitized.

As regards prejudice per se, eighteen of twenty-seven officers interviewed openly admitted a dislike for Negroes. However, they attributed their dislike to experiences they had, as policemen, with youths from this minority group. The officers reported that Negro boys were much more likely than non-Negroes to "give us a hard time," be unco-operative, and show no remorse for their transgressions. Recurrent exposure to such attitudes among Negro youth, the officers claimed, generated their antipathy toward Negroes. The following excerpt is typical of the views expressed by these officers:

They (Negroes) have no regard for the law or for the police. They just don't seem to give a damn. Few of them are interested in school or getting ahead. The girls start having illegitimate kids before they are 16 years old and the boys are always "out for kicks." Furthermore, many of these kids try to run you down. They say the damnedest things to you and they seem to have absolutely no respect for you as an adult. I admit I am prejudiced now, but frankly I don't think I was when I began police work.

IMPLICATIONS

It is apparent from the findings presented above that the police officers studied in this research were permitted and even encouraged to exercise immense latitude in disposing of the juveniles they encountered. That is, it was within the officers' discretionary authority, except in extreme limiting cases, to decide which juveniles were to come to the attention of the courts and correctional agencies and thereby be identified officially as delinquents. In exercising this discretion policemen were strongly guided by the demeanor of those who were apprehended, a practice which ultimately led, as seen above, to certain youths (particularly Negroes[21] and boys dressed in the style of "toughs") being treated more severely than other juveniles for comparable offenses.

But the relevance of demeanor was not limited only to police disposition practices. Thus, for example, in conjunction with police crime statistics the criterion of demeanor led police to concentrate their surveillance activities in areas frequented or inhabited by Negroes. Furthermore, these youths were accosted more often than others by officers on patrol simply because their skin color identified them as potential troublemakers. These discriminatory practices — and it is important to note that they are discriminatory, even if

---

[21] An unco-operative demeanor was presented by more than one-third of the Negro youths but by only one-sixth of the white youths encountered by the police in the course of our observations.

based on accurate statistical information — may well have self-fulfilling consequences. Thus it is not unlikely that frequent encounters with police, particularly those involving youths innocent of wrongdoing, will increase the hostility of these juveniles toward law-enforcement personnel. It is also not unlikely that the frequency of such encounters will in time reduce their significance in the eyes of apprehended juveniles, thereby leading these youths to regard them as "routine." Such responses to police encounters, however, are those which law-enforcement personnel perceive as indicators of the serious delinquent. They thus serve to vindicate and reinforce officers' prejudices, leading to closer surveillance of Negro districts, more frequent encounters with Negro youths, and so on in a vicious circle. Moreover, the consequences of this chain of events are reflected in police statistics showing a disproportionately high percentage of Negroes among juvenile offenders, thereby providing "objective" justification for concentrating police attention on Negro youths.

To a substantial extent, as we have implied earlier, the discretion practiced by juvenile officers is simply an extension of the juvenile-court philosophy, which holds that in making legal decisions regarding juveniles, more weight should be given to the juvenile's character and life-situation than to his actual offending behavior. The juvenile officer's disposition decisions — and the information he uses as a basis for them — are more akin to the discriminations made by probation officers and other correctional workers than they are to decisions of police officers dealing with non-juvenile offenders. The problem is that such clinical-type decisions are not restrained by mechanisms comparable to the principles of due process and the rules of procedure governing police decisions regarding adult offenders. Consequently, prejudicial practices by police officers can escape notice more easily in their dealings with juveniles than with adults.

The observations made in this study serve to underscore the fact that the official delinquent, as distinguished from the juvenile who simply commits a delinquent act, is the product of a social judgment, in this case a judgment made by the police. He is a delinquent because someone in authority has defined him as one, often on the basis of the public face he has presented to officials rather than of the kind of offense he has committed.

The Working Policeman,
Police "Professionalism,"
and the Rule of Law

JEROME H. SKOLNICK

The traditional concern of criminology and of writers on "social control" is the maintenance of order in society. This study suggests that such a view is limited both philosophically and sociologically. "Social control" must deal not merely with the maintenance of order, but with the quality of the order that a given system is capable of sustaining and the procedures appropriate to the achievement of such order. Thus, a given set of social and legal conditions may lead to order in a stable democracy but not in a stable totalitarianism. Meaningful sociological analysis of order cannot, therefore, be value-free, because such a posture falsely assumes the equivalence of all types of order.

This research rejects the "value-free" approach, and concentrates instead upon the social foundations of legal procedures designed to protect democratic order. In the workings of democratic society, where the highest stated commitment is to the ideal of legality, a focal point of tension exists between the substance of order and the procedures for its accomplishment. "The basic and anguishing dilemma of form and substance in law can be alleviated, but never resolved, for the structure of legal domination retains its distinguishing features only as long as this dilemma is perpetuated."[1] This dilemma is most clearly manifested in law enforcement organizations, where both sets of demands make forceful normative claims upon police conduct.

In addition to this fundamental dilemma, there are further complications. Neither form nor substance, law nor order, is an entirely clear conception; and what it means for police to use law to enforce order is also somewhat problematic. The empirical portion of this study looked into the question of how the police themselves conceive the meaning of "law" and "order" to find out how these conceptions develop and are implemented in police practices. Social conditions in the varying assignments of police heightened or diminished the conflict between the obligations of maintaining order and observing the rule of law.

Here we consider the implications of the research. First we summarize findings about these issues and suggest that the dilemma of the police in

Reprinted from *Justice Without Trial: Law Enforcement in Democratic Society,* by Jerome H. Skolnick, pp. 203–245 (New York: 1966), by permission of the author and John Wiley & Sons, Inc., Publishers.

[1] Reinhard Bendix, *Nation-Building and Citizenship* (New York: John Wiley and Sons, 1964), p. 112.

democratic society arises out of the conflict between the extent of initiative contemplated by nontotalitarian norms of work and restraints upon police demanded by the rule of law. Second, we consider the meaning of police professionalization, pointing out its limitations according to the idea of managerial efficiency. Finally, we discuss how the policeman's conception of himself as a craftsman is rooted in community expectations, and how the ideology of police professionalization is linked to these expectations. Thus, the focus is upon the relation between the policeman's conception of his work and his capacity to contribute to the development of a society based upon the rule of law as its master ideal.

OCCUPATIONAL ENVIRONMENT AND THE RULE OF LAW

Five features of the policeman's occupational environment weaken the conception of the rule of law as a primary objective of police conduct. One is the social psychology of police work, that is, the relation between occupational environment, working personality, and the rule of law. Second is the policeman's stake in maintaining his position of authority, especially his interest in bolstering accepted patterns of enforcement. Third is police socialization, especially as it influences the policeman's administrative bias. A related factor is the pressure put upon individual policemen to "produce" — to be efficient rather than legal when the two norms are in conflict. Finally, there is the policeman's opportunity to behave inconsistently with the rule of law as a result of the low visibility of much of his conduct.

Although it is difficult to weigh the relative import of these factors, they all seem analytically to be joined to the conception of policeman as *crafts-man* rather than as *legal actor,* as a skilled worker rather than as a civil servant obliged to subscribe to the rule of law. The significance of the conception of the policeman as a craftsman derives from the differences in ideology of work and authority in totalitarian and nontotalitarian societies. Reinhard Bendix has contended that the most important difference between totalitarian and nontotalitarian forms of subordination is to be found in the managerial handling of problems of authority and subordination.[2]

Subordinates in totalitarian society are offered little opportunity to introduce new means of achieving the goals of the organization, since subordination implies obedience rather than initiative. As Bendix says, ". . . managerial refusal to accept the tacit evasion of rules and norms or the uncontrolled exercise of judgment is related to a specific type of bureaucratization which

---

[2] See his *Work and Authority in Industry* (New York: Harper Torchbook, 1963); and *Nation-Building and Citizenship* (New York: John Wiley and Sons, 1964).

constitutes the fundamental principle of totalitarian government."[3] By contrast, in non-totalitarian society, subordinates are encouraged to introduce their own strategies and ideas into the working situation. Bendix does not look upon rule violation or evasion as necessarily subverting the foundations of bureaucratic organization, but rather sees these innovations as "strategies of independence" by which the employees "seek to modify the implementation of the rules as their personal interests and their commitment (or lack of commitment) to the goals of the organization dictate."[4] In brief, the managerial ideology of nontotalitarian society maximizes the exercise of discretion by subordinates, while totalitarian society minimizes innovation by working officials.[5]

This dilemma of democratic theory manifests itself in every aspect of the policeman's work, as evidenced by the findings of this study. In explaining the development of the policeman's "working personality," the dangerous and authoritative elements of police work were emphasized. The combination of these elements undermines attachment to the rule of law in the context of a "constant" pressure to produce. Under such pressure, the variables of danger and authority tend to alienate the policeman from the general public, and at the same time to heighten his perception of symbols portending danger to him and to the community. Under the same pressure to produce, the policeman not only perceives possible criminality according to the symbolic status of the suspect; he also develops a stake in organized patterns of enforcement. To the extent that a suspect is seen as interfering with such arrangements, the policeman will respond negatively to him. On the other hand, the "cooperative" suspect, that is, one who contributes to the smooth operation of the enforcement pattern, will be rewarded. Accordingly, a detailed investigation was made of exchange relations between police and informers, in part to ascertain how informers are differentially treated according to the extent to which they support enforcement patterns, and partly to analyze how the policeman creates and uses the resources given to him.

In attempting to enrich his exchange position, the policeman necessarily involves the prosecutor in supporting his enforcement needs. The prosecutor, of course, also has a stake in the policeman's work performance, since the policeman provides him with the raw materials of prosecutorial achievement. Our observations suggested, however, that although he is ultimately the

[3] *Work and Authority*, p. 446.

[4] *Ibid.*, p. 445.

[5] There is, perhaps, some ambiguity in this posing of the situation of the worker in totalitarian society. Police in a totalitarian society may have the opportunity to exercise a great deal of "initiative." See Simon Wolin and Robert M. Slusser (eds.), *The Soviet Secret Police* (New York: Frederick A. Praeger, 1957), *passim;* and Jacques Delarue, *The Gestapo* (trans. Mervyn Sevill) (New York: William Morrow and Company, 1964), *passim.*

policeman's spokesman, the prosecutor performs a quasi-magisterial function by conveying a conception of legality to the policeman.

Most interesting, of course, is the basis on which the prosecutor's greater attachment to legality rests. We may point here to pertinent differences between policeman and prosecutor. One, of course, has to do with socialization. The prosecutor is a product of a law school, with larger understanding and appreciation of the judiciary and its restraints, especially constitutional ones. The policeman, on the other hand, generally has less formal education, less legal training, and a sense of belonging to a different sort of organization. Such differences in background go far to explain the development of the policeman's conception of self as a craftsman, coupled with a guildlike affirmation of worker autonomy. The policeman views himself as a specialist in criminological investigation, and does not react indifferently either to having his conclusions challenged by a distant judiciary or to having "obstacles" placed in his administrative path. He therefore views the judiciary, especially the appellate courts, as saboteurs of his capacity to satisfy what he sees as the requirements of social order. Each appellate decision limiting police initiative comes to be defined as a "handcuffing" of law enforcement, and may unintentionally sever further the policeman's attachment to the rule of law as an overriding value. In addition, the policeman is offended by judicial assumptions running contrary to probabilistic fact — the notion of due process of law staunchly maintains a rebuttable presumption of innocence in the face of the policeman's everyday experience of an administrative presumption of regularity.

Although the prosecutor is legally accorded a wider area of discretion than the policeman, the setting of the policeman's role offers greater opportunity to behave inconsistently with the rule of law. Police discretion is "hidden" insofar as the policeman often makes decisions in direct interaction with the suspect. The prosecutor typically serves at most as advisor to these dealings. Whether it is a question of writing out a traffic citation, of arresting a spouse on a charge of "assault with a deadly weapon," or of apprehending an addict informer, the policeman has enormous power; he may halt the legal process right there. Such discretionary activity is difficult to observe. By contrast, prosecutorial discretion frequently takes place at a later stage in the system, after the initial charge has been made public. The public character of the charge may restrict the prosecutor's discretion in practice more than the policeman's, even though the scope of the prosecutor's discretion is far wider in theory.

Internal controls over policeman reinforce the importance of administrative and craft values over civil libertarian values. These controls are more likely to emphasize efficiency as a goal rather than legality, or, more precisely, legality as a means to the end of efficiency. Two analyses were made along these lines. One was of the clearance rate as an internal control process. Here it was suggested that the policeman operates according to his most concrete and specific understanding of the control system, and that the clearance rate control system emphasizes measures stressing the detective's ability to "solve" crimes. It was further shown how it is possible for this control system to reverse the penalty structure associated with substantive criminal law by rewarding those evidencing a high degree of criminality. Thus, persons with greater criminal experience are frequently better "equipped" to contribute to the "solution" of crimes, thereby enhancing the policeman's appearance as a competent craftsman. The introduction of this control system into police work was analyzed to illustrate a response to the difficulties experienced by organizations that produce a fundamentally intangible service, or at least where "output" is subject to a variety of interpretations. Such an organization requires internal measures of the competence of employees, plus a set of measures (which may be the same) for assessment by outside evaluators.

The dilemma of democratic society requiring the police to maintain order and at the same time to be accountable to the rule of law is thus further complicated. Not only is the rule of law often incompatible with the maintenance of order but the principles by which police are governed by the rule of law in a democratic society may be antagonistic to the ideology of worker initiative associated with a nontotalitarian philosophy of work. In the same society, the ideal of legality rejects discretionary innovation by police, while the ideal of worker freedom and autonomy encourages such initiative. Bureaucratic rules are seen in a democracy as "enabling" regulations, while the regulations deriving from the rule of law are intended to constrain the conduct of officials.

The conflict between the democratic ideology of work and the legal philosophy of a democracy brings into focus the essential problem of the role of the police. The police are not simply "bad guys" or "good guys," authoritarians or heroes. Nor are they merely "men doing their jobs." They are legal officials whose tendencies to be arbitrary have roots in a conception of the freedom of the worker inhering in the nontotalitarian ideology of the relation between work and authority, a conception carried out in the context of police work. Seeing themselves as craftsmen, the police tend to conduct themselves according to the norms pertaining to a working bureaucracy in democratic society. Therefore, the more police tend to regard themselves as "workers" or "craftsmen," the more they demand a lack of constraint upon initiative. By contrast, *legal actors* are sympathetic toward the necessity for constraint and review.

PROFESSIONALISM
AND POLICE CONDUCT

The idea of professionalism is often invoked as the solution to the conflict between the policeman's task of maintaining order and his accountability to the rule of law. The meaning of this idea, however, is by no means clear. In sociology, there have been two main traditions, one emphasizing professional ideals and values, the other stressing technical competence. In Durkheim's view, what is distinctive about the idea of "professional" groups is not merely that such groups have high status, or high skill, or a politically supported monopoly over certain kinds of work, or a distinctive structure of control over work — most important is an infusion of work and collective organization with moral values, plus the use of sanctions to insure that these moral values are upheld. Arguing against the laissez-faire doctrines of the classical economists, for example, Durkheim pleaded for the introduction of morality into economic life:

> [W]hen we wish to see the guilds reorganized on a pattern we will presently try to define, it is not simply to have new codes superimposed on those existing; it is mainly so that economic activity should be permeated by ideas and needs other than individual ideas and needs . . . with the aim that the professions should become so many moral *milieu* and that these (comprising always the various organs of industrial and commercial life) should constantly foster the morality of the professions. As to the rules, although necessary and inevitable, they are but the outward expression of these fundamental principles. It is not a matter of coordinating any changes outwardly and mechanically, but of bringing men's minds into mutual understanding.[6]

An alternative concept of "professionalism" is associated with a managerial view emphasizing rationality, efficiency, and universalism. This view envisages the professional as a bureaucrat, almost as a machine calculating alternative courses of action by a stated program of rules, and possessing the technical ability to carry out decisions irrespective of personal feelings. As Weber says:

> Above all, bureaucratization offers the optimal possibility for the realization of the principle of division of labor in administration according to purely technical considerations, allocating individual tasks to functionaries who are trained as specialists and who continuously add to their experience by constant practice. "Professional" execution in this case means primarily execution "without regard to person" in accordance with calculable rules.[7]

---

[6] Emile Durkheim, *Professional Ethics and Civic Morals* (trans. Cornelia Brookfield) (Glencoe: The Free Press, 1958), p. 29.

[7] *Max Weber on Law in Economy and Society* (ed. Max Rheinstein, trans. Max Rheinstein and Edward Shils) (Cambridge: Harvard University Press, 1954), p. 350.

In the effort to introduce fairness, calculability, and impersonality into an American administration of criminal justice that was often riddled with corruption and political favoritism, most writers who have seriously examined police have also tended to subscribe to reforms based upon the managerial conception of "professional." Reviewing the works of such police reformers as O. W. Wilson or William Parker, we find that the conception of "professional" emphasizes managerial efficiency based upon a body of "expert" knowledge. A recently completed volume by law professor Wayne LaFave contains a similar point of view. In his concluding chapter, LaFave advocates a conception of the police as an administrative agency, with, presumably, the presumptions of regulation associated with such "expertise." He writes:

> The development of police expertness should be encouraged, and its existence should be recognized when appropriate. . . . There is need, and ample precedent in other fields, for the development of methods of communicating the existence of police expertness to trial or appellate courts which are called upon to decide arrest issues. The relationship between the court and the economic regulatory agency might serve as a model in the absence of a more highly developed proposal.[8]

There are, however, costs in developing a professional code based upon the model of administrative efficiency. Such a conception of professionalism not only fails to bridge the gap between the maintenance of order and the rule of law; in addition it comes to serve as an ideology undermining the capacity of police to be accountable to the rule of law. The idea of organization based on principles of administrative efficiency is often misunderstood by officials who are themselves responsible for administering such organizations. In practice, standardized rules and procedures are frequently molded to facilitate the tasks of acting officials. The materials of this study have clearly demonstrated that the policeman is an especially "nonmechanical" official. As Bruce Smith says:

> The policeman's art . . . consists in applying and enforcing a multitude of laws and ordinances in such degree or proportion and in such manner that the greatest degree of protection will be secured. The degree of enforcement and the method of application will vary with each neighborhood and community. There are no set rules, nor even general principles, to the policy to be applied. Each policeman must, in a sense, determine the standard to be set in the area for which he is responsible. Immediate superiors may be able to impress upon him some of the lessons of experience, but for the most part such experience must be his own. . . . Thus he is a policy-forming police administrator in miniature, who operates beyond the scope of the usual devices for control. . . .[9]

---

[8] Wayne R. LaFave, *Arrest: The Decision to Take a Suspect into Custody* (Boston: Little, Brown and Company, 1965), pp. 512–513.

[9] Bruce Smith, *Police Systems in the United States* (New York: Harper and Brothers, 1960), p. 19.

Smith may be making his point too strongly. Nevertheless, as a system of organization, bureaucracy can hope to achieve efficiency only by allowing officials to initiate their own means for solving specific problems that interfere with their capacity to achieve productive results. Some of these procedures may arise out of personal feelings — for example, relations between police and traffic violators — while others may become a routine part of the organizational structure. Examination of a procedural code, for example, would disclose no reference to the systematic use of informants. Given the task of enforcing crimes without citizen complainants, however, it becomes necessary for police to develop alternative methods to those used to apprehend violators in "standard" or "victimizing" crimes. These techniques of apprehension may demand considerable organization and skill on the part of the individual official, skill not so much in a formal administrative sense as in the sense of knowledge and ability to work within the effective limits of formal organization. As described, for example, the informer system requires so much ability that an aesthetic of execution has come to be associated with its use; it has become such an intrinsic component of police work that the abilities of the "professional" detective have come to be defined in terms of capacity to utilize this system.

As a bureaucratic organization, however, the police and governmental institutions, increasingly and generally, have a distinctive relationship to the development of the rule of law. The rule of law develops in response to the innovations introduced by officials to achieve organizational goals. It is certainly true, as Bendix asserts, that "A belief in legality means first and foremost that certain formal procedures must be obeyed if the enactment or execution of a law is to be considered legal."[10] At the same time, while legality may be seen as comprising a set of unchanging ideals, it may also be seen as a working normative system which develops in response to official conduct. The structure of authoritative regulations is such that legal superiors are not part of the same organization as officials and are expected to be "insensitive" to "productive capacity" as contrasted with legality. Thus, for example, a body of case law has been emerging that attempts to define the conditions and limits of the use of informants. Legality, therefore, develops as the other side of the coin of official innovation. As such, it is both a variable and an achievement. To the extent that police organizations operate mainly on grounds of administrative efficiency, the development of the rule of law is frustrated. Therefore, a conception of professionalism based mainly on satisfying the demands of administrative efficiency also hampers the capacity of the rule of law to develop.

The police are increasingly articulating a conception of professionalism

[10] Bendix, *op. cit.*, p. 112.

based on a narrow view of managerial efficiency and organizational interest. A sociologist is not surprised at such a development. Under the rule of law it is not up to the agency of enforcement to generate the limitations governing its actions, and bureaucrats typically and understandably try to conceal the knowledge of their operations so that they may regulate themselves unless they are forced to make disclosures. But the police in a democracy are not merely bureaucrats. They are also, or can be conceived of as, legal officials, that is, men belonging to an institution charged with strengthening the rule of law in society. If professionalism is ever to resolve some of the strains between order and legality, it must be a professionalism based upon a deeper set of values than currently prevails in police literature and the "professional" police department studied, whose operations are ordered on this literature.

The needed philosophy of professionalism must rest on a set of values conveying the idea that the police are as much an institution dedicated to the achievement of legality in society as they are an official social organization designed to control misconduct through the invocation of punitive sanctions. The problem of police in a democratic society is not merely a matter of obtaining newer police cars, a higher order technical equipment or of recruiting men who have to their credit more years of education. What must occur is a significant alteration in the ideology of police, so that police "professionalization" rests on the values of a democratic legal order, rather than on technological proficiency.

No thoughtful person can believe that such a transformation is easily achieved. In an article estimating the prospects for the rule of law in the Soviet Union, Leonard Schapiro has written, "It is perhaps difficult for dictators to get accustomed to the idea that the main purpose of law is, in fact, to make their task more difficult."[11] It is also hard for police officials in a democracy to accept this idea. In the same article, Schapiro reports the case of two professors who were criticized for urging the desirability of adopting certain principles of bourgeois law and criminal procedure, arguing that observance of legal norms must prevail over expediency in government legislation and administration. They were officially criticized for incorrectly understanding "the role of legal science in the solution of the practical tasks of government,"[12] a criticism not too different from the sort often leveled by "professional" police administrators in the United States against those who, for example, insist that the police must act legally for their evidence against the accused to be admitted. The argument is always essentially the same: that the efficient administration of criminal law will be hampered by the adoption of procedures designed to protect individual liberties. The police ad-

[11] Leonard Schapiro, "Prospects for the Rule of Law," *Problems of Communism,* 14 (March-April, 1965), 2.
[12] *Ibid.,* p. 7.

ministrators on the whole are correct. They have been given wide and direct responsibility for the existence of crime in the community, and it is intrinsically difficult for them to accustom themselves to the basic idea of the rule of law: "that the main purpose of law is, in fact, to make their task more difficult."

THE COMMUNITY
AND POLICE CONDUCT

If the police are ever to develop a conception of *legal* as opposed to *managerial* professionalism, they will do so only if the surrounding community demands compliance with the rule of law by rewarding police for such compliance, instead of looking to the police as an institution solely responsible for controlling criminality. In practice, however, the reverse has been true. The police function in a milieu tending to support, normatively and substantively, the idea of administrative efficiency that has become the hallmark of police professionalism. Legality, as expressed by both the criminal courts community with which the police have direct contact, and the political community responsible for the working conditions and prerogatives of police, is a weak ideal. This concluding section will attempt to locate the main sources of support for the managerial concept of police professionalism.

A posthumously published article by Professor Edmond Cahn distinguishes between "the imperial or official perspective" on law and "the consumer perspective."[13] The official perspective, according to the author, is so called "because it has been largely determined by the dominant interests of rulers, governors, and other officials.[14] In contrast, the "consumer" perspective reflects the interests and opinion of those on the receiving end of law. In the "consumer" view, therefore, constraints on the decision-making powers of officials are given more importance than the requirements of the processing system and those who carry out its administration. Cahn adds, in addition, that "A free and open society calls on its official processors to perform their functions according to the perspective of consumers."[15] At the same time that he argues against it, however, Cahn demonstrates in his own article the empirical strength of the presumption of correctness in official conduct. So in large part do the materials in this study.

The "official perspective" is most persuasive because it operates as the "established" mode of law enforcement, in the broadest sense of that term. The administration of criminal justice has become a major industry in modern

---

[13] "Law in the Consumer Perspective," *University of Pennsylvania Law Review*, 112 (November, 1963), 1–21.
[14] *Ibid.*, p. 4.
[15] *Ibid.*, p. 9.

urban society. FBI data show that during 1963 there were 4,437,786 arrests reported by 3,988 police agencies covering areas totaling 127 million in population. In California alone during 1963 there were 98,535 adult felony arrests and 595,992 adult misdemeanor arrests. There were in addition 244,312 arrests of juveniles.[16] During 1962 to 1963, the District Attorney of Los Angeles County had a staff of 546 (with 180 lawyers) and a budget of just over $4,800,000.[17]

Under these circumstances of mass administration of criminal justice, presumptions necessarily run to regularity and administrative efficiency. The negation of the presumption of innocence permeates the entire system of justice without trial. All involved in the system, the defense attorneys and judges, as well as the prosecutors and policemen, operate according to a working presumption of the guilt of persons accused of crime. As accused after accused is processed through the system, participants are prone to develop a routinized callousness, akin to the absence of emotional involvement characterizing the physician's attitude toward illness and disease. That the accused is entitled to counsel is an accepted part of the system, but this guarantee implies no specific affirmation of "adversariness" in an interactional sense. Indeed, the most respected attorneys, prosecuting and defense alike, are those who can "reasonably" see eye to eye in a system where most defendants are guilty of some crime.

The overwhelming presence of the "official" system of justice without trial provides normative support for the policeman's own attachment to principles of administrative regularity in opposition to due process of law. Under such circumstances, it should not be surprising to find the policeman adopting the "official" perspective too, since his role is to make the initial decision as to whether a charge has been warranted. Having made the charge, he of all people can hardly be expected to presume the innocence of the defendant. He has, in practice, listened to the defendant's story and assured himself of the latter's culpability. In his own mind, there are numerous guilty parties whom he has not arrested because he does not feel their cases will hold up in court, even though he is personally convinced of their guilt to a moral certainty. Police may feel most strongly about the "irrationality" of due process, but in fact other role players in the system of criminal justice may also be observed to be more concerned with efficiency than legality. If the policeman is the strongest advocate of a "rational bureaucratic" system emphasizing factual over legal guilt, he may well be simply because it is the definition of his ability as a worker that is most affected by the application of the rule of law.

An "order" perspective based upon managerial efficiency also tends to be

---

[16] Edward L. Barrett, "Criminal Justice and the Problem of Mass Production," in Harry W. Jones (ed.), *The Courts, and the Public, and the Law Explosion* (Englewood Cliffs, N.J.: Prentice-Hall, 1965), p. 95.
[17] *Ibid.,* p. 98.

supported by the civic community. The so-called power structure of the community, for example, often stresses to the police the importance of "keeping the streets clear of crime." The La Loma County Grand Jury, composed of "prominent" citizens — mainly businessmen and bankers — typically expresses concern not over violations of due process of law, but over a seemingly ever-rising crime rate and the inability of police to cope with it. Similarly, the Westville *Courier,* the city's only newspaper, makes much of the crime news, exaggerating criminality and deploring its existence. The police, quite sensitive to press criticism, find little support for the rule of law from that quarter. Indeed, when a newspaper runs an editorial, or a political figure emphasizes the importance of "making the streets safe for decent people," the statements are rarely qualified to warn law enforcement officials that they should proceed according to the rule of law. On the contrary, such injunctions are typically phrased as calls for zealous law enforcement or strict law enforcement. James Q. Wilson has described this as the "problem of the crusade." As he says:

Even if the force has but one set of consistent ends specified for it by the commissioner or superintendent, and even if adherence to those ends is enforced as far as possible, it is almost inevitable that there will come a time when the commissioner will decide that something must be done "at all costs" — that some civic goal justifies any police means. This might be the case when a commissioner is hard pressed by the newspapers to solve some particularly heinous crime (say, the rape and murder of a little girl). A "crusade" is launched. Policemen who have been trained to act in accord with one set of rules ("Use no violence." "Respect civil liberties." "Avoid becoming involved with criminal informants.") are suddenly told to act in accord with another rule — "catch the murderer" — no matter what it costs in terms of the normal rules.[18]

The emphasis on the maintenance of order is also typically expressed by the political community controlling the significant rewards for the police — money, promotions, vacations. Mayors, city councilmen, city managers draw up police budgets, hire and fire chiefs of police, and call for "shake-ups" within the department. Even the so-called "liberal" politician is inclined to urge police to disregard the rule of law when he perceives circumstances as exceedingly threatening. Thus, Wilson adds:

When Fiorello La Guardia became mayor of New York City he is said to have instructed his police force to adopt a "muss 'em up" policy toward racketeers, to the considerable consternation of groups interested in protecting civil liberties. The effort to instill one set of procedural rules in the force was at cross-purposes with the effort to attain a certain substantive end.[19]

In contrast to that of political authority, the power of appellate courts over the police is limited. In practice, the greatest authority of judges is to

---

[18] James Q. Wilson, "The Police and Their Problems: A Theory," *Public Policy,* 12 (1963), p. 199.
[19] *Ibid.*

deny the merit of the prosecution. Thus, by comparison to the direct sanctions held by political authority, the judiciary has highly restricted *power* to modify police behavior. Not only do appellate courts lack direct sanctions over the police but there are also powerful political forces that, by their open opposition to the judiciary, suggest an alternative frame of reference to the police. By this time, however, the police have themselves become so much a part of this same frame of reference that it is often difficult to determine whether it is the political figure who urges "stricter law enforcement" on the policeman, or the law enforcement spokesman who urges the press and the politician to support his demands against laws "coddling criminals," by which he typically means rulings of appellate courts upholding constitutional guarantees, usually under the Fourth, Fifth, Sixth, and Fourteenth Amendments. Whether the policeman is the "man in the middle," as Wilson portrays him, and as police prefer to present themselves, or whether police have by this time come to be the tail wagging the press and the politician, is the subject for another study. Beyond doubt, however, there are enough forces within the community, perhaps by now including the police themselves, to provide the working policeman with a normative framework praising managerial efficiency and opposing due process of law.

CONCLUSION

We have indicated how the police respond to the pressures of the dilemma of having two sets of ideals thrust upon them. As workers in a democratic society, the police seek the opportunity to introduce the means necessary to carry out "production demands." The means used to achieve these ends, however, may frequently conflict with the conduct required of them as legal actors. In response to this dilemma, police "experts" have increasingly adopted a philosophy of professionalism based upon managerial efficiency, with the implied hope that advancing technology will somehow resolve their dilemma. As indicated, it has not, and by its very assumptions cannot. First of all, in those areas where violations of the rule of law occur, advanced technology often results in greater violation. Technological advances in the form of wiretaps, polygraphs, stronger binoculars, and so forth only make the police more competent to interfere with individual liberty. Secondly, the model of efficiency based on bureaucracy simply does not work out in practice. Warren Bennis has catalogued the limitations of bureaucracy in general, and such limits are certainly applicable to large urban police forces. The following is a sample:

1. Bureaucracy does not adequately allow for personal growth and development of mature personalities.

2. It develops conformity and "group-think."
3. It does not take into account the "informal organization" and the emergent and unanticipated problems.
4. Its systems of control and authority are hopelessly outdated.
5. It has no adequate juridical process.
6. It does not possess adequate means for resolving differences and conflicts between ranks, and most particularly, between functional groups.
7. Communication (and innovative ideas) are thwarted or distorted due to hierarchical division.[20]

The working policeman is well aware of the limitations of "scientific" advances in police work and organization. He realizes that his work consists mostly of dealing with human beings, and that these skills are his main achievement. The strictures of the rule of law often clash with the policeman's ability to carry out this sort of work, but he is satisfied to have the argument presented in terms of technological achievement rather than human interaction, since he rightly fears that the public "will not understand" the human devices he uses, such as paying off informers, allowing "fences" to operate, and reducing charges, to achieve the enforcement ends demanded of him.

Police are generally under no illusions about the capacity of elected officials and the general public to make contradictory demands upon them. A certain amount of lip-service may be paid to the need for lawful enforcement of substantive criminal law, but the police are rarely, if ever, rewarded for complying with or expanding the area of due process of law. On the contrary, they are rewarded primarily for apprehension of so-called "notorious" criminals, for breaking "dope-rings," and the like. As a matter of fact, police are often much more sophisticated about their practices than the politicians who reward them. Police, for example, generally recognize the complexities of the meaning of such a term as "hardened criminal" and of the difficulties involved in carrying out a system of enforcement in line with the strictures of due process of law. The working detective who has used an individual as an informant for years, who has developed a relationship with the man in which each can depend on the word of the other, is not taken in by newspaper exaggerations of the man's "criminal" character.

Finally, the dilemma can never be resolved since it contains a built-in dialectic. Appellate decisions upholding the integrity procedural requirements may well move large segments of the community to a greater concern for the security of the substantive ends of criminal law. Especially when the police are burdened with the responsiblity of enforcing unenforceable laws,

[20] Warren Bennis, "Beyond Bureaucracy," *Trans-action,* 2 (July-August, 1965), 32.

thereby raising the spectre of a "crime-ridden" community,[21] decisions that specifically protect individual liberty may increase the pressure from an anxious community to soften these, and thus contain the seeds of a more "order-oriented" redefinition of procedural requirements. Over the past twenty years, courts have been increasingly indulgent of the rights of the accused. Whether this trend will continue, or whether the court will redefine "due process of law" to offer legitimacy to what is presently considered unlawful official behavior may well be contingent upon the disposition of the civic community.

If this analysis is correct in placing ultimate responsibility for the quality of "law and order" in American society upon the citizenry, then the prospects for the infusion of the rule of law into the police institution may be bleak indeed. As an institution dependent on rewards from the civic community, police can hardly be expected to be much better or worse than the political context in which they operate. When the political community is itself corrupt, the police will also be corrupt. If the popular notion of justice reaches no greater sophistication than that "the guilty should not go free," then the police will respond to this conception of justice. When prominent members of the community become far more aroused over an apparent rise in criminality than over the fact that Negroes are frequently subjected to unwarranted police interrogation, detention, and invasions of privacy, the police will continue to engage in such practices. Without widespread support for the rule of law, it is hardly to be expected that the courts will be able to continue advancing individual rights, or that the police will themselves develop a professional orientation as *legal* actors, rather than as efficient administrators of criminal law.

[21] Police statistics also contribute to this perception. See Gilbert Geis, "Statistics Concerning Race and Crime," *Crime and Delinquency* (April, 1965), 142–150.

3

JUDICIAL ADMINISTRATION

The Criminal Court as Organization and Communication System

ABRAHAM S. BLUMBERG

The fastening of the label "criminal" upon an individual, even by virtue of information that may be fragmentary in all respects, is a major institutional enterprise.

The screening device which sifts . . . the person's overall performance . . . is a very important instrument of social control. We know very little about the properties of this screen, but we do know that it takes many factors into account which are not directly related to the deviant act itself: it is sensitive to the suspect's social class, his past record as an offender, the amount of remorse he manages to convey, and many similar concerns which take hold in the shifting moods of the community. This may not be so obvious when the screen is dealing with extreme forms of deviance like serious crimes, but in the day-by-day filtering processes which take place throughout the community this feature is easily observable. Some men who drink too much are called alcoholics and others are not, some men who act oddly are committed to hospitals and others are not, some men who have no visible means of support are hauled into court and others are not — and the difference between those who earn a deviant label and those who go their own way in peace depends almost entirely on the way in which the community sifts out and codes the many details of behavior to which it is witness. In this respect, the community screen may be a more relevant subject for sociological research than the actual behavior which is filtered through it.[1]

The criminal court is that part of the "community screen" which sifts out and labels the accused person. Metropolitan Court, the subject of this case study, is probably one of the largest criminal courts in the world in terms of numbers of cases processed each year and personnel engaged in the enterprise. It is the highest court of original criminal jurisdiction in one of the largest cities in America, empowered to deal with all serious offenses known as felonies, and with lesser crimes.

The defendant population of Metropolitan Court is drawn largely from the lower socio-economic strata — the usual pattern in a criminal court. Minority groups tend to be over-represented, including Negroes, but not nearly to the extent that they are in national data. Virtually every major ethnic

[1] Howard S. Becker, *The Other Side: Perspectives on Deviance* (New York, 1964), pp. 11–12.

group in the United States is represented to some extent, although skin color continues to be a critical factor in one's vulnerability.

It is interesting that "white collar" criminals do not appear to have the extensive immunity to prosecution that sociologists have believed. During 1964 the court's probation division investigated 3,643 persons; of these approximately 8 per cent, by virtue of their education, occupation, income, and nature of their offense, would qualify as "white collar" criminals. While these offenders might ultimately have fared better by plea or sentence, they could not by virtue of a more favorable social position overcome the organizational mechanism of the court entirely — contrary to a rather shopworn notion among criminologists. In addition, the probation division collected more than $250,000 in restitution money during the year, a substantial amount of that sum being amounts returned to their victims by "white collar" offenders.

Metropolitan Court has been in existence since colonial days and has an annual operating budget in excess of $3 million. Salaries of its nine judges are among the highest in the world, averaging $35,000 a year. An elaborate court staff is at the judges' disposal, including a chief clerk and assistants and deputies performing all sorts of functions from clerical duties to that of court crier, wardens of the grand jury, court reporters, and court attendants. The attendants are armed and "protect" the physical environment of the court-room. There are also many stenographers, typists, and interpreters. Each judge has in his personal entourage a law assistant, a confidential attendant, and a law secretary or clerk. The secretaries fill patronage positions, for the judge himself is of course very much a political figure, being elected for a term of years. Lately, in the city where Metropolitan Court is located, both major parties have entered into arrangements where certain judicial candidates run unopposed as part of a political "swap."

The other patronage jobs are the chief clerk and certain other clerical positions. Almost all of the lower-level positions in the court structure are filled through civil service, but any of these personnel are of course available to a judge for tasks which may be beyond their ordinary duties. For example, a civil service attendant, because of his political activity or even his special skills, may be asked to perform more prestigious and less onerous duties.

The nine justices constitute a board of judges who, in addition to their judicial functions in the courtroom, have administrative responsibility and overall control of the major activities of the court. There are three major court functions, each with its own staff of professionals and clerical, service personnel. One is fundamental case record keeping and processing, which is the function of the clerk of the court and his staff of assistant and deputy clerks, interpreters, stenographers, and court attendants. This office also furnishes interpreting, stenography, typing, and policing services for the entire court. Some few members of the clerk's office, as previously indicated, may augment the personal staffs of retainers assigned to each judge. The word "retainers" is used deliberately, because the judge's personal staff has many of the qualities of organization and personal fealty that characterized the feudal lord and his staff of retainers. The relationship is one of extreme deference and fierce loyalty based not so much on any charismatic quality of the judge but rather on the largesse and privileges he bestows and dispenses. This feature sets the judge's personal entourage apart from the ordinary court staff.

The "clerk," of course, is not necessarily an unskilled, low-paid menial. Many clerks in the clerk's office are lawyers who perform the various ministerial and record processing tasks that are critical to the functioning of the court. Many have substantial local political party clubhouse ties, even though they have attained their positions through civil service promotions. In this almost all-male world in the clerk's office, the entering rank is that of court attendant; the line of promotion leads to deputy and assistant clerk positions paying in excess of $16,000 a year. The chief clerk and his assistant, as political appointees, receive considerably higher salaries. The usual profusion of typists and stenographers, mainly female, are relatively low-paid civil service personnel.

The second important segment of the court structure is the probation division. This unit is headed by a chief, his two deputies, and an administrative assistant, who are responsible for a staff of supervisors and approximately sixty probation officers. The probation division also has its own clerical services — some fifty typists, clerks, statisticians, stenographers, and receptionists. Again, most of the personnel, except for the typing and clerical staff, are males.

The third court segment, the psychiatric clinic, employs five psychiatrists, two of whom are employed on a per diem or part-time basis. There are also a number of clinical psychologists whose function is largely diagnostic testing. The clinic also has at its disposal a major public psychiatric hospital with all its resources for special tests and such periods of observation as may be required. And the clinic has its own filing, clerical, and stenographic personnel facilities.

Physically quartered in the same building but not part of the court budget or having any formal and *direct* administrative relationship with the court, is a legal aid defender service. It is largely privately endowed and employs a staff of fifteen to eighteen full-time lawyers. This unit has its own quarters in the building and maintains a clerical staff and other supportive services with its own budget. Its function is to provide legal services to persons arraigned in Metropolitan Court who are unable to retain private counsel for a fee. The city in which Metropolitan Court is located pays part of the budgetary requirements of this legal service, and in this sense the agency is no longer a private legal aid service but is more in the nature of a "public defender" service for those of limited financial means. Thus, unlike most of the rest of the nation prior to the *Gideon v. Wainwright* decision requiring counsel in all felony cases, no person who appears in Metropolitan Court is ever without the assistance of a lawyer at every stage of his case.

During 1964 this legal defense unit acted as counsel for approximately 70 per cent of the Metropolitan Court case load. There is no formal administrative connection between the unit and the court, but the service plays a vital function in the court's daily operations and in realizing its organizational goals. As a consequence, there is really a close, continuing liaison between the defender service and all court officials from the judge down to even the most minor functionary.

Also quartered in the court building is the office of the district attorney, which has its own budget and personnel. This office has direct formal and informal relations with the court structure and the legal aid unit, for it is the source of the court's business. While specific organizational features and characteristics of the office of the district attorney are beyond the scope of this book, one significant aspect of its organization must at least be mentioned so that we may understand how it affects the larger court through which it funnels its cases.

After decades of unsavory and corrupt practices at the county and municipal level in the city in which Metropolitan Court is located, there was concerted public pressure to remove certain municipal and county offices from the political patronage system. Both major political parties, anxious to avoid scandal and to improve at least superficially the tarnished image of municipal government, agreed to sponsor joint candidates for some judicial and prosecutor posts. Qualities of personal integrity, honesty, intellectual achievement, and dedication to public service were to be the ideal characteristics of potential candidates, regardless of party label.

As a result, the office of the district attorney has in the past twenty-five years taken on the character of a civil service post. The chief prosecutor has always enjoyed the political endorsement of both major parties and, in furtherance of the public service image, has recruited assistant district attorneys from among the graduates of leading law schools. There are still a number of patronage people in the office and even civil service personnel with strong clubhouse ties. Indeed, many of the bright young men recruited from the better law schools usually seek political affiliation to further their careers in the office or afterward, in private practice or some other post, in or out of government. But in the main, politics is much less a part of the district attorney's office than it once was.

The office employs a full-time staff of approximately seventy assistant district attorneys. Six bureau heads are responsible for the major activities of the office, and they supervise the daily work of the assistants who in turn file a brief report on each plea of guilty accepted, proposed, or negotiated. Each case must be accounted for as a unit of production. At the annual office banquet, it is customary for the district attorney to praise his staff in glowing terms, especially for their "batting average," which is an omnipresent standard of performance.

Most assistants remain in the office from three to five years until they make a "connection" or some other appropriate step upward in the career line. Usually it is the "failures" who remain behind to become bureau heads in the office or assume other supervisory functions. As a result the office takes on a more rational-impersonal orientation, geared to aggressive prosecution without "fear or favor." This is not to say that political concerns and pressures are not present. But they have in large measure been concealed by an impartial civil servant organization and a public service image, which is vigorous in maximizing production to justify its budget, and which does not as readily lend itself to informal political considerations at the beck and call of the "political club."

The assistant district attorneys operate within the confines of office policy enforced by bureau heads. Not only must the total output of cases be maximized, but the "batting average" must reflect the kind of superior efficiency supposedly present in the impartial, public-service type of district attorney's office. This perception of the office contrasts to the old-fashioned "political" model based on patronage with its personal and informal commitments, now for the most part rejected. Of course, the office of the district attorney still retains the traditional ideology that its function is not simply to prosecute but more important to "protect the innocent" and to exercise great care and prudence in its decisions to prosecute. The public prosecutor has a unique role in our system of jurisprudence. He is required to be "impartial" in the sense that he must try to determine whether the accused is really guilty of the crime charged. He must not only use facts unfavorable to an accused but must also not conceal facts favorable to him. The stated measure of success is not the number of convictions but their "fairness." Thus the district attorney is not an ordinary party to a criminal controversy but has a higher standard, an impartial concern with "fairness" and "justice." As a practical matter, however, prosecutors have great discretion and power to use their office for idiosyncratic, nonorganizational ends, or to use it in a manner that overrides obligations to the accused in order to meet unstated requirements of the organization.[2]

[2] See Paul W. Tappan, *Crime, Justice and Correction* (New York, 1960), pp. 342–344; David Fellman, *The Defendant's Rights* (New York, 1958), p. 63; Ernst W. Puttkammer, *Administration of Criminal Law* (Chicago, 1963), pp. 190–193; Lewis Mayers, *The Machinery of Justice* (Englewood Cliffs, N.J.), 1963, pp. 104–105.

As a practical matter, self-imposed organizational pressures, such as getting the most for each prosecution dollar and demonstrating the superiority of the public-service model of the office, direct all energies toward maximum production. The new type of assistant district attorney is far less politically connected and is wholly dependent upon his superiors for their employment recommendations when he moves on — whether to another political office or to private practice. As in any other bureaucratic setting, the rewards are dispensed only to those who have "played the game" and have conformed to the expectancies of their superiors.

The criterion of office efficiency becomes the number of convictions (or pleas) produced, which in turn are built and based upon the growth of impersonal, rational procedures which energize and amplify bureaucratic structures. Max Weber has written:

> The more bureaucracy is "dehumanized," the more completely it succeeds in eliminating from official business love, hatred, and all purely personal, irrational elements which escape calculation. This is the specific nature of bureaucracy and it is appraised as its special virtue.[3]

In reality, therefore, an accused is, so to speak, ground between the millstones of the district attorney and of the court. Both have their respective organizational requirements of maximum production.

Figure 1, [see page 273], depicts some of the structural relationships in the system.

Note that counsel, whether privately retained or of the legal aid variety, have close and continuing relations with the prosecuting office and the court itself. Indeed, lines of communication, influence, and contact with those offices, as well as with the other subsidiary divisions of the office of the clerk and the probation division and with the press, are essential to the practice of criminal law. Accused persons come and go in the court system, but the structure and its personnel remain to carry on their respective career, occupational, and organizational enterprises. The individual stridencies, tensions, and conflicts which certain cases may generate within the system are overcome, because the relations of all the groups in the court setting require it. They must preserve their own relations and interaction at all costs.

In some modern bureaucratic settings, the organization appears to exist to serve the needs of its personnel rather than its clients.[4] The client becomes a secondary figure in the court system as in other large organizational settings. He is a means to other, larger ends of the organization's incumbents. He may present doubts, contingencies, and pressures which challenge or disrupt exist-

---

[3] H. H. Gerth and C. Wright Mills, *From Max Weber: Essays in Sociology* (New York, 1958), p. 211.
    [4] Amitai Etzioni, *Modern Organizations* (Englewood Cliffs, N.J., 1964), pp. 94–104.

Figure 1: Some Structural Relationships in the Metropolitan Court Organization

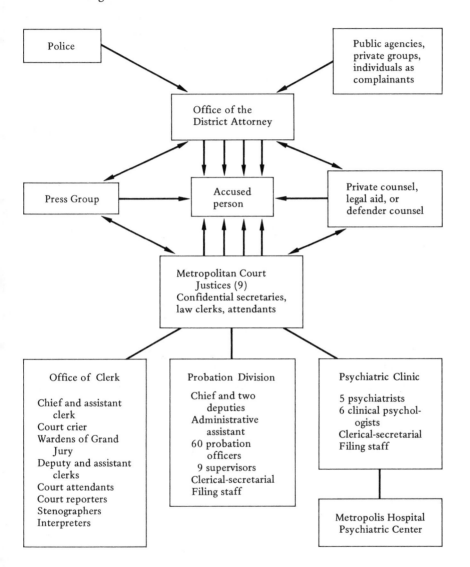

ing informal networks, but they are usually resolved in favor of the organization. Even the accused's lawyer has far greater professional, economic,
intellectual, and other ties to the various elements of the court system than
to his own client. Yet the lawyer is the only member of the system who is
officially recognized as having a special status and obligations. He is an
"officer of the court," and he is expected to maintain a standard of ethical
performance and duty to his client, as well as to the court, which is far higher
than that expected of ordinary individuals occupying the various occupational
statuses in the court community.

One other aspect of organizational structure must be considered in attempt-
ing to measure a social reality such as the "closed community" of a court.
And the essence of this aspect of the problem has been captured by Aaron
Cicourel:

> Most of the data that sociologists honor as "given" . . . are largely the product
> of bureaucratically organized activities, for example census bureaus, vital statistics
> bureaus, correctional agencies, welfare agencies, and business agencies. The multi-
> tudinous perceptions and interpretations that went into the assembly of such data
> are invariably lost to the reader or user of such materials. The quantitative features
> must be accepted by fiat. The fact that even factual data are subject to perceptions
> and interpretations which may vary with the actor's biography, the occasion of
> recording, the explicit or implicit rules employed for deciding the sense of the ob-
> jects or events categorized, and the stated language and unstated meanings which
> were relevant to the particular observer, means that these are variables to consider
> in assessing the relevance and importance of such data.[5]

Every public agency or privately owned corporation interprets its past,
present, and future operations through the medium of the annual, semi-
annual, or quarterly report. Sometimes an elaborate affair with color plates,
intricate charts, and impressive tables, it is essentially a brief for the agency
or corporation. In effect it advises the publics concerned that the operation
is in good hands and merits confidence. It is the "official" window through
which the author-agency wishes to present itself. It is an important vehicle
of justification for public or private funds already spent and requested for
expanding future budgets.

In the case of a public agency, the "report" justifies its budget. In essence
it says, "Look, how busy we are!" Figures on how many cases were processed
or clients served are usually accurate, as are most of the other innocuous items
in the report of Metropolitan Court and similar courts. Any organization,
public or private, whose flow of funds depends largely upon production data
as evidence of its efficiency and social utility, will find it hard to resist pressures to tamper with the figures. It is a basic fact of bureaucratic life that

[5] Aaron V. Cicourel, *Method and Measurement in Sociology* (New York,
1964), pp. 36–37.

production and production figures are a fetish. Nothing demolishes criticism faster than a robust set of production figures which reflect an ever onward and upward increase, and they are therefore almost blindly worshiped. Reports may be slanted, certain data may be highlighted or "puffed up" to meet felt needs for additional budget and staff, but reports of public agencies usually reveal nothing of social consequence about the real organizational world they come from.

An agency's published data are of course never adequate or appropriate for the sociologist, except as a point of beginning. Sociological perspective involves a process of "seeing through" the façades of social structures. The official data are an organizational curtain to be drawn aside so that the important network of human activities may be laid bare. For all the personnel of Metropolitan Court — judges, lawyers, down to the most menial clerk — the fact that more than 90 per cent of its clients plead guilty each year rather than stand trial arouses no curiosity, interest, or surprise. In fact, it is never mentioned. It is a "world taken for granted." It is statistical evidence of the agency's high efficiency in giving the public maximum service for each tax dollar spent. In similar fashion, the police and prosecution seek "successful" cases as grist for their respective enforcement and production "mills," in part to justify their budgets and in part as ego-satisfying evidence of workmanship and professional expertise. Thus the policeman seeks the "good pinch"[6] and the prosecutor the "airtight case."

THE SIEVE EFFECT

Each enforcement agency seeks to maximize its viability with a set of "successful" prosecution figures. Nevertheless, it is an interesting study in contrasts to observe the incredible statistical difference between the number of crimes committed or reported and the number of persons actually dealt with officially in the law enforcement machinery. Criminal and delinquent activity has a rather small overall liability of being subjected to official action — that is, of the offender being detected, apprehended, and convicted. The FBI reports on a rather consistent basis that only about 25 per cent of all crimes reported are actually cleared by arrest.[7]

The police have wide powers of discretion in selecting persons for processing. Similarly, prosecutors may choose to ignore offenses or to prosecute, and

---

[6] See Jerome H. Skolnick, *Justice Without Trial* (New York, 1966), pp. 142–155, 174–175; Richard C. Donnelly, "Police Authority and Practices," *The Annals* (January, 1962), pp. 90–110; Joseph Goldstein, "Police Discretion Not to Invoke the Criminal Process: Low Visibility Decisions in the Administration of Criminal Justice," *Yale Law Journal*, LXIX (March, 1960), pp. 543–594.

[7] *Uniform Crime Reports* — 1963, Table 8, p. 93; 1964, Table 8, p. 95; 1965, Table 8, p. 97.

grand juries and courts of preliminary hearing are also engaged in a selection-sifting process of some kind. There is therefore a sieve effect in the criminal process, and it is directly relevant to the organizational analysis of one of the most important elements in the whole process — the court.

Some aspects of the preliminary sifting of potential accused clients have already been discussed. We have not noted that a fundamental character-istic of the sieve effect is that initially its escape holes are somewhat broad and coarse. They begin to sift in an increasingly finite manner as we move structurally from the initial point of police handling to the court of pre-liminary hearing, then to the arena of the criminal court where felonies are tried. There the process almost freezes, and only infrequently from then on can the accused free himself from the procedural engine in which he is en-meshed. It is as though he had been, in social-psychological terms, prepared and shaped for his ultimate disposition and presented to the court in a crude fashion for final processing. In these final steps the accused person is helped to redefine and restructure his concept of "presumed to be innocent" to that of a "guilty" person. Figure 2, [see page 277], examines in cursory fashion the gross possibilities as they may terminate at any point in the processing of a felony case, either in being "sifted" to the next step or in freedom.[8]

The virtual freezing of the sifting process occurs in phases IV and V of Figure 2, when a maximum of organizational structure, personnel, and skills are brought to bear upon the individual.

Table 1 confirms our contention that once the case of an accused reaches the Metropolitan Court level in his "career," the possibility of freedom be-comes problematic, if not slight. These data draw upon a different geographic universe (the Kings County Criminal Court of Brooklyn, New York), but deal with a population similar in size and composition to that of Metropolitan Court. The Kings County court also has many structural and procedural similarities, as well as similarities in case load composition and volume, which would make for a valid comparison.

Justice Sobel of the court, who collected the data, did so largely to demon-strate that relatively few persons who are initially charged with a crime are indeed found to have committed the original version of the crime charged. It is a not uncommon administrative device of the police to couch the original version of their charge against an accused in the most extreme form possible within the confines of a given set of facts. Thus, very often, an original charge of felonious assault (with a weapon) is reduced at the initial hearing to a more realistic one of simple assault, or even to disorderly conduct. In part,

[8] Adapted from Donald R. Cressey, "Crime," in Robert K. Merton and Robert A. Nisbet, eds., *Contemporary Social Problems* (New York, 1961), p. 29. Cressey based his version of Figure 2 on Walter A. Lunden, "How to Beat the Rap," *American Journal of Correction,* XIX (May–June, 1957), p. 13.

Figure 2: The Sieve Effect

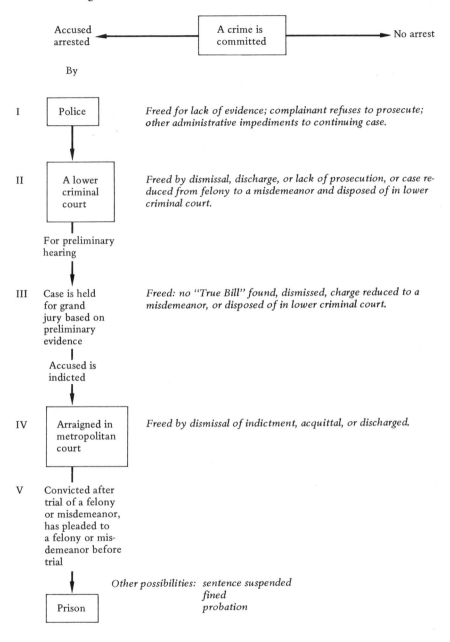

Table 1: Disposition of Adult Felony Arrests, Kings County (1960-1962)

Stage of proceeding	Number of cases	Percentage of total	Percentage remaining
1. Preliminary arraignment in a lower criminal court	32,000	100	100
2. Discharged, dismissed on technical or procedural grounds or otherwise adjusted at preliminary arraignment	2,000	6.2	93.8
3. Dismissed on merits (case was not proven) at preliminary arraignment	6,000	18.6	75.2
4. Reduced to misdemeanor charge at preliminary arraignment	12,000	37.6	37.6
5. Held for grand jury	12,000	37.6	37.6
6. Dismissed by grand jury	1,000	3.1	34.5
7. Charge reduced by grand jury to a misdemeanor	1,000	3.1	31.4
8. Indicted by grand jury	10,000	31.4	31.4
9. Indictments dismissed for procedural reasons as defective	320	1.0	30.4
10. Indictments dismissed on facts and law of case	640	2.0	28.4
11. Adjudged youthful offender	860	2.6	25.8
12. Pleas before trial to a felony	3,200	10.0	15.8
13. Pleas before trial to a misdemeanor	4,280	13.4	2.4
14. Convicted after trial of a felony	350	1.2	1.3
15. Convicted after trial of a misdemeanor	50	.3	1.0
16. Acquitted	300	1.0	0.0

this is the sort of activity to which Sobel refers in his data, but he also empirically spells out the wide disparity in the number accused and those actually ultimately convicted in our courts. Also to be noted is the manner in which the situation becomes firm after one is indicted and begins his processing in a court dealing with felonies, such as the Brooklyn court or Metropolitan Court.

The data are given in the form of round numbers and approximate percentages. The format has been altered slightly to promote clarity, and some of the "stages" of the data have been relabeled. The figures all refer to adult felony arrests in cases for the years 1960 through 1962.[9]

Two almost casual observations can be made about Table 1 which further support the concept of a diminution in the sifting process as a case reaches the level of indictment and beyond. Of the total of ten thousand persons indicted by the grand jury (item 8), 8,740 either pleaded guilty or were adjudged or convicted after trial (total of items 11 through 15), or approximately 87 per cent of all those ultimately indicted. This approximate figure is not significantly different from the Metropolitan Court figures for 1950–1964, which were of course precise figures and not rounded off as are the data in Table 1.

The sieve effect is the result of the increase in personnel and the greater intricacy of structure brought to bear on the accused as he moves toward and into the court for the felony trial itself.

INSTRUMENTS AND PRESSURES
PROMOTING PLEAS OF GUILTY

During the course of Anglo-American history, convicted persons have sometimes been burned at the stake, drawn and quartered, or pressed to death (also known as *peine forte et dure*). This last mode of execution was an excruciating style of death employed especially in cases where an individual refused to plead guilty or not guilty to an indictment.[10] Nothing so appalling or violent has been used in the contemporary administration of criminal law. But the basic overriding concern is still with a *plea*, rather than anything more elaborate, by way of disposing of a criminal case. The methodology employed to get that plea has undergone the kind of subtle refinement and elaboration that only the modern features of formal organization can provide.

The fundamental event which places an accused upon the horns of a dilemma, leading to his ultimate desire for a negotiated or bargained lesser plea, is very simply the decline of the jury system. Whatever that system's

---

[9] Nathan R. Sobel, *Brooklyn Law Review*, XXX, No. 1 (December, 1963), p. 13.
[10] Hugo A. Bedau, ed., *The Death Penalty in America* (Chicago, 1964), pp. 15–16.

merits or drawbacks may be, the fact is that defendants shun a jury trial.[11] This is borne out by Metropolitan Court data, attesting to the dearth of jury trials in that court. But an even more critical factor for the individual accused is his knowledge (whether he senses it intuitively or has learned it from his jail companions or his lawyer) that juries are notoriously prone to convict. In simple terms, the outcome of any jury trial often turns upon the question of whom the jury will believe — the assertions of the police, law enforcement officials and their witnesses, or the accused. The answer forthcoming with frequent regularity is: the police and those offering testimony in their behalf. This fact lies at the root of an accused's reluctance to risk a jury trial and in part accounts for the consequent decline of the jury as an important feature of the system.

An accused is confronted with a formidable barrier at the very outset of his passage as an indicted person (Table 1, stage 8), in that he is perceived as a far more serious offender than if he had been sifted out at an earlier stage in his career. The charges he now faces are those of a felony. This fact alone helps to determine the kinds of pressures he will face and how the staff of Metropolitan Court will react to his processing. And, at the outset, the accused's position is complicated by still another factor which dissuades him from braving the possible consequences of a trial by jury — the multiple-count indictment.

An indictment is a list of criminal charges. Its purpose is to notify an accused of the precise nature of his alleged offenses so that he may prepare a defense. But a law violation which occurs through a single act can legally result in one being charged with several offenses. A typical indictment for, let us say, possession of more than an eighth of an ounce of heroin, will read as follows:

Count #1.   Felonious possession of a narcotic drug.
Count #2.   Felonious possession of a narcotic drug with intent to sell.
Count #3.   Unlawfully possessing a narcotic drug.

A quite common indictment for burglary may read:

Count #1.   Burglary 3rd degree.
Count #2.   Possession of burglar's instruments.
Count #3.   Unlawful entry of a building.

---

[11] E. H. Sutherland and D. R. Cressey, *Principles of Criminology* (Philadelphia, 1960), pp. 385–386; Charles Winick, "The Psychology of Juries," in Hans Toch, ed., *Legal and Criminal Psychology* (New York, 1961), pp. 96–120; Charles L. Newman, "Trial by Jury: An Outmoded Relic?", *Journal of Criminal Law, Criminology and Police Science*, XLVI, No. 4 (November–December, 1955), pp. 512–518.

Or one for armed robbery:

Count #1. Robbery 1st degree.
Count #2. Assault 2nd degree.
Count #3. Assault 3rd degree.
Count #4. Grand larceny 1st degree.
Count #5. Carrying a dangerous weapon.
Count #6. Petit larceny.

Another quite common illustration of the force and effectiveness of the multiple-count indictment occurs in connection with so-called "white collar" offenses. Modern commercial transactions and enterprises have been so rationalized that they are conducted largely with letters of credit, notes, checks, elaborate records, securities, mortgages, bonds, stocks, certificates, and other documents. These of course are subject to theft, forgery, manipulation, and fraud. It is therefore not uncommon for a case of embezzlement or theft based on a series of forgeries to result in an indictment containing more than a hundred counts of forgery, grand larceny, and other charges of theft and fraud. Each count is grounded upon an individual document connected with a particular person who used it in the course of his thefts. The pressure on the accused to seek some sort of compromise of all these charges becomes intense, to say the least. Conviction by a jury on all counts could result in an accused spending the rest of his life in prison.

There are, therefore, depending on the alleged facts in each case, many combinations available which result in an accused being charged with multiple felonies and lesser misdemeanors growing out of the same event. Using the Robbery 1st degree indictment as an example, if an accused were to "gamble" and proceed to a jury trial, it is quite possible (indeed, probable) that he could be convicted on each and every count of the indictment and face many years in prison if the sentences were fixed to run consecutively instead of concurrently on each count. In some states the Robbery 1st degree count *alone* would warrant a sentence of up to thirty years. But typically in Metropolitan Court, if an accused has had no prior record and if he has capably performed the defendant role, he probably will receive a lesser plea of, let us say, a misdemeanor such as simple assault or petit larceny.

The impulse to seek a negotiated plea at this point, in view of the dire possibilities of going to trial and losing, is almost impossible for an accused to overcome. The "benefits" and advantages of a lighter sentence for a lesser plea, or even the possibility of a suspended sentence, become overwhelmingly attractive. For example, as subsequent data will indicate, the possibilities of a defendant being placed on probation are far greater if he has pleaded to a lesser offense, rather than having been convicted after a trial. An accused's fears of harsh treatment if he does not plead are hardly groundless, considering what courts and judges do to defendants who remain recalcitrant and go to trial.

The jury system and the multiple indictment, then, are used as the initial blows to further collapse an accused's will to resist at this phase of his processing. The district attorney is the moving force, the upper of the millstones, as we have indicated, between which the defendant is ground. The prosecutor calls all the strategic plays:

1. He decides when the case will appear on the calendar for any particular stage of the proceeding.
2. He recommends the amount of bail, if any is to be granted (although final discretion is up to the judge).
3. He selects the particular term or part — that is, which judge will hear or try the case.
4. He has virtually complete discretion as to whether to prosecute and on what legal grounds (of course, subject to restriction of law).
5. He often determines what lesser plea, if any, will be accepted in lieu of the case going to trial.[12]

This last prerogative is the most important weapon in the prosecutor's arsenal, for it furnishes his basis for power in negotiations with the significant "others" in the court. The district attorney is the one court figure most aggressively interested in obtaining a negotiated plea rather than a case culminating in a combative trial. First, there is the almost impossible administrative task of going through the elaborate procedures of a court trial for each case. The personnel and other resources of the prosecutor's office simply could not carry such an impossible burden. And the prosecutor would lose a degree of dominance over those variables essential to the maintenance of his "public image" and the "batting average." In those cases which end in a plea, the prosecutor usually retains a far greater influence over the ultimate sentence or disposition. Indeed, the very plea which is finally negotiated and accepted by the accuser and the accused fairly well defines the limits of punishment ultimately involved.

But even the civil-service model prosecutor is subject to political and bureaucratic pressures of important "others." He is himself observed by the police, judges, lawyers, and lesser officials in the court community, such as those who administer the short-term prison housing for persons awaiting disposition of their cases. This last is a frequently overlooked element of internal

---

[12] Clarence C. Ferguson, Jr., "Formulation of Enforcement Policy: An Anatomy of the Prosecutor's Discretion Prior to Accusation," *Rutgers Law Review,* II (Spring, 1957), p. 507; Newman F. Baker, "The Prosecutor — Initiation of Prosecution," *Journal of Criminal Law, Criminology and Police Science,* XXIII (January–February, 1933), pp. 770–796.

pressure in the court system. Accused who are not released on bail are housed in the short-term prison; as a rule it is overpopulated in terms of its capacity. Each day a statistical resumé of the jail population is sent to the prosecutor, the judges, and the probation division. Its message is not lost upon its recipients: faster production.

The short-term prison attached to Metropolitan Court was built to house approximately nine hundred males. The average population awaiting disposition there is double that number and often far more. The conditions at the prison, even if improved, would still be onerous in view of the overcrowding. At times, bail practices become a function of the extent of crowding in the short-term prison. The prison is used in still another way, namely, to further soften defendants reluctant to plead. In short, crowded conditions in the short-term prison become an extremely functional adjunct for the total administrative process of the court system.

The external pressures on the prosecutor depicted in Figure 3 are set out in terms of intensity and proximity of the pressures they exert. Of greater intensity and proximity are those of the short-term prison population (a substantial part of the case load), as represented by the warden of that institution. Police officials and personnel who are moved by pressures and demands of their own organization for production, are a second important source of pressure on the district attorney for production results, as are the judges. Politically visible defense lawyers, unlike attorneys who appear only casually and irregularly in Metropolitan Court and who have therefore failed to de-

Figure 3: Proximate and More Remote Pressures on the Prosecutor

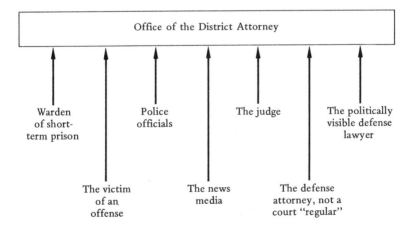

velop political or informal relationships with the district attorney, must be accommodated somehow or at least extended certain courtesies.

More remote, and exerting pressures of less immediate intensity, are the victims of offenses committed by accused persons, the news media, and the defense attorney who is not part of the intimate circle of official persons who make up the tight-knit, xenophobic community of the court. Victims who may be seeking restitution, the return of stolen property, or just revenge or retaliation are a constant source of minor harassment, but they are easily put off or somehow pacified. The news media and those attorneys who are not "regulars" are dealt with on a quid pro quo basis of "favors" given and returned, and while they exert pressure, their placation is not insurmountable.

On the other hand, of more intimate concern to the prosecutor are pressures from those with whom he lives in a virtually symbiotic professional relationship in order to maintain his own organizational equilibrium. Thus, although the prosecutor has many powers and prerogatives, and possesses the initiative at virtually all times, he nevertheless depends upon the close, continuing help of the police, judges, lawyers, and other lesser functionaries to attain his ends. And they in turn depend upon him for the identical objectives they desire, namely, as few trials as possible.

Besides the time, energy, and resources that the court organization is reluctant to expend on trials, as a bureaucracy it is loath to engage in activity whose predictability it is unable to control. The rational component of formal organization avoids the fortuitous, the random, and the contingent, such as a jury trial. Greater faith is placed upon symbiotic relationships and structured expectancies to meet the individual and group needs of the court participants, rather than a working through of legal abstractions such as due process. The deviant or even maverick individual who predicates his official conduct solely on accepted notions of due process, or chooses possibilities of action which run counter to normatively established routines, is quickly isolated, neutralized, or re-socialized.

Professionals of the older variety (for example, lawyers) or of the "new" professions (for example, social workers, probation officers, psychologists), have increasingly become part of an occupational mass known as a "salariat," employed and seeking employment in large-scale organizations.[13] This development has created conflict between the professionally oriented individual who seeks satisfaction and recognition outside the immediate, narrow confines of his organization, and the specific task requirements of his organization. Two types of professionals emerge: the "cosmopolitan" seeks satisfaction and recognition outside the organization; the "local" perfects his relationships and rituals within the organization. The "local" develops a method of or-

---

[13] Everett C. Hughes, *Men and Their Work* (Glencoe, Ill., 1958), pp. 131–138.

ganizational maneuver, promoting at all times his idiosyncratic career interests but at the same time showing a seemingly passionate, loyal concern for the organization. His "career" rises or falls with the organization, in contrast to the "cosmopolitan," whose interests range beyond the organization — even though he may be just as zealously concerned with career escalation.

Even though the organizational world of the court — which is in many respects unique — contains an ongoing struggle between a legal due process perception and an ameliorative-therapeutic perception of the court's function, these are overridden by the superordinate requirements of efficiency and production. The usual staff-line struggles of quality versus quantity, the divergent concerns, professional commitments and interests, occupational goals, values, and perspectives of those engaged in the enterprise are overcome, harnessed, and coordinated into a working consensus to alter effectively the accused's view of himself as "presumed to be innocent."

Individuals with a professional orientation or worldly concerns are considered deviants and are not tolerated if they are discovered invoking other than ritualized organization means and objectives. The standard of performance, the model of commitment and loyalty becomes the "local" — the bureaucratically oriented routineer. Because the individual in organizational society is so dependent upon the various bureaucratic enclaves for material goods and services, he is motivated to conform to their expectancies and demands. Individuals are thereby motivated to "play the game" rather than deviate. (The court organization, as we shall see later, invokes still other controls and motivations for compliance by group members.)

Those professionals in the court, such as probation officers, psychologists, and psychiatrists, who believe they will manipulate the legal structures in line with their orientations, discover too late that they are mere instruments to be utilized for larger organizational ends. They find that their body of professional skills cannot be autonomously employed but must be exercised within the framework of precise organizational limits and objectives.

THE "MORAL CAREER"
OF AN ACCUSED PERSON

We have described the journey of an accused person through the sifting process of the court system as a "career." Sociologists use the term not necessarily to describe conventional notions of occupational careers but to delineate the social-psychological steps in transition from one status to another.[14]

---

[14] Erving Goffman, *Asylums*, pp. 127–169. See also a most recent example of the use of the "career" concept by a sociologist whose basic focus is the tuberculosis patient, but who also employs it in an analysis of prisoners, airline pilots, and business executives. Julius A. Roth, *Timetables: Structuring the Passage of Time in Hospital Treatment and Other Careers* (New York, 1963).

Erving Goffman speaks of "the moral aspects of career — that is, the regular sequence of changes that career entails in the person's self and in his framework of imagery for judging himself and others."[15] Goffman elaborates:

> The moral career of a person of a given social category involves a standard sequence of changes in his way of conceiving of selves, including, importantly, his own. . . . Each moral career, and behind this, each self, occurs within the confines of an institutional system, whether a social establishment such as a mental hospital or a complex of personal and professional relationships. The self, then, can be seen as something that resides in the arrangements prevailing in a social system for its members. The self in this sense is not a property of the person to whom it is attributed, but dwells rather in the pattern of social control that is exerted in connection with the person by himself and those around him. This special kind of institutional arrangement does not so much support the self as constitute it.[16]

One can apply Goffman's analysis to the case of the accused person who moves from civilian to criminal, or is convicted. We begin with a complainant, who may be a private individual, a policeman, the district attorney, or an administrative agency. If the gravamen of his complaint is sustained in a lower criminal court of first instance, the individual complained of has become an accused person. Henceforth the accused will be dealt with and processed by a variety of mediators and agencies who will relay him along. But already he has marked the first milestone in his career — he has become an accused person.

He may now face an assistant district attorney who will point to the multiple counts of an indictment and ask whether the accused would rather go to trial than plead to some proposed lesser offense. Even the most obtuse accused will understand the full import of this.

To police administrations, a plea of guilty is a welcome addition to the statistical evidence of their effectiveness, for they correlate a favorable public image and a high conviction rate. Equally important is the fact that valuable police time that would be spent in trial testimony is freed for other activities.

Much police work at every level — federal, state, and local — is conducted on the basis of information furnished by informers and paid agents. Because of the nature of this mode of operation, which encroaches on dearly held ethical values, police work and negotiation with other agencies is best carried on in relative secrecy. Thus the kind of informal negotiations which are conducted by police, district attorney, defense counsel, and judge in connection with a negotiated plea are best performed in virtual secrecy. In bargaining with an accused, the police use the possibility of a negotiated plea as leverage, usually to get further information. Of course, at times they are com-

15 *Ibid.*, p. 128.
16 *Ibid.*, p. 168.

pletely out of bounds in their zeal, making offers of immunity or threats of punishment wholly beyond their authority or function.

The vested interest of the district attorney and the police, and their role as agents, is readily perceived and understood by an accused person. He will have sensed certain negative attitudes toward police and will have internalized them long before he has ever been arrested. The agent-mediator roles of judges, lawyers, probation officers, psychiatrists, and members of his own family are not so easily understood. The accused could reasonably define them as allies.

But some of the same reasons which serve as the basis for the district attorney's actions apply also to the judge. According to the ideology of the law, the judge is required to be not only impartial but active in seeking out and preserving the rights of all offenders. Nevertheless, he also has a vested interest in a high rate of negotiated pleas. He shares the prosecutor's earnest desire to avoid the time consuming, expensive, unpredictable snares and pitfalls of an adversary trial. He sees an impossible backlog of cases, with their mounting delays, as possible public evidence of his "inefficiency" and failure. The defendant's plea of guilty enables the judge to engage in a social-psychological fantasy — the accused becomes an already repentant individual who has "learned his lesson" and deserves lenient treatment. Indeed, as previously indicated, many judges give a less severe sentence to a defendant who has negotiated a plea than to one who has been convicted of the same offense after a trial.[17]

The lawyer, whether a public defender or a privately retained defense counsel, is subject to pressures peculiar to his role and organizational obligations. But ultimately he is also concerned with strategies leading to a plea. Again, impersonal elements prevail — the economics of time, labor, expense, and the commitment of the defense counsel to the rationalistic values of the court organization; the accused who expects a personal, affective relationship with his lawyer is likely to be disappointed. The lawyer "regulars" of Metropolitan Court are frequently former staff members of the prosecutor's office. They utilize the charisma, "know-how," and contacts of their former affiliation as part of their stock in trade. An accused and his kin, as well as others outside the court community, are unable to comprehend the nature and dimensions of the close relations between the lawyer "regular" and his former colleagues in the prosecutor's office. Their continuing colleagueship is based on real professional and organizational needs of a quid pro quo, which goes beyond the limits of an accommodation one might ordinarily expect in a seem-

---

[17] Lloyd E. Ohlin and Frank J. Remington, "Sentencing Structure: Its Effects Upon Systems for the Administration of Criminal Justice," *Law and Contemporary Problems,* XXIII (Summer, 1958), pp. 495–507.

ingly adversary relationship. Indeed, adversary features are for the most part
muted and exist in their attenuated form largely for external consumption.
The principals — lawyer and assistant district attorney — rely upon each
other's cooperation for their continued professional existence, and so the
bargaining between them usually is "reasonable" rather than fierce.

In his relations with his counsel, the accused begins to experience his first
sense of "betrayal." He had already sensed or known that police and district
attorneys were adversaries, and perhaps even a judge might be cast in such a
role, but he is wholly unprepared for his counsel's performance as an agent or
mediator.

It is even less likely to occur to an accused that members of his own family
may become agents of the court system. Upon the urging of other agents or
mediators, relatives may believe they are really helping an accused negotiate
the best possible arrangement under the circumstances. Usually the lawyer
will activate next of kin in this role, his ostensible motive being to arrange
for his fee. But soon counsel will suggest that they appeal to the accused to
"help himself" by pleading. Gemeinschaft sentiments are to this extent exploited by a defense lawyer (or even at times by a district attorney) to
achieve specific secular ends, to conclude the matter with all possible dispatch.

Sooner or later the probation officer becomes an agent in an accused's
processing, depending upon when his services are invoked by judicial requisi-
tion. In his role as an agent-mediator there is a fundamental theme — the
professional self-conception of a "case worker in an authoritative setting."
Probation officers and psychiatrists in the court must, according to established procedures, accept as a "given" the facts of a defendant's case as they
are presented by the police and the district attorney. This has specific consequences in their relations with an accused. In other words, they view important aspects of a defendant's social biography in terms and meanings
defined for them by agents hostile to the accused. Thus they see him, whether
before or after he has pleaded, as already "in treatment."

The accused is usually unable to understand that he does not enjoy the
worker-client or doctor-patient relationship with these functionaries. On the
contrary, their professional services are pre-empted by the court organization,
and they tend to impute primacy to the organization for the content and
meaning of their roles. Usually, a defendant speaks much more freely and
reveals a good deal more about himself to psychiatrists and probation officers
than he would to other agent-mediators. But he can also reveal too much; he
overlooks the lack of real confidentiality present in his relationship with them,
and this too has consequences in terms of his ultimate disposition. The court
organization may rely heavily on probation and psychiatric reports, especially
in those cases where there are no other firm or compelling legal, political,

personal, or other criteria to use as a basis for disposing of a case. Bear in mind that the justifications and rationales employed by these agents are grounded in a stock of knowledge about the accused that is pre-cast by police and prosecutor, whose objectivity may be problematic. So, to a large extent, probation and psychiatric reports reaffirm and recirculate the same knowledge about the accused originally furnished by police and prosecutor — refurbished in the patois and argot of social work and psychiatry.

The probation officer has an important function as an agent-mediator, especially after the accused has pleaded and has begun to have second thoughts about the matter. This function may be best described as "cooling the mark out." The phrase was originally used to describe that part of a confidence game in which the operatives leave one of their number behind to discourage the victim from going to the police and to help him accept his new social situation. The victim of, let us say, a swindle must be furnished with a set of apologia or rationales so that he can redefine himself in suitable and defensible terms, instead of going to the police to complain. His embarrassment and defeat are assuaged by the operative who is "cooling him." In similar fashion, in other social matrices, losers and defeated persons must be somehow "cooled out" in order to avoid some sort of social explosion. Erving Goffman furnishes an illustration in which one spouse "decourts" another by maneuvering the marital partner into a divorce without incurring undue hostility. Or in the case of a dying person, the cooling role is assumed by a doctor or priest.[18] Helping an accused person to accept defeat is another aspect of the agent-mediator role which is thus of great significance. The lawyer, probation officer, psychiatrist, and next of kin perform important "cooling out" functions. Even the police, prosecutor, and judge may occasionally find it necessary to perform such a function as an accused is processed toward a reconceptualization of self, in the course of changing his initial plea of "not guilty" to one attesting guilt.

We have previously noted that the short-term jail which houses defendants awaiting disposition is frequently crowded to double the intended capacity. Although this is a state of affairs not deliberately created, the discomforts occasioned thereby are employed as a weapon against the accused by the prosecutor and judge. A recalcitrant accused can be socialized relatively quickly by an extended sojourn in the remand jail, including setting bail at a level high enough so that he cannot meet it. The common refrain heard in the remand jail, from those who have been there for an extended period, is a desire to plead quickly and get sentenced, so that they can be moved to a

---

[18] Erving Goffman, "On Cooling the Mark Out: Some Aspects of Adaptation to Failure," in Arnold M. Rose, ed., *Human Behavior and Social Processes* (Boston, 1962), pp. 482–505.

more commodious prison. The greatly crowded conditions, while unintended and unforeseen, are used as part of the process of reducing an accused's resistance to the various agent-mediators.

While it is true that efforts have been made to simplify and develop less onerous bail procedures,[19] most defendants are still subject to the usual difficulties connected therewith. The bail or jail feature of the system is not the crucial one in terms of an accused's defeat; it is only one feature in the total array of structure and personnel in the prosecutor's arsenal of weapons.

Although many accused persons are never confronted with the problem, their alleged wrongdoing being unsung in the press, there are instances in which the news media serve in an agent-mediator role. Obviously this is not their intention, for they desire to serve publics and ends of their own. But it is virtually impossible for an accused to receive a fair trial by "an impartial jury," should he elect to do so, because an "impartial jury" could never be constituted if the press, radio, and television have established for weeks in advance of his "trial" that a defendant is guilty.

In summary, the accused is confronted by definitions of himself which reflect the various worlds of the agent-mediators — yet are consistent for the most part in their negative evaluation of him. The agent-mediators have seized upon a wholly unflattering aspect of his biography to reinterpret his entire personality and justify their present attitude and conduct toward him. Even an individual with considerable personal and economic resources has great difficulty resisting pressures to redefine himself under these circumstances. For the ordinary accused of modest personal, economic, and social resources, the group pressures and definitions of himself are simply too much to bear. He willingly complies with the demands of agent-mediators, who in turn will help "cool him out."

Figure 4, [see page 291], does not spell out the interrelationships of the various agent-mediators, but it depicts the accused's ultimate situation. Of course, he does not initially assume that all these pressures are allied against him.

One of the major requisites of due process is a "public trial," but justice by negotiation avoids public scrutiny. Technically, it may meet the minimum requirements of due process (the defendant having waived jury trial), but whether it meets the ideological and historical criteria of due process is at least an open question.

The court, unlike most other formal organizations, functions as a genuinely "closed community" in that it successfully conceals the true nature of its

---

[19] See, for example, one major effort in this direction which is summarized in Charles E. Ares, Anne Rankin, and Herbert Sturz, "The Manhattan Bail Project: An Interim Report on the Use of Pre-Trial Parole," *New York University Law Review* (January, 1963), pp. 67–95.

Figure 4: The Accused vis-à-vis His Agent Mediators

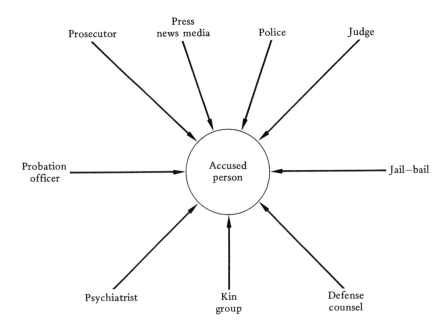

routine operations from the view of outsiders — and sometimes even from some of the participants themselves. It socializes its members and participants toward compliance with specific objectives which are not part of the official goals of justice and due process.

But the usual organizational use of ideological goals and internal discipline are inadequate in the court situation. They must be augmented and implemented. In dealing with this problem the court is unique in a number of respects, and the organizational solutions that have been elaborated are calculated to overcome not only the resistance of the accused but the possible reluctance and work alienation of his accusers.

Bail Setting:
A Study of
Courtroom Interaction

FREDERIC SUFFET

In the past ten years there has been an upsurge in empirical studies of the bail system in the United States. Some of them helped trigger the bail reform movement now underway across the nation,[1] and some were done in response to this movement. Most of them, based on data collected from court records, have sought to determine the factors which underlie the amount of bail set in various cases.[2] Many features of the bail system *qua* system still remain relatively unexplored by sociological research. Something is known of the standards which guide the judge in setting bail, but no systematic research has been done on the standards employed by bondsmen in accepting or rejecting potential clients.[3] Research has been done into the legal consequences of pretrial detention,[4] but the social consequences to those detained are all but unknown.[5] Nonfinancial reasons for the failure to post bail have been

Reprinted from *Crime and Delinquency,* October 1966, pp. 318–331, by permission of the author and the National Council on Crime and Delinquency.

[1] For a review of this movement, see *Proceedings and Interim Report of the National Conference on Bail and Criminal Justice* (Washington, D.C., 1965), hereinafter cited as *Proceedings.* See also, Bernard Botein, "The Manhattan Bail Project: Its Impact on Criminology and the Criminal Law Processes," *Texas Law Review* (February, 1965), p. 319.

[2] See, e.g., C. Foote, J. Markle, and E. Woolley, "Compelling Appearance in Court: Administration of Bail in Philadelphia," *University of Pennsylvania Law Review* (June, 1954), p. 1031. See also, "A Study of the Administration of Bail in New York City," *University of Pennsylvania Law Review* (March, 1958), p. 693.

[3] Bondsmen have occasionally been interviewed by reform or study groups in an effort to determine such standards. *The Bail System of the District of Columbia: Report of the Committee on the Administration of Bail* (Washington, D.C., 1963) says (p. 12): "Employment, length of residence, presence of relatives or responsible persons who will vouch for him, and family ties were frequently mentioned [by bondsmen] as criteria." However, how universal these criteria are among bondsmen and whether their application varies according to certain characteristics of the defendants, such as race, are not known.

[4] See Anne Rankin, "The Effect of Pretrial Detention," *New York University Law Review* (June 1964), p. 641.

[5] Occasional cases come to light which illustrate the negative social consequences of detention. For example, there is the oft cited case of Daniel Walker, a victim of mistaken identity, who spent fifty-five days in detention and lost his home and job. (For one account, see Senator Robert Kennedy's statement in the *Hearings on S. 2838, S. 2839 and S. 2840 before the Subcommittee on Constitutional Rights and the Subcommittee on Improvements in the Judicial Machinery of the Committee on the Judiciary,* U.S. Senate, 88th Cong., 2nd Sess. [1964], p. 13.) It is not known, however, how widespread such consequences are.

investigated,[6] but the social mechanisms which release a defendant on bail have not been fully described.[7]

This study will examine a hitherto uncharted process: what happens in the courtroom when bail is being set. The remarks by the judge when he sets bail have been reported in occasional studies,[8] but they have been used to illustrate the factors he takes into account in arriving at a bail figure. Our present concern extends beyond this to the following questions:

1. What are the typical patterns of interaction between the judge, the prosecutor, and the defense attorney at bail setting?

2. How much disagreement over bail is there between these parties? What is the effect of disagreement on bail amount, and whose side will the judge usually take?

3. Who wields the greatest influence at bail setting?

METHOD

The study is based on 1,473 bail settings observed during October, November, and December, 1964, in Part 1A of the New York County Criminal Court.[9] In each case an observer positioned near the judge's bench recorded verbatim what was said by the judge, the prosecutor, and the defense attorney when bail was set.[10] He noted the person initially suggesting a bail amount, the amount suggested, countersuggestions, and the amount finally set. The defendant's prior criminal record and the current charge against him were determined from the case papers. For purposes of the study, two categories for each of these variables were created. Criminal record was dichotomized as *no record* (never arrested) and *prior record* (any record of arrest, conviction, or imprisonment).[11] Charges were dichotomized as *major* (homicide, forcible rape, and robbery) and *minor* (assault, burglary, carrying a concealed weapon, forgery, larceny, receiving stolen property, and statutory rape).[12]

[6] Suffet, "Patterns of Failure to Raise Bail" (unpublished ms., Vera Foundation, 1965).

[7] No studies have been done of the referral processes which lead clients to bondsmen. Kickback arrangements between bondsmen and jailers are noted in the catalogue of abuses of the bail system, but little is known of the legitimate modes of referral.

[8] Foote, Markle, and Woolley, *supra* note 2, p. 1039.

[9] During this period there were an additional 181 arraignments not included in the study. In 79 cases observers were not present in the court, and in 102 cases essential items of information were not available from the case papers at the time of the analysis.

[10] The observation procedure did not noticeably affect the observed interactions. The observers were Manhattan Bail Project staff members whose presence in court was a regular occurrence and who normally stood in the spot used for the observations when discharging their Bail Project duties.

[11] Among those defendants having a prior criminal record, the extent of this record affects bail disposition. However, the major distinction is between (a) having no record and (b) having a record, no matter how small.

[12] These categories were determined from the bail distributions for each

Whether there was positive recommendation by the Office of Probation for release on recognizance (hereinafter, *r.o.r.*) was also recorded. The Manhattan Bail Project, a three-year experiment designed to increase the use of r.o.r., was undertaken in Part 1A of the Court. The Project provided the judge with a positive recommendation for r.o.r. — which the judge could accept or reject — when the community ties (family, employment, residence) of the defendant had been verified, he was not accused of a major crime, and he did not have an extensive prior record.[13] In no case was a recommendation made *against* r.o.r. The Project was adjudged a success by the city government,[14] and the pre-arraignment investigation into the defendant's community ties was made a permanent city-wide court procedure administered by the Office of Probation.

All observations were made at arraignment, the defendant's first court appearance. If the case was continued — for trial, for sentencing (if the accused pleaded guilty), or for obtaining private counsel — bail was set. Three general bail dispositions are possible: (a) the defendant may be r.o.r.'d; or (b) bail may be set in some dollar amount; or (c) under certain conditions the defendant may be remanded to jail.[15] Overall, 19 per cent of the defendants observed were r.o.r.'d, 77 per cent had bail set in an average amount of $1,822, and 4 per cent were remanded.

BAIL SETTING STANDARDS

The New York statute clearly specifies the conditions under which a defendant may be admitted to bail, but it carries only the following note on the amount of bail:

Elements properly considered in fixing amount of bail are nature of offense, penalty imposed, probability of defendant's appearance or flight, pecuniary and social condition, and apparent nature and strength of proof as bearing on the probability of his conviction.[16]

charge. The term "minor" is used as a complement to "major"; the charges here called minor are not necessarily the least serious in the overall scale of criminal offenses. The minor category includes both felonies and misdemeanors; less serious charges — the disorderly conduct offenses — are arraigned in another court.

[13] For a description of the operating procedures of the Manhattan Bail Project, see *Proceedings, op. cit. supra* note 1, pp. 43–46. See also, "The Manhattan Bail Project: An Interim Report on the Use of Pretrial Parole," *New York University Law Review* (January, 1963), p. 67.

[14] In three years 3,505 defendants were r.o.r.'d on the recommendation of the Manhattan Bail Project, and the rate of r.o.r. rose from 6 per cent to 19 per cent. On Sept. 1, 1964, the Project's procedures were taken over by the Office of Probation.

[15] The exact conditions under which a defendant is bailable are set down in §550-556 of the New York Code of Criminal Procedure.

[16] New York Code of Criminal Procedure, §550, case note 2.

As to how these elements are to be related to the amount of bail, another note says:

Amount of bail is a question of sound discretion and judgment, depending upon primary conditions in the particular case.[17]

These notes give little clue to a bail standard since (a) no instruction is given on how the various elements are to be weighted vis-a-vis one another and (b) the direction in which bail is to vary according to these elements is not specified (although perhaps it should be regarded as implicit that the worse an element, the higher the bail).

A clear conception of the standards which govern bail setting in this court is of signal importance, for these standards define the boundaries of the interactions to be examined. No institutionalized social interaction takes place without explicit or implicit "rules of the game." The principal actors in the bail-setting process interact with the standards as well as with each other; the standards set the limits to their initial bail suggestions and to the frequency of and occasions for, their disagreements. Since the statute does not take us very far toward identifying the standards in the court under observation, we must turn to the cases themselves and let the standards emerge from the data at hand.

The bases ("elements properly considered") of the standards must be known to the actors so that inappropriate behavior will be constrained and interaction facilitated; as reflected in particular cases, they must be matters of fact, not opinion. Charge, prior record, and the presence or absence of an r.o.r. recommendation are all facts of variable status known in each case to the judge and the opposing attorneys, and it is expected that bail is related to these variables. Table 1 shows the final bail dispositions for each combination of charge, record, and r.o.r. recommendation. In cases where bail was set in dollars, the average amount is given in brackets.

The table shows that the three selected variables are related to bail disposition in predictable ways. The presence of a major charge, a prior record, and the absence of an r.o.r. recommendation all increase the chances of an unfavorable bail disposition. Of the three variables, charge has the strongest influence. There is less overall variation in bail disposition according to record and r.o.r. recommendation *within* each of the categories of charge than there is *between* the charge categories when record and r.o.r. recommendation are held constant. A defendant in the major charge category stands a greater chance of being remanded than one in the minor charge category; few defendants accused of a major charge are r.o.r.'d (few are recommended); and bail averages are uniformly high.

A defendant in the minor charge category who has a prior record *and* a

[17] *Ibid.*, case note 3.

Table 1: Bail Disposition according to Charge, Prior Record, and Presence of R.O.R. Recommendation

Major charge[a]

Disposition	Prior record[b]				No prior record			
	No r.o.r. rec'd.		R.o.r. rec'd.		No r.o.r. rec'd.		R.o.r. rec'd.	
	%	No.	%	No.	%	No.	%	No.
Remand	10.0	18			14.0	8	0.0	
Bail	89.4	161	c	1	82.5	47	87.5	7
[Average amount]	[$3,863]				[$3,085]		[$2,714]	
R.o.r.	0.6	1	c	2	3.5	2	12.5	1
	100.0	180		3	100.0	57	100.0	8

Minor charge

Disposition	Prior record				No prior record			
	No r.o.r. rec'd.		R.o.r. rec'd.		No r.o.r. rec'd.		R.o.r. rec'd.	
	%	No.	%	No.	%	No.	%	No.
Remand	4.1	29	1.3	1	2.2	6	0.6	1
Bail	92.1	654	49.4	39	68.3	185	21.2	35
[Average amount]	[$1,587]		[$732]		[$961]		[$760]	
R.o.r.	3.8	27	49.4	39	29.5	80	78.2	129
	100.0	710	100.1	79	100.0	271	100.0	165

[a]Major charges include homicide, forcible rape, and robbery. Minor charges include assault, burglary, carrying a deadly weapon, forgery, larceny, receiving stolen property, and statutory rape.

[b]Prior record includes any record of arrest, conviction, or prison. No prior record means never previously arrested.

[c]Number of cases is too small for percentage to be meaningful.

positive r.o.r. recommendation is likely to get a more favorable disposition than the defendant who has no prior record but also does not have an r.o.r. recommendation. Furthermore, a positive r.o.r. recommendation which is not accepted by the judge has the effect of keeping the bail amount low, regardless of prior record. In general, then, the demonstration of verified community ties is of considerable benefit to the defendant at his arraignment.

The standards which govern bail setting emerge as relatively clear and unequivocal. The more serious the charge, the more extensive the prior record, and the weaker the defendant's community ties, the greater is the chance for high bail or remand and the smaller is the chance for r.o.r. It is assumed that the prosecutor and the defense attorney develop a clear sense of this formula, since over the course of many cases they can relate the bail that is set to the charge, the record, and the recommendation in each case.

PATTERNS OF INTERACTION

Social interaction of any kind is a complex phenomenon which may proceed at many levels. It may be physical, nonverbal, verbal, or any combination of the three. The regular spatial arrangement of the various parties at arraignment — direct physical interaction — is not relevant to bail setting. Nonverbal expressions — the nod, the raised eyebrow, the scowl — are all part of courtroom interaction, but are easily missed by an observer and in the end do not lend themselves easily to interpretation or statistical analysis.[18] In this study we have had to limit our observations to the verbal level. Within the limits of the data employed, verbal statements reveal quite well the basic patterns of interaction at bail setting.

The interactions described are those which take place between the judge, the prosecutor, and the defense attorney. The defendant himself is, to a striking degree, a passive bystander. He does not act; he is acted upon. Occasionally a question is put to him by the judge.

The interactions examined are those between *role actors*, not the often important individual variations between particular judges or attorneys. To focus on the latter would obscure the way in which roles cohere into broader identifiable social patterns. There is a relatively high degree of interchangeability among the persons who play each role. Individual variations (e.g., "Judge X is tough on car thieves") are taken into account by the various actors, but the variations are seen as departures from the expected "normal" behavior prescribed by mutually recognized standards.

During the period studied the average number of cases per day on the

---

[18] The author holds no brief for statistical analysis as the only proper mode of analysis. It is, however, the best method for dealing with a large number of cases.

court calendar, including arraignments, hearings, and sentencings, was 146 (some with multiple defendants). Given this press of business, the possible patterns of interaction are not infinite. The injunction to keep things moving — "Counselor, the calendar is heavy today" — is often voiced by the judge, and accordingly bail setting interactions tend to be brief. The charge, the defendant's prior record as shown in the case papers, and the r.o.r. recommendation, if any, provide the judge with most of the information on which he bases his decision. The modal pattern of bail setting is for the judge simply to fix bail without discussing the matter with either of the attorneys. This occurs in 49 per cent of the cases. Sometimes one of the attorneys, usually the prosecutor, gives verbal assent to the decision, but the central characteristic of this dominant pattern is that the judge makes the first bail suggestion and meets with no objection from either side.

In the second major pattern, either the prosecutor or the defense attorney suggests a bail amount, often with supporting reasons, and then, without an objection from the opposing attorney, the judge fixes the bail. This pattern occurs in 38 per cent of the cases. The judge does not always follow the original suggestion in this simple suggestion-decision pattern: he disagreed with 9 per cent of the prosecutor's 374 suggestions, usually setting bail lower than the initial suggestion, and he disagreed with 24 per cent of the defense attorney's 189 suggestions, invariably setting higher bail.

The third pattern of interaction is more complex. Here the first bail suggestion is followed by an objection to it and a countersuggestion from one of the attorneys, after which the judge sets bail. This pattern, manifesting an overt verbal "conflict," occurs in 9 per cent of the cases. The conflict is of two kinds: one attorney or the other may object to (a) a bail suggestion by the judge or (b) a suggestion by the other attorney. Here, too, the prosecutor's countersuggestions are followed more often.

These three interactional patterns — *decision, suggestion-decision,* and *suggestion-objection-decision* — account for the great majority of bail settings. In only 3 per cent of the observed cases does the sequence of interaction extend further; these cases, too, are examples of conflict and often involve considerable argument. Though in many ways the most dramatic they are the least typical.

CONFLICT

The corollary of short bail-setting interactions is the low incidence of disagreement between the judge and the two attorneys. In only 18 per cent of the cases is there disagreement of any kind, either when the judge changes the bail amount first suggested by one of the attorneys, or when an attorney objects to an amount suggested by the judge or the opposing counsel. The general lack of disagreement probably reflects the clarity of the bail-setting standards; neither attorney, knowing the relevant facts in the case, suggests an amount greatly different from that usually set, given a particular charge, prior record, and r.o.r. recommendation.

Cases in which a verbal objection is made by one of the attorneys to a bail amount initially suggested by someone else have been labeled "conflict." These cases are instructive, for they provide a measure of the prestige structure in the court. When the attorneys conflict with the judge or with each other, the prosecutor, as expected, asks for higher bail and the defense attorney asks for lower bail. Table 2 shows how often these conflicts occur, in cases manifesting the *suggestion-objection-decision* pattern. (Longer interactions have been omitted so that the eventual effect of the objection in these cases can be ascertained without "contamination" from succeeding objections which mediate between the orignal objection and the final bail decision.)

Table 2 reveals a number of points. First, the prosecutor always asks for higher bail and the defense attorney always asks for lower bail. Since they represent opposing interests, any other configuration of data would be surprising.

Second, the attorneys conflict with each other more often than they do with the judge. To some extent this fact may reflect the normal disinclination of a lower-status person to argue with the decisions of his superior; it is easier to disagree with someone at one's own level. While more prestige is often attributed to the prosecutor than to the defense attorney, in terms of the formal court hierarchy the judge is superior to both. (The difference between the frequency with which the attorneys conflict with each other and the frequency with which either attorney conflicts with the judge may also point to the conflict that more often produces the intended result.)

Table 2: Reaction to First Bail Suggestion according to Person Reacting and Person Making First Bail Suggestion

| | *Prosecutor* | | | | *Defense attorney* | | | |
| | *Reacts to judge* | | *Reacts to defense attorney* | | *Reacts to judge* | | *Reacts to prosecutor* | |
Reaction	%	No.	%	No.	%	No.	%	No.
Asks lower bail	0.0		0.0		3.5	25	11.7	45
Does not object	97.5	756	81.5	189	96.5	706	88.3	341
Asks higher bail	2.5	19	18.5	43	0.0		0.0	
	100.0	775	100.0	232	100.0	731	100.0	386

Note: *Omitted from the table are 78 cases in which the defendant was not represented by counsel at arraignment.*

Table 3: Bail Differential according to Person Disagreeing and Person Making First Bail Suggestion

| | Prosecutor asks higher bail | | | | Defense attorney asks lower bail | | | |
| | 1st suggestion by judge | | 1st suggestion by def. attorney | | 1st suggestion by judge | | 1st suggestion by prosecutor | |
Differential	%	No.	%	No.	%	No	%	No.
Lower	0.0		2.3	1	28.0	7	57.8	26
None	15.8	3	14.0	6	72.0	18	40.0	18
Higher	84.2	16	83.7	36	0.0		2.2	1
	100.0	19	100.0	43	100.0	25	100.0	45

Third, the prosecutor objects to the first bail suggestion of the defense attorney somewhat more often than the defense attorney objects to the prosecutor's first suggestion. The explanation for this, it turns out, lies in the fact that the objection of the prosecutor is more likely to be heeded by the judge than the defense attorney's objection. Knowing that his objection will often have no effect, the counsel for the defendant will less often argue with his opponent's first suggestion. The conflict cases are presented in Table 3, which shows the effect of the attorneys' objections according to whom each is in conflict with. The term "bail differential," as used in the table, refers to the direction of the difference between the first bail amount suggested and the bail finally set. The differential may be "lower," "higher," or "none" (no difference).

Table 3 reveals that the prosecutor's request for higher bail will achieve the desired results in over four out of five cases no matter to whose original suggestion he is objecting. The defense attorney has no comparable success. In arguing against a first suggestion by the prosecutor, slightly more than half the time he will get the bail amount lowered, and in a direct conflict with the judge his objection will affect the bail decision a little more than a fourth of the time.

The overall difference in their ability to affect a change in bail amount lends credence to the notion that the prosecutor has somewhat more prestige in the courtroom than the defense attorney. Of course, to say "more prestige" is simply another way of saying that he stands a better chance of getting his way. In light of the relative inability of the defense attorney to make his objection count, it is not surprising that he does not conflict with the judge very often; he realizes that to raise an objection to a bail amount suggested by the judge is generally useless. He has more success against the prosecutor, but not as much as the prosecutor has against him. This explains why the prosecutor is the more likely of the two to object to a bail suggestion

Table 4: First Bail Suggestion according to Person Suggesting

	Judge		Prosecutor		Defense attorney	
Suggestion	*%*	*No.*	*%*	*No.*	*%*	*No.*
Remand	6.0	47	3.2	14	0.0	
Bail	84.9	664	76.9	333	17.8	46
R.o.r.	9.1	71	19.9	86	82.2	212
	100.0	782	100.0	433	100.0	258

by the opposing counsel. What remains unexplained is why he so infrequently objects to the judge's first bail suggestion, especially since the judge usually follows his countersuggestion. The answer, as Table 4 indicates, is that he and the judge make much the same kinds of initial bail suggestions; in short, they have little to disagree about.

It is revealing of where the judge's sympathies lie to note that he is somewhat stricter in his initial bail suggestions than the prosecutor. This holds true for particular combinations of charge record and r.o.r. recommendation. When we examine the initial suggestions of the judge and the prosecutor in even the "best" cases — defendants with a minor charge, no prior record, and a recommendation for r.o.r. — we find that the judge suggests r.o.r. 69 per cent of the time (total cases, 54) and that the prosecutor suggests r.o.r. 73 per cent of the time (total cases, 40). Needless to say, when the defense attorney makes the first suggestion, he recommends r.o.r. for *all* such defendants (total cases, 71).

The totals at the bottom of the columns in Table 4 show that the judge makes the first bail suggestion most of the time (53 per cent of all cases), followed by the prosecutor (29 per cent), and then by the defense attorney (18 per cent). This order of frequency of initial bail suggestion holds in most kinds of cases, except for those described just above, where the defendant shows the most favorable combination of characteristics. Here the defense attorney is more likely than the judge or the prosecutor to make the first suggestion as these defendants offer him the opportunity to make the strongest case for r.o.r.

The defense attorney is expected to make the best suggestion he can on behalf of his client. Four-fifths of his initial suggestions are for r.o.r.; in the remaining cases the suggestion is invariably phrased as a request for "low" bail or "cash" bail. In theory, it may be that the best first suggestion he can make is not that which simply falls at the bottom of the scale of bail amounts, but that which is lower than the bail amount normally anticipated in a given type of case. For example, the defense attorney might first try to suggest $2,500 in a case which often calls for $5,000. His strategy in limiting himself

Table 5: Bail Differential according to Person Making First Suggestion and Content of First Suggestion

	Judge suggests			Prosecutor suggests			Defense attorney suggests		
	remand	bail	r.o.r.	remand	bail	r.o.r.	remand	bail	r.o.r.
Differential	%	%	%	%	%	%	%	%	%
Lower	0.0	2.1	0.0	0.0	17.4	0.0	0.0	6.5	0.0
None	100.0	96.1	90.1	100.0	80.2	100.0	0.0	52.2	59.9
Higher	0.0	1.8	9.9	0.0	2.4	0.0	0.0	41.3	40.1
	100.0	100.0	100.0	100.0	100.0	100.0		100.0	100.0
Total no.	47	664	71	14	333	86		46	212

to relatively infrequent suggestions for r.o.r. and low bail is a forced one: (a) suggesting bail in a specific dollar amount forecloses the possibility that the judge or the prosecutor would have suggested bail in a lower amount and (b) most of the cases do not qualify for r.o.r. under the prevailing standards. Thus, he must let one of the other parties take the lead most of the time and "save" his initial suggestions for situations where, presumably, they would do the most good. The prosecutor can afford to let the judge make most of the initial suggestions, for, as the table shows, the judge makes stronger suggestions on behalf of the people than the prosecutor does himself.

INFLUENCE

Do the defense attorney's initial suggestions "do any good"? How often will they be followed, compared to the suggestions of the judge and the prosecutor? Overall, whose first suggestion is the most influential — that is, will result in the amount suggested being set?

Table 5 presents the bail differential according to the person making the first bail suggestion and the content of the suggestions.[19] It shows that the first suggestions of the judge and the prosecutor carry far more weight than the defense attorney's; neither is likely to have his first suggestion changed very often. On the other hand, the defense attorney's first suggestion is changed 42 per cent of the time, with the change almost always going in an upward direction.

The table shows that no suggestion for remand is ever lowered to a dollar

[19] Since the defense attorney rarely specifies an amount in those cases where he suggests bail, we have had to assign a dollar amount to his suggestion in order to calculate the differential. Where "low" bail is asked, the amount of $500 has been taken as the starting point; where "cash" bail is asked, the amount of $100 has been substituted. In this manner the structure of the interaction is preserved for purposes of analysis without, it is hoped, the introduction of a radical bias. Fortunately, cases in which the defense attorney asks for bail are rare.

bail amount, no matter who makes it. And a check of these cases revealed that in only one case did the defense attorney object to a remand suggestion. Since the defendants who are remanded are usually charged with a serious offense, and since charge is the primary determinant of bail, it may be assumed that the defense attorney knows he cannot force the issue with any chance of success. It is better, from his point of view, not to take up court time with futile moves.

Where bail differentials do appear, they are often the result of counter-suggestions from one or the other of the opposing attorneys. Such counter-suggestions accounted for over two-fifths of the cases in which the prosecutor's first suggestion was lowered, and a third of the cases in which the defense attorney's first suggestion was raised. However, the area in which an objection is made to the initial suggestion is limited. When the prosecutor makes an objection it is usually to a suggestion of r.o.r. From his point of view there is no need to object to bail suggestions above r.o.r., since these are either made by himself or by the judge, who tends to make similar suggestions. The counsel for the defendant tends to make his objections in cases where the initial suggestion falls toward the lower end of the scale of bail amounts. Seventy-one per cent of the bail suggestions to which he objects are $1,000 or less. Thus, his strategy in making countersuggestions is to take certain cases which are treated relatively leniently to begin with and press for slightly more lenience. The characteristics of these cases — a minor charge, no prior record, or a positive r.o.r. recommendation — give the defense attorney a base from which to make his objection in some hope that it will count.

It is interesting that *all* of the prosecutor's suggestions for r.o.r. are followed, whereas the result of the defense attorney's suggestions for r.o.r. is that two-fifths of the time bail is set in a dollar amount. The suggested r.o.r. cases of the two attorneys bear no substantial difference; both groups have similar charges, prior records, and r.o.r. recommendations.[20] In spite of the similarities, the judge accepts all of the prosecutor's r.o.r. suggestions and rejects a good part of those made by the defense attorney. An examination of the latter's cases showed that when his r.o.r. suggestion is rejected by the judge, the reason usually given is that the defendant has no positive r.o.r. recommendation from the Office of Probation or that he has a prior record. These deficiencies are, apparently, offset when the prosecutor makes the r.o.r. suggestion.

[20] Of the prosecutor's cases, 44 per cent are backed by a positive probation recommendation for r.o.r., 69 per cent have no prior record, and 95 per cent are accused of a minor offense. Of the defense attorney's cases, 51 per cent have a positive r.o.r. recommendation, 64 per cent have no prior record, and 93 per cent are accused of a minor offense.

In sum, the defense attorney is the least influential member of the court; not only is he the least likely to make the initial bail suggestion, but he has the least chance of making his suggestion stick. The judge and the prosecutor are reciprocally supportive. They subscribe to the same bail-setting standards, they disagree with each other far less often than either disagrees with the defense attorney, and they show the same concern for the people's interest. The role of the prosecutor is prescribed: he represents the public. But the judge is supposed to be, in theory, a neutral "referee" between the two sets of interests. I suggest that the judge's concern for the people's side springs from another source, which I shall now examine.

A LATENT FUNCTION OF BAIL

Sociologists make a distinction between those functions of a social practice which are "manifest" and those which are "latent." Manifest functions are intended consequences of the practice; latent functions are consequences which are not originally intended and are often unrecognized. Put another way, manifest functions are "purposes," and latent functions roughly correspond to "side effects" or "by-products."[21]

The major manifest function of setting bail is to guarantee the appearance of the defendant at subsequent court proceedings. Some hold that this is its only legitimate function.[22] Be that as it may, legal officials acknowledge other manifest functions of bail setting, including the following: "To prevent release where flight is likely; to prevent a recurrence of criminal conduct by an accused believed to be dangerous to the community; and to punish the accused by giving him a taste of jail."[23] Whether any of these functions are legitimate under our system of law is a current subject of debate.[24]

A number of critics of the bail system maintain that bail does not truly function to guarantee the appearance of the defendant in court.[25] They point out that, though in theory the defendant's financial stake in posting bail is supposed to assure his appearance, the bondsman's fee is not returnable and full collateral is not often demanded by New York City bondsmen; thus, the

---

[21] For a definitive discussion of manifest and latent functions, see Robert K. Merton, *Social Theory and Social Structure* (New York: Free Press, 1957), ch. I.

[22] For example, Daniel J. Freed and Patricia M. Wald, *Bail in the United States: 1964* (Washington, D.C.: National Conference on Bail and Criminal Justice, 1964, p. 8): "Bail in America has developed for a single lawful purpose: to release the accused with assurance he will return for trial."

[23] *Ibid.,* p. 49.

[24] For a statement by a proponent of preventive detention, see the address by Garrett H. Byrne, president of the National District Attorneys Association, *Proceedings, op. cit. supra* note 1, pp. 160–68.

[25] See, e.g., Botein, *supra* note 1, p. 326.

presumed financial stake is virtually nonexistent.[26] Assuming that the criticism is valid, the question arises why bail setting persists as a social practice. The function of preventive detention — setting high bail to prevent release and thus deter flight or recidivism — is not a sufficient explanation since far too many of these defendants raise bail.[27]

Social practices may persist because of their latent functions. One latent function of bail setting is to diffuse the responsibility for the release of the defendant, and we shall argue that this explains, at least in part, why the practice persists and why the judge consistently sides with the prosecutor in fixing bail.

The bail setting interactions between the judge and the two attorneys cannot be understood if the court is viewed as a closed system. In order to make sense out of what happens in the court, we must take the role of the public into account. Judges are sensitive to public pressure, and some will admit they fear an adverse reaction from the press should they make a mistake. Their position was stated succinctly at the National Conference on Bail and Criminal Justice by Judge Francis Morrissey, who said: "If you let [the defendant] out on personal recognizance, with the understanding that he would reappear again for trial, and then the victim was badly injured, or killed, you have the problem of the newspapers coming in a very critical vein. You have to have some security for the particular judge."[28] In short, judges have a natural reluctance to be responsible for releasing defendants who commit deeds which outrage public opinion.

Fixing high bail to prevent release may explain why $5,000 bail is set in a given case instead of $500, but it does not explain why a judge will set $25 cash bail rather than r.o.r. the defendant. An answer emerges if "responsibility" is seen as coming into play not only when high bail is set, but throughout the range of bail settings, from remand to r.o.r. In this view, the judge who sets $25 cash bail is shifting part of the responsibility for the release of the defendant to the defendant himself. Stated more generally, bail setting serves the latent function of diffusing the responsibility for releasing the defendant,

[26] This position is taken by Richard H. Kuh, formerly chief of the Criminal Division, New York County District Attorney's Office. Kuh estimates that in 95 per cent of the cases, no collateral is asked. (See *Proceedings, op. cit. supra* note 1, pp. 234–35.) A report in the *New York Times* on a one-week bondsmen's "strike" in New York City agrees that 100 per cent collateral is not demanded, although it is at variance with Kuh on exactly how much is asked. The report implies that 20 per cent of the face value of the bond is normally demanded in collateral. ("Bondsmen Relax Security Demand," *New York Times,* Jan. 1, 1964.)

[27] The observed cases were not followed to establish the rate of bail raising. The latest available figures for this court show that approximately half the defendants on whom dollar bail is set manage to post it. (Rankin, *supra* note 4, table 2, p. 645.)

[28] *Proceedings, op. cit. supra* note 1, p. 184.

and the three bail dispositions — remand, dollar bail, and r.o.r. — indicate different degrees in the judge's share of this responsibility. (a) When the judge remands the defendant, foreclosing the possibility that the defendant will commit an additional offense, he assumes no responsibility for the release. (b) When the judge sets bail in some dollar amount, he shares the responsibility for releasing the defendant with the bondsman, the defendant's family, or the defendant himself. The higher the amount of the bail, the greater is the share of the others' responsibility. (c) When the judge grants r.o.r., he has the entire responsibility for releasing the defendant.

The setting of dollar bail implicitly condones the release of the defendant. Even in cases where high bail is set to prevent the release of the accused, it is possible that the bail will somehow be raised. The reluctance expressed by some officials at the thought of granting r.o.r. to a dangerous defendant (hark back to Judge Morrissey's statement) can be easily explained: if such a defendant commits a crime while free on r.o.r., the judge may be pilloried. If, on the other hand, he sets such a defendant free on bail, he cannot be held strictly to account; the responsibility for the defendant's release is not exclusively his.

By permitting different degrees of judicial responsibility to be attached to the release of the defendant, bail setting functions as a protective device for the court. Thus, where the judge has the slightest hesitation about utilizing r.o.r., he can share the responsibility for release by setting minimal bail. And even where he does grant r.o.r., the judge does not assume the full responsibility for releasing the defendant, as might first appear. One function of the Manhattan Bail Project, which formerly operated in the court studied, was to share this responsibility by providing recommendations for good r.o.r. risks. This function continues now under the Office of Probation. Of the 281 cases of r.o.r. falling into the sample, 61 per cent were backed by a Probation Office recommendation. Virtually all of the remainder were granted r.o.r. on the recommendation of one of the attorneys. Only eighteen defendants — approximately 1 per cent of all cases observed — were given r.o.r. without a recommendation from someone other than the judge. Thus, the judge almost never takes absolute, complete responsibility for releasing a defendant outright. Even in the r.o.r. cases the judge is sharing the responsibility, no matter to how small a degree, with someone else.

The reason why the judge adheres to the same bail standards as the prosecutor now becomes clear. Handing down bail dispositions which fall toward the severe end of the bail setting scale (much in line with the kinds of dispositions suggested by the prosecutor) more broadly diffuses the responsibility for releasing the defendant. If the judge were to make more frequent use of r.o.r. or set generally lower bail amounts, he would not be sharing the responsibility for the defendant's release quite as much. If, as we assume, the judge is aware of the ever present possibility of negative public response should a case go wrong, it is to his interest to increase others' share in the responsibility for release by being more severe. Thus, he finds himself in the same position as the prosecutor but for different reasons. The prosecutor is supposed to represent the public interest according to the prescriptions of his role; the judge, however, must keep the public in mind because, as the final decision-maker, he is the most vulnerable target of criticism.

Bail-setting's latent function of diffusing the responsibility for the release of the accused puts a buffer between the court and the potential outraged response of the public to crimes which may be committed by persons at liberty pending court appearance. As long as the courts need such a buffer, it is doubtful that bail-setting as a social practice will entirely disappear.

Normal Crimes:
Sociological Features
of the Penal Code
in a Public Defender Office

DAVID SUDNOW

Two stances toward the utility of official classificatory schema for criminological research have been debated for years. One position, which might be termed that of the "revisionist" school, has it that the categories of the criminal law, e.g., "burglary," "petty theft," "homicide," etc., are not "homogeneous in respect to causation."[1] From an inspection of penal code descriptions of crimes, it is argued that the way persons seem to be assembled under the auspices of criminal law procedure is such as to produce classes of criminals who are, at least on theoretical grounds, as dissimilar in their social backgrounds and styles of activity as they are similar. The entries in the penal code, this school argues, require revision if sociological use is to be made of categories of crime and a classificatory scheme of etiological relevance is to be developed. Common attempts at such revision have included notions such as *"white collar* crime," and *"systematic* check forger," these conceptions constituting attempts to institute sociologically meaningful specifications which the operations of criminal law procedure and statutory legislation "fail" to achieve.

The other major perspective toward the sociologist's use of official categories and the criminal statistics compiled under their heading derives less from a concern with etiologically useful schema than from an interest in understanding the actual operations of the administrative legal system. Here, the categories of the criminal law are not regarded as useful or not, as objects to be either adopted, adapted, or ignored; rather, they are seen as constituting the basic conceptual equipment with which such people as judges, lawyers, policemen, and probation workers organize their everyday activities. The study of the actual use of official classification systems by actually employed administrative personnel regards the penal code as data, to be pre-

Reprinted from *Social Problems,* Vol. 12, No. 3, pp. 255–276, by permission of the author and The Society for the Study of Social Problems.

[1] D. R. Cressey, "Criminological Research and the Definition of Crimes," *American Journal of Sociology,* Vol. 61, No. 6 (1951), p. 548. See also, J. Hall, *Theft, Law and Society,* second edition (Indianapolis: Bobbs-Merrill, 1952) ; and E. Sutherland, *Principles of Criminology,* review (New York: Lippincott, 1947), p. 218. An extensive review of "typological developments" is available in D. C. Gibbons and D. L. Garrity, "Some Suggestions for the Development of Etiological and Treatment Theory in Criminology," *Social Forces,* Vol. 38, No. 1 (1959).

served intact; its use, both in organizing the work of legal representation, accusation, adjudication, and prognostication, and in compiling tallies of legal occurrences, is to be examined as one would examine any social activity. By sociologically regarding, rather than criticizing, rates of statistics and the categories employed to assemble them, one learns, it is promised, about the "rate producing agencies" and the assembling process.[2]

While the former perspective, the "revisionist" position, has yielded several fruitful products, the latter stance (commonly identified with what is rather loosely known as the "labelling" perspective), has been on the whole more promissory than productive, more programmatic than empirical. The present report will examine the operations of a Public Defender system in an effort to assess the warrant for the continued theoretical and empirical development of the position argued by Kitsuse and Cicourel. It will address the question: what of import for the sociological analysis of legal administration can be learned by describing the actual way the penal code is employed in the daily activities of legal representation? First, I shall consider the "guilty plea" as a way of handling criminal cases, focusing on some features of the penal code as a description of a population of defendants. Then I shall describe the Public Defender operation with special attention to the way defendants are represented. The place of the guilty plea and penal code in this representation will be examined. Lastly, I shall briefly analyze the fashion in which the Public Defender prepares and conducts a "defense." The latter section will attempt to indicate the connection between certain prominent organizational features of the Public Defender system and the penal code's place in the routine operation of that system.

GUILTY PLEAS,
INCLUSION,
AND NORMAL CRIMES

It is a commonly noted fact about the criminal court system generally, that the greatest proportion of cases are "settled" by a guilty plea.[3] In the county from which the following material is drawn, over 80 per cent of all cases "never go to trial." To describe the method of obtaining a guilty plea disposition, essential for the discussion to follow, I must distinguish between what shall be termed "necessarily-included-lesser-offenses" and "situationally-

---

[2] The most thorough statement of this position, borrowing from the writings of Harold Garfinkel, can be found in the recent critical article by J. I. Kitsuse and A. V. Cicourel, "A Note on the Official Use of Statistics," *Social Problems,* Vol. 11, No. 2 (Fall, 1963), pp. 131–139.

[3] See D. J. Newman, "Pleading Guilty for Considerations," 46 *J. Crim. L. C. and P.S.* Also, M. Schwartz, *Cases and Materials on Professional Responsibility and the Administration of Criminal Justice* (San Francisco: Matthew Bender and Co., 1961), esp. pp. 79–105.

included-lesser-offenses." Of two offenses designated in the penal code, the lesser is considered to be that for which the length of required incarceration is the shorter period of time. *Inclusion* refers to the relation between two or more offenses. The "necessarily-included-lesser-offense" is a strictly legal notion:

Whether a lesser offense is included in the crime charged is a question of law to be determined solely from the definition and corpus delicti of the offense charged and of the lesser offense. . . . If all the elements of the corpus delicti of a lesser crime can be found in a list of all the elements of the offense charged, then only is the lesser included in the greater.[4]

Stated alternatively:

The test in this state of necessarily included offenses is simply that where an offense cannot be committed without necessarily committing another offense, the latter is a necessarily included offense.[5]

The implied negative is put: could Smith have committed A and not B? If the answer is yes, then B is not necessarily included in A. If the answer is no, B is necessarily included. While in a given case a battery might be committed in the course of a robbery, battery is not necessarily included in robbery. Petty theft is necessarily included in robbery but not in burglary. Burglary primarily involves the "intent" to acquire another's goods illegally (e.g., by breaking and entering); the consummation of the act need not occur for burglary to be committed. Theft, like robbery, requires that some item be stolen.

I shall call *lesser* offenses that are not necessarily but "only" *actually* included, "situationally-included-lesser-offenses." By statutory definition, necessarily included offenses are "actually" included. By actual here, I refer to the "way it occurs as a course of action." In the instance of necessary inclusion, the "way it occurs" is irrelevant. With situational inclusion, the "way it occurs" is definitive. In the former case, no particular course of action is referred to. In the latter, the scene and progress of the criminal activity would be analyzed.

The issue of necessary inclusion has special relevance for two procedural matters:

A. A man cannot be charged and/or convicted of two or more crimes any one of which is necessarily included in the others, unless the several crimes occur on separate occasions.

If a murder occurs, the defendant cannot be charged and/or convicted of both "homicide" and "intent to commit a murder," the latter of which is

    [4] C. W. Fricke, *California Criminal Law* (Los Angeles: The Legal Book Store, 1961), p. 41.
    [5] *People v. Greer*, 30 Cal. 2d 589.

necessarily included in first degree murder. If, however, a defendant "intends to commit a homicide" against one person and commits a "homicide" against another, both offenses may be properly charged. While it is an extremely complex question as to the scope and definition of "in the course of," in most instances the rule is easily applied.

B. The judge cannot instruct the jury to consider as alternative crimes of which to find a defendant guilty, crimes that are not necessarily included in the charged crime or crimes.

If a man is charged with "statutory rape" the judge may instruct the jury to consider as a possible alternative conviction "contributing to the delinquency of a minor," as this offense is necessarily included in "statutory rape." He cannot however suggest that the alternative "intent to commit murder" be considered and the jury cannot find the defendant guilty of this latter crime, unless it is charged as a distinct offense in the complaint.

It is crucial to note that these restrictions apply only to (a) the relation between several charged offenses in a formal allegation, and (b) the alternatives allowable in a jury instruction. At any time before a case "goes to trial," alterations in the charging complaint may be made by the district attorney. The issue of necessary inclusion has no required bearing on (a) what offense(s) will be charged initially by the prosecutor, (b) what the relation is between the charge initially made and "what happened," or (c) what modifications may be made after the initial charge and the relation between initially charged offenses and those charged in modified complaints. It is this latter operation, the modification of the complaint, that is central to the guilty plea disposition.

Complaint alterations are made when a defendant agrees to plead guilty to an offense and thereby avoid a trial. The alteration occurs in the context of a "deal" consisting of an offer from the district attorney to alter the original charge in such a fashion that a lighter sentence will be incurred with a guilty plea than would be the case if the defendant were sentenced on the original charge. In return for this manipulation, the defendant agrees to plead guilty. The arrangement is proposed in the following format: "if you plead guilty to this new lesser offense, you will get less time in prison than if you plead not guilty to the original, greater charge and lose the trial." The decision must then be made whether or not the chances of obtaining complete acquittal at trial are great enough to warrant the risk of a loss and higher sentence if found guilty on the original charge. As we shall see below, it is a major job of the Public Defender, who mediates between the district attorney and the defendant, to convince his "client" that the chances of acquittal are too slight to warrant this risk.

If a man is charged with "drunkenness" and the Public Defender and Public Prosecutor (hereafter P.D. and D.A.) prefer not to have a trial, they seek to have the defendant agree to plead guilty. While it is occasionally possible, particularly with first offenders, for the P.D. to convince the defendant to plead guilty to the orginally charged offense, most often it is felt that some "exchange" or "consideration" should be offered, i.e., a lesser offense charged.

To what offense can "drunkenness" be reduced? There is no statutorily designated crime that is necessarily included in the crime of "drunkenness." That is, if any of the statutorily required components of drunk behavior (its *corpus delicti*) are absent, there remains no offense of which the resultant description is a definition. For drunkenness there is, however, an offense that while not necessarily included is "typically-situationally-included," i.e., "typically" occurs as a feature of the way drunk persons are seen to behave — "disturbing the peace." The range of possible sentences is such that, of the two offenses, "disturbing the peace" cannot call for as long a prison sentence as "drunkenness." If, in the course of going on a binge, a person does so in such a fashion that "disturbing the peace" may be employed to describe some of his behavior, it would be considered as an alternative offense to offer in return for a guilty plea. A central question for the following analysis will be: in what fashion would he have to behave so that disturbing the peace would be considered a suitable reduction?

If a man is charged with "molesting a minor," there are not any necessarily included lesser offenses with which to charge him. Yet an alternative charge — "loitering around a schoolyard" — is often used as a reduction. As above, and central to our analysis the question is: what would the defendant's behavior be such that "loitering around a schoolyard" would constitute an appropriate alternative?

If a person is charged with "burglary," "petty theft" is not necessarily included. Routinely, however, "petty theft" is employed for reducing the charge of burglary. Again, we shall ask: what is the relation between burglary and petty theft and the *manner in which the former occurs* that warrants this reduction?

Offenses are regularly reduced to other offenses the latter of which are not necessarily or situationally included in the former. As I have already said the determination of whether or not offense X was situationally included in Y involves an analysis of the course of action that constitutes the criminal behavior. I must now turn to examine this mode of behavioral analysis.

When encountering a defendant who is charged with "assault with a deadly weapon," the P.D. asks: "what can this offense be reduced to so as to arrange for a guilty plea?" As the reduction is only to be proposed by the P.D. and accepted or not by the D.A., his question becomes "what reduction will be allowable?" (As shall be seen below, the P.D. and D.A. have institutionalized a common orientation to allowable reductions.) The method of reduction involves, as a general feature, the fact that the particular case in question is scrutinized to decide its membership in a class of similar cases. But *the penal code does not provide the reference for deciding the correspondence between the instant event and the general case; that is, it does not define the classes of offense types.* To decide, for purposes of finding a suitable reduction, if the instant case involves a "burglary," reference is not made to the statutory definition of "burglary." To decide what the situationally included offenses are in the instant case, the instant case is not analyzed as a *statutorily* referable course of action; rather, reference is made to a *non-statutorily* conceived class "burglary" and offenses that are typically situationally included in it, taken as a class of behavioral events. Stated again: in searching an instant case to decide what to *reduce it to,* there is no analysis of the statutorily referable elements of the instant case; instead, its membership in a class of events, the features of which cannot be described by the penal code, must be decided. An example will be useful. If a defendant is charged with burglary and the P.D. is concerned to propose a reduction to a lesser offense, he might search the elements of the burglary at hand to decide what other offenses were committed. The other offenses he might "discover" would be of two sorts: those necessarily and those situationally included. In attempting to decide those other offenses situationally included in the instant event, the instant event might be analyzed as a statutorily referable course of action. Or, as is the case with the P.D., the instant case might be analyzed to decide if it is a "burglary" in common with other "burglaries" conceived of in terms other than those provided by the statute.

Burglaries are routinely reduced to petty theft. If we were to analyze the way burglaries typically occur, petty theft is neither situationally or necessarily included; when a burglary is committed, money or other goods are seldom illegally removed from some person's body. If we therefore analyzed burglaries, employing the penal code as our reference, and then searched the P.D.'s records to see how burglaries are reduced in the guilty plea, we could not establish a rule that would describe the transformation between the burglary cases statutorily described and the reductions routinely made (i.e., to "petty theft"). The rule must be sought elsewhere, in the character of the non-statutorily defined class of "burglaries," which I shall term *normal burglaries.*

NORMAL CRIMES

In the course of routinely encountering persons charged with "petty theft," "burglary," "assault with a deadly weapon," "rape," "possession of marijuana," etc., the P.D. gains knowledge of the typical manner in which offenses of given classes are committed, the social characeristics of the persons who regularly commit them, the features of the settings in which they occur, the types of victims often involved, and the like. He learns to speak knowledgeably of "burglars," "petty thieves," "drunks," "rapists," "narcos," etc., and to attribute to them personal biographies, modes of usual criminal activity, criminal histories, psychological characteristics, and social backgrounds. The following characterizations are illustrative:

Most ADWs (assault with deadly weapon) start with fights over some girl.

These sex fiends (child molestation cases) usually hang around parks or schoolyards. But we often get fathers charged with these crimes. Usually the old man is out of work and stays at home when the wife goes to work and he plays around with his little daughter or something. A lot of these cases start when there is some marital trouble and the woman gets mad.

I don't know why most of them don't rob the big stores. They usually break into some cheap department store and steal some crummy item like a $9.95 record player you know.

Kids who start taking this stuff (narcotics) usually start out when some buddy gives them a cigarette and they smoke it for kicks. For some reason they always get caught in their cars, for speeding or something.

They can anticipate that point when persons are likely to get into trouble:

Dope addicts do O.K. until they lose a job or something and get back on the streets and, you know, meet the old boys. Someone tells them where to get some and there they are.

In the springtime, that's when we get all these sex crimes. You know, these kids play out in the schoolyard all day and these old men sit around and watch them jumping up and down. They get their ideas.

The P.D. learns that some kinds of offenders are likely to repeat the same offense while others are not repeat violators or, if they do commit crimes frequently, the crimes vary from occasion to occasion:

You almost never see a check man get caught for anything but checks — only an occasional drunk charge.

Burglars are usually multiple offenders, most times just burglaries or petty thefts. Petty thefts get started for almost anything — joy riding, drinking, all kinds of little things.

These narcos are usually through after the second violation or so. After the first time some stop, but when they start on the heavy stuff, they've had it.

I shall call *normal crimes* those occurrences whose typical features, e.g., the ways they usually occur and the characteristics of persons who commit them (as well as the typical victims and typical scenes), are known and attended to by the P.D. For any of a series of offense types the P.D. can provide some form of proverbial characterization. For example, *burglary* is seen as involving regular violators, no weapons, low-priced items, little property damage, lower class establishments, largely Negro defendants, independent operators, and a non-professional orientation to the crime. *Child molesting* is seen as typically entailing middle-aged strangers or lower class middle-aged fathers (few women), no actual physical penetration or severe tissue damage, mild fondling, petting, and stimulation, bad marriage circumstances, multiple offenders with the same offense repeatedly committed, a child complainant, via the mother, etc. *Narcotics* defendants are usually Negroes, not syndicated, persons who start by using small stuff, hostile with police officers, caught by some form of entrapment technique, etc. *Petty thefts* are about 50-50 Negro-white, unplanned offenses, generally committed on lower class persons and don't get much money, don't often employ weapons, don't make living from thievery, usually younger defendants with long juvenile assaultive records, etc. *Drunkenness* offenders are lower class white and Negro, get drunk on wine and beer, have long histories of repeated drunkenness, don't hold down jobs, are usually arrested on the streets, seldom violate other penal code sections, etc.

Some general features of the normal crime as a way of attending to a category of persons and events may be mentioned:

1. The focus, in these characterizations, is not on particular individuals, but offense types. If asked "What are burglars like?" or "How are burglaries usually committed?", the P.D. does not feel obliged to refer to particular burglars and burglaries as the material for his answer.

2. The features attributed to offenders and offenses are often not of import for the statutory conception. In burglary, it is "irrelevant" for the statutory determination whether or not much damage was done to the premises (except where, for example, explosives were employed and a new statute could be invoked). Whether a defendant breaks a window or not, destroys property within the house or not, etc., does not affect his statutory classification as a burglar. While for robbery the presence or absence of a weapon sets the degree, whether the weapon is a machine gun or pocket knife is "immaterial." Whether the residence or business establishment in a burglary is located in a higher income area of the city is of no issue for the code requirements. And, generally, the defendant's race, class position, criminal history (in most offenses), personal attributes, and particular style of committing offenses are features specifically not definitive of crimes under the auspices of the penal code. For deciding "Is this a 'burglary' case I have before me," however, the P.D.'s reference to this range of non-statutorily referable personal and social attributes, modes of operation, etc., is crucial for the arrangement of a guilty plea bargain.

3. The features attributed to offenders and offenses are, in their content, specific to the community in which the P.D. works. In other communities and historical periods the lists would presumably differ. Narcotics violators in certain areas, for example, are syndicated in dope rackets or engage in sys-

tematic robbery as professional criminals, features which are not commonly encountered (or, at least, evidence for which is not systematically sought) in this community. Burglary in some cities will more often occur at large industrial plants, banking establishments, warehouses, etc. The P.D. refers to the population of defendants in the county as "our defendants" and qualifies his prototypical portrayals and knowledge of the typically operative social structures, "for our county." An older P.D., remembering the "old days," commented:

We used to have a lot more rapes than we do now, and they used to be much more violent. Things are duller now in. . . .

4. Offenses whose normal features are readily attended to are those which are routinely encountered in the courtroom. This feature is related to the last point. For embezzlement, bank robbery, gambling, prostitution, murder, arson, and some other uncommon offenses, the P.D. cannot readily supply anecdotal and proverbial characterizations. While there is some change in the frequencies of offense-type convictions over time, certain offenses are continually more common and others remain stably infrequent. The troubles created for the P.D. when offenses whose features are not readily known occur, and whose typicality is not easily constructed, will be discussed in some detail below.

5. Offenses are ecologically specified and attended to as normal or not according to the locales within which they are committed. The P.D. learns that burglaries usually occur in such and such areas of the city, petty thefts around this or that park, ADWs in these bars. Ecological patterns are seen as related to socio-economic variables and these in turn to typical modes of criminal and non-criminal activities. Knowing where an offense took place is thus, for the P.D., knowledge of the likely persons involved, the kind of scene in which the offense occurred, and the pattern of activity characteristic of such a place:

Almost all of our ADWs are in the same half dozen bars. These places are Negro bars where laborers come after hanging around the union halls trying to get some work. Nobody has any money and they drink too much. Tempers are high and almost anything can start happening.

6. One further important feature can be noted at this point. Its elaboration will be the task of a later section. As shall be seen, the P.D. office consists of a staff of twelve full time attorneys. Knowledge of the properties of offense types of offenders, i.e., their normal, typical, or familiar attributes, constitutes the mark of any given attorney's competence. A major task in socializing the new P.D. deputy attorney consists in teaching him to recognize these attributes and to come to do so naturally. The achievement of competence as a P.D. is signalled by the gradual acquisition of professional

command not simply of local penal code peculiarities and courtroom folk-lore, but, as importantly, of relevant features of the social structure and criminological wisdom. His grasp of that knowledge over the course of time is a key indication of his experience. Below, in our brief account of some relevant organizational properties of the P.D. system, we shall have occasion to re-emphasize the competence-attesting aspects of the attorney's proper use of established sociological knowledge. Let us return to the mechanics of the guilty plea procedure as an example of the operation of the notion of normal crimes.

Over the course of their interaction and repeated "bargaining" discussions, the P.D. and D.A. have developed a set of unstated recipes for reducing original charges to lesser offenses. These recipes are specifically appropriate for use in instances of normal crimes and in such instances alone. "Typical" burglaries are reduced to petty theft, "typical" ADWs to simple assault, "typical" child molestation to loitering around a schoolyard, etc. The character of these recipes deserves attention.

The specific content of any reduction, i.e., what particular offense class X offenses will be reduced to, is such that the reduced offense may bear no obvious relation (neither situationally nor necessarily included) to the orig-inally charged offense. The reduction of burglary to petty theft is an example. The important relation between the reduced offense and the original charge is such that the reduction from one to the other is considered "reasonable." At this point we shall only state what seems to be the general principle in-volved in deciding this reasonableness. The underlying premises cannot be explored at the present time, as that would involve a political analysis beyond the scope of the present report. *Both P.D. and D.A. are concerned to obtain a guilty plea wherever possible and thereby avoid a trial. At the same time, each party is concerned that the defendant "receive his due." The re-duction of offense X to Y must be of such a character that the new sentence will depart from the anticipated sentence for the original charge to such a degree that the defendant is likely to plead guilty to the new charge and, at the same time, not so great that the defendant does not "get his due."*

In a homicide, while battery is a necessarily included offense, it will not be considered as a possible reduction. For a conviction of second degree murder a defendant could receive a life sentence in the penitentiary. For a battery conviction he would spend no more than six months in the county jail. In a homicide, however, "felony manslaughter," or "assault with a deadly weapon," whatever their relation to homicide as regards inclusion, would more closely approximate the sentence outcome that could be expected on a trial conviction of second degree murder. These alternatives would be considered. For burglary, a typically situationally included offense might be "disturbing the peace," "breaking and entering" or "destroying public property." "Petty theft," however, constitutes a reasonable lesser alternative to burglary as the sentence for petty theft will often range between six months and one year in the county jail and burglary regularly does not carry higher than two years in the state prison. "Disturbing the peace" would be a thirty-day sentence offense.

While the present purposes make the exposition of this calculus unnecessary, it can be noted and stressed that the particular content of the reduction does not necessarily correspond to a relation between the original and altered charge that could be described in either the terms of necessary or situational inclusion. Whatever the relation between the original and reduced charge, its essential feature resides in the spread between sentence likelihoods and the reasonableness of that spread, i.e., the balance it strikes between the defendant "getting his due" and at the same time "getting something less than he might so that he will plead guilty."

The procedure we want to clarify now, at the risk of some repetition, is the manner in which an instant case is examined to decide its membership in a class of "crimes such as this" (the category *normal crimes*). Let us start with an obvious case, burglary. As the typical reduction for burglary is petty theft and as petty theft is neither situationally nor necessarily included in burglary, the examination of the instant case is clearly not undertaken to decide whether petty theft is an appropriate statutory description. The concern is to establish the relation between the instant burglary and the normal category "burglaries" and, having decided a "sufficient correspondence," to now employ petty theft as the proposed reduction.

In scrutinizing the present burglary case, the P.D. seeks to establish that "this is a burglary just like any other." If that correspondence is not established, regardless of whether or not petty theft in fact was a feature of the way the crime was enacted, the reduction to petty theft would not be proposed. *The propriety of proposing petty theft as a reduction does not derive from its in-fact-existence in the present case, but is warranted or not by the relation of the present burglary to "burglaries," normally conceived.*

In a case of "child molestation" (officially called "lewd conduct with a minor"), the concern is to decide if this is a "typical child molestation case." While "loitering around a schoolyard" is frequently a feature of the way such crimes are instigated, establishing that the present defendant *did in fact loiter around a schoolyard* is secondary to the more general question "Is this a typical child molestation case?" What appears as a contradiction must be clarified by examining the status of "loitering around a schoolyard" as a typical feature of such child molestations. The typical character of "child molesting cases" does not stand or fall on the fact that "loitering around a schoolyard" is a feature of the way they are in fact committed. It is *not* that "loitering around a schoolyard" as a *statutorily referable behavior sequence* is part of typical "child molesting cases" but that "loitering around a school-yard" as a *socially distinct mode of committing child molestations typifies the way such offenses are enacted.* "Strictly speaking," i.e., under the auspices of the statutory corpus delicti, "loitering around a schoolyard," requires *loitering, around, a schoolyard;* if one loiters around a ball park or a public recreation area, he "cannot," within a proper reading of the statute, be charged with loitering around a *schoolyard.* Yet "loitering around a school-yard," as a feature of the typical way such offenses as child molestations are committed, has the status not of a description of the way in *fact* (*fact,* statutorily decided) it occurred or typically occurs, but "the kind-of-social-activity-typically-associated-with-such-offenses." It is not its statutorily conceived features but its socially relevant attributes that gives "loitering around a schoolyard" its status as a feature of the class "normal child molestations." Whether the defendant loitered around a schoolyard or a ball park, and whether he loitered or "was passing by," "loitering around a schoolyard" as a reduction will be made if the defendant's activity was such that "he was hanging around some public place or another" and "was the kind of guy who hangs around schoolyards." As a component of the class of normal child molestation cases (of the variety where the victim is a stranger), "loitering around a schoolyard" typifies a mode of committing such offenses, the class of "such persons who do such things as hang around schoolyards and the like." A large variety of actual offenses could thus be nonetheless reduced to "loitering" if, as kinds of social activity, "loitering," conceived of as typifying a way of life, pattern of daily activity, social psychological circumstances, etc., characterized the conduct of the defendant. The young P.D. who would object "You can't reduce it to 'loitering' — he didn't really 'loiter,' " would be reprimanded: "Fella, you don't know how to use that term; he might as well have 'loitered' — it's the same kind of case as the others."

Having outlined the formal mechanics of the guilty plea disposition, I shall now turn to depict the routine of representation that the categories of crime, imbued with elaborate knowledge of the delinquent social structure, provide for. This will entail a brief examination of pertinent organizational features of the P.D. system.

PUBLIC "DEFENSE"

Recently, in many communities, the burden of securing counsel has been taken from the defendant.[6] As the accused is, by law, entitled to the aid of

---

[6] For general histories of indigent defender systems in the United States, see The Association of the Bar of the City of New York, *Equal Justice for the Accused* (Garden City, N.Y.: 1959) ; and E. A. Brownell, *Legal Aid in the United States* (Rochester, N.Y.: The Lawyers Co-operative Publishing Company, 1951).

counsel, and as his pocketbook is often empty, numerous cities have felt obliged to establish a public defender system. There has been little resistance to this development by private attorneys among whom it is widely felt that the less time they need spend in the criminal courts, where practice is least prestigeful and lucrative, the better.[7]

Whatever the reasons for its development, we now find, in many urban places, a public defender occupying a place alongside judge and prosecutor as a regular court employee. In the county studied, the P.D. mans a daily station, like the public prosecutor, and "defends" all who come before him. He appears in court when court begins and his "clientele," composed without regard for his preferences, consists of that residual category of persons who cannot afford to bring their own spokesmen to court. In this county, the "residual" category approximates 65 per cent of the total number of criminal cases. In a given year, the twelve attorneys who comprise the P.D. Office "represent" about 3,000 defendants in the municipal and superior courts of the county.

While the courtroom encounters of private attorneys are brief, businesslike and circumscribed, interactionally and temporally, by the particular cases that bring them there, the P.D. attends to the courtroom as his regular work place and conveys in his demeanor his place as a member of its core personnel.

While private attorneys come and leave court with their clients (who are generally "on bail"), the P.D. arrives in court each morning at nine, takes his station at the defense table, and deposits there the batch of files that he will refer to during the day. When, during morning "calendar,"[8] a private attorney's case is called, the P.D. steps back from the defense table, leaving his belongings in place there, and temporarily relinquishes his station. No private attorney has enough defendants in a given court on a given day to claim a right to make a desk of the defense table. If the P.D. needs some information from his central office, he uses the clerk's telephone, a privilege that few private lawyers feel at home enough to take. In the course of calendar work, a lawyer will often have occasion to request a delay or "continuance" of several days until the next stage of his client's proceedings. The private attorney addresses the prosecutor via the judge to request such an alteration; the P.D. talks directly over to the D.A.:

Private attorney: "If the prosecutor finds it convenient your Honor, my client would prefer to have his preliminary hearing on Monday, the 24th."

---

[7] The experience of the Public Defender system is distinctly different in this regard from that of the Legal Aid Societies, which, I am told, have continually met very strong opposition to their establishment by local bar associations.

[8] "Calendar part" consists of that portion of the court day, typically in the mornings, when all matters other than trials are heard, e.g., arraignments, motions, continuances, sentencing, probation reports, etc.

Judge: "Is that date suitable to the district attorney?"
Prosecutor: "Yes, your Honor."
Private attorney: "Thank you, your Honor."

Public Defender: "Bob (D.A.), how about moving Smith's prelim up to the 16th?"
Prosecutor: "Well, Jim, we've got Jones on that afternoon."
Public Defender: "Let's see, how's the 22nd?"
Prosecutor: "That's fine, Jim, the 22nd."

If, during the course of a proceeding, the P.D. has some minor matter to tend to with the D.A., he uses the time when a private attorney is addressing the bench to walk over to the prosecutor's table and whisper his requests, suggestions or questions. The P.D. uses the prosecutor's master calendar to check on an upcoming court date; so does the D.A. with the P.D.'s. The D.A. and P.D. are on a first name basis and throughout the course of a routine day interact as a team of co-workers.

While the central focus of the private attorney's attention is his client, the courtroom and affairs of court constitute the locus of involvements for the P.D. The public defender and public prosecutor, each representatives of their respective offices, jointly handle the greatest bulk of the court's daily activity.

The P.D. office, rather than assign its attorneys to clients, employs the arrangement of stationing attorneys in different courts to "represent" all those who come before that station. As defendants are moved about from courtroom to courtroom throughout the course of their proceedings (both from municipal to superior courtrooms for felony cases, and from one municipal courtroom to another when there is a specialization of courts, e.g., jury, non-jury, arraignment, etc.), the P.D. sees defendants only at those places in their paths when they appear in the court he is manning. A given defendant may be "represented" by one P.D. at arraignment, another at preliminary hearing, a third at trial and a fourth when sentenced.

At the first interview with a client (initial interviews occur in the jail where attorneys go, *en masse*, to "pick up new defendants" in the afternoons) a file is prepared on the defendant. In each file is recorded the charge brought against the defendant and, among other things, his next court date. Each evening attorneys return new files to the central office where secretaries prepare court books for each courtroom that list the defendants due to appear in a given court on a given day. In the mornings, attorneys take the court books from the office and remove from the central file the files of those defendants due to appear in "their court" that day.

There is little communication between P.D. and client. After the first interview, the defendant's encounters with the P.D. are primarily in court. Only under special circumstances (to be discussed below) are there contacts between lawyers and defendants in the jail before and after appearances in court. The bulk of "preparation for court" (either trials or non-trial matters) occurs at the first interview. The attorney on station, the "attending attorney," is thus a stranger to "his client," and vice versa. Over the course of his proceedings, a defendant will have several attorneys (in one instance a man was "represented" by eight P.D.'s on a charge of simple assault). Defendants who come to court find a lawyer they don't know conducting their trials, entering their motions, making their pleas, and the rest. Often there is no introduction of P.D. to defendant; defendants are prepared to expect a strange face:

Don't be surprised when you see another P.D. in court with you on Tuesday. You just do what he tells you to. He'll know all about your case.

P.D.'s seldom talk about particular defendants among themselves. When they converse about trials, the facts of cases, etc., they do so not so much for briefing, e.g., "This is what I think you should do when you 'get him'," but rather as small talk, as "What have you got going today." The P.D. does not rely on the information about a case he receives from a previous attending attorney in order to know how to manager his "representation." Rather, the file is relied upon to furnish all the information essential for making an "appearance." These appearances range from morning calendar work (e.g., arraignments, motions, continuances, etc.) to trials on offenses from drunkenness to assault with a deadly weapon. In the course of a routine day, the P.D. will receive his batch of files in the morning and, seeing them for the first time that day, conduct numerous trials, preliminary hearings, calendar appearances, sentencing proceedings, etc. They do not study files overnight. Attorneys will often only look over a file a half hour or so before the jury trial begins.

THE FIRST INTERVIEW

As the first interview is often the only interview and as the file prepared there is central for the continuing "representation" of the defendant by other attorneys, it is important to examine these interviews and the file's contents. From the outset, the P.D. attends to establishing the typical character of the case before him and thereby instituting routinely employed reduction arrangements. The defendant's appearance, e.g., his race, demeanor, age, style of talk, way of attending to the occasion of his incarceration, etc., provides the P.D. with an initial sense of his place in the social structure. Knowing only that the defendant is charged with section 459 (Burglary) of the penal code, the P.D. employs his conception of typical burglars against which the character of the present defendant is assessed.

. . . he had me fooled for a while. With that accent of his and those Parliaments he was smoking I thought something was strange. It turned out to be just another burglary. You heard him about New York and the way he had a hold on him there that he was running away from. I just guess N.Y. is a funny place, you can never tell what kinds of people get involved in crimes there.

The initial fact of the defendant's "putting in a request to see the P.D." establishes his lower position in the class structure of the community:

We just never get wealthier people here. They usually don't stay in jail overnight and then they call a private attorney. The P.D. gets everything at the bottom of the pile.

Searching over the criminal history (past convictions and arrests) the defendant provides when preliminary face sheet data is recorded in the file, the P.D. gets a sense of the man's typical pattern of criminal activity. It is not the particular offenses for which he is charged that are crucial, but the constellation of prior offenses and the sequential pattern they take:

I could tell as soon as he told me he had four prior drunk charges that he was just another of these skid row bums. You could look at him and tell.

When you see a whole string of forgery counts in the past you pretty much know what kind of case you're dealing with. You either get those who commit an occasional forgery, or those that do nothing but. . . . With a whole bunch of prior checks (prior forgery convictions) you can bet that he cashes little ones. I didn't even have to ask for the amount you know. I seldom come across one over a hundred bucks.

From the looks of him and the way he said "I wasn't doing anything, just playing with her," you know, its the usual kind of thing, just a little diddling or something. We can try to get it out on a simple assault.

When a P.D. puts questions to the defendant he is less concerned with recording nuances of the instant event (e.g., how many feet·from the bar were you when the cops came in, did you break into the back gate or the front door), than with establishing its similarity with "events of this sort." That similarity is established, not by discovering statutorily relevant events of the present case, but by locating the event in a sociologically constructed class of "such cases." The first questions directed to the defendant are of the character that answers to them either confirm or throw into question the assumed typicality. First questions with ADWs are of the order: "How long had you been drinking before this all started?"; with "child molestation cases": "How long were you hanging around before this began?"; with "forgery" cases: "Was this the second or third check you cashed in the same place?"

We shall present three short excerpts from three first interviews. They all begin with the first question asked after preliminary background data is gathered. The first is with a 288 (child molestation), the second with a 459 (burglary) and the last with a 11530 (possession of marijuana). Each interview was conducted by a different Public Defender. In each case the P.D.

had no information about the defendant or this particular crime other than
that provided by the penal code number:

288

P.D.: O.K., why don't you start out by telling me how this thing got started?

Def.: Well, I was at the park and all I did was to ask this little girl if she wanted
to sit on my lap for awhile and you know, just sit on my lap. Well, about
twenty minutes later I'm walkin' down the street about a block away from
the park and this cop pulls up and there the same little girl is, you know,
sitting in the back seat with some dame. The cop asks me to stick my head
in the back seat and he asks the kid if I was the one and she says yes. So
he puts me in the car and takes a statement from me and here I am in the
joint. All I was doin was playin with her a little. . . .

P.D.: (interrupting) . . . O.K. I get the story, let's see what we can do. If I can
get this charge reduced to a misdemeanor then I would advise you to plead
guilty, particularly since you have a record and that wouldn't look too well
in court with a jury.

(the interview proceeded for another two or three minutes and the decision
to plead guilty was made)

459

P.D.: Why don't you start by telling me where this place was that you broke into?

Def.: I don't know for sure . . . I think it was on 13th street or something like
that.

P.D.: Had you ever been there before?

Def.: I hang around that neighborhood you know, so I guess I've been in the place
before, yeah.

P.D.: What were you going after?

Def.: I don't know, whatever there was so's I could get a little cash. Man, I was
pretty broke that night.

P.D.: Was anyone with you?

Def.: No, I was by myself.

P.D.: How much did you break up the place?

Def.: I didn't do nothing. The back window was open a little bit see and I just
put my hand in there and opened the door. I was just walking in when I
heard police comin so I turn around and start to run. And, they saw me
down the block and that was that.

P.D.: Were you drunk at the time?

Def.: I wasn't drunk, no, I maybe had a drink or two that evening but I wasn't
drunk or anything like that.

11530

P.D.: Well Smith, why don't you tell me where they found it (the marijuana)?

Def.: I was driving home from the drugstore with my friend and this cop car pulls
me up to the side. Two guys get out, one of them was wearing a uniform
and the other was a plain clothes man. They told us to get out of the car
and then they searched me and then my friend. Then this guy without the

uniform he looked over into the car and picked up this thing from the back floor and said something to the other one. Then he asked me if I had any more of the stuff and I said I didn't know what he was talking about. So he wrote something down on a piece of paper and made me sign it. Then he told my friend to go home and they took me down here to the station and booked me on possession of marijuana. I swear I didn't have no marijuana.

P.D.: You told me you were convicted of possession in 1959.

Def.: Yeah, but I haven't touched any of the stuff since then. I don't know what it was doing in my car, but I haven't touched the stuff since that last time.

P.D.: You ought to know it doesn't make any difference whether or not they catch you using, just so as they find it on your possession or in a car, or your house, or something.

Def.: Man, I swear I don't know how it got there. Somebody must have planted it there.

P.D.: Look, you know as well as I do that with your prior conviction and this charge now that you could go away from here for five years or so. So just calm down a minute and let's look at this thing reasonably. If you go to trial and lose the trial, you're stuck. You'll be in the joint until you're 28 years old. If you plead to this one charge without the priors then we can get you into jail maybe, or a year or two at the most in the joint. If you wait until the preliminary hearing and then they charge the priors, boy you've had it, it's too late.

Def.: Well how about a trial?

(After ten minutes, the defendant decided to plead guilty to one charge of possession, before the date of the preliminary hearing)

Let us consider, in light of the previous discussion, some of the features of these interviews.

1. In each case the information sought is not "data" for organizing the particular facts of the case for deciding proper penal code designations (or with a view toward undermining the assignment of a designation in an anticipated trial). In the 288 instance, the P.D. interrupted when he had enough information to confirm his sense of the case's typicality and construct a typifying portrayal of the present defendant. The character of the information supplied by the defendant was such that it was specifically lacking detail about the particular occurrences, e.g., the time, place, what was said to the girl, what precisely did the defendant do or not do, his "state of mind," etc. The defendant's appearance and prior record (in this case the defendant was a fifty-five year old white, unemployed, unskilled laborer, with about ten prior drunk arrests, seven convictions, and two prior sex offense violations) was relied upon to provide the sense of the present occasion. The P.D. straightforwardly approached the D.A. and arranged for a "contributing to the delinquency of a minor" reduction. In the burglary case, the question, "Had you ever been there before?", was intended to elicit what was received, e.g.,

that the place was a familiar one to the defendant. Knowing that the place was in the defendant's neighborhood establishes its character as a skid row area business; that the First Federal Bank was not entered has been confirmed. "What were you going after?", also irrelevant to the 459 section of the penal code, provides him with information that there was no special motive for entering this establishment. The question, "Was anyone with you?", when answered negatively, placed the event in the typical class of "burglaries" as solitary, non-coordinated activities. The remaining questions were directed as well to confirming the typical character of the event, and the adequacy of the defendant's account is not decided by whether or not the P.D. can now decide whether the statutory definition of the contemplated reduction or the original charge is satisfied. Its adequacy is determined by the ability with which the P.D. can detect its normal character. The accounts provided thus may have the character of anecdotes, sketches, phrases, etc. In the first instance, with the 288, the prior record and the defendant's appearance, demeanor and style of talking about the event was enough to warrant his typical treatment.

2. The most important feature of the P.D.'s questioning is the presupposition of guilt that makes his proposed questions legitimate and answerable at the outset. To pose the question, "Why don't you start by telling me where this place was that you broke into?" as a lead question, the P.D. takes it that the defendant is guilty of a crime and that the crime for which he is charged probably describes what essentially occurred.

The P.D.'s activity is seldom geared to securing acquittals for clients. He and the D.A., as co-workers in the same courts, take it for granted that the persons who come before the courts are guilty of crimes and are to be treated accordingly:

Most of them have records as you can see. Almost all of them have been through our courts before. And the police just don't make mistakes in this town. That's one thing about —, we've got the best police force in the state.

As we shall argue below, the way defendants are "represented" (the station manning rather than assignment of counselors to clients), the way trials are conducted, the way interviews are held and the penal code employed — all of the P.D.'s work is premised on the supposition that people charged with crimes have committed crimes.

This presupposition makes such first questions as "Why don't you start by telling me where this place was . . ." reasonable questions. When the answer comes: "What place? I don't know what you are talking about," the defendant is taken to be a phony, making an "innocent pitch." The conceivable first question: "Did you do it?", is not asked because it is felt that this gives the defendant the notion that he can try an "innocent pitch":

I never ask them, "did you do it?", because on one hand I know they did and mainly because then they think that they can play games with us. We can always check their records and usually they have a string of offenses. You don't have to, though, because in a day or two they change their story and plead guilty. Except for the stubborn ones.

Of the possible answers to an opening question, bewilderment, the inability to answer or silence are taken to indicate that the defendant is putting the P.D. on. For defendants who refuse to admit anything, the P.D. threatens:

Look, if you don't want to talk, that's your business. I can't help you. All I can say is that if you go to trial on this beef you're going to spend a long time in the joint. When you get ready to tell me the story straight, then we can see what can be done.

If the puzzlement comes because the wrong question is asked, e.g., "There wasn't any fight — that's not the way it happened," the defendant will start to fill in the story. The P.D. awaits to see if, how far, and in what ways the instant case is deviant. If the defendant is charged with burglary and a middle class establishment was burglarized, windows shattered, a large pay-roll sought after and a gun used, then the reduction to petty theft, generally employed for "normal burglaries," would be more difficult to arrange.

Generally, the P.D. doesn't have to discover the atypical kinds of cases through questioning. Rather, the D.A., in writing the original complaint, provides the P.D. with clues that the typical recipe, given the way the event occurred, will not be allowable. Where the way it occurs is such that it does not resemble normal burglaries and the routinely used penalty would reduce it *too far* commensurate with the way the crime occurred, the D.A. frequently charges various situationally included offenses, indicating to the P.D. that the procedure to employ here is to suggest "dropping" some of the charges, leaving the originally charged greatest offense as it stands.

In the general case he doesn't charge all those offenses that he legally might. He might charge "child molesting" and "loitering around a school-yard" but typically only the greater charge is made. The D.A. does so so as to provide for a later reduction that will appear particularly lenient in that it seemingly involves a *change* in the charge. Were he to charge both molesting and loitering, he would be obliged, moreover, should the case come to trial, to introduce evidence for both offenses. The D.A. is thus always constrained not to set overly high charges or not situationally included multiple offenses by the possibility that the defendant will not plead guilty to a lesser offense and the case will go to trial. Of primary importance is that he doesn't charge multiple offenses so that the P.D. will be in the best position vis-à-vis the defendant. He thus charges the first complaint so as to provide for a "setup."

The alteration of charges must be made in open court. The P.D. requests to have a new plea entered:

P.D.: Your honor, in the interests of justice, my client would like to change his plea of not guilty to the charge of burglary and enter a plea of guilty to the charge of petty theft.

Judge: Is this new plea acceptable to the prosecution?

D.A.: Yes, your honor.

The prosecutor knows beforehand that the request will be made, and has agreed in advance to allow it.

I asked a P.D. how they felt about making such requests in open court, i.e., asking for a reduction from one offense to another when the latter is obviously not necessarily included and often (as is the case in burglary-to-petty theft) not situationally included. He summarized the office's feeling:

. . . in the old days, ten or so years ago, we didn't like to do it in front of the judge. What we used to do when we made a deal was that the D.A. would dismiss the original charge and write up a new complaint altogether. That took a lot of time. We had to re-arraign him all over again back in the muni court and everything. Besides, in the same courtroom, everyone used to know what was going on anyway. Now, we just ask for a change of plea to the lesser charge regardless of whether it's included or not. Nobody thinks twice about asking for petty theft on burglary, or drunkenness on car theft, or something like that. It's just the way it's done.

Some restrictions are felt. Assaultive crimes (e.g., ADW, simple assault, attempted murder, etc.) will not be reduced to or from "money offenses" (burglary, robbery, theft) unless the latter involve weapons or some violence. Also, victimless crimes (narcotics, drunkenness) are not reduced to or from assaultive or "money offenses," unless there is some factual relation, e.g., drunkenness with a fight might turn out to be simple assault reduced to drunkenness.

For most cases that come before their courts, the P.D. and D.A. are able to employ reductions that are formulated for handling typical cases. While some burglaries, rapes, narcotics violations and petty thefts, are instigated in strange ways and involve atypical facts, some manipulation in the way the initial charge is made can be used to set up a procedure to replace the simple charge-alteration form of reducing.

RECALCITRANT DEFENDANTS

Most of the P.D.'s cases that "have to go to trial" are those where the P.D. is not able to sell the defendant on the "bargain." These are cases for which reductions are available, reductions that are constructed on the basis of the typicality of the offense and allowable by the D.A. These are normal crimes committed by "stubborn" defendants.

So-called "stubborn" defendants will be distinguished from a second class of offenders, those who commit *crimes which are atypical in their character (for this community, at this time, etc.) or who commit crimes which while typical (recurrent for this community, this time, etc.) are committed atypically.* The manner in which the P.D. and D.A. must conduct the representation and prosecution of these defendants is radically different. To characterize the special problems the P.D. has with each class of defendants, it is first necessary to point out a general feature of the P.D.'s orientation to the work of the courts that has hitherto not been made explicit. This orientation will be merely sketched here.

As we noticed, the defendant's guilt is not attended to. That is to say, the presupposition of guilt, as a *presupposition,* does not say "You are guilty" with a pointing accusatory finger, but "You are guilty, you know it, I know it, so let's get down to the business of deciding what to do with you." When a defendant agrees to plead guilty, he is not *admitting* his guilt; when asked to plead guilty, he is not being asked, "Come on, admit it, you know you were *wrong,*" but rather, "Why don't you be sensible about this thing?" What is sought is not a *confession,* but reasonableness.

The presupposition of guilt as a way of attending to the treatment of defendants has its counterpart in the way the P.D. attends to the entire court process, prosecuting machinery, law enforcement techniques, and the community.

For P.D. and D.A. it is a routinely encountered phenomenon that persons in the community regularly commit criminal offenses, are regularly brought before the courts, and are regularly transported to the state and county penal institutions. To confront a "criminal" is, for D.A. and P.D., no special experience to tell their wives about, nothing to record as outstanding in the happenings of the day. Before "their court" scores of "criminals" pass each day.

The morality of the courts is taken for granted. The P.D. assumes that the D.A., the police, judge, the narcotics agents and others all conduct their business as it must be conducted and in a proper fashion. That the police may hide out to deceive petty violators; that narcotics agents may regularly employ illicit entrapment procedures to find suspects; that investigators may routinely arrest suspects before they have sufficient grounds and only later uncover warrantable evidence for a formal booking; that the police may beat suspects; that judges may be "tough" because they are looking to support for higher office elections; that some laws may be specifically prejudicial against certain classes of persons — whatever may be the actual course of charging and convicting defendants — all of this is taken, as one P.D. put it, "as part of the system and the way it has to be." And the P.D. is part of the team.

While it is common to overhear private attorneys call judges "bastards," policemen "hoodlums" and prosecutors "sadists," the P.D., in the presence of such talk, remains silent. When the P.D. "loses" a case — and we shall see that *losing* is an adequate description only for some circumstances — he is likely to say "I knew *he* couldn't win." Private attorneys, on the other hand, will not hesitate to remark, as one did in a recent case, "You haven't got a fucking chance in front of that son-of-a-bitch dictator." In the P.D. office, there is a total absence of such condemnation.

The P.D. takes it for granted and attends to the courts in accord with the view that "what goes on in this business is what goes on and what goes on is the way it should be." It is rare to hear a public defender voice protest against a particular law, procedure, or official. One of the attorneys mentioned that he felt the new narcotics law (which makes it mandatory that a high minimum sentence be served for "possession or sale of narcotics") wasn't too severe "considering that they wanted to give them the chair." Another indicated that the more rigid statute "will probably cure a lot of them because they'll be in for so long." One P.D. feels that wiretapping would be a useful adjunct to police procedure. It is generally said, by everyone in the office, that ". . . is one of the best cities in the state when it comes to police."

In the P.D.'s interviews, the defendant's guilt only becomes a topic when the defendant himself attempts to direct attention to his innocence. Such attempts are never taken seriously by the P.D. but are seen as "innocent pitches," as "being wise," as "not knowing what is good for him." Defendants who make "innocent pitches" often find themselves able to convince the P.D. to have trials. The P.D. is in a professional and organizational bind in that he requires that his "clients" agree with whatever action he takes "on their behalf":

Can you imagine what might happen if we went straight to the D.A. with a deal to which the client later refused to agree? Can you see him in court screaming how the P.D. sold him out? As it is, we get plenty of letters purporting to show why we don't do our job. Judges are swamped with letters condemning the P.D. Plenty of appeals get started this way.

Some defendants don't buy the offer of less time as constituting sufficient grounds for avoiding a trial. To others, it appears that "copping out" is worse than having a trial regardless of the consequences for the length of sentence. The following remarks, taken from P.D. files, illustrate the terms in which such "stubborn" defendants are conceived:

Def wants a trial, but he is dead. In lieu of a possible 995, DA agreed to put note in his file recommending a deal. This should be explored and encouraged as big break for Def.

Chance of successful defense negligible. Def realizes this but says he ain't going to cop to no strong-arm. See if we can set him straight.

Dead case. Too many witnesses and . . . used in two of the transactions. However, Def is a very squirmy jailhouse lawyer and refuses to face facts.

Possibly the DA in Sup/Ct could be persuaded into cutting her loose if she took the 211 and one of the narco counts. If not, the Def, who is somewhat recalcitrant and stubborn, will probably demand a JT (jury trial).

The routine trial, generated as it is by the defendant's refusal to make a lesser plea, is the "defendant's fault":

What the hell are we supposed to do with them. If they can't listen to good reason and take a bargain, then it's their tough luck. If they go to prison, well, they're the ones who are losing the trials, not us.

When the P.D. enters the courtroom, he takes it that he is going to lose, e.g., the defendant is going to prison. When he "prepares" for trial, he doesn't prepare to "win." There is no attention given to "how am I going to construct a defense in order that I can get this defendant free of the charges against him." In fact, he doesn't "prepare for trial" in any "ordinary" sense. (I use the term *ordinary* with hesitation; what *preparation for trial* might in fact involve with other than P.D. lawyers has not, to my knowledge, been investigated.)

For the P.D., "preparation for trial" involves, essentially, learning what "burglary cases" are like, what "rape cases" are like, what "assaults" are like. The P.D.'s main concern is to conduct his part of the proceedings in accord with complete respect for proper legal procedure. He raises objections to improper testimony; introduces motions whenever they seem called for; demands his "client's rights" to access to the prosecution's evidence before trial (through so-called "discovery proceedings"); cross examines all witnesses; does not introduce evidence that he expects will not be allowable; asks all those questions of all those people that he must in order to have addressed himself to the task of insuring that the *corpus delicti* has been established; carefully summarizes the evidence that has been presented in making a closing argument. Throughout, at every point, he conducts his "defense" in such a manner that no one can say of him "He has been negligent, there are grounds for appeal here." He systematically provides, in accord with the prescriptions of due process and the fourteenth amendment, a completely proper, "adequate legal representation."

At the same time, the district attorney, and the county which employs them both, can rely on the P.D. not to attempt to morally degrade police officers in cross examination; not to impeach the state's witnesses by trickery; not to attempt an exposition of the entrapment methods of narcotics agents; not to condemn the community for the "racial prejudice that produces our criminals" (the phrase of a private attorney during closing argument); not to challenge the prosecution of "these women who are trying to raise a family without a husband" (the statement of another private attorney during closing argument on a welfare fraud case); in sum, not to make an issue of the moral character of the administrative machinery of the local courts, the community or the police. He will not cause any serious trouble for the routine motion of the court conviction process. Laws will not be challenged, cases will not be tried to test the constitutionality of procedures and statutes, judges will not be personally degraded, police will be free from scrutiny to decide the legitimacy of their operations, and the community will not be condemned for its segregative practices against Negroes. The P.D.'s defense is completely proper, in accord with correct legal procedure, and specifically amoral in its import, manner of delivery, and perceived implications for the propriety of the prosecution enterprise.

In "return" for all this, the district attorney treats the defendant's guilt in a matter-of-fact fashion, doesn't get hostile in the course of the proceedings, doesn't insist that the jury or judge "throw the book," but rather "puts on a trial" (in their way of referring to their daily tasks) in order to, with a minimum of strain, properly place the defendant behind bars. Both prosecutor and public defender thus protect the moral character of the other's charges from exposure. Should the P.D. attend to demonstrating the innocence of his client by attempting to undermine the legitimate character of police operations, the prosecutor might feel obliged in return to employ devices to degrade the moral character of the P.D.'s client. Should the D.A. attack defendants in court, by pointing to the specifically immoral character of their activities, the P.D. might feel obligated, in response, to raise into relief the moral texture of the D.A.'s and police's and community's operations. Wherever possible, each holds the other in check. But the "check" need not be continuously held in place, or even attended to self consciously, for both P.D. and D.A. trust one another implicitly. The D.A. knows, with certainty, that the P.D. will not make a closing argument that resembles the following by a private attorney, from which I have paraphrased key excerpts:

If it hadn't been for all the publicity that this case had in our wonderful local newspapers, you wouldn't want to throw the book at these men.

If you'd clear up your problems with the Negro in . . . maybe you wouldn't have cases like this in your courts.

(after sentence was pronounced) Your honor, I just would like to say one thing —that I've never heard or seen such a display of injustice as I've seen here in this court today. It's a sad commentary on the state of our community if people like yourself pay more attention to the local political machines than to the lives of our defendants. I think you are guilty of that, your Honor.

(At this last statement, one of the P.D.'s who was in the courtroom turned to me and said, "He sure is looking for a contempt charge.")

The P.D. knows how to conduct his trials because he knows how to conduct "assault with deadly weapons" trials, "burglary" trials, "rape" trials, and the rest. The corpus delicti here provides him with a basis for asking "proper questions," making the "proper" cross examinations, and pointing out the "proper" things to jurors about "reasonable doubt." He need not extensively gather information about the specific facts of the instant case. Whatever is needed in the way of "facts of the case" arise in the course of the D.A.'s presentation. He employs the "strategy" of directing the same questions to the witness as were put by the D.A. with added emphasis on the question mark, or an inserted "Did you really see . . .?" His "defense" consists of attempting to "bring out" slightly variant aspects of the D.A.'s story by questioning his own witnesses (whom he seldom interviews before beginning trial but who are interviewed by the Office's two "investigators") and the defendant.

With little variation the same questions are put to all defendants charged with the same crimes. The P.D. learns with experience what to expect as the "facts of the case." These facts, in their general structure, portray social circumstances that he can anticipate by virtue of his knowledge of the normal features of offense categories and types of offenders. The "details" of the instant case are "discovered" over the course of hearing them in court. In this regard, the "information" that "comes out" is often as new to him as to the jury.

Employing a common sense conception of what criminal lawyers behave like in cross examination and argument, and the popular portrayal of their demeanor and style of addressing adversary witnesses, the onlooker comes away with the sense of having witnessed not a trial at all, but a set of motions, a perfunctorily carried off event. A sociological analysis of this sense would require a systematic attempt to describe the features of adversary trial conduct.

A NOTE ON SPECIAL CASES

To conduct trials with "stubborn" defendants, so-called, is no special trouble. Here trials are viewed as a "waste of time." Murders, embezzlements, multiple rape cases (several defendants with one victim), large scale robberies, dope ring operations, those cases that arouse public attention and receive special notice in the papers — these are cases whose normal features are not constructed and for which, even were a guilty plea available, both parties feel uncomfortably obliged to bring issues of moral character into the courtroom. The privacy of the P.D.-D.A. conviction machinery through the use of the guilty plea can no longer be preserved. Only "normal defendants" are accorded this privacy. The pressure for a public hearing, in the sense of "bringing the public in to see and monitor the character of the proceedings," must be allowed to culminate in a full blown jury trial. There is a general preference in the P.D. office to handle routine cases without a jury, if it must go to trial at all. In the special case the jury must be employed and with them a large audience of onlookers, newspaper men, and daily paper coverage must be tolerated.

To put on a fight is a discomforting task for persons who regularly work together as a team. Every effort is made to bind off the event of a special case by heightened interaction outside the courtroom. In the routine case, with no jury or at least no press coverage, the whole trial can be handled as a backstage operation. With special cases there can be no byplay conversation in the courtroom between D.A. and P.D., and no leaving court together, arm in arm. Metaphorically, two persons who regularly dance together must now appear, with the lights turned on, to be fighting.

The P.D. Office reserves several of its attorneys to handle such cases. By keeping the regular personnel away from particular courtrooms, their routine interactions with the D.A. can be properly maintained. An older, more experienced attorney, from each side, comes to court to put on the show. The device of so handling the assignment of attorneys to cases serves to mark off the event as a special occasion, to set it outside the regular ordering of relationships that must resume when the special, and dreaded, case becomes a statistic in the penal institution records.

With the special cases, the client-attorney assignment procedure is instituted. The head of the P.D. Office, along with a coterie of older attorneys, goes to the first interview in the jail, and these same attorneys, or some of them, take over the case and stay with it, handling its development with kid gloves. The concern to provide "adequate legal representation" may be relegated to a back seat. Both P.D. and D.A. must temporarily step outside their typical modes of mutual conduct and yet, at the same time, not permanently jeopardize the stability of their usual teamlike relationship.

SOME CONCLUSIONS

An examination of the use of the penal code by actually practicing attorneys has revealed that categories of crime, rather than being "unsuited" to sociological analysis, are so employed as to make their analysis crucial to empirical understanding. What categories of crime are, i.e., who is assembled under this one or that, what constitute the behaviors inspected for deciding such matters, what "etiologically significant" matters are incorporated within their scope, is not, the present findings indicate, to be decided on the basis of an *a priori* inspection of their formally available definitions. The sociologist who regards the category "theft" with penal code in hand and proposes necessary, "theoretically relevant" revisions, is constructing an imagined use of the penal code as the basis for his criticism. For in their actual use, categories of crime, as we have reiterated continuously above, are, at least for this legal establishment, the shorthand reference terms for that knowledge of the social structure and its criminal events upon which the task of practically organizing the work of "representation" is premised. That knowledge includes, embodied within what burglary, petty theft, narcotics violations, child molestation and the rest *actually stand for,* knowledge of modes of criminal activity, ecological characteristics of the community, patterns of daily slum life, psychological and social biographies of offenders, criminal histories and futures; in sum, practically tested criminological wisdom. The operations of the Public Defender system, and it is clear that upon comparative analysis with other legal "firms" it would be somewhat distinctive in character, are routinely maintained via the proper use of categories of crime for everyday decision making. The proprieties of that use are not described in the state criminal code, nor are the operations of reduction, detailed above.

A cautionary word is required. It will appear as obvious that the system of providing "defense" to indigent persons described above is not representative of criminal defense work generally. How the penal code is employed, i.e., how behaviors are scrutinized under its jurisdiction and dispensations made via operations performed on its categories, in other kinds of legal establishments, has not been investigated here. The present case, albeit apparently specialized, was chosen as an example only. It may well be that, in certain forms of legal work, the penal code as a statutory document is accorded a much different and more "rigorous" scrutiny. The legalistic character of some criminal prosecutions leads one to suspect that the "letter of the law" might constitute a key reference point in preparing for a criminal defense, aiming for acquittal, or changing a statutory regulation.

Current Psychiatric Roles
in the
Legal Process

SEYMOUR L. HALLECK

Unlike most other medical specialists, the psychiatrist has not restricted himself to the treatment of those who seek his services but has deeply involved himself in the legal and social problems of controlling disturbed people. One of the major functions of the nineteenth- and twentieth-century psychiatrist has been to assist judicial authorities in making decisions as to who is to be punished and who is to be treated as a mental patient. The modern psychiatrist is frequently a participant in the insanity trial, a social ritual which has a profound impact upon the community and upon those of its members who have violated the law.

So much has been written about the role of psychiatry in determining the legal status of offenders that it would be presumptuous to offer a comprehensive summary in one brief article. Instead, the purpose here is to describe a few of the basic principles and theoretical orientations which underlie psychiatric involvement in the insanity trial and to present a consistently critical view of current practices.

PUNISHMENT
AND RESPONSIBILITY

Psychiatric involvement in criminal court proceedings is intimately linked to the question of punishment. If society did not wish to punish those who have transgressed against it, there would be little need for the psychiatrist to enter the courtroom. It is not essential to review the historical origins of punishment nor attempt to document the extent to which punitive measures are directed against the criminal in American society; it need merely be noted that punishment in America is severe. Our prison sentences are longer than those imposed in most other countries. Our correctional techniques are relatively harsh. And most discouragingly, we probably execute more people for nontreasonous behavior than any other nation in the world.[1]

Reprinted from *Wisconsin Law Review,* 379 (Spring 1966), pp. 379–401, by permission of the author and publisher.

[1] There are three reasons why society might choose to punish its offenders. It is sometimes assumed that punishment helps to rehabilitate the offender. Penitence is believed to be good for people; it hopefully cleanses them of their sins and makes them recognize and cling to "good" instead of "evil." A second reason for punishment is retribution. The society which has been attacked has some need to retaliate. Vengeance is a powerful

In spite of the many questions that could be raised as to the utilitarian or moral value of punitive attitudes toward the criminal, punishment for antisocial behavior has been with us since the dawn of history, is especially characteristic of American criminology, and will very likely be with us for many generations to come. Punishment of offenders is, however, flexible. If the society would simply agree to punish any person who committed an antisocial act irrespective of his intent, his age, his mental status, or his socioeconomic class, there would be no need for psychiatric testimony. But such a state of affairs obviously cannot be. A democratic society is guided by the principle that "our collective conscience does not allow punishment where it cannot impose blame."[2] It inevitably moves to temper cruelty or indiscriminate punishment. Humanitarian sentiments have become inextricably interwoven with punitive goals. Since the nineteenth century, for example, few civilized nations have punished children under the age of seven. People who commit crimes under duress or under reasonable apprehension of immediate danger of death or grievous bodily harm (self-defense) are not likely to be punished harshly. Similarly, the person who accidentally injures another (as in an auto accident) is not likely to be subjected to stern measures. The guiding principle in determining who should be punished has been that those who of their own free will and with evil intent (sometimes called *mens rea*)[3] commit acts which violate the law shall be criminally responsible for such acts.[4] Presumably the child under seven, the person who accidentally violates the law, or the person who violates the law under duress does not have criminal intent.

As early as the seventeenth century, English jurists such as Coke and Hale proposed that mental illness could totally or partially preclude the possibility

motivation and the psychological need of society to punish its criminals has been well documented. A third reason for punishing criminals is the belief that punishment has a deterrent value. It is hoped that the person who is disciplined will not be inclined to commit a similar crime. It is also believed that he will serve as an example to the rest of the population who will be sufficiently encouraged to resist temptation. If the commitment of a criminal act carries with it the threat of punishment, we assume that most rational people would be less inclined to behave in an antisocial manner.

Whether punishment helps to rehabilitate the majority of criminals is certainly debatable on scientific grounds. The need for society to gain vengeance against the criminal can be questioned on moral grounds. A rational justification of the value of punishment must primarily be based upon its deterrent effect. There is probably agreement that fear of punishment deters many people from committing crimes. It should be emphasized, however, that the deterrent value of punishment has a direct relationship to the degree of rationality of the prospective criminal. The unreasonable offender would be less likely to be favorably influenced.

[2] *Holloway v. United States,* 148 F.2d 665, 666–67 (D.C. Cir. 1945).

[3] It should be noted, however, that not all crimes involve the element of intent or mens rea. See, *e.g.,* Myers, "Reasonable Mistake of Age: A Needed Defense to Statutory Rape," 64 *Mich. L. Rev.,* 105, 109–19 (1965).

[4] Rubin, *Psychiatry and Criminal Law,* 52 (1965).

of an individual having felonious intent.[5] Over the past three centuries jurists and psychiatrists have continued to examine the proper punishability of a criminal offender who is adjudged to be mentally ill. The extent to which mental illness has been thought to preclude criminal intent has been greatest at those times when humanistic principles have been in ascendency. It is tempting and not too difficult to convince ourselves that the person who is intoxicated or organically confused cannot have evil intent when he commits a criminal act.[6] If we can believe that a mentally ill person is under duress, is compelled to commit a criminal act, or cannot help himself, we are less inclined to punish him.

Another way of looking upon our legal codes is to note that punishability is equated with the criminal's responsibility for his actions. The psychiatrist is directed toward the specific task of examining the emotional status of the allegedly mentally ill offender and toward assisting the court in determining whether or not he can be held responsible for his actions. If the offender is judged to have been too emotionally disturbed at the time of the crime to have possessed evil intent (or sometimes if the evil intent is based on a presumption of severe mental illness), he is not responsible and not punishable. Without, for the moment, commenting on the social practicability of this arrangement, the writer will briefly examine some positions that have been taken on the issue of responsibility and ask, does the psychiatrist possess any special knowledge or skills which enable him to judge an individual's responsibility for a given act?

The extent to which man can be considered responsible for his behavior is a broad philosophical question which transcends legalistic considerations. If a person is assumed to be morally, personally, religiously, or legally responsible for his behavior, it must be assumed that he has some freedom of action. Whether man's behavior is completely determined by hereditary and environmental circumstances beyond his control or whether he actually possesses "choice" or "free will" is a question which has preoccupied theologians, philosophers, and other scholars for centuries. There is clearly much variation between scientific and legalistic or theological viewpoints. The behavioral scientist most often is a "hard" determinist.[7] He believes that all behavior is determined by the impact of uncontrollable environmental experiences upon

[5] Guttmacher & Weihofen, *Psychiatry and the Law,* 433–34 (1952).

[6] The writer takes a somewhat different stand. While certain kinds of external conditions may be necessary causes of some crimes, other determinants must include motivations which arise out of the organism's need to maintain a state of equilibrium. We all have antisocial impulses. It can be argued that the most seriously confused man who commits a crime such as murder did indeed intend to kill even if his act was unreasonable and would not have occurred if he had been well. The act belongs to the man. He could have been confused and behaved in a thousand different ways.

[7] For a firm exposition of the "hard"-determinist viewpoint, see Eysenck, *Crime and Personality, passim* (1964).

inherited personality characteristics. If he were to be consistent, he might argue that ultimately no person is responsible for his behavior.

Yet, no society which follows a doctrine of nonresponsibility has ever been known to exist. The existence of a legal code implies that man must be held accountable for his actions. All theology teaches us that man has choice. Indeed, it seems impossible for man to survive without some belief in his capacity to exercise free will. The determinist might argue that social change and the fullest kind of human development could take place in a society which denied the existence of free will, but man has never been willing to give up his belief in the notion.

For most of us the absence of free will implies a degraded or subhuman condition. If we argue that the child under seven, the lunatic, or the imbecile cannot be held responsible for his behavior, we also seem to be saying that they cannot be looked upon as real people. It is of interest to note that even those individuals who are defined as having minor forms of mental illness (such as neurotics who claim to be unable to help themselves) are usually looked down upon by the rest of society when they imply that they are not responsible for their behavior. To communicate that one does not have choice (in the absence of measurable interfering factors such as a clearly defined physical illness) admits weakness and requires an abdication of status.[8]

It has been argued that it is society's need to punish which brings psychiatry face to face with the philosophical question of man's responsibility and his capacity to exercise free will. Particularly where the death penalty is involved, however, punishment makes the question of responsibility and free will more than a philosophical exercise. The criminal's life may depend upon the psychiatrist's assessment of his responsibility. Yet, any definitive statement which the psychiatrist offers as to the responsibility of the offender must have a certain inconsistency. If he argues that a man is responsible for his behavior, he begins to compromise certain tenets of scientific determinism. If he insists that a man is not responsible, he argues against ethical codes and traditions which seem to have always been necessary to preserve a smoothly functioning society. The existence of this dilemma is rarely acknowledged and many psychiatrists continue to believe that psychiatric examination and certain psychiatric concepts help to clarify decisions as to man's responsibility. Society unfortunately encourages the psychiatrist to participate in such decisions by setting up legal rules which seek to test the

---

[8] No amount of education or "brainwashing" can convince the public that the neurotic person should not be held responsible for his behavior. This may be a manifestation of society's demand that such a person rejoin the rest of us and assume his responsibilities as a whole man. Whether or not free will actually exists, a belief in its existence and an assumption of personal responsibility on the part of all citizens seems to be essential to the survival of any society.

degree of man's responsibility in terms of the degree of his psychological impairment.

RESPONSIBILITY
AND MENTAL ILLNESS

Perhaps the earliest measure which psychiatrists utilized to assess responsibility was the degree of unreasonableness of the offender's behavior. A criminal act which seems totally alien to any goal that a rational man would pursue has traditionally been looked upon as a sign of illness. Both psychiatry and the culture as a whole are often willing to assume that the unreasonable man is a sick man and that a sick man is not responsible for his actions. Depending upon prevailing concepts of mental illness, a characterization of unreasonableness as sickness has often led to an assumption that unreasonable behavior is determined by external and mysterious agents. In eras when mental illness was approached from a more theological standpoint, efforts were made to place the responsibility for sick behavior on external "devils" such as incubi or succubi.[9] With the advent of Kraepelinian psychiatry, responsibility for sick behavior was placed upon physical disease. Mental illness was thought of as being caused by hereditary or acquired organic impairment and the structural defect was held responsible for such an individual's unreasonable behavior.[10] Even today unreasonable behavior is often blandly described as mental illness and that illness is characterized as a separate, viable, and pernicious external agent. Such a demonological concept of mental illness has never been supported by scientific data and represents a form of psychiatric thinking which is totally inconsistent with modern adaptational or homeostatic viewpoints. Unreasonable behavior is not an external happening and can be quite adequately understood in terms of the individual's conflict with his society.

With the growth of psychoanalytic knowledge many psychiatrists have sought answers to the degree of man's responsibility in terms of the unconscious component in human behavior. The argument here is that if an individual behaves in an unreasonable manner because of motivations of which he is unaware, then he cannot really help himself and should not be held responsible for his actions. Thus some psychoanalytic observers have argued that free will exists only to the extent that a person is aware of his motivations. Choice, according to this viewpoint, is available in inverse proportion to the amount of behavior or thinking which is dominated by unconscious processes.[11]

---

[9] Zilboorg & Henry, *History of Medical Psychology,* 145 (1941).

[10] Veith, "Psychiatric Nosology: From Hypocrates to Kraepelin," 114 *American J. Psychiatry,* 385 (1957).

[11] Overholser, *The Psychiatrist and the Law,* 42 (1953); Zilboorg, *The Psychology of the Criminal Act and Punishment,* 92 (1954).

While the writer is deeply impressed with the role of the unconscious in determining behavior, he can see little value in utilizing this concept to clarify the problem of responsibility or free will. First of all, the degree to which motivation is unconscious is always relative. Psychiatrists have devised no means of measuring how close to the surface awareness may be, and it must be acknowledged that every act carries with it a mixture of conscious and unconscious elements. Any psychiatrist is, therefore, on highly tenuous grounds when he uses this criterion to say that a man is responsible for one of his acts but not for another. Furthermore, the concept of out-of-awareness forces mitigating responsibility subtly personifies the unconscious and relegates it to the role of a dangerous and unpredictable external agent. Used in this sense, it is as though the unconscious is a lurking shadow hidden somewhere in the soul of each individual, waiting only for the opportunity to commit some heinous act. This kind of thinking might lead to regrettable statements such as, "It was not I that committed this offensive act but my unconscious mind." Such a notion assumes that a person's unconscious motivations are not a part of the individual in the same sense as his conscious motivations. It is in effect a denial of the existence of the organism as an integrated unit.[12]

Another way of looking at the psychoanalytic viewpoint is that an individual should not be held responsible for his actions if he is responding to internalized conflicts or misperceived oppression. While this at first glance appears to be a humanitarian notion, it could in practice grossly discriminate against the offender who is responding to more readily observable stress. Actually, the person whose criminal behavior is primarily engendered by poverty or persecution may be motivated by forces which are just as powerful and unrelenting as those which motivate the emotionally disturbed offender. Crime may be necessary for survival in either case. If the psychiatrist can be persuaded to argue that the presence of unreasonable behavior which is largely determined by unconscious factors makes a man nonresponsible, then perhaps the sociologist should be urged to argue that poverty, discrimination, and delinquent associations would also make the criminal nonresponsible. Either observation would be compatible with a deterministic viewpoint.

Paradoxically, the psychiatrist who would excuse the criminal from responsibility for his unconscious motivations cannot allow the same luxury to those patients he hopes to treat. Psychotherapy requires the patient to adhere

---

[12] It should be noted that while some psychiatrists have placed themselves in the position of arguing that he who is primarily motivated by unconscious forces should not be punished, this same logic could be utilized to come up with an opposite answer. It could be argued, for example, that a person who is not familiar with his unconscious and who is not able to make free choices represents a greater danger to his fellow man. Since he has not familiarized himself with his unconscious, he has neglected an obligation to a free society and should be punished.

to a code of responsibility. Responsibility in this sense may be divorced from the issue of punishment and can be thought of more accurately as personal accountability. The psychiatrist expects each of his patients to be willing to account for his behavior, to try to explain why he acts in a given way, to accept the praise of others when he acts favorably, and to accept the censure or disapproval of others when he is offensive. Although the patient is sometimes reassured that he cannot help himself, he is more frequently told that his eventual cure or rehabilitation lies within himself. Psychiatrists regularly remind their patients that getting well is dependent upon how determined they are to change, how willing they are to work on their problems, and how much responsibility they assume for their own behavior.

The psychoanalytic movement is dominated by the values of individualism, freedom, and maturity. It attempts to do away with the vision of gargantuan forces moving man, trying rather to teach the patient that he is capable of controlling his behavior. No psychiatrist would allow a patient to disavow responsibility for an aggressive or erotic thought or act. Even in a classical psychoanalytic situation the patient is taught that his unconscious wishes are his own productions and that they are not the visitations of an external devil.[13] Freud at one time stated:

> Obviously one must hold oneself responsible for the evil impulses of one's dreams. What else is one to do with them? Unless the content of the dream (rightly understood) is inspired by alien spirits, it is a part of my own being. If I seek to classify the impulses that are present in me according to social standards into good and bad, I must assume responsibility for both sorts; and if, in defense, I say that what is unknown, unconscious and repressed in me is not my "ego" then I shall not be basing my position upon psychoanalysis.[14]

The psychoanalytic movement is not alone in holding to such beliefs. Existential schools of therapy are similarly concerned with the needs of the patient to recognize and "be at one" with his feelings and impulses.[15] Progress is measured by such therapists in terms of their patients' movement toward fully knowing, accepting, and taking responsibility for their thoughts and actions. This applies to the most disturbed patients — those labelled as

---

[13] It might be noted that such an orientation is not necessarily contradictory to a deterministic viewpoint. By asking the patient to behave "as though" he were responsible, the psychiatrist changes one of the factors which might determine that person's future behavior. In the same manner society's insistence on personal responsibility is one of the factors which determines the behavior of its citizens. Behavior would be quite different if our society gave up its belief in free will. Yet the behavior of a society which either believed or disbelieved in the concept could be looked upon in similar deterministic terms.

[14] Freud, "Moral Responsibility for the Content of Dreams," in 19 *Complete Psychological Works of Sigmund Freud,* 131 (1961).

[15] See, e.g., Boss, *Psychoanalysis and Daseinsanalysis, passim* (1963); Rogers, *On Becoming a Person, passim* (1961).

psychotic — as well as to those who are better integrated. When psychiatrists enter the courtroom and testify that certain mentally ill people are not responsible for their behavior, they speak against philosophies which many of them feel are essential to therapeutic effectiveness. This inconsistency or effort to "have it both ways" is confusing and illogical.

Familiarity with the dynamics of unreasonable behavior or of the unconscious does not endow the psychiatrist with any special insights into the controversy between determinism and free will. In fact his statements in court are often inconsistent with his practice in the consultation room or hospital. The psychiatrist can describe why a person behaves in a certain way, but he is in no better position to judge that man's moral or legal responsibility than any other citizen. Unfortunately, the rules by which he is allowed to present his information to the court confuse the whole issue even further.

COURTROOM TESTS
OF RESPONSIBILITY

In most jurisdictions the rule by which a mentally ill person is adjudged legally responsible or not responsible is derived from nineteenth-century English law. This rule, enunciated in *M'Naghten's Case* over a hundred years ago, states that

to establish a defence on the ground of insanity, it must be clearly proved that, at the time of the committing of the act, the party accused was labouring under such a defect of reason, from disease of the mind, as not to know the nature and quality of the act he was doing; or, if he did know it, that he did not know he was doing what was wrong.[16]

The psychiatrist who testifies in a case in which the plea of insanity has been raised is asked to give his opinion as to whether at the time of the crime the offender knew the nature and quality of the act and knew that it was wrong. If the patient is presumed to know the nature and quality of his act and recognizes its wrongness, he is presumed to be responsible. If the psychiatrist answers these questions negatively, there is a possibility that the offender will not be held responsible for his behavior. Although the final decision is made by a judge or jury, the psychiatrist who responds to the *M'Naghten* test (whether he is the witness of the defendant or the state) is really asked to make a judgment as to the responsibility and hence the guilt or innocence of the offender.[17]

---

[16] M'Naghten's Case, 10 Cl. & F. 200, 210, 8 Eng. Rep. 718, 722 (H.L. 1843).

[17] It can be argued that the psychiatrist is not too different from other expert witnesses, but this is not the case. Most expert winesses testify only

The *M'Naghten* rule has been a subject of almost endless controversy.[18] Since it deals with the question of intent, it has a great deal of appeal to attorneys. It is, however, so alien to current concepts of human behavior that it has been vigorously attacked by psychiatrists. The obvious difficulty with the rule is that practically everyone, regardless of the degree of his emotional disturbance, knows the nature and quality and rightness or wrongness of what he is doing. Stated differently, almost any offender knows what he is doing when he commits a criminal act, and although he may feel that he is without choice, he also knows that his fellow citizens will be critical of his actions. Efforts have been made to extend the limits of meaning of the word "know" so that emotional as well as intellectual aspects of behavior can be introduced into the psychiatrist's testimony.[19] Psychiatrists, however, have rightly pointed out that it is almost impossible for them to testify honestly under this rule.[20] Bernard Diamond has stated:

> Whenever a psychiatrist is called upon to testify, under the *M'Naghten* Rule of a knowledge of right and wrong, as to the sanity or insanity of a defendant, the psychiatrist must either renounce his own values with all their medical-humanistic implications, thereby becoming a puppet doctor, used by the law to further the punitive and vengeful goals demanded by our society; or he must commit perjury if he accepts a literal definition of the *M'Naghten* Rule. If he tells the truth — stating on the witness stand that just about every defendant, no matter how mentally ill, no matter how far advanced his psychosis, knows the difference between right and wrong in the literal sense of the phrase — he becomes an expeditor to the gallows or gas chamber.[21]

In 1954 a different rule was enunciated by Judge Bazelon, Chief Judge of the United States Court of Appeals in the District of Columbia. In ruling on the case of Monte Durham, the court of appeals said:

> [The rule we now hold] is simply that an accused is not criminally responsible if his unlawful act was the product of mental disease or mental defect.

as to facts and opinions in their own field of knowledge and are not regularly required to answer philosophical questions.

[18] See, e.g., Biggs, *The Guilty Mind*, 79 (1955); Glueck, *Mental Disorder and the Criminal Law*, 161 (1925); Hall, *Studies in Jurisprudence and Criminal Theory*, 275 (1958); Louisell & Diamond, "Law and Psychiatry: *Détente, Entente or Concommitance?*", 50 *Cornell L.Q.*, 217 (1965).

[19] Efforts to tamper with the meaning of the word "know" bring one deeper into the realm of arbitrariness. The writer has made it a practice to question inmates at a hospital for the criminally insane as to the rightness or wrongness of their act. A few (just like many criminals) will insist that their act was justified, but even the most deluded are able to verbalize that they have always known that their act was illegal and would lead to punishment.

[20] See, e.g., Diamond, "Criminal Responsibility of the Mentally Ill," 14 *Stan. L. Rev.*, 59 (1961); Waelder, "Psychiatry and the Problem of Criminal Responsibility," 101 *U. Pa. L. Rev.*, 378 (1952).

[21] Diamond, *supra* note 20, at 60–61.

We use "disease" in the sense of a condition which is considered capable of either improving or deteriorating. We use "defect" in the sense of a condition which is not considered capable of either improving or deteriorating and which may be either congenital, or the result of injury, or the residual effect of a physical or mental disease.[22]

The *Durham* rule is quite similar to that which has been applied in New Hampshire since 1869.[23] Many psychiatrists at first welcomed this ruling as a forward movement in the enlightened treatment of the criminal. It was believed that it would simplify psychiatric testimony and would allow for rational utilization of psychiatric knowledge. There has, however, been much disillusionment. Initially the *Durham* rule was criticized mainly by attorneys, but more recently psychiatrists as well have become skeptical of its value.[24] In spite of many efforts to extend it to other jurisdictions, its use has been almost entirely confined to the District of Columbia. Only a few of the major criticisms concerning the *Durham* rule will be listed and briefly discussed.

The rule is not concerned with the issue of *mens rea* or intent. It replaces a rule that can be understood and debated by laymen with a more nefarious and professionalized concept. As such it may present the psychiatrist with too much power to decide who is going to be punished or not punished.[25]

Durham reifies mental illness as a distinct condition and seems to assume that it can be readily defined. If the psychiatrist testifies that a crime is a product of mental illness, this almost implies that mental illness is a distinct force which exerts an external influence upon the organism. Such a notion is not consistent with current psychiatric concepts of behavior.[26]

There is a danger of circularity in the rule. If an offender is defined as mentally ill, this designation is largely based upon his unreasonable behavior during the crime. Both crime and mental illness are forms of adaptation and if the same behavior is used to diagnose both conditions, and if we then state that one condition causes the other, we are in a logically absurd position.[27]

Although the *Durham* decision has been hailed as a humanitarian achievement, it also makes a very sharp distinction between those criminals who are mentally ill and those who are not. It expresses little or no concern for the disturbed offender who may not be seen as mentally ill. In a sense it condones

[22] *Durham v. United States,* 214 F.2d 862, 874–75 (D.C. Cir. 1954).
[23] *State v. Pike,* 49 N.H. 399 (1869).
[24] Roche, "Criminal Responsibility and Mental Disease: Medical Aspects," 26 *Tenn. L. Rev.,* 222, 230 (1959); Savage, "Discussion of Watson's Article," 116 *American J. Psychiatry,* 297 (1959).
[25] Rubin, *op. cit. supra* note 4, at 81.
[26] Halleck, "Juvenile Delinquents: 'Sick' or 'Bad'?", *Social Work* (April 1962), p. 58.
[27] Szasz, "Psychiatry, Ethics and the Criminal Law," 58 *Colum. L. Rev.* 183, 190 (1958).

punishment of the ordinary offender and may distract from a humanitarian concern for the overwhelming majority of offenders.[28]

Durham opens the possibility of keeping people in mental hospitals for long periods of time even though they have not demonstrated evidence of social dangerousness or social violence. Some legal experts have argued that the *Durham* rule is so concerned with the interests of psychiatry that it neglects the humanitarian needs of potential offenders and can result in serious abridgement of civil liberties.[29]

SOME PRACTICAL CRITICISMS OF PSYCHIATRIC PARTICIPATION IN THE INSANITY TRIAL

In addition to criticisms of the theoretical basis of psychiatric testimony and the deficiencies of any legal test of criminal responsibility, it must be noted that many practical inconsistencies and injustices can arise through psychiatric involvement in the courtroom. Specifically, the writer wishes to elaborate upon the following three points. (1) For any form of criminal justice to be effective it must be consistently applied to all men regardless of race or social or economic status. The writer will note that the issue of criminal responsibility is raised with unusual selectivity. (2) Implied in any legal contest of criminality and criminal responsibility is an assumption that to find a man not guilty by reason of insanity and to send him to a state hospital is a merciful and humane act. In practice this is a highly questionable as-

---

[28] Rubin, *op. cit. supra* note 4, at 25.

[29] Szasz, *Law, Liberty and Psychiatry,* 70 (1963); Hall, "The Scientific and Humane Study of Criminal Law," 42 *B.U.L. Rev.,* 267 (1962).
    There are a number of other rules for determining criminal responsibility which have had sporadic usage or have been recommended by interested agencies. For a brief review of alternative proposals, see Rubin, *op. cit. supra* note 4, at 62. A list of these can be set out with the notation that all rules for determining responsibility can be subjected to the same criticisms which have been leveled against either *M'Naghten* or *Durham.*
    The irresistible impulse test has sometimes been added to *M'Naghten* as a test of responsibility. Under this test a defendant is not criminally liable if he "was unable to refrain from doing wrong in the commission of the acts charged." *Argent v. United States,* 325 F.2d 162, 172 (5th Cir. 1963). A different federal test of criminal responsibility is found in *United States v. Currens,* 290 F.2d 751, 774 (3d Cir. 1961): "The jury must be satisfied that at the time of committing the prohibited act the defendant, as a result of mental disease or defect, lacked substantial capacity to conform his conduct to the requirements of the law which he is alleged to have violated." The *Currens* statement is based in part on the test suggested by the *Model Penal Code* § 4.01 (Proposed Official Draft 1962), which states in its first subsection: "A person is not responsible for criminal conduct if at the time of such conduct as a result of mental disease or defect he lacked substantial capacity either to appreciate the criminality [wrongfulness] of his conduct or to conform his conduct to the requirements of the law." Finally, there has been some support for the use of a concept of diminished responsibility as set out in *People v. Gorshen,* 51 Cal. 2d 716, 336 P.2d 492 (1959).

sumption. (3) Effective utilization of the plea of criminal insanity implies that psychiatrists will come to eventual agreement on a workable definition of terms such as psychosis or mental illness. The writer contends that this is unlikely.

First, the use of psychiatric testimony to determine criminal responsibility is greatest in those states which have capital punishment. Here it should be noted, however, that not every emotionally disturbed offender who is on trial for his life uses this defense. Many factors other than the degree of emotional disturbance enter into the introduction of the insanity plea. Much depends on the circumstances of the crime, the availability of forensic psychiatrists,[30] the laws of the state, the attitude of the community, and the offender's socioeconomic class. In many jurisdictions, for example, it would be quite unlikely that an uneducated Negro offender would plead insanity or be found not guilty by reason of insanity.

Even in states which do not have a death penalty, the plea of not guilty by reason of insanity is not invoked in a consistent manner. In the State of Wisconsin there are at the present time eleven inmates confined to the state hospital for the criminally insane who have been found not guilty by reason of insanity. Of this number eight are murderers. There are probably no more than ten to twenty individuals who are currently free (some of whom have spent many years in a mental hospital) who have been acquitted by reason of insanity. This is a very small group when compared with the total number of offenders in the state, and is made up mainly of individuals who have murdered or committed other violent crimes. What is important to note here is that the plea of insanity is practically never raised unless there has been a violent crime. If some murderers are not responsible for their behavior, then it is difficult to understand why there are not forgers, burglars, car thieves, and sex offenders who are similarly nonresponsible. The explanation must be that the plea of insanity is raised only when there is a possibility of a long prison sentence.

[30] The guilt or innocence of an emotionally disturbed offender may become highly dependent upon the skills of the defendant's psychiatrist. The psychiatrist's manner of presentation, his personality, and his credentials may have as much influence upon the jury as his scientific data. In this sense having a good psychiatrist becomes quite similar to having a good defense attorney. Unfortunately, a good psychiatrist — like a good attorney — costs money. In many jurisdictions it is extremely difficult for a poor person to find competent psychiatric assistance.

It is only fair to note also that some jurisdictions do provide psychiatric assistance for the offender who wishes to plead insanity. In some states an impartial panel of psychiatrists may provide testimony as to the defendant's sanity. The State of Massachusetts goes even further — under the Brigg's law anyone charged with a capital offense and most felons are automatically examined to determine their sanity. See *Mass. Ann. Laws* ch. 123, § 100A (1965).

Several years ago the author and a colleague[31] studied the records of a group of offenders who were at that time committed to the Wisconsin State Hospital for the Criminally Insane after having been transferred from the Wisconsin State Prison. The issue of not guilty by reason of insanity had *never* been raised for these offenders, but they had nevertheless been too emotionally disturbed to remain in a prison. At the time of the study there were sixty such inmates living at the state hospital. Offhand, it might be assumed that these were relatively normal men who broke down under the stress of incarceration. This, however, was not the case. Over half of the inmates studied had a history of having spent time in a mental hospital before the commission of a criminal act. An additional twenty per cent, although not having a history of previous hospitalization, had revealed such overt peculiar behavior that the issue of insanity had been raised in the probation officer's presentence report. A number of these men had to be transferred to the state hospital almost immediately after their arrival at the prison.

It must be repeated that the emotional state of these men was never raised as a legal issue. Although even the most cursory kind of examination would have revealed the presence of what most psychiatrists would call mental illness, apparently nobody even wondered if these men were responsible for their acts. Since Wisconsin is an enlightened state which has an excellent tradition of social welfare, it is difficult to rationalize the cavalier disposition of these cases. Obviously, it must be that factors other than the degree of emotional disturbance preceding the criminal act operate in the selection of those who plead insanity. Whether these factors are the economic status of the offender, the type of crime he commits, his race, the attitude of local psychiatrists, the type of negotiated plea which is made with the district attorney, or the whim of the community, psychiatrists cannot be too proud of contributing to a system which offers one kind of justice for some men and another kind for others.

If one were to argue that although these men were defined as criminals they eventually ended up in the appropriate institution anyway, it would be difficult to disagree. The point is that if only a few offenders are found nonresponsible and if other disturbed offenders must find a circuitous route to the hospital, there is reason to be skeptical as to the value of psychiatry's humanitarian contribution in the courtroom. Those who support our current system of correctional justice should be troubled by the likelihood that the majority of emotionally disturbed offenders are never given an opportunity to plead insanity. The noble victories for humanism claimed when an occasional offender is found not guilty by reason of insanity pale in comparison to the grim indifference which society accords to a much larger group of men.

[31] Dr. Richard Thurrell, Assistant Professor of Psychiatry, University of Wisconsin.

Second, at the conclusion of a recent widely publicized trial in the State of Wisconsin,[32] some of the writer's colleagues were jubilant over what they perceived to be a victory for the forces of social welfare and righteousness. In this case a man had been found not guilty of murder by reason of insanity and was returned to the state hospital for the criminally insane. In spite of the enthusiasm which so many psychiatrists show for this kind of decision, there is reason to be skeptical of its humanitarian value. This particular offender had already spent several years at the hospital for the criminally insane, having been legally confined until he had shown sufficient improvement to be psychologically competent to stand trial. He was returning to an institution where he would continue to be deprived of freedom.

It is sometimes difficult to see what advantages are offered to the man who is committed to a hospital for the criminally insane. In the State of Wisconsin (which has one of the best of such hospitals) he is still sent to a heavy security institution. His cell is located behind several formidable locked doors and he is rarely allowed to leave the hospital grounds. Opportunities for receiving help are limited because the institution is chronically understaffed. (At the time of the particular case we are referring to, the state prison had approximately three times the amount of psychiatric and psychological help available as the state hospital.) Many of the men who are sent to the state hospital are retained for as long a period or longer than they would have been if given a criminal commitment.

It is true that punitive elements are less emphatically stressed at hospitals for the criminally insane than in prisons. Both types of institutions, however, are theoretically devoted to a program of rehabilitation. It is also true that in our society there may be punitive aspects to commitment to a state hospital which are reflected in social attitudes and which may be more devastating than legally codified punishment. For many the stigma of the mental hospital is more feared than the restraints of prison. Even seriously disturbed prison inmates may be reluctant to be transferred to a hospital setting. The mental illness role is resisted on the basis that dignity, self-esteem, and chances for an earlier release would be seriously compromised. Prison inmates sense that confinement to a hospital for the criminally insane is not an evasion of punishment nor a soft touch and that continued loss of freedom by confinement to an understaffed institution is a grim prospect whether it is called punishment or treatment.

Third, terms such as insanity, mental illness, psychosis, and neurosis may be definable for purposes of professional communication but they can never be refined so that they describe concrete categories. Value judgments invariably enter into any categorization of the individual patient, and although

---

[32] *State v. Esser*, 16 Wis. 2d 567, 115 N.W.2d 505 (1962).

there are criteria by which attempts can be made to separate the mentally
ill from the normal or the psychotic from the neurotic, these criteria are
necessarily vague and equivocal. They serve best in separating obvious disorders; they are of little value when applied to the borderline cases.

Criminal offenders tend to have personality disorders which are not readily
classifiable. The psychiatrist rarely sees offenders who are either overtly disorganized or who are in good psychological health. Because of the criminal's
propensity for action and because he is exposed to so many different kinds
of environments, he will show unusual variation in his mental status. It is not
uncommon, for example, to find an offender who is grossly disorganized
while awaiting trial, who is then fully coherent during court proceedings, who
later decompensates at the prison, and who still later appears to reintegrate
his personality when transferred to the state hospital. In cases such as this
the diagnosis of psychosis becomes almost a matter of chance. It is dependent
on the training, experience, and personal philosophies of the particular
psychiatrist who examines the offender and the circumstances under which
the offender is examined. Attempts to use such examinations to speculate as
to the offender's emotional state at the time of the crime are extremely un-
reliable. What too often happens is that the judge and jury are subjected to
a variety of opinions all of which may disagree and all of which may have
a certain relevance.

The problem can be illustrated more clearly by a hypothetical case. While
the example is fictional, everything recorded here has actually happened
more than once in the State of Wisconsin and certainly must have occurred
in other states.

Mr. K was arrested for the crime of forgery. While in the county jail he
was observed behaving peculiarly and the sheriff requested a psychiatric examination. A psychiatrist examined the patient and stated that he was
undergoing an acute schizophrenic reaction, that he was psychotic, and that
he needed immediate hospitalization. The judge then committed Mr. K to
hospital X for thirty days. At that institution a thorough examination was
conducted and it was concluded that Mr. K was suffering from a chronic
schizophrenic reaction, undifferentiated type and that he was not able to stand
trial. The judge then committed Mr. K to hospital Y (a hospital for the
criminally insane) until he was felt to be sufficiently recovered to stand trial.
After he had spent two months at hospital Y, the staff felt that the patient
was no longer psychotic and in their report expressed the view that he would
be more correctly labeled a passive-aggressive personality, aggressive type.
Mr. K was then returned to court to stand trial for his offense. At the time of
the trial, the patient's attorneys raised the plea of not guilty by reason of
insanity. Two psychiatrists testified that Mr. K was sane at the time of his
offense and two testified that he was not. During the course of a lengthy trial

a great amount of psychiatric testimony was heard, and in some ways there was considerable agreement among the psychiatric witnesses. They all agreed that Mr. *K* was a seriously disturbed person. They agreed that at times his behavior was ineffective and peculiar. There was further agreement that Mr. *K* needed treatment and that it would be of benefit to him. Yet when forced to strait-jacket their testimony into issues such as responsibility and mental illness, the psychiatrists disagreed violently. The judge found that Mr. *K* was sane and sentenced him to the state prison. Within two weeks after his arrival at the prison the patient became extremely disturbed, hallucinated, and unable to function. The prison psychiatrist found him to be psychotic and he was immediately transferred to state hospital *Y*. Within a month he appeared to have recovered and hospital psychiatrists recommended his return to the prison.

There are two problems here. One is that disturbed offenders show rapid fluctuations in their emotional state. The patient's immediate environment plays a major role in whatever psychological picture predominates at a given moment. A second problem is that even though Wisconsin psychiatrists are no less homogeneous than those in other states, they do differ widely in their concepts of psychosis and mental illness, particularly as applied to so-called borderline states. As human beings who hold to a variety of ethical positions, they also differ as to the degrees to which they would hold a man responsible for his behavior. These differences characterize not only individual psychiatrists but are also true at an institutional level. Thus one hospital may regularly utilize criteria of psychosis which are quite different from those preferred by another institution which may be located just a few miles away.

It is hoped the reader has noted that in the example given psychiatrists may have disagreed as to philosophical issues and problems of categorization, but there was general agreement as to what was wrong with the patient. The writer is not arguing that psychiatry is an inconsistent discipline nor that psychiatrists must always disagree with one another. When the psychiatrist confines himself to simply trying to understand and treat the disturbed individual, he uncovers dynamic patterns and uses techniques which are relatively consistent. In the courtroom, however, it often appears that psychiatrists are a group of inconsistent, disagreeable, and even ludicrous amateur philosophers.

THE URGE TO TESTIFY

At a time when attacks on the specialty of psychiatry and particularly forensic psychiatry are coming from so many directions, it might be useful to examine some of the possible motivations for psychiatric involvement in the problem of criminal responsibility. This writer is in strong disagreement with those authorities, psychiatric or otherwise, who speak of a conspiracy of forensic psychiatry to broaden its influence in the legal process and to gain financial rewards or status.[33] It is hard to believe that status or prestige seekers would be willing to risk the tremendous buffeting and criticism which is associated with courtroom testimony. The psychiatrist who enters the courtroom may receive a great deal of publicity but he is rarely likely to survive the experience without having to fend off serious attacks upon his dignity, his honesty, and his intelligence. It is also difficult to believe that the forensic psychiatrist is interested in money. As medical specialties go, forensic psychiatry does not pay very well. Courtroom work requires many hours of arduous preparation and the fees are rarely comparable to what the average psychiatrist can earn in private practice.

The most important reason for psychiatric participation in the criminal trial is humanitarian zeal to temper the harshness of punishment. Psychiatrists, perhaps more than other individuals, are repelled by cruelty, even when it is imposed by society. They are familiar with the malignant effects of arbitrary punishment and are deeply aware of the limitations of punishment in controlling behavior. In a case where capital punishment is at stake, the forensic psychiatrist fights to preserve the life of the disturbed offender. The passion and the degree of involvement which characterize all psychiatric writing and participation in legal issues serves as an indication of how deeply committed most psychiatrists are to social change in accordance with their own ethical and political principles.

A second possible reason for this dedication which characterizes forensic psychiatry seems to be more defensive. If one reads through psychiatric forensic literature, he gains the distinct impression that the authors feel that criticism of psychiatric intervention in the legal processes is criticism of psychiatry as a whole. It is as though psychiatry must justify itself by proving that it is capable of determining which offenders are mentally ill and nonresponsible. Of course, vigorous and sometimes vicious attacks upon forensic psychiatry have contributed to this attitude. Such attacks help to crystallize an evangelistic attitude towards the law and the correctional system. When psychiatrists respond so defensively to criticisms of their role in the legal process, they forget that it is neither their profession nor their knowledge which is being attacked. In fact the criticism is aimed at the particular social function or philosophical position assumed by those psychiatrists who react to the criminal trial as though it were a battleground upon which they must prove their mettle rather than a social ritual which meets the needs of a particular society.

---

[33] Hakeem, "A Critique of the Psychiatric Approach to Crime and Correction," 23 *Law & Contemp. Prob.*, 650 (1958); Hall, "The Scientific and Humane Study of Criminal Law," 42 *B.U.L. Rev.*, 267, 274 (1962).

The final and perhaps least admirable reason for psychiatric participation in the insanity trial might be that it affords an exciting distraction from the sometimes tedious medical work of diagnosis and treatment. While the psychiatrist certainly undertakes serious risks to his dignity and status when he enters the courtroom, he also becomes a participant in one of the most exciting rituals our society is capable of creating. There is no mistaking the fantastic intellectual and emotional appeal of a public trial in which the defendant pleads not guilty by reason of insanity. A number of bestselling novels have been written on the subject and the tremendous amount of newspaper space devoted to such trials testifies to their seductive quality. Where the entire future of a man is at stake and where the deepest secrets of his intimate life are to be revealed in public, other men become involved, take sides, and hold and express opinions.

The psychiatrist is not immune from these temptations. If he is a person who enjoys intellectual challenge, who is articulate, and who is not too shy to participate in public debate, he may well find his involvement to be extraordinarily meaningful. If together with these marvelously exciting qualities the psychiatrist is convinced that he is promoting social reform and helping his own profession, the urge to testify may overcome his intellectual doubts or his fears of public humiliation.

In spite of a high level of enthusiasm and commitment, it appears that the psychiatrist has been rather ineffective in influencing the law or promoting change in social attitudes toward the criminal. If the plea of not guilty by reason of insanity is now invoked with more frequency and is more often found to be an excusing condition, it is probably because society has independently changed some of its attitudes toward the criminal, and is willing to utilize psychiatry to provide a rationale for its wish to excuse certain offenders. In most sanity trials it is extremely easy to predict the outcome if even minimal information is available as to the type of crime committed, the status of the criminal in the community, and the attitudes of that community toward the offender. The psychiatrist is used to lend scientific authenticity to a social ritual; he is much more a pawn than a knight.

ARE THERE ALTERNATIVES?

Much of what is decided in the courtroom is influenced by an awareness of what happens to the offender once he is convicted. If our correctional system were more concerned with rehabilitation than with punishment, society would not be so preoccupied with finding the mentally ill nonresponsible. If we knew that the disturbed offender would be subjected to real treatment rather than neglect or cruelty, we would have little need to wrestle with unanswerable philosophical questions. One recourse for providing a rational role for psychiatry in the legal and correctional process is, therefore, dependent upon a radical alteration of many correctional practices.

An enlightened correctional system would employ psychiatrists for only two purposes: to help diagnose, treat, and rehabilitate all classes of offenders; and to help control dangerous offenders. If punishment were not the major issue, the criminal offender believed to be emotionally disturbed would be tried in court only with regard to the question of his actual commission of the crime. Mental illness would not mitigate criminal intent. All persons found to have committed a crime (except where *mens rea* did not exist for reasons other than mental illness) would be considered fully responsible. Psychiatrists and other behavioral scientists would be able to confine their role to assisting in the determination of what is to be done with the individual offender.[34]

Many systems have been proposed which would not allow the psychiatrist to testify as to responsibility, but would use him to aid in disposition and treatment. Even a brief list of psychiatrists who have advocated such changes is impressive. It would include men of such diverse orientations as Menninger, Roche, Haines, and Cameron.[35] These systems could be unwieldy, would certainly pose many new problems, and might require radical alterations in some of our laws and attitudes. We can note, however, that such systems have had some success in European countries, and there is no reason why they would not have similar value in this country.

Any radical change in our legal system would be subjected to vigorous scrutiny, and it is unlikely that the above-mentioned suggestions would be easily accepted by many segments of our society. Even if such changes are many years away, however, there are available to us today less radical means by which the psychiatrist could assist the judicial process and still not involve himself in the unresolvable question of man's responsibility. These methods would not tamper with the concept of *mens rea* applied to the seriously emotionally disturbed and would require only minimal alterations in our legal code.

The psychiatrist is the only expert witness who is asked to form opinions as to man's responsibility and man's punishability. The toxicologist may testify as to the amount of poison in a victim's body and give an opinion as

---

[34] An enlightened system of justice would have to do away with the death penalty. As long as we continue to execute people, psychiatrists and others will be tempted to perjure themselves for humanitarian purposes.

[35] See Roche, *The Criminal Mind,* 271 (1958) ; Cameron, "Did He Do It? If So, How Shall He Be Managed?" in *Proceedings of Midwestern Governors' Conference Interstate Workshop on the Mentally Disordered Offender,* 72 (1964) ; Haines, "The Future of Court Psychiatry" in *Criminal Psychology,* 282 (Nice ed. 1962) ; Menninger, "Verdict Guilty — Now What?", *Harper's* (Aug. 1959), p. 60.

to cause of death. The orthopedic surgeon testifies as to the degree of motor incapacitation and its possible causes. The fingerprint or ballistics expert gives opinions which are strictly limited to his field of competence. None of these experts is ever asked to give an opinion as to the guilt or responsibility of the offender. Only the psychiatrist is asked to testify and answer questions which go beyond his own training or competence.

There is no reason why the psychiatrist could not be allowed to testify like other expert witnesses: he could present all of the information available as to why a man committed a certain crime and as to the extent of his psychological impairment, without having to ponder whether the offender knew right from wrong or if one of his behaviors was the product of another. Under such a directive the psychiatrist would describe in detail the emotional state of the offender at the time of the crime without answering the impossible questions posed by *M'Naghten* or *Durham*. The judge or the jurors could then make up their own minds as to whether the offender possessed evil intent and should be punished. In making such decisions they would be assisted by psychiatric facts and opinions and not directed by the philosophical speculations of a single professional discipline. Ultimately, if the decision of responsibility is to be made at all, it must be entirely in the hands of the judge or the jurors. This form of psychiatric participation would facilitate their task by providing information instead of value judgments.

There are undoubtedly some who would argue that lay people could not decide on the responsibility of mentally ill offenders without receiving considerable direction from psychiatrists. The writer would strongly disagree with this view. If the community wishes to punish some and excuse others, it could just as easily make such decisions itself without forcing the problem upon the psychiatrist. As things stand today, the psychiatrist is often exploited to provide a pseudoscientific rationalization for actions which the community would take anyway. Changes in the current legal code which would make the psychiatrist more of an expert witness and the judge or jury more of a decision-making body would simply put each group into its proper and traditional role.

THE PROBLEM OF
PRETRIAL COMMITMENTS

One practical legal issue which society must face is what to do with the offender who does not appear to be well enough to stand trial. Irrespective of the stand it takes on the issue of criminal responsibility, a humane society cannot afford to have confused or disorganized citizens tried in its courts. It is unlikely that such persons could adequately defend themselves and receive a fair trial. In most jurisdictions an alleged offender who is unable to understand the charges against him, is unable to understand the proceedings which are to be invoked, or is unable to assist his counsel is judged incompetent. He is then committed to a unit for the criminally insane until he regains his competency. All such commitments are based upon psychiatric testimony which is heard by a judge.

On the face of it this appears to be a straightforward and humane procedure. One major problem, however, is that confinement to an institution for the criminally insane represents a loss of freedom and is experienced as a form of punishment. If the individual does not recover he can spend the rest of his life behind bars. If he recovers slowly he will still be spending time in confinement without having been convicted of a crime. Given the deplorable condition of so many of our hospitals for the criminally insane, opportunities for recovery may be sorely limited. This is complicated by the fact that some judges and district attorneys are quite reluctant to try certain individuals and therefore they subtly encourage their continued confinement in a hospital. Obviously, in such a situation the civil liberties of an emotionally disturbed offender are in great jeopardy. He may be deprived of constitutional guarantees for a speedy trial, and he is placed in a kind of double jeopardy since time spent in the hospital is not considered in terms of a future sentence. The gruesome kinds of injustice which have been perpetrated under this system have been exceptionally well described by Hess and Thomas, Szasz, and Rubin.[36]

Again we find that humanistic and conscientious psychiatrists have unwittingly contributed to social injustices. Many of the psychiatrists who testify on the issue of competency to stand trial are unfamiliar with conditions in hospitals for the criminally insane. Their frequent diagnoses of incompetency are intended to help sick people, but too often they result in only an arbitrary restriction of freedom. Part of the problem lies in the vagueness of terms such as ability to understand charges, ability to understand legal proceedings, or ability to assist counsel. Obviously these terms can only be defined quantitatively. Given a group of either normal or disturbed people, there are all degrees of ability to comprehend charges and proceedings or to co-operate.

In the writer's view, psychiatrists, particularly those who are psychoanalytically oriented, expect too much of a man before they call him competent. The greater proportion of the mentally ill and mentally defective who are now judged incompetent could probably do as good a job of protecting their interests in the courtroom as most other offenders of a similar socioeconomic class. It seems that with the enormous potential threat to civil

---

[36] See Rubin, *op. cit. supra* note 4, at 154; Szasz, *Law, Liberty and Psychiatry,* 159 (1963); Hess & Thomas, "Incompetency to Stand Trial: Procedures, Results, and Problems," 119 *American J. Psychiatry,* 713 (1963).

liberties involved, psychiatrists would do better to define incompetency only as the most severe case of deficiency, confusion, or disorganization. Under our current system it might be argued that this would result in a number of disturbed persons having to reach the mental hospital only after a criminal commitment. This, however, might be preferable to the frightening possibility of endless incarceration without trial.

Actually, if our hospitals for the criminally insane were upgraded to the level possible in modern psychiatry, the great majority of incompetent offenders (even if our definition of incompetency were restricted as above) would be able to recover sufficiently to return to court in a few months. The only major exceptions would be the brain-damaged and the severely defective. Unfortunately no hospital for the criminally insane approaches the adequacy of private psychiatric hospitals or even public ones. There is also great variability of policy in these hospitals. Some superintendents of hospitals for the criminally insane work diligently to return their patients to court as soon as it is humanistically possible; others do not. Some jurisdictions encourage the hospitals to return offenders as rapidly as possible; others do not. In order to improve the plight of the noncompetent offender there would not only be a need for better hospitals but also a need to exert moral pressure upon psychiatrists, judges, and attorneys to more diligently guard the right to a speedy trial.

Even if psychiatrists were more careful in defining competency and even if psychiatrists and attorneys were more diligent in returning offenders to court, there would still be serious problems. A certain number of the severely disturbed and the severely retarded would still not recover. After a year or two in a hospital for the criminally insane, some offenders simply do not change. What is to be done with this small but troublesome group?[37] One possibility would be to release these individuals from all criminal proceedings and give them a civil commitment. This would at least entitle them to the possibility of parole and release. A mentally defective person, for example, might never be legally competent but could become sufficiently well socialized so that he could live in his community. While the writer is not unaware of some of the hazards and potential injustices of civil commitment (especially when proof of deviant behavior is not established), this does seem like a more humane approach. It would allow the psychiatrist and the community to continue to restrain truly dangerous offenders in a method similar to that by which dangerous patients not faced with criminal charges are currently restrained.

---

[37] In the State of Wisconsin, the Department of Public Welfare can parole an incompetent offender at any time, providing the committing court does not object. This practice works well in the majority of cases. Sometimes, however, the court is reluctant to parole men who could be safely released without endangering others.

Status and Competence of Jurors

RITA JAMES SIMON

The determining of eligibility for jury service has been a problem of the legal profession since the inauguration of the jury as an integral part of our legal system. In recent years a series of cases concerned in part with the basis of jury selection have come before the courts.[1] The nature of the controversy over jury eligibility may be illustrated by Supreme Court and appellate court decisions, the former emphasizing representativeness, the latter, qualifications:

> The American tradition of trial by jury, considered in connection with either criminal or civil proceedings, necessarily contemplates an impartial jury drawn from a cross-section of the community. This means that prospective jurors shall be selected without systematic and intentional exclusion of economic, racial, political, and geographic groups [Mr. Justice Murphy in *Smith v. Texas*].

> Nobody contends that the jury list must be a sample of the whole community. Minors and the aged are excluded, as are the infirm and those of unsound mind, and practically so are all the exempt. . . . Not only does the law exclude those groups we have just mentioned, but it excludes those who do not satisfy the very modest financial minimum still retained; and those also who cannot pass an examination as to the other prescribed qualities — intelligence, character, and information [Judge Learned Hand in *United States v. Dennis*].

Those who believe that the jury should be representative of the total adult population frequently urge criteria of jury service paralleling those of voting. They argue that the two are comparable instances of popular participation in a democratic society. Those, on the other hand, who believe that the jury should be composed of persons who have shown themselves to be capable of carrying out the assigned task compare the jury to the judge and argue that special qualifications are necessary. Locating the jury somewhere in between the voting public and the judge helps us to state the problem more concretely. It is true that, if we consider the functions jurors are expected to perform, there does appear to be a closer affinity with the judge than with the voting public, in that jurors are expected to decide problems that are dependent

Reprinted from *American Journal of Sociology*, 64 (May 1959), pp. 563–570, by permission of the author and The University of Chicago Press. Copyright 1959 by The University of Chicago.

[1] *Smith v. Texas*, 311 U.S. 128, 130 (1940); *Fay v. New York*, 332 U.S. 261 (1947); and *United States v. Dennis*, 183 F.2d 201. In addition, see W. S. Robinson, "Bias, Probability and Trial by Jury," *American Sociological Review*, XV (1950), 73–78; and John H. Wigmore, *American Judicature Society*, XVII (January, 1914), 15–17.

upon points of law. The similarity between jurors and voting public is not so dependent on function as it is on the principle that representation in law and government is a right of all citizens of a democratic society.

Those in favor of establishing criteria of competency have the additional obligation of presenting evidence of a significant relationship between competency and socioeconomic characteristics. Thus far there have been no data to indicate that restricting persons eligible for jury service on the basis of social or economic characteristics would have the effect of upgrading the level of jury competency. If, on the other hand, they argue that competency is unrelated to socioeconomic or demographic considerations, then they are obliged to suggest a tool for predicting competency that would have no implication for selection but which could be utilized after the jurors are already in the pools. Some gross notions of incompetency are already controlled, such as age, residence, physical or mental incapacity, and literacy; but no additional bases for delimiting competence have been suggested.

The data relevant to the problem of representativeness as against competency to be presented here have been gathered and analyzed as a part of the experimental jury research at the Law School of the University of Chicago. We shall present indexes of the performance of jurors of a range of status. Our aim is not to assign grades to jurors. We have not formulated correct responses to the resolution of a problem, nor have we determined beforehand what the right verdict in a given case should be. In fact, we are almost wholly concerned with differences, by status, in the performance of jurors. In this article we shall report our findings for three types of behavior: the content and quality of jurors' contribution to the deliberation; the quality of the contribution as perceived by fellow jurors; and ability of jurors to withstand, accept, or succumb to group pressure. In addition, we seek knowledge of the relative performance of persons, classified by status, as they reach consensus in a face-to-face group, both to illuminate a little-studied phenomenon of stratification and to provide a factual basis for procedural decisions in the management of juries.

The two hundred and forty jurors to be discussed in this article heard a criminal trial in which a plea of insanity had been entered in defense of an act of housebreaking. They were selected at random from the jury pools of the Chicago and St. Louis Circuit and municipal courts. Their instructions were: "Today you will listen to a recorded trial and deliberate, just as you would on any other case." Before the trial began, they were asked to fill out a questionnaire eliciting the same information as that obtained by lawyers during the pretrial, or voir dire, examination.

The deliberations of ten of the twenty juries who listened to the case have been transcribed, and their content has been analyzed.[2] Each "burst" of

---

[2] These deliberations were selected so as to maintain the proportion of

Table 1: Relative Participation, by Education and Sex (Percentage)

Education	Male	Female	Combined
College	14 (23)[a]	10 (9)	13 (32)
High school	9 (31)	7 (20)	8 (51)
Grade school	4 (27)	5 (9)	4 (36)
Combined	9 (81)	7 (38)	8 (119)

[a]*Frequencies are in parentheses.*

speech was scored into four mutually exclusive categories: originator re-cipient; content usage; verdict implication; and active-passive quality. The analytic unit, a "burst" of speech, is the successive remarks of a speaker before he is interrupted by another. A measure of participation was obtained as a by-product of the content analysis. Differences in performance at-tributable to status will be sought by comparing thirty-two jurors with col-lege educations with thirty-six jurors who went no further than grade school. In the final section, when the number of jurors increases from one hundred and twenty to our full set of two hundred and forty (12×20), the two groups we are comparing increases from thirty-six to seventy-six and from thirty-two to fifty-eight.

It is the male jurors and jurors with a college education who participate most in the group discussion (Table 1), corroborating the relationship be-tween participation and status previously reported of civil actions.[3] In the previous paper we reported that, in jury deliberations, participation is an indicant of power, that high participation and high status are positively cor-related, and that jurors with high participation are perceived by their fellows as helpful during the deliberation. In this article, using a different set of juries, we shall examine the quality of participation to provide further in-formation on the competence of jurors, according to status.

The categories described below were evolved to parallel this conception of the jurors' task. Members of the jury were instructed by the court that they were to deliberate on a case until they arrived at a unanimous verdict. Dur-ing the deliberation they were expected to review accurately the testimony

"Guilty" and "Not guilty by insanity" verdicts obtained under the alternative instruction forms for the full set of twenty deliberations.

[3] F. L. Strodtbeck, R. M. James, and C. Hawkins, "Social Status in Jury Deliberations," *American Sociological Review,* XXII (1957), 713–19; re-printed in E. Maccoby, T. Newcomb, and E. Hartly (eds.), *Readings in Social Psychology* (New York: Henry Holt & Co., 1958), pp. 379–88.

they heard, share with their colleagues relevant personal experiences, and, when necessary, accurately apply the rule of law given to them by the court. The categories employed are:

1. *Reference to the court's instructions.* A speech is scored "instruction" when it refers to any phase of the instruction which the court has read to the jurors, informing them which law is to govern them in their deliberations. Such a reference may be accurate or inaccurate. [Accurate — Inaccurate.]

2. *Reference to the testimony.* A speech is scored "testimony" when it refers to any fact which was brought out during the trial. Such a reference may be accurate or inaccurate. [Accurate — Inaccurate.]

3. *Opinion on the facts of the case.* A speech is scored "opinion" when it refers to a juror's opinion on some piece of information which was brought out during the trial. It may be pertinent or not. [Pertinent — Non-pertinent.]

4. *Experiences from personal and daily life.* A speech is scored "experience" if it refers to an event or opinion not mentioned during the trial or if it is not based on information brought out during the trial. It is an observation or an opinion emanating from the juror's experience which he carried with him into the courtroom. It may be pertinent or not. [Pertinent — Non-pertinent.]

5. *Procedural.* A speech is scored "procedural" when it is concerned with the form or movement rather than the substance of the discussion. A comment concerned with keeping the discussion going is scored "facilitative," while a comment which hinders it is scored "disruptive." [Facilitative — Disruptive.]

It is plausible to believe that college-educated persons are probably accustomed to formal group discussion; business conferences, for example, may well be part of their daily work activities. On the other hand, persons with grade-school educations who work as manual laborers or who are housewives will probably find their roles in the deliberation relatively new and uncomfortable. How do these predispositions affect the quality of their participation as jurors? Do highly educated jurors respond more to the rule of law; that is, do they spend more of their time on the court's instructions? Do they assume greater responsibility for maintaining an orderly discussion and therefore devote more of their comments to procedure? Do less-educated jurors lean more heavily on insight derived from personal experiences, thereby participating more in opinion and experience?

The figures in the "Combined" column (Table 2) show that jurors spend at least half their time exchanging experiences and opinions either directly or indirectly related to the trial. About a quarter of the time is spent on procedural matters, and, of the remaining quarter, 15 per cent is spent reviewing the facts of the case and 8 per cent on the court instructions. Jurors with grade-school educations differ significantly from jurors with high-school and college educations in that they place greater emphasis on the substantive

Table 2: Relative Content Usage, by Education (Percentage)[a]

Content category	Grade school	High school	College	Combined
		Education		
Instruction	6	8	8	8
Testimony	18	15	15	15
Personal and daily life-experience	26	22	21	22
Opinions on trial	32	27	30	29
Procedural	18	28	26	26
Total	100	100	100	100
Bursts	766	3,092	2,024	5,882

[a] $[\chi^2_{8d.f.} (.99) = 20.1, \chi^2 = 40.88\ P < .01.]$

categories concerned with testimony, personal and daily life-experiences, and opinions based on the trial and less on procedure and instruction. Jurors with high-school and college educations are similar to each other, save for the fact that the former contribute fewer comments in the "opinion" category.

We reported in the earlier paper that the foreman was usually a person of higher social status than his fellow jurors. In these deliberations six of the foremen had a college education and four had a high-school education. In addition, the foreman contributed a disproportionately high percentage of his comments to the instructions and procedure. When the foreman's participation is removed, the total chi-square contribution is reduced, but the lesser participation of the jurors with grade-school education in the procedural and legal categories remains significant.[4]

Along with observing the substance of the participation, we were interested in providing some bases for evaluating the quality of each contribution. Does the contribution have a positive or negative implication for carrying out the jury's task? Of each factual or informational contribution, we asked: "Is this accurate?" (i.e., "Does the statement appear in essentially the same context in the trial or the judge's instructions?"). Of each opinion we asked: "Is this pertinent?" (i.e., "Does the comment have implications for solving the group problem?"). And of each procedural comment we asked: "Is this facilitative?" (i.e., "Does it keep the discussion moving toward consensus?"). If differences do exist in the quality of contributions, are they attributable to variations in the jurors' education?

Perhaps the most striking fact about Table 3 is the high percentage of

[4] $\chi^2_{8d.f.} (.99) = 20.1, \chi^2 = 33.13\ P < .01.$

Table 3: Qualitative Content Usage, by Education (Percentage)

Content category	Education Grade school	High school	College
Instruction (percentage accurate)[a]	41	68	60
Testimony (percentage accurate)	71	78	78
Personal and daily life-experience (percentage pertinent)	61	55	57
Opinions on trail (percentage pertinent)	78	82	83
Procedural (percentage facilitative)[b]	74	74	80

$$^a[x^2_{2d.f.} (.99) = 9.2, x^2 = 11.39 \ P < .01.]$$

$$^b[x^2_{2d.f.}(.95) = 6.0, x^2 = 7.61 \ P < .05.]$$

accurate and pertinent comments made by all the jurors in each category, especially in the categories concerned with the recall of testimony and in the opinions derived from the facts of the case. Even the level of pertinency of comments based upon personal experiences does not fall below 55 per cent; only in the references to court instructions is there a cell below 50 per cent. The accuracy of the grade-school jurors' interpretation of the court's instructions is significantly less than that of the high-school and college jurors; and the concern for facilitating the group discussion is significantly greater in the college-educated jurors than in any of the others. There are no significant differences in pertinency of opinion or accuracy in recall of testimony.

As noted, there were two other categories into which each burst of speech was scored: the verdict implication and the active-passive quality of the comment. In contrast to the adversary tone of the trial, more than half of the jurors' contribution to the deliberation is the exchange of information and opinions that has no immediate implication for or against the defendant. The neutral comments predominated in all three groups:

Education	Percentage neutral
College	60
High school	68
Grade school	60

While high-school jurors do tend to make slightly more neutral comments, the differences among the three groups are not significant.

Concerning the active-passive dimension, which is based upon whether the

Education	Percentage active
College	64
High school	64
Grade school	50

$$x^2_{2d.f.} \, (.99) = 92, \, x^2 = 36 \; P < .01.$$

comment represents an idea or opinion or mere agreement with a previous speaker, there is the following distribution:

While at least 50 per cent of the contributions to the deliberation have been scored as active, the grade-school jurors' contributions are significantly less so than that of the others.

The differences based on education described in the content analysis do not fully determine the quality of the deliberations. This type of analysis does not, for example, describe the process whereby the inaccurate comments of one juror are corrected by another; or the relative attentiveness with which different comments are received; or how the timing of a comment is likely to effect the final decision. For these reasons the information in the content analysis was supplemented by consideration of the ratings jurors received from their fellows on the post-deliberation questionnaire.[5] In the previous paper, as well as more generally in the literature on small groups, level of participation is reported as being positively associated with votes received. In the present case we wish to determine if the same relative amount of participation produces comparable votes for jurors of different educational levels.

Table 4 indicates two things. Jurors who rank first, second, and third in participation receive the highest rating; jurors who rank tenth, eleventh, and twelfth, the lowest. In addition, the less-educated jurors who are in the top half of the participation ranking receive a slightly higher rating than the more highly educated jurors of the same rank, while less-educated jurors in the bottom half receive a lower rating than their more-educated colleagues.

In the American system each juror is expected to have a vote in the decision, and in most jurisdictions, especially in a criminal case, the verdict must be unanimous.[6] Phrased as they are, these two requirements leave un-

---

[5] Within each jury, half the jurors were asked to circle the location on the seating chart of "the four jurors whom you feel really helped the group arrive at a verdict." The other half were asked to circle the seats of "the four jurors whom you feel you would like to have serve if you were on trial." The sum of the votes received is the acceptance score.

[6] The unanimity rule applies to a wide range of civil cases; where it does not apply, a strong majority of jurors, nine or ten of the twelve, is required.

Table 4: Acceptance Rating, by Participation Rank and Education

Participation rank	College	Education High school	Grade School
1-2-3	6.4 (15)[a]	6.4 (13)	7 (2)
4-5-6	3.6 (9)	3.6 (13)	4.1 (7)
7-8-9	4.5 (6)	4.1 (12)	2.3 (12)
10-11-12	3 (1)	2 (13)	.7 (16)

[a]*Frequencies are in parentheses.*

resolved the difficult question of what a juror is (or, as is more frequently the case, a group of jurors are) to do when he finds himself at odds with the more pervasive opinions of the group. Is he expected to abide by his own convictions even if by so doing he "hangs" the jury? Or should he concede to the wisdom of his colleagues and resolve his differences in favor of the majority? This is a difficult decision, especially since the members of the jury may have argued for several hours, and both sides may have presented reasonable arguments and may be in agreement concerning the facts they have heard. Which jurors fulfil more appropriately the role expectations — the jurors who concede to their colleagues or those who stand resolute in face of strong opposition? The court tells members of the jury that cases which result in a "hung" jury are usually retried, which is costly. On the other hand, the court also tells the jurors that a quotient verdict in civil cases (i.e., a verdict that is reached by taking the average of the award favored by each of the twelve jurors) is not a proper verdict. In other words, the norms are broad and ambiguous enough to provide support for being reasonably persuaded or for holding one's own position.

To examine better the problem of persuasion and coercion, we first divided the two hundred and forty persons who sat on the twenty criminal juries into five mutually exclusive patterns based on verdict.[7]

Taking first just those whose individual pre-verdict concurred with the group, we asked: "Within each jury how many of their fellow jurors was it necessary to win over before the group arrived at a unanimous decision?" We

---

[7] Two jurors did not fit into any of the categories because the pattern of their verdicts was:

Pre-Verdict	Group	Post-Verdict
NGI	NGI	Guilty

We believe that this somewhat illogical pattern may be attributed to a coding error, and, in the absence of any other explanation, they have not been included.

Table 5: Verdict Patterns of Unanimous and Hung Juries

Designation	Pre-deliberation	Verdict pattern Group	Post-deliberation
		Unanimous juries	
1. Concurred	{ NGI[a]	NGI	NGI
	{ Guilty	Guilty	Guilty
2. Pressured	{ NGI	Guilty	NGI
	{ Guilty	NGI	Guilty
3. Convinced	{ NGI	Guilty	Guilty
	{ Guilty	NGI	NGI
		Hung juries	
4. Reversed	{ NGI	Hung	Guilty
	{ Guilty	Hung	NGI
5. Resisted	{ NGI	Hung	NGI
	{ Guilty	Hung	Guilty

[a]*NGI = Not guilty by reason of insanity.*

then examined, jury by jury, the number in the opposition, keeping separate the educational groups.

As indicated in Table 6, the greater the number of jurors in the opposition, the less the likelihood of winning them over. This seems to hold across educational categories with minor fluctuations. When the juries are divided almost evenly, college-educated jurors appear to be slightly more effective persuaders; but, when the opposition is either very strong or very weak, the jurors with a high school education are most effective. Grade school persons

Table 6: Percentage of "Concurred" Jurors, by Education and Opposition

No. opposing jurors	Education Grade school	High school	College	Combined
0-4	76 (25)[a]	81 (37)	77 (13)	79 (75)
5-6	29 (31)	31 (45)	43 (28)	34 (104)
7-11	17 (12)	33 (27)	21 (19)	26 (58)
Combined	14 (68)	48 (109)	43 (60)	237[b]

[a]*Frequencies are in parentheses.*

[b]*Three jurors did not check both of their individual verdicts; thus there are 237 rather than 240 respondents.*

Table 7: Jurors, by Verdict Pattern and by Education

Category	Education Grade school	High school	College	Combined percentage
		Unanimous juries		
Concurred	44	48	43	46 (109)[a]
Pressured	9	6	15	9 (21)
Convinced	16	23	18	20 (47)
		Hung juries		
Reversed	9	2	5	4 (11)
Resisted	22	21	19	21 (49)
Combined	100 (68)	100 (109)	100 (60)	(237)

[a] Frequencies are in parentheses.

appear to be consistently, but not significantly, less effective in winning over dissenters to their views. It appears then that the relative incidence in the juror-opposed categories is not significantly different; and thus the remaining patterns of verdicts may be viewed simultaneously.

The combined percentages (Table 7) show that almost half of the jurors, 46 per cent, had in fact reached consensus before the deliberation began and that during the discussion an additional 29 per cent were persuaded, at least to the extent that a unanimous verdict could be reported. In addition, it may be noted that jurors in each educational group are randomly distributed across the categories. There is no tendency for any group to be overrepresented in the concurred, pressured, or convinced groups; nor is there a tendency for any class of juror to be overrepresented in the hung juries. The above statement is accurate with one slight exception. In the reversed group, that is, persons who participated in hung juries but who shifted their individual verdicts during or after the discussion, there is some tendency toward the overrepresentation of grade-school jurors. However, since they comprise only 4 per cent of all jurors, there is no adequate reason for rejecting the null assumption of equal representation in all verdict patterns.

The indexes of competence reported in this article have been derived from the experiences of twenty juries all of whom were exposed to the same criminal trial, involving a plea of insanity. The fact that the defendant committed the act of housebreaking was stipulated at the outset by the defense attorney. Much of the testimony that the jury heard was by expert witnesses — in this case, psychiatrists. The jurors' task was to determine whether or not the defendant should be held responsible for his actions; and, unlike the typical criminal trial, his guilt was not disputed.

Whether this kind of case with its heavy dependence on psychiatric information is the most suitable instrument for testing the relative performance of jurors of different status has not been demonstrated. One could argue that the specialized testimony would make it an extremely sensitive instrument for evaluating status differences. On the other hand, national surveys indicate that the general public's knowledge of psychiatry is very limited.[8] To the extent that the jury is representative of the general public and does not include the professions, one could expect that the differences in performance would be relatively slight. We do know that the task jurors were asked to perform in this case was a special one, considering the wide variety of tasks jurors are expected to perform. It is premature and unwise to generalize until further work has been carried out on civil and other types of criminal trials.

Concerning this set of data, the general and most significant impression that we are left with is that all jurors, regardless of status, indicate a real concern for carrying out the prescribed task in a thorough and conscientious manner. During the deliberation the evidence presented in the trial is reviewed and evaluated. The personal experiences of individual jurors are taken into account, and the discussion maintains a degree of tentativeness quite unlike the adversary nature of the trial. For the fear that, although the jury numbers twelve, the decision, or basis of power, rests with one or two "strong men" we found no substantial ground.

Grade-school jurors speak less frequently in the "instructions" and "procedural" categories, and, when they do speak, their remarks are significantly less accurate and more disruptive. In addition, grade-school jurors' contributions are more frequently passive than are the contributions of their more-educated colleagues. Nevertheless, jurors who are high participators are rewarded by their fellow jurors without regard for their educational attainment. To this extent, the participants in the deliberation set the standards. Participation is valued, and those who are allowed by the group to contribute to producing it are rewarded. Those who hang back or who are forced out of the discussion receive few votes; and, among the low participating, combination of low participation and low education results in low acceptance.

It is when we turn to the institution to supply indexes of competency that our task becomes considerably more difficult. The directives from the court are broad and ambiguous enough to legitimate a great variety of behavior. For example, the responses of jurors in the "pressured" category might be interpreted by the court to mean that these jurors were shirking their responsibility, as formulated: "Each juror shall have an equal vote, and the

[8] Shirley A. Star, "The Place of Psychiatry in Popular Thinking" (paper given at the annual meeting of the American Association for Public Opinion Research, Washington, D.C., May, 1957).

decision must represent the unanimous thinking of all the jurors." Or they might be interpreted as acting wisely and rationally; recognizing that it is impossible to convert the others to their view, they fell in with the majority verdict rather than hang the jury. Then, given the opportunity, they expressed their differences in private. The responses of jurors in the "concurred" category might be interpreted by the court to mean that they were assuming a disproportionate share of the responsibility for determining the verdict or that the effect they had on their fellow jurors was untestable. The responses of jurors in hung juries might be interpreted by the court as a failure on the part of some to enter the deliberation with an open mind, or they might be taken to mean that, having listened and weighed carefully everything that was said during the deliberation, they could not in good conscience relinquish their own position. The experimental finding tells us that, whatever the interpretation, it is applicable to jurors irrespective of education, since there is no tendency for the college or the grade-school jurors to be overrepresented in any category.

In attempting to derive indexes of competence, we have not, as trial lawyers might have done, examined the relative strength of the defendant's in contrast to the prosecution's case, nor have we attempted to determine the "just verdict." We have gone instead to the deliberations themselves and derived measures of competency unrelated to the substantive issues of the case and based on a concept of the jury as confronting a problem whose solution they are to determine by means only broadly prescribed.

The Pattern
of Disagreement Between
Jury and Judge

HARRY KALVEN, JR. AND HANS ZEISEL

This study seeks to answer two basic questions: First, what is the magnitude and direction of the disagreement between judge and jury? And, second, what are the sources and explanations of such disagreement?. . .

Although any distinctive function of the jury must be found in the possibility of disagreement between judge and jury, there is something curious in the question how much judge and jury agree and disagree. No prior expectations exist either among the legal profession or in legal tradition as to what a proper amount of disagreement between judge and jury should be. We lack a pre-existing context in which to place the measurements. You may find it amusing to make your own private guess and to see whether it overestimates or underestimates the amount of actual disagreement.

Table 1 reports for the full sample of 3576 cases the actual verdict of the jury and the matching hypothetical verdict of the judge. Since the jury may acquit, convict, or hang, where realistically the judge may only acquit or convict, the verdicts distribute in six cells.[1]

Table 1 thus furnishes the basic measure of the magnitude of judge-jury disagreement. Reading the two shaded cells first, we obtain the percentage of cases in which judge and jury agree. They agree to acquit in 13.4 per cent of all cases and to convict in 62.0 per cent of all cases, thus yielding a total agreement rate of 75.4 per cent.

Looking next at the four unshaded cells, we see that the total disagreement, 24.6 per cent of all cases, consists of $(16.9 + 2.2 =)$ 19.1 per cent of cases in which judge and jury disagree on guilt, and $(1.1 + 4.4 =)$ 5.5 per cent of cases in which the jury hangs.[2]

Reprinted from *The American Jury,* by Harry Kalven, Jr. and Hans Zeisel, pp. 55–63, 106–117 (Boston, 1966), by permission of the authors and Little, Brown and Company.

[1] Though to be precise Table 1 is a sixfold table (2 x 3), it can serve to introduce its simpler prototype, the fourfold (2 x 2) contingency table (see Table 2 below). It matches the verdicts of jury and judge by confronting two dichotomies: *jury acquits* or *convicts* with *judge acquits* or *convicts.* Such a matrix is a remarkably economic expositive device. It enables us to see not only what juries and judges do independently (this is reflected in the pair of marginal percentages outside the quadrangle), but simultaneously, what they decide as against each other. See Zeisel, *Say It With Figures,* Chs. VIII and IX (4th ed., 1957). Table 1 has, of course, no provision for judges who "hang," but not surprisingly we had two cases (excluded from the sample) in which the judges stated that they simply could not make up their minds.

[2] The figure of 5.5 per cent hung juries conceivably understates somewhat

Table 1: Verdict of Jury and Judge (*in percentage of 3576 trials*)

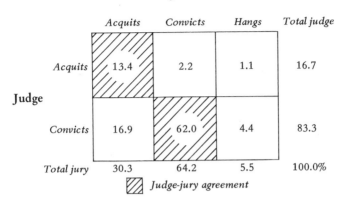

JURY

	Acquits	Convicts	Hangs	Total judge
Acquits	13.4	2.2	1.1	16.7
Convicts	16.9	62.0	4.4	83.3
Total jury	30.3	64.2	5.5	100.0%

(Judge, on left side)

▨ Judge-jury agreement

It is not easy to know what to make of these figures. To some, no doubt, the fact that judge and jury agree some 75 per cent of the time will be read as a reassuring sign of the competence and stability of the jury system; to others the fact that they disagree 25 per cent of the time will be viewed as a disturbing sign of the anarchy and eccentricity of the jury. We would suggest that the significance of these figures for any judgment about the jury must depend on the reasons for these disagreements and must wait upon the detailed examination of those reasons.

The inclusion of hung juries makes Table 1 somewhat awkward to handle. At times it will prove useful to employ the following convention in the counting of hung juries: a hung jury will be considered as in effect half an acquittal.[3] Accordingly in Table 2, Table 1 is rewritten by redistributing

the true frequency of hung juries. Since our instructions to the judges as to what constitutes a reportable jury trial were perhaps imprecise on the point, it is possible that some felt no need to report on what is technically a mistrial. However, the total lack of more reliable data on this point moved us to accept our figure.

[3] Before the hung juries are redistributed, it is worth noting that the judge's ratio of acquittals to convictions is roughly the same for cases where the jury reaches a verdict as for cases where the jury does not:

	Jury hangs	Jury decides
Judge acquits	1.1	15.6
Judge convicts	4.4	78.9
	5.5	94.5

Table 2: Verdict of Jury and Judge—Consolidated (*percentage of 3576 trials*)

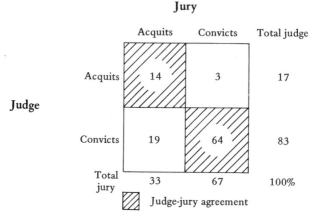

Jury

	Acquits	Convicts	Total judge
Acquits	14	3	17
Convicts	19	64	83
Total jury	33	67	100%

Judge

▨ Judge-jury agreement

the hung juries half to the acquittals and half to the convictions and rounding off to integers.[4]

It is immediately apparent in Table 2 that the jury's disagreement with the judge is massively in one direction, and the direction is the expected one. The jury has long been regarded as a bulwark of protection for the criminal defendant, and Table 2 can be taken to retell this story. There is some puzzle, however, as to how best to state the extent of this imbalance in favor of the defendant. After considerable deliberation over the point, we now conclude that the most meaningful statement is the simplest. The jury is less lenient than the judge in 3 per cent of the cases and more lenient than the judge in 19 per cent of the cases. Thus, the jury trials show on balance a net leniency

---

[4] This distribution is predicated on the experience that, as a practical matter, roughly half the hung jury cases end up having the same consequences for the defendant as an acquittal, either because his prosecution is dropped or because he is acquitted in a subsequent trial. This is based on an estimate we were given by an experienced prosecutor. We were unable to obtain reliable statistics on the final disposition of the hung juries. The practice varies according to jurisdiction. The Los Angeles Municipal Court, for instance, considers the final vote, and if a clear majority found the defendant guilty the case is retried. For data on that court, see generally, Holbrook, *A Survey of Metropolitan Trial Courts — Los Angeles Area* (1956). And, of course, some of the retried cases end in acquittal, if not in a second hung jury.

Compare also the English practice: "There is . . . no compulsion upon the Crown to re-indict a man, after a disagreement of the jury, but it is the usual practice to re-indict once, and then, if the jury disagree a second time, to enter a *nolle prosequi* or consent to a directed acquittal. Sometimes, for special reasons, the Crown abandons a case after a single disagreement of the jury." Williams, *The Proof of Guilt,* p. 283 (London, 1955).

of 16 per cent. This means that in the cases which the defendant decides to bring before the jury, on balance, he fares better 16 per cent of the time than he would have in a bench trial.[5]

But this figure must not be made the basis for a general probability calculus by *any* defendant, because the cases to which this 16 per cent applies have been selected for jury trial *because* they are expected to evoke pro-defendant sentiments.[6]

Tables 1 and 2 summarize the most important area of disagreement between judge and jury, namely disagreement on acquittal and conviction. There are, however, further ways in which judge and jury can disagree in criminal cases, and, to round out the picture, we look now at the possibilities of disagreements on charge and on penalty. Such subsidiary disagreements arise from special characteristics of the case and from special provisions of the law which vary from one jurisdiction to another.

In a fair number of cases more than one charge is presented to the jury; hence, judge and jury can agree to convict but may disagree as to the charge.[7] Again, in some jurisdictions the jury is given the power to set the penalty, as in many southern states with respect to all crimes, and in almost all states with respect to the death penalty. Here, judge and jury may agree to convict and even agree on the charge (if there is more than one) but still disagree as to the level of penalty. In Tables 1 and 2 both these subsidiary disagreements are concealed as agreements to convict.

Table 3 provides the relevant data for disagreements on charge.

While the picture is somewhat complicated by the circumstance that almost forty per cent of the cases offer no possibility of disagreement on charge, nevertheless in these disagreements the jury once again shows a marked imbalance (4.5 per cent to 0.7 per cent) in favor of the defendant.

In an important sense, the 5.2 per cent enlarges the amount of disagreement between jury and judge and hence will be added to the universe of

---

[5] Another way of stating this is by comparing the marginal figures in Table 2. The jury acquits in 33 per cent, the judge in only 17 per cent of all trials. Thus, if all these cases had been tried without a jury, the acquittal ratio would be cut in half.

[6] This marked balance of leniency toward the defendant should not, however, be read as rendering unimportant the 3 per cent of the cases in which the jury reverses itself and is less lenient than the judge.

Essentially, we suspect the jury is non-rule minded. The fact that the jury's pro-prosecution sentiments do not come into play more often is due primarily to the selection of cases that come before it.

[7] The multiple charge may either be concurrent, such as assault and carrying a concealed weapon, where the defendant may be convicted or acquitted on either or both of the charges; or the multiple charge may arise from a doubt as to whether the defendant committed only a "lesser included offense," such as manslaughter instead of murder. Here the defendant can be found guilty of only one of these crimes, not of both. Lesser offenses are included most frequently where a specific intent is at issue, e.g., intention to kill as against intention only to harm.

Table 3: Jury and Judge Agree to Convict, May Disagree on Charge
(Percentage of 3576 Trials)

Verdict	Single charge cases	Multiple charge cases	Total
Judge more lenient[a]	—	.7	.7
Both agree	38.2	18.6	56.8
Jury more lenient[b]	—	4.5	4.5
Total	38.2	23.8	62.0[c]

[a]*Judge, in disagreement with the jury, would have found for lesser charge.*

[b]*Jury, in disagreement with the judge, finds for lesser charge.*

[c]*This 62.0 per cent appears in Table 1 and represents the trials in which judge and jury agree to convict.*

disagreement cases which it is the central objective of this study to analyze. For almost all purposes hereafter disagreements on charge will be considered as full units of disagreement.

The final opportunity for disagreement between judge and jury arises in those cases where the law allows the jury to set the penalty. To trace disagreements on penalty we need carry forward from Table 3 only the 56.8 per cent of all cases in which there was agreement on charge as well as on guilt; it is only in these cases that an independent disagreement on penalty can arise. Table 4 provides the relevant data. While the directionality is the same, the ratio of jury leniency to severity is more evenly balanced for disagreements on penalty than for those on guilt or charge.[8]

. . . Table 5 gives one last view of the full range of disagreement between judge and jury. Beginning with the disagreements on guilt and hung juries, it separates out from the agreements to convict the disagreements on charge, and finally from the agreements to convict on the same charge, the disagreements on penalty.

This then is the summary report on the magnitude and direction of judge-jury disagreement in criminal cases, in all its dimensions. Table 5 shows that

[8] The disagreement ratios for the four types of issues are as follows:

Area of Disagreement	Jury more lenient, percentage	Judge more lenient, percentage	Approximate ratio
Guilt	16.9	2.2	(8:1)
Charge	4.5	.7	(6:1)
Hung jury	4.4	1.1	(4:1)
Penalty	2.5	1.5	(2:1)

Table 4: Jury and Judge Agree on Conviction and Charge, May Disagree on Penalty (Percentage of 3576 trials)

	Percentage
Judge gives more lenient penalty	1.5
Jury and Judge agree on penalty	5.4
Jury gives more lenient penalty	2.5
Total	9.4[a]

[a]*In 47.4 per cent of the trials, judge and jury convict on the same charge, but since the judge sets the penalty no penalty disagreement can occur. Adding to these 47.4 per cent the 9.4 per cent penalty disagreement and the 5.2 per cent charge disagreement, we obtain the 62.0 per cent of the trials in which judge and jury agree to convict. See Table 1.*

even when hung juries, disagreements on charge, and disagreements on penalty are included, the general impression left by Table 1, is not substantially altered. . . .

What are the reasons or sources of the disagreement between jury and judge? The reasons seemed to fall into the following categories:

Evidence factors
Facts only the judge knew
Disparity of counsel
Jury sentiments about the individual defendant
Jury sentiments about the law

Since these labels are not self-explanatory, a brief description of each is provided. It should be stressed that, in each instance, the category locates a generic source of disagreement, without regard to whether it is the judge or the jury who is the more lenient.

Evidence factors. Although the traditional view of the jury is that it is largely concerned with issues of fact, it turns out to be surprisingly difficult to give a thumbnail sketch of evidence as a category of judge-jury disagreement. At times the jury may evaluate specific items of evidence differently; at other times the jury might simply require a higher degree of proof. Frequently evidentiary disagreement, in our usage, refers simply to the closeness of the case, which liberated the jury to respond to non-evidentiary factors. Under these special circumstances, issues of evidence, as we were able to handle them, are properly speaking not so much a cause for disagreement as a condition for it.

Table 5: Summary View of Judge-Jury Disagreement (Percentage of 3576 Trials)

Disagreement on *guilt*		19.1
Judge acquits	2.2	
Jury acquits	16.9	
Jury *hangs* while judge—		5.5
would have acquitted	1.1	
would have convicted	4.4	
Disagreement on *charge* only		5.2
Judge for lesser offense	.7	
Jury for lesser offense	4.5	
Disagreement on *penalty* only		4.0
Judge more lenient	1.5	
Jury more lenient	2.5	
Total disagreement		33.8%[a]
Judge more lenient	5.5%	
Jury more lenient	28.3%	

[a]The figures for disagreements on guilt and for the hung juries are taken from Table 1. The figures for disagreements on charge from Table 3 and those on penalty from Table 4. The figure which complements the 33.8 per cent disagreement for 100.0 per cent is 66.2 per cent; it represents the number of trials in which there is no disagreement between jury and judge, neither on guilt nor on charge nor on penalty.

Facts only the judge knew. Here the concern is with the occasional circumstance that, during or prior to the trial, an important fact will become available to the judge but not to the jury, such as whether the defendant had a prior specific criminal record or not. Whenever the judge notes such special knowledge on his part in a disagreement case, it has been taken as a reason for his disagreement. The rationale is that judge and jury were, in fact, trying different cases, and had the jury known what the judge knew, it would have agreed with him.

Disparity of counsel. It was possible to collect data systematically on how evenly counsel for prosecution and for defense were matched. This category covers the instances in which the superiority of either defense or prosecution counsel was given as one of the reasons for the jury's disagreement with the judge.

Jury sentiments about the individual defendant. The type of defendant involved in a criminal case can vary across the entire spectrum of human personality and background, from the crippled war veteran who evokes intense sympathy to the loud mouth who alienates the jury. In this category are included all reasons for judge-jury disagreement attributable to the personal characteristics of the defendant.

Jury sentiments about the law. This category includes particular instances of "jury equity," reasons for disagreement that imply criticism of either the law or the legal result. For example, the jury may regard a particular set of facts inappropriately classified as rape, because it perceives what might be called contributory negligence on the part of the victim. A similar notion may operate in fraud cases in which the victim first hoped for an improper gain. Thus, a broader concept, contributory fault of the victim, evolves as a defense to a crime. This general category of jury sentiments about the law includes roughly a dozen sub-categories of such jury sentiments.

There must remain, of course, a certain blandness and ambiguity about the major categories for the present. Since the purpose here is only to provide an over-all summary view of the explanations for judge-jury disagreement, these sketches will have to suffice. At this point the categories simply provide a handy device for summarizing the data. . . .

We are now ready to quantify the explanations for judge-jury disagreement. We begin with a revised version of the basic table of disagreement.[9]

The universe of disagreement can now be defined with precision. It comprises the disagreements on guilt, disagreements on charge, and the cases in which the jury hangs. Reading off the relevant figures from Table 6, it can be seen that this total universe of disagreement consists of 1063 instances that fall conveniently into six groups as follows. With Table 7 we establish a usage already adverted to which it will be convenient to follow henceforth. Cases of disagreement where *the jury is more lenient* than the judge will be called *normal* disagreements; cases where, in the less frequent situation, *the judge is more lenient* will be called *cross-over* disagreements. The precise quest of this study then is to explain what caused the disagreements in these 1063 instances, constituting 30 per cent of all trials.

We must adjust now for the circumstance that it was not possible to find an explanation for every case of disagreement. Table 8 presents the basic tabulation of success and failure in obtaining explanations.

No explanation was forthcoming in 101 out of 1063 cases, or about 10 per cent of all disagreements. The percentage is smallest for the disagreements on guilt and largest, as might be expected, for hung juries. The percentage of failures is, on the average, smaller for the cross-over cases than it is for the normal disagreements, suggesting that the reversal of the jury's normal response is so exceptional that explanations for it are easier to see. Sub-

---

[9] This table has not appeared previously in quite this form. It is a composite of Table 1 and Table 3.

Table 6: Judge-Jury Disagreements in the 3576 Trials

Jury

		Acquits	*Convicts*	*Hangs*
Judge	*Acquits*	Agreement	77	40
			2.2%	1.1%
	Convicts	603	26[a] 0.7%	157
			Agreement	
		16.9%	160[b] 4.7%	4.4%

[a] *Jury convicts of* major *offense; judge of lesser.*
[b] *Jury convicts of* lesser *offense; judge of major.*

tracting 101 from 1063 leaves 962 instances, or 90 per cent of all disagreement for which we have an explanation.

An exhaustive comparison of the 101 unexplained cases with the 962 explained cases revealed no marked differences between the two groups such as would suggest any peculiarities in the unexplained cases. We will therefore disregard these cases in future discussion, on the assumption that even if we knew the answers, they would not represent new sources of disagreement but would have satisfied some one of the established categories of explanation without changing their relative frequency.

In the future discussion, then, the relevant universe will be the 962 disagreements for which it proved possible to find an explanation. Table 9 reports the basic data for these cases in terms of the five basic reason categories.

The last column of Table 9 yields the first over-all measure of the relative

Table 7: Type and Direction of Disagreement

	Percentage	*Number*
Normal disagreements on—		
Guilt	57	603
Charge	15	160
Hung Jury	15	157
Cross-over disagreements on—		
Guilt	7	77
Charge	2	26
Hung Jury	4	40
Total disagreements	100%	1063

Table 8: Percentage of Unexplained Disagreements

Normal disagreements on			Cross-overs on			Total
Guilt	Charge	Hung	Guilt	Charge	Hung	disagreements
7%	11%	19%	3%	4%	15%	10%

roles of the five major reason categories in explaining the judge-jury disagreement. As might more or less be expected, in 79 per cent of all cases, or in four out of every five cases, the disagreement in whole or in part derives from evidence problems. At the other extreme, the over-all roles of disparity of counsel and of differential knowledge to which the judge is privy are low (8 per cent and 5 per cent), a result which in the case of disparity of counsel may cause surprise. A second result that may be unexpected is that in 50 per cent of the cases there is found a jury sentiment at odds with the law.

By way of gaining a preliminary perspective on the broader sources of disagreement, we see that, apart from evidence difficulties, the primary sources of disagreement are the jury sentiments about the law and about the defendant. Thus, the data in Table 9 give focus to a general theory of judge-jury disagreement.

The data permit another basic observation. The rank order of reasons which we obtained for the Total column, representing all cases of disagreement, remains the same for all six types of disagreements, whether it concerns guilt, charge, or the hung jury, and whether it is in the direction of greater

Table 9: Summary Explanation of Disagreement

	Normal disagreements on			Cross-overs on			Total disagreements
	Guilt	Charge	Hung	Guilt	Charge	Hung	
	%	%	%	%	%	%	%
Sentiments on the law	53	59	32	49	72	26	50
Sentiments on the defendant	23	27	17	28	20	3	22
Evidence factors	78	62	84	93	100	100	79
Facts only the judge knew	7	3	3	4	4	—	5
Disparity of counsel	9	6	9	5	4	—	8
Average number of reasons per case[a]	1.7	1.6	1.5	1.8	2.0	1.3	1.6
Number of cases	559	142	127	75	25	34	962

[a]Percentages add to more than 100 because, as indicated in the Average line, some cases have more than one reason, e.g., column one adds to 170 per cent or 1.7 reasons per case.

or of lesser jury leniency. But although the rank order remains the same, there is a difference in emphasis: sentiments on the law are most important in respect to disagreements on charge and least important to hung juries; hung juries show a higher level of evidence issues than do the other disagreements on guilt and charge.

Thus far we have counted each reason as one. It is helpful, however, to adjust for multiple reasons and reach a more precise estimate of the roles of the five categories. This is the function of Tables 10, 11, and 12.

Table 10 shows that for roughly half the disagreements there is more than one reason, but in no case were all five reason categories required, and in only 1 per cent of the cases were there four reasons.

Next we explore whether the five basic reason categories differ from each other in the degree to which they combine with other reasons as sources of explanation. Table 11 shows how dependent each of the five basic categories is.

Each of the reason categories appears more frequently in combination with other reasons than it does alone. Interestingly enough, it is the evidence category that appears alone most frequently, a point on which more will be said later.

The sharing of reasons is particularly interesting with respect to disparity of counsel and jury sentiments about the defendant, both of which combine with other reasons over 90 per cent of the time they operate. This fact has broad implications. Disparity of counsel, for the most part, will not make a difference by itself but will require materials which superior counsel can exploit; the implication is that the cases do not present such material evenly.

Table 10: Frequency of Multiple Reasons

Number of reasons[a] per case	Percentage	Number of cases
1	47	456
2	41	395
3	11	105
4	1	6
5	—	—
Total disagreements	100	962

[a]*The term "reason" refers here only to the five major categories. The multiplicity of reasons within one of these categories is ignored. One reason is treated as sufficient to bring the category into play. For example, the defendant may be a mother in one case, and a mother, a widow, and poor in a second case. Yet in each case Sentiments on the Defendant would be counted only once as a reason for disagreement.*

Table 11: Frequency With Which Major Reasons Appear Alone or With Other Reasons

	Sentiment on law	Sentiment on defendant	Issues of evidence	Facts only judge knew	Disparity of counsel
	%	%	%	%	%
Appears— alone	22	8	43	2	8
with other reasons	78	92	57	98	92
Total	100	100	100	100	100
Number of cases[a]	484	213	758	52	78

[a] *The number of cases adds to 1585 although there are actually 962 cases because the same case may appear again in two or more of the five columns.*

Again, sentiments about the individual defendant are seldom powerful enough to cause disagreement by themselves; rather, they gain their effectiveness only in partnership with some other factor in the case. The implication again is that for the defendant to be poor and crippled or beautiful and blonde is by itself rarely a sufficient stimulus for the jury to disagree with the judge.

Putting together the sheer frequency with which the reason categories appear in Table 9 and the perspective on multiple reasons gained in Tables 10 and 11, it is possible to show the *power* of each reason category in explaining disagreement. We have adverted earlier to the process by which multiple reasons would be weighed; they are valued inversely to their frequency in the particular case. Making these weighting computations, one obtains the profile presented in Table 12.

Table 12 permits a major conclusion for a theory of judge-jury disagreement. By giving weights to each of the major reason categories, it states in the large, but with precision, the answer to the question: what causes jury and judge to disagree? Slightly over half the job of explanation falls to the evidence category. Apart from evidence factors, the explanation for disagreements resides principally in jury sentiments on the law or jury sentiments about the defendant. Perhaps the most interesting aspect of Table 12 is the salient role played by jury sentiments on the law in causing disagreements; jury equity looms as a significant factor.

The reason data can be arranged into one further profile. Reducing the categories to two, as in Table 13, by simply placing the evidence category on one side and the other four categories on the other, one gets a crucial image of the jury's performance in terms of *facts* on one hand and *values* on the other.

Table 12: Summary of Weighted Reasons

	Percentage
Sentiments on the law	29
Sentiments on the defendant	11
Issues of evidence	54
Facts only the judge knew	2
Disparity of counsel	4
Total	100
Number of cases	*962*

The conventional and official role of the jury, although it is not clear that anyone believes this, is that it is the trier of the facts and nothing else. Table 13 tells us that in only one third of the cases is the jury's fact-finding the sole source of judge-jury disagreement; in the remaining two thirds of the cases the sources of disagreement are to be seen fully only by looking beyond the official role of the jury. On the other hand, only 21 per cent of the disagreements arise from a source having nothing to do with the facts, but purely with values or sentiments. Thus, Table 13 serves to spotlight the peculiar difficulty that attends any effort to isolate the causes of judge-jury disagreement. The difficulty arises because to a considerable extent, or in exactly 45 per cent of the cases, the jury in disagreeing with the judge is neither simply deciding a question of fact nor simply yielding to a sentiment or a value; it is doing both. It is giving expression to values and sentiments under the guise of answering questions of fact. If the factual leeway is not present, the sentiments or values will as a rule have to be particularly strong to move the jury to disagree. Conversely, if only ambiguity in the facts is present, and the directionality of the sentiment is absent, the jury will be less likely to disagree with the judge. The decision-making patterns we are pursuing are subtle ones.

In one sense the basic task of this inquiry is now completed. Answers have been given to the question of how often judge and jury disagree and to the

Table 13: Values and Facts as Causes of Disagreement

Disagree on—	*Percentage*	
Facts alone	34	Total facts, 79
Values and facts	45	Total values, 66
Values alone	21	
Total	100	
Number of cases	*962*	

question of why they disagree. In another sense, of course, this presentation has served simply as an extended preface. There is an inescapable blandness about any discussion of jury behavior at such a level of abstraction and generality. The remainder of our book will be devoted to the task of giving precise content to these general findings.[10]

[10] Kalven and Zeisel, *The American Jury*, chapters 9–39.

Judicial Backgrounds
and Criminal Cases

STUART S. NAGEL

Various scholars of the judicial process have compiled data on differences in the backgrounds of American judges, but they have not shown that these background characteristics correlate with differences in the decisions of the judges analyzed.[1] Various other scholars of the judicial process have compiled data on the different decisional tendencies of American judges, but they similarly have not shown that these decisional propensities correlate with differences in the backgrounds of the judiciary.[2] It is the purpose of this paper to explore the empirical relationships between various background and attitudinal characteristics of judges and their decisions in criminal cases.[3]

THE RESEARCH DESIGN[4]

The judges analyzed consist of the 313 state and federal supreme court judges listed in the 1955 *Directory of American Judges;*[5] 15 judges so listed left the bench before the end of the year, however, and as a result were included in only certain portions of the study.[6] The background characteristics

Reprinted by special permission of the author and *The Journal of Criminal Law, Criminology and Police Science,* Copyright © 1962 by the Northwestern University School of Law, Vol. 53 (September 1962), pp. 333–339.

[1] *E.g.,* Schmidhauser, "The Justices of the Supreme Court: A Collective Portrait," 3 *M.W.J. of Pol. Sci.* 1 (1958); Ewing, *The Judges of the Supreme Court 1787–1937* (1938); Mott, "Judicial Personnel," 167 *Annals* 143 (1933).

[2] *E.g.,* Gaudet, "Individual Differences in Sentencing Tendencies of Judges," 32 *Archives of Psychology* 1 (1938); Iverson, "Human Element in Justice," 10 *J. Crim. L. & C.* 90 (1919); Pritchett, *The Roosevelt Court* (1948); Schubert, *Quantitative Analysis of Judicial Behavior* (1959).

[3] Non-statistical speculations on the relations between judicial characteristics and judicial decisions include Haines, "General Observations on the Effects of Personal, Political, and Economic Influences on the Decisions of Judges," 17 *Ill. L. Rev.* 96 (1922); Frank, *Courts on Trial,* 146–56, 165–85 (1950); Carr, *The Supreme Court and Judicial Review,* 231–57 (1942); and Hall, "Determination of Methods for Ascertaining the Factors that Influence Judicial Decisions in Cases Involving Due Process of Law," 20 *Am. Pol. Sci. Rev.* 127 (1926).

[4] For a more detailed analysis and justification of the judges, the cases, and the analysis used in the research design than can be given here see Nagel, "Testing Relations Between Judicial Characteristics and Judicial Decision-Making" (a mimeographed paper presented at the 1961 Midwest Conference of Political Scientists). Copies of this paper are available on request from the writer.

[5] *Directory of American Judges* (Liebman, ed., 1955). This source is sometimes referred to herein as the *Directory.*

[6] The term "supreme court" is used as synonym for "highest court" or

of the judges were determined by consulting the *Directory of American Judges, Who's Who in America,*[7] the *Martindale-Hubbell Law Directory,*[8] and the governmental directories published by many of the states. The attitudinal characteristics of the judges were determined on the basis of their answers to mailed questionnaires.

The cases analyzed consist of the full-court criminal cases which these judges heard in 1955. By full-court cases is meant cases heard by all judges in the sample from the court involved. By criminal cases is meant cases in which one party was charged with an act subject to fine, imprisonment, or other penalty owed to the collectivity rather than to the individuals who may have been particularly harmed. The cases involved both appeals and habeas corpus proceedings, and they centered around questions of guilt, punishment, or procedure. Tax and business regulation cases were excluded because they were analyzed separately in the larger study of which this paper is a part.

Each judge was given a decision score representing the proportion of times he voted for the defense out of all the times he voted in the criminal cases. For example, in the 21 Pennsylvania criminal cases,[9] Justice Arnold voted 3 times for the defense, resulting in a decision score of .14. Sometimes a judge did not vote clearly for either the prosecution or the defense, as where he concurred in part and dissented in part. In one Pennsylvania case,[10] Justice

"court of last resort." Statements in this paper describing the background characteristics of the judges are based on all 313 judges, except for those who did not supply the relevant background information. Statements describing the relations between backgrounds and decisional tendencies, however, are based on 298 judges (313 minus the 15 judges who left the bench before the end of the year), except for those who did not supply the relevant background information, who sat only on unanimous cases, or who sat on courts that were homogeneous as to the relevant background characteristics.

[7] 26, 27, 28 *Who's Who in America* (Sammons, ed., 1954, 1956, 1958).

[8] Martindale-Hubbell Inc., *Martindale-Hubbell Law Directory* (1955).

[9] *Commonwealth v. Burdell,* 380 Pa. 43, 110 A.2d 193 (1955); *Commonwealth v. Edwards,* 380 Pa. 52, 110 A.2d 216 (1955); *Commonwealth v. Mackley,* 380 Pa. 70, 110 A.2d 172 (1955); *Commonwealth v. Grays,* 380 Pa. 77, 110 A.2d 422 (1955); *Commonwealth ex rel. Dunn v. Ruch,* 380 Pa. 152, 110 A.2d 240 (1955); *Commonwealth ex rel. Lane v. Baldi,* 380 Pa. 201, 110 A.2d 409 (1955); *Commonwealth v. Chaitt,* 380 Pa. 532, 112 A.2d 379 (1955); *Commonwealth v. LaRue,* 381 Pa. 113, 112 A.2d 362 (1955); *Commonwealth v. Lane,* 381 Pa. 293, 113 A.2d 290 (1955); *Commonwealth v. Thompson,* 381 Pa. 299, 113 A.2d 274 (1955); *Commonwealth v. Mason,* 381 Pa. 309, 112 A.2d 174 (1955); *Commonwealth v. Cisneros,* 381 Pa. 447, 113 A.2d 293 (1955); *Commonwealth v. Bolish,* 381 Pa. 500, 113 A.2d 464 (1955); *Commonwealth ex rel. Matthews v. Day,* 381 Pa. 617, 114 A.2d 122 (1955); *Commonwealth v. Farrow,* 382 Pa. 61, 114 A.2d 170 (1955); *Commonwealth v. Capps,* 382 Pa. 72, 114 A.2d 338 (1955); *Commonwealth v. Wable,* 382 Pa. 80, 114 A.2d 334 (1955); *Commonwealth ex rel. Taylor v. Superintendent of the County Prison,* 382 Pa. 181, 114 A.2d 343 (1955); *Commonwealth ex rel. Bishop v. Maroney,* 382 Pa. 324, 114 A.2d 906 (1955); *Commonwealth v. Thomas,* 382 Pa. 639, 117 A.2d 204 (1955); *Commonwealth v. Moon,* 383 Pa. 18, 117 A.2d 96 (1955).

[10] *Commonwealth v. Edwards,* 380 Pa. 52, 110 A.2d 216 (1955).

Musmanno cast such a half-way vote, resulting in a decision score of 11½ out of 21 or .55.

The data were analyzed to determine what judicial characteristics, if any, were associated with a decision score above the average for a given court. For example, the question was posed whether being a Democrat rather than a Republican is associated with a decision score above the average for one's court. The answers to this and similar questions for the data used as presented in the Table which accompanies this paper.

The Table includes data for only those courts on which both groups compared are present, because if, for example, there are all Democrats or all Republicans on a court, then comparisons within the court between judges from the two parties cannot be made. The Table also includes data for only non-unanimous cases, because the unanimous cases have no bearing on who is above or below the average decision score of a court.

The probability scores listed in the far right column represent the probability of the observed differences occurring merely by chance, given the number of judges involved in each group.[11] Where the scores are less than .05 (i.e., less than 5 out of 100), the differences have been regarded as statistically significant and not merely attributable to chance, in accordance with conventional statistical procedures. In the discussion which follows, each row will be discussed separately, and an illustrative court will be described for each relationship which falls below the .05 level of chance probability.

THE RESEARCH FINDINGS

POLITICAL PARTY AFFILIATION

The first row of the Table tends to indicate that on the bipartisan supreme courts Democratic and Republican judges do differ from one another in deciding criminal cases. In 1955, 15 bipartisan state and federal supreme courts decided at least one non-unanimous criminal case on which all their judges sat. These courts were comprised of 85 judges who gave a party affiliation in the sources consulted. Fifty-five per cent of the 40 Democrats were above the average of their respective courts on the decision score, whereas only 31 per cent of the 45 Republicans were above the average of their respective courts on the decision score.

The California Supreme Court illustrates this statistically significant difference. Two of the California judges, Justices Carter and Traynor, declared themselves as Democrats in the *Directory*, and 2, Justices Shenk and Spence, declared themselves as Republicans. Justices Edmonds, Gibson, and Schauer

---

[11] Yuker, *A Guide to Statistical Calculations*, 64–66 (1958); Siegel, *Non-Parametric Statistics for the Behavioral Sciences*, 13–14 (1956).

did not indicate party affiliation. It is unusual for so many judges on a supreme court not to give party affiliation. The California Supreme Court, however, is not an elected court. Partly to eliminate partisan influence, the judges are appointed initially by the governor with the approval of a Commission on Qualifications, and they appear on the ballot for voter approval every 12 years thereafter. In 1955 only Missouri had a similar system of judicial election. In spite of this attempt to eliminate partisan divisions, Democrats Carter and Traynor were on opposite sides of Republicans Shenk and Spence in a large number of cases of different types. All 7 judges of the court heard 14 criminal cases together in which non-unanimous decisions were reached.[12] The 2 Democrats had an average decision score in these cases of 85 per cent for the defense, whereas the 2 Republicans had an average decision score in the same cases of only 18 per cent for the defense. In the famous Chessman case of 1955, for example, the only 2 dissenters in favor of the defense were Democrats Carter and Traynor.

Other supreme courts in which the Democrats had a higher decision score for the defense than did the Republicans include the supreme courts of Colorado, Idaho, Maryland, Michigan, Montana, New Jersey, Rhode Island, North Dakota, and Pennsylvania. Of the 15 courts with qualifying criminal cases, only the Illinois, New York, Ohio, Utah, and federal supreme courts followed an opposite pattern, although not to as great extent as the 10 courts which followed the general pattern.

PRESSURE GROUP AFFILIATIONS

Many of the judges were members of pressure groups which endorse various kinds of legislation. The types of pressure groups most frequently mentioned were professional groups (e.g., the American Bar Association), veterans' groups (e.g., the American Legion), business groups (e.g., chambers of commerce), and nativist groups (e.g., the Sons of the American Revolution). Decision scores of the judges who were members of these groups did not differ to a statistically significant extent from the decision scores of the non-member judges, with the exception of the scores pertaining to membership in the American Bar Association. The Table shows that 52 per cent of

[12] *Lyons v. Superior Court,* 43 Cal. 2d 755, 278 P.2d 681 (1955); *In re Chessman,* 44 Cal. 2d 1, 279 P.2d 24 (1955); *People v. Sykes,* 44 Cal. 2d 166, 280 P.2d 769 (1955); *Bompensiero v. Superior Court,* 44 Cal. 2d 178, 281 P.2d 250 (1955); *In re Bartges,* 44 Cal. 2d 241, 282 P.2d 47 (1955); *People v. Cavanaugh,* 44 Cal. 2d 252, 282 P.2d 53 (1955); *People v. Terry,* 44 Cal. 2d 371, 282 P.2d 19 (1955); *People v. Cahan,* 44 Cal. 2d 434, 282 P.2d 905 (1955); *People v. Berger,* 44 Cal. 2d 459, 282 P.2d 509 (1955); *People v. Jackson,* 44 Cal. 2d 511, 282 P.2d 898 (1955); *In re Hess,* 45 Cal. 2d 171, 288 P.2d 5 (1955); *People v. Acosta,* 45 Cal. 2d 538, 290 P.2d 1 (1955); *People v. Tarantino,* 45 Cal. 2d 590, 290 P.2d 505 (1955); *Calhoun v. Superior Court,* 46 Cal. 2d 18, 291 P.2d 474 (1955).

Table: How Judges of Differing Backgrounds and Attitudes Differ in Their Criminal Case Decisions; based on the non-unanimous cases of the state and federal supreme courts of 1955 on which both groups being compared are present.

Group 1 (hypothesized to be less defense minded)	Group 2 (hypothesized to be more defense minded)	Number of judges involved in each group		% of group 1 above their court average on the decision score[a]	% of group 2 above their court average on the decision score[a]	Difference	Probability of the positive difference being due to chance
		(1)	(2)				
Party							
Republicans	Democrats	45	40	31%	55%	+14	Less than .05
Pressure groups							
Members of a business group	Did not indicate such membership	15	71	47	52	+ 5	.20 to .50
Members of ABA	Did not indicate such membership	105	88	37	52	+15	Less than .05
Members of a nativist group	Did not indicate such membership	11	33	36	48	+12	.20 to .50
Occupations							
Former businessmen	Did not indicate such occupation	22	71	32	40	+ 8	.05 to .20
Former prosecutors	Did not indicate such occupation	81	105	36	50	+14	Less than .05

Characteristic					Difference	Significance
Education						
Attended high tuition law school	24	22	54	59	+ 5	.20 to .50
Attended low tuition law school						Negligible diff.
Age						
Over age 65	67	66	43	42	− 1	Negligible diff.
Under age 60						
Geography						
Practiced initially in small town	31	37	35	35	0	Negligible diff.
Practiced initially in large city						
Religion and Ancestral nationality						
Protestants	39	18	31	56	+25	Less than .05
Catholics						
High income Prot. denomination	54	54	41	50	+ 9	.05 to .20
Low income Prot. denonination						
Only British Ancestry	96	97	38	47	+ 9	.05 to .20
Part non-British ancestry						
Attitudes						
Low general liberalism score	22	23	27	57	+30	Less than .05
High general liberalism score						
Low criminal liberalism score	26	17	27	59	+32	Less than .05
High criminal liberalism score						

[a] *Decision score: proportion of times voting for the defense in criminal cases.*

the judges who indicated (in the *Directory, Who's Who,* or *Martindale-Hub-bell*) that they were not members of the ABA had decision scores above the average for their respective courts, whereas only 37 per cent of the judges who indicated that they were members of the ABA had such scores.

On the United States Supreme Court, for instance, Justices Black, Douglas, Frankfurter, and Minton did not indicate ABA membership, while Mr. Chief Justice Warren and Justices Burton, Clark, Harlan, and Reed, did indicate such membership. In the 9 full-court non-unanimous criminal cases of 1955, the 4 non-ABA members had an average decision score of 70 per cent for the defense, whereas the 5 ABA members had only an average decision source of 51 per cent.[13] Subsequent to 1955 the Chief Justice withdrew from the ABA on ideological grounds. If Warren were considered a non-ABA member in 1955, then the average decision score of the non-ABA group would move up to 71 per cent for the defense, and the average decision score of the ABA group would move down to 45 per cent for the defense.

PRE-JUDICIAL OCCUPATIONS

Many of the judges indicated that they had formerly held occupations other than the private practice of law. The types of occupations most frequently mentioned were prosecuting attorney, legislator, corporation counsel, business-man, teacher, public administrator, attorney general, and regulatory agency attorney. The pre-judicial occupations thought to have the most relevance to decisional differences among judges in criminal cases were those of busi-nessman and prosecuting attorney. Although judges who were former busi-nessmen tended to have a lower decision score for the defense in criminal cases than did judges who were not, the difference was not quite statistically significant. However, 50 per cent of the judges who did not indicate being former prosecutors had decision scores above the average for their respective courts, whereas only 36 per cent of the judges who did indicate being former prosecutors had such scores.

The Pennsylvania Supreme Court exemplifies the general pattern found on supreme courts having some judges who were former prosecutors. On this court, 3 of the judges (Justices Arnold, Bell, and Chidsey) indicated they had been prosecutors before becoming judges. In the 9 non-unanimous crim-inal cases which the full court heard in 1955, the other 4 judges in the court (Justices Jones, Musmanno, Stearne, and Stern) had an average decision score of 26 per cent for the defense, whereas the 3 judges who were former

---

[13] *Bell v. United States,* 349 U.S. 81 (1955); *In the Matter of Murchison,* 349 U.S. 133 (1955); *Quinn v. United States,* 349 U.S. 155 (1955); *Emspak v. United States,* 349 U.S. 190 (1955); *Bart v. United States,* 349 U.S. 219 (1955); *Williams v. Georgia,* 349 U.S. 375 (1955); *Donaducy v. Pennsyl-vania,* 349 U.S. 913 (1955); *United States ex rel. Toth v. Quarles,* 350 U.S. 11 (1955); *Michel v. Louisiana,* 350 U.S. 91 (1955).

prosecutors had an average decision score for the defense of only 7 per cent.[14] Mr. Justice Musmanno, the famous defense lawyer in the Sacco-Vanzetti case and other criminal cases, alone had a decision score of 94 per cent for the defense in these cases.

EDUCATION, AGE, AND GEOGRAPHY

Approximately one-third of the 313 supreme court judges serving in 1955 went to law schools whose annual tuition was under $120 in 1927 (the earliest year for which school-by-school tuition figures are available), and approximately one-third went to law schools whose annual tuition was over $240.[15] A higher percentage of judges who went to low tuition law schools (under $120) had decision scores above the average for their respective courts than did judges who went to high tuition law schools (over $240). This difference, however, was not statistically significant. Likewise there was no statistically significant difference between judges in the bottom third age group (under 60) and judges in the top third age group (over 65).

There was also no statistically significant difference between judges who practiced law initially in small towns with populations under 5,000 (the bottom third among the judges) and judges who practiced initially in large cities with populations over 100,000 (the top third among the judges).[16]

Because in this study comparisons are made only within courts, comparisons are not made between judges of different regions. If southern supreme courts were compared with northern supreme courts, however, one might hypothesize that the southern courts would have a higher per cent of judgments granted to the defense than would the northern courts because (1) violence is possibly more condoned in the south than in the north, except violence by a Negro against a white, (2) less efficient southern police are possibly more likely to bring innocent persons to trial than are northern police, and (3) southern lower courts are possibly more likely to commit reversible error than are northern lower courts.

[14] *Commonwealth v. Edwards,* 380 Pa. 52, 110 A.2d 216 (1955); *Commonwealth ex rel. Dunn v. Ruch,* 380 Pa. 152, 110 A.2d 240 (1955); *Commonwealth ex rel. Lane v. Baldi,* 380 Pa. 201, 110 A.2d 409 (1955); *Commonwealth v. Chaitt,* 380 Pa. 532, 112 A.2d 379 (1955); *Commonwealth v. LaRue,* 381 Pa. 113, 112 A.2d 362 (1955); *Commonwealth v. Mason,* 381 Pa. 309, 112 A.2d 174 (1955); *Commonwealth v. Cisneros,* 381 Pa. 447, 113 A.2d 293 (1955); *Commonwealth ex rel. Taylor v. Superintendent of the County Prison,* 382 Pa. 181, 114 A.2d 343 (1955); *Commonwealth v. Thomas,* 382 Pa. 639, 117 A.2d 204 (1955).

[15] Tuition figures for the last law school each judge attended were taken from Reed, *Review of Legal Education in the United States and Canada for the Year 1928* (1929).

[16] Population figures for the place of initial law practice of each judge were taken from 1 U.S. Bureau of the Census, Dep't of Commerce, *Census of Population,* 178–320 (1920). The year 1920 was the census year nearest to the year when the average judge among the 313 judges began practicing law.

RELIGION AND ANCESTRAL NATIONALITY

Most of the judges with entries in the *Directory of American Judges* listed their religion in response to the *Directory* questionnaire. There were too few Jewish supreme court judges to make comparisons between Jewish and non-Jewish judges. There were 11 supreme courts, however, which had some Catholic and some Protestant judges, and which heard some non-unanimous who indicated they were either Catholics or Protestants. Fifty-six per cent of the 18 Catholic judges had decision scores above the average for their respective courts, whereas only 31 per cent of the 39 Protestants had such scores.

This statistically significant difference is illustrated by the New Jersey Supreme Court. Justices Brennan and Heher indicated they were Catholics; Justices Oliphant, Vanderbilt, and Wachenfeld indicated they were Protestants; and Justices Burling and Jacobs gave no religious affiliation. In the 12 non-unanimous criminal cases which the full New Jersey Supreme Court heard in 1955, the 2 Catholics had an average decision score for the defense of 52 per cent, whereas the 3 Protestants had an average decision score for the defense of only 28 per cent.[17]

The members of certain Protestant denominations are traditionally thought to have a higher average income than that of members of other Protestant denominations. The relatively high income denominations are the Congregationalist, Episcopalian, Presbyterian, and Unitarian; and the relatively low income denominations are the Baptist, Lutheran, and Methodist.[18] When judges from each of the two groups sitting on the same supreme court criminal cases were compared, the judges from the relatively low income denominations tended to have a higher decision score for the defense than did the judges from the relatively high income denominations. The difference, however, was not quite statistically significant.

The ancestral nationality of each judge can be roughly determined by taking each judge's paternal and maternal family names or their component parts to Elsdon C. Smith's *Dictionary of Family Names* (1956), which in dictionary form gives the nationality origin of over 10,000 family names. If one compares judges whose ancestral nationality is exclusively British (which

[17] *State v. Schmelz,* 17 N.J. 227, 111 A.2d 50 (1955); *State v. Newton,* 17 N.J. 271, 111 A.2d 272 (1955); *State v. Low,* 18 N.J. 179, 113 A.2d 169 (1955); *State v. Cianoi,* 18 N.J. 191, 13 A.2d 176 (1955); *Johnson v. State,* 18 N.J. 422, 114 A.2d 1 (1955); *In the Matter of White,* 18 N.J. 449, 114 A.2d 261 (1955); *State v. Haines,* 18 N.J. 550, 115 A.2d 24 (1955); *State v. Wise,* 19 N.J. 59, 115 A.2d 62 (1955); *State v. Fary,* 19 N.J. 431, 117 A.2d 499 (1955); *State v. D'Ippolita,* 19 N.J. 540, 117 A.2d 592 (1955); *State v. DeMeo,* 20 N.J. 1, 118 A.2d 1 (1955); *State v. Kociolek,* 20 N.J. 92, 118 A.2d 812 (1955).

[18] Allinsmith, "Religious Affiliation and Politico-Economic Attitudes," 12 *Public Opinion Q.* 377 (1948).

includes English, Scotch, or Welsh) with judges on the same court whose ancestral nationality is at least partly non-British (to the extent determinable in the Smith book), one finds that the judges of partially non-British derivation tend to have higher decision scores for the defense than do the judges of wholly British derivation on the same courts. This difference, however, is not quite statistically significant.

OFF-THE-BENCH ATTITUDES

In the spring of 1960 a mailed questionnaire was sent to each of the 313 state and federal supreme court judges of 1955 in order to determine their attitudes on various issues. One hundred and nineteen of the judges returned answered questionnaires. The questionnaire represented a condensed and revised version of a liberalism-conservatism questionnaire written by H. J. Eysenck.[19] The judges were asked to indicate whether on the whole they agreed a lot, agreed a little, neither agreed nor disagreed, disagreed a little, or disagreed a lot with a list of statements. The questionnaire was primarily designed to measure the degree of sympathy a respondent has for less privileged groups and the degree of acceptance he has toward long run social change. These two components make up what is generally referred to as liberalism.[20] The questionnaire was scored in such a way that a respondent could receive a liberalism score ranging from 41 to 195. The median liberalism score actually received was 109. Seventeen supreme courts that heard full-court non-unanimous criminal cases had at least one judge with a score over 109 and at least one judge with a score at or below 109. Fifty-seven per cent of the judges scoring above 109 were above the average of the respondents of their respective courts on the decision score, whereas only 27 per cent of the judges scoring at or below 109 were above the average of the respondents of their respective courts on the decision score. This difference is statistically significant, but a specific example cannot be given because the judges were promised anonymity if they responded to the questionnaire.

There was one particularly relevant statement to which the judges were asked to respond by indicating whether and how much they agreed or disagreed. This statement read "Our treatment of criminals is too harsh; we should try to cure not to punish them." Twenty-four of the 119 responding judges indicated they strongly disagreed on the whole with the statement, 48 disagreed but not strongly, 22 neither disagreed nor agreed, 20 agreed on the whole but not strongly, and 5 agreed strongly. The average responding judge was thus in between disagreeing mildly and being neutral. Fifty-nine per cent of those who were neutral or who agreed with the statement were

---

[19] Eysenck, *Psychology of Politics,* 122–24 (1954).
[20] Maciver, *The Web of Government,* 215–17 (1951).

above the average of the respondents of their respective courts on the decision score, whereas only 27 per cent of those who disagreed with the statement were above the average of the respondents of their respective courts on the decision score. This difference is statistically significant.

REASONS AND REMEDIES

How might one account for the relationships between judicial characteristics and judicial decision-making that have been described? Some of the relationships found are easily attributable to chance. Others, however, are not. The latter are those where the odds are more than 95 to 5, or 19 to 1, of obtaining the differences purely by chance given the size of the differences and the size of the groups. They include the differences between Democratic and Republican judges, non-ABA members and ABA members, non-former prosecutors and former prosecutors, Catholic judges and Protestant judges, and relatively liberal judges and relatively conservative judges as measured by their off-the-bench attitudes.

To some extent a criminal case represents a conflict of social groups, in that the defendant generally tends to be a member of the lower-middle or working class (particularly if tax and business regulation cases are analyzed separately),[21] and the prosecutor tends to be a member of the upper-middle or upper class, enforcing laws promulgated by upper-middle and upper class legislators and judges.[22] Mass data show that persons holding certain positions (e.g., being a Democrat or a Catholic) with respect to background characteristics (e.g., party or religion) tend to have greater sympathy for lower economic and social groups than do persons holding obverse positions.[23] Given the nature of the average criminal case, judges holding such positions with respect to background characteristics are therefore likely to have a higher decision score for the defense than do judges holding obverse background positions. The correlation between a judge's position on background characteristics and his relative degree of sympathy for lower economic and social groups may account for the differences found concerning party, pressure groups, religion, and liberal-conservative attitudes.

However, it probably does not account for the differences found between former prosecutors and their opposite number; judges who are former prosecutors are probably on the average not substantially more or less ideologically liberal than judges who have not been prosecutors. Their lower decision scores for the defense are possibly more attributable to a relatively pro-

[21] Taft, *Criminology*, 131–33 (1950).

[22] Matthews, *The Social Background of Political Decision-Makers*, 23–30 (1954).

[23] Campbell, Gurin & Miller, *The Voter Decides* (1954); Turner, *Party and Constituency: Pressures on Congress* (1951).

prosecution frame of reference which caused them to become prosecutors or which they acquired or had reinforced when they served as prosecutors.

Many devices are available for minimizing the influence of judicial backgrounds, including the availability to defendants of easy appeals, the requirement that judges write opinions to justify their decisions, the use of multi-judge courts with judges of diversified backgrounds, and the drafting of clearer and more detailed substantive statutes thereby limiting the area of judicial discretion.

Because criminal cases frequently involve value-oriented controversies, however, and because different background and attitudinal positions tend to correspond to different value orientations, there will probably always be some correlation between judicial characteristics and judicial decision-making in criminal cases.

Some Factors in
Sentencing Policy

ROBERT M. CARTER AND LESLIE T. WILKINS

The probation officer as a member of the court staff has two major functions to fulfill. The first is to conduct an investigation of an offender which culminates in a presentence or probation report. This report is frequently accompanied by a recommendation to the court as to the selection of an appropriate sentence. The second function is to provide supervision for offenders placed on probation or some other form of conditional liberty. Despite the recent focus of correctional interest and attention, and a considerable volume of literature, the terms and conditions of these functions remain relatively vague. It is proposed to examine here a segment of one of these, namely the presentence report recommendation and its relationship to the court disposition. Our purpose is not so much to provide data, but to make explicit some questions about presentence report recommendations and their relation to court dispositions.

Even though corrections is a relatively new field in the United States, some of its components have already become so institutionalized that they form a cornerstone for the development of a correctional folklore or mythology. In essence, it appears that the increasing problem of crime and delinquency is being addressed by the application of principles and practices which have not been substantially modified, or even questioned, since their inception. Yet, the correctional systems must change if for no other reason than that of the increasing number of offenders processed. Tradition would have it that the changes be in the direction of increased probation and parole staff, prison personnel, new institutions, and related services. If these be the sole nature of the changes — more of what already exists — there will be a reliance upon a view of the past without a realistic vision of the future.

CASE LOAD SIZE

The fifty-unit workload as the standard for probation and parole supervision is an example of one of the myths. Where did this number come from? On what empirical data is it based? Is it an appropriate limitation of case load size? If it is not appropriate, what should be the workload for corrections? A search of the literature dates the fifty-unit concept back to at least 1922, when Charles L. Chute, then President of the National Probation As-

Reprinted by special permission of the authors and *The Journal of Criminal Law, Criminology and Police Science,* Copyright © 1967 by the Northwestern University School of Law, Vol. 58 (December 1967), pp. 503–514.

sociation, observed: "To this end fifty cases is as many as any probation officer ought to carry."[1] The fifty-unit concept found its way in the prestigious academic literature when Sutherland[2] in 1934, and Tannenbaum[3] in 1938, suggested that fifty cases "is generally regarded as the maximum number" and "the best practice would limit the caseload of a probation officer to fifty cases." The concept of fifty entered the professional literature when the American Prison Association in 1946 indicated that a probation officer "should not have more than fifty cases under continuous supervision."[4] An almost identical statement appears in the 1954 revision of the Manual of Correctional Standards.[5] Not until 1966 (while still suggesting a fifty-unit workload) did the American Correctional Association indicate that "where methods of classification for case loads have been developed through research, varying standards of workloads may prevail."[6]

The institutionalization of the fifty-unit concept is now firmly entrenched. Budgets for operating agencies, testimony before legislative bodies, standards of practice, and projections for future operational needs all center around this number. There is no evidence of any empirical justification for fifty, nor for that matter, any other number.

The following discussion relates mainly to the federal probation system, and we are indebted to the Administrative Office of the United States Courts for furnishing pertinent data. Information has also been drawn from the San Francisco Project, a study of the federal probation system, supported by the National Institute of Mental Health.[7] It should be noted that these data cover different populations over different periods of time, and are not to be seen as interesting in themselves, but as throwing light on the presentence report recommendation and court disposition.

RECOMMENDATIONS AND DISPOSITIONS: THE RELATIONSHIP

The presentence report is a document basic to the functioning of both judicial and correctional administrations. The contents of the report, including the recommendation, assist the court in making a judgment consistent with its dual responsibilities to society and the defendant. Within the federal system the report aids the institutions within the Bureau of Prisons in deter-

---

[1] Chute, "Probation and Suspended Sentence," 12 *J. Crim. L. & C.* 562 (1922).

[2] Sutherland, *Principles of Criminology*, 359 (1934).

[3] Tannenbaum, *Crime and the Community*, 462 (1938).

[4] *Manual of Suggested Standards for a State Correctional System* (Am. Pris. Assn.) 13 (1946).

[5] *Manual of Correctional Standards* (Am. Corr. Assn.) 43 (1954).

[6] *Ibid.* 109 (1966).

[7] See Lohman, Wahl & Carter, "A Non-Technical Description of the San Francisco Project," *The San Francisco Project* series (April 1965).

mining classification and treatment programs and also in planning for subsequent release. The report provides information to the Board of Parole, furnishing information believed to be pertinent to its deliberations. Furthermore, the report contributes to the probation officer's rehabilitative efforts while an offender is under his supervision.[8]

In February, 1965, with the publication of a 39-page monograph entitled *The Presentence Investigation Report,* a standard outline and format was adopted for the preparation of presentence reports in the federal courts.[9] The final paragraph headings of the report are "Evaluative Summary" and "Recommendation." The importance of these paragraphs is recognized by the American Correctional Association which includes among its standards for the preparation of presentence reports a "recommendation for or against probation, or for other disposition according to court policy."[10]

The fact that there is a substantial number of sentencing alternatives available to federal judges also means that an equal number of possible recommendations may be considered by the probation officer. The selection ranges, of course, from probation with or without a fine or restitution, and/or a jail sentence, and imprisonment under various statutes which determine parole eligibility, to other dispositions which include commitment for observation and study and continuances for community observation.

Because of this variety of available disposals, the relationship between a recommendation and a disposition may be more simply considered from one of two directions. The first method would be to contrast recommendations for probation made by probation officers with actual court dispositions resulting in probation. The second would be from an opposite direction, viewing recommendations against probation (or for imprisonment) with actual court dispositions for probation.

Data developed during the San Francisco Project contrast recommendations and dispositions for 500 consecutive cases processed through the United States District Court in the Northern District of California between September 1964 and August 1965.[11] These data indicate that:

. . . there is a close relationship between the recommendation of probation and the actual granting of probation. Probation was recommended in 227 cases and was granted in 212 of those cases. If the 7 cases of "observation and study" are not included, probation was granted, when recommended, in 212 of the 220 cases or in 96 per cent of the cases. In only 2 of the 227 cases was there a substantial dif-

---

[8] The federal probation officer supervises persons released on parole or mandatory release from federal correctional institutions or the United States Disciplinary Barracks.

[9] *The Presentence Investigation Report* (Adm. Off. U. S. Cts.) (1965).

[10] *Manual of Correctional Standards* (Am. Corr. Assn.) 521 (2d ed. 1959).

[11] Carter, "It is Respectfully Recommended . . . ," 30 *Fed. Prob.* 2 (1966).

Table I: Percentage of Probation Officer Recommendations for Probation Followed by California Superior Courts

1959	95.6
1960	96.4
1961	96.0
1962	96.5
1963	97.2
1964	97.3
1965	96.7

Source: State of California, Department of Justice. *Delinquency and Probation in California, 1964, p. 168; and Crime and Delinquency in California, 1965, pp. 98-99.*

ference between the probation officer's recommendation and the court's disposition of the cases. In these instances, prison sentences were ordered where probation had been recommended.[12]

These data closely parallel the California data. The percentages of probation officer recommendations for probation followed by California Superior Courts, for the years cited, are shown in Table I.

Data on the federal system, arranged by the ten judicial circuits, indicate the relationship, shown in Table II, between probation officer recommendations for probation and such dispositions in court for Fiscal Year 1964.

The patterns in these first two tables exhibit almost total agreement between a probation officer's recommendation for probation and an actual disposition of probation. However, this trend appears less stable when viewed from the opposite perspective — the relationship between recommendations against probation (or for imprisonment) and court dispositions of probation. California data reveal, in Table III, the percentages of "against probation" recommendations and probation dispositions in court.

It is noteworthy that California authorities indicate the "superior court judges are more lenient than probation officers as to who should be granted probation."[13] This pattern has already been observed by one of the authors,[14] and by others,[15] in respect to the federal probation officer. Further confirmation of this pattern is found throughout the federal system as indicated by a review, in Table IV, of "against probation" recommendations and probation dispositions according to the ten judicial circuits for Fiscal Year 1964.

As already indicated, the probation officer has a wide latitude in his choice

[12] *Ibid.* 41.
[13] *Delinquency and Probation in California, 1964* (Calif. Dept. of Justice) 166 (1964).
[14] Carter, *supra* note 11.
[15] Lohman, Wahl & Carter, *San Francisco Project* series, Report #2, 8 (Berkeley: June 1965).

Table II: Percentage of Probation Officer Recommendations for Probation Followed by Ten Judicial Circuits, Fiscal Year 1964

First Circuit	99.4
Second Circuit	96.0
Third Circuit	93.2
Fourth Circuit	93.3
Fifth Circuit	95.2
Sixth Circuit	93.9
Seventh Circuit	89.9
Eighth Circuit	95.0
Ninth Circuit	93.5
Tenth Circuit	97.8
Overall	94.1

Source: Data furnished by the Administrative Office of the United States Courts.

of a recommendation. Table V presents data on the specific recommendations of probation officers in the Northern District of California between September 1964 and February 1967, and shows the wide variety of possible recommendations.

Table VI presents overall data on the relationship between recommendations and dispositions of 1,232 cases processed through the District Court in Northern California. The reader will note that of 601 cases recommended for probation, 15 were ordered imprisoned; of 334 cases recommended for imprisonment, 31 were placed on probation.

These data seem to support certain generalizations about the nature of the relationship between probation officer recommendations and court dispositions. We have seen that there is a very strong relationship between recommendations *for probation* and court dispositions of probation, an average agreement of about 95 per cent. It has also been observed that the strength of the relationship diminishes slightly when recommendations *against proba-*

Table III: Percentage of Probation Officer Recommendations Against Probation Not Followed by California Superior Courts

1959	13.5
1960	12.8
1961	14.8
1962	17.4
1963	21.6
1964	21.1
1965	19.9

Source: State of California, Department of Justice. Delinquency and Probation in California, 1964, p. 168; and Crime and Delinquency in California, 1965, pp. 98-99.

Table IV: Percentage of Probation Officer Recommendations Against
Probation Not Followed by Ten Judicial Circuits, Fiscal Year 1964

First Circuit	7.3
Second Circuit	9.5
Third Circuit	27.4
Fourth Circuit	31.8
Fifth Circuit	11.5
Sixth Circuit	19.3
Seventh Circuit	15.9
Eighth Circuit	16.5
Ninth Circuit	23.3
Tenth Circuit	9.2
Overall	19.7

*Source: Data furnished by the Administrative Office of the United States
Courts.*

tion (or for imprisonment) are contrasted with court dispositions of probation. Thus, it may be concluded that where disagreements exist between
recommendations and dispositions, they occur when the officer recommends
imprisonment. In a sense, if this relationship measures "punitiveness" then
it may be concluded that the probation officer is more punitive than the
judge.

OUTCOME OF SUPERVISION ACCORDING
TO THE RECOMMENDATION

Very limited data are available on the outcome of supervision, i.e., the violation rate, according to recommendations of probation officers. The 1964
cohort study of Davis[16] examined the violation status of 11,638 adult defendants granted probation in California Superior Courts between 1956 and
1958. Davis showed that 27.1 per cent of the defendants recommended for
and placed on probation were "revoked," while 36.7 per cent of the defendants placed on probation against the recommendation of the probation officer were revoked. Davis concluded that the "difference in revocation rates
was very significant and indicates that the two groups were not alike in their
tendency to recidivism."

It is questionable that this single explanation for the ten per cent differential in revocation rates occurs simply because of differences in the two groups.
There are two other possible explanations for this. One explanation may be
that subtle differences exist in the supervision provided by a probation officer
who may feel "resentful" in having an individual placed on probation against

[16] Davis, "A Study of Adult Probation Violation Rates by Means of the
Cohort Approach," 55 *J. Crim. L., C. & P.S.* 70 (1964).

Table V: Probation Officers' Recommendations as to Sentence, Northern District of California, September, 1964 to February, 1967

Recommendation	Total	Percentage of total
All cases	1,232	100.0
No recommendation	67	5.4
Mandatory sentence (under certain narcotic law violations)	45	3.6
Probation	601	48.9
Regular	(284)	(23.1)
With fine and/or restitution	(197)	(16.0)
Split sentence (imprisonment up to six months followed by probation)	(49)	(4.0)
Under Youth Corrections Act	(71)	(5.8)
Fine only	38	3.1
Jail only	35	2.8
Imprisonment	334	27.1
Parole eligibility after 1/3 sentence	(234)	(19.0)
Parole eligibility at any time	(64)	(5.2)
Under Youth Corrections Act	(36)	(2.9)
Observation and study	51	4.2
Adult	(39)	(3.2)
Youth	(12)	(1.0)
Continuance for 90 days observation	16	1.3
Deferred prosecution	3	.2
Commitment under Federal Juvenile Delinquency Act	2	.2
Other recommendations	40	3.3

Source: Unpublished San Francisco Project data.

his recommendation. The second possibility is that the defendant's attitude toward a probation officer who recommended that he be imprisoned instead of placed on probation may affect the outcome of supervision. While there are no measures of these two negative factors, it is possible that they account for a large portion of the observed differential. There are other interesting studies which support the hypothesis of self-fulfilling prophecies.

Another way of viewing Davis' data is to emphasize that 63.3 per cent of those who received an unfavorable probation recommendation but were placed on probation completed their probation without revocation. Thus, to deny probation to all those with negative recommendations from probation officers would suggest that approximately two out of every three defendants with such recommendations would be denied the opportunity to complete probation successfully. Davis inquired as to the number of defendants who, denied probation on unfavorable recommendations, would have succeeded on proba-

Table VI: Probation Officers' Recommendation and Subsequent Court Dispositions, Northern District of California, September, 1964 to February, 1967

Recommendation	Total	Manda-tory	Proba-tion	Fine only	Jail only	Im-prison-ment	Obser-vation and study	Contin-uances	De-ferred prose-cution	Other
All cases	1,232	45	671	30	27	337	73	18	2	29
No recommendation	67	—	44	2	2	14	1	—	—	4
Mandatory	45	45	—	—	—	—	—	—	—	—
Probation	601	—	551	5	3	15	17	2	—	8
Fine only	38	—	14	22	—	1	—	—	—	1
Jail only	35	—	5	1	19	8	2	—	—	—
Imprisonment	334	—	31	—	2	281	13	5	—	2
Observation and study	51	—	3	—	—	9	38	1	—	—
Continuances	16	—	6	—	—	—	—	10	—	—
Deferred prosecution	3	—	—	—	—	—	—	—	2	1
Federal Juvenile Delinquency Act	2	—	1	—	—	—	2	—	—	1
Other	40	—	16	—	1	9	2	—	—	12

Source: Unpublished San Francisco Project data.

tion if given the opportunity. There are, at this time, no data to answer this question.[17]

Other data are available from the Administrative Office of the United States Courts which indicate that despite considerable variation in the use of probation, the overall violation rates, or the rates broken down by "major," "minor," or "technical" are almost identical. Table VII of the Administrative Office report is reproduced here to show probation violation rates for 1965, according to the actual percentage of persons placed on probation by the 88 U.S. District Courts, arranged by quartiles.

The data in Table VII reveal that approximately 19 per cent of those placed under probation supervision violate the terms of this conditional liberty, regardless of the percentage of the offender population on probation.

FACTORS AFFECTING THE AGREEMENT BETWEEN RECOMMENDATIONS AND DISPOSITIONS

Reverting to the possible explanations for the high degree of agreement between probation officer recommendations and court dispositions, it is possible that four factors, operating independently, but more probably simultaneously, account for this relationship:

1. The court, having such high regard for the professional qualities and competence of its probation staff, "follows" the probation recommendation — a recommendation made by the person (probation officer) who best knows the defendant by reason of the presentence investigation;
2. There are many offenders who are "obviously" probation or prison cases;
3. Probation officers write their reports and make recommendations anticipating the recommendation the court desires to receive. (In this situation, the probation officer is quite accurately "second-guessing" the court disposition.);
4. Probation officers in making their recommendations place great emphasis on the same factors as does the court in selecting a sentencing alternative.

Data from the San Francisco Project confirm the fact that probation officers and judges apply approximately equal significance to similar factors.[18] Examination of 500 probation officer recommendations according to the major categories of recommendations for probation and recommendations for

---

[17] Wilkins, "A Small Comparative Study of the Results of Probation," 8 *British J. Crimino.* 201 (1958).

[18] See Lohman, Wahl & Carter, *San Francisco Project* series, Reports 4 and 5 (Berkeley: December 1965, February 1966).

Table VII: (Table A 18 of the Administrative Office of the U.S. Courts covering 88 United States District Courts) Comparison of the Use of Probation in District Courts, by Type of Violation, Fiscal Year 1965 (Excludes violators of immigration laws, wagering tax laws and violators of Federal regulatory acts)

Item	88 District courts	Quartile groups of District Courts			
		First 22 District Courts	Second 22 District Courts	Third 22 District Courts	Fourth 22 District Courts
Average					
Actual percentage placed on probation	49.0	65.9	53.8	47.2	36.9
Total removed	11,259	2,263	2,759	3,678	2,559
No violations	9,157	1,843	2,267	2,973	2,074
Violated probation	2,102	420	492	705	485
Technical violation	344	78	85	106	75
Minor violation	577	111	120	216	130
Major violation	1,181	231	287	383	280
Percentage					
Violated probation	18.7	18.5	17.8	19.2	18.9
Technical violation	3.1	3.4	3.1	2.9	2.9
Minor violation	5.1	4.9	4.3	5.9	5.1
Major violation	10.5	10.2	10.4	10.4	10.9

Source: Administrative Office of the United States Courts, *Persons Under the Supervision of the Federal Probation System* (*Washington, D.C., 1965*), *p. 33.*

imprisonment (or against probation), produced data on the legal and demographic characteristics of the offender population which had an important effect upon the recommendation selected. In general terms, the proportion of recommendations for probation increased with the number of years of education, average monthly income, higher occupational levels, residence, marital and employment stability, participation in church activities, and a good military record. Recommendations for imprisonment (or against probation) increased proportionately when offenders exhibited such characteristics as homosexuality, alcoholic involvement, the use of weapons or violence in the commission of the offense, the existence of family criminality, and drug usage. Age (in the range examined) did not significantly distinguish between the two recommendations, and racial and religious affiliation differences were absent. The female, however, was more likely to be recommended for probation than the male offender.

Certain offense categories (e.g., embezzlement, theft from interstate shipments or theft of government property, and false statement) usually produced recommendations for probation, while other offense categories (e.g., bank robbery, the interstate transportation of stolen motor vehicles [Dyer Act], and National Defense law violation) usually resulted in recommendations for imprisonment. Offenders who entered a plea of guilty, retained their own attorneys, or who were released to the community on bail, bond, or personal recognizance while the presentence investigation was being conducted, had significantly greater chances of being recommended for probation. It is recognized, of course, that a recommendation for or against probation is generally based upon some combination of characteristics — some obvious, others subtle — rather than upon any single characteristic or piece of information.

It is apparent that not all factors are of equal significance in determining the probation officer's recommendation. Accordingly, statistical computations produced a general ranking of the significance or importance of various factors.[19]

A further examination of the 500 cases was made, reviewing the selection of the sentencing alternative by the court. Again, statistical computations were completed and a second rank order of the significant or important factors was produced.

These two sets of data — one relating to the recommendation, the other to the disposition — are summarized in Table VIII. The rankings were based on probability and contingency coefficient values. A correlation was computed and a significant value of .90 was obtained. These data indicate that there is considerable agreement between probation officers and judges as to the sig-

[19] *Id.*

nificance of certain factors and characteristics for decisions relating to probation or imprisonment recommendations and dispositions.

Another possible explanation of the close agreement between recommendations and dispositions is certainly that some cases are clearly probation or imprisonment cases. However, there are no "hard" data to identify which cases are "clearly" probation or prison cases. An actual, but extreme example

Table VIII: Rank of Demographic Factors Utilized by Probation Officers for Recommendations and District Court Judges for Sentencing Alternatives, According to Probability and Contingency Coefficient Values, 500 Federal Offenders, Northern District of California, September, 1964 to August, 1965

Demographic factors	Probation officers' ranking	District Court judge's ranking
Prior record	1	3
Confinement status	2	2
Number of arrests	3	4
Offense	4	1
Longest employment	5	5
Occupation	6	8
Number of months employed	7	6
Income	8	10
Longest residence	9	7
Military history	10	9
Number of residence changes	11	17
Distance to offense	12	14
Number of aliases	13	24
Marital status	14	11
Legal representation	15	13
Weapons and violence	16	15
Family criminality	17	21
Plea	18	18
Education	19	12
Church attendance	20	16
Narcotics usage	21	23
Sex	22	19
Alcoholic involvement	23	25
Crime partners	24	20
Homosexuality	25	26
Race	26	28
Age	27	22
Religion	28	27

Source: Joseph D. Lohman, Albert Wahl and Robert M. Carter, San Francisco Project *series, Report 5 (Berkeley, February 1966), p. 68.*
Spearman's p = .90

of an "imprisonment case" is the bank robber who, armed with an automatic pistol and with an accomplice waiting in a stolen automobile, robbed a bank of $35,000, pistol-whipped a teller, and in the flight from the scene, engaged in a gun battle with pursuing police. It is doubtful that probation officers or judges would be inclined to see probation as a suitable disposition for such a case, regardless of any other factors involved. An example of the "probation case" is the young married offender, who, unemployed prior to the Christmas season, made a false statement to the Post Office for employment, concealing a prior misdemeanor arrest. In general terms, this type of offender would normally be seen as a suitable candidate for probation.

From observation and conversations with judges and probation officers during the past years, it appears that judges do indeed have a high regard for their probation staff and value their professional judgment as to the disposition of a case. It is suspected that this is especially true in the federal system in which probation officers are appointed by the court and serve at its pleasure. This esteem for probation officers and their services by the court may also contribute to the high agreement between recommendations and dispositions, even though there are no statistical data to support this.

The fourth potential explanation for the close agreement between recommendations and dispositions — probation officers anticipating the recommendation the court desires — is now to be discussed.

VARIATION AMONG PROBATION OFFICERS AND PROBATION OFFICES

Disparities in sentencing have been of considerable interest in recent years and attempts to reduce these frequently observed differentials have normally been focused on judges. For example, sentencing institutes for judges have been developed at the federal and state level, as well as training programs for newly appointed or elected judges. That attention should be directed toward judges — for they impose the sentences — is certainly normal and, on the surface, a logical approach to resolving disparities. However, this pattern ignores one of the facts of community life — in this case the judicial community and its social system — that many persons play a part in the functioning of the community. Included in the judicial community are probation officers, prosecutors, defense attorneys, perhaps to a lesser extent the law enforcement agencies, and other judges on the same bench.

It seems to have been generally assumed that the judges are solely responsible for the disparities and that the remainder of the judicial community plays only a minor role which remains constant, neither supporting or contributing to the disparities. Although we do not have complete data upon which a judicial "community-effect" can be shown to be a basis for disparities, there are data available which demonstrate the supporting role of at least one member, namely the probation officer.

If we assume that probation officers are "constant" and that judges are "variable," we would expect to find significant differences in the relationship between officer recommendations and court dispositions as we move toward extremes in the use of probation or imprisonment. We would not, in the federal system for example, expect to find the more than 94 per cent agreement between recommendations and dispositions spread uniformly throughout the system, for some courts use probation frequently, others infrequently. In Fiscal Year 1965, individual federal courts had a range of probation usage in excess of 50 per cent, with one court using probation for 23.8 per cent of its cases, another for 75.7 per cent of its cases. The percentage of defendants on probation in Fiscal Year 1965 by the ten judicial circuits is shown in Table IX.

Thus, on a circuit-wide basis, there is a high of 63.8 per cent in the usage of probation ranging to a low of 43.7 per cent, an overall spread of twenty per cent, and as noted above, the variation is even more marked among individual courts. Six of the eighty-eight district courts used probation in excess of 70 per cent for their defendants; twelve courts used probation for less than 40 per cent of their defendants.

Despite the variation among courts, individually or circuit wide, the relationship between probation officer recommendations and court dispositions is generally quite constant, whether there is high, moderate, or low usage of probation. This may be seen more precisely in Table X which provides data for Fiscal Year 1964 on sixteen selected federal courts: the five with the highest

Table IX: Percentage of Use of Probation in Ten Federal Judicial Circuits

First Circuit	53.0
Second Circuit	45.2
Third Circuit	63.8
Fourth Circuit	60.8
Fifth Circuit	44.8
Sixth Circuit	44.3
Seventh Circuit	44.4
Eighth Circuit	49.9
Ninth Circuit	49.0
Tenth Circuit	43.7
Overall	49.0

Source: Administrative Office of the United States Courts. Persons Under the Supervision of the Federal Probation System, Fiscal Year 1965, *pp. 103-105.*

Table X: Use of Probation and Recommendations for and against Probation by Selected United States District Courts, Fiscal Year 1964

	Percentage use of probation	Recommended for probation			Recommended against probation			Recommendations given by probation officers: percentage of total cases
		Number of defendants	Number granted probation	Percentage granted probation	Number of defendants	Number granted probation	Percentage granted probation	
A	78.3	147	143	97.3	55	20	36.4	73.2
B	71.4	144	137	95.1	90	31	34.4	88.0
C	70.7	27	26	96.3	7	0	—	82.9
D	70.4	20	19	95.0	11	2	18.2	43.7
E	70.2	125	125	100.0	28	1	3.6	77.3
F	50.8	106	100	94.3	112	17	15.2	89.3
G	50.0	16	16	100.0	17	1	5.9	82.5
H	50.0	152	145	95.4	149	19	12.8	80.9
I	50.0	14	13	92.9	9	0	—	60.5
J	49.7	12	12	100.0	36	6	16.7	15.4
K	49.6	29	28	96.6	36	0	—	47.4
L	36.8	28	28	100.0	19	0		13.6
M	36.5	61	61	100.0	117	14	12.0	73.0
N	35.6	158	148	93.7	310	21	6.8	87.8
O	28.5	92	82	89.1	74	25	33.8	35.1
P	26.3	44	38	86.4	174	24	13.8	90.8
Total for all District Courts	50.2	6868	6463	94.1	7691	1518	19.7	63.1

Source: Data furnished by the Administrative Office of the United States Courts.

usage of probation, the five with the lowest use of probation, and the six courts which were within 1 per cent of the national average for use of probation.

It will be seen, for example, that in District *A*, probation was recommended for approximately three of each four defendants (147–55); in District *H*, the recommendations are about equal (152–149), while in District *N*, probation is recommended for about one defendant in three (148–310). However, the "agreement" rate between probation recommendations and dispositions in District *A* is 97.3 per cent, in District *H*, 95.4 per cent, and in District *N*, 93.7 per cent.

These data indicate clearly that the recommendation-disposition relationship does not vary greatly from court to court, and that disparities in sentencing are supported, at least in terms of recommendations, by the probation officer member of the judicial "influence group." To be sure, there may be differences in the Districts which justify high or low use of probation, but thus far these have not been demonstrated. These data raise some interesting and important questions regarding the utility of sentencing institutes for judges, by themselves, as the solution to disparities, and suggest that probation officers, and perhaps prosecuting and defense attorneys, be included in such institutes.

The data in Table X have indicated that there is considerable variation in officer recommendations for or against probation in different Districts, but that rate of agreement between recommendations and dispositions is relatively constant between Districts. Accordingly, we would expect to find a common frame of mind, or "influence group set," among officers in a single District which leads to the agreement in that District, regardless of the frequency of probation or imprisonment dispositions. Thus, where probation is used frequently, we would expect the officers in that court to be sympathetic to such usage and we would anticipate that little variation would exist among officers. If this is the case, we would not expect to find much significant variation among probation officers in a single District. We would not expect to find large differences among colleagues appointed by the same court, operating in a similar fashion as regards court and office policies and directives, appointed under uniform standards, paid identical salaries, and theoretically sharing similar views of the correctional process.

Let us return to our data on the 1,232 recommendations made by the probation officers in the Northern District of California as shown in Table V. By restricting ourselves to a probation-imprisonment dichotomy, we observe that probation was recommended 64.3 per cent of the time (601 of 935 cases) and that imprisonment was recommended 35.7 per cent (334 of 935 cases). The recommendations of 19 probation officers in Northern California for probation or imprisonment are presented in Table XI. (Officers who made less than 15 recommendations are excluded.)

Table XI: Individual Probation Officer Recommendations for Probation and Imprisonment, Northern District of California, September, 1964 to February, 1967

Probation officer	Number of Recommendations	Number of probation recommendations	Number of prison recommendations	Percentage of probation recommendations
1	55	40	15	72.7
2	39	25	14	64.1
3	46	21	25	45.7
4	57	35	22	61.4
5	16	14	2	87.5
6	20	13	7	65.0
7	55	22	33	40.0
8	38	22	16	57.9
9	22	17	5	77.3
10	58	46	12	79.3
11	59	32	27	54.2
12	57	35	22	61.4
13	54	42	12	77.8
14	36	17	19	47.2
15	56	34	22	60.7
16	46	31	15	67.4
17	60	43	17	71.7
18	18	16	2	88.9
19	42	24	18	57.1

Source: Unpublished San Francisco Project data.

The percentage of recommendations for probation is almost 50 per cent — from a low of 40.0 to a high of 88.9 per cent. Three officers recommended probation for less than 50 per cent of their cases; three officers between 50 and 60 per cent, six between 60 and 70 per cent, five between 70 and 80 per cent, and two in excess of 80 per cent.

While this individual variation may be attributed, in part, to the geographic basis for assignment of cases or to other administrative reasons, it is statistically significant and suggests that probation officers, even in the same District do not view the correctional process from identical perspectives.

What accounts for this variation among officers? In part, administrative and geographic considerations may be an explanation. There may be differences in probation-suitability among persons from metropolitan areas (e.g., San Francisco-Oakland) and less developed or rural areas such as the northern coast or central valleys of California. But it is equally possible that these variations are due to personal characteristics, including academic training, age, and vocational background. Some general, but not conclusive observations can be made based on the probation officers in Northern California. For example, probation officers with graduate training or graduate degrees in social work or social welfare recommended probation for 56.3 per cent of their cases; officers with graduate work or graduate degrees in criminology in 69.6 per cent of their cases, and officers with graduate work or graduate degrees in sociology in 67.7 per cent of their cases. Officers with the longest service recommended probation for 54.0 per cent of their cases, while the "newer" officers recommended probation for 68.4 per cent. Three hypotheses are suggested by these and other data:

1. Some of the variation in probation officer recommendations is a product of the individual background of the officer and includes vocational experience and academic training.
2. The differences or variations tend to diminish with the period of employment; that is, officers with different backgrounds are far more dissimilar upon entering the probation service than after exposure to the agency.
3. With an increase in the period of service (i.e., more experience) there is a decrease in recommendations for probation. This may represent a more "realistic" or less "optimistic" view of the benefits of probation treatment for a greater number of offenders, than was the view held by the officer earlier in his professional career.

"SECOND-GUESSING" OR "FOLLOWING"

There is, in our search for variation, the possibility that the probation officer attempts to second-guess the court by making recommendations which are anticipated to be those desired by the court. If this were the case, one measure of this factor would be that different judges receive different rates or percentages of probation or imprisonment recommendations. Thus, properly "second-guessing" a punitive judge would require a larger proportion of imprisonment recommendations; second-guessing a "lenient" judge would require more probation recommendations. Returning to the data on the 1,232 cases in the Northern District of California, and again restricting ourselves to a probation-imprisonment dichotomy, we find some, but not significant variation in the percentage of probation recommendations to individual judges. These data are in Table XII. Since none of these judges has a reputation of being punitive or lenient, we can only surmise that in this District, there is little if any second-guessing.

A review of Table XII will also indicate that individual judges are equally receptive to recommendations for probation; the relationship between recommendations for probation and such dispositions being 97.2 per cent over-all and constant between judges.

Table XII: Recommendations for and against Probation according to United States District Court Judges, Northern District of California, September, 1964 to February, 1967

Judge	Number of cases disposed of in court	Number of recommendations for probation	Number of recommendations against probation	Percentage of cases recommended for probation	Number of cases granted probation	Number of cases denied probation	Percentage agreement between probation recommendations and dispositions
Total	831	527	304	63.4	512	278	97.2
1	64	40	24	62.5	38	23	95.0
2	58	30	28	51.7	29	23	96.7
3	160	103	57	64.4	99	53	96.1
4	156	114	42	73.1	111	38	97.4
5	88	57	31	64.8	57	30	100.0
6	100	58	42	58.0	56	36	96.6
7	60	39	21	65.0	38	18	97.4
8	73	46	27	63.0	44	26	95.7
9	72	40	32	55.6	40	31	100.0

Source: Unpublished San Francisco Project data.

It appears that judges "follow" probation officer recommendations; there is no other ready explanation of the individual officer variation in probation recommendations and the high over-all relationship between recommendations and dispositions. This also tends to confirm the observation that probation officers contribute to the problems of disparities in sentencing. From these data, all four previously suggested explanations of the close agreement between recommendation and disposition (probation officers and judges giving approximately equal weight to similar factors, the "following" of recommendations by the court, the presence of "obvious" probation or imprisonment cases, and some "second-guessing") appear appropriate.

SUMMARY

In this paper, some of the dangers of continued reliance on tradition and the development of a body of correctional folklore have been pointed out. It has been determined that the relationship between recommendations for and dispositions of probation are high and that the relationship diminishes when viewed from the recommendations against and the subsequent grant of probation perspective. Limited data on the outcome of supervision by recommendation and by percentage use of probation are provided. We have inquired into the reasons for the close agreement between recommendation and disposition and suggest that four factors, in varying degrees, account for it. We have observed that the overall relationship between recommendation and disposition does not vary from District Court to District Court, but rather remains relatively constant, regardless of the percentage use of probation. We suggest that disparities in sentencing are supported by the probation officer and it appears that these differences, in part, are a reflection of the officer's individual academic training and experience. Length of service brings about a trend toward conformity with colleagues and the development of a more conservative perspective toward the use of probation.

There are other segments of the presentence report process to which questions should be addressed. These include operational and administrative considerations, the decision-making processes of probation officers, and an examination of the nature and impact of the social system of correctional agencies. Within the operational considerations would be inquiries as to the role of subprofessionals in presentence investigations, the rearrangement of the standard presentence format to provide a developmental sketch instead of the current segmented report, a determination as to the appropriateness of "confidential" presentence reports, the collection of presentence data in a fashion which allows computer analysis, and the separation of the investigation and supervision functions. Although some examination has been made of the decision-making process,[20] we need additional information about the sequence of data collection, the relative importance of certain kinds of data, and the eventual use of the data for decision-making within the correctional system. We find almost a complete void in knowledge on the social systems of correctional agencies, although available data indicate that the system itself has a profound influence on job behavior, beliefs, values, and the definition and achievement of correctional goals. Indeed, we know more about the social systems of the offenders with whom we deal than about the systems of the agencies which provide correctional services.

There are vast gaps in our knowledge about the entire correctional process, but these gaps may be closed by imaginative, innovative, and creative research and operational designs and programs. This requires a willingness to subject our current traditional, correctional models to scrutiny and a willingness to set aside those features, cherished though they may be, which are inefficient and ineffective.

[20] *Id.*

Significance of the Racial Factor in the Length of Prison Sentences

HENRY ALLEN BULLOCK

Sociologists have given some attention to the problem of accounting for the Negro's disproportionate representation in the records of police departments, courts, and prisons. Many, accepting the record at face value, have sought an explanation on the basis of the Negro's greater exposure to the social and cultural conditions that foster criminal behavior.[1] Others, more critical in their evaluation of the record, have sought an explanation in the inadequacy of available criminal statistics. This paper represents an exploratory inquiry growing out of the latter approach. It attempts specifically to test the significance of the racial factor in the length of assessed prison sentences under conditions that control many of the other factors which also appear to be influential in determining such sentences.

The idea that racial discrimination exists in the administration of criminal law has been suggested indirectly through theoretical attacks upon the validity of criminal statistics and directly through field evidence charging racial discrimination at various levels of law enforcement.

The theoretical attack has been largely directed against the confusions inherent in the definition of "crime." One of the great barriers to adequate crime reporting has been unstable definitions of the kinds of behavior identified in criminal records. Some scholars have persistently located this instability in the area of human judgment, where perceptual qualities are refracted by social values and attitudes. An examination of the literature dealing with the concept "crime" reveals a considerable amount of confusion among scholars who have attempted to clarify this term.[2] And writers have warned that interpretations and implementations of the law vary widely from place to place and from time to time even within a particular jurisdiction.[3] Sutherland's studies of "white collar" crime demonstrate that not *all* unlawful behavior is treated as criminal behavior; that an entire social class enjoys

Reprinted by special permission of the author and *The Journal of Criminal Law, Criminology and Police Science,* Copyright © 1961 by the Northwestern University School of Law, Vol. 52 (November-December 1961), pp. 411–417.

[1] See Reid, *In a Minor Key* (1940); McKeown, "Poverty, Race, and Crime," 39 *J. Crim. L. & C.* 480 (1948); Reckless, *The Crime Problem,* 37 (1955); Bernard, *Social Problems at Mid-Century,* 518 (1957); Merrill, *Society and Culture,* 293 (1957).

[2] For a summary of this type of literature, see Wilber, "The Scientific Adequacy of Criminological Concepts," 28 *Social Forces* 165 (1949).

[3] Sutherland, *Principles of Criminology,* 18 (1947).

protection from criminal treatment for offenses committed in connection with their occupations and that criminologists have derived theories of criminal behavior from statistics loaded against the lower class and in favor of the upper.[4] Sellin has also based his conception of the inadequacy of criminal statistics upon our variable attitudes toward crime and what it is. He has contended that the nature of such statistics varies with social status, social customs, and social sensitivity; that a dependable crime index cannot be derived from criminal records unless they are sufficiently free of these variations to reflect real criminality.[5]

Field evidence of racial discrimination in the administration of criminal justice has generally indicated that public officials, under the influence of their prejudices, tend to make decisions that exaggerate Negro criminality. It is generally concluded that Negroes receive differential treatment in arrest, sentencing, and imprisonment;[6] apparently even Negro juveniles receive such treatment.[7] This type of differential treatment, some authors conclude, artificially increases the Negro's *apparent* criminality and makes any comparison of criminal statistics between the two races exceedingly hazardous.[8] Generally, therefore, observations of the Negro's contacts with all stages of criminal treatment suggest that statistics exaggerate his criminality because the prejudices of public officials give members of the race a higher risk of being included in the record.[9]

THE PROCEDURE

These two sets of criticisms — the charges of faulty statistics and racial discrimination in law enforcement — have one implication in common; they imply that equality before the law is impaired because decisions about criminal behavior are influenced by other than recognized legal considerations, namely racial prejudice. Is this implication supported by fact? The study reported in this paper tests this implication as regards racial bias at the judicial level of law enforcement.

Many factors affect the decisions of public officials concerning a subject and his criminal behavior. The type of offense, number of previous felonies, nature of the plea, and nature of community sensitivity are factors that enter at

---

[4] Sutherland, "Is 'White Collar Crime' Crime?", 10 *Am. Soc. Rev.* 132 (1945); Sutherland, "Crime and Business," 217 *Annals* 112 (1941).

[5] Sellin, "The Basis of a Crime Index," 22 *J. Crim. L. & C.* 335 (1931).

[6] Weaver, *Social Problems,* 596 (1951). See also Donald, "The Negro Migration of 1916–1918," 4 *J. Negro Hist.* 383 (1921).

[7] Axelrod, "Negro and White Male Institutionalized Delinquents," 47 *Am. J. Soc.* 569 (1952).

[8] Sellin, "The Negro Criminal," 140 *Annals* 52 (1928).

[9] Taft, *Criminology,* 134 (1956).

various stages of law enforcement.[10] It is possible, therefore, that previous studies that failed to control these variables have derived conclusions concerning racial bias from comparisons of white and Negro subjects whose characteristics differed significantly in factors other than race.

We have attempted to make an objective study of racial and non-racial bias at the judicial level of law enforcement by seeking to test these assumptions:

1. The length of prison sentence will be found significantly associated with non-racial characteristics of the offender, of both legal and "extra-legal" nature.
2. Negro prisoners will be found to possess these non-racial characteristics in greater proportion to their number than will white prisoners.
3. Negro prisoners will be found to receive long sentences in greater proportion to their number than will white prisoners, even when the two groups are similar in other characteristics found to be associated with length of prison sentence.

Our data were provided through a survey of prisoners in the Texas State Prison at Huntsville in 1958.[11] Specific facts designed to characterize each prisoner were secured from the Prison Classification and Identification Department concerning 3,644 white and Negro inmates who had been committed for burglary, rape, and murder.[12] These facts were: (1) his racial identity, (2) type of offense for which he was committed, (3) number of previous felonies for which he had been convicted, (4) nature of his plea before the court, (5) county from which he was committed, and (6) number of years to which he was sentenced.

Prisoners were classified on the basis of these facts to test the significance of racial differences in length of sentence for each class. The data were coded, placed on IBM cards, and sorted according to the above characteristics. A series of dichotomous tables was constructed, first resulting in a classification of prisoners according to length of sentence and their characteristics excluding race, and later according to length of sentence and race under conditions that held other characteristics constant. Sentences representing less than ten years were defined as "short"; those ten years and over were defined as "long." By this method we were able to observe the number and per cent of prisoners in each racial group actually receiving short or long

---

[10] See Walter, *Race and Culture Relations,* 436 (1952); Johnson, "The Negro and Crime," 217 *Annals* 93 (1941).

[11] The survey was made by Professor R. C. Koeninger and students of the Department of Sociology at Sam Houston State Teachers College, Huntsville, Texas.

[12] Prisoners awaiting the death sentence were omitted. All subjects included in the study were male.

sentences as compared with the quantity expected to receive such sentences if judgments were not passed on the basis of race. We used values of chi square to determine the statistical significance of differences in observed and expected frequencies, and we used the contingency coefficient of association, represented by the symbol Q, to measure the degree of relationship existing between the main variables.

THE FINDINGS

Absolute equality before the law is difficult to realize. The imprecise nature of legal norms allows the values, attitudes, and prejudices of individuals to influence their responses to criminal behavior. The statutes of many states, including Texas, not only set a relatively wide range within which punishment for a given felony may fall, but also empower juries to assess a particular punishment within that range.[13] The assessment tends to vary significantly according to characteristics not necessarily involved by law in criminal punishment. One of these characteristics is a prisoner's racial identity.

THE INFLUENCE OF
NON-RACIAL CHARACTERISTICS

The assumption that non-racial factors of both legal and "extra-legal" nature influence the length of prison sentences is validated by the stable relationship existing between these sentences and certain traits that may characterize a prisoner at the bar. Obviously, the first sign that the validation is likely appears in the close relationship between length of sentence and type of offense. The Texas Penal Code provides that one found guilty of burglary shall be confined to the penitentiary not less than two nor more than twelve years.[14] It specifies that punishment for rape or murder shall be death, life imprisonment, or prison sentences for any term of years not less than five for rape nor less than two for murder.[15] According to the statutes, therefore, juries could assess the same penalty for each of these offenses. As one would expect, however, they exact the shorter sentences for burglary; the longer ones are for rape and murder. Prisoners convicted of burglary constituted 40.7 per cent of our study group, but 57.7 per cent of those receiving short sentences. Those committed for murder formed 49.1 per cent of the total group, but 65.2 per cent of those receiving long sentences. Similar disproportion existed among those committed for rape. The chi square value of

13 See Texas Code Crim. Proc. art. 693 (1950).
14 See Tex. Pen. Code art. 1397 (Vernon, 1948).
15 See Tex. Pen. Code arts. 1188–89, 1257 (Vernon, 1948).

Table 1: Percentage Distribution of 3,644 Prisoners according to Select Characteristics and Length of Sentence

Select characteristics	Percentage short sentences	Percentage long sentences	Total prisoners
Type of offense			
Burglary	77.0	23.0	1,482
Rape	36.1	63.9	374
Murder	39.3	60.7	1,788
Total	54.3	45.7	3,644
$\chi^2 = 521.67$, P $<$ .001, 2-df			
Type of Plea			
Guilty	64.5	35.5	2,118
Not guilty	40.1	59.9	1,526
Total	54.3	45.7	3,644
$\chi^2 = 211.96$, P $<$ .001, 1-df			
No. of previous felonies			
Less than two	53.9	46.1	3,063
Two and over	56.3	43.7	581
Total	54.3	45.7	3,644
$\chi^2 = 1.21$, P $<$ .300, 1-df			

521.67, computed from data presented in Table 1, virtually eliminates the probability that these variations are due to chance.[16] The dichotomous distribution resulting from a combination of those committed for rape and those committed for murder yields a coefficient of association ($Q = .68$) that indicates a substantial relationship between length of sentence and type of offense.

The variation of length of sentence with type of offense indicates, not surprisingly, that the sentences studied and the Texas Penal Code reflect like views concerning the relative seriousness of the offenses involved.

In contrast, despite statutory recognition of previous conviction as a factor tending to increase the length of sentence, this factor does not appear to influence significantly the length of sentence which a jury imposes. The Texas Penal Code stipulates that a second felonious offender be given the maximum rather than the minimum sentence; and that a third be given a life sentence.[17] However, the length of sentence received by our study group did not vary significantly when prisoners were classified according to this factor. Slightly more than four-fifths of them had been convicted of less than two previous felonies, and relatively the same proportion received long sentences. It should

[16] In all tables chi square accepted as indicating genuine association if large as 3.84 for probability of .05 with one degree of freedom.
[17] Tex. Pen. Code art. 62–64 (Vernon, 1952).

Table 2: Percentage Distribution of 3,644 Prisoners according to
Type of Area and Length of Sentence

Type of area	Percentage short sentences	Percentage long sentences	Total prisoners
Type of region			
East Texas	51.8	48.2	2,526
West Texas	59.8	40.2	1,118
Total	54.3	45.7	3,644

$$\chi^2 = 19.99, P < .001, \text{1-df}$$

Type of area	Percentage short sentences	Percentage long sentences	Total prisoners
Degree of urbanization			
Large cities	51.5	48.5	1,548
Small cities	56.3	43.7	2,096
Total	54.3	45.7	3,644

$$\chi^2 = 8.37, P < .010, \text{1-df}$$

be noted that juries tended to favor shorter sentences for those convicted of the greater number of previous felonies, but the differences were apparently an accident of sampling.

More important to our view is the variation of length of sentence with factors not reflected in the penal code. One such factor is the nature of the offender's plea before the court. Prisoners pleading "guilty" were given short sentences in a significantly greater proportion to their number than were those pleading "not guilty."[18] As an index of this imbalance, prisoners pleading "guilty" composed 69.1 per cent of those receiving short sentences, but only 58.1 per cent of the total group. The chi square value of 211.96 validates the statistical significance of these differences, and the coefficient Q = .46 indicates a fairly high degree of relationship between the two variables. These facts tend to support the view that bargaining between the prosecution and the offender operates through the plea, and those pleading guilty are rewarded for their cooperation.

Another set of non-racial factors apparently associated with length of prison sentence pertains to the type of area from which prisoners are committed. Assuming community sensitivity to criminal behavior to be based upon the type of culture area in which the prisoner is tried, we grouped the counties from which our prisoners were committed according to the cultural regions of Texas and the degree of urbanization characterizing these counties. As shown in Table 2, those committed from counties composing the traditional East Texas region tended to get long sentences in greater proportion

---

[18] "Guilty" also includes those pleading guilty to one charge though "not guilty" to another.

to their representation in the total group, while those from West Texas tended to get short sentences.[19] Likewise, prisoners committed from counties having large cities tended to get long sentences in greater proportion than did those committed from counties having small cities.[20] Although the coefficients of association were low, the chi square value in each instance indicates that such areal factors are significantly associated with the length of sentences which juries of these areas tend to assess.

It appears, therefore, that established legal norms are not the only grounds upon which juries decide the fate of an offender. Whether he pleads guilty or not guilty and whether he is committed from a highly urbanized area or one less urbanized also operate as factors determining how long a prison sentence he will be required to serve.

EXPOSURE OF NEGRO PRISONERS TO EFFECTIVE NON-RACIAL FACTORS

Because of the inclination of jurors to be influenced by these particular characteristics of prisoners, Negroes who possess such characteristics to a greater degree than do white prisoners would be expected to receive longer sentences, even when their racial identity is not being considered. From the point of view of expressed criminality, Negro prisoners do run such a "risk." They appear more likely than white prisoners to be committed for a type of offense for which juries usually assess long sentences. According to Table 3, a greater proportion of them were committed for murder. Approximately 60 per cent of the Negro prisoners were committed for this offense as compared with 39 per cent of the whites. On the other hand, only one-third of them were committed for burglary, while 47.5 per cent of the white prisoners were committed for this offense. Approximately the same proportion of the prisoners of each racial group entered pleas of guilty and not guilty, and a smaller proportion of the Negro prisoners had committed two or more previous felonies.

Negro prisoners also run a greater confinement risk from the point of view of the areal factor. They were committed from the East Texas region in greater proportions than were whites, and a greater proportion of them were committed from counties having large cities. It should be recalled that these

---

[19] Geographically, the line which divides East and West Texas is hazy. It may be said to follow roughly the 98th meridian. Culturally, it is more definite. It separates two different types of economies — East Texas, the region of lumbering, small farms and oil industries; West Texas, the region of large ranches. For cultural descriptions, see Steen, *The Texas Story*, 290–305 (1948) ; Goodwyn, *Lone Star Land*, 39–47 (1955).

[20] A county was identified as a "large city" county if it had one or more cities 50,000 or over in population size. Others were identified as "small city" counties.

Table 3: Percentage Distribution of 3,644 Prisoners according to Select Characteristics and Race

Characteristics	Percentage Negro	Percentage white	Total
Type of offense			
Burglary	38.6	61.4	1,482
Rape	31.8	68.2	374
Murder	58.0	42.0	1,788
Total	47.4	52.6	3,644

x^2 = 78.28, P < .001, 2-df

Type of plea			
Guilty	47.7	52.3	2,118
Not guilty	47.0	53.0	1,526
Total	47.4	52.6	3,644

x^2 = 0.22, P < .634, 1-df

No. of previous felonies			
Less than two	48.5	51.5	3,063
Two and over	41.8	58.2	581
Total	47.4	52.6	3,644

x^2 = 8.94, P < .010, 1-df

Type of region			
East Texas	51.5	48.5	2,526
West Texas	38.1	61.9	1,118
Total	47.4	52.6	3,644

x^2 = 55.98, P < .001, 1-df

Urbanization			
Large cities	52.0	48.0	1,548
Small cities	44.0	56.0	2,096
Total	47.4	52.6	3,644

x^2 = 22.71, P <.001, 1-df

are the kinds of areas in which juries tend to give long sentences. These are the kinds of factors which must be controlled if the influence of the racial factor is to be objectively tested. When the effects of these factors are eliminated, the association of race and length of prison sentence should decrease and become less significant.

SIGNIFICANCE OF THE RACIAL FACTOR UNDER CONTROLLED CONDITIONS

However, control of these non-racial factors fails to reduce the gross association which we observe to exist between race and length of prison sentence. Instead, it increases the degree of this association, changes its direction, and strengthens its validity. Although the total coefficient is low, "being black" generally means one type of sentence while "being white" means another. This conclusion, however, is much more valid when observed through white and Negro prisoners who were committed for the same offense. Table 4 shows that there is a slightly higher degree of association between race and length of sentence among prisoners who were committed for burglary and murder. Juries tended to give Negro prisoners committed for murder shorter sentences than they gave whites who were committed for the same offense. They gave Negroes committed for burglary longer sentences than they gave whites committed for this offense. These judicial responses possibly represent the indulgent and non-indulgent patterns that characterize local attitudes concerning property and interracial morals. Murder is an intra-racial crime.[21] Since the victims of most of the Negroes committed for this offense were also Negroes, local norms tolerate a less rigorous enforcement of the law; the disorder is mainly located within the Negro society. On the other hand, burglary is mainly an interracial offense. When a Negro is an offender, his attack is usually against the property of a white person.[22] Local norms are less tolerant, for the motivation to protect white property and to protect "white" society against disorder is stronger than the motivation to protect "Negro" society.

These indulgent and non-indulgent patterns of racial discrimination are even more firmly established when other variables are controlled. In three of the four types of areas a significantly greater proportion of Negroes received short sentences for murder. Only in the cases of prisoners from East Texas committed for murder were racial differences in length of sentence not statistically significant. However, the higher coefficients of association derived from a comparison of white and Negro prisoners committed for burglary from East and West Texas counties indicate that the greater risk which Negroes run with regard to this offense persists under the control of areal variables. This is also true for those counties that have small cities.

Although juries generally favor with short sentences those who plead guilty of the charges held against them, their attitude appears different when their judgments are observed through the influence of the racial factor. Negro prisoners who entered a plea of guilty received long sentences in greater proportion than did whites who entered this plea. When racial differences were observed under conditions that controlled both type of offense and plea, as shown in Table 6, the degree and significance of the association increased while the direction remained the same. Negro offenders who plead guilty of murder

---

[21] Bullock, "Urban Homicide in Theory and Fact," 45 *J. Crim. L., C. & P.S.* 565 (1955).

[22] That burglary offenses committed by Negroes are usually or more often directed against the property of whites than the property of Negroes has been verified by evidence secured from the District Attorney's offices of sample counties.

Table 4: Percentage Distribution of 3,644 Prisoners according to Type of Offense, Length of Sentence, and Race

Offense	Short			Long			Q	x^2	$p^a<$
	Percentage Negro	Percentage white	Total	Percentage Negro	Percentage white	Total			
Burglary	35.9	64.1	1,141	47.5	52.5	341	.23	14.45	.001
Rape	36.3	63.7	135	29.3	70.7	239	.16	1.92	.250
Murder	62.1	37.9	702	55.3	44.7	1,086	.14	8.10	.010
Total	45.2	54.8	1,978	50.0	50.0	1,666	.10	8.20	.010

[a]*With one degree of freedom.*

Table 5: Coefficient of Association Between Race and Length of Sentence for Prisoners Classified by Area and Type of Offense

Area and type of offense	Q	x^2 1-df	P <
1—East Texas Counties			
a. Burglary	.25	5.36	.050
b. Rape	.27	2.32	.200
c. Murder	.10	1.57	.300
2—West Texas counties			
a. Burglary	.33	5.43	.020
b. Rape	.00	0.00	
c. Murder	.15[a]	4.12	.050
3—Large city counties			
a. Burglary	.10	2.55	.200
b. Rape	.13[a]	0.55	.500
c. Murder	.23[a]	7.70	.010
4—Other city counties			
a. Burglary	.31	12.62	.001
b. Rape	.18	1.46	.300
c. Murder	.12[a]	3.91	.050

[a] *"Being Negro" and receiving shorter sentences.*

also get shorter sentences than do whites who plead guilty of this offense, and those who plead guilty of burglary get longer sentences. The indulgent and non-indulgent patterns appear to operate undisturbed by the nature of an offender's plea.

According to Table 7, racial differences in the assessment of prison sentences tend to persist even though the prisoners are alike in all effective characteristics except race. Negro prisoners committed for murder get short sentences more often than whites committed for this offense even when prisoners of the two racial groups are alike in terms of plea and area from which they were committed. Those committed from East Texas counties and from counties having large cities also received short sentences in greater proportion than did white prisoners of similar characteristics.

Rape, too, is a form of intra-racial crime that elicits short sentences when Negroes are the offenders. Despite the wide publicity given interracial cases, the victim and the assailant are usually of the same race. That Negroes are given short sentences in greater proportion that are whites is probably another expression of the employment of a double standard of moral expectation from the Negro society. In addition to responding to the law, jurors appear also to respond to the race of an offender. If his offense carries him

Table 6: Coefficient of Association Between Length of Sentence and Race for Prisoners Classified by Type of Offense and Plea

Type of offense and plea	Q	$\chi^2_{1\text{-}df}$	p <
1—Total prisoners:			
a. Plea of guilty	.24	29.75	.001
b. Plea of not guilty	.08	2.46	.200
2—Committed for burglary:			
a. Plea of guilty	.31	14.00	.001
b. Plea of not guilty	.03	0.01	.900
3—Committed for rape:			
a. Plea of guilty	.40[a]	4.79	.050
b. Plea of not guilty	.12[a]	0.82	.800
4—Committed for murder:			
a. Plea of guilty	.28[a]	8.40	.010
b. Plea of not guilty	.12[a]	3.69	.100

[a]*"Being Negro" and receiving shorter sentences.*

across racial lines, his penalty is heavier than that given whites who appear in court under the same circumstances. If his offense remains within the confines of his segregated community life, his punishment is less than that imposed upon his white counterpart. These patterns, indulgent and non-indulgent, seem to operate irrespective of the area from which he was committed, the nature of his plea, or the number of previous felonies for which he was convicted.

SUMMARY AND CONCLUSIONS

In light of basic criticisms directed against criminal statistics, and certain charges directed against the agencies of law enforcement, an exploratory study designed to observe the significance of racial differences in length of prison sentences was undertaken. Certain factors other than those specified in the law were found significantly associated with the length of sentences imposed by a jury upon an offender. Negro prisoners were observed to be more greatly exposed to these factors than white prisoners, but were also observed to receive sentences significantly different from those given white prisoners even when these factors were controlled. Assuming indulgent and non-indulgent patterns in which Negro offenders are apparently under-penalized for one type of offense and over-penalized for another, racial discrimination appears to be motivated more by the desire to protect the order of the white community than to effect the reformation of the offender. If the study

Table 7: Coefficient of Association Between Race and Length of Sentences for Prisoners Classified by Area of Origin, Type of Offense and Plea

Area, type of plea and offense	Q	x^2 1-df	P <
1—East Texas counties:			
a. Burglary, guilty	.33	5.78	.02
b. Rape, guilty[b]	.61[a]	5.02	.05
c. Murder, guilty	.31[a]	4.64	.05
d. Murder, not guilty	.09	0.88	.80
2—West Texas counties:			
a. Burglary, guilty	.53	15.64	.001
b. Rape, guilty	.00	0.00	
c. Murder, guilty	.23[a]	4.38	.05
d. Murder, not guilty	.00	0.00	
3—Large city counties:			
a. Burglary, guilty	.09	0.80	.80
b. Rape, guilty	.22[a]	4.31	.05
c. Murder, guilty	.27[a]	4.48	.05
d. Murder, not guilty	.15[a]	2.20	.20
4—Other city counties:			
a. Burglary, guilty	.43	24.87	.001
b. Rape, guilty	.15[a]	0.78	.50
c. Murder, guilty	.75[a]	111.99	.001
d. Murder, not guilty	.15[a]	2.19	.20

[a]*"Being Negro" and receiving shorter sentences:*

[b]*Those pleading not guilty except in the case of murder, when distributed for these variables, yielded frequencies smaller than 10 for the different cells of our tables.*

has any theoretical suggestion at all, it is this: Those who enforce the law conform to the norms of their local society concerning racial prejudice, thus denying equality before the law. That criminal statistics reflect social customs, values, and prejudices appears to be further validated.

Sentencing Practices of Criminal Court Judges

EDWARD GREEN

I. THE PROBLEM

What determines the severity of the sentences meted out by judges to convicted offenders? How consistent are different judges attached to the same court in sentencing offenders whose crimes and past records in crime are similar? Prior investigations of these questions have presented a picture of the sentencing process that is highly incongruent with the legalistic conception of the law as a rational science. They convey the notion that the deliberations of the sentencing judge are unduly influenced by his prejudices against certain classes of persons or by personality factors stemming from his social origins and life experience. None of them, however, has undertaken a systematic study of the sentencing process as a whole. Their investigations center primarily upon the influence of psychologic and sociologic factors on sentencing while juridical factors are neglected. Thus in comparing different categories of offenders with respect to the gravity of the penalties received, they do not give due consideration to possible differences among them in the legal make-up of the cases. The controls which are imposed for variations in the gravity of the offenses or in the recidivism of the convicted offenders are conjectural and lack precision and completeness.[1] The research summarized in this article has sought to present a more balanced outline of the sentencing process by investigating the criteria of sentencing more comprehensively than hitherto has been done.

II. THE METHOD

The data for this study were derived from official court and police records of the City of Philadelphia, Pennsylvania. The research sample comprises all of the cases resulting in conviction recorded in a single volume of the docket of a non-jury prison court of the Philadelphia Court of Quarter Sessions. The cases, totaling 1,437, are divided among eighteen judges, and were tried within a period of seventeen months during the years 1956-1957.

Reprinted by special permission of the author and *The American Journal of Correction,* official publication of The American Correctional Association, July-August 1960, pp. 32–35.

[1] Edward Green, *An Analysis of the Sentencing Practices of Criminal Court Judges in Philadelphia* (unpublished Ph.D. dissertation, Univ. of Pennsylvania, 1959).

The variables which were studied for their effect upon variations in the severity of the sentences comprise the following three sets of factors:

Legal factors: the crime, the number of bills of indictment on which the offender is convicted, and the prior criminal record.

Non-legal factors: sex, age, race, and place of birth.

Factors in the criminal prosecution: the sentencing judge, the prosecuting attorney, and the plea of the defendant.

The types of sentences in the order of their severity are imprisonment, probation, fine, and suspended sentence. The measure of the severity of prison sentences adopted for purposes of this study is the minimum term which, for reasons pertaining to· procedures of release from prison, is a more realistic estimate of the actual weight of the sentence than the maximum term or some point between the two limits. Prison sentences are classified according to whether the minimum term is 12 months or more, 3-11½ months, or under 3 months. The first and second categories consist of commitments to the state penitentiary and to the county prison (or workhouse) respectively. Minimum terms of less than 3 months are generally fixed at the period of days spent in detention awaiting the completion of trial whereupon the defendant is released on a bench parole. Although prison sentences in form, they are equivalent to probation in substance; hence they are combined with probations, fines, and suspensions into the category of "non-imprisonment."

III. THE FINDINGS

A. LEGAL FACTORS

The crime. The penal statutes which set the maximum permissible penalties for the various crimes provide an official measure of the relative gravity of the different kinds of offenses. The judges, however, apply this scale somewhat loosely. As the accompanying Table shows, there are many discrepancies between the statutory ranks of the various crimes and the ranks based upon the proportion of penitentiary sentences imposed for each type of crime. Burglary and statutory rape, for example, rank higher according to statute but lower in the severity of the sentences imposed than narcotics violations or felonious assault. In other instances, crimes of the same statutory rank receive widely dissimilar sentences. This observation raises the question: What are the standards by which the judges rank the gravity of the various crimes and which prevail over the statutory scale of crimes? An analysis of the data on the distribution of sentences for the various types of crimes indicates that they consist of three variables, each an aspect of the offender-victim relationship, described as follows.

The specificity of the victim. Of broadest range, taking in the entire continuum of crimes, is whether the victim of an offense is diffuse ("the public") or specific (a person or a business). Crimes against the public which do not involve a specific victim, such as liquor and gambling violations, receive the lowest penalties of all. Those which entail a potential physical threat to a possible victim, carrying concealed deadly weapons and drunken driving, receive the next higher penalties.

Personal contact between the offender and the victim. Where the victim is specific but the element of personal contact is not germane to the definition of the crime, as in property crimes of misdemeanor grade and felonious crimes against personal property (except fraud), the penalties are less severe than where personal contact is implicit in the definition of the crime. Where personal contact is lacking but is a potentiality inherent in the nature of the criminal act, as in burglary (the illegal entry of a premises with the intent to commit a felony), the sentences are heavier. Fraud and statutory rape, crimes which involve personal contact between the offender and the victim, are more stringently punished than any of the preceding ones.

Bodily harm. Among crimes involving personal contact between the offender and his victim, those including the element of bodily harm receive higher penalties than those lacking it. The least severely punished of these is narcotic drug violations wherein bodily injury is presumed to be a by-product of the criminal act rather than an intended result. Ranking next higher is robbery, in which the element of bodily harm enters the offender's designs but is secondary to the intent to deprive the victim of his property. The sentences for felonious crimes against the person wherein the essence of the offense is menace or violence directed at the victim, are higher yet. And finally, the degree of bodily harm intended and the degree inflicted are important criteria as revealed by the differences between felonious assault and homicide in the proportions of penitentiary sentences dealt out. (See Table.)

The derivation of these standards for weighting the gravity of the various crimes is implicit in the data of the Table. Within the separate categories of felonies and misdemeanors, the offender-victim relationship in each type of crime receiving a higher proportion of penitentiary sentences than another entails a greater degree of personalization which follows a gradient of the extent to which the element of bodily injury enters into the definition of the crime.

Thus it appears that the present-day administrators of the criminal law, compared to the legislators who framed the penal statutes, place a relatively higher premium on personality values than upon property values. This conclusion finds additional support in the observation that in theft cases differences in the value of stolen property do not affect the severity of the sentences which the judges impose.

Percentage of Cases in Each Crime Category Receiving Penitentiary
Sentences

Crime	Maximum sentence (in years) according to statute	Percentage of penitentiary sentences
Felonies		
Homicide	12-life	96.0
Felonious assault	5-10	58.5
Robbery	10-20	45.2
Narcotics	5 (for 1st offense)	39.9
Fraud	5	38.1
Statutory rape	15	35.6
Burglary	20	29.1
Personal property	5 (except forgery: 10)	19.4
Misdemeanors		
Person	2-3	16.7
Property	2-3	15.7
Public: drunken driving, carrying concealed weapons	1-3	7.5
Public: others	1-3	3.1

The number of bills of indictment. This variable reflects the number of
separate criminal acts for which a defendant is convicted in the same legal
action. The data show that in each crime category, except felonious homicide, there is a marked association between the number of bills of indictment
for which a verdict of guilty is found and the severity of the sentences. For
the cases as a whole, defendants charged in one, two, three, and four or more
bills of indictment receive penitentiary sentences in 15.2 per cent, 27.1 per
cent, 40.4 per cent, and 57.8 per cent of cases, respectively.

The prior criminal record. The criterion of recidivism showing the greatest association with variations in the severity of the sentences is the number
of prior convictions of felonies; defendants with none, one, two or three, four
or more prior convictions of felonies receive penitentiary sentences in 14.4 per
cent, 27.0 per cent, 33.9 per cent, and 50.7 per cent of cases, respectively. In
cases involving prior convictions of felonies, prior convictions of crimes at
the misdemeanor level have no effect upon the severity of the sentences. But
in cases lacking prior felony convictions, the number of prior convictions of
misdemeanors resulting in penitentiary sentences significantly influences the
severity of the sentences. In cases involving no prior convictions of felonies
and no prior convictions of misdemeanors resulting in penitentiary sentences,
the number of prior convictions of misdemeanors disposed of by milder penalties becomes a significant criterion for sentencing. The number of arrests

not resulting in convictions and the recency of the last prior conviction of a felony have no effects upon the sentences. In short, the judges tend to use the highest criterion in the prior criminal record which is applicable to a case, ignoring those which are lesser or irrelevant.

Factors affecting the length of penitentiary sentences. Since the length of the minimum terms of penitentiary sentences ranges broadly from one year to life imprisonment, a separate analysis was made for this group of cases. The findings are briefly summarized as follows:

The rank order of gravity of the crimes according to the term of the minimum penitentiary sentences imposed is similar to the rank order based upon the severity of the sentences generally. A single exception is the reduction in the position of crimes of felonious assault from next to the highest crime of felony grade to next to the lowest. This shift is most likely to be due to the relatively low statutory ceilings on the maximum terms of imprisonment for these offenses (5-10 years). The effect of the prior criminal record on the length of penitentiary sentences is negligible. This implies that, once the offenses achieve a high level of gravity, the condition of the offender is no longer a major concern of the sentencing judge. The number of bills of indictment in the accusation continues to exert a strong effect upon the severity of the sentences except within the categories of felonious assault and homicide. It is likely that the utter gravity of these offenses tends to overshadow the influence of other factors upon the judges' deliberations.

B. Non-legal Factors

Sex. The female defendants receive significantly milder sentences than the men; but the women's offenses involve a smaller proportion of serious crimes — 54.4 per cent of the females, compared to 65.4 per cent of the males, were convicted of felonies. Upon controlling for this difference in the proportions of serious crimes, the difference in sentences between the sexes declines to a level of non-significance.

Age. The cases are classified into three age groups: under 21, 21-29, and over 29. A preliminary analysis shows that the offenders in the under 21 category are favored with greater leniency than the older offenders. However, there are crucial differences among the three age groups in the variables that constitute the legal criteria for sentencing. The youthful offenders have lesser prior criminal records than the older offenders. The proportion of cases in each age category involving more than one prior conviction of a felony is 11.7 per cent for the under 21 group, 25.7 per cent for the 21-29 group, and 39.0 per cent for the over 29 group. The young offenders tend to commit the more serious crimes in greater proportion. Indictments for felonious crimes against the person and robbery account for 24.8 per cent of the cases in the under 21 group but only for 14.5 per cent and 12.1 per cent of the cases in the 21-29 group and over 29 group, respectively. The younger offenders are also more active in certain kinds of criminal activities. This is illustrated by the fact that 75 per cent of the cases of burglary committed by offenders under 21 are charged in two or more bills of indictment, whereas the proportions for the 21-29 and over 29 age groups are 43.5 per cent and 30.0 per cent, respectively. By holding constant these factors — the type of crime, the number of prior convictions of felonies, and the number of bills of indictment — the differences in sentences among the age categories declines to a level of non-significance.

Race. The initial investigation of the differences in sentences according to race shows that the whites receive generally milder penalties than the Negroes. The greatest difference is in the proportion of probations, whites receiving this disposition in 20.1 per cent of cases, and Negroes in 12.8 per cent of cases. However, there are marked differences between the two groups in age distribution — a much larger proportion of the whites is in the younger age categories. Thus — recalling that young offenders have lesser prior criminal records than older offenders — there is likely to be a higher proportion of recidivists among the Negroes. Moreover, within each age category, there are marked differences between whites and Negroes in the proportions of the various types of crimes. In the under 21 group, the Negroes, compared to the whites, were convicted of proportionately two and a half times as many robberies, twice as many felonious crimes against the person, but only half as many burglaries. In the 21-29 group these differences decline considerably, but the Negroes were convicted of proportionately three times as many narcotics violations as the whites. The smallest differences between the races in criminal behavior patterns occur in the over 29 group. When these race-linked differences in the legal make-up of the cases are taken into consideration, there is no evidence whatever of racial discrimination in sentencing. Likewise, the differences between the two racial groups in the length of the penitentiary sentences received turns out to be negligible.

Place of birth. The effect of nativity upon variation in the severity of sentences is explored by comparing the sentences of Negroes born in the northern states with the sentences of those who have migrated from the South. The differences obtained are too slight to be of any consequence.

C. Factors in the Criminal Prosecution

The judge. The effect of the "personal equation" on the dispensation of criminal justice is investigated by determining the extent to which the judges differ among themselves in sentencing cases of similar gravity. The gravity of the cases is controlled by assigning to each case a score based upon the observed relationship between each of the legal criteria for sentencing and the severity of the sentences — the higher the score, the more serious the case. The sentencing records of the eighteen judges are compared within three categories of cases: high-score cases, intermediate-score cases, and low-score cases.

The results yielded by the procedure described above show that in the cases at each level of gravity there are statistically significant differences among the judges in the severity of the sentences imposed. However, the degree of disparity is not uniform at all levels of cases. In the category of low-score cases, two groups of judges emerge: six impose sentences of "non-imprisonment" in no more than half of their respective cases, and twelve impose such sentences in more than half of their respective cases. In the cases of intermediate gravity, three groups of judges take form. One group of three judges metes out penitentiary sentences in the range of 0.0 per cent to 11.8 per cent; the range for the second group of eight judges is 18.4 per cent to 34.2 per cent; and for a third group of six judges, it is 38.0 per cent to 57.1 per cent. Within the high-score cases, the major division occurs between the fourteen judges who sentence over half of their respective cases to penitentiary terms and the four who impose such sentences in less than half of their cases. Within each of the subgroups in the three score categories, there are no statistically significant differences among the judges in sentencing.

A similar procedure is employed in investigating the degree of consistency among the judges in the length of the penitentiary sentences imposed. The results show an unexpectedly high degree of similarity. In the cases scoring above the median score, only one of the judges is appreciably out of line with the others; his sentences are more severe. In the cases falling below the median score, there are no statistically significant differences among all of the judges in sentencing.

Thus we see that in cases which are patently either mild or grave, there tends to be a relatively high degree of consensus among the judges on the standards for gauging the gravity of the cases. As the cases move from either extreme toward intermediacy, group standards become less stable and sentencing practices more individualized.

The prosecuting attorney. In view of the importance attached to the role of the prosecuting attorney in the American legal system, it is reasonable to suppose that a judge's sentences may vary according to differences among district attorneys in the quality or vigor of their presentations. A statistical test of this hypothesis is made by analyzing the dispositions of each of seven judges. In all instances, the differences in the prosecuting attorneys have a negligible effect.

The plea. The belief is prevalent that offenders who plead guilty and thereby save the state the expense of a lengthy trial, receive lighter sentences than those who plead not guilty and are subsequently convicted. Surprisingly, the data offer no evidence that differences in plea affect the severity of the sentences. Only in cases of convictions of crimes against personal property, which are commonly accompanied by offers to make restitution, is it clear that the defendants accrue any benefit by a plea of guilty.

IV. CONCLUSIONS

The results of the investigation of the influence of legal and non-legal factors upon variations in the severity of the sentences offer the reassurance that the deliberations of the sentencing judges are not at the mercy of passions and prejudices but rather mirror the operation of rational processes. The criteria for sentencing recognized in the law, the nature of the offense and the offender's prior criminal record, make a decisive contribution to the determination of the weight of the penalties; and in applying these criteria, the judges display a sensibility for the relative importance of each. The marked variations in sentences according to sex, age, and race are due to differences in criminal behavior patterns associated with these bio-social variables, not to hidden prejudice.

The findings concerning the differences in sentences among the various judges are not clear in their implications. Although they reveal wide disparities, they show also an impressive degree of uniformity. Undoubtedly, individual differences in social background, personality, and penal philosophy sensitize the various judges differently to cases of a similar kind; but without specific information on these factors for each judge, the precise nature and extent of their influence is problematic. It appears, however, that whatever proclivities they generate are appreciably checked by the legal criteria. Perhaps of even greater significance is the fact that the disparities do not occur uniformly in cases at all levels of seriousness but rather follow a distinctive pattern. The tendency toward consistency as cases approach the poles of pettiness or seriousness indicates that only in cases of intermediate gravity could individual differences in legal philosophy and other factors less susceptible to analysis be a prominent factor in producing the disparities. It also suggests that the judges need more background information on convicted offenders or supplemental standards for sentencing, particularly in cases that are clearly neither mild nor grave.

4

ADMINISTRATION OF PENAL AND CORRECTIONAL POLICY

Correctional Systems and National Values

NORMAN S. HAYNER

The correctional systems of different countries can be compared statistically. Many will have unusual features. These can be analysed in terms of the distinct cultural settings. It is the purpose of this paper to make an attempt (1) to place five selected systems on a theoretical continuum from extreme emphasis on punishment of offenders to extreme emphasis on treatment and (2) to explain unique features of these systems in terms of national or regional values.

To determine the position of a given country or state on the punishment-treatment continuum the following empirical criteria have been used:

1. *Sentencing.* Extent to which pre-sentence investigations were used by judges. It was assumed that this was an index to the consideration. of personality and social background in addition to the crime.
2. *Probation.* The ratio of probationers to prisoners, the quality of probation officers, as measured by training and experience, and the caseloads which they carry.
3. *Architecture.* Size of correctional buildings and degree of departure from traditional Pennsylvania or Auburn types of architecture.
4. *Personnel.* Method of selection and training of correctional personnel.
5. *Maternal and child care.* The methods used in handling women prisoners who are pregnant or mothers of small children.
6. *Classification.* The degree to which the admission study is professional and the extent to which it is followed by the classification authority.
7. *Work by prisoners.* Extent to which prisoners are employed, the diversification of this employment and the degree to which remuneration approaches that for similar work outside the prison.
8. *Education.* The variety of educational services and the percentage of prisoners who participate.
9. *Handling of escapees.* The extent of individualisation and the severity of punishment for escapees.
10. *Visits and letters.* The frequency, length, and informality of visits and the frequency of letters.
11. *Parole.* The percentage of prisoners released under supervision; the caseloads and the quality (training and experience) of parole officers.

Reprinted from *British Journal of Criminology,* 3 (October 1962), pp. 163–175, by permission of the author and the Institute for the Study and Treatment of Delinquency.

12. *Statistics and research.* The standards reached by correctional statistics and research.

By means of long interviews with key officials or through first-hand experience[1] data on each of these criteria have been gathered from the various jurisdictions. These facts have been evaluated by the writer to determine where the political entity should be placed on a seven-point punishment-treatment scale. A score of one means extreme emphasis on punishment; seven, extreme emphasis on treatment. On the basis of judgments made by five European correctional administrators all items have been given a double weighting except 3, 5, 9 and 12. The results are shown in Table 1.

It will be noted that the governmental units included in Table 1 have been limited to Mexico, Spain, West Germany, Western United States and England. Spain and England have national prison systems; the United States and Mexico have both federal and state systems; Germany has a federally established body of criminal law, but administration is in the hands of the states.

The two German states (*Länder*) of Baden-Württemberg and Hessen were studied independently and given ratings of 77 and 93. They were then averaged to get the score for Germany. The correctional system of the former is considered by administrators about average; of the latter, better than average for Germany. If data were available for all the Länder, the city-state of Hamburg would probably be at the top; Rheinland-Pfalz, near the bottom.[2]

On the basis of many contacts with the correctional system for the state of Oaxaca in southern Mexico, the rating was 48. A three-hour inspection in 1960 of the penitentiary at Ciudad Victoria, capital of the state of Tamaulipas in northern Mexico, supplemented by information from a local judge and from a representative of the prosecutor's office, suggested a rating of 56. Extended study of the correctional system of the Federal District (includes Mexico City) gave a score of 73. The ratings listed for Mexico are, therefore, averages for these three jurisdictions.

The Western Region of the United States includes both the Mountain

---

[1] Four weeks were spent in 1954 and 1960 studying the correctional institutions of Spain with visits to ten establishments; an equal time in England with inspections of eleven prisons and borstals; and five weeks in Germany with visits to fifteen institutions. Between 1941 and 1961 the writer visited fifteen correctional facilities in Mexico — two of them many times. He has taught courses in criminology at the University of Washington in Seattle for thirty-seven years and was on leave for five years (1951–56) to serve full time as member and chairman of the Washington State Board of Prison Terms and Paroles.

[2] In 1958 Hamburg had one probation officer for every 62,331 of the estimated population for that year; Hessen, one for 98,968; Baden-Württemberg, one for 158,161; Rheinland-Pfalz, one for 209,669; Saarland, one for 346,733. The ratio for West Germany was one for 140,512.

Table I: Punishment-Treatment Ratings for Selected
Correctional Systems

Criterion		Mexico	Spain	West Germany	Western United States	England
[a]1.	Sentencing	6	6	9	10	8
[a]2.	Probation	4	4	5	10	10
3.	Architecture	3.7	4	5	4.3	6
[a]4.	Personnel	4.7	10	11	10	12
5.	Mothers	4.3	7	2.5	1.3	4
[a]6.	Classification	4.7	10	9	10.7	12
[a]7.	Work	8	12	12	8.7	10
[a]8.	Education	6	8	8	10	12
9.	Escapees	3.3	3	5	3	5
[a]10.	Visits	10.7	4	7	8.7	12
[a]11.	Parole	2	2	7	10.7	10
12.	Statistics	1	3	4.5	4.7	6
	Total	59[b]	73	85	92[b]	107

[a]*Double weighting for this criterion.*

[b]*Corrected for error of .1 due to rounding.*

and Pacific Divisions with a total of thirteen states. The correctional system of California easily ranks at the top from the standpoint of emphasis on treatment with a score of 122 points out of a possible 140. It was given the top evaluation for sentencing, personnel, classification, education, and statistics. It would be matched by the U.S. Bureau of Prisons which has thirteen institutions and many probation departments in this Western Region. The Bureau may be a little higher in probation and architecture but slightly lower in sentencing, education and statistics. The state of Washington with a rating of 107 is probably a bit more treatment-oriented than five other states in the region (not counting California). Montana with a rating of 47[3] (the lowest possible score is 20) is roughly similar in punitive emphasis to the five remaining states. This low score pulls down the average for the Western United States to 92.

As to the economic, social and criminal situations in the regions included, Mexico is a country in transition with a low average standard of living and a preponderance of crimes against the person, but in the rapidly growing cities increasing rates for offences against property. The Western portion of the United States has a high standard of living, high urbanisation (especially on the Pacific Coast), a high degree of residential mobility in its population, and high rates for such crimes as robbery and burglary. England and Ger-

---

[3] Benjamin W. Wright, graduate student in sociology at the University of Washington and formerly Director of Parole in Montana, provided the ratings on the twelve criteria for his home state.

many are in the northern belt of Western European countries which in general are more industrialised, have higher standards of living, and higher rates for crime and imprisonment than countries like Spain which are located in the less industrialised and less prosperous Mediterranean belt.

Examination of the ratings for specific criteria in Table 1 reveals that the sharpest gradients between the five jurisdictions are to be found in the handling of pregnant offenders and for statistics, visits, parole, probation and education.[4] Comments are made below on the handling of mothers, visits and education. Correctional statistics and research are almost absent in Mexico, but they profit from a million-dollar annual budget in California. Except for the possibility of revocation and incarceration if caught by the police in a criminal act, supervision for adult probationers and parolees is lacking in Mexico and Spain and insufficiently provided in most of Germany. Mexicans, Spaniards and many Germans in these statuses are, therefore, actually free men. But supervision by trained and experienced salaried officers is generally regarded as essential for adequate treatment of persons on probation or parole.

Probably more interesting than this attempt to make general comparisons between governmental areas is the fact that different countries or regions tend to have unique correctional practices. An attempt is made below to explain such differences in terms of national or regional values.

In Mexico, for example, it is the custom to permit well-behaved prisoners to have conjugal visits. This means that these prisoners are permitted to have sexual contact with their wives either in their cells or in a designated section of the prison. The new penitentiary for sentenced offenders in the Federal District provides special rooms for the purpose. This custom appears to be rooted in the strong emphasis on family in Mexican life and a feeling that conjugal visits keep couples together. Marital rights here take precedence over punishment of the criminal, whereas the reverse is true in most other countries. Home visits are, however, permitted in Sweden, Poland, Argentina and (once during a prison term) in England.[5]

---

[4] In Germany, England, Mexico, and Spain escape by a prisoner alone is not a crime. It is regarded as something to be expected of confined men and is punishable by some such method as isolation on reduced rations for two weeks. The ratings for this criterion were complicated by lack of individualisation in the handling of escapees in certain prisons and the extreme measures taken by some directors to prevent escapes.

[5] See Ruth Shonle Cavan and Eugene S. Zemans, "Marital Relationships of Prisoners in Twenty-Eight Countries," *Journal of Criminal Law, Criminology and Police Science*, XLIX, 133–139 (July-August, 1958). Conjugal visits are permitted in Cuba, in certain other Latin American countries, and in selected prisons of Sweden and Yugoslavia. Upper-class prisoners are probably permitted such visits in all Latin American prisons. Some prison directors in Mexico also permit prostitutes. This seems to reflect admiration for the person who is *macho, i.e.,* exhibits physical courage, loyalty to a group, and sexual prowess.

Spaniards, in contrast to Mexicans, are horrified at the idea of conjugal visits. Visiting arrangements for husbands and wives usually give emphasis to physical separation. The most unusual feature of Spanish corrections is in the handling of women with small children. The Centre for Care of Mothers and Children (Centro de Maternología y Puericultura) in Madrid is the outstanding institution of this type in Western Europe. From all over Spain pregnant felons with sentences of three years or more are sent here. Excellent facilities and medical care are provided for these women. Mothers who nurse their children sleep in a separate dormitory and get one day off their sentence for every day they continue nursing. If satisfactory provision for the children cannot be made by families outside, mothers are permitted to keep their youngsters with them for as long as four years. In special cases the children may stay until seven years of age. They do not hear the word "prison." They think of the institution as a hospital. Girls and boys sleep in separate dormitories while their mothers sleep near them in open-top cubicles containing three beds each. Spaniards feel that keeping the children and mothers together does something constructive for both.

As compared with other European countries, juvenile delinquency rates are low in Spain. Spaniards believe that anything which will strengthen the bond between parents and children should be encouraged. On the Day of Our Lady of Merced, for example, all young children of prisoners are permitted to visit their parents within walls. Toys are given and entertainment provided. Although the importance of family is stressed in both Spain and Mexico, the stronger control exercised by the Roman Catholic Church in Spain is probably one factor accounting for the greater emphasis there on the parent-child rather than the husband-wife relationship.

A distinctive feature of the German system of corrections is the persistence of a programme of isolation. The so-called Pennsylvania style of prison architecture, with its separation of prisoners night and day, was introduced first into England and shortly afterwards (1846) into Germany. Thirty years ago in England there was a strong movement away from this programme. Such a movement is more recent in Germany. When each prisoner is sleeping, eating and working alone in his cell, it seems to satisfy the systematic and orderly qualities so prevalent in German life. It is like the precise arrangement of every object in the typical middle-class German household.

The movement away from this emphasis on isolation was facilitated by the prison division of the American occupation government in conjunction with the English occupation group. Modifications have been faster for youths than for adults, however. This trend is illustrated by the institution for older delinquent boys at Hahnöfersand near Hamburg with its stress on education, and by the open, borstal-like school for youths at Staumühle in Westphalia. The new Gustav Radbruch-Haus in Frankfurt (Hessen) represents the most radical departure from isolation-oriented corrections for adults. A transfer institution, it houses prisoners for an average of three months prior to release. Many of its inmates work under supervision in local factories or farms during the day and sleep in the prison at night. In fact the shift in major institutions for adults in Hessen and in the Schwäbisch-Hall Youth Prison and the Bruchsal Landesstrafanstalt of Baden-Württemberg is toward isolation at night for sleeping, but toward working, eating and getting their recreation together during the day.

In addition to the orderliness appeal made by the Pennsylvania system, there is also a general feeling on the part of German citizens that what happens behind prison walls "is not our business." An old proverb is pertinent: "Do not go to your Prince when you are not called" ("Geh nicht zu deinem Fürst wenn du nicht gerufen wirst"). It has been a Prussian idea that you should do what you are supposed to do and not bother about other people. During the Hitler régime perhaps 90 per cent. of the Germans, so they affirm, did not know or think about the concentration camps. Methods of measuring the extent of detachment from public view would be the number of visits to prisons by distinguished persons (ordinarily not many) or the items about prisons in the newspapers of a state (also not many). The development of a multi-party prison commission in the Hessen parliament is one move away from this attitude.

One of the most unusual correctional practices in the states of Washington, California and Hawaii is sentencing by an administrative board. In Washington State, for example, judges set the maximum sentence, largely under control of statutory provisions for each crime, but the minimum sentence is set by a full-time board of five members appointed for staggered terms of five years each by the governor. The board is aided in this decision by an admission summary prepared by a professional staff and by an interview with each prisoner. Although the trend is toward appointment of men of competence on this board, many purely political appointments have been made. The method makes possible, however, consideration of personality and situational factors as well as the specific crime and criminal record. It has to a considerable extent equalised the widely varying sentences of individual judges for similar patterns of crime, personality and social situation.

This method of sentencing was established in 1935 after a bloody riot at the penitentiary. Inmates had complained bitterly about sentencing by judges. More recent improvements in the quality and training of personnel for probation, institutional treatment, and parole also followed serious riots at both the reformatory (1953) and the penitentiary (1955). These riots served to focus public attention and to convince both political parties of the need for improvements. Changes were facilitated also by the lesser importance of tradition and the greater willingness to experiment that characterise the Pacific Division of the United States.[6]

England provides a noteworthy programme of education for its prisoners with a rich variety of courses taught by competent teachers from the outside community and participated in by a high proportion of inmates.[7] More unusual, however, is one aspect of its work and classification programme. As long ago as 1954 the writer visited a small, barrack-like structure in the yard, but inside the wall, of the Bristol local prison. From here a small group of long-term, recidivist prisoners, in the third and last stage of England's preventive detention programme, went out each work-day morning to jobs in the city of Bristol and came back each evening. They earned the same wages as employees who were not prisoners; they were able to resume responsibility for the support of their families; and they saved a substantial sum toward eventual release. Occasionally one of these men would become too drunk or in some other way violate this privilege and have to be returned to close confinement, but in general the results have been sufficiently encouraging to enable establishment of eight such centres by 1960 with six additional "hostels" planned.

There were twenty-three prisoners housed in the "hostel" of the Wakefield Prison in August of 1960. They bring their wages intact to the supervisor who pays for the support of families that had been on national assistance, gives the prisoner his expense money for midday meals and transportation, allows him up to 30 shillings (4.20 American dollars) per week pocket money. Income averages £9 15s. (27.44 American dollars) per week. Average amount saved for release is £57 or 159.60 American dollars. All prisoners with sentences of over four years spend their last nine months here. Out of fifty who have been released for twelve months or more, only one has been reconvicted.

At the women's open prison at Askham Grange the writer met informally

[6] In Hawaii an administrative board sets the minimum sentence, but its decisions are subject to review by judges. Due to the predominance of highly indeterminate sentences, such as one year to life, the California Adult Authority has what amounts to sentencing power.

[7] For additional information on England and the other countries discussed the following articles by the author are pertinent: "English Schools for Young Offenders," *Journal of Criminal Law and Criminology,* XXVII: 696–705 (Jan.-Feb., 1937); "Recent Observations of Mexican Prisons," *Proceedings of the American Prison Association,* 1941 (Spanish translation: *Revista Mexicana de Sociología,* IV: 73–83, 1942); "German Correctional Procedures: Impact of the Occupation," *National Probation and Parole Association Journal,* I: 167–173 (October, 1955); "Notes on the Spanish Correctional System," *Federal Probation,* XIX: 48–51 (December, 1955); "Sentencing by an Administrative Board," *Law and Contemporary Problems,* XXIII: 477–494 (Summer, 1958); "Why Do Parole Boards Lag in the Use of Prediction Scores?" *Pacific Sociological Review,* I: 73–76 (Fall, 1958).

with twelve members of the "going out group." The group showed a surprising degree of ease in conversation and of self-confidence. They not only talked briefly concerning themselves but also asked questions about prisons in America. One older woman, a "nine-time loser," was now waiting on tables in a restaurant. A well-educated younger woman, who had acquired £800 (2,240 American dollars) through some "cock and bull story," was receiving good pay in a factory and saving money so that she could support her two children when released. Another woman working as a gardener was an alcoholic. Three worked in nursing jobs at local hospitals; another worked at a race track; still another as a hotel maid; and one even worked in a brewery. They were housed separately from the other women. It was the writer's impression that this combination of supervision at night with work outside during the day was making a contribution to their reformation. In the words of the governor, "they gain new life and new hope."

The development of "hostels" in England seems to be tied up with a willingness to experiment which has characterised the English correctional system during its last fifty years. The Borstal institutions for young adults which reached a high state of rehabilitative efficiency in the 1930s are another example of this principle.[8] More recently the Norwich plan has given prison officers more responsibility for the individual rehabilitation of the prisoners under their care. Certain personalities such as Alexander Paterson, W. W. Llewellin, and Lionel Fox have won public confidence and contributed much to improving the personnel and encouraging experimentation. Members of the House of Commons do ask questions of the responsible minister, but they place trust in civil servants and do not interfere politically with their work.

To conclude, it has been demonstrated in an exploratory way that correctional systems can be placed on a punishment-treatment continuum. Mexico, Spain, West Germany, Western United States and England were distributed in that order on such a scale. Attention has been given also to the relation between certain unique correctional practices and distinctive values held by the people in the jurisdictions where these practices have developed. Additional studies in other political entities would help to test and sharpen these ideas.

[8] See William Healy and Benedict S. Apler, *Criminal Youth and the Borstal System* (New York: The Commonwealth Fund, 1941). "Flexibility is a cardinal principle," they write, "reflected in every feature and department of the system" (p. 85).

Criminal Justice, Legal Values and the Rehabilitative Ideal

FRANCIS A. ALLEN

Although one is sometimes inclined to despair of any constructive changes in the administration of criminal justice, a glance at the history of the past half-century reveals a succession of the most significant developments. Thus, the last fifty years have seen the widespread acceptance of three legal inventions of great importance: the juvenile court, systems of probation and of parole. During the same period, under the inspiration of continental research and writing, scientific criminology became an established field of instruction and inquiry in American universities and in other research agencies. At the same time, psychiatry made its remarkable contributions to the theory of human behavior and, more specifically, of that form of human behavior described as criminal. These developments have been accompanied by nothing less than a revolution in public conceptions of the nature of crime and the criminal, and in public attitudes toward the proper treatment of the convicted offender.[1]

This history with its complex developments of thought, institutional behavior, and public attitudes must be approached gingerly; for in dealing with it we are in peril of committing the sin of oversimplification. Nevertheless, despite the presence of contradictions and paradox, it seems possible to detect one common element in much of this thought and activity which goes far to characterize the history we are considering. This common element or theme I shall describe, for want of a better phrase, as the rise of the rehabilitative ideal.

The rehabilitative ideal is itself a complex of ideas which, perhaps, defies completely precise statement. The essential points, however, can be articulated. It is assumed, first, that human behavior is the product of antecedent causes. These causes can be identified as part of the physical universe, and it is the obligation of the scientist to discover and to describe them with all possible exactitude. Knowledge of the antecedents of human behavior makes possible an approach to the scientific control of human behavior. Finally and

Reprinted by special permission of the author and *The Journal of Criminal Law, Criminology and Police Science,* Copyright © 1959 by the Northwestern University School of Law, Vol. 50 (September-October 1959), pp. 226–232.

[1] These developments have been surveyed in Allen, "Law and the Future: Criminal Law and Administration," 51 *Nw. L. Rev.* 207, 207–208 (1956). See also Harno, "Some Significant Developments in Criminal Law and Procedure in the Last Century," 42 *J. Crim. L., C. and P.S.* 427 (1951).

of primary significance for the purposes at hand, it is assumed that measures employed to treat the convicted offender should serve a therapeutic function, that such measures should be designed to effect changes in the behavior of the convicted person in the interests of his own happiness, health, and satisfactions and in the interest of social defense.

Although these ideas are capable of rather simple statement, they have provided the arena for some of the modern world's most acrimonious controversy. And the disagreements among those who adhere in general to these propositions have been hardly less intense than those prompted by the dissenters. This is true, in part, because these ideas possess a delusive simplicity. No idea is more pervaded with ambiguity than the notion of reform or rehabilitation. Assuming, for example, that we have the techniques to accomplish our ends of rehabilitation, are we striving to produce in the convicted offender something called "adjustment" to his social environment or is our objective something different from or more than this? By what scale of values do we determine the ends of therapy?[2]

These are intriguing questions, well worth extended consideration. But it is not my purpose to pursue them in this paper. Rather, I am concerned with describing some of the dilemmas and conflicts of values that have resulted from efforts to impose the rehabilitative ideal on the system of criminal justice. I know of no area in which a more effective demonstration can be made of the necessity for greater mutual understanding between the law and the behavioral disciplines.

There is, of course, nothing new in the notion of reform or rehabilitation of the offender as one objective of the penal process. This idea is given important emphasis, for example, in the thought of the medieval churchmen. The church's position, as described by Sir Francis Palgrave, was that punishment was not to be "thundered in vengeance for the satisfaction of the state, but imposed for the good of the offender: in order to afford the means of amendment and to lead the transgressor to repentance, and to mercy."[3] Even Jeremy Bentham, whose views modern criminology has often scorned and more often ignored, is found saying: "It is a great merit in a punishment to contribute to the *reformation of the offender,* not only through fear of being punished again, but by a change in his character and habits."[4] But this is far

---

[2] "We see that it is not easy to determine what we consider to be the sickness and what we consider to be the cure." Fromm, *Psychoanalysis and Religion* (1950) 73. See also the author's development of these points at 67–77.

[3] Quoted in Dalzell, *Benefit of Clergy and Related Matters* (1955) 13.

[4] Bentham, *The Theory of Legislation* (Ogden, C. K., ed., 1931) 338–339. (Italics in the original.) But Bentham added: "But when [the writers] come to speak about the means of preventing offenses, of rendering men better, of perfecting morals, their imagination grows warm, their hopes excited; one would suppose they were about to produce the great secret, and that the human race was going to receive a new form. It is because we have a more magnificent idea of objects in proportion as they are less familiar, and because the imagination has a loftier flight amid vague projects which have never been subjected to the limits of analysis." *Id.* at 359.

from saying that the modern expression of the rehabilitative ideal is not to be sharply distinguished from earlier expressions. The most important differences, I believe, are two. First, the modern statement of the rehabilitative ideal is accompanied by, and largely stems from, the development of scientific disciplines concerned with human behavior, a development not remotely approximated in earlier periods when notions of reform of the offender were advanced. Second, and of equal importance for the purposes at hand, in no other period has the rehabilitative ideal so completely dominated theoretical and scholarly inquiry, to such an extent that in some quarters it is almost assumed that matters of treatment and reform of the offender are the only questions worthy of serious attention in the whole field of criminal justice and corrections.

THE NARROWING OF
SCIENTIFIC INTERESTS

This narrowing of interests prompted by the rise of the rehabilitative ideal during the past half-century should put us on our guard. No social institutions as complex as those involved in the administration of criminal justice serve a single function or purpose. Social institutions are multi-valued and multi-purposed. Values and purposes are likely on occasion to prove inconsistent and to produce internal conflict and tension. A theoretical orientation that evinces concern for only one or a limited number of purposes served by the institution must inevitably prove partial and unsatisfactory. In certain situations it may prove positively dangerous. This stress on the unfortunate consequences of the rise of the rehabilitative ideal need not involve failure to recognize the substantial benefits that have also accompanied its emergence. Its emphasis on the fundamental problems of human behavior, its numerous contributions to the decency of the criminal-law processes are of vital importance. But the limitations and dangers of modern trends of thought need clearly to be identified in the interest, among others, of the rehabilitative ideal, itself.

My first proposition is that the rise of the rehabilitative ideal has dictated what questions are to be investigated, with the result that many matters of equal or even greater importance have been ignored or cursorily examined. This tendency can be abundantly illustrated. Thus, the concentration of interest on the nature and needs of the criminal has resulted in a remarkable absence of interest in the nature of crime. This is, indeed, surprising, for on reflection it must be apparent that the question of what is a crime is logically the prior issue: how crime is defined determines in large measure who the criminal is who becomes eligible for treatment and therapy.[5] A related ob-

---

[5] Cf. Hart, "The Aims of the Criminal Law," 23 *Law and Cont. Prob.* 401 (1958).

servation was made some years ago by Professor Karl Llewellyn, who has done as much as any man to develop sensible interdisciplinary inquiry involving law and the behavioral disciplines:[6] "When I was younger I used to hear smuggish assertions among my sociological friends, such as: 'I take the sociological, *not* the legal, approach to crime'; and I suspect an inquiring reporter could still hear much the same (perhaps with 'psychiatric' often substituted for 'sociological') — though it is surely somewhat obvious that when you take 'the legal' out, you also take out 'crime'."[7] This disinterest in the definition of criminal behavior has afflicted the lawyers quite as much as the behavioral scientists. Even the criminal law scholar has tended, until recently, to assume that problems of procedure and treatment are the things that "really matter".[8] Only the issue of criminal responsibility as affected by mental disorder has attracted the consistent attention of the non-lawyer, and the literature reflecting this interest is not remarkable for its cogency or its wisdom. In general, the behavioral sciences have left other issues relevant to crime definition largely in default. There are a few exceptions. Dr. Hermann Mannheim, of the London School of Economics, has manifested intelligent interest in these matters.[9] The late Professor Edwin Sutherland's studies of "white-collar crime"[10] may also be mentioned, although, in my judgment, Professor Sutherland's efforts in this field are among the least perceptive and satisfactory of his many valuable contributions.[11]

The absence of wide-spread interest in these areas is not to be explained by any lack of challenging questions. Thus, what may be said of the relationships between legislative efforts to subject certain sorts of human behavior to penal regulation and the persistence of police corruption and abuse of power?[12] Studies of public attitudes toward other sorts of criminal legislation might provide valuable clues as to whether given regulatory objectives are more likely to be attained by the provision of criminal penalties or by other kinds of legal sanctions. It ought to be re-emphasized that the question, what sorts of behavior should be declared criminal, is one to which the behavioral sciences might contribute vital insights. This they have largely failed to do, and we are the poorer for it.

[6] See Llewellyn and Hoebel, *The Cheyenne Way* (1941). See also "Crime, Law and Social Science: A Symposium," 34 *Colum. L. Rev.* 277 (1934).

[7] "Law and the Social Sciences — Especially Sociology," 62 *Harv. L. Rev.* 1286, 1287 (1949).

[8] Allen, *op. cit. supra,* note 1, at 207–210.

[9] See, especially, his *Criminal Justice and Social Reconstruction* (1946).

[10] *White-Collar Crime* (1949). See also Clinard, *The Black Market* (1952).

[11] Cf. Caldwell, "A Re-examination of the Concept of White-Collar Crime," 22 *Fed. Prob.* 30 (March, 1958).

[12] An interesting question of this kind is now being debated in England centering on the proposals for enhanced penalties for prostitution offenses made in the recently-issued Wolfenden Report. See Fairfield, "Notes on Prostitution," 9 *Brit. J. Delin.* 164, 173 (1959). See also Allen, "The Borderland of the Criminal Law: Problems of 'Socializing' Criminal Justice," 32 *Soc. Ser. Rev.* 107, 110–111 (1958).

Another example of the narrowing of interests that has accompanied the rise of the rehabilitative ideal is the lack of concern with the idea of deterrence — indeed the hostility evinced by many modern criminologists toward it. This, again, is a most surprising development.[13] It must surely be apparent that the criminal law has a general preventive function to perform in the interests of public order and of security of life, limb, and possessions. Indeed, there is reason to assert that the influence of criminal sanctions on the millions who never engage in serious criminality is of greater social importance than their impact on the hundreds of thousands who do. Certainly, the assumption of those who make our laws is that the denouncing of conduct as criminal and providing the means for the enforcement of the legislative prohibitions will generally have a tendency to prevent or minimize such behavior. Just what the precise mechanisms of deterrence are is not well understood. Perhaps it results, on occasion, from the naked threat of punishment. Perhaps, more frequently, it derives from a more subtle process wherein the mores and moral sense of the community are recruited to advance the attainment of the criminal law's objectives.[14] The point is that we know very little about these vital matters, and the resources of the behavioral sciences have rarely been employed to contribute knowledge and insight in their investigation. Not only have the criminologists displayed little interest in these matters, some have suggested that the whole idea of general prevention is invalid or worse. Thus, speaking of the deterrent theory of punishment, the authors of a leading textbook in criminology assert: "This is simply a derived rationalization of revenge. Though social revenge is the actual psychological basis of punishment today, the apologists for the punitive regime are likely to bring forward in their defense the more sophisticated, but equally futile, contention that punishment deters from [*sic*] crime."[15] We are thus confronted by a situation in which the dominance of the rehabilitative ideal not only diverts attention from many serious issues, but leads to a denial that these issues even exist.

DEBASEMENT OF THE REHABILITATIVE IDEAL

Now permit me to turn to another sort of difficulty that has accompanied the rise of the rehabilitative ideal in the areas of corrections and criminal justice. It is a familiar observation that an idea once propagated and introduced into the active affairs of life undergoes change. The real significance

[13] But see Andenaes, "General Prevention — Illusion or Reality?", 43 *J. Crim. L., C. and P.S.* 176 (1952).

[14] This seems to be the assertion of Garafalo. See his *Criminology* (Millar trans., 1914) 241–242.

[15] Barnes and Teeters, *New Horizons in Criminology* (2nd ed., 1954) 337. The context in which these statements appear also deserves attention.

of an idea as it evolves in actual practice may be quite different from that intended by those who conceived it and gave it initial support. An idea tends to lead a life of its own; and modern history is full of the unintended consequences of seminal ideas. The application of the rehabilitative ideal to the institutions of criminal justice presents a striking example of such a development. My second proposition, then, is that the rehabilitative ideal has been debased in practice and that the consequences resulting from this debasement are serious and, at times, dangerous.

This proposition may be supported, first, by the observation that, under the dominance of the rehabilitative ideal, the language of therapy is frequently employed, wittingly or unwittingly, to disguise the true state of affairs that prevails in our custodial institutions and at other points in the correctional process. Certain measures, like the sexual psychopath laws, have been advanced and supported as therapeutic in nature when, in fact, such a characterization seems highly dubious.[16] Too often the vocabulary of therapy has been exploited to serve a public-relations function. Recently, I visited an institution devoted to the diagnosis and treatment of disturbed children. The institution had been established with high hopes and, for once, with the enthusiastic support of the state legislature. Nevertheless, fifty minutes of an hour's lecture, delivered by a supervising psychiatrist before we toured the building, were devoted to custodial problems. This fixation on problems of custody was reflected in the institutional arrangements which included, under a properly euphemistic label, a cell for solitary confinement.[17] Even more disturbing was the tendency of the staff to justify these custodial measures in therapeutic terms. Perhaps on occasion the requirements of institutional security and treatment coincide. But the inducements to self-deception in such situations are strong and all too apparent. In short, the language of therapy has frequently provided a formidable obstacle to a realistic analysis of the conditions that confront us. And realism in considering these problems is the one quality that we require above all others.[18]

There is a second sort of unintended consequence that has resulted from the application of the rehabilitative ideal to the practical administration of criminal justice. Surprisingly enough, the rehabilitative ideal has often led to increased severity of penal measures. This tendency may be seen in the opera-

---

[16] See note 25, *infra.*

[17] As I recall, it was referred to as the "quiet room." In another institution the boy was required to stand before a wall while a seventy pound fire hose was played on his back. This procedure went under the name of "hydrotherapy."

[18] Cf. Wechsler, "Law, Morals and Psychiatry," 18 *Colum. L. School News* 2, 4 (March 4, 1959): "The danger rather is that coercive regimes we would not sanction in the name of punishment or of correction will be sanctified in the name of therapy without providing the resources for a therapeutic operation."

tion of the juvenile court. Although frequently condemned by the popular press as a device of leniency, the juvenile court, is authorized to intervene punitively in many situations in which the conduct, were it committed by an adult, would be wholly ignored by the law or would subject the adult to the mildest of sanctions. The tendency of proposals for wholly indeterminate sentences, a clearly identifiable fruit of the rehabilitative ideal,[19] is unmistakably in the direction of lengthened periods of imprisonment. A large variety of statutes authorizing what is called "civil" commitment of persons, but which, except for the reduced protections afforded the parties proceeded against, are essentially criminal in nature, provide for absolutely indeterminate periods of confinement. Experience has demonstrated that, in practice, there is a strong tendency for the rehabilitative ideal to serve purposes that are essentially incapacitative rather than therapeutic in character.[20]

THE REHABILITATIVE IDEAL
AND INDIVIDUAL LIBERTY

The reference to the tendency of the rehabilitative ideal to encourage increasingly long periods of incarceration brings me to my final proposition. It is that the rise of the rehabilitative ideal has often been accompanied by attitudes and measures that conflict, sometimes seriously, with the values of individual liberty and volition. As I have already observed, the role of the behavioral sciences in the administration of criminal justice and in the areas of public policy lying on the borderland of the criminal law is one of obvious importance. But I suggest that, if the function of criminal justice is considered in its proper dimensions, it will be discovered that the most fundamental problems in these areas are not those of psychiatry, sociology, social case work, or social psychology. On the contrary, the most fundamental problems are those of political philosophy and political science. The administration of the criminal law presents to any community the most extreme issues of the proper relations of the individual citizen to state power. We are concerned here with the perennial issue of political authority: Under what circumstances is the state justified in bringing its force to bear on the individual human being? These issues, of course, are not confined to the criminal law, but it is in the area of penal regulation that they are most dramatically manifested. The criminal law, then, is located somewhere near the center of the political problem, as the history of the twentieth century abundantly reveals. It is no accident, after all, that the agencies of criminal justice and law enforcement

[19] Cf. Tappan, "Sentencing under the Model Penal Code," 23 *Law and Cont. Prob.* 538, 530 (1958).
[20] Cf. Hall, Jerome, *General Principles of Criminal Law* (1947) 551. And see Sellin, *The Protective Code: A Swedish Proposal* (1957) 9.

are those first seized by an emerging totalitarian regime.[21] In short, a study of criminal justice is most fundamentally a study in the exercise of political power. No such study can properly avoid the problem of the abuse of power.

The obligation of containing power within the limits suggested by a community's political values has been considerably complicated by the rise of the rehabilitative ideal. For the problem today is one of regulating the exercise of power by men of good will, whose motivations are to help not to injure, and whose ambitions are quite different from those of the political adventurer so familiar to history. There is a tendency for such persons to claim immunity from the usual forms of restraint and to insist that professionalism and a devotion to science provide sufficient protections against unwarranted invasion of individual right. This attitude is subjected to mordant criticism by Aldous Huxley in his recent book, *Brave New World Revisited*. Mr. Huxley observes: "There seems to be a touching belief among certain Ph.D.'s in sociology that Ph.D.'s in sociology will never be corrupted by power. Like Sir Galahad's, their strength is the strength of ten because their heart is pure — and their heart is pure because they are scientists and have taken six thousand hours of social studies."[22] I suspect that Mr. Huxley would be willing to extend his point to include professional groups other than the sociologists. There is one proposition which, if generally understood, would contribute more to clear thinking on these matters than any other. It is not a new insight. Seventy years ago the Italian criminologist, Garafalo, asserted: "The mere deprivation of liberty, however benign the administration of the place of confinement, is undeniably punishment."[23] This proposition may be rephrased as follows: Measures which subject individuals to the substantial and involuntary deprivation of their liberty are essentially punitive in character, and this reality is not altered by the facts that the motivations that prompt incarceration are to provide therapy or otherwise contribute to the person's well-being or reform. As such, these measures must be closely scrutinized to insure that power is being applied consistently with those values of the community that justify interferences with liberty for only the most clear and compelling reasons.

But the point I am making requires more specific and concrete application to be entirely meaningful. It should be pointed out, first, that the values of individual liberty may be imperiled by claims to knowledge and therapeutic technique that we, in fact, do not possess and by failure candidly to concede what we do not know. At times, practitioners of the behavioral sciences have been guilty of these faults. At other times, such errors have supplied the as-

---

[21] This development in the case of Germany may be gleaned from Crankshaw, *Gestapo* (1956).

[22] Huxley, *Brave New World Revisited* (1958) 34–35.

[23] *Op. cit. supra*, note 14, at 256.

sumptions on which legislators, lawyers and lay people generally have proceeded. Ignorance, in itself, is not disgraceful so long as it is unavoidable. But when we rush to measures affecting human liberty and human dignity on the assumption that we know what we do not know or can do what we cannot do, then the problem of ignorance takes on a more sinister hue.[24] An illustration of these dangers is provided by the sexual psychopath laws, to which I return; for they epitomize admirably some of the worst tendencies of modern practice. These statutes authorize the indefinite incarceration of persons believed to be potentially dangerous in their sexual behavior. But can such persons be accurately identified without substantial danger of placing persons under restraint who, in fact, provide no serious danger to the community? Having once confined them, is there any body of knowledge that tells us how to treat and cure them? If so, as a practical matter, are facilities and therapy available for these purposes in the state institutions provided for the confinement of such persons?[25] Questions almost as serious can be raised as to a whole range of other measures. The laws providing for commitment of persons displaying the classic symptoms of psychosis and advanced mental disorder have proved a seductive analogy for other proposals. But does our knowledge of human behavior really justify the extension of these measures to provide for the indefinite commitment of persons otherwise afflicted? We who represent the disciplines that in some measure are concerned with the control of human behavior are required to act under weighty responsibilities. It is no paradox to assert that the real utility of scientific technique in the fields under discussion depends on an accurate realization of the limits of scientific knowledge.

There are other ways in which the modern tendencies of thought accompanying the rise of the rehabilitative ideal have imperiled the basic political values. The most important of these is the encouragement of procedural laxness and irregularity. It is my impression that there is greater awareness of these dangers today than at some other times in the past, for which, if true, we perhaps have Mr. Hitler to thank. Our increased knowledge of the functioning of totalitarian regimes makes it more difficult to assert that the insistence on decent and orderly procedure represents simply a lawyer's quibble or devotion to outworn ritual. Nevertheless, in our courts of so-called "socialized justice" one may still observe, on occasion, a tendency to assume that, since the purpose of the proceeding is to "help" rather than to "pun-

---

[24] I have developed these points in Allen, *op. cit. supra,* note 12, at 113–115.

[25] Many competent observers have asserted that none of these inquiries can properly be answered in the affirmative. See, e.g., Sutherland, "The Sexual Psychopath Laws," 40 *J. Crim. L., C. and P.S.* 543 (1950) Hacker and Frym, "The Sexual Psychopath Act in Practice: A Critical Discussion," 43 *Calif. L. Rev.* 766 (1955). See also Tappan, *The Habitual Sex Offender* (Report of the New Jersey Commission) (1950).

ish," some lack of concern in establishing the charges against the person before the court may be justified. This position is self-defeating and otherwise indefensible. A child brought before the court has a right to demand, not only the benevolent concern of the tribunal, but justice. And one may rightly wonder as to the value of therapy purchased at the expense of justice. The essential point is that the issues of treatment and therapy be kept clearly distinct from the question of whether the person committed the acts which authorize the intervention of state power in the first instance.[26] This is a principle often violated. Thus, in some courts the judge is supplied a report on the offender by the psychiatric clinic before the judgment of guilt or acquittal is announced. Such reports, while they may be relevant to the defendant's need for therapy or confinement, ordinarily are wholly irrelevant to the issue of his guilt of the particular offense charged. Yet it asks too much of human nature to assume that the judge is never influenced on the issue of guilt or innocence by a strongly adverse psychiatric report.

Let me give one final illustration of the problems that have accompanied the rise of the rehabilitative ideal. Some time ago we encountered a man in his eighties incarcerated in a state institution. He had been confined for some thirty years under a statute calling for the automatic commitment of defendants acquitted on grounds of insanity in criminal trials. It was generally agreed by the institution's personnel that he was not then psychotic and probably had never been psychotic. The fact seemed to be that he had killed his wife while drunk. An elderly sister of the old man was able and willing to provide him with a home, and he was understandably eager to leave the institution. When we asked the director of the institution why the old man was not released, he gave two significant answers. In the first place, he said, the statute requires me to find that this inmate is no longer a danger to the community; this I cannot do, for he may kill again. And of course the director was right. However unlikely commission of homicide by such a man in his eighties might appear, the director could not be certain. But, as far as that goes, he also could not be certain about himself or about you or me. The second answer was equally interesting. The old man, he said, is better off here. To understand the full significance of this reply it is necessary to know something about the place of confinement. Although called a hospital, it was in fact a prison, and not at all a progressive prison. Nothing worthy of the name of therapy was provided and very little by way of recreational facilities.

---

[26] A considerable literature has developed on these issues. See, e.g., Allen, "The Borderland of the Criminal Law: Problems of 'Socializing' Criminal Justice," 32 *Soc. Ser. Rev.* 107 (1958), Diana, "The Rights of Juvenile Delinquents: An Appraisal of Juvenile Court Proceedings," 44 *J. Crim. L., C. and P.S.* 561 (1957), Paulsen, "Fairness to the Juvenile Offender," 41 *Minn. L. Rev.* 547 (1957); Waite, "How Far Can Court Procedures Be Socialized without Impairing Individual Rights?", 12 *J. Crim. L. and C.* 430 (1921).

This case points several morals. It illustrates, first, a failure of the law to deal adequately with the new requirements being placed upon it. The statute, as a condition to the release of the inmate, required the director of the institution virtually to warrant the future good behavior of the inmate, and, in so doing, made unrealistic and impossible demands on expert judgment. This might be remedied by the formulation of release criteria more consonant with actuality. Provisions for conditional release to test the inmate's reaction to the free community would considerably reduce the strain on administrative decision-making. But there is more here. Perhaps the case reflects that arrogance and insensitivity to human values to which men who have no reason to doubt their own motives appear peculiarly susceptible.[27]

CONCLUSION

In these remarks I have attempted to describe certain of the continuing problems and difficulties associated with, what I have called, the rise of the rehabilitative ideal. In so doing, I have not sought to cast doubt on the substantial benefits associated with that movement. It has exposed some of the most intractable problems of our time to the solvent properties of human intelligence. Moreover, the devotion to the ideal of empirical investigation provides the movement with a self-correcting mechanism of great importance, and justifies hopes for constructive future development.

Nevertheless, no intellectual movement produces only unmixed blessings. It has been suggested in these remarks that the ascendency of the rehabilitative ideal has, as one of its unfortunate consequences, diverted attention from other questions of great criminological importance. This has operated unfavorably to the full development of criminological science. Not only is this true, but the failure of many students and practitioners in the relevant areas to concern themselves with the full context of criminal justice has produced measures dangerous to basic political values and has, on occasion, encouraged the debasement of the rehabilitative ideal to produce results, unsupportable whether measured by the objectives of therapy or of corrections. The worst manifestations of these tendencies are undoubtedly deplored as sincerely by competent therapists as by other persons. But the occurrences are neither so infrequent nor so trivial that they can be safely ignored.

[27] One further recent and remarkable example is provided by the case, *In re Maddox,* 351 Mich. 358, 88 N.W. 2d 470 (1958). Professor Wechsler, *op. cit. supra,* note 18, at 4, describes the facts and holding as follows: "Only the other day, the Supreme Court of Michigan ordered the release of a prisoner in their State prison at Jackson, who had been transferred from the Ionia State Hospital to which he was committed as a psychopath. The ground of transfer, which was defended seriously by a State psychiatrist, was that the prisoner was 'adamant' in refusing to admit sexual deviation that was the basis of his commitment; and thus, in the psychiatrist's view, resistant to therapy. The Court's answer was, of course, that he had not been tried for an offense."

Limitations on Organization of Treatment in the Modern Prison

DONALD R. CRESSEY

In the past decade American sociology has seen a tremendous growth of interest and specialization in the theory and study of organization. Variations in the effectiveness and efficiency of different kinds of organization and in the conditions under which these arise, persist, and change have been studied in many settings, ranging from broad administrative systems to specific governmental and military hierarchies, factories, and hospitals. The theory and research results are directly applicable to the study of prisons, which contain systems of a military type designed to keep inmates within the walls, factory systems to produce goods, and professional or "service" systems to treat and rehabilitate inmates. The prison as a whole is a governmental organization designed to administer the activities of the persons in the various roles in these subsidiary systems. Thus, all the types of organization studied in other settings can be studied in a prison.

Prisons, however, provide more than a convenient opportunity for verifying observations already made by students of social organization. In two principal respects prisons seem to differ significantly from factories and similar organizations. First, the administrative hierarchies of prisons are organized *down to the lowest level.* In factories there are separate hierarchies of management personnel and of workers (and research has been concerned with the relations of these roles to each other and to their organizational purpose, production). The lowest-status employee in a prison, in contrast, is both a manager and a worker. He is managed in a system of regulations and controls from above, but he also manages in a presumably concordant system the inmates who are in his charge. He is a low-status worker in interaction with management, but a higher-status foreman, "officer," or treatment agent in interaction with inmates. The guard, who in traditional prisons is at the bottom of a hierarchical system which manages his job of managing men, has no counterpart in the business and industrial world. The closest analogy would be the overseer of a crew of slaves, who would be viewed as "outside" the organization designed to utilize their labor effectively. Even this analogy is fallacious except as guards may serve as foremen of inmate industrial or maintenance crews. Most guards have nothing to do but guard; they do not "use" inmates productively any more than they themselves are used pro-

Reprinted from *Theoretical Studies in Social Organization of the Prison,* Richard A. Cloward, *et al.,* pp. 78–110 (New York: 1960), by permission of the author and the Social Science Research Council.

ductively by prison managers. Guards manage and are managed in organizations where management is an end, not a means.

Second, as prisons have grown in size and as concepts of good penology have changed, new services and roles have been added without regard for those already existing. This process seems different from that accompanying similar growth of other bodies, for the new roles have been organized around purposes that are little related to each other. In all prisons there is a line organization of custodial ranks, ranging from warden to guard, and salary differentials and descriptive titles indicate that a chain of command is expected within this hierarchy. However, while all employees are responsible to the warden, there is no clear expectation that the institution shall consist *solely* of a hierarchy of custodial ranks in reference to which all positions are integrated. Systems of nonline positions, such as those of professional personnel and industrial foremen and superintendents, are essentially separate and have their own salary differentials and titles. They are neither part of the custodial chain of command nor staff organizations. Noncustodial personnel are not advisers to the custodians in the sense that the experts of various sorts who make up the staff organization of factories are advisers, providing specialized knowledge to assist the line organization with its task of production.[1] The structure of prisons provides for three principal hierarchies — devoted respectively to *keeping, using,* and *serving* inmates — but not for the integration of their divergent purposes. The separate organizations concerned with keeping and with serving inmates, for example, are not merely overlapping, but have entirely different and partly contradictory purposes.

The objectives of each hierarchy require that its roles and processes of role integration take definite forms. The model of an organization for giving help and treatment to inmates is an archetypal mental hospital; for using them, an industrial organization, such as a lumber camp, where employees both work and live together; for keeping them, a prison on the order of the early Pennsylvania institutions. Each organization includes a specific kind of relationship between employees and inmates; a specific pattern of communication, authority, and decision making; and a specific system for distributing rewards and punishments. These features vary significantly among the three kinds of organization.

Little is known about the processes of modification and accommodation taking place when the three hierarchies are expected to function as parts of an over-all organization. There has been little systematic observation of the resulting consequences for each subsidiary organization. There is need for description and analysis of organizational problems stemming from admin-

[1] Melville Dalton, "Conflicts Between Staff and Line Managerial Officers," *American Sociological Review,* 15:342–351 (June, 1950).

istrative attempts to transform the total system into an organization consistent with only one or another of the subsidiaries. For example, some prison administrators seem committed to establishing, in the presence of treatment and productive organizations, a total system modeled on the custodial archetype.[2] Other administrators, in the presence of productive and custodial organizations, strain toward establishing and maintaining a total system consistent with the treatment archetype. This report is focused on development of the latter kind of system and is concerned with some theoretical considerations regarding the limitations on the service or treatment model imposed by the reality of custodial and production functions.

The discussion which follows is organized in six parts, of which the first two are introductory. The first deals with the conflicting implications of contemporary attitudes about punishment and treatment in our society for prison organization; the second, with the historical development of the treatment-oriented prison, where high priority is given to nonpunitive treatment of inmates. The third part reviews the theory that ideally is used in reforming prisoners. The fourth identifies some organizational conflicts that necessarily arise when this theory is extended as an ideology for administration of an organization that must perform custodial and productive as well as treatment operations. In the fifth part the administrators' method of "resolving" these conflicts by transferring them to nonprofessional employees is discussed. Finally, some implications of this type of resolution for behavior of nonprofessional employees are explored, and types of resolution or "adjustment" by employees are specified.

ATTITUDES TOWARD CRIME
AND IMPLICATIONS
FOR PRISON ORGANIZATION

In American society there are at least four distinguishable attitudes about control of crime, and each implies a specific program of action for prisons. First, retribution is regarded as desirable and just. At least since the time of Hammurabi it has been generally accepted that the criminal deserves to suffer simply because he is a criminal. Second, imposition of suffering is regarded as a deterrent. In this view the future effect of punishment on society, rather than on the criminal, is most important. It is believed that infliction of pain on offenders inculcates in others fear of the consequences of per-

---

[2] For preliminary analyses of organizational strain stemming from such attempts see Harvey Powelson and Reinhard Bendix, "Psychiatry in Prison," *Psychiatry,* 14:73–86 (February, 1951); Louis N. Robinson, "Contradictory Purposes in Prisons," *Journal of Criminal Law and Criminology,* 37:449–457 (March-April, 1947); and R. L. Jenkins, "Treatment in an Institution," *American Journal of Orthopsychiatry,* 11:85–91 (January, 1941).

petrating like offenses or at least has long-range effects on public morality.[3] Third, protection from the criminal is desired and demanded. Whether punished or not, the offender must be physically isolated so that the community is safe from him. Finally, there is interest in reforming criminals, particularly in order to reduce the incidence of crime. Punishment of offenders may deter potential criminals, but reform or rehabilitation of the imprisoned is also important if crime is to be substantially reduced. This attitude is congruent with the notion that society must be protected from criminals but implies a variation of the action to be taken in order to achieve protection.

In contemporary democratic societies, prison administrators are charged with implementing programs compatible with each of these attitudes about crime control, so that the structure of a prison is expected to be adequate for performing four functions: the direct and immediate functions of retribution, incapacitation, and reformation, and the indirect one of deterrence. Prison programs are to make life unpleasant for persons who have made others' lives unpleasant, to isolate offenders so they cannot commit crimes during certain periods of time, to reform them, and to have a deterrent effect on criminal behavior in the general population as well.

THE PAIN OF RESTRICTION

In early American prisons few organizational problems arose in meeting society's expectations with respect to these four functions. Each could be fulfilled by an organization designed to inflict punishment.[4] The prison walls protected society from criminals; and within the walls a rigorous, monotonous, and unpleasant regime, including corporal punishments, filled the social and organizational demands for retribution, deterrence, and reformation. Gradually, however, organizational strain was introduced, first as a consequence of serious doubts about the social need for retribution and deterrent punishments more severe than "mere" deprivation of liberty, and more recently by doubts that reformation can be achieved by punishment of any kind, including deprivation of liberty. The fundamental organizational problem in progressive contemporary prisons arises from the directive to inflict punishment by custodianship while maintaining a program based on a new conception of the process of reformation, namely, rehabilitation through treatment.

It must be emphasized that punishment is still an unequivocal function

---

[3] See Emile Durkheim, *The Division of Labor in Society,* trans. by George Simpson (Glencoe: Free Press, 1947), pp. 70–110.

[4] Punishment as an instrument of public justice is pain and suffering purposively inflicted by the state because of some value that they are assumed to have. Significantly, they need not be physical but can be inflicted through deprivation of anything the society cherishes, such as money or liberty.

of prisons. All criminal laws specify that any person behaving in a stipulated manner shall be punished, and imprisonment is identified as a proper punishment. Although the punishment in many kinds of criminal cases may be only threatened, as in probation, and although a few states have made legislative provision for psychiatric treatment of certain adult criminals, such as sex offenders, commitment to prison must always be primarily for the purpose of punishment, regardless of whether it is considered essential in reformation. This is a fundamental tenet of the criminal law, and to modify it to any significant degree would shake the foundations of our democratic legal system, for civil rights — such as the right to be tried by a jury, to confront witnesses, and to have counsel — are predicated on the assumption that imprisonment must be a painful experience, inflicted only on persons proved guilty. A prison administration that attempted to overthrow this tenet openly would be quickly dissolved for having taken revolutionary action.

Changing Conceptions
of the Process of Reformation

The general trend toward the position that men are sent to prison *as* punishment rather than *for* punishment has two distinct aspects. First, there has been a trend toward the view that mere incarceration continues to be painful and hence to be reformative in itself. Although the view that men are imprisoned *for* punishment has not been completely abandoned, the conditions of punishment have been altered considerably in most prisons during the past half-century. The changes have followed changing conceptions of the "proper" punishment to be used to bring about reform. Whereas corporal punishments formerly were considered proper, deprivation of freedom — with all that it entails — has been increasingly advocated as a substitute for physical pain. The controversy has been about alternative kinds and degrees of punishment, not about the relative merits of punitive and nonpunitive devices for reforming criminals.

Second, there has been a trend toward the view that incarceration can at best have a neutral effect and that positive steps must be taken if the prison is to carry out its reformative function. Here, the controversy is between alternative theories to be followed in reformative programs. The theory that criminals can be changed by punitive measures of any kind has been increasingly challenged by the theory that change can be induced only by nonpunitive "treatment."

As a result of these concurrent trends, prison discipline generally has become more relaxed and, simultaneously, positive rehabilitation measures have been introduced. However, this does not mean that prisons have been increasingly viewed as places of treatment. Rather, they are seen as places where both punitive and nonpunitive measures must be used. In prisons of the traditional type the mechanism assumed to be most effective for reform was likely to be the same used in performing other functions: almost complete totalitarian control over inmates, with corporal punishment and extreme isolation imposed for violation of rules. Little organizational strain could occur in connection with the punitive and reformative functions of such a prison. Even when the restrictive and punitive conditions in a prison are made less severe, they still may be assumed to be reformative in themselves, so that a minimum of functional conflict occurs. According to modern rehabilitation theory, however, punitive restriction is by definition antagonistic to reformation and rehabilitation. An institution organized to inflict suffering is, therefore, contra-indicated if treatment is a goal. If this theory is followed some degree of organizational conflict is inevitable, for prisons then are to inflict pain on criminals and at the same time to reform them by nonpunitive measures.

The fact that the theory of reformation through punishment has not been replaced by that of reformation through treatment means that directives for administration of the prison are necessarily contradictory and that personnel must work out some means of reconciling them. The conditions essential for implementing treatment in prisons are fundamentally different from those essential for retribution, deterrence, and reformation through punishment.

INMATE LABOR

As when it was assumed that the proper mechanism for reformation was imposition of pain, now when this assumption is being challenged, prisoners are expected to work. Systems for occupying the time of prisoners developed when prisons became places of punishment, rather than of detention of men awaiting trial. At first, work was regarded primarily as a means of imposing physical discomfort and was not economically useful. Offenders were sentenced to confinement at hard labor and they walked treadmills, turned cranks, and did other uncomfortable tasks. As the notion that imprisonment per se *is* punishment has developed, this conception of prison labor has lost ground. Work activities have been economically useful, and forced participation in them is considered part of incarceration, not purposively inflicted physical discomfort.

In a society where work often is viewed as a means for achieving the "independence" and "freedom" of retirement, however, the conception of prison labor as a painful experience can hardly disappear entirely. The activities that in many contemporary prisons are directed and regulated as part of the system for imposing punishment by mere restriction of freedom are primarily *work*. Inmates have the status of slaves, and almost all their conduct is considered part of the master-servant (work) relationship. These prisons are said to perform the functions of retribution and deterrence by restricting freedom to choose one's work, among other things. In prisons of an earlier type the official reaction to unsatisfactory work was corporal punishment, whereas in present-day prisons it is more likely to be greater curtailment of freedom in more uncomfortable surroundings. The restriction of choices regarding work and the consequent requirement that inmates perform tasks perhaps not to their liking are expected to be reformative — to instill habits of industry, obedience, perseverance, and conformity. Regulated work activity also is defended on the ground that it "keeps inmates out of mischief" and thus contributes to the incapacitation function. Prison labor systems, then, are expected to contribute to accomplishment of the major tasks that society has assigned to prisons.

The economic value of prison labor rarely has been overlooked.[5] In various periods inmates have been leased to private entrepreneurs, goods have been made on contract for private companies, and prison administrators themselves have operated elaborate industrial enterprises, all to produce goods that could be sold at a profit. While recent restrictive legislation has greatly curtailed the amount of wealth that can be produced by prisoners, they are expected at least to "pay part of their way" by producing goods and performing housekeeping and maintenance tasks, which reduce the number of tax dollars necessary for support of the institutions. Thus, the penological services prisons perform for society are to be carried on at least cost. Stated positively, this is a mandate to prison administrators to maintain profitable productive enterprises.

DEVELOPMENT OF THE TREATMENT-ORIENTED PRISON

The modern prison, designed to punish inmates and at the same time to reform them by nonpunitive measures, is a logical outcome of earlier practices. Even the first prisons used some nonpunitive measures believed to have a reformative effect on prisoners, such as haphazard religious and secular education, and exhortations in the name of God, mother, and country. An important characteristic of Elmira, the first American "reformatory," established in 1876, was provision of educational classes and vocational training, which were believed to be reformative. Yet this first reformatory was constructed as a maximum-security *penal* institution, and the educational and vocational efforts at rehabilitation were made in that setting. The conflicting punitive and treatment conceptions of reformation thus became institutionalized, for almost all prisons in the United States have followed the Elmira pattern.

[5] See Georg Rusche and Otto Kirchheimer, *Punishment and Social Structure* (New York: Columbia University Press, 1939).

USE OF PROFESSIONAL PERSONNEL

If the entire system of imprisonment is observed, it appears that over the years more and more emphasis has been given to nonpunitive measures. Classification of inmates has been introduced, and standard-setting groups such as the American Prison Association have insisted that inmates should be differentiated on the basis of individual needs for treatment services of various kinds, rather than on criteria such as age, nature of offense, or custodial risk.[6] From a conception of classification as a system of segregation for purposes of administrative control, prison leaders have moved to a new conception, which has developed in the last few decades, of classification as the entire process by which the prison attempts to attain the objective of reformation through individualized treatment.[7] With the adoption of this conception psychiatrists, social workers, and sociologists have been employed in some prisons to provide treatment services which are more directly aimed at altering criminals' personalities than are academic classes and vocational training. These professionally trained workers have become the symbols of reformation through treatment, for they diagnose each incoming inmate's needs, prescribe the necessary treatment, and see that it is provided.

A few administrators continue to deny the legitimacy of the contention that inmates should be treated and try to maintain old-type prisons where efforts to reform by nonpunitive measures are negligible. Even educational classes, let alone psychotherapeutic counseling, may be viewed as unnecessary and unwarranted frills. Prisons administered on the basis of this ideology are occasionally attacked as cruel, vicious, and inhumane. However, most wardens who are directed both to treat and to punish employ treatment specialists and set up treatment programs on paper, administer so-called treatment activities as measures to help insure security, or define as treatment the distribution of "amenities" or "privileges." (Such programs may make prison life more comfortable but not necessarily any more conducive to reformation.) In these custodially oriented prisons, administrators who are admonished to punish and incapacitate criminals and also to treat them try to mitigate the inevitable organizational strain by transforming treatment roles into custodial roles.[8] Treatment specialists here are subordinate to officials who emphasize the necessity for maintaining order and for motivating inmates to work, even if their work interferes with desirable treatment practices. A psychiatrist, for

---

[6] American Prison Association, Committee on the Model State Plan, *Manual of Suggested Standards for a State Correctional System* (New York, 1946), p. 21.

[7] American Prison Association, Committee on Classification and Case Work, *Handbook on Classification in Correctional Institutions* (New York, 1947), p. 2.

[8] See Lloyd E. Ohlin, *Sociology and the Field of Corrections* (New York: Russell Sage Foundation, 1956), pp. 15–16.

example, may not be expected to rehabilitate inmates; his task may be to stop *rumbles* (complaints and disturbances) and to *cool out* inmates who are becoming threats to peaceful routines. In this situation both the administrator and the psychiatrist may have difficult problems of adjustment, for introduction of nonpunitive treatment roles in an organization where other roles are designed to insure the maintenance of punitive restriction means that there will be conflicts of functions.

THE PROFESSIONAL AS ADMINISTRATOR

One consequence of the growing expectation that prisons will utilize specialists to rehabilitate inmates, as well as custodians to restrict and punish them, has been that a few prison administrations are directed by treatment specialists themselves. Their introduction into the *administration* of prisons has come as a logical consequence of the now popular notion that criminals cannot be reformed by punitive measures. In these relatively rare treatment-oriented institutions,[9] administrators are committed to alter custodial roles so that they are at least in part treatment roles; e.g., a guard is to contribute to treatment of inmates as well as to custody. The conflict of functions is similar to that in custodial prisons, but efforts to resolve it take a different form. The psychiatrist who has been expected to be a psychiatrist but also to behave custodially now expects the custodian to be a custodian but also to behave psychiatrically. In this kind of institution, treatment personnel have become the policy makers, and treatment functions have been assigned a priority that has marked consequences for the custodial and production organizations.

The term "treatment orientation" is used advisedly, to indicate that the transition of the prison from a place of punitive restriction to one of treatment is incomplete, even when administered by professional personnel. Since influential groups outside the prison continue to expect it to punish, punitive conditions cannot be abolished; they can only be mitigated in favor of treatment. Conversely, ideal treatment programs must be modified in favor of the punitive and productive aspects of imprisonment, just as in custodial institutions. Other groups outside the prison, or perhaps the same groups at different times, may demand that it perform nonpunitive treatment functions. There is societal resistance to changing prisons into places of treatment, as well as societal stimuli to change. The general problem confronting professionally trained administrators who are attempting to transform their organizations into therapeutic and rehabilitative communities is that of over-

---

[9] It is estimated that only about a dozen American prisons now qualify as treatment oriented. A much larger proportion of the institutions for youthful offenders are administered by professional specialists.

coming resistance to change in the larger community that supports the prison system.[10]

PREMISES
OF INDIVIDUALIZED TREATMENT

Professional personnel who act as prison administrators apparently have as their long-range goal a system that is completely treatment-centered. Their model is a mental hospital, and this model is based on an assumption that criminals are mentally ill and in need of treatment for that illness:

Imprisonment and punishment do not present themselves as the proper methods of dealing with criminals. We have to treat them physically as sick people, which in every respect they are. It is no more reasonable to punish these individuals for behavior over which they have no control than it is to punish an individual for breathing through his mouth because of enlarged adenoids. . . . It is the hope of the more progressive elements in psychopathology and criminology that the guard and the jailer will be replaced by the nurse and the judge by the psychiatrist, whose sole attempt will be to treat and cure the individual instead of merely to punish him.[11]

In the actual administration of a prison, however, professional personnel ordinarily recognize external demands for custody and restriction. As in custodial prisons, a line organization of ranks is accepted as part of current institutional organization, even if often characterized as undesirable. Although according to the professional ideology the line organization in an ideal institution would be composed of treatment specialists — not lieutenants and guards — most professional administrators consider their basic duties to be administrative, not political. Their administrative task is thus not to replace the custodians and foremen with treatment specialists, but rather to modify custodial roles so that they include treatment or at least do not interfere with it.

The assumption made by specialists in individualized treatment is that each role in the prison must be integrated as far as possible into an organization directed toward a single goal, treatment of inmates according to their individual needs. The conception is of a "stream of action" in which criminals, like raw material, pass through the organization and have various re-

[10] Although we cannot discuss the problem here, it is apparent that factionalism among employees, which develops in the early stages of transition from a custodial to a treatment orientation, is closely linked with changing interests among authorities external to the organization. For description of a comparable situation see Paula Brown and Clovis Shepherd, "Factionalism and Organizational Change in a Research Laboratory," *Social Problems,* 3:235–243 (April, 1956).

[11] Benjamin Karpman, "Criminality, Insanity and the Law," *Journal of Criminal Law and Criminology,* 39:584–605 (January-February, 1949).

habilitative operations performed on them, each according to his needs. The custodial organization is no more than a framework in which these operations take place — somewhat analogous to the physical plant of a factory. In this view, treatment personnel are more than advisers to a quasi-military custodial hierarchy. They are technical experts who stand above the other employees because of professional competence. They are to diagnose the specific ailments of incoming inmates, make prescriptions, and decide when the ailments have been cured and, therefore, when each inmate is ready for release. In the interim they must have the administrative capacity to direct the "stream of action," to see that their prescriptions are followed and that progress is made in each case.

CONCEPTION OF INMATE NEEDS

While the theory underlying the specific practices that have been devised to treat inmates may not have been rationalized, in the professional conception of inmate needs there seems to be a mixture of social-work and psychiatric theory, humanitarianism, and ethics of the middle class. These elements are welded into a general policy for handling inmates by the assertion that almost all inmates need treatment and by the following negative definition of treatment: *A method of dealing with inmates that involves purposive infliction of pain and suffering is not treatment.* This premise obviously must create strain in an organization that by definition is expected to be painful to inmates, even if mere incarceration — the framework within which treatment is to be given — is the sole instrument for inflicting the pain.

Psychiatric and Social Work Theory. The purely professional conception of what should be done for inmates stems from psychiatric and social work theory, which cannot be reviewed in detail here. The body of theory lies near one pole of a continuum on which can be ordered theories about the relation between personality and "organization" of social relationships. As Stanton and Schwartz have suggested, social scientists at one extreme think of organization much as anthropologists view culture — as a way of living in which group and individual needs are both satisfied.[12] The person is a product of his culture and obtains his satisfactions and his essence from participation in rituals, schedules, customs, and regulations of various sorts — in the "orderliness" with which his society is endowed. He behaves according to the rules of this large organization in which he participates. Behavioral sci-

---

[12] Alfred H. Stanton and Morris S. Schwartz, *The Mental Hospital* (New York: Basic Books, 1954), pp. 37–38. See also Saul D. Alinsky, "The Philosophical Implications of the Individualistic Approach in Criminology," *Proceedings of the American Prison Association, 1937*, pp. 156–171.

entists at the opposite extreme think of the individual as essentially autonomous and view his relation to rules and regulations as *submission* rather than participation. They emphasize individual self-determination and attempt to distinguish between the "real" or "natural" part of the person and the "spurious," "artificial," or "consensual" part. The former is free and spontaneous, the latter (obtained from society), formal and restrictive. In discussing prison organization these students are likely to emphasize its rigidity, cruelty, unresponsiveness, and sadism, without recognizing the usefulness of the organization for the larger society or for the inmates.[13]

Theories of personality are certainly more complex than this simple statement indicates, and probably no social scientist subscribes to either position with no reservations. But the professional administrators of treatment-oriented prisons incline more toward the second theory than the first. The extreme view is that imprisonment is a system for imposing punitive restrictions on individuals who need just the opposite — an opportunity to be "spontaneous" and self-directing; and that enforced conformity to formal prison regulations is an undesirable (though perhaps necessary) restriction of individuals whose criminality is evidence of a need for opportunities for self-expression (e.g., in the form of "sublimation," "ventilation," and "acting out" of psychological conflicts). More simply stated, prisoners are regarded as personalities whose emotional needs have not been met in the free community, and their criminality is a consequence of this deprivation. It is illogical and inefficient to deprive them further while they are incarcerated. Rather, institutional routines must be arranged to provide both a minimum of deprivation and adequate opportunity for clinical treatment. Prison programs must be designed to help inmates become psychologically mature, rather than to reduce them to dependency. To facilitate clinical handling of cases there must be a supportive "therapeutic" community in which individual differences are recognized, rather than a restrictive or repressive system. Further, inmates must be handled individually because the psychological need-deprivations and emotional conflicts suffered by one may be quite different from those suffered by another. Here, the position is that treatment is what takes place in the psychotherapeutic interchange, which the rest of the institution must be arranged to facilitate.

[13] Parsons has pointed out that organizations are always part of a larger social structure and he has classified them in terms of the type of societal goal or function about which they are organized. His classification includes organizations oriented to economic production, those oriented to political goals, integrative organizations, and pattern-maintenance organizations. Prisons are "integrative organizations," for they (like mental hospitals) are mechanisms of social control which contribute to the efficiency of the larger society. They help adjust conflicts and attempt to stimulate motivation toward fulfillment of societal expectations. See Talcott Parsons, "Suggestions for a Sociological Approach to the Theory of Organizations — II," *Administrative Science Quarterly*, 1:225–239 (September, 1956).

Humanitarianism. Inmates are also viewed, consistently, as in need of simple humanitarian consideration. Amenities, as Reckless calls them, are granted to all inmates to reduce the deprivations stemming from institutional confinement.[14] Thus, privileges, such as the use of a canteen, payment of wages, smoking, radios in cells and shops, movies, and recreational activities, usually are considered parts of an institution's treatment program, just as they are in custodially oriented prisons. Each privilege is viewed as providing opportunities for making individual choices, for "releasing tensions," or for "channeling aggressions," among other purposes. The principle seems to be that treatment in the form of psychotherapeutic counseling is desirable for all inmates. However, since the reality of prison organization severely limits administration of this purely professional view, an alternative position is taken: the prison should have an essentially nonpunitive atmosphere, and inmates should have at least *some* opportunities for expressing themselves and meeting their psychological needs. Negatively, prisoners should not be subjected to punitive restriction that will make their emotional problems worse.[15] This view extends treatment beyond the professional staff's offices, into the institution as a whole. It puts emphasis on *administration of treatment in a community,* for the institution must be organized so that the individual can be "free" and can exercise numerous choices.

Middle-Class Ethics. Intermingled with these two views of inmate needs are assumptions that prisoners need what middle-class citizens consider the "good things of life." Cleanliness, deferring gratifications, nonaggressiveness, educational accomplishment, steady work habits, and contributing to charity are all attributes of good men; and acquisition of such characteristics by prisoners is, therefore, evidence of rehabilitation. While inmates may be permitted to "find themselves" in the school and work programs, for example, the man who settles down to a rational, planned sequence for self-improvement or "getting ahead" probably is regarded with approval. Especially important is the view that incarceration shall not prohibit participation in the kind of activity considered good in the middle-class world: the *opportunity* for satisfying individual needs in a socially acceptable manner must always be available to inmates and must not be limited solely by their in-

---

[14] Walter C. Reckless, *The Crime Problem,* 2nd ed. (New York: Appleton-Century-Crofts, 1955), pp. 572–573.

[15] "Modern correctional administrators, who believe that the emphasis in institutions should be on rehabilitation, put much stress on making the institutional atmosphere as much like ordinary living as possible. They feel that too much regimentation militates against successful adjustment after release and that a prisoner is better prepared to assume his responsibilities in the community if he has the self-respect that comes from having been treated like a grown man instead of a caged animal or unruly child." — Robert G. Caldwell, *Criminology* (New York: Ronald Press Company, 1956), p. 494.

carceration.[16] This assumption is consistent with the view that "amenities" are rehabilitative, and with their use because of their possible effects on individual psychological adjustment.

These three interrelated notions of what inmates need have one common implication for policy: that inmates should be given as much freedom as possible. A program of "relaxed discipline," as it may be called, based on this policy is rehabilitative because it is nonpunitive, if for no other reason. Yet it is axiomatic that the discipline cannot be relaxed nor the prisoners granted freedom to the degree stipulated as necessary to rehabilitation.

ORGANIZATION OF TREATMENT
AND RESULTING CONFLICTS

The premises on which individualized institutional treatment is based imply organizational chaos, for time schedules, coordination of activities, and group norms are disdained. If each inmate were handled individually, according to his needs, in a setting in which formal regulations were viewed as undesirable, motivating inmates to perform maintenance and housekeeping activities and otherwise to be cooperative in the production and custodial programs of the prison would be impossible. The organizational necessities of coordination, cooperation, and integration could not be achieved. In reality, such disorganization cannot be tolerated. Any prison must maintain the minimum conditions of orderliness and security that are demanded by groups outside the prison and dictated by other than theoretical considerations. Administrators of treatment-oriented prisons, therefore, must work out a system for reconciling their commitments to individualized treatment and their commitments to their administrative role.[17] They must rely on guards and other nonprofessional employees for carrying out administrative policy; yet the conflict between organizational and professional ideologies is such that administrative rules cannot be clearly formulated, instructions cannot be understood, and enforcement of rules and "understanding" cannot be achieved by invoking punitive measures for nonconformity.

ROLES OF NONPROFESSIONAL EMPLOYEES

As professionals the members of the administrative staff are expected to be experts at "doing something" rehabilitative to inmates. The institutional

[16] See Gordon Fuller, "Value to Prisoners of Participation in Public Service Projects," *Federal Probation,* 20:52–54 (December, 1956).

[17] Their dilemma is in principle almost identical with that of social workers who as parole officers must participate in a process of individualized treatment but also work in an agency that has to adapt itself to the threat of powerful groups who want it to act as a law-enforcement agency. See Lloyd E. Ohlin, Herman Piven, and Donnell M. Pappenfort, "Major Dilemmas of the Social Worker in Probation and Parole," *National Probation and Parole Association Journal,* 2:211–225 (July, 1956).

program ideally becomes one in which nonprofessional employees, who remain as custodians or foremen, assist the professional staff in this rehabilitative work. Hence the administrative job becomes one of modifying all the roles in the institution so that they *include* treatment but are not treatment roles, and integrating them in an organization whose aim is rehabilitation. This is usually what is meant when professionals say, as one official did, that their goal is "coordination of all the institution's facilities in a program of individualized treatment."

Once this commitment has been made, treatment becomes organizational since procedures assuring coordination must be developed. However, in the "pure" view of treatment (what takes place in the psychotherapeutic interchange), there are no positive directives for its organization, nor for integrating the institution's three subsidiary organizations so that the treatment job gets done. Furthermore, application of the clinical principle on which nonpunitive individualized treatment is based[18] is restricted by various limitations on the professional staff's activities. For example, they have time for psychotherapeutic interviews with only a small minority of the inmates. If the program is to affect many inmates there must be assistance from the nonprofessional staff, especially from the guards. The implication is that the guard must do more than guard.

There are two principal views of what guards should do: (1) They should act as referral agents for the professionally trained staff — discuss inmates' problems with them, in a broad sense diagnose surface problems of adjustment, and on the basis of amateur diagnoses refer each inmate to the proper professional personnel. This plan is favored by treatment personnel when they are acting in professional rather than administrative roles. Counseling and treatment are professional tasks for qualified personnel. (2) As administrators, the treatment specialists are likely to take the position that the guards should participate more in treatment: under professional direction they should deal with inmates' minor emotional problems, advise and encourage them to "talk out" their difficulties with the law and with institutionalization, and inspire them by personal example to lead law-abiding lives.

In either case the guard must be receptive, passive, and relaxed. If he emphasizes his superior position in the relationship, if he ridicules, represses, or punishes inmates, or if he "blames" them for their faults, they will not be receptive to his further surface diagnoses or therapeutic counseling, and the

---

[18] An analogy with the procedures of clinical medicine and psychiatric practice is apparent; even the *theories* of clinical medicine have been adopted. See Donald R. Cressey, "Changing Criminals: The Application of the Theory of Differential Association," *American Journal of Sociology,* 61:116–120 (September, 1955), and "Contradictory Theories in Correctional Group Therapy Programs," *Federal Probation,* 18:20–26 (June, 1954).

ensuing hostility could interfere with treatment being given by a professional person. All personnel are expected to recognize that inmates will behave in unnatural ways because imprisonment is strange and unnatural in a democratic society. Guards thus are expected to behave like those "ideal" psychiatrists, social workers, and experienced mental hospital workers who without personal tension can listen to bizarre language, witness "indecent" behavior, watch patients attempt to escape, or withstand violent verbal and physical attacks.

CONCEPTIONS OF DEVIATIONS
BY INMATES AND EMPLOYEES

Since coordination and direction of guards' activities are necessary if this general plan for treatment is to be effective, formal and explicit rules for the administration of policy would be expected. However, the premises of individualized treatment make it practically impossible for administrators to state explicitly what guards should do to make relationships with inmates therapeutic. This may be illustrated by the consequences of viewing inmates as patients or clients. In the interests of extratheoretical concepts such as "justice," some rules for inmates must be maintained, but violations of rules are ascribed to *inability* to conform, rather than to deliberate intent. Deviations from prison rules, like deviations that result in arrest for crime, are viewed as the consequence of psychological illness, not intentional badness. This is highly significant, for when nonconformity is viewed as unintentional in our culture the response is one of "treatment" or "education," whereas the response to intentional nonconformity is punishment and close surveillance.[19] Since inmate deviation from custodial and work rules is unintentional, then, guards and foremen must be nonpunitive and "professional" in their handling of it.

This expectation regarding the conduct of employees makes it necessary for professional administrators to rely on *professional authority* rather than *administrative rules* (enforced by punishment) for diffusing the treatment orientation to the nonprofessional employees. The establishment of professional authority in reference to proper views of *inmate* deviation (through in-service training sessions in which psychologists are the faculty, and guards and foremen the students) gives the treatment personnel the same authority in handling employee relationships. The authority that in custodial prisons

---

[19] This principle is illustrated in criminal law, which exempts from liability insane and very young persons whose deviation is assumed to be unintentional. Thus, a person whose deviant behavior is perceived as a consequence of inability to conform has committed no crime, whereas one whose deviant behavior is perceived as willful nonconformity is viewed as a proper object of punishment.

rests on rank or position is supplemented by authority based on *technical competence* in the professional function of the organization.[20]

ENFORCEMENT OF EXPECTATIONS

In custodial prisons, employees are expected to conform to the rules for their behavior because it is their duty; in treatment-oriented prisons, however, decision making is decentralized and they are expected to think for themselves, to use discretion, and to be "professional" and flexible. Rather than rules, there are mere expectations that each employee will accept professional standards and make decisions consistent with them.

It is significant for the functioning of the total organization that these expectations cannot be effectively communicated to employees or enforced. There are four principal reasons for this difficulty. First, as indicated previously, the professional treatment ideology has no positive implications for administration, and professional administrators thus cannot devise specific rules for the professional conduct of nonprofessionals. "Administration" in the usual sense of securing compliance with pre-existing rules cannot be achieved. Violation of specific rules for treatment becomes impossible. But the clinical theory does have the important negative implication that guards and foremen are *not to do anything* that will increase inmates' emotional problems. The general order to guards and foremen therefore is to "relax." Understandings based on this negative order cannot be enforced by punishing violations, however, because that in itself would violate the theoretical premises. The failure of employees to behave according to expectations must, like inmates' deviations from rules, be viewed as unintentional; guards who are punitive or repressive must be considered *unable* to exhibit affective neutrality in relation to inmates because of some personality characteristic. The usual diagnoses are "rigid," "punitive," "sadistic," "maladjusted," and "neurotic" — terms that are used somewhat opprobriously. But such difficulties call for education and therapy, not punishment. Imposition of punishment would be illegitimate and most inconsistent, for employees would be punished for behaving punitively.[21]

---

[20] For elaboration of this difference, see Weber's discussion in *The Theory of Social and Economic Organization,* trans., ed. by A. M. Henderson and Talcott Parsons (New York: Oxford University Press, 1947), pp. 337–339; Parsons' discussion, *ibid.,* p. 59; H. H. Gerth and C. W. Mills, eds., *From Max Weber: Essays in Sociology* (New York: Oxford University Press, 1946), p. 254; and Alvin W. Gouldner, *Patterns of Industrial Bureaucracy* (Glencoe: Free Press, 1954), pp. 18–27.

[21] Professional personnel do sometimes maintain a double standard, inconsistently viewing deviations of inmates as unintentional and those of employees as deliberate. This makes establishment of a treatment orientation impossible, for employees are explicitly held responsible for the irresponsibility of inmates. To a degree, this occurs in all treatment-oriented prisons: inmates are considered not responsible, but guards are responsible for seeing

Second, institutional organization itself blocks the communication processes necessary for correction of unintentional deviation from the negative understandings derived from the treatment ideology — i.e., educating and administering therapy to nonprofessional employees. Professionals who do not have enough time for necessary diagnostic and therapeutic interviews with inmates of course do not have time to "treat" employees. Even if legislators could be persuaded to provide funds for enough professional personnel to administer therapy to both groups, nonprofessional employees would have to be relieved of some of their duties in order to participate. Since this is not feasible in an organization that must be custodial and productive, nonprofessional supervisors from the custodial and industrial hierarchies must be relied on for diffusion of the treatment orientation. The limited effectiveness of this system is discussed below (pages 482–485).

Third, supervisors, guards, and foremen are not trained for social work or psychiatric practice, nor are they prepared to receive a professional education even if there were time to provide it. They cannot be expected to understand the theoretical premises on which they are expected to operate. Because of their different general orientations toward prison work, one basic requirement for acceptance of administrative direction — the understanding of communication — is absent.[22]

Fourth, and perhaps most important, while nonprofessional employees are relaxing so as to contribute to inmate rehabilitation, they are also expected to maintain order and to see that inmates perform the work tasks necessary to the continued functioning of the institution. Inmates are not only perceived as in need of treatment, but also, significantly, as in need of justice and control. As *professionals,* front-office workers may think that nonconformity to institutional rules is usually the result of "acting out" emotional conflicts and problems. For example, aggressive behavior by inmates is to be *expected* as a response to even those minimal restrictions that must be imposed if the institution is to perform a nonpunitive incapacitating function, in the manner of a mental hospital. Yet as *administrators* these workers recognize that aggression cannot be tolerated in an institution where hundreds

that these inmates are cooperative and that they perform assigned work tasks. For discussion of this kind of inconsistency in correctional agencies, see John F. Perkins, "Common Sense and Bad Boys," *Atlantic Monthly* (May 1944), pp. 43–47.

[22] "A communication that cannot be understood *can* have no authority. An order issued, for example, in a language not intelligible to the recipient is no order at all — no one would so regard it. Now, many orders are exceedingly difficult to understand. They are often necessarily stated in general terms, and the persons who issued them could not themselves apply them under many conditions. Until interpreted they have no meaning. The recipient either must disregard them or merely do anything in the hope that that is compliance." — Chester I. Barnard, "A Definition of Authority," in Robert K. Merton and others, eds., *Reader in Bureaucracy* (Glencoe: Free Press, 1952), p. 181.

of inmates live in close association, for security might be threatened. Direct attempts are made to channel aggressions — through grudge fights, athletics, painting, and other "media of expression" — but there also are specific rules for inmate conduct, violation of which is threatened with punishment. Disciplinary courts are established on the assumption that, whatever the cause, aggression that is not channeled will be reported and punished, not treated. Similarly, stealing, homosexuality, and refusal to work might be viewed as the consequence of personal problems which are treatable; nevertheless, any such offenses reported to the court are punished even if the punishment interferes with treatment.

It should be emphasized that disciplinary courts are seldom considered either therapeutic or consistent with the ideology of individualized treatment. They exist in deference to the necessity for order and justice and can operate only if the administrators make the traditional assumption that deviation is deliberate and that recalcitrant inmates can be reformed and other inmates deterred by punishment. We have emphasized that professional administrators are likely to take the position that nonconformity is an unintentional consequence of emotional disturbance and therefore should not be punished. But they also know that if riots and other disorders are to be prevented, inmates who violate rules must be handled "justly"; and this practice rests on the assumption that the defendant who is found guilty will be made to suffer.[23] Intention, responsibility for deviation, and punishment as a consequence of deviation are assumed in the definition of "maintaining discipline." In a situation where "discipline" is required, then, expectations that guards will behave professionally cannot be stipulated or enforced: they cannot be explicitly instructed to behave therapeutically and to handle deviation as if it were unintentional. Yet, if the treatment ideology is to be maintained, neither can they be ordered to report all deviations to the disciplinary court for punishment. They can only be instructed to be professional, to relax, and to use discretion in reporting violations of rules to the court. This directive decentralizes decision making without providing explicit criteria on which decisions are to be based.

---

[23] Writing on the more general effects of introducing the theory of individualized treatment, a juvenile-court judge has said: "Stripped of all its elaborate wrappings, the doctrine of individual treatment may be expressed by one word — *injustice*. Its basic principle is arbitrary discrimination, discrimination unsupported by tangible evidence. Without reference to any standard of conduct, a public official will determine whether we are deserving . . ., as he sees fit. There is to be only one restriction. He is not allowed to be fair. He must base his decision on his estimate of our personal characteristics — and no two of us are alike. The word *merit* will become obsolete. All signs of a government of laws will disappear. We shall have a personal government. Equality under the law will go out the window, and with it all hope of equality of opportunity in the future." — Perkins, *op. cit.*, p. 47.

Sources of Problems in
Handling the "Special Case"

The four organizational blocks to effective diffusion and enforcement of the treatment ideology have their sources in the larger society. That is, in a society where only men "guilty" of "intentionally bad" behavior are sent to prison, even the treatment-oriented prison must restrain and punish inmates if it is to maintain itself; and in this situation instructions given to nonprofessional employees tend to be vague and contradictory. The externally imposed requirement that the treatment-oriented prison restrain and punish the inmates who are being treated also creates *internal* conditions that make transformation of the organization into a true treatment center extremely difficult. Even if all employees of a prison accepted the individualized treatment ideology, the institution probably would continue to be punitive.

In the first place, the attitudes and demands of inmates are involved. The hostile procedures of criminal justice are interpreted as personally beneficial by only a few criminals, and incarceration is viewed by inmates as part of this hostile process. Even in a treatment-oriented prison, they are not convinced that the institution is being run to treat or help them, rather than to punish them. They are being held against their will; that is the basic reason for their opposition to incarceration. They do not believe that necessary rules are for their benefit and consequently have no personal, internalized sense of duty to keep the institution running, work hard, or be cooperative.[24] Neither are inmates convinced that they need the treatment offered. They cooperate with employees not to get treatment, but to avoid institutional punishments and to secure a release from the punitive aspects of imprisonment as soon as possible. Thus, the essential custodial and punitive functions of a prison make inmates hostile to it even if they are understood and treated there.

In an environment characterized by inmate hostility and desire to avoid the pain of restriction, attempts by employees to apply individualized treatment criteria in dealing with inmates will almost surely be interpreted by them and even by some employees as administration of special favors and

---

[24] One ex-convict writes: "The prisoner in the modern liberal and scientific institution has most of the same frustrations as the man in the old-style prison or modern county jail — but with this added disadvantage: he is now managed 'scientifically' from some remote-control board to which he does not have access. No prisoner has any confidence that the immense amount of data which is collected on him will be used for his benefit. Most prisoners know that the subtle pressures constantly put upon them have nothing to do with their welfare but much to do with 'prison security' — and with the job security of the penologist. The prisoner's need to live and the system's attempt to live for him (and off him) can never be reconciled." — W. H. Kuenning, "Letter to a Penologist," in Holley Cantine and Dachine Rainer, eds., *Prison Etiquette* (Bearsville, N. Y.: Retort Press, 1950), p. 132.

privileges. An inmate who becomes "adjusted," shows evidence of rehabilitation, and is therefore released on parole is freed from institutional punishment as well as treatment. He escapes from the suffering imposed on inmates, and those who remain behind are more interested in this fact than in evidence of his rehabilitation. For example, granting parole to a man who the inmates expect will return to crime immediately or who has a reputation as a violator of prison rules is considered unjust and a special privilege even though the personnel authorizing the release believe he is adjusted or "cured." Similarly, if a "bad actor" in the prison is assigned, as part of the therapy for misconduct, a responsible job that is a "good job" from the inmates' standpoint, he is viewed as *rewarded* for misconduct. If this attitude were held by many inmates, it would be a serious threat to institutional security, and so cannot be allowed to develop.

Second, it is impossible for either professional or other employees to accept a system of special treatment that does not explicitly recognize that inmates must contribute to the maintenance of the prison. Guards and foremen who are to use work crews efficiently and to maintain peaceful routines, as well as to treat inmates, cannot accept a system of discharges, job transfers, and other treatment activities that ignores the institutional necessities and operates solely on the basis of individual needs of inmates. We have seen that the professionals' conception of the proper system for dealing with inmates must be modified by the necessity of discipline. Where authoritarian direction and regulation of inmate conduct are essential to the accomplishment of nontreatment organizational purposes, the employee — whether administrator or worker—cannot give unqualified support to practices that reduce such direction significantly, even if his theoretical orientation calls for extensive "relaxation" and nondirectiveness. This is important, for it indicates that even if guards and foremen were replaced by professionally trained specialists, the problems stemming from the attempt to administer treatment in a punitive setting would not be resolved. The handling of prisoners as individualized treatment cases, unlike that of probationers and parolees, is limited by the necessity of meeting the inmate community's demands for justice and the employee's needs for cooperation of inmates.

ADMINISTRATIVE RESOLUTION OF
PROBLEMS OF INDIVIDUALIZED TREATMENT

Two principal systems are used by professional personnel for administering individualized treatment in a community that views this as special privilege. One is to conduct the treatment activities so that any special consideration that might be interpreted as a reward for misconduct is kept relatively secret. Such a practice, of course, is an admission of a measure of defeat;

it means that only in certain organizationally limited circumstances will inmates be handled according to their individual needs. For example, an "early parole" was granted an inmate whose background was not especially criminogenic but whose behavior in the institution was abominable. From the time he arrived he was in trouble; he got into fights with inmates, cursed and attacked staff members, broke up his cell, and refused to go to work or to school. His case was reviewed, and immediate parole was recommended on the ground that his adjustment in the free community had been adequate but that he was incapable of adjusting to institutional life. However, because it was feared that other inmates might start misbehaving if they learned that one had been "rewarded" for misconduct, precautions were taken to see that the case did not attract attention. His name was not on the list of men going before the parole board that month, and he left the institution a few days after the hearing, rather than after the customary two or three weeks. The attempt to maintain secrecy revealed suspicion that violation of rules might be directed toward "using" the staff. It also indicated that neither inmates nor employees would be explicitly instructed that only individual needs for treatment were to be considered in handling inmates. Organizational demands for inmate cooperation make it impossible to publicize the notion that an inmate who needs a specific kind of treatment will be given it regardless of his cooperation.

The more popular system is to keep administrative roles and professional roles separate. Thus, the administrator overlooks violations of his own official rules while he is acting in his professional capacity. For example, in individual or group therapy the confidential relationship requires an administrator who is serving as a therapist to take no punitive action on discovered or reported violations of rules. In more general institutional settings, professional administrators often overlook such violations because they are considered part of an inmate's personality. There may be explicit or tacit agreements with inmates that rule violations will be acted on only if, in the words of one professional, "they come to my *official* attention in some way." Thus professional administrators prohibit violation of rules in one role and, in effect, sanction it in another; and both inmates and employees frequently complain of such inconsistency.

The contradiction in the treatment and administrative roles and the attempt to separate them are significant, for they have caused to be shifted to *nonprofessional* employees the task of deciding any priority to be given to either special treatment or conformity to administrative rules. This is a general phenomenon in treatment-oriented institutions: the "treatment versus punishment" dilemma is shifted from the administrative officials to the guards and industrial foremen.

Resolution of the administrators' problem in this way may be illustrated by the system for handling the type of rule violation by inmates that is a direct consequence of violation by professional personnel of their own administrative orders. A well-understood administrative order in almost all prisons, whether treatment-oriented or not, is that no employee shall give anything to an inmate or bring anything in from the outside. Most institutions, for public relations reasons, also have rules that inmates may not possess certain kinds of literature, such as detective stories and nudist magazines. But in a treatment-oriented prison these rules may be violated frequently both by professional personnel who give or loan such literature to inmates and by inmates who receive it. Conceivably, reading matter is brought in by the professional illicitly because of some therapeutic value it is believed to have *for a particular inmate.* The professional, to maintain his conception of himself as such and his conception of the prison as a treatment agency, thus conveniently ignores the institutional needs for justice and uniform enforcement of rules.

Whenever the professional behaves in this way, special treatment becomes the custodians' problem, for the organization continues to need orderliness and uniformities. The custodians are expected to overlook the violations of both inmates and employees (some inmates are given the literature, on treatment grounds), and simultaneously to enforce rules pertaining to inmates (no literature of this kind allowed). The custodians, then, must "use discretion" and somehow behave both custodially and therapeutically. Yet, as we have seen, they cannot be given explicit criteria on which to base this discretion. If they enforce the rules, they risk being diagnosed as "rigid" and "just a guard" because such enforcement interferes with individualized treatment. But if their failure to enforce rules creates a threat to institutional security, orderliness, or maintenance, they are not "doing their job."[25]

SOME EFFECTS ON NONPROFESSIONAL EMPLOYEES

Maintenance of the treatment orientation is complicated by the fact that the nonprofessional supervisors, such as captains and industrial superinten-

---

[25] The dilemma of other persons who have to judge workers' performance according to multiple criteria is similar. As Ridgway has said, "Without a single over-all composite measure of performance, the individual is forced to rely upon his judgment as to whether increased effort on one criterion improves over-all performance, or whether there may be a reduction . . . on some other criterion which will outweigh the increase in the first." — V. F. Ridgway, "Dysfunctional Consequences of Performance Measurements," *Administrative Science Quarterly,* 1:245 (September, 1956). Since punitive restriction by definition interferes with treatment, guards are frequently confronted with the necessity for making judgments of the second type. See also Peter M. Blau, *The Dynamics of Bureaucracy* (Chicago: University of Chicago Press, 1955) ; and Burleigh B. Gardner, *Human Relations in Industry* (Chicago: Richard D. Irwin, 1945), p. 174.

dents, who are expected to insure the achievement of the goals of the custodial and industrial organizations, also must be relied upon for diffusing treatment values to guards and foremen. But positive instructions for handling guards in a therapeutic manner are as difficult to formulate and communicate as are positive instructions to guards for handling inmates. Negatively, just as the guard or foreman is expected not to do anything punitive, the supervisor is expected to do nothing that will make the workers tense. The membership of the guard in the subsidiary custodial organization and that of the foreman in the production organization mean that they are held responsible for custodial and production goals; but if they are to relax and use discretion, they must greatly reduce custodial and work supervision of inmates. Because of this contradiction, explication of custodial and production duties through rules is impossible. Explicit rules for use by supervisors in regulating the conduct of employees in regard to custody and work of inmates cannot be formulated, let alone enforced, for these relationships are precisely those in which the employees are to relax and use discretion.

Neutralization of Nonprofessional Supervisory Authority

Under such conditions the supervisors' superiority is neutralized. They are not treatment specialists and therefore cannot rely on professional, technical authority in the supervisory relationship. But the expectation that guards and foremen will "treat" inmates deprives the supervisors of any bureaucratic authority to secure compliance with routines that they or the administrators might consider desirable from the standpoint of security or production. Thus, their authority is neutralized: they can scarcely judge an employee *either* unable or unwilling to "do his job"; they have neither the ability to evaluate his "professional" conduct nor a set of enforceable rules with which to regiment his custodial or work relations with inmates.

This process of neutralizing supervisors' authority is possible only in an organization where the work tasks of participants cannot be explained in definite rules. Rules specify the obligations of the worker and indicate management's expectations as to minimal performance. In a "service bureaucracy," such as a treatment-oriented prison, a welfare agency, a mental hospital, or any other agency where rapport, discretion, finesse, subtleness, and insight are work requirements, the explicational function of rules is lost. Since an end product cannot be specified, a supervisor can judge a worker's performance only by professional standards, and then only if he is professionally trained and if there are verbatim records or informal reports from clients.[26]

---

[26] Professional staff members in treatment-oriented institutions un-

The extent of supervisors' neutrality can be shown by comparing them with factory foremen who, by contrast, can tell when a worker is unmotivated or unwilling to do his job. They have explicit criteria by which to judge his competence and can respond to poor performance by directing him more closely, watching him carefully, outlining his work obligations in detail, and punishing him for serious deviation. This procedure, however, may enmesh management in a vicious cycle, for the close supervision may arouse the worker's ire and accentuate his apathy, putting the supervisor back where he started.[27] The alternative is for the foreman to believe that workers *want* to do what is expected of them. If they are motivated but *unable* to do their jobs, the job of supervision is much easier and consists of improving performance by teaching rather than supervising.

Supervisors in treatment-oriented prisons *necessarily* assume that workers are motivated to perform their tasks. Since neither guards nor supervisors know precisely how guards are to be both custodial and therapeutic, their behavior cannot be judged by supervisors as either unmotivated or the consequence of ignorance or personality make-up. Therefore they can neither supervise closely and punish nor improve performance by education and therapy. Both their superiority of rank and the superiority stemming from their knowledge of custody and production are lost because of the institution's treatment functions.

The supervisor does not have opportunity to segregate — in time, place, or circumstances — the behavior congruent with each of his two conflicting roles. Rather, each of his acts is supposed to achieve contradictory results, stimulating the guards and foremen to behave both custodially and therapeutically.[28] Since that is impossible, supervisors frequently fail to act, and neither treatment nor custodial tasks, as ideally conceived, are accomplished. A pattern of "indulgency" develops and this may be conducive to high em-

doubtedly sometimes act as supervisors and rely on this device, as well as on diffusion, for administering the treatment ideology. They have ready access to inmates for counseling and therapy purposes and thus are in a position to receive confidential reports on the actions of individual guards and other employees. If an employee's reported behavior gives evidence of being punitive or rigid, it can be quietly investigated and corrected by educational discussions with the offender, or in an extreme case the offender can be transferred to a post where he will have no contact with inmates and where he will be "better adjusted." Thus, the professional personnel have direct "educational control" — a system for securing employees' consent to the plans for the institution — over some guards as well as over non-professional supervisors. Use of this device in relations with guards, however, is evidence of inadequate diffusion of the treatment ideology through the custodial and production hierarchies.

[27] Gouldner, *op. cit.,* p. 160.

[28] This may be perceived as "inconsistency" by outsiders and by the employee who tries to get direction from it, but it is not necessarily so interpreted by the actor. See Georg Simmel, *Conflict,* trans. by Kurt H. Wolff (Glencoe: Free Press, 1955), p. 24.

ployee morale but not necessarily to efficient accomplishment of administrators' goals.[29] The absence of rules stimulates the development of an unofficial system for meeting the organizational need for a minimal custodial routine, and the unofficial system in turn makes bureaucratic allocation of specific custodial responsibilities seem unnecessary. Supervisors maintain personal, friendly, and equalitarian relations with workers rather than formal, bureaucratic, professional, or other types of relations ordinarily existing between managers and workers.

NEUTRALIZATION OF THE AUTHORITY OF GUARDS AND FOREMEN

The indulgency pattern of relations between supervisors and guards has a direct counterpart in the relations between guards and inmates. Just as the dual role of the guard makes impossible evaluation of his general effectiveness in the organization by the supervisor — because expertness as a treatment agent necessarily involves a degree of inefficiency as a custodian and vice versa — so the dual role of the inmate (as patient and prisoner) makes it impossible for the guard to behave ideally either in treating or repressing him. The guard can fulfill neither the professional expectations that he will behave therapeutically nor the administrative expectations that he will maintain order and insure accomplishment of essential work tasks. His response to the joint expectations that he will be therapeutic, use discretion about reporting inmates for misconduct, and relax is likely to be one of relaxation only, the precise counterpart of his supervisor's relation with him.

We have already emphasized the impossibility of communicating to guards and foremen what is expected of them as treatment agents. Because they are not professionals, can be given no rules to apply as nonprofessionals, and have custodial and maintenance as well as treatment tasks, they can be expected to base a minimal number of decisions explicitly on individual inmates' needs. Even referrals to the professional staff are limited by the nonprofessionals' needs for assistance in essential maintenance tasks. For example, an inmate who performs a coordinating function in a prison shop is not likely to be referred for treatment that will take him out of the shop. He may even be discouraged from participation in such treatment if his absence from the shop seriously interferes with the productive or cooperative activities of other inmates.

The discretion accorded guards and foremen in the interests of therapy is not necessarily used for therapeutic purposes. Rather, it is highly probable

---

[29] Conditions of employment in treatment-oriented prisons are remarkably similar to the indulgency pattern that Gouldner found in an industrial plant, where workers considered the discipline lenient, the rules flexible, and the relations with supervisors friendly (*op. cit.*, pp. 45–46).

that the official decentralization of decision making, introduced so that individualized treatment could be administered, has as one consequence the decentralization of *punishment*. From the guards' viewpoint, introduction of the treatment ideology has transferred administration of the traditional incentives for securing cooperation, such as the promise of parole, "good time" allowances, and special privileges, from the custodians to the professionals. Guards believe that the official system for administering these incentives cannot be relied on to motivate inmates to cooperate and work hard, and the need for some system to insure a minimum of orderliness has continued. The treatment ideology also has sharply limited the official use of punishment. As noted earlier, when the administrative view that rule breaking shall not be "rewarded" prevails, the custodian is admonished to report offenders to the disciplinary court for punishment. But the professional view that punishment is incompatible with treatment blocks extensive use of this device — guards and foremen are to use discretion in reporting offenses. If an employee does not use this discretion "properly" and frequently reports uncooperative inmates to the court, he risks being diagnosed unfavorably himself.

Faced, then, with a perceived need for stimulating conformity and productiveness in a situation in which both positive and negative official sanctions are denied him, the guard unofficially administers punishments and rewards to get the cooperation he needs. Inmates may be given dirty or unpleasant duty, deprived of recreational privileges, or demoted from high-status jobs without going either to a professional specialist or to disciplinary court. Probably there are few guards who do not resort to this course, even if they accept the notion that inmates should be understood rather than punished.

Even unofficial punishments cannot be imposed extensively, however, so guards and foremen must relax. One effect of unofficial administration of punishment is the personalization of custodial measures. Thus, behavior that a guard seriously believes is undesirable or even dangerous may simply be overlooked, because he wants neither to report it to the disciplinary court nor to punish it unofficially and thereby arouse the animosity of inmates against him personally. By officially overlooking all but the most serious deviation, the guard in effect unofficially *rewards* inmates for general cooperativeness in matters of security or production.

Because the guard has been granted freedom to use discretion in handling inmates, and is not "backed" by an impersonal official hierarchy which demands that custodial rules be routinely administered, when he behaves punitively the inmates, like the front-office workers, are likely to attribute his behavior to personal vindictiveness or maladjustment. This is true whether he officially reports misconduct to the disciplinary court or unofficially punishes the inmate in question. Relaxation by guards, then, is stimulated by an undercurrent of fear, as well as by treatment considerations.

To avoid the risk of gaining a bad reputation among the inmates, most guards carefully examine the circumstances and the inmate before taking unofficial action or writing an official conduct report. They cannot avoid behaving inconsistently, overlooking and thereby rewarding misconduct in some circumstances and punishing it or reporting it in others. This closely parallels the behavior of the professional administrators when they separate their unofficial and official roles. The principal difference is that their unofficial role is primarily a therapeutic one, while that of the guard is ordinarily a neutral one, in which he neither punishes nor treats.

In summary, guards and foremen seem to use their discretion chiefly for securing cooperation in work and custodial matters, not for surface diagnosis and counseling. The professional ideology emphasizes understanding inmate misconduct and applying nonpunitive measures in cases of nonconformity, and this course is followed in some circumstances. But the guards also use their decision-making power to impose unofficial punishments and, more significantly, to do nothing, to *overlook* what in custodial institutions might be rather serious infractions of rules.

EMPLOYEE MORALE

The treatment-oriented prison is a pleasant place in which to work. Although guards and foremen, like inmates, often complain of inconsistency and lack of direction from the professional or the supervisory staff, they respond positively to the friendly relations characteristic of the organization. The employee turnover rate is likely to be lower than in more traditionally organized prisons, where employees are closely supervised. Speaking relatively, in treatment-oriented institutions each employee is to a large extent his "own boss." He is given few orders, is not supervised closely or required to be prompt or efficient, has a "clean job," and usually has what are ordinarily considered good working conditions in his social group. Prior discussion has implied that this pattern of indulgency for employees is directly linked to the pattern of relaxed discipline for inmates. The attempt to administer individualized treatment to inmates is responsible for the individual handling of *guards* in a relaxed atmosphere, instead of their control by a rank-oriented system for enforcing bureaucratic rules. The desired relaxed relationship between guard and inmate must be accompanied by a similar relaxed relationship between guard and supervisor.

Few guards or foremen show evidence of resisting the system of relaxed discipline *as it pertains to employees*. However, it is significant that the older guards and foremen in treatment-oriented prisons do not consider their present conditions of employment preferable in all respects to the earlier ones, when the institutions' goals were more directly custodial. Occasionally they look back wistfully to "the good old days," when, as one guard said, "The inmates always knew where you stood and you always knew where they stood." Since guards are responsible for stimulating inmates to work and be cooperative, the relaxed discipline for inmates can only be perceived by guards as undesirable. They would much prefer a central system for punitive enforcement of specific rules and for rewarding cooperative, hard-working inmates without regard to evidence of their rehabilitation.

Few employees recognize that what they consider the good aspects of their employment are directly linked to what they view as the bad aspects — the difficulties of trying to handle recalcitrant inmates without recourse to traditional incentives or to punitively enforceable rules. Guards who have never worked in any but a relaxed system cannot be expected to observe, as one older guard did, that employees "have swapped the easy job we used to have with inmates for good hours and working conditions." As recipients of relaxed discipline, they find their work easy and enjoyable; but as treaters and controllers of inmates, they find it difficult and nonrewarding.

A high level of employee morale can be maintained in these circumstances only because the guards can administer unofficial rewards and punishments to the degree necessary to motivate inmates and to avoid gross injustices and can overlook deviations insofar as necessary to avoid the open hostility of inmates. In other words, guards can develop with the inmates the same kind of friendly relations that exist between supervisors and guards. The professional personnel take these relaxed relationships as evidence that individualized treatment of inmates is being accomplished. This is necessarily a correct interpretation by professional personnel, for, as has been indicated, they view a system of relaxed discipline as therapeutic simply because it does not make inmates' emotional problems worse. The conditions that in a custodial prison would be viewed as evidence of disorganization or even corruption are interpreted as evidence of a treatment orientation and officially approved.

When Weber wrote that "the choice is only between bureaucracy and dilettantism in the field of administration,"[30] he could not have had in mind an organization where roles of supervisors and workers have characteristics such that the behavior of persons occupying them cannot be ordered, disciplined, or directed toward administrative goals. Such conditions probably could exist only in an organization established not for profit or production but "to do something," in an organization where "success" is absence of trouble, in an organization administering the activities of workers who cannot be expected to be technically efficient in doing the "something" they are expected to do. Each of these features implies an organization with contradictory ends, which are not merely the ends of different people in the system but are representative of the attitudes of all the people involved. Each also characterizes the treatment-oriented prison.

[30] Henderson and Parsons, *op. cit.,* p. 337.

The Parole Supervisor
in the Role of
Stranger

ELMER H. JOHNSON

Parole is a link in a chain of experiences the parolee has undergone involuntarily, with his own self-interest and personal wishes subordinated to the interests and needs of the total society. As such a link, parole represents a transitional period between the regimentation of a correctional institution and the freedom of the normal community life. This transition requires that the supervisor govern his interaction with the parolee to be consistent with the objectives of the earlier incarceration and the ultimate purpose of developing in the parolee self-reliance and identification with the community norms.

This function complicates the definition of the proper role for the supervisor. Authoritarian elements exist in the role because: First, to be consistent with the objectives of imprisonment, the supervisor supports the use of force by the state in a positive way as a means for treating criminals; secondly, the effectiveness of parole lies in its restrictions on the parolee's freedom. Although he is outside prison walls, the parolee still is under sentence and subject to certain conditions in his use of his limited freedom. Parole is a period of guidance and supervision which continues the correctional treatment begun in prison. The supervisor's responsibility is to protect society by assuring that the parolee is fulfilling his obligations.

DIFFERENCES FROM
OTHER SIMILAR ROLES

The authoritarian qualities cause some to confuse this role with that of a policeman or prison custodial officer. In contrast to the policeman, who is charged with the duty of apprehending criminals, the supervisor uses his authority to create a favorable attitude in the parolee and a favorable situation in the parolee's environment for the assuming of self-control by the parolee. The objective is to bridge the gap between purely externalized authority over the parolee and the achievement by the parolee of a capacity for self-direction. This bridging requires the parolee's participation in the process of change in his own behavior. This difficult task can be accomplished only if the supervisor uses his authority with firmness and consistency, but without rigidity, by limiting restrictions to those which are essential and can be understood by the parolee, and through avoidance of unnecessary humiliation or irritation.

The supervisor's role also resembles that of a social caseworker. Both roles involve concern with environmental effects upon personality and with ways of erasing personality defects. To change behavior patterns, individualized treatment is sought through insights into the unique qualities of the parolee and of his environment. Insights require rapport between parolee and his supervisor. However, his role differs from that of the social worker to the extent that the attempts to establish and maintain rapport jeopardize the supervisor's responsibilities stemming from authoritarian elements of his role. This does not imply that the caseworker does not represent and apply authority[1] but his authority differs in degree and, to some extent, in the type of client to which it is applied. The social caseworker and the parole supervisor often deal with the same kinds of personalities among their respective clients, but personality factors in crime causation and the offender's response to the stimuli of conviction and imprisonment can produce personalities and situations not to be found in social casework.

PATTERN FOR
REHABILITATION STRATEGY

The two major elements of the supervisor's role are united by the common objective of instilling self-discipline in the parolee. This gives the supervisor's role the aforementioned transitional quality. Contacts with the parolee are to be used to create a relatively stable relationship for him within his community which will encourage him to internalize the norms supporting the social order. The strategy is to use the contacts as units for creating new patterns of association. It is helpful to conceive of these patterns to be differentiated along a continuum beginning with the parolee's isolation from the social order and culminating in his amalgamation within law-abiding society. The stages along this continuum can be described as follows: *Advance,* tentative admission of the officer by the parolee to the parolee's private and personal world of thoughts and aspirations; *Adjustment,* recognition by the parolee that differences exist between his value system and that of the total social order; *Accordance,* mutual participation by the parolee and the supervisor becomes possible because of common experiences, emotions, and attitudes created during the adjustment period, but full identification of the parolee with the values of the total social order is not attained; and *Amalgamation,* the devia-

---

[1] For a discussion of case work in an authoritarian setting, see Richard A. Chappell, "Probation: Case Work and Current Status," in Paul W. Tappan (editor), *Contemporary Correction* (New York: McGraw-Hill, 1951), pp. 386–88.

tion of the parolee from the social norms of total society is eliminated through his internalization of those norms.[2]

This paper is concerned primarily with the first of these stages. However, effective supervision requires that the contacts which contribute to the attainment of this first stage must not jeopardize the attainment of later stages. Of course, the essence of advance is the creation of rapport between officer and parolee by minimizing social distance through establishment of free communication. Rapport is a prerequisite for later stages, but it is of little value as an end in itself, insofar as the objectives of supervision are concerned. It is possible that close rapport could be established easily if the supervisor accepts the parolee's values, but the costs would be loss of a professional relationship and of the possibility of rehabilitation. The supervisor would find himself enmeshed in a social situation pushing him toward amalgamation with the parolee's norms. Then, who would be "rehabilitating" whom?

The officer enters into social interaction with the parolee within a community environment made up of third parties who can influence the quality of the parolee-supervisor relationship. Such third parties include social workers, law enforcement officers, court officials, ministers, and members of service clubs. Other third parties will be in more direct contact with the parolee; these include his employer, members of his family, his neighbors, and members of his work and recreational groups. The supervisor must establish and maintain rapport with these third parties so that they may be his allies in amalgamating the parolee within the community. Therefore, the officer, assuming his responsibility in a community new to him, will find that he must proceed through the stages from advance to amalgamation with these third parties. Even when the supervisor has had previous experiences in the community, each new case will bring contacts with new third parties.

In his efforts to attain the stage of advance, the officer can be defined as a sociological stranger. The remainder of this paper will be devoted to assessing the limitations and advantages given the supervisor by his role as stranger in initial contacts.

CHARACTERISTICS
OF THE STRANGER

What is this role of stranger? It exists because the individual is in an alien land, away from his own people, and consequently not subject completely to the subtle controls exerted by the culture of the people among whom he now lives. Simmel pointed out that this mobility of the stranger makes him

---

[2] Adapted from Howard Becker, *Systematic Sociology on the Basis of the Beziehungslehre and Begildelehre of Leopold von Wiese* (New York: Wiley, 1932).

physically near but socially remote in his relationships within the community.[3] Because his mobility has made him an exception to the personality-conditioning processes experienced by the orthodox members of the community, the stranger is objective in his attitude toward the values of the people among whom he lives. His objectivity, if coupled with personal ties with the individual concerned, fits the stranger for the role of confidant to an orthodox member of the community. Unlike the wanderer, the stranger has a place in the social structure of the community because of his economic, political, or social functions. In history, we find the stranger often served as a trader, a middleman between peoples who stand in a producer-consumer relationship. Although his differences may bar him from full acceptance into the community, the stranger must be recognized as a participant in the community life to the extent that his function contributes to community life.

The height of the social barriers erected against the stranger will vary with the intensity of the in-group ties uniting the members of the community. We are bound in personal relations to other members of our in-group through common characteristics and common possession of culture and cultural equipment. The greater the similarity, the greater is the warmth of the social bonds of the individual to his group. The less the similarity, the weaker are the social bonds. If the group defines such similarities as unique to itself, a greater barrier is erected against the stranger because his freedom from the group's conventions makes him dissimilar. However, if the group defines the similarities as peculiar to the individual as individual rather than to the group, the stranger exhibiting such similarities has a greater chance of gaining social acceptance. This possibility is enhanced if the group is so large numerically in membership that the warmth of the emotional ties with fellow group members is reduced. The stranger could be similar to other members of the community in nationality, religion, social position, racial criteria, educational attainment, or personality.

Because of his freedom from local conventions, the stranger is more likely to exhibit "sanctioned rationality," rather than the "affective rationality" characteristic of natives of the community. "Sanctioned rationality" is the pursuit of ends by means regarded as conforming to the principles of economy of effort, efficiency, and absence of undesirable effects, but limited by the character of the ends sought. In "affective rationality," the means and ends are fused emotionally on the basis of unquestioned acceptance of the traditions of one's people.[4]

---

[3] See George Simmel, *Soziologie* (Leipzig: Duncker and Humblot, 1908), pp. 685–691.

[4] See Howard Becker, "Interpretive Sociology and Constructive Typology," in George Gurvitch and Wilbert E. Moore, *Twentieth Century Sociology* (New York: The Philosophical Library, 1945), pp. 78–81.

HOW THE SUPERVISOR
QUALIFIES AS STRANGER

The supervisor qualifies as a stranger in these ways:

1. He is a functionary within the state-wide parole system, with his jurisdiction usually extending beyond the bounds of the local community. As a middleman, he implements the policies and expresses the authority of an extra-community agency. Ethnocentric attitudes against extra-community agencies are barriers to rapport.

2. The combination of authoritarian and rehabilitation-oriented elements in his role makes him the ally of both law enforcement and social workers in the community, but his dissimilarity from each in objectives and functions requires that he resist stereotyping of his role in terms of either element. Therefore, he may appear at times to these allies to be representing a program disruptive, or at least contrary, to the objectives of the community agencies whose support and services are essential to effective parole supervision.

3. To achieve rehabilitation, the supervisor must implement moral norms which, presumably, differ from those expressed by the parolee in the anti-social act which occasioned imprisonment. The supervisor applies sanctioned rationality toward the end that contacts of the parolee with the supervisor and with members of the community will contribute to the parolee's amalgamation within the community. Those agencies and individuals in the community who oppose the techniques and/or objectives of parole would consider his rationality to oppose their affective rationality. Thus, the officer may be cast as a stranger by some members of the very community within which the parolee should be integrated.

4. Similarly, the supervisor may be cast as a stranger to the parolee. If the anti-social norms of the offender stem from a sub-culture, he may be motivated by an affective rationality not shared by the total community. Then the officer is a stranger to the group sharing that sub-culture.

5. The supervisor may be cast as a stranger because he differs from the residents in characteristics he has attained through previous membership in ethnic, religious, social class, racial, educational attainment, or rural-urban residence groupings.

SUPERVISOR'S CHARACTERISTICS
AND COMMUNITY'S REACTION

The quality of the initial reaction to the officer can be a barrier to, or can be a factor favorable for, rapport. The result depends in part upon his awareness of his place in the social situation and his skill in turning the sociological factors operating to the advantage of his objectives. He should be aware of his own contribution to the "chemistry" of the situation. His introspective analysis is aided if he realizes that the conception of the supervisor's role held by the parolee and the various third parties is at least as important as his own view of that role. Their conceptions are reactions to three inter-dependent sets of characteristics exhibited by the supervisor. The first set is related to his status as an institutional functionary within the parole system. The second set stems from his membership in various groupings based on criteria such as social class, religion, race, educational attainment, or rural-urban residence. His behavior, mental make-up, and dress will reflect values and attitudes he has internalized through socialization while he has partici-pated in such groupings. His uniqueness as an individual will be reflected in the third set of characteristics.

It has been noted that newcomers frequently evoke no perceivable prefer-ence or distaste on their first appearance.

Reaction is more objective: rational criteria or accepted social standards inhibit emotions linked with sympathy or antipathy. The stranger is promptly labeled or assigned a niche in a familiar plurality pattern. His social affiliations with a class, a cultural or racial group, etc., are matters of primary interest for the observer. In Shaler's terminology, this is categoric contact; it is markedly in contrast to the emotional attraction and repulsion sometimes called forth in the observer as a re-sult of the newcomer's relation to his own tastes, inclinations, desires, and experi-ences — in brief, to positive or negative sympathetic contacts. . . .[5]

As a newcomer, the supervisor appears to be making contacts of a categoric nature in many instances. This would be most true for initial contacts based on his status as institutional functionary. The validity of this statement for the second set of characteristics would depend upon the degree of his simi-larity in group affiliations with natives of the community and the relative importance placed upon such similarities by the natives. The contribution of the third set of characteristics to the rehabilitative process depends on the sympathetic contacts it makes possible.

SUPERVISOR AS
INSTITUTIONAL FUNCTIONARY

The status of institutional functionary is likely to be a dominant factor in the initial contacts of the officer with the parolee and the third parties. The initial response is to the supervisor's office, rather than to him as an individual personality. The quality of the response to the office varies with the respon-dent's conception of the parole program and its effect upon his own activities.

---

[5] Wiese-Becker, *op. cit.,* p. 158.

One possibility is that the response to the office will place the case automatically beyond the stage of advance. Local agencies may accept the supervisor as an ally with a similar occupation. Some parolees will welcome him as a guide along the route toward successful termination of parole. The parolee and the third parties accept the supervisor's conception of parole.

Another possibility is that the supervisor is welcomed but on the basis of an erroneous conception of role and of parole itself. The office permits easy establishment of rapport, but the attainment of later stages of adjustment and accordance is blocked because the rapport is based on a stereotyped conception of the supervisor's role. Such stereotyping can create false expectations of parole which later brings disenchantment to the parolee and third parties.

A third possibility is that the categoric nature of initial contact is obscured by antipathies aroused by the supervisor's office. Because the emotional response is to the office rather than to the supervisor as an individual, the initial contact appears to be categoric. However, the antipathies make this a negative sympathetic contact, impeding progress toward advance and subsequent stages of association.

SOCIAL CLASS AND EDUCATIONAL CHARACTERISTICS

Social class attributes are included in the second set of characteristics of the officer which affect the initial response given him. This probably is the most important of the characteristics included in this set. The difference in socio-economic status can be a real obstacle to the communication essential to the establishment of rapport. This point has been established by Johnston.[6] He noted that the professional in the correctional institution finds it difficult to project himself into the social situations common to his lower class inmate and much of the clinical literature deals with middle-class patients who are more amenable to treatment than those from the lower class. Johnston wrote:

. . . Social scientists have discovered that, due to values, childrearing patterns, and circumstances in lower class homes, these children tend to grow up with lower levels of aspiration, a lessened ability to defer gratification for future gains, and generally a lower level of "push" to succeed in a given task, than persons raised in middle class homes. . . . The professional man in the prison setting may find himself unable, then, to understand a prisoner's preference for a job in the officer's kitchen to an opportunity to learn the machinists' trade — a choice which is hedonistic and opportunistic but which in no way deviates from what seems to be typical reactions found in the social strata from which most of our prisoners are

[6] Norman Johnston, "Sources of Distortion and Deception in Prison Interviewing," *Federal Probation* (March, 1956), pp. 46–47.

recruited. In other areas such as early sexual experiences, the amount of physically aggressive behavior manifested by the prisoner in previous life, etc., it is imperative that the evaluator shun his own middle class value system and appraise the behavior of the inmate in light of what we know about standards of behavior and customs in other segments of society. . . .

Although social class differences may be a barrier to rapport with the parolee, the similar difference between parolee and various third parties can expedite establishment of communication between the supervisor and these third parties. If the rapport is consistent with the objectives of parole, the officer finds advance easily established with these third parties. However, the opposite result is to be expected if rapport is based on faulty premises held by the third parties or if the third parties place the parolee outside their in-group as unacceptable for integration into the community as a law-abiding citizen.

Because of his presumably advanced education, the supervisor can gain acceptance by community residents with similar educational attainments. However, the supervisor has attained an educational level higher than that of most of his parolees and some of the third parties. An important function of formal education is socialization, including development of such elements of personality as philosophy, recreational interests, vocabulary, accent, and taste in dress. Differences of this sort can be the basis of ethnocentric reaction against the supervisor.

As one criterion of social status, high educational attainment sometimes stimulates antipathy in persons with an inferior education because the difference symbolizes the inferiority they feel. On the other hand, superior educational attainment is regarded automatically by some with less schooling as proof of great ability. Therefore, formal educational status, in and of itself, can stimulate either a negative or a positive sympathetic contact.

Thirdly, the curriculum of formal education is an abstraction from the past experience of man presented in a "hot house" environment in order to increase the quality and quantity of facts and insights learned in a given time over that available through unplanned and uncoordinated individual experience. Presumably, the supervisor has been found qualified as an institutional functionary because his formal education has given him a reservoir of facts and insights for carrying out his responsibilities. Therefore, he can win support for parole objectives from the parolee and the third parties because he has such a reservoir to draw upon as he applies his "sanctioned rationality." His educational attainment is a means for achieving rapport because it enables him to demonstrate greater skills and knowledge, not just because it is a "calling card" for the impersonal granting of superior status in a world of hasty and transitional contacts between persons.

Racial, religious, and ethnic qualities of the officer may be the basis for categoric contacts if these qualities are criteria for social stratification within the community. It is likely that these qualities were taken into consideration in his selection as an institutional functionary so that they would not be serious barriers to establishment of rapport in the community as a whole. However, varying with the heterogeneity of the community in terms of these qualities, achievement of rapport through conformity of the supervisor's characteristics with those of one segment of the community could mean creation of barriers to rapport with other segments.

The stereotypes of the "city slicker" and the "country hick" are exaggerations of dissimilarities in personal traits between urban and rural people derived from difference in such sociological factors as degree of cultural homogeneity, pecuniary nexus, division of labor, population density, and pace of life. The supervisor conditioned to urban life is likely to find his personal traits a barrier to free communication with individuals conditioned to rural life. The supervisor with a rural heritage may find the same situation in dealing with urban people. He must acculturize himself consciously and deliberately to folkways, mores, vocabulary, and traditions others have learned unconsciously and informally as a part of daily life since childhood.

SUPERVISOR AS AN INDIVIDUAL PERSONALITY

The third set of characteristics are those unique to each supervisor as an individual. The personality of the officer is the key to effective parole because individualized treatment requires a personal relationship between parolee and officer based on mutual confidence, trust, and respect. Burbank and Goldsborough have pointed out that the probation officer must have these abilities: To form and sustain wholesome interpersonal relationships, to accept responsibility for the authority he carries, to work with aggressive persons, to work with other agencies and people, and to improve in performance through self-analysis.[7] Of course, the same can be said for the parole officer. Flexibility, objectivity, patience, persistence, and a sophisticated grasp of the crucial factors in each case are essential qualities in the officer. His professional competency should include the understanding of the sociological potentialities of his role as stranger and capacity to exploit them.

ADVANTAGES GIVEN BY ROLE OF STRANGER

Although his office gives him a place and function in the community, the parole officer is free comparatively from the affective rationality of the native

---

[7] Edmund G. Burbank and Ernest W. Goldsborough, "The Probation Officer's Personality: A Key Factor in Rehabilitation," *Federal Probation* (June, 1954), pp. 11–13.

residents. He does not share community attitudes derived from previous behavior of the parolee which would conflict with objective application of techniques appropriate for the case. Because amalgamation with the community is a prerequisite to lasting rehabilitation, the supervisor must give heed to the affective rationality of the community in his contacts. However, in his professional role, he must be sufficiently detached from his "patient" and the community to be able to diagnose, prescribe, and administer the proper treatment. The objectivity inherent in the role of stranger contributes to this end.

In attempting rehabilitation, the supervisor is seeking to construct a social environment most conducive to behavior changes in the specific parolee with his own unique personality and his own special constellation of environmental factors. The parolee and the third parties have certain attitudes which affect the possibility of amalgamating the parolee into the community in a new role consistent with society's interests. As a newcomer, the officer represents a new element in the "social chemistry" of the group encompassing the parolee and the third parties. In the process of readjustment of interpersonal relationships within the group to this new element, the attitudes and behavior of the group members may be modified. If the supervisor has the necessary insights and leadership skills, the role of stranger gives him an opportunity to inject the seed of change into this group environment to the end that rehabilitation becomes possible.

To carry out his responsibilities effectively, the supervisor must elicit the support of various third parties and of the parolee for both authoritarian and rehabilitation-oriented elements of his office. He must achieve rapport with the individuals concerned, but it must be rapport which contributes to modification of the parolee's behavior and his environment consistent with rehabilitation. As a newcomer, the supervisor has the opportunity to build a foundation of attitudes towards himself and his objectives consistent with this type of rapport. As an established member of the community, he would face the added burden of revising prior definitions of himself and his role before creating more appropriate attitudes.

Earlier we noted that objectivity fits the stranger for the role of confidant. This role is appropriate for the task of reducing the deviation of the parolee from the community norms. As an outsider, the supervisor can be a more acceptable confidant to the parolee than members of the community. He is a passerby in the sociological sense; the members of the community have a more permanent place in the parolee's social world. The officer does not share the affective rationality of the community. His professional attitude and his objectivity as stranger can encourage the parolee to express doubts about the validity of this affective rationality, thereby opening the way to adjustment and accordance. Such confidences with more permanent members of his group invite retaliation or future embarrassment for the parolee.

SUMMARY

In summary, the parole supervisor faces the problem of integrating authoritarian and rehabilitation-oriented elements of his role. To achieve rehabilitation, he must elicit the participation of the parolee and of other members of the community in creating new interpersonal relationships which integrate the parolee into community life. The supervisor will find his role of stranger both a handicap and a resource in attaining rapport as an essential prerequisite. If it is to be a resource, he must understand the nature of his role and the sociological implications of his personal and professional characteristics within the social context of community life.

Comparison of the Executed
and the Commuted Among
Admissions to Death Row

MARVIN E. WOLFGANG, ARLENE KELLY, AND HANS C. NOLDE

BASIS FOR THE STUDY

The purpose of this study is to analyze statistically the social characteristics of those persons who have been sentenced to death for the crime of murder since introduction of the electric chair in Pennsylvania. The basic data consist of the case records of 439 persons sentenced to death for first degree murder[1] and detained under custody on death row between 1914 and 1958.[2] These records are filed at the State Correctional Institution at Rockview, Pennsylvania, the only place in the state where the death penalty is administered. Because an offender sentenced to die is transported there only as his date of execution approaches, there are a number of offenders who were sentenced to die during the 1914–1958 period who do not appear in the present study because their sentences were commuted before being placed on death row at Rockview. Of those who did reach Rockview, 341

Reprinted by special permission of the authors and *The Journal of Criminal Law, Criminology and Police Science,* Copyright © 1962 by the Northwestern University School of Law, Vol. 53 (September 1962), pp. 301–311.

[1] "All murder which shall be perpetrated by means of poison, or by lying in wait, or by any other kind of wilful, deliberate and premeditated killing, or which shall be committed in the perpetration of, or attempting to perpetrate any arson, rape, robbery, burglary, or kidnapping, shall be murder in the first degree." Pa. Penal Code art. XII, § 701.

The first statute to divide the crime of murder into degrees was enacted in Pennsylvania on April 22, 1794. Many other states of the union adopted this model with slight changes in the substantive law but with considerable variations in judicial interpretations. See, e.g., Keedy, "History of the Pennsylvania Statute Creating Degrees of Murder," 97 *U. Pa. L. Rev.* 759 (1949); Keedy, "A Problem of First Degree Murder: *Fisher v. United States,*" 99 *U. Pa. L. Rev.* 267 (1950); Keedy, "Criminal Attempts at Common Law," 102 *U. Pa. L. Rev.* 464 (1954).

[2] A recent review of data in the archives of the State Correctional Institution at Rockview, furnished by W. W. Thomas to the Bureau of Corrections, indicates that there were 433 total dispositions from death row in that institution between 1915 and 1959; of these, 347 were executed (80 per cent), and 86 were commuted (20 per cent). *Populations in the Bureau of Correction During 1960,* p. 3 (Directorate of Research and Statistics, Pa. Dep't of Justice, Bureau of Correction) (unpublished).

For an interesting historical survey of early executions in Pennsylvania, see Teeters, "Public Executions in Pennsylvania 1682 to 1834," 64 *J. Lancaster County Hist. Soc'y* 85 (No. 2, 1960).

Especially stimulating and useful for its comparative data is the study reported by Johnson, "Selective Factors in Capital Punishment," 36 *Social Forces* 165 (1957).

were executed and 71 were commuted; the remaining 27 included persons who either died of natural causes on death row or for whom it has not been possible to determine the final disposition.

Although the amount and kind of information on individual cases varies greatly, most records provide sufficient data for analysis of the following major attributes of the convicted offender: age, sex,[3] race, nativity, occupation, and marital status. Additional information usually obtainable and secured from examination of the original bill of indictment and of the Pennsylvania Legislative Journal includes: type of counsel for the defendant (private or court-appointed); type of murder (felony or non-felony); reasons for commutation of the death sentence.

There is a growing body of literature concerned with differential treatment of offenders who have committed similar offenses, but discussion usually centers around the sentencing problem, and judicial caprice in sentencing is contrasted with the need for individual treatment.[4] It is a widely held belief that minority groups, particularly Negroes, suffer discrimination in the courts, but there are few studies that examine this hypothesis empirically.[5] Because there are always many difficulties encountered when seeking to hold constant a variety of factors in the personal and social background of offenders who appear before the courts, carefully controlled research in this area of differential judicial treatment is still in its nascency.

The present study does not pretend to overcome these difficulties. We are required to assume, in the absence of detailed psychological analyses and other kinds of data regarding the specific character of the murder, the offender, and his victim, that there has been some randomness in the distribution of known factors. Hence, we are able to work only with the accessible gross social variables in the records. However, there is one common underlying factor, it must be remembered, that is socially and legally visible and that

[3] The number of females sentenced to die is too small to analyze separately, so that for all intents and purposes we are referring to males throughout the study. In only 4 cases during the entire period were females detained on death row; and of these, 2 were executed and 2 were commuted.

[4] For cogent discussions of these matters, see S. Glueck, "The Sentencing Problem," 20 *Fed. Prob.* 15 (Dec., 1956); Edward Green, *Judicial Attitudes in Sentencing* (XV Cambridge Studies in Criminology, London, 1961); *What's New in Sentencing* (Bul. No. 7 Correctional Research, Morris, ed., Oct., 1957).

[5] Gaudet, Harris & St. John "Individual Differences in the Sentencing Tendencies of Judges," 23 *J. Crim. L. & C.* 811 (1933); Lane, "Illogical Variations in Sentences of Felons Committed to Massachusetts State Prison," 32 *J. Crim. L. & C.* 171 (1941); Frankel, "The Offender and the Court: A Statistical Analysis of the Sentencing of Delinquents," 31 *J. Crim. L. & C.* 448 (1940); Lemert & Rosberg, "The Administration of Justice to Minority Groups in Los Angeles County," 2 *U. Calif. Publications in Culture and Society* 1 (No. 1, 1948); Bullock, "Significance of the Racial Factor in the Length of Prison Sentences," 52 *J. Crim. L., C. & P.S.* 411 (1961); Edward Green, *op. cit. supra* note 4.

permits us to examine the present cases as a homogeneous group already controlled for the most significant attribute: all of these persons have been convicted — justly or unjustly — of having committed first degree murder and have been sentenced to death.

There are, of course, many social and legal forces that function selectively prior to this stage and that have produced many differences in the conditions surrounding commission of the crime. Age, race, sex, social status, and other factors have long been recognized as functioning selectively in the commission of this and other types of crime.[6] Moreover, the youthful first offender, even though having committed a heinous murder, is rarely sentenced to death.

The reasons and emotions involved in court decisions that refrain from legally permitted use of the death penalty are so numerous that research has only scratched the surface of these phenomena. There are no official public national statistics on the number of capital crimes committed in the United States each year, but good estimates suggest that not more than 15 per cent of all criminal homicides are capital crimes. In any case, the *Uniform Crime Reports* for 1959 reveal that there were 8,583 murders and non-negligent manslaughters throughout the country.[7] For the same year *National Prisoner Statistics* reported only 49 executions for the nation.[8] In 1959 there were 285 murders and non-negligent manslaughters reported in Pennsylvania, and the state executed three persons during that year. Because only nine states presently have abolished the death penalty by statute, it is obvious that executions are disappearing de facto if not de jure and that a variety of factors in concatenation function to spare most convicted murderers from execution.

We are not here analyzing the factors that determine whether a penalty of death or some lesser penalty is more likely to be the sentence of the court. We recognize that from the total population capable of committing murder, selective forces are operating to "cause" some persons rather than others to commit the crime of murder, to be detected, to be prosecuted, to be convicted, to be sentenced to death, and to be held in custody on death row. The cases presently under analysis are taken from this last level of the whole cultural and judicial process of selectivity. We begin with all persons who have been sentenced to die and who have been detained on death row. We then dichotomize this group into (a) those persons who actually were executed (whose sentences were in fact carried out) and (b) those whose sentences of death were commuted to a lesser penalty (usually life imprison-

---

[6] Wolfgang, *Patterns in Criminal Homicide* (1958).
[7] U. S. Dep't of Justice, *Uniform Crime Reports — 1959*, 33 (1960).
[8] Fed. Bureau of Prisons, *Executions 1959* (Nat'l Prisoner Statistics No. 23, Feb., 1960).

ment).[9] Whether there was legal or moral justification for the sentences of death is not our immediate concern. We may even assume (for lack of primary evidence upon which to base any other assumption) that all of these persons were equally guilty of first degree murder and were given equal treatment by the courts. At any rate, all of these offenders received identical sentences for their crimes. This element of homogeneity is one of the most severe that our society can place upon its citizens, but our judicial machinery permits reconsideration of the sentence in the form of a pardon or commutation. It is important, therefore, for us to know something about any differences that may exist between those persons who suffer the full extent of the law through death and those who have enjoyed the privilege of administrative reconsideration and retraction of the original sentence.

COMPARISON OF THE EXECUTED AND THE COMMUTED

Because our political institutional machinery does provide a means for mitigating the severity of a death sentence pronounced in the judicial process, we should expect some differences to be apparent between offenders who have been executed and those who were commuted. However, assuming that this legal machinery functions on the basis of rational and legal principles and discriminates among convicted offenders only on such basis, any class or racial differences that are noted between the executed and commuted cast doubt on the basic principles.

Only a minimal number of factors can presently be examined in this kind of comparison because of the paucity of data available to the researcher. But statistical analysis even on a macroscopic level is useful for it provides a point of departure for more intensive examination of the refined differentials that are placed in focus in this way.

To assure elimination of spurious associations due to chance operation we have employed common devices for testing the data. These include the chi-square (χ^2) with correction for continuity and the test of significance of differences between proportions, both with a probability level (P value) of less than .05. The total N, or number of cases possible for comparison among each of the variables under analysis, differs from one table to another because not all of the same information was available for all 439 cases. Among those cases for which data are available, we have used test statistics to determine whether statistically significant differences occur between the executed and

---

[9] For discussion and research on pardons and commutations, see "Pardon and Commutation," 39 *Prison J.* 1 (Pa. Prison Soc'y, April, 1959); Wolfgang, "Murder, the Pardon Board, and Recommendations by Judges and District Attorneys," 50 *J. Crim. L., C. & P.S.* 338 (1959).

commuted, and where the P value is less than .05 we are in effect saying that the difference is not due to chance factors, or that some selectivity is functioning that differentiates those who were put to death from those who were spared the ultimate penalty.

TYPE OF MURDER

Although all of these cases are defined in Pennsylvania as first degree murder, an important legal and social difference is whether the death occurred in conjunction with, or as a result of, commission of another type of felony.[10] In Pennsylvania any death that occurs during the commission of arson, burglary, robbery, rape, or kidnapping is by statute classified as first degree murder, whether or not the felon committed, intended, or premeditated the slaying. This type of slaying is referred to as "felony murder," and all other types of murder are "non-felony murder." While extenuating circumstances may have been involved in commission of a non-felony murder, nonetheless there can be little doubt in a capital conviction that the court found the defendant guilty of a premeditated, intentional killing. A felony murder may involve deliberate killing concomitant to another felony, but usually this type of slaying is incidental and peripheral to the principal purpose of another crime, which most commonly is some form of theft or other crime for financial profit.[11]

Relative to these two types of murder a null hypothesis states: Among felony and non-felony murderers sentenced to death and detained on death row there are no significant differences in the proportions who are subsequently executed or commuted. Table I presents the distribution of these cases, and a test for significance of difference reveals that there is an association between felony murder conviction and execution for the crime. Not only are there absolutely more felony murderers (184) than non-felony murderers (125) among the total cases for which information is available, but also proportionately more felony murderers than non-felony murderers actually suffered the death penalty; contrariwise, more non-felony cases had their sentences commuted. We shall later examine these relationships by holding constant the factor of race.

These findings are interesting simply as descriptive statistics of the disposition of capital crimes, but they take on important meaning because of wide state variations in the definition of felony murder.[12] Moreover, suggestions

---

[10] Savitz, "Capital Crimes as Defined in American Statutory Law," 46 *J. Crim. L., C. & P.S.* 355 (1955). See also Wolfgang, *Patterns in Criminal Homicide* ch. 13 (1958).

[11] *Id.* at 238–44.

[12] Savitz, *supra* note 10.

Table I: Type of Murder, by Final Disposition

| | Type of murder | | | | | |
| | Felony murder | | Non-felony murder | | Total | |
Final disposition	N	%	N	%	N	%
Executed	159	86.4	92	73.6	251	81.2
Commuted	25	13.6	33	26.4	58	18.8
Total	184	100.0	125	100.0	309	100.0

$\chi^2 = 7.14; P$ *less than .01.*

have recently been made to eliminate from the penal code an automatic charge of first degree murder in felony homicide cases. The felony murder rule has been abrogated in England, from which country our own use of this rule has evolved.[13] An act that is by statute labeled "first degree murder" is consequently a capital crime and subjects the offenders, whether principals in the first or second degree, to the maximum penalty. Thus, all other things being equal a state such as Kansas that considers as a felony murder a death occurring during *any* felony has a proportionately greater number of capital offenders involved in the administration of justice than does a state such as Massachusetts that considers as felony murder a death occurring only during a crime punishable by death or life imprisonment. On the basis of the experience in Pennsylvania, one convicted of a felony murder, regardless of the kind of felony in which he participated concurrent to the death and irrespective of how the death occurred (by accident, by a police officer, or by the offender directly), has less probability of having his death sentence commuted. Although we cannot speak conclusively about experience in other states, it would appear that states with felony murder statutes so broad in scope as to include a death during any felony would have an even higher proportion of executions than we have found in Pennsylvania. This assumption leads to a generalization requiring further study; namely, that the more inclusive the definition of felony murder, the higher the proportion of execu-

---

[13] The English Homicide Act, enacted in 1957, provides as follows:
"§ 1. *Abolition of 'constructive malice.'* — (1) Where a person kills another in the course or furtherance of some other offense, the killing shall not amount to murder unless done with the same malice aforethought (express or implied) as is required for a killing to amount to murder when not done in the course or furtherance of another offense.
"(2) For the purpose of the foregoing subsection, a killing done in the course or for the purpose of resisting an officer of justice, or of resisting or avoiding or preventing a lawful arrest, or of effecting or assisting an escape or rescue from legal custody, shall be treated as a killing in the course or furtherance of an offense."

tions and the greater the differential in final disposition between felony and non-felony murderers.

We cannot know what would have been the fate of the 184 felony murderers sentenced to death had there been no statutory definition of felony homicide as first degree murder; but it is probably safe to say that more than a few of the 159 defendants who were executed under this ruling would have been convicted of less serious forms of criminal homicide and consequently would not have received sentences of death and would not have been executed.[14] It appears, then, that abolition of the felony murder rule would reduce the number of executions if the past proportion of commutations for non-felony cases should continue. At any rate, nearly half a century of Pennsylvania history indicates that a significantly higher proportion of felony murder than of non-felony murder cases provoked the full extent of society's negative reaction to homicide.

Age of the Offender

Table II shows the distribution of 407 cases for whom age at time of arrival on death row was known. As might be expected, the polar ends of the age groups (15–19 years, and those 55 years and over) have the lowest frequency of execution and consequently the highest frequency of commutation. As a matter of fact, an equal number in each of these age groups was executed as was commuted. The highest frequency (92 per cent) of execution occurs in the age group 20–24 years. Although the highest rate of criminal homicide occurs in this same age group,[15] this fact does not explain their highest proportion of executions. The answer seems to lie in the fact that this age group contributes most disproportionately to felony murders.[16] Of the 160 felony murderers executed, 57, or 36 per cent, were aged 20–24 years; while of the 99 non-felony murderers executed, only 16, or 16 per cent, were aged 20–24. Although persons in the youngest (15–19 years) and the oldest (55 years and over) age groups may be treated differentially because of age, it appears that within the age range from 20 through 54, age per se has little or no influence on final disposition. Rather, it is the higher frequency of felony murders that most directly affects the final disposition, as is indicated by the association between felony murder, execution, and the age class 20–24 years. This age group has the highest frequency among all felony murderers; consequently, any change in the statutes regarding felony murder would most

---

[14] Especially would this statement be valid for at least 20 persons executed who were not directly responsible for the deaths which occurred.

[15] Wolfgang, *Patterns in Criminal Homicide* 65–78 (1958).

[16] Among those cases for whom information was available for both age and type of murder (N = 317), there are 185 felony murderers and 132 non-felony murderers; of the felony murderers, 160, or 87%, were executed compared to 99, or 75%, of non-felony murderers.

Table II: Final Disposition, by Age of Offender

	Final disposition			
Age of offender	*Executed N*	*Commuted N*	*Percentage executed*	*Total N*
15-19	7	7	50.0	14
20-24	96	8	92.3	104
25-29	71	21	77.2	92
30-34	58	12	82.9	70
35-39	48	9	84.2	57
40-44	26	6	81.3	32
45-49	18	2	90.0	20
50-54	7	1	87.5	8
55+	5	5	50.0	10
Total	336	71	82.6	407

directly affect homicide offenders in their early twenties. Non-felony murders appear to be more evenly distributed throughout the age groups from 15–19 to age 55 and over. Finally, the median age for executed felony murderers is 27.5 years, and the median age for executed non-felony murderers is 35.7 years. The interrelationship therefore is strikingly obvious between the proportion of persons convicted of murder who (a) are executed, (b) are young adults, and (c) have committed felony murder.

RACE OF THE OFFENDER

Much previous research in criminal homicide, which includes murder in the first degree, has demonstrated that a disproportionate contribution to the homicide rate is made by Negroes.[17] It is no surprise, therefore, that as many as 36 per cent of the persons placed on death row are Negro. Consistent with independent research and the *Uniform Crime Reports,* Negroes comprise between three and four times more of the criminal homicide cases (either as offenders or as victims) than they do of the general population.

What interests us in the present analysis, however, is not the rate of criminal homicide but the ratio of executed-to-commuted Negroes compared to this same ratio among whites. Using the null hypothesis again, we may assert that there is no significant difference between Negroes and whites in the proportionate distributions of capital offenders who are ultimately executed and those who are commuted. Table III indicates that this hypothesis is rejected and that there is an association between race and type of disposition. The probability value resulting from the χ^2 reveals in this table that compared to

[17] For an analysis of criminal homicide rates by race both in Philadelphia and in other community studies, see Wolfgang, *Patterns in Criminal Homicide* 31–46 (1958).

Table III: Race of the Offender, by Final Disposition

Race

Final disposition	Negro		White		Total	
	N	%	N	%	N	%
Executed	130	88.4	210	79.8	340	82.9
Commuted	17	11.6	53	20.2	70	17.1
Total	147	100.0	263	100.0	410	100.0

$x^2 = 4.33$; P less than .05.

whites a significantly higher proportion of Negroes are executed instead of commuted.

Although there may be a host of factors other than race involved in this frequency distribution, something more than chance has operated over the years to produce this racial difference. On the basis of this study it is not possible to indict the judicial and other public processes prior to the death row as responsible for the association between Negroes and higher frequency of executions; nor is it entirely correct to assume that from the time of their appearance on death row Negroes are discriminated against by the Pardon Board. Too many unknown or presently immeasurable factors prevent our making definitive statements about the relationship. Nevertheless, because the Negro/high-execution association is statistically present, some suspicion of racial discrimination can hardly be avoided. If such a relationship had not appeared, this kind of suspicion could have been allayed; the existence of the relationship, although not "proving" differential bias by the Pardon Boards over the years since 1914, strongly suggests that such bias has existed.

Within 'the confines of the data available examination has been made of race and type of final disposition by holding constant the factor of age. Of the total number of cases for which there is information for each of these variables ($N = 308$), no significant differences emerged. When tests were run to determine association only between race and type of murder (excluding final disposition), both among Negroes and among whites a little over six out of ten had been convicted of felony murder.[18] (See Table IV.) No significant differences occurred in this comparison; hence, the previously noted significant association between felony murder and a high proportion of executions could not account for the proportionately greater number of Negro offenders who are executed. Furthermore, there are no important differences in the distributions of Negro and white offenders among non-felony murder cases according to the type of disposition (Table IV). In short, although among non-felony

[18] Of 207 whites, 121, or 59%, had been convicted of felony murder; of 101 Negroes, 63, or 63%, had been convicted of felony murder.

Table IV: Race of Offender, by Type of Murder and Final Disposition

	Negro				White					
	(A)		*(B)* Non-felony		*(C)*		*(D)* Non-felony			
Final disposition	*Felony murder*		*felony murder*		*Felony murder*		*felony murder*		*Total*	
	N	%	N	%	N	%	N	%	N	%
Executed	59	93.7	30	79.0	100	82.6	61	70.9	250	81.2
Commuted	4	6.3	8	21.0	21	17.4	25	29.1	58	18.8
Total	63	100.0	38	100.0	121	100.0	86	100.0	308	100.0

For columns (A) and (C): $\chi^2 = 4.27$; P less than .05
For columns (B) and (D); (A) and (B); (C) and (D): not significant.

cases a higher percentage of Negroes (79 per cent) than of whites (71 per cent) are executed, it is not a statistically significant difference and could be due to chance.

But, as Table IV indicates, it is among felony murder cases that major differences may be noted when type of disposition is examined: 94 per cent of Negro felony murderers are executed compared to 83 per cent of white felony murderers. Thus, we see that the earlier statistical association between executions and felony murder is principally due to the fact that proportionately a much greater number of Negro felony murderers are executed. In terms of final disposition, no significant differences occur when Negro felony murder is compared with Negro non-felony murder; and no significant differences occur when white felony murder is compared with white non-felony murder.

Here, then, is a point at which the lack of statistical significance carries important meaning when placed side by side with a relationship that is significant. Thus, the fact that Negroes on death row do not comprise a significantly higher proportion of felony murderers than do whites, combined with the fact that a significantly higher proportion of Negro felony murderers are executed than are white felony murderers focuses the direction of differential treatment. It is the Negro felony murderer more than any other type of offender who will suffer the death penalty. Especially is this finding striking when we note that nearly three times more white (17.4 per cent) than Negro (6.3 per cent) felony murderers have their sentences commuted.

NATIVITY

Although differentials between the native-born and the foreign-born have been noted relative to the commission of certain types of crime[19] our point

---

[19] For a general survey of nativity and crime, see Donald R. Taft, *Criminology* 152–66 (3d ed., 1956); Sutherland & Cressey, *Principles of Criminology* 143–50 (5th ed., 1955).

Table V: Nativity of Offender, by Final Disposition

Final disposition	Native born		Foreign born	
	N	%	N	%
Executed	127	80.9	83	79.8
Commuted	30	19.1	21	20.2
Total	157	100.0	104	100.0

Chi-square test not significant.

of reference once again is executions and commutations among those who have been sentenced to death and have been held in custody on death row. A null hypothesis states: There is no significant difference between native-born and foreign-born in the proportions executed and commuted. (Negro males have been eliminated from this particular analysis for obvious reasons.) Table V presents data by nativity and disposition and shows that the hypothesis generally is accepted. Too many national groups are involved to analyze these cases statistically by country of origin.

In order to determine whether there are inter-relationships obscured by the factor of type of murder, Table VI is presented below. Among those on death row, proportionately and significantly more native-born than foreign-born offenders committed felony murder. Of the 123 native-born offenders two-thirds had committed felony murder; whereas, among the 82 foreign-born offenders less than half had committed felony murder. We should expect, on the basis of our previous finding of a relationship between felony murder and higher frequency of executions, that significantly more native-born than foreign-born offenders would be executed. Therefore, the observed absence of any significant association between nativity and final disposition (as shown in Table V) is meaningful and Table VI indicates that proportionately fewer native-born than foreign-born felony murderers are executed.

Table VI: Nativity, by Type of Murder

Type of murder	Native born		Foreign born	
	N	%	N	%
Felony	83	67.5	38	46.3
Non-felony	40	32.5	44	53.7
Total	123	100.0	82	100.0

$x^2 = 8.25$; P less than .01.

Table VII: Nativity of Offender, by Type of Murder and
Final Disposition

	Native born				Foreign born			
	(A) Felony murder		(B) Non-felony murder		(C) Felony murder		(D) Non-felony	
Final disposition	N	%	N	%	N	%	N	%
Executed	66	79.5	30	75.0	34	89.5	30	68.2
Commuted	17	20.5	10	25.0	4	10.5	14	31.8
Total	83	100.0	40	100.0	38	100.0	44	100.0

For columns (C) and (D): $\chi^2 = 4.14$; *P less than .05*
For columns (A) and (B); (A) and (C); (B) and (D): not significant.

Table VII should help to clarify the relationships among these various attributes. As it indicates, nearly 90 per cent of foreign-born felony murderers are executed compared to slightly less than 80 per cent of native-born felony murderers. However, the difference does not quite reach the level of statistical significance. It is important to recognize what cannot be asserted statistically from this table. We cannot say, for example, that compared with the native-born significantly more foreign-born felony murderers are executed (columns A and C); nor that more foreign-born non-felony murderers are executed (columns B and D); nor that among the native-born more felony murderers than non-felony murderers are executed (columns A and B). The only statistically significant difference that emerges from this particular analysis is that among the foreign-born more felony murderers (90 per cent) than non-felony murderers (68 per cent) are executed (columns C and D). A statement about commutations is, of course, equally true; that is, among the foreign-born significantly more non-felony murderers (32 per cent) than felony murderers (11 per cent) have their sentences commuted. This finding suggests that there may have been some kind of conflict between the communal mores of the foreign-born who committed non-felony murder and the legal codes of the host cultures to which the immigrants came, and that the Pardon Boards (if not the courts) recognized this culture conflict as a basis for mitigation of the severity of the sentence.[20]

RACE AND NATIVITY COMPARED

At this point in our analysis we can make some interesting generalizations about the various sets of attributes consisting of ethnic status (Negro, white,

[20] Sellin, *Culture Conflict and Crime* (Social Science Research Council Bul. No. 41, 1938).

native-born, foreign-born); type of murder (felony, non-felony); and type of final disposition (execution, commutation).

1. If an offender commits a first degree murder, he is more likely to be executed than commuted (in a ratio between three and four to one) regardless of his ethnic affiliation.

2. Negroes (in a ratio of five to one) more than whites (in a ratio of four to one) are more likely to be executed than commuted.

3. If the offense is a non-felony first degree murder, there are no statistically significant differences among ethnic groups in the proportions that are executed, although a higher proportion of foreign-born (32 per cent) than of native-born (25 per cent) or of Negroes (21 per cent) have their sentences commuted.

4. If the offense is a felony murder, a significantly higher proportion of Negroes (94 per cent) than of whites (83 per cent) are executed.

5. If the offense is a felony murder, there is no significant difference in the proportion of offenders executed when Negroes (94 per cent) are compared with the foreign-born whites (90 per cent), nor when the foreign-born whites are compared with the native-born whites (80 per cent).

6. If the offense is a felony murder, there is a significant difference between the proportion of Negroes (94 per cent) and of native-born whites (80 per cent) executed.

7. The statistically greatest likelihood of being executed occurs among Negro felony murderers (94 per cent).

8. The statistically greatest likelihood of being commuted occurs among foreign-born white non-felony murderers (32 per cent).

OCCUPATION AND MARITAL STATUS

Our null hypothesis again states that there are no significant differences in the distribution by occupational status of capital offenders who have been executed, compared to capital offenders who have been commuted. Table VIII presents these distributions, and analysis accepts this hypothesis. Moreover, no significant differences occur when the table is compressed into relatively similar occupational groupings, or when race or type of murder is held constant. It cannot be said, therefore, on the basis of these data, that differential application of the death penalty among those persons who ultimately reach death row is due to social class variation as represented by occupation. The race differential previously noted remains therefore unaffected by the factor of social class.

Similarly, no important differences appear between the executed and commuted when examined in terms of marital status. One interesting feature is that there are five times as many widowers among the commuted as among

Table VIII: Final Disposition, by Occupation of Offender[a]

	Final disposition		
Occupation of offender	*Executed*	*Commuted*	*Total*
Professional	5	0	5
Farmers and farm managers	0	2	2
Managers, officials, proprietors	7	0	7
Clerical, sales	5	1	6
Craftsmen, foremen	60	9	69
Operatives, kindred workers	75	20	95
Laborers, incl. farm	122	21	143
Service workers, household	51	15	66
Total	325	68	393

[a]*Adapted from occupational categories in* Alphabetical Index of Occupations and Industries *at vi (United States Department of Commerce, Bureau of Census, 1950).*

the executed, even though the executed outnumbered the commuted nearly five to one. The major reason appears to be that many of the commuted had slain their wives in non-felony murders.

COUNSEL

An a priori assumption suggests that a private counsel will devote more attention and energy to his client's case than will a court-appointed attorney. A variety of reasons may be offered to explain why this assumption appears valid, although we are not necessarily casting any derision on capable court-appointed attorneys. However, the expenses incurred in pursuing a murder case through the judicial process from indictment to petition for commutation would seem to handicap the court-appointed counsel in preparation of his case. If incentive to work diligently on the case is present, expenses usually are not; and lack of the latter may sometimes reduce the former. Moreover, it is suggested that younger lawyers eager or willing to accept these cases for experience are often appointed by the courts to act as counsel for persons indicted for murder. More thorough analysis of the system of court-appointed counsel, the methods of selection of counsel, and the qualification of the appointed attorneys are needed before any valid assertions can be made that the defendant with a court-appointed counsel is at a definite disadvantage.

However, the data presented in Table IX indicate that there is a significant relationship between type of counsel and final disposition, for less than 15 per cent of the death-row offenders with a court-appointed counsel received commutation of sentence compared to over 25 per cent of those offenders with private counsel. Refined examination of the data leads us to conclude that

Table IX: Race of Offender and Type of Counsel, by Final Disposition

	Negro				White			
	(A) Court-appointed counsel		(B) Private counsel		(C) Court-appointed counsel		(D) Private counsel	
Final disposition	N	%	N	%	N	%	N	%
Executed	93	91.2	9	69.2	121	81.2	53	75.7
Commuted	9	8.8	4	30.8	28	18.8	17	24.3
Total	102	100.0	13	100.0	149	100.0	70	100.0

For columns (A) + (C) and (B) + (D): $\chi^2 = 4.14$; P less than .05
For columns (A) and (B): $\chi^2 = 5.40$; P less than .05
For columns (A) and (C): $\chi^2 = 4.04$; P less than .05
For columns (C) and (D); (B) and (D): not significant.

race is the major factor influencing this association. Among whites, no significant differences are noted in the final disposition according to whether the defendant had a private or a court-appointed counsel; but among Negroes, a decided relationship is discernible. It appears that if a Negro offender has a private counsel he is much more likely to have his death sentence commuted than if he has a court-appointed attorney. The number of cases (13) of Negroes on death row having a private attorney is so small that statistical analysis must be viewed with much caution. If the counsel is private, no significant differences are noted between whites and Negroes in the final disposition; hence, the race differential under private counsel disappears. But if the counsel is court-appointed, the race differential is again evident, for proportionately twice as many whites (19 per cent) have sentences commuted as do Negroes (9 per cent).

REASONS FOR COMMUTATION

Of the total 71 commutations over the period examined, information was available regarding the reasons for commutation in 62 cases. The number is too small for more refined analysis than the frequencies presented in Table X. (Overlapping in these commutation themes means that the total percentage is more than one hundred.) The 71 cases represent over 17 per cent of the total 407 persons sent to death row between 1914 and 1958. Thus, in nearly one out of six cases in which a court had pronounced the death sentence and the defendant had moved as close to the electric chair as being in custody at the center for executions, a politically designated body — the Board of Pardons — found legally justifiable reasons to impose limits on the courts' decisions.

Table X: Number and Percentage Commuted, according to Reason for Commutation[a]

Reason for commutation	Number commuted	Percentage commuted
A. Relative to crime:		
Lack of premeditation	16	25.8
Provocation by victim	7	11.3
Not directly responsible for death	5	8.0
Possibility of mistaken identity	3	4.8
	31	49.9
B. Relative to defendant:		
Previous good record	9	14.7
Mentally deficient or diseased	9	14.7
Intoxication at time of crime	8	12.9
Comparative youth	7	11.3
Lacking or poor family background	3	4.9
	36	58.5
C. Relative to court trial:		
Accomplices received lesser sentences	13	20.9
Deprivation of right to fair trial	4	6.4
	17	27.3

[a]*More than one reason was given for some of the 62 persons commuted; hence, the percentage commuted on the table totals more than one hundred. Our interest, however, is in the frequency with which each reason for commutation occurred among the total persons commuted.*

It is especially interesting to note that of the eleven reasons given for commuting sentences, four involve serious doubts about the circumstances of the slaying so that the status of first degree murder is legally in question. These items include: lack of premeditation (26 per cent), provocation by victim (11 per cent), not directly responsible for the death (8 per cent), and the possibility of mistaken identity (5 per cent). All told, these items (under "A" in Table X) related to the crime itself account for 50 per cent of the reasons for commutation.[21] In another 59 per cent the commutation themes ("B" in Table X) are related to the character of the defendant rather than to aspects of the crime and include such items as the comparative youthfulness of the offender, his previous good record, poor family background, mental condition,

[21] It is conceivable that "intoxication at time of crime" could be added to this list of items that relate to the crime instead of being listed under items related to the defendant. However, drunkenness is not generally a legally justifiable basis for reduction of the seriousness of the crime nor for mitigation of the penalty.

and intoxication at the time of the crime. Finally, in 27 per cent of these commutation statements ("C" in Table X) the reason given was most directly related to the conduct of the trial, for in 21 per cent it was noted that accomplices had received lesser sentences and in 6 per cent the defendants had been considered as having been deprived of fair trials.

SUMMARY AND CONCLUSION

An attempt has been made in the foregoing analysis to examine the application of the death penalty in Pennsylvania since introduction of electrocutions in 1914. The original group studied consisted of 439 persons who were held in custody awaiting final disposition at the state center for execution. This number was reduced as additional variables were introduced for analysis, for all data were not available for each case. The major focus of attention has been on the proportion of persons whose sentences were executed and those whose sentences were commuted. Significant relationships (P less than .05) were found to exist between the type of final disposition and several attributes summarized under A and B below. The numbered item under A was compared with the same numbered item under B relative to final disposition.

A Attributes associated with execution	*B* Attributes associated with commutation
1. Felony murder	1. Non-felony murder
2. Offenders 20–24 years of age	2. Offenders 15–19 yrs. or 55+ yrs.
3. Negro offenders	3. White offenders
4. Negro felony offenders	4. White felony offenders
5. Foreign-born white felony offenders	5. Foreign-born white non-felony offenders
6. Offenders with court-appointed counsel	6. Offenders with private counsel
7. Negro offenders with court-appointed counsel	7. Negro offenders with private counsel
8. Negro offenders with court-appointed counsel	8. White offenders with court-appointed counsel

No significant differences in distributions were noted when the following were analyzed:

Age and race with type of murder
Race and felony murder
Race and non-felony murder
Among Negroes, type of murder and final disposition
Among whites, type of murder and final disposition
Among native-born whites, type of murder and final disposition

Non-felony murder, by nativity and final disposition
Occupation and final disposition
Occupation, by race and type of murder
Marital status and final disposition
Among whites, type of counsel and final disposition
Among offenders with private counsel, race and final disposition

The quality and quantity of the data available for research do not permit more refined analysis, but on the basis of what we have, it appears that the three significant findings are intricately inter-related: type of murder, race of the offender, and type of counsel. The one factor that links each of the others together is race; for while more offenders convicted of felony murder and offenders with court-appointed counsel are executed than offenders convicted of non-felony murder and offenders with private counsel, respectively, these differences are produced by the fact that significantly more Negroes than whites are executed. This race differential bears no relationship to the fact that the homicide rate (or perhaps even the murder rate) is higher for Negroes than for whites in the general population. We have consistently posed the question: After the pre-death-row factors have selectively functioned to produce a group possessing the major element of homogeneity characterized by being convicted of first degree murder and held in custody at the center for execution, what measureable factors differentiate those who are executed from those who are commuted? While the present study has not been able to draw any conclusions regarding differential treatment of Negroes in the courts, and although there may be many factors obscured by the available gross data, there is reason to suspect — and statistically significant evidence to support the suspicion — that Negroes have not received equal consideration for commutation of the death penalty.

Thus, although differences in the disposition of capital offenders probably function to the greatest extent before sentencing, differences may be found even after offenders have been committed to death. This study of the Pennsylvania data has discovered nothing new; Johnson's analysis in North Carolina has many similarities and also used death-row data.[22] But any empirical verification of previously assumed differences among persons who received society's ultimate sanction should be of value in understanding the operation of our legal principles. That race is one of these significant differences constitutes a social and political violation of the principle of equal justice and is an obvious argument for those who favor abolition of the death penalty.

[22] Johnson, *supra* note 2.

Index
to Authors

Index
to Subjects